BUDDHA
OSAMU TEZUKA

VERTICAL.

1: *Kapilavastu*

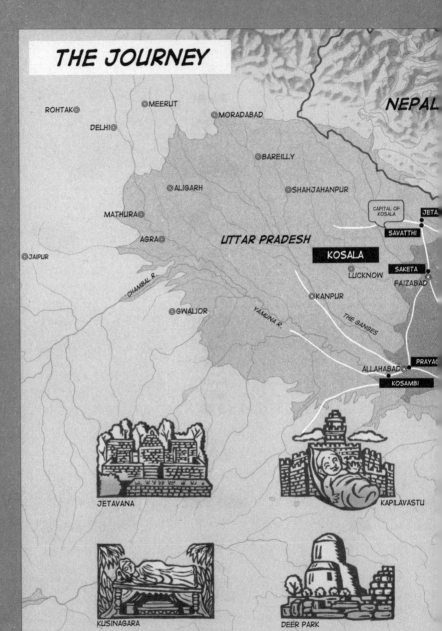

THE JOURNEY

NEPAL

ROHTAK◎   ◎MEERUT
      ◎MORADABAD
DELHI◎

            ◎BAREILLY

      ◎ALIGARH   ◎SHAHJAHANPUR
                              CAPITAL OF
                              KOSALA   JETA
MATHURA◎
                              SAVATTHI
AGRA◎   *UTTAR PRADESH*
                    KOSALA
◎JAIPUR   SAKETA
              ◎LUCKNOW   FAIZABAD
      CHAMBAL R.   ◎KANPUR
      ◎GWALIOR   *YAMUNA R.*   THE GANGES

                              PRAYAG
                    ALLAHABAD◎
                        KOSAMBI

JETAVANA   KAPILAVASTU

KUSINAGARA   DEER PARK

LUMBINI ANCIENT   ———— MAJOR ROUTES   ● PLACES VISITED BY THE BUDDHA
        PLACE NAMES

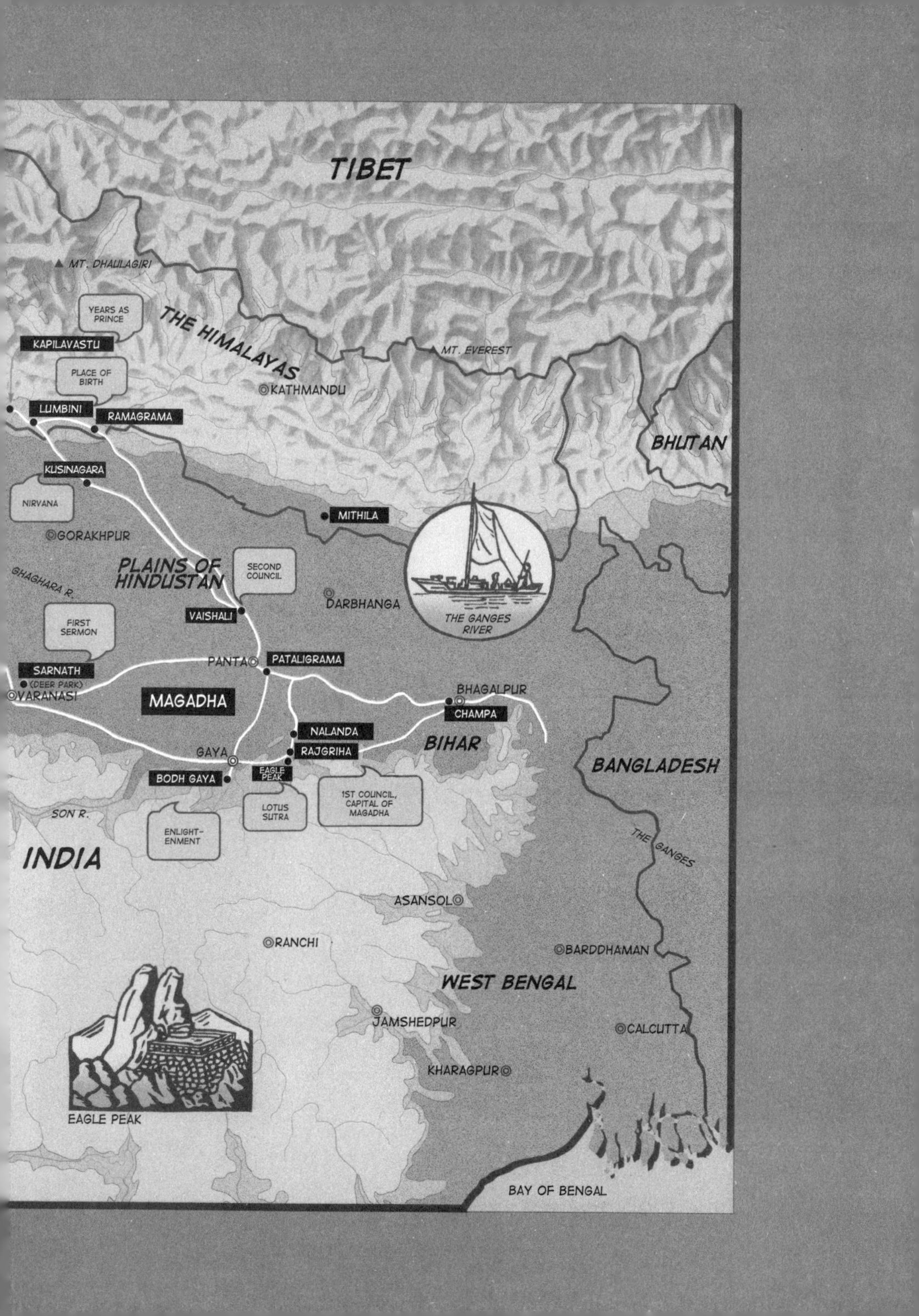

TIBET
MT. DHAULAGIRI
YEARS AS PRINCE
KAPILAVASTU
THE HIMALAYAS
MT. EVEREST
PLACE OF BIRTH
KATHMANDU
LUMBINI
RAMAGRAMA
BHUTAN
KUSINAGARA
NIRVANA
MITHILA
GORAKHPUR
PLAINS OF HINDUSTAN
SECOND COUNCIL
GHAGHARA R.
DARBHANGA
VAISHALI
FIRST SERMON
THE GANGES RIVER
PANTA
PATALIGRAMA
SARNATH
(DEER PARK)
VARANASI
MAGADHA
BHAGALPUR
CHAMPA
NALANDA
BIHAR
GAYA
RAJGRIHA
BANGLADESH
BODH GAYA
EAGLE PEAK
SON R.
1ST COUNCIL, CAPITAL OF MAGADHA
LOTUS SUTRA
ENLIGHT-ENMENT
INDIA
THE GANGES
ASANSOL
RANCHI
BARDDHAMAN
WEST BENGAL
JAMSHEDPUR
CALCUTTA
KHARAGPUR
EAGLE PEAK
BAY OF BENGAL

COPYRIGHT © 2006 BY TEZUKA PRODUCTIONS
TRANSLATION COPYRIGHT © 2006 BY VERTICAL

ALL RIGHTS RESERVED.

PUBLISHED BY VERTICAL, AN IMPRINT OF
KODANSHA USA PUBLISHING, LLC.

ORIGINALLY PUBLISHED IN JAPANESE AS *BUDDA DAI IKKAN
KAPIRAVASUTU* BY USHIO SHUPPANSHA, TOKYO, 1987.

ISBN 978-1-932234-56-5

MANUFACTURED IN CANADA

FIRST PAPERBACK EDITION. THE ARTWORK OF THE ORIGINAL HAS BEEN
PRODUCED AS A MIRROR-IMAGE IN ORDER TO
CONFORM WITH THE ENGLISH LANGUAGE. THIS WORK OF
FICTION CONTAINS CHARACTERS AND EPISODES THAT ARE
NOT PART OF THE HISTORICAL RECORD.

NINTH PRINTING

KODANSHA USA PUBLISHING, LLC.
451 PARK AVENUE SOUTH 7TH FLOOR
NEW YORK, NY 10016
WWW.VERTICAL-INC.COM

CONTENTS

PART ONE

PART ONE

CHAPTER ONE

BRAHMIN

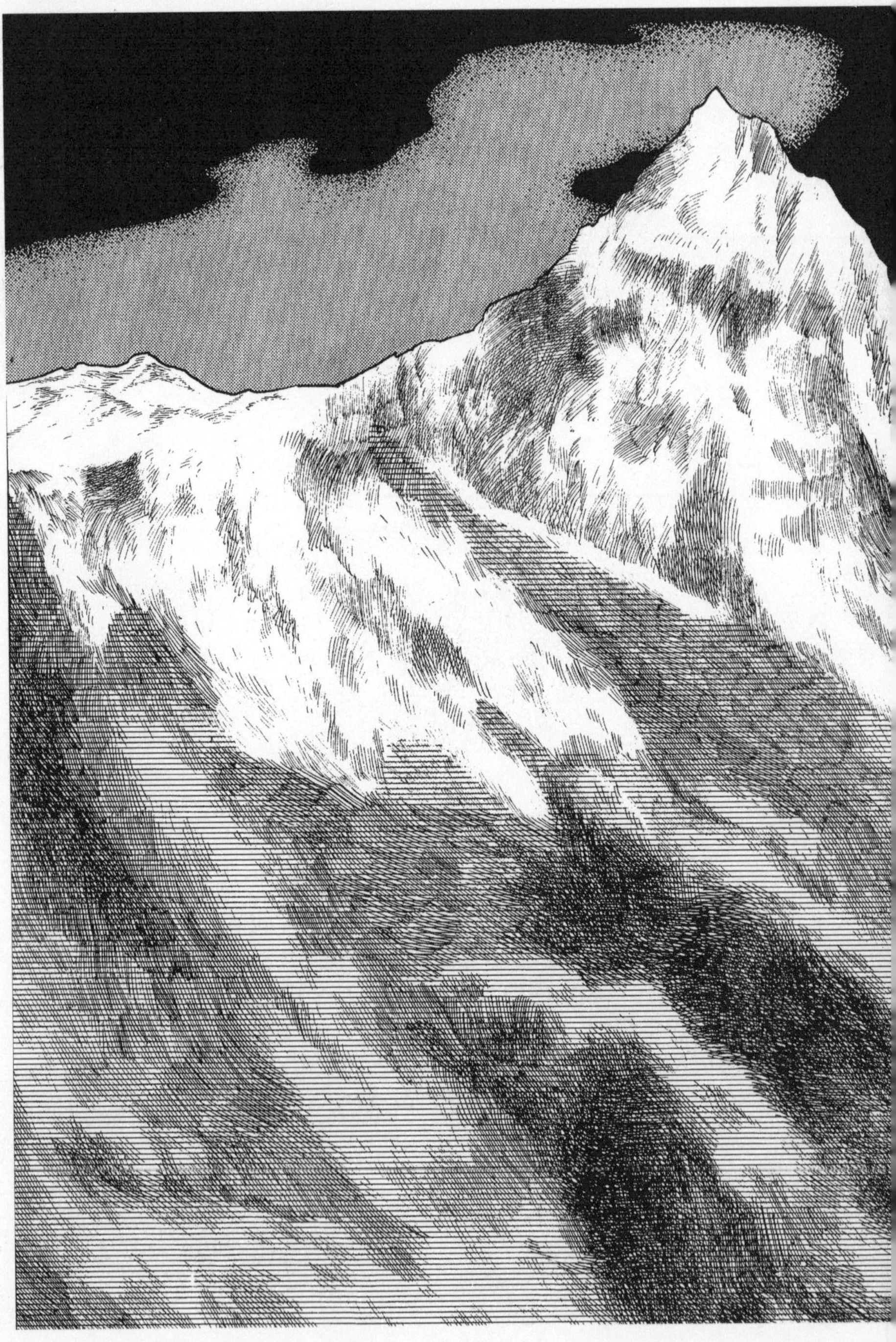

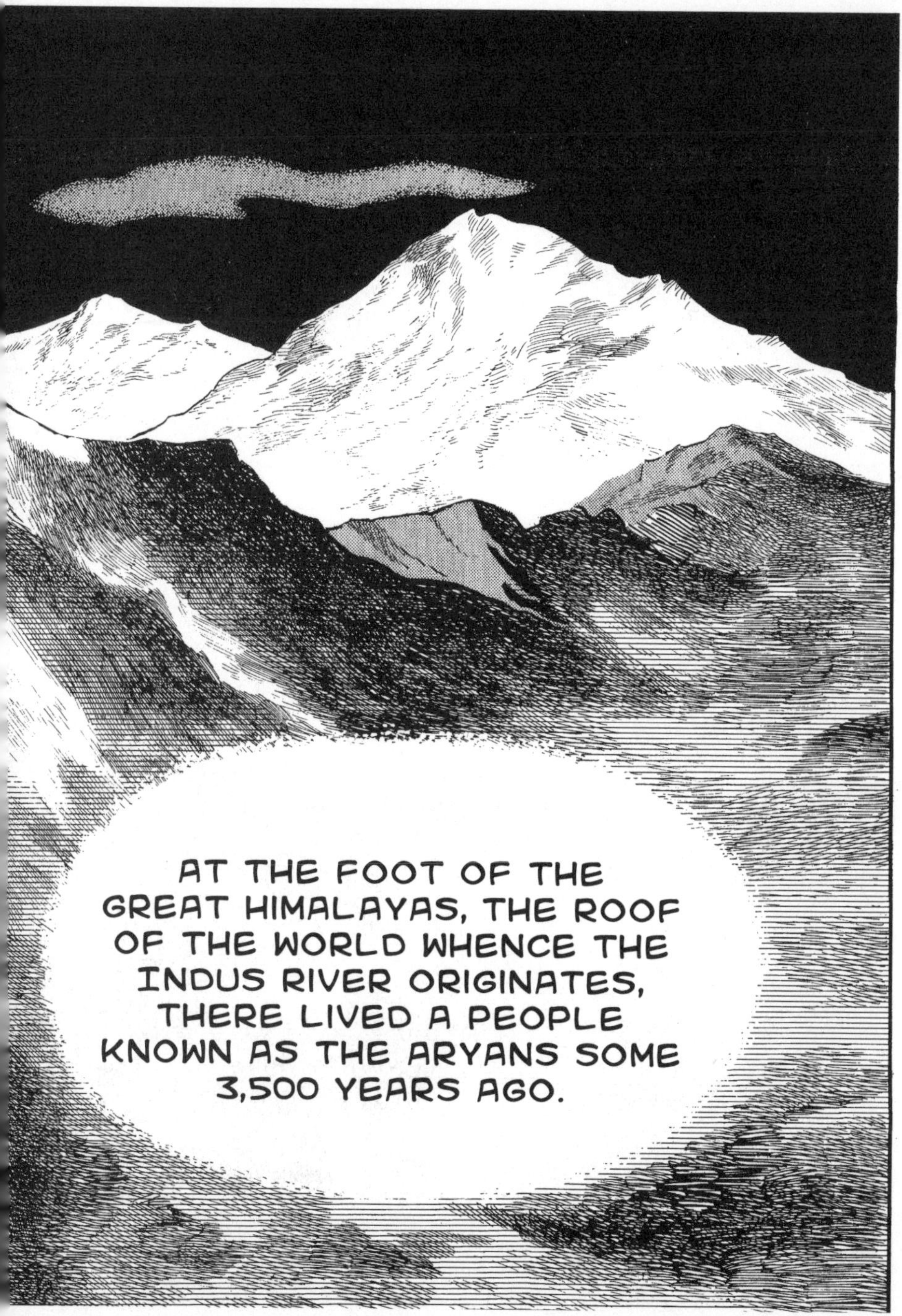
AT THE FOOT OF THE GREAT HIMALAYAS, THE ROOF OF THE WORLD WHENCE THE INDUS RIVER ORIGINATES, THERE LIVED A PEOPLE KNOWN AS THE ARYANS SOME 3,500 YEARS AGO.

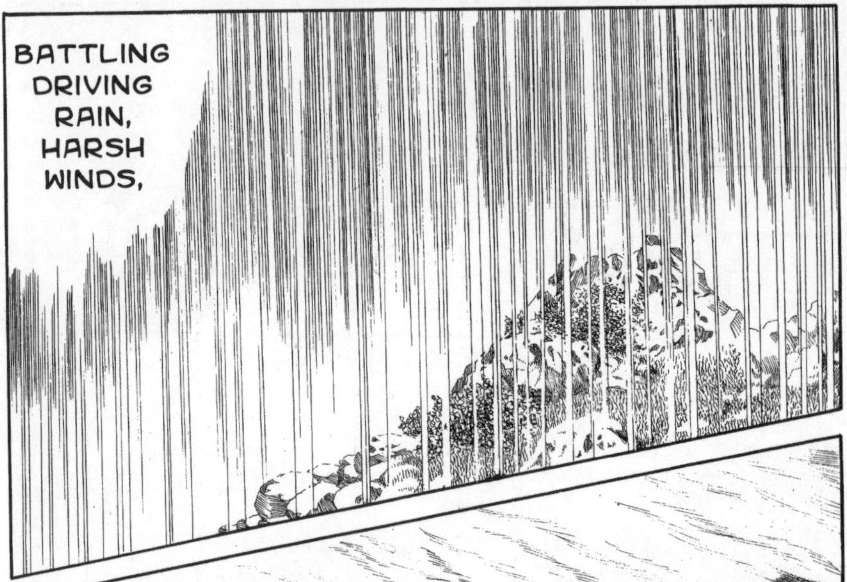
BATTLING DRIVING RAIN, HARSH WINDS,

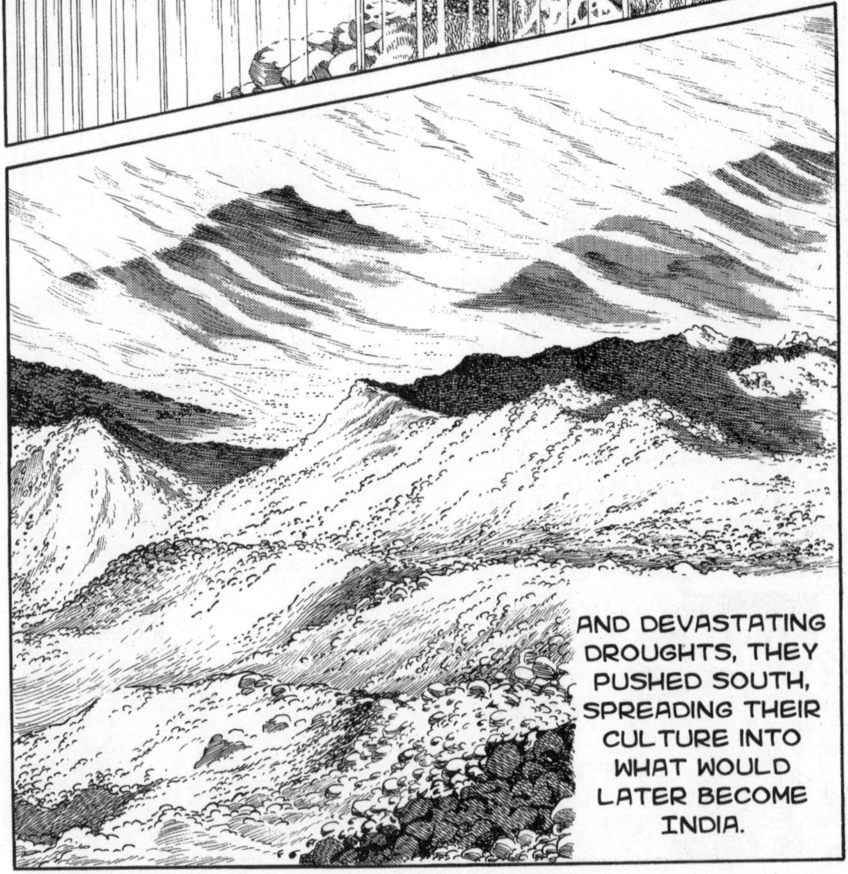
AND DEVASTATING DROUGHTS, THEY PUSHED SOUTH, SPREADING THEIR CULTURE INTO WHAT WOULD LATER BECOME INDIA.

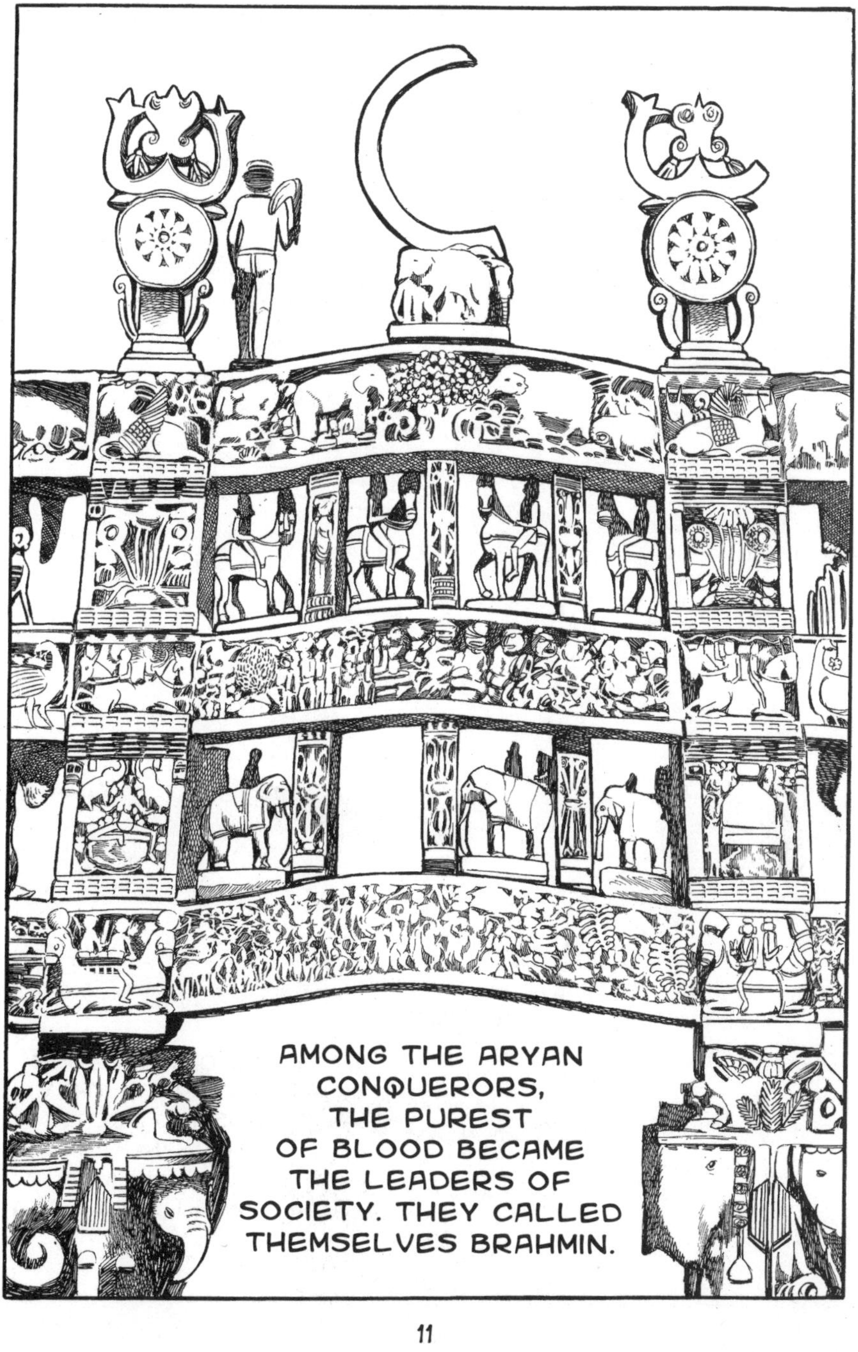
AMONG THE ARYAN CONQUERORS, THE PUREST OF BLOOD BECAME THE LEADERS OF SOCIETY. THEY CALLED THEMSELVES BRAHMIN.

BRAHMIN! THE VERY NAME WAS AN EMBLEM
OF INVINCIBLE POWER IN INDIAN SOCIETY
FOR CENTURIES.

UNDERNEATH THEM THE BRAHMIN
CREATED CLASSES LIKE
"WARRIOR," "COMMONER," AND "SLAVE,"
INTRODUCING DISCRIMINATION AMONG
FELLOW HUMANS.

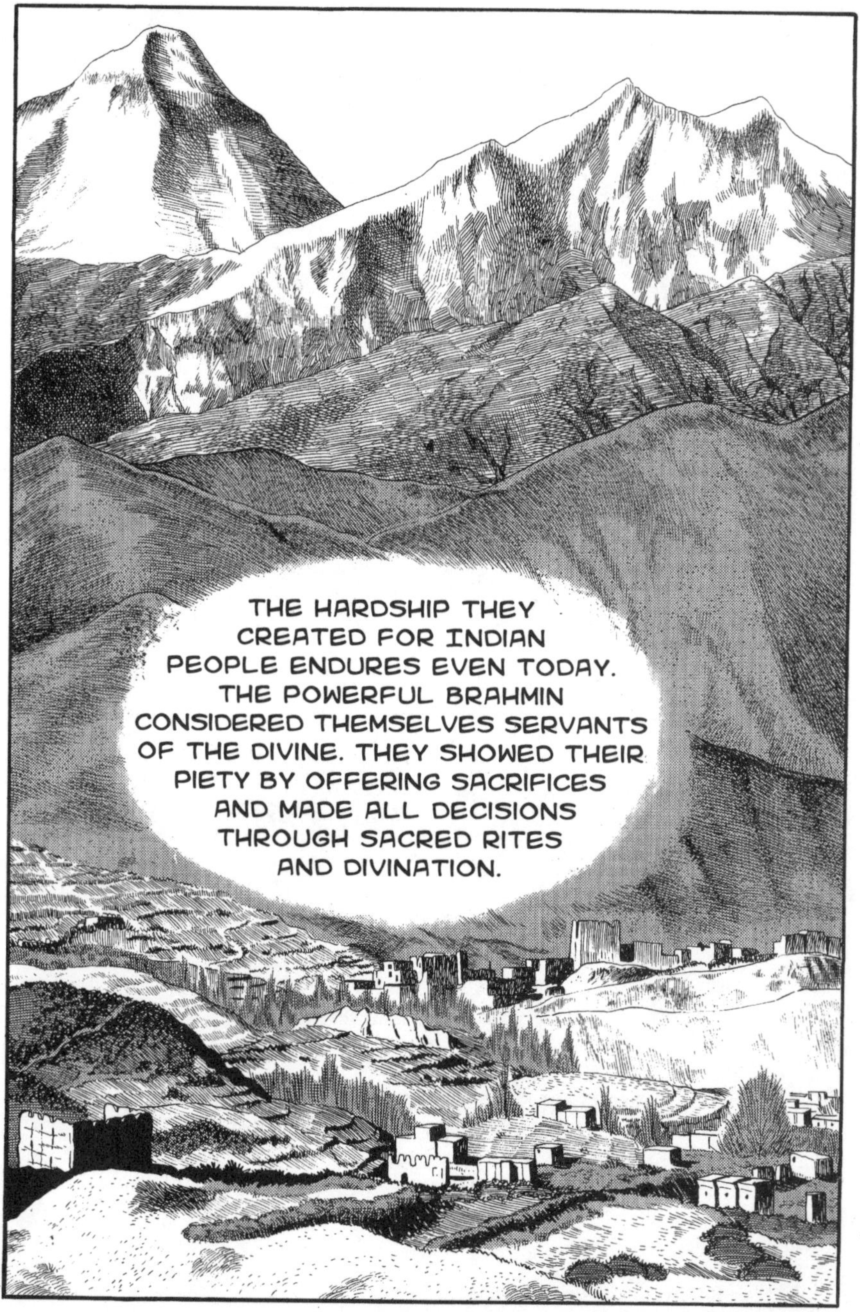
THE HARDSHIP THEY CREATED FOR INDIAN PEOPLE ENDURES EVEN TODAY. THE POWERFUL BRAHMIN CONSIDERED THEMSELVES SERVANTS OF THE DIVINE. THEY SHOWED THEIR PIETY BY OFFERING SACRIFICES AND MADE ALL DECISIONS THROUGH SACRED RITES AND DIVINATION.

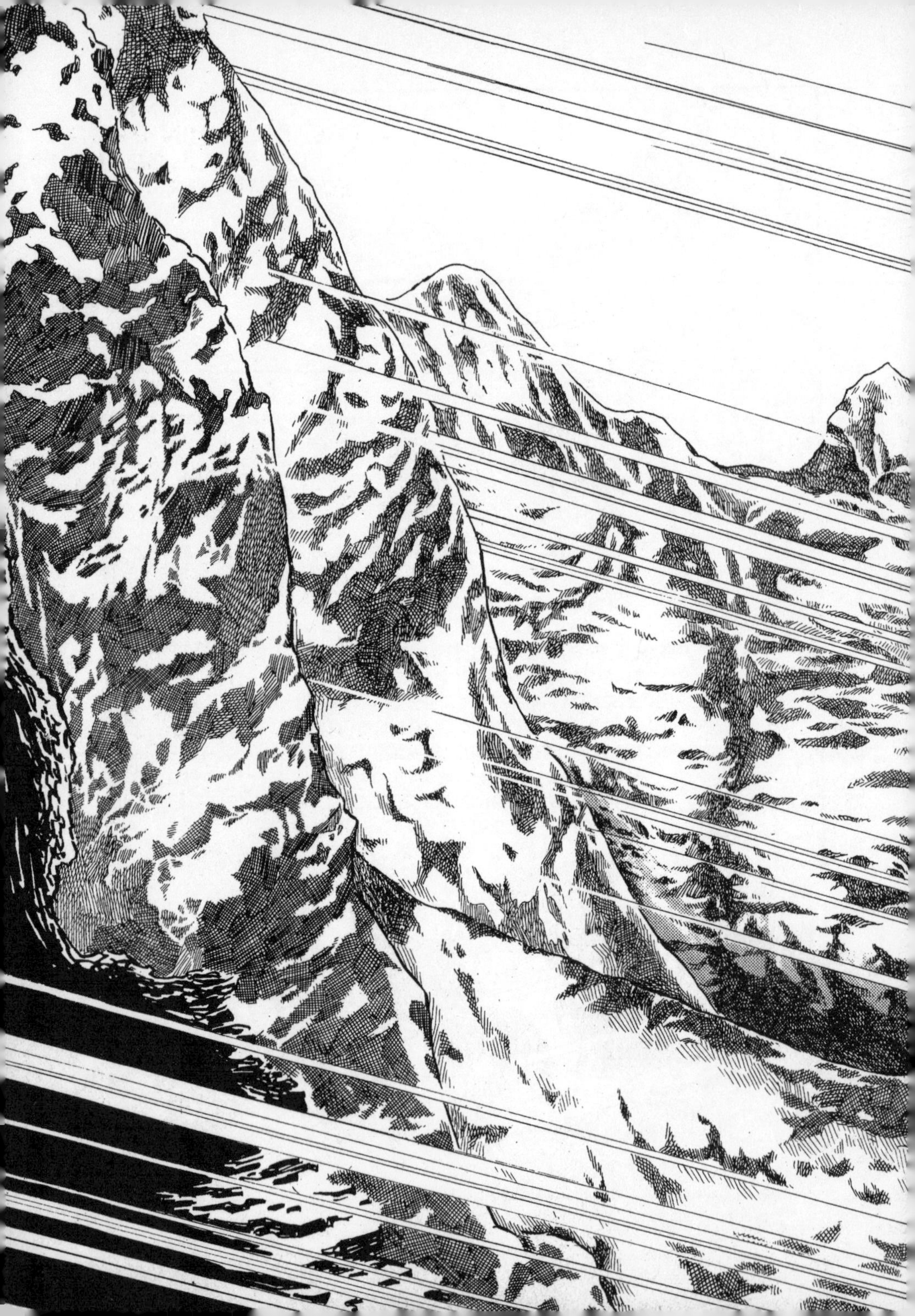

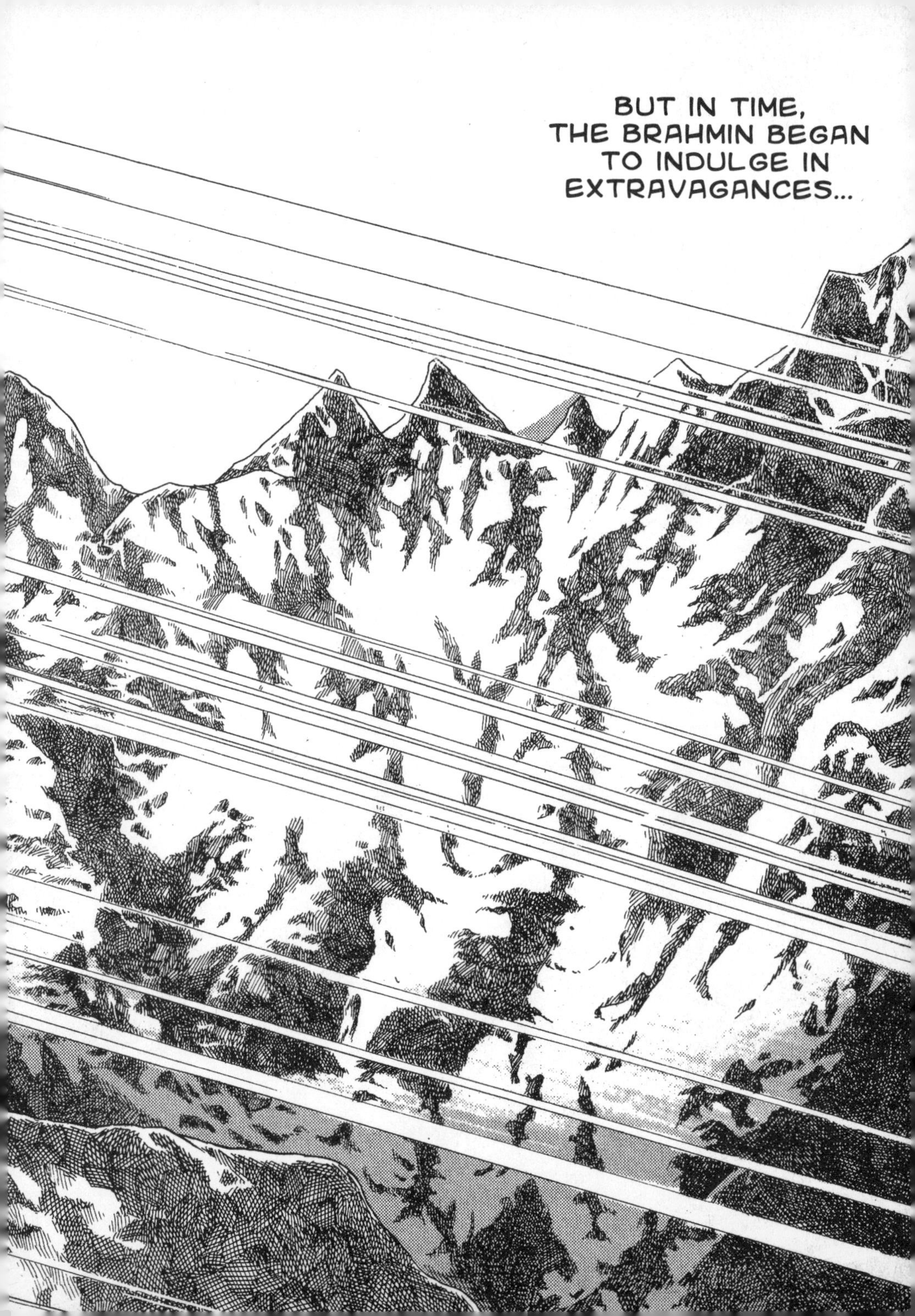
BUT IN TIME,
THE BRAHMIN BEGAN
TO INDULGE IN
EXTRAVAGANCES...

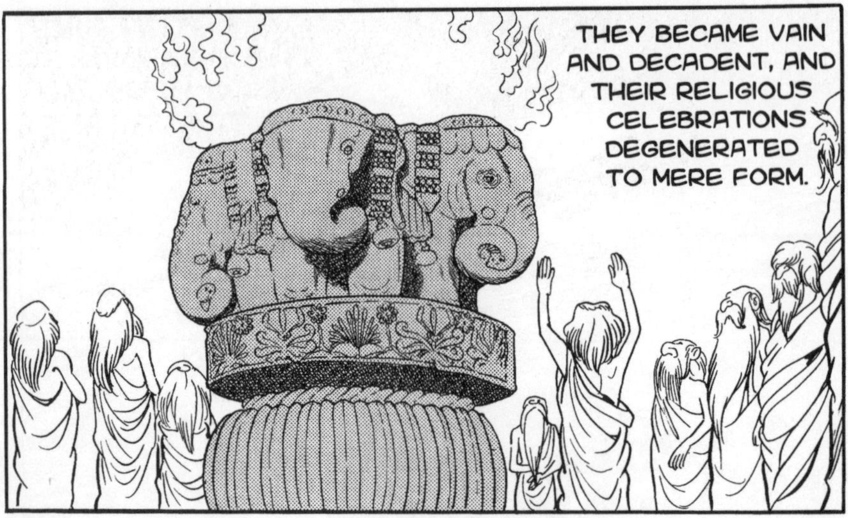
THEY BECAME VAIN AND DECADENT, AND THEIR RELIGIOUS CELEBRATIONS DEGENERATED TO MERE FORM.

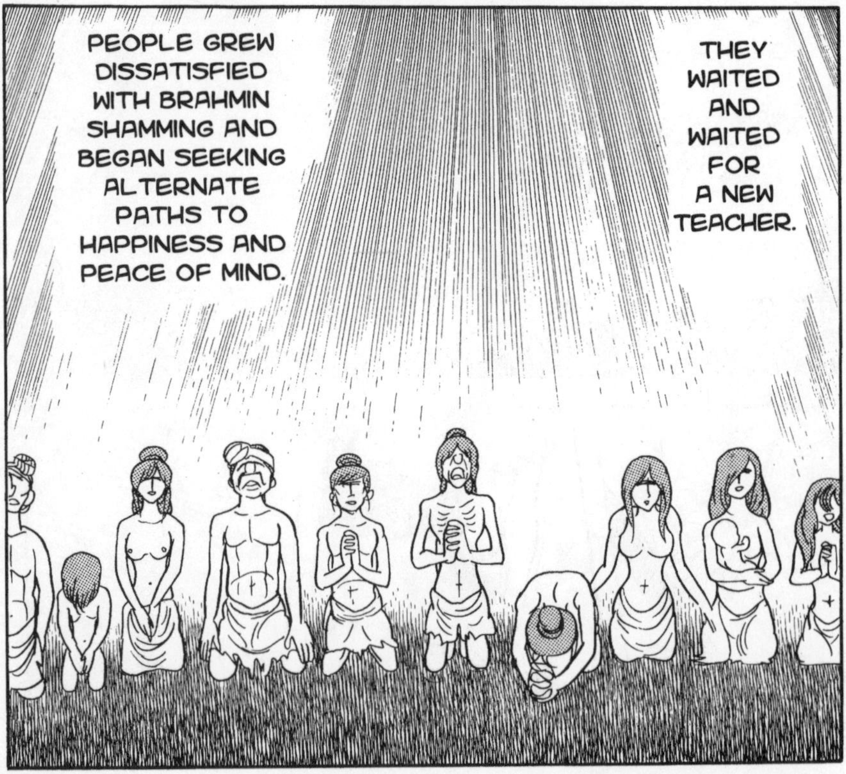
PEOPLE GREW DISSATISFIED WITH BRAHMIN SHAMMING AND BEGAN SEEKING ALTERNATE PATHS TO HAPPINESS AND PEACE OF MIND.
THEY WAITED AND WAITED FOR A NEW TEACHER.

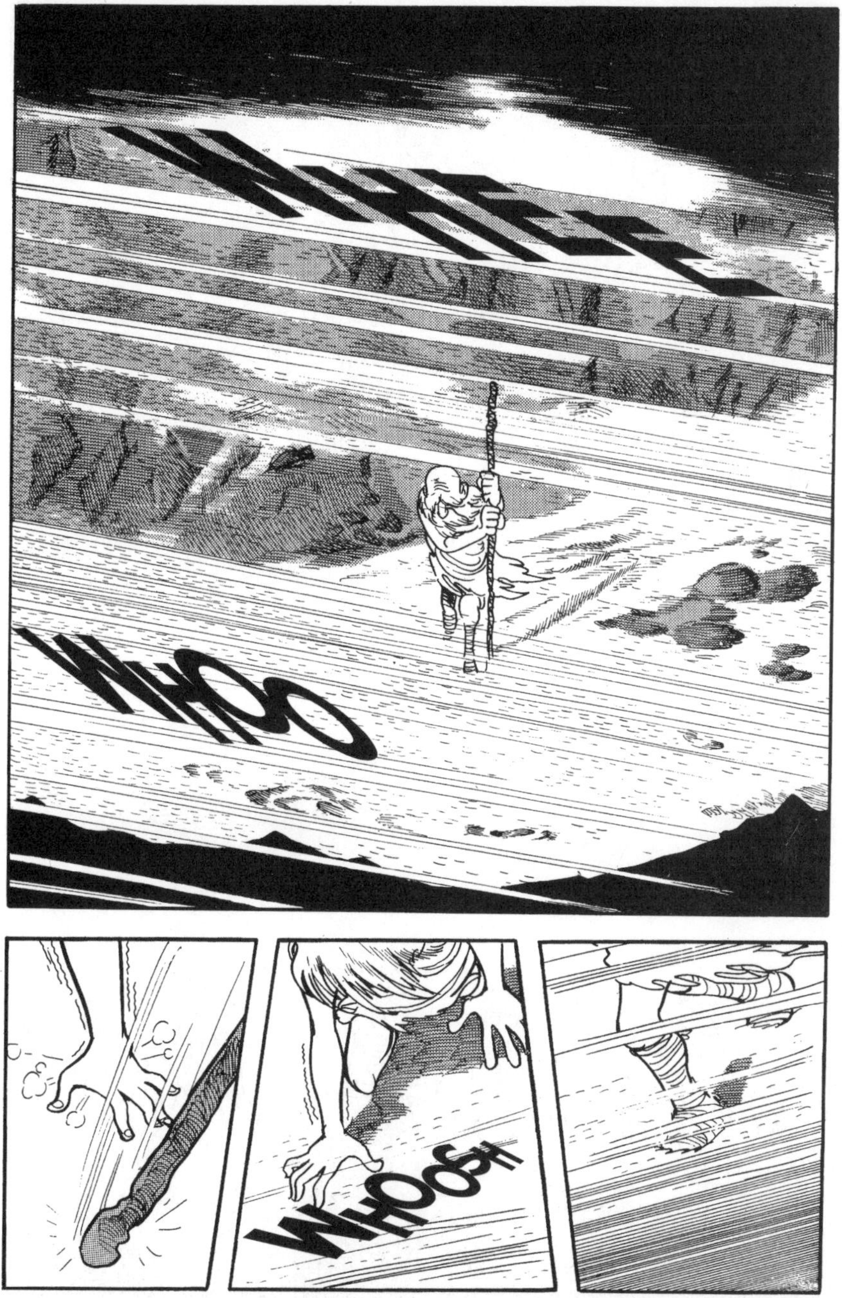
WHEEE
WHOO
WHOOSH

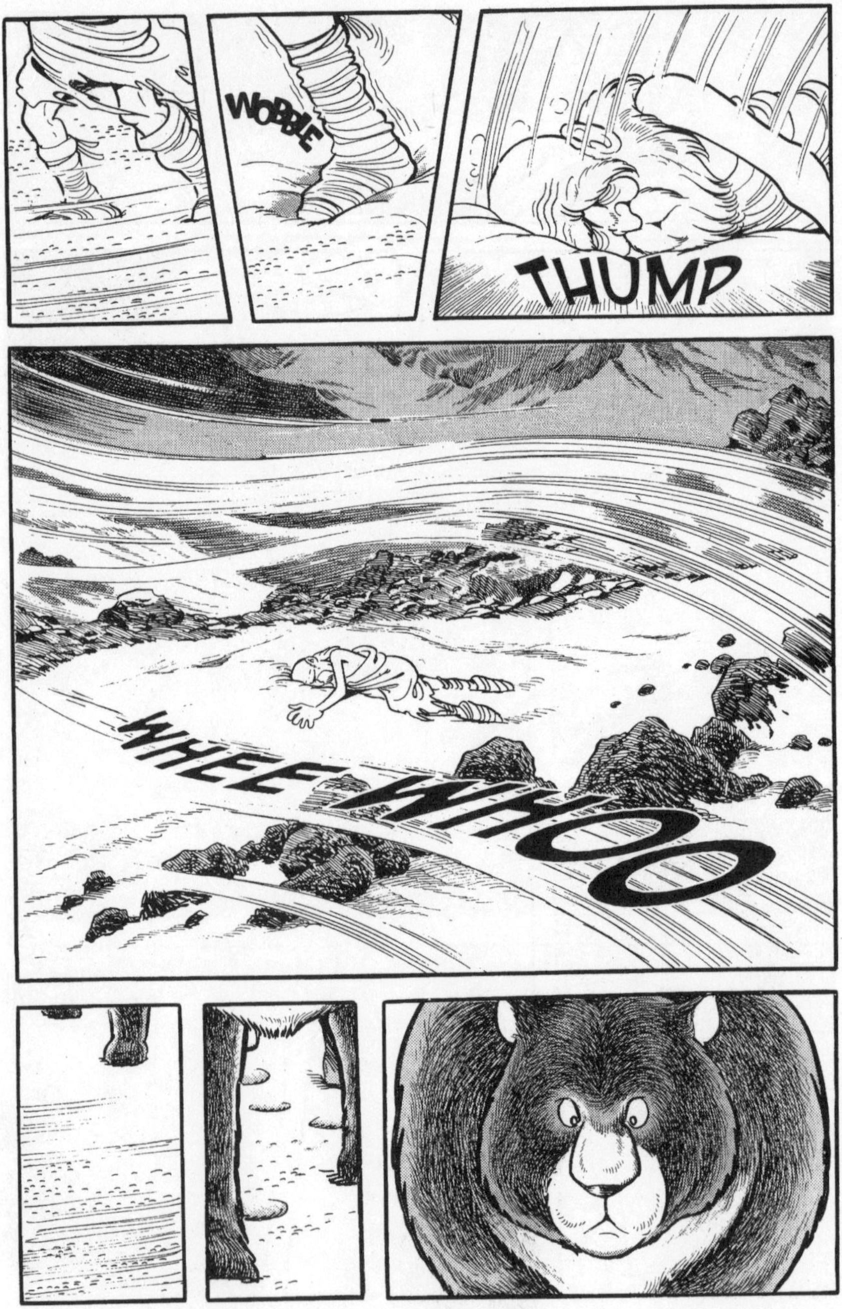
WOBBLE
THUMP
WHEE-WHOO

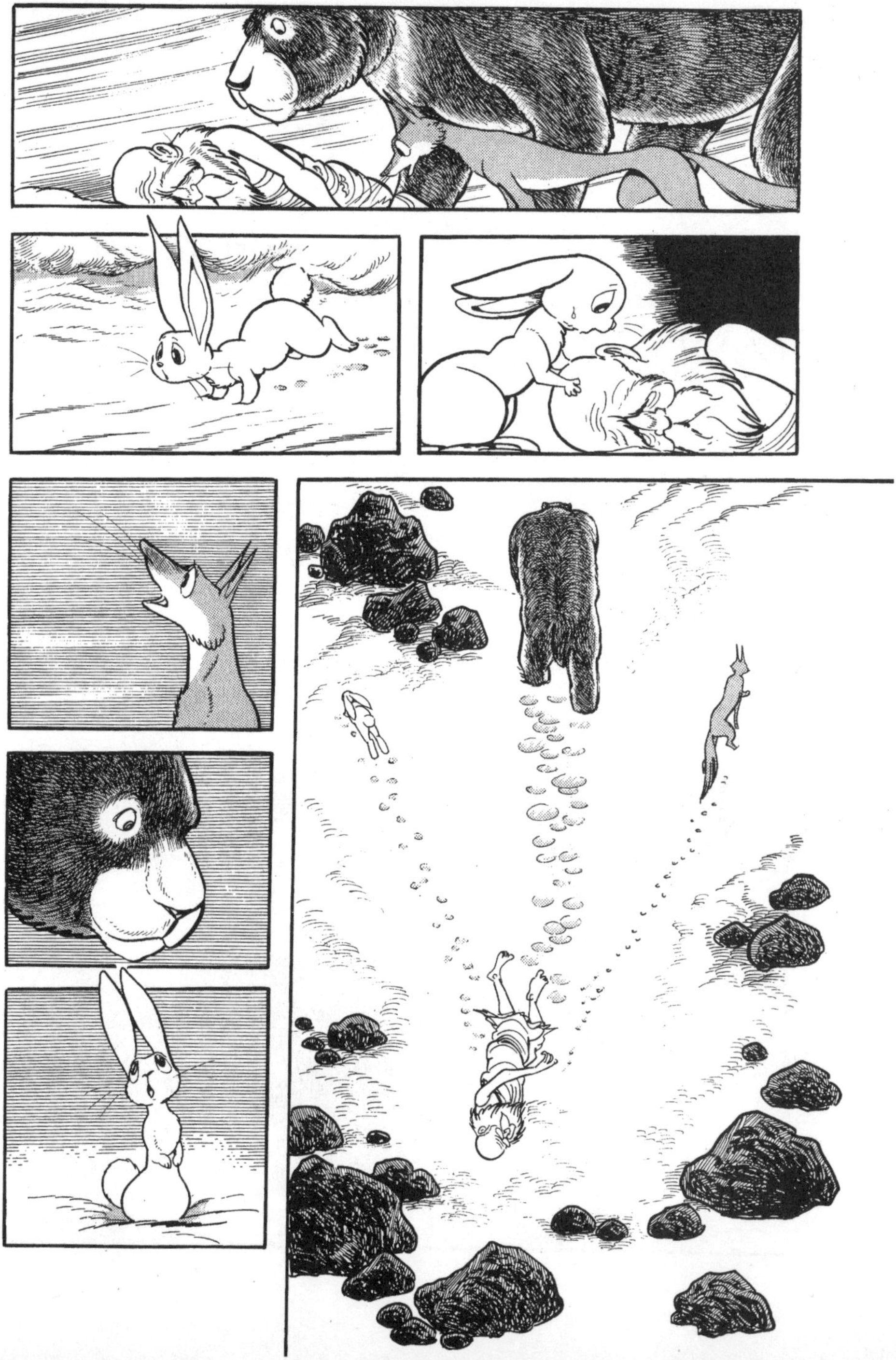

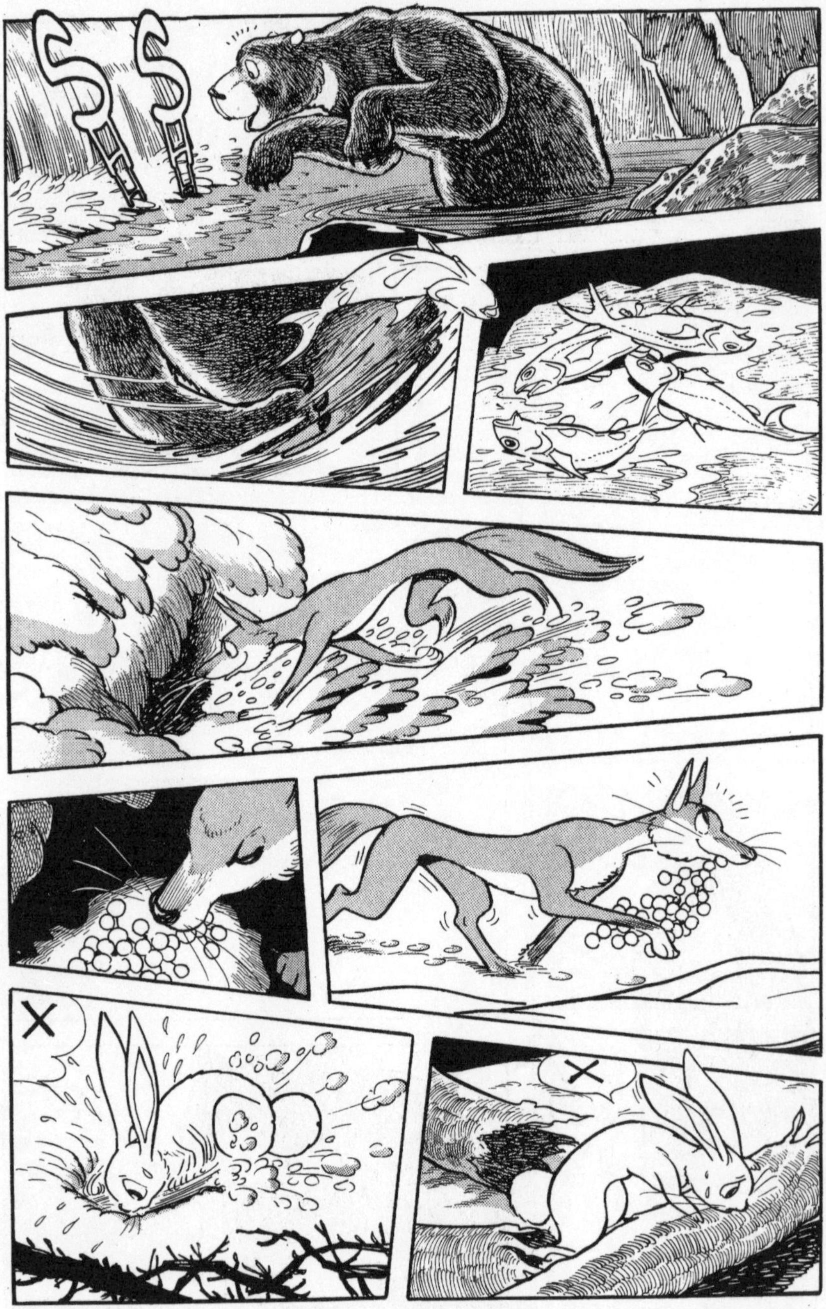

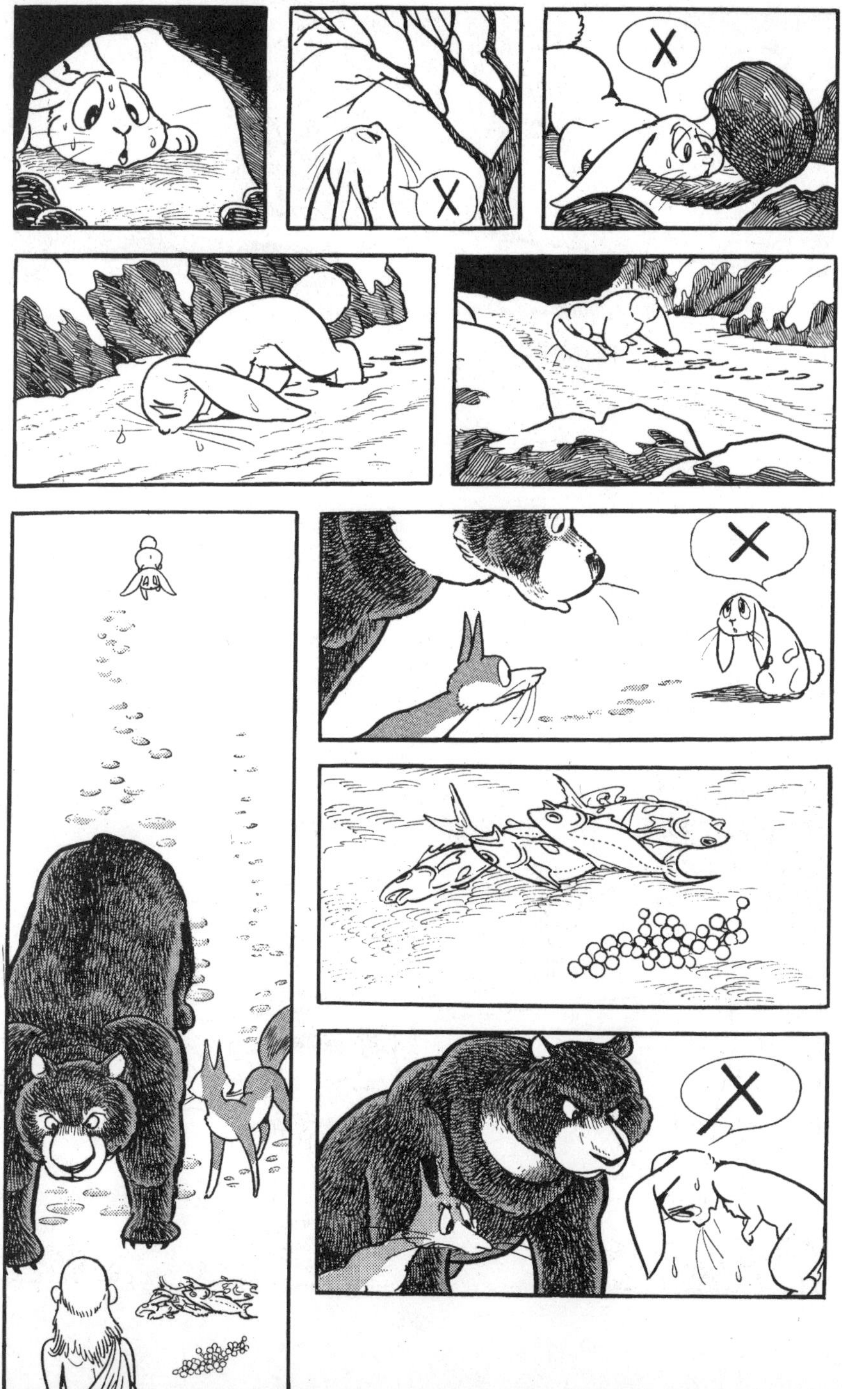

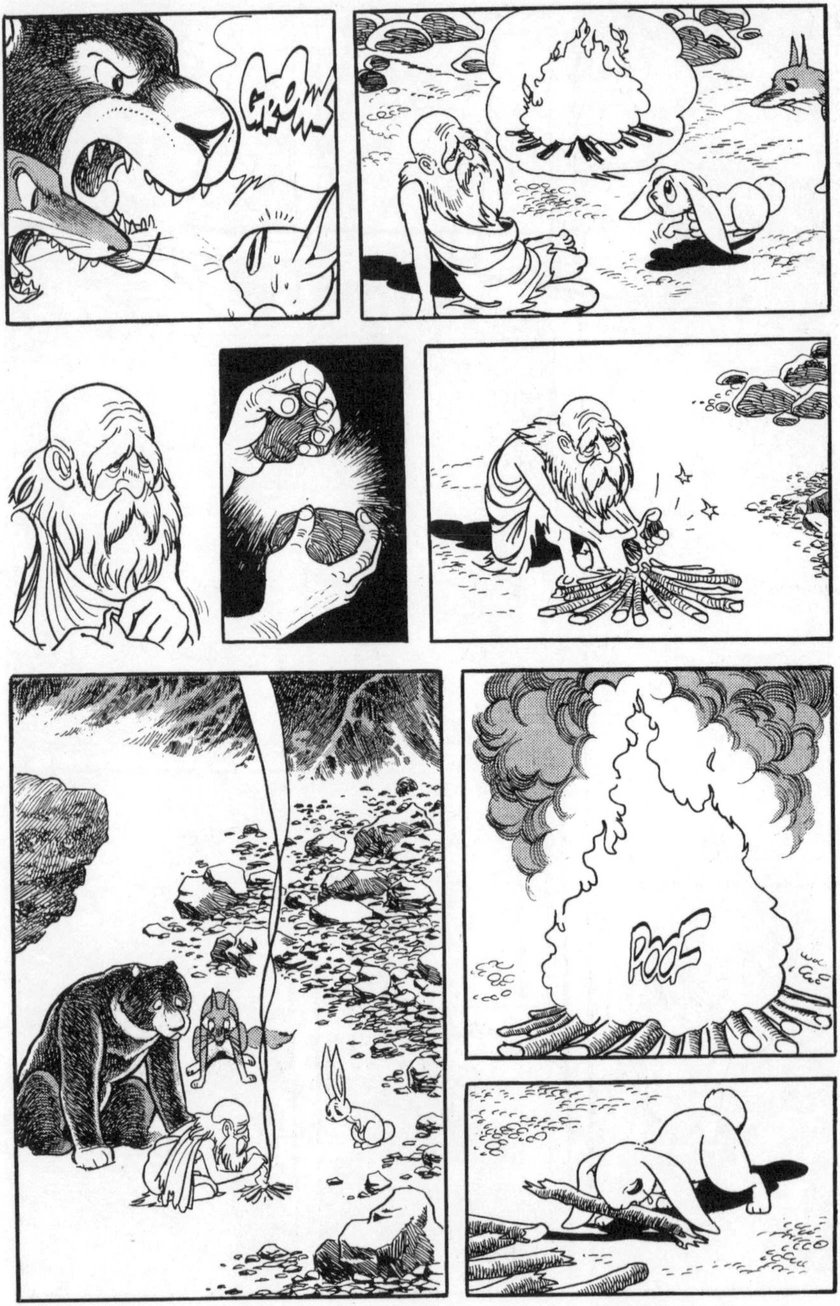
GROWL
POOF

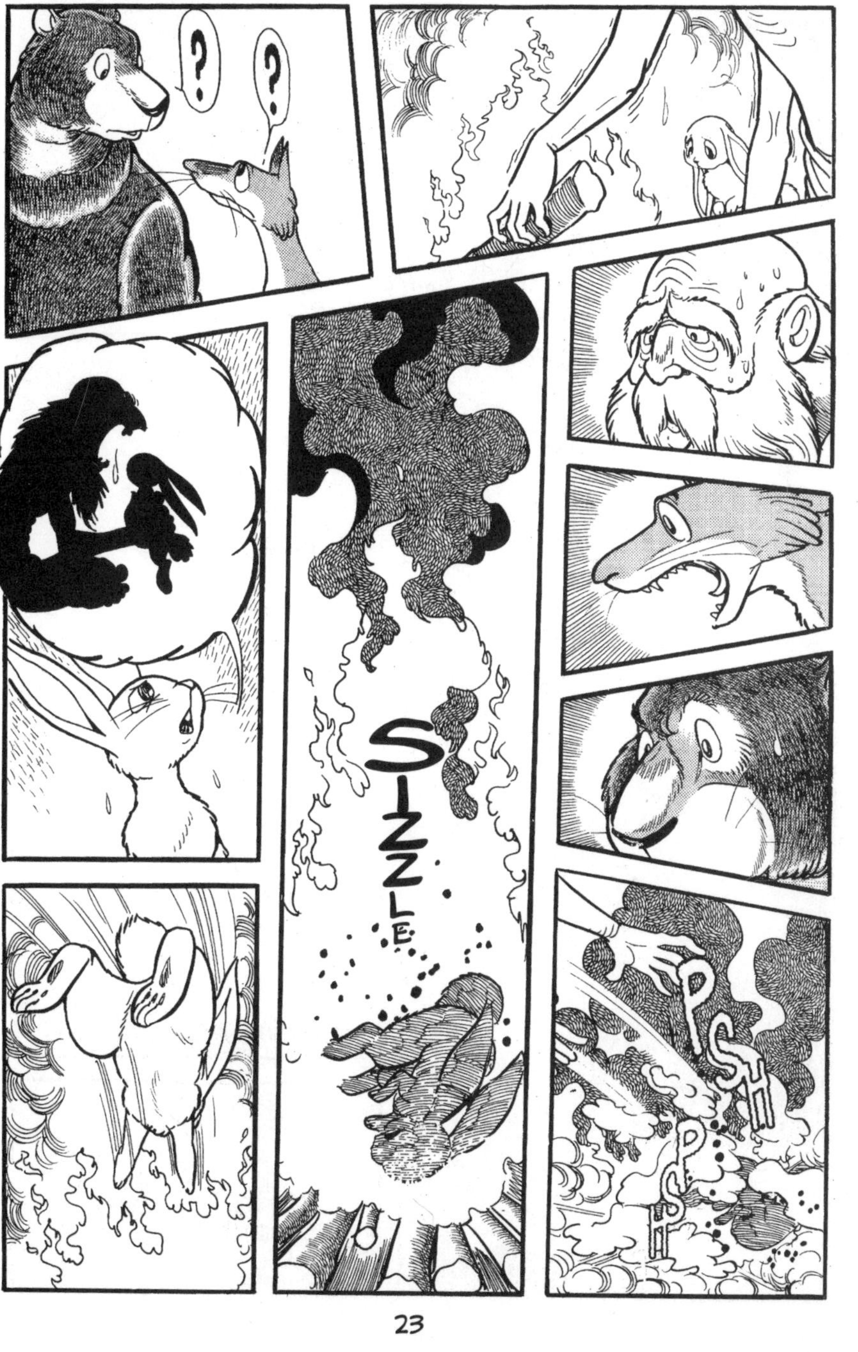
?
?
SIZZLE
PSH
PSH

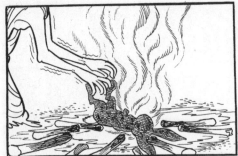

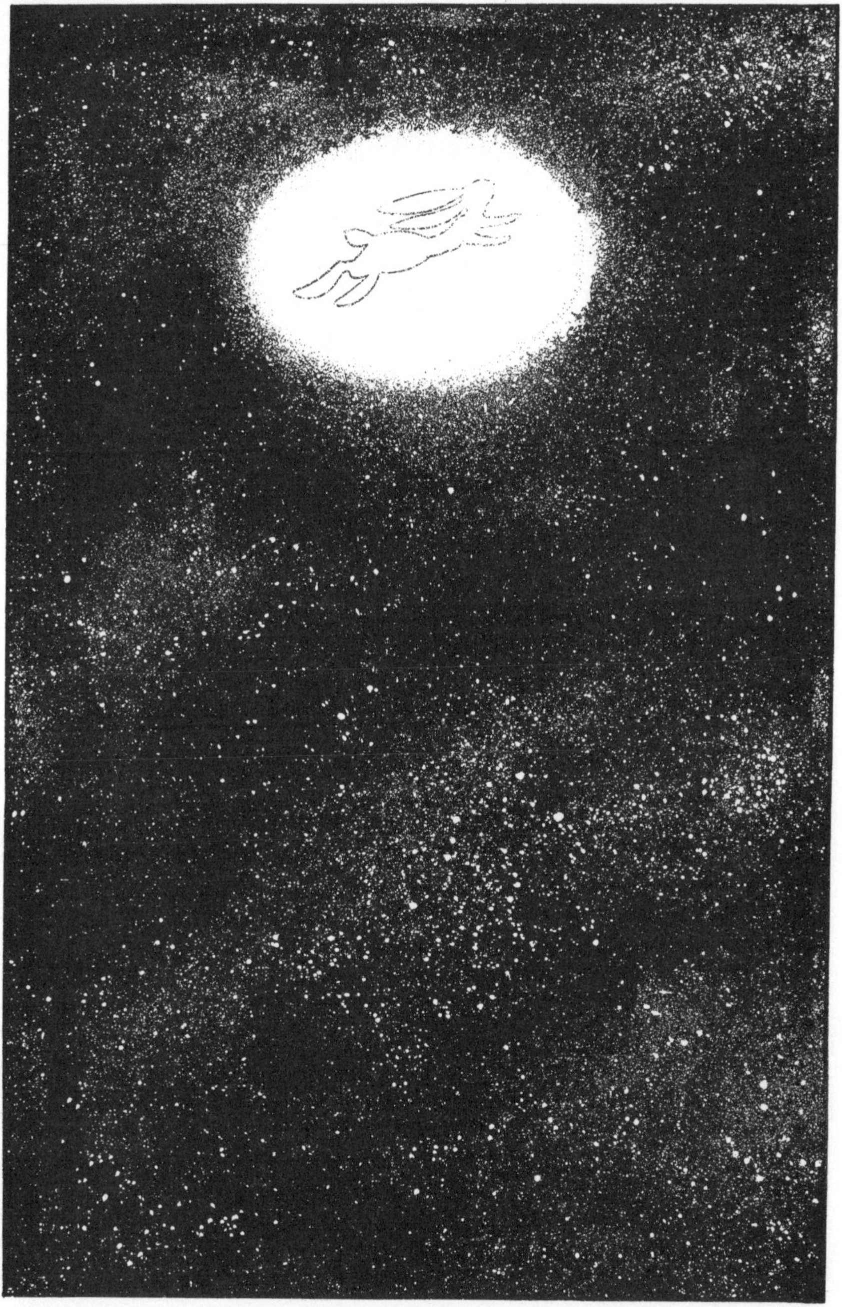

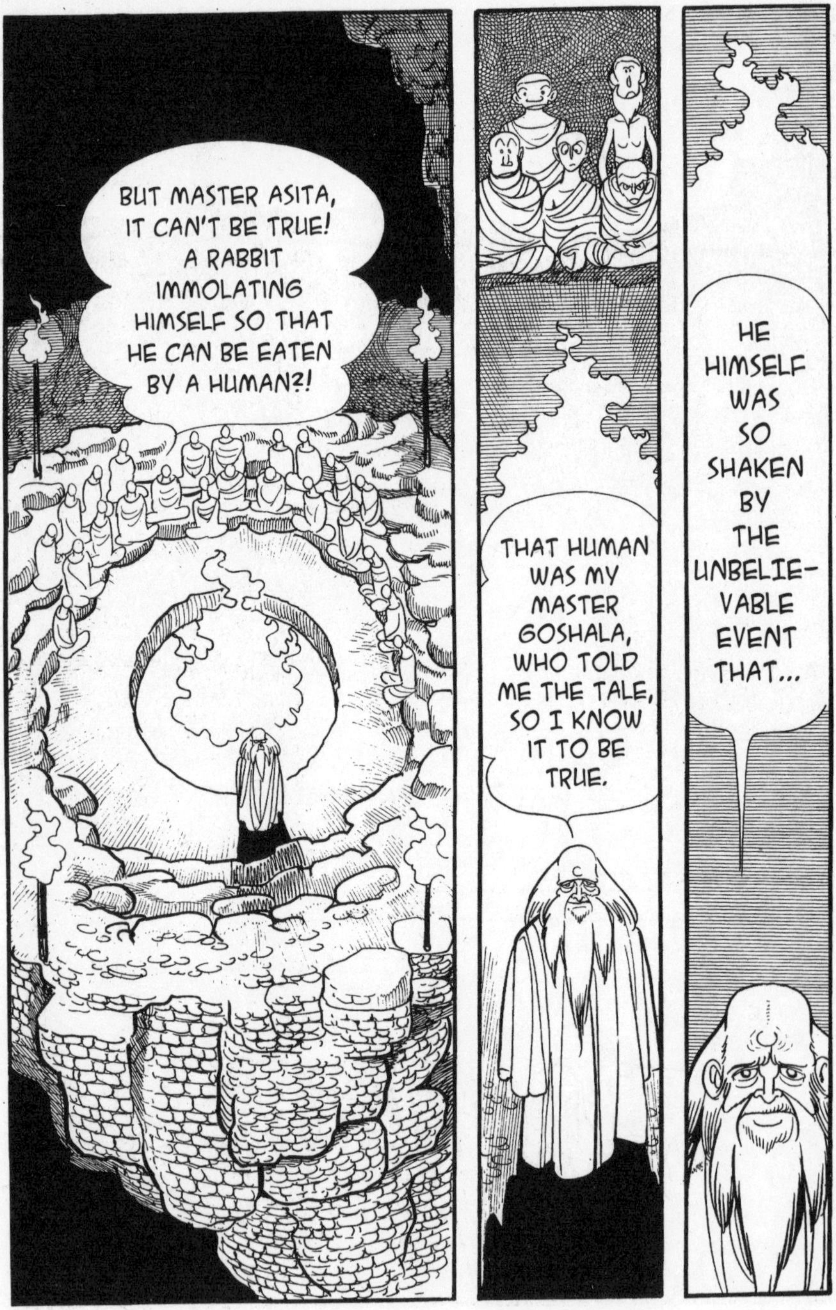
BUT MASTER ASITA, IT CAN'T BE TRUE! A RABBIT IMMOLATING HIMSELF SO THAT HE CAN BE EATEN BY A HUMAN?!
THAT HUMAN WAS MY MASTER GOSHALA, WHO TOLD ME THE TALE, SO I KNOW IT TO BE TRUE.
HE HIMSELF WAS SO SHAKEN BY THE UNBELIEVABLE EVENT THAT...

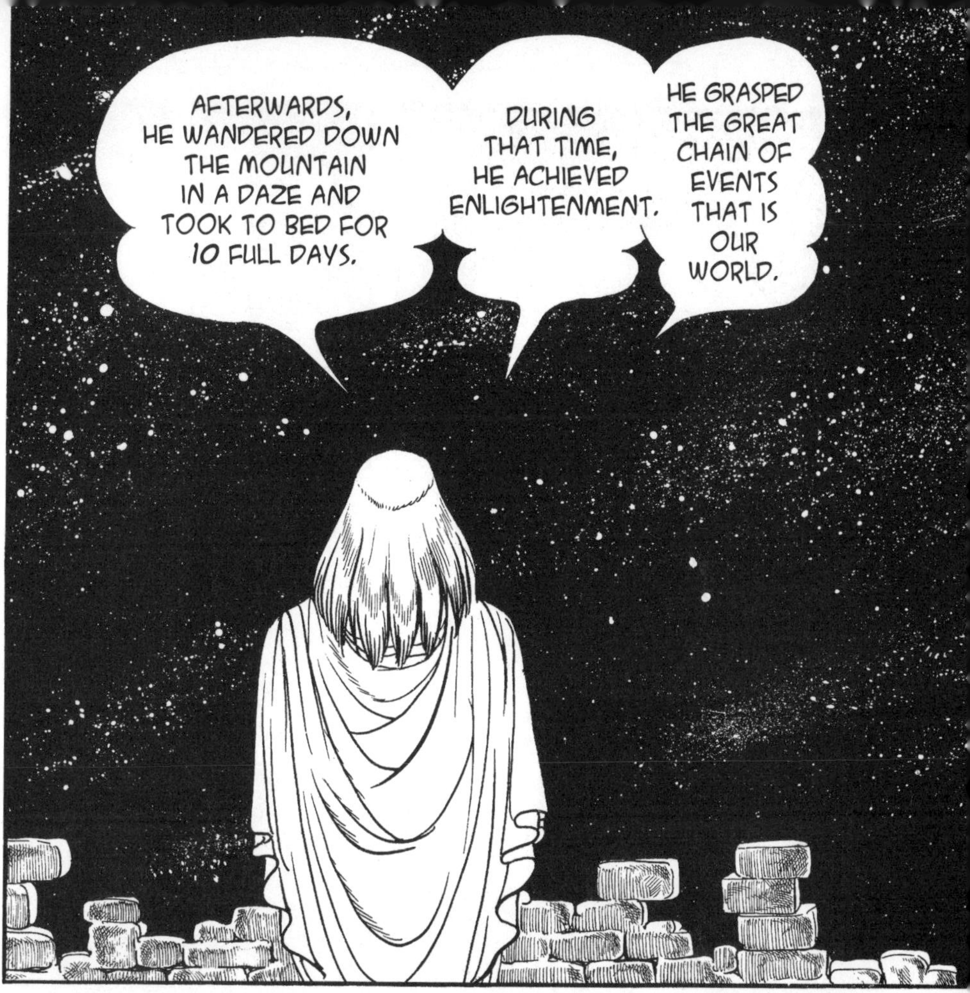
AFTERWARDS, HE WANDERED DOWN THE MOUNTAIN IN A DAZE AND TOOK TO BED FOR 10 FULL DAYS.
DURING THAT TIME, HE ACHIEVED ENLIGHTENMENT.
HE GRASPED THE GREAT CHAIN OF EVENTS THAT IS OUR WORLD.

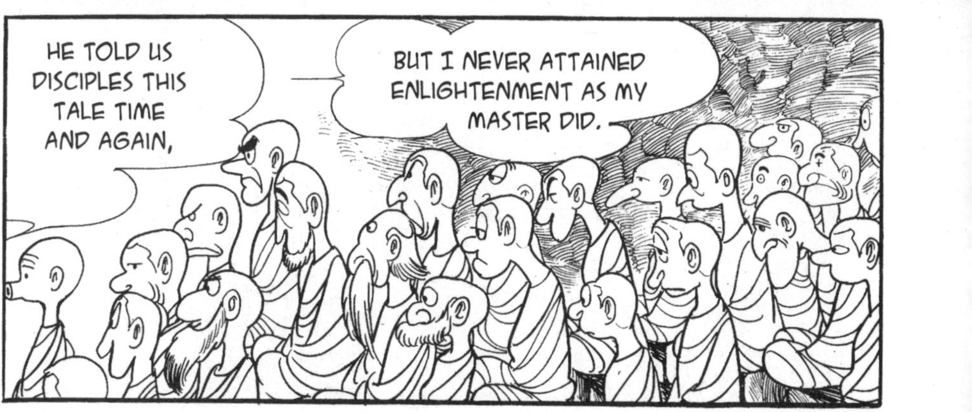
HE TOLD US DISCIPLES THIS TALE TIME AND AGAIN,
BUT I NEVER ATTAINED ENLIGHTENMENT AS MY MASTER DID.

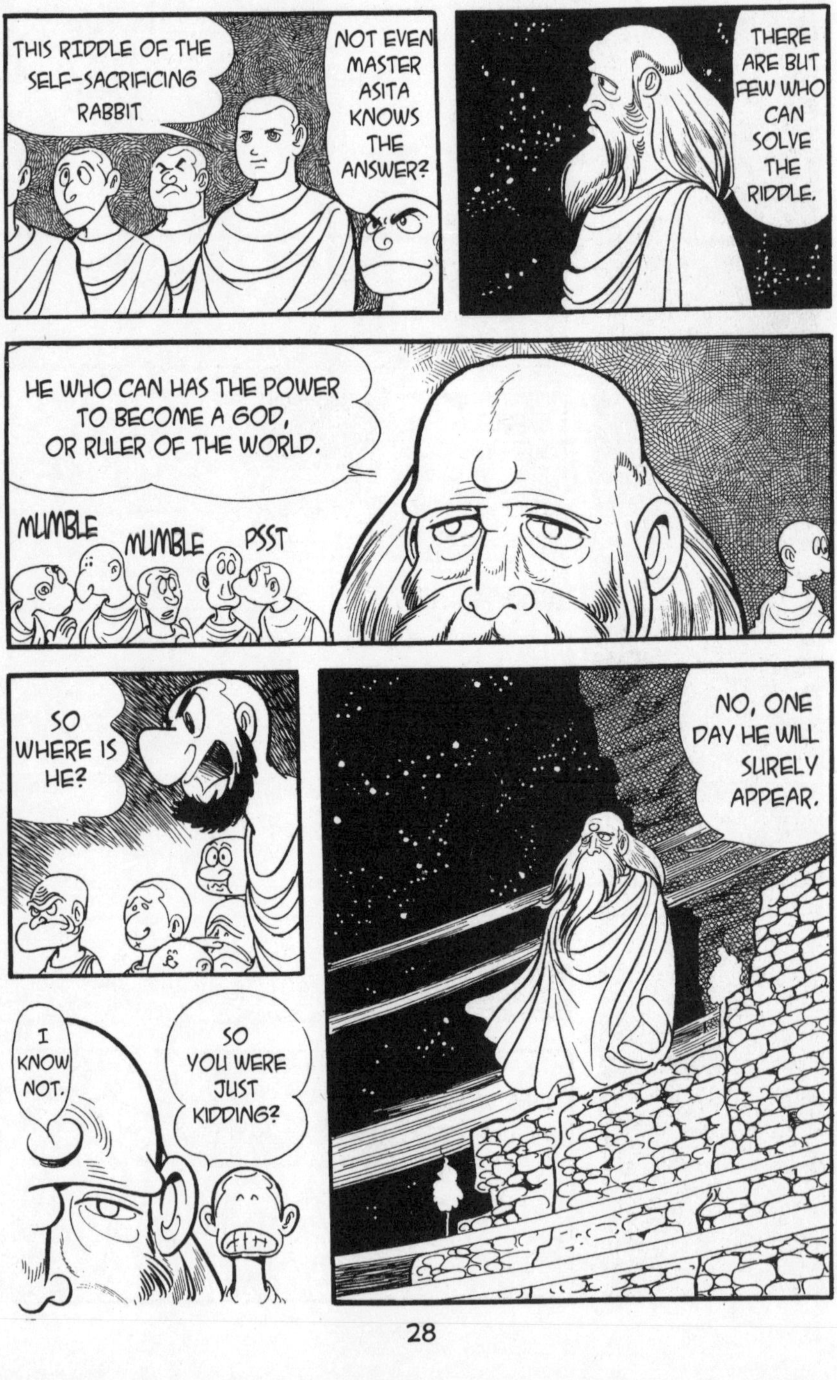
THIS RIDDLE OF THE SELF-SACRIFICING RABBIT
NOT EVEN MASTER ASITA KNOWS THE ANSWER?
THERE ARE BUT FEW WHO CAN SOLVE THE RIDDLE.
HE WHO CAN HAS THE POWER TO BECOME A GOD, OR RULER OF THE WORLD.
MUMBLE
MUMBLE
PSST
SO WHERE IS HE?
I KNOW NOT.
SO YOU WERE JUST KIDDING?
NO, ONE DAY HE WILL SURELY APPEAR.

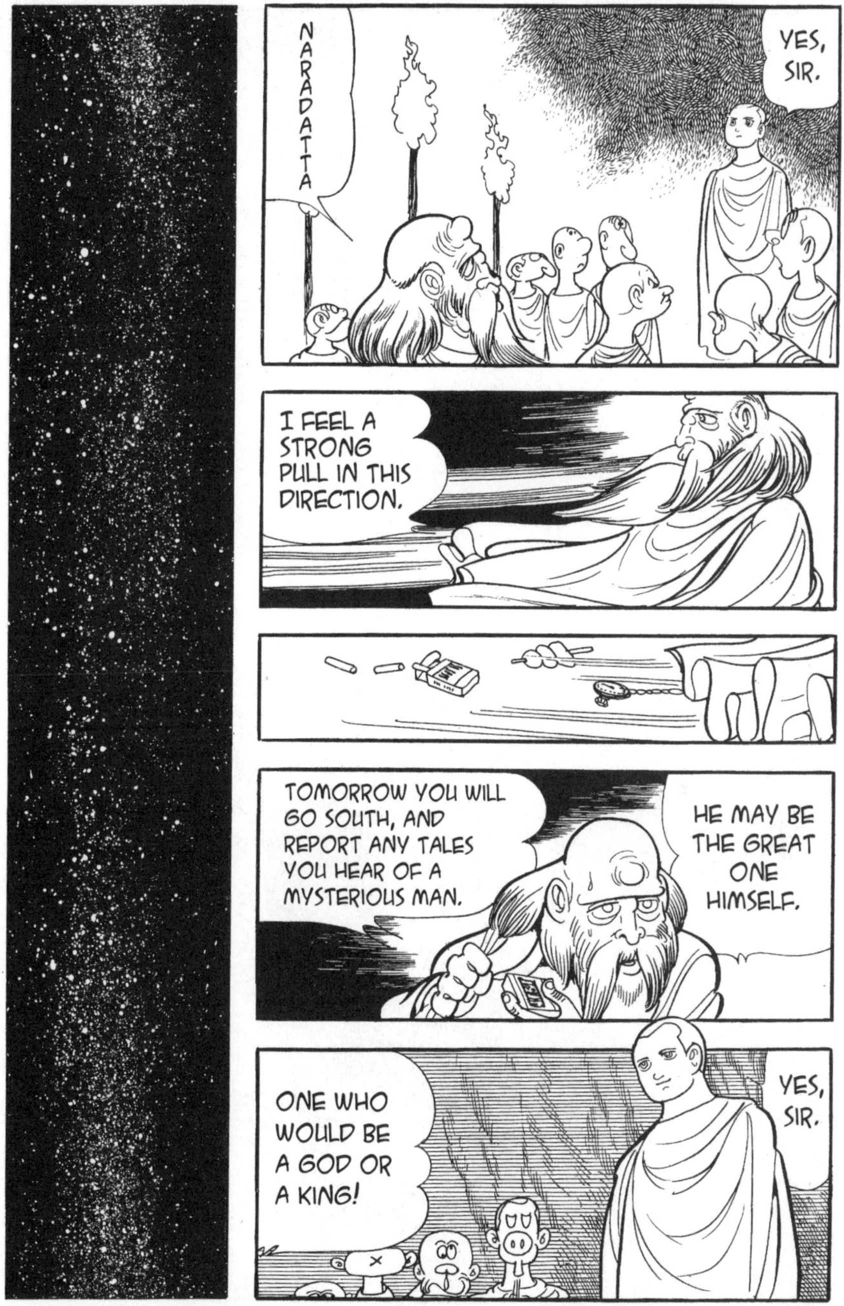
NARADATTA
YES, SIR.
I FEEL A STRONG PULL IN THIS DIRECTION.
TOMORROW YOU WILL GO SOUTH, AND REPORT ANY TALES YOU HEAR OF A MYSTERIOUS MAN.
HE MAY BE THE GREAT ONE HIMSELF.
ONE WHO WOULD BE A GOD OR A KING!
YES, SIR.

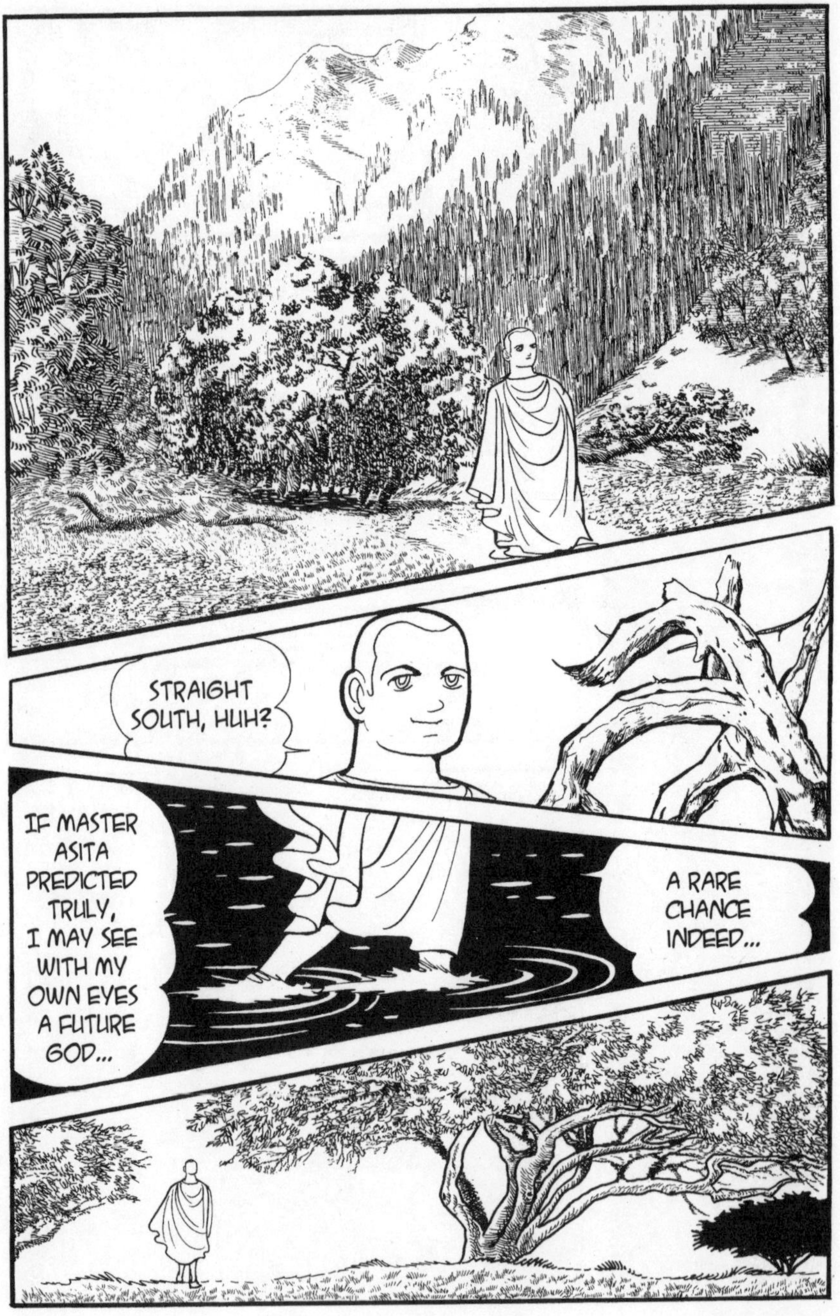
STRAIGHT SOUTH, HUH?
IF MASTER ASITA PREDICTED TRULY, I MAY SEE WITH MY OWN EYES A FUTURE GOD...
A RARE CHANCE INDEED...

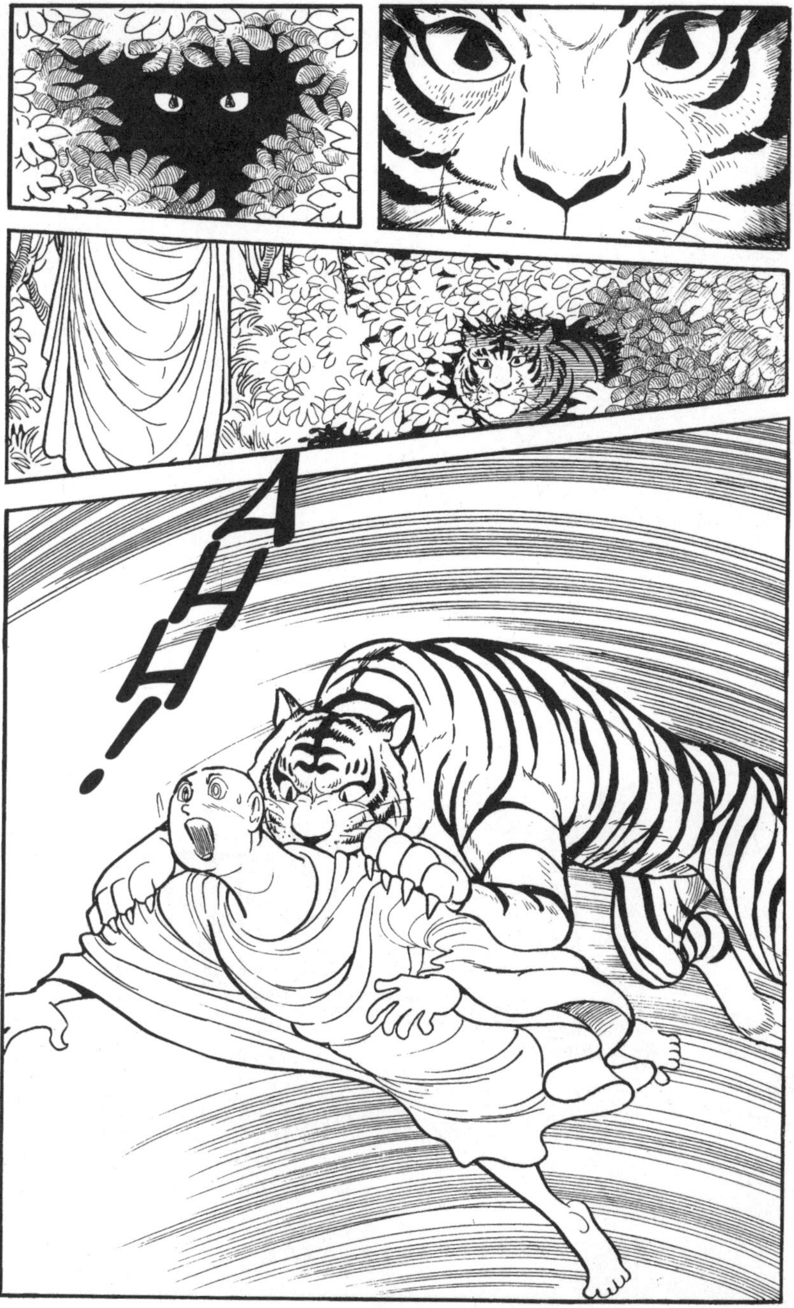
AHH!

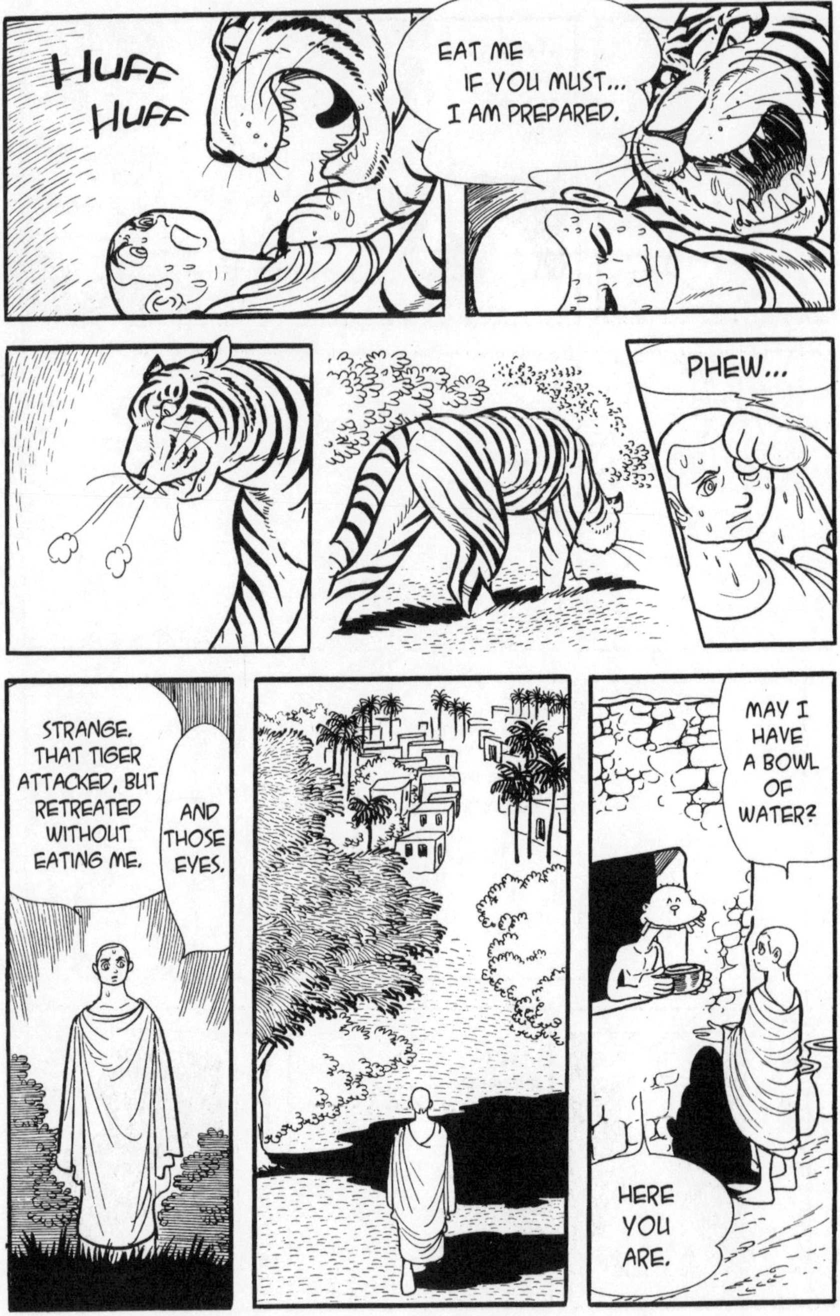
HUFF HUFF
EAT ME IF YOU MUST... I AM PREPARED.
PHEW...
STRANGE. THAT TIGER ATTACKED, BUT RETREATED WITHOUT EATING ME.
AND THOSE EYES.
MAY I HAVE A BOWL OF WATER?
HERE YOU ARE.

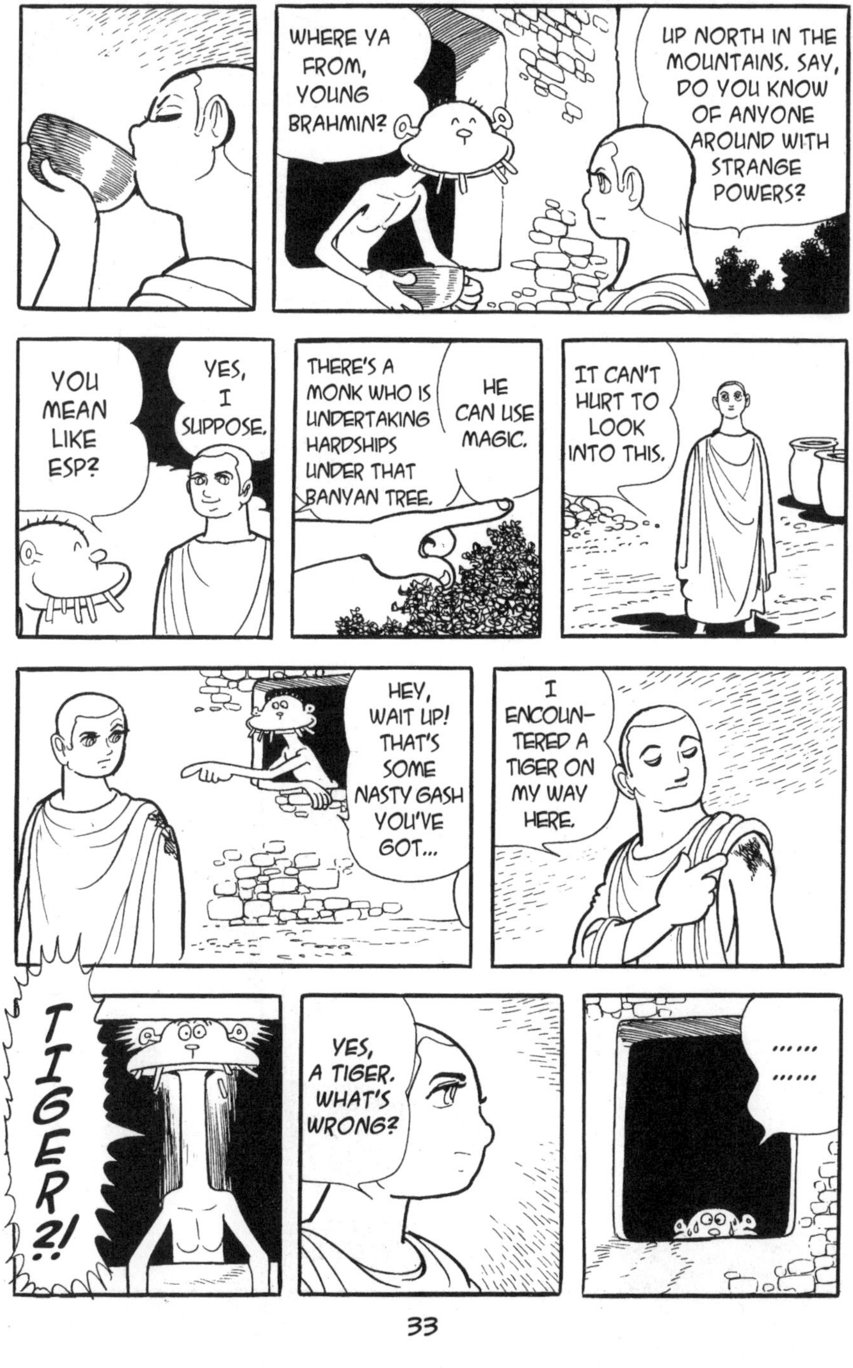
WHERE YA FROM, YOUNG BRAHMIN?
UP NORTH IN THE MOUNTAINS. SAY, DO YOU KNOW OF ANYONE AROUND WITH STRANGE POWERS?
YOU MEAN LIKE ESP?
YES, I SUPPOSE.
THERE'S A MONK WHO IS UNDERTAKING HARDSHIPS UNDER THAT BANYAN TREE.
HE CAN USE MAGIC.
IT CAN'T HURT TO LOOK INTO THIS.
HEY, WAIT UP! THAT'S SOME NASTY GASH YOU'VE GOT...
I ENCOUN-TERED A TIGER ON MY WAY HERE.
TIGER?!
YES, A TIGER. WHAT'S WRONG?
......
......

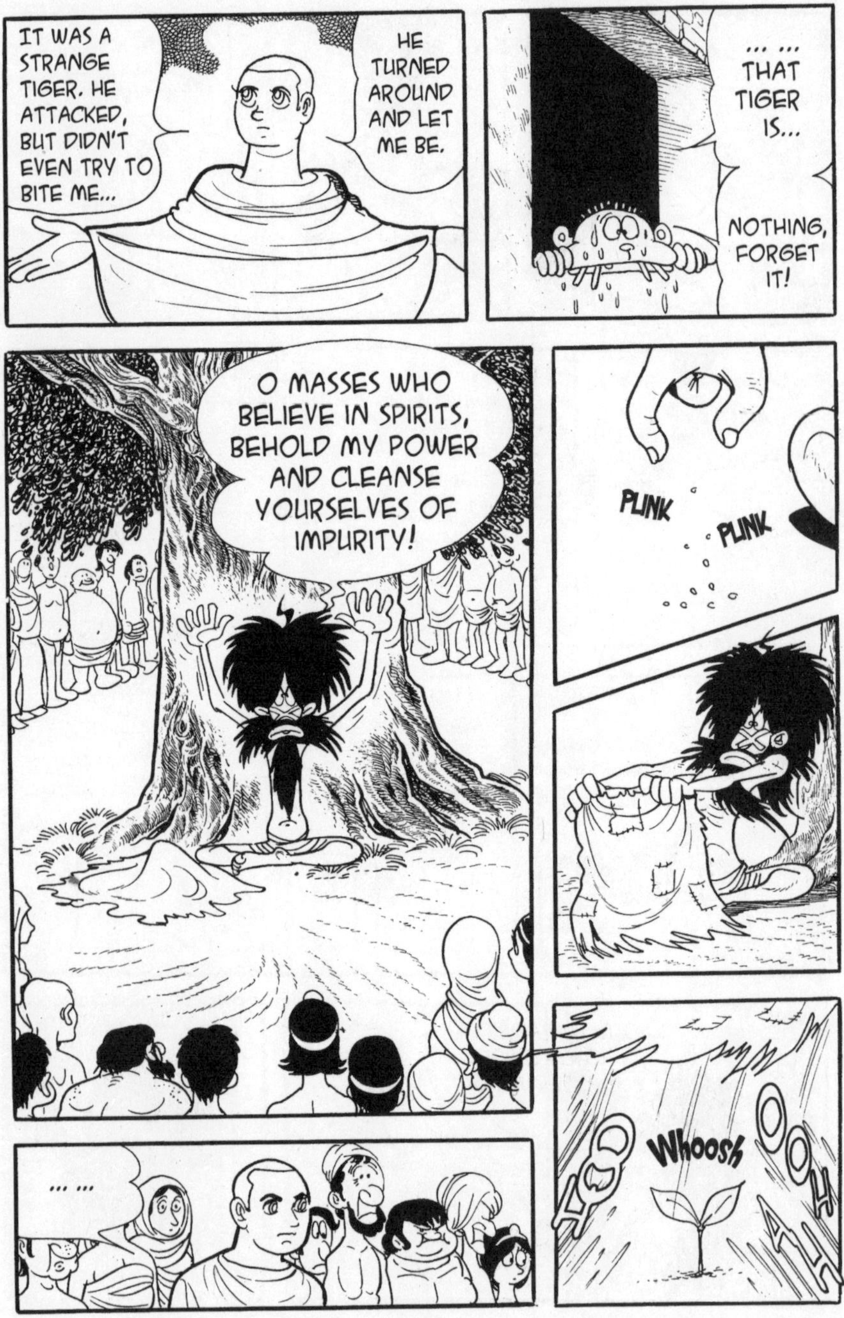
IT WAS A STRANGE TIGER. HE ATTACKED, BUT DIDN'T EVEN TRY TO BITE ME...
HE TURNED AROUND AND LET ME BE.
... ... THAT TIGER IS...
NOTHING, FORGET IT!
O MASSES WHO BELIEVE IN SPIRITS, BEHOLD MY POWER AND CLEANSE YOURSELVES OF IMPURITY!
PLINK
PLINK
Whoosh
OOOH
AAH
... ...

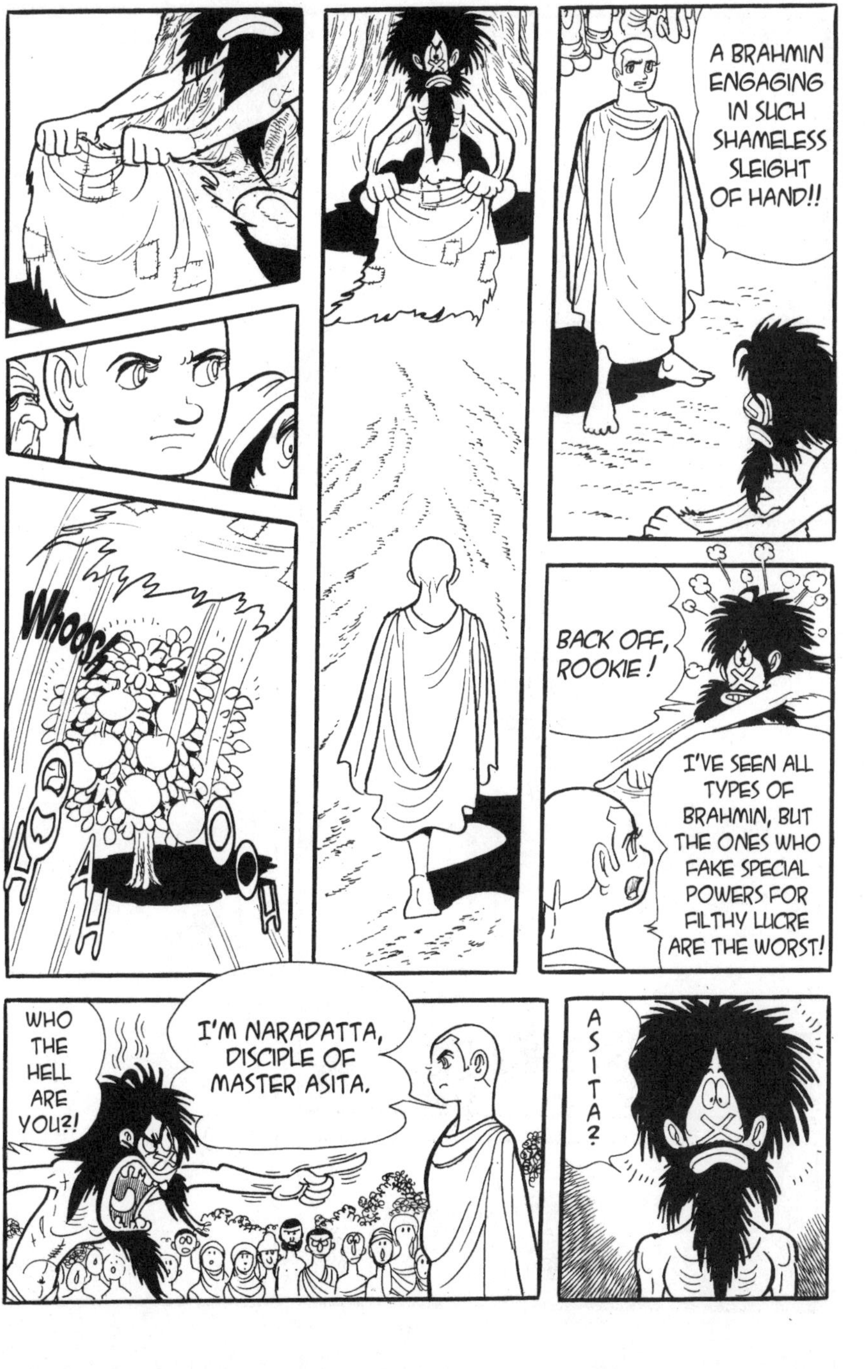
Whoosh
A BRAHMIN ENGAGING IN SUCH SHAMELESS SLEIGHT OF HAND!!
BACK OFF, ROOKIE!
I'VE SEEN ALL TYPES OF BRAHMIN, BUT THE ONES WHO FAKE SPECIAL POWERS FOR FILTHY LUCRE ARE THE WORST!
WHO THE HELL ARE YOU?!
I'M NARADATTA, DISCIPLE OF MASTER ASITA.
ASITA?

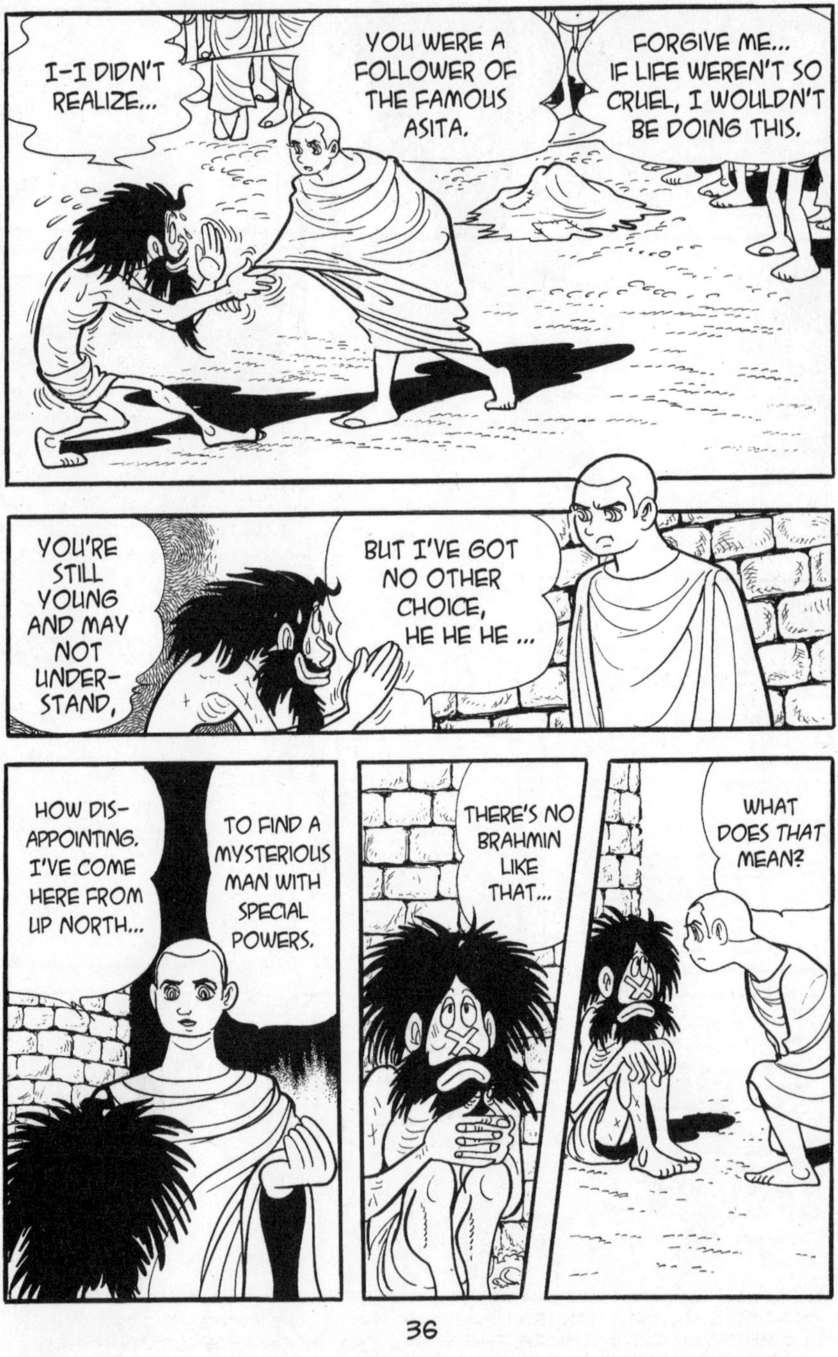

I-I DIDN'T REALIZE...
YOU WERE A FOLLOWER OF THE FAMOUS ASITA.
FORGIVE ME... IF LIFE WEREN'T SO CRUEL, I WOULDN'T BE DOING THIS.
YOU'RE STILL YOUNG AND MAY NOT UNDER-STAND,
BUT I'VE GOT NO OTHER CHOICE, HE HE HE ...
HOW DIS-APPOINTING. I'VE COME HERE FROM UP NORTH...
TO FIND A MYSTERIOUS MAN WITH SPECIAL POWERS.
THERE'S NO BRAHMIN LIKE THAT...
WHAT DOES THAT MEAN?

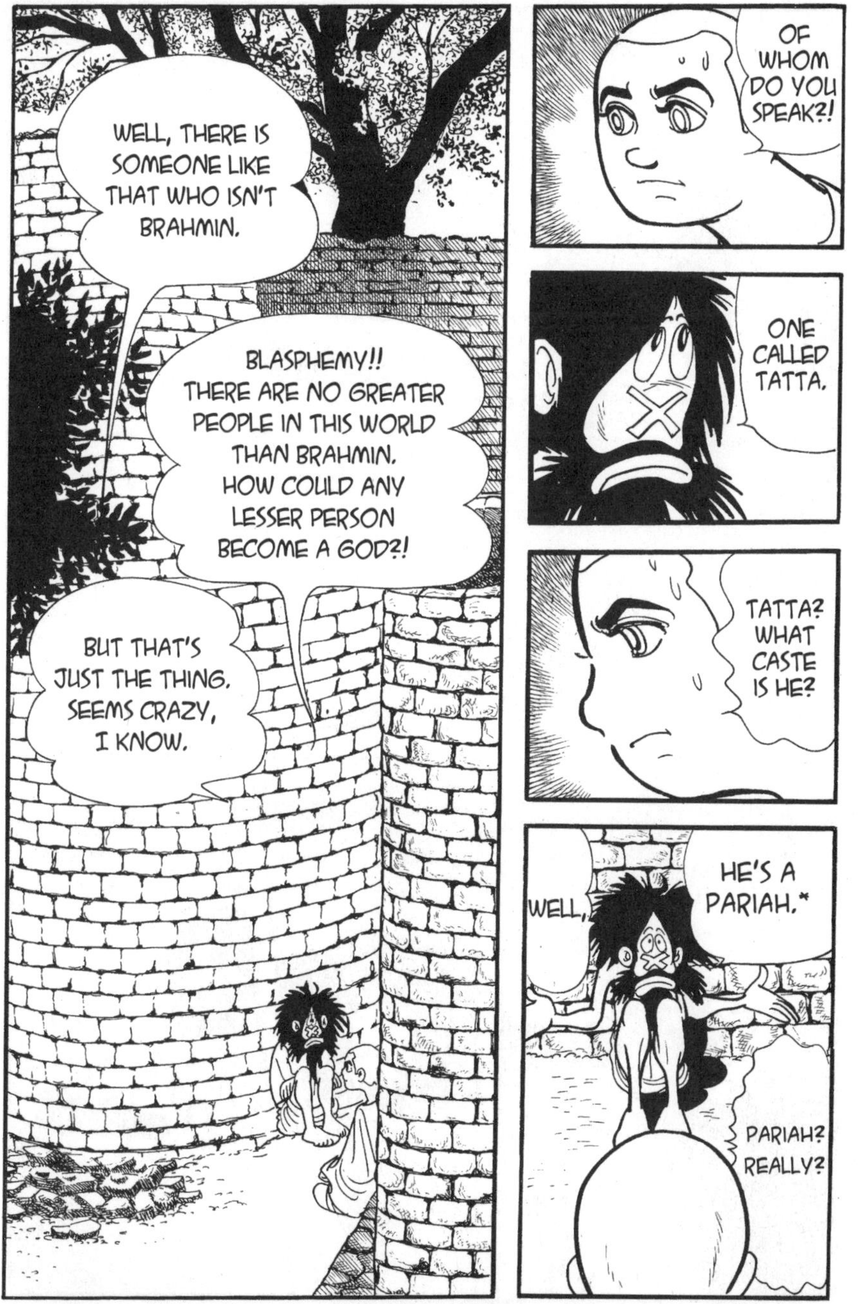
WELL, THERE IS SOMEONE LIKE THAT WHO ISN'T BRAHMIN.
BLASPHEMY!! THERE ARE NO GREATER PEOPLE IN THIS WORLD THAN BRAHMIN. HOW COULD ANY LESSER PERSON BECOME A GOD?!
BUT THAT'S JUST THE THING. SEEMS CRAZY, I KNOW.
OF WHOM DO YOU SPEAK?!
ONE CALLED TATTA.
TATTA? WHAT CASTE IS HE?
WELL,
HE'S A PARIAH.*
PARIAH? REALLY?

*THESE OUTCASTS RANKED LOWEST IN THE CLASS SYSTEM OF THE TIME, LOWER EVEN THAN SHUDRA, THE SLAVE CASTE. CONSIDERED SUBHUMAN, PARIAHS SUFFERED TERRIBLE DISCRIMINATION.

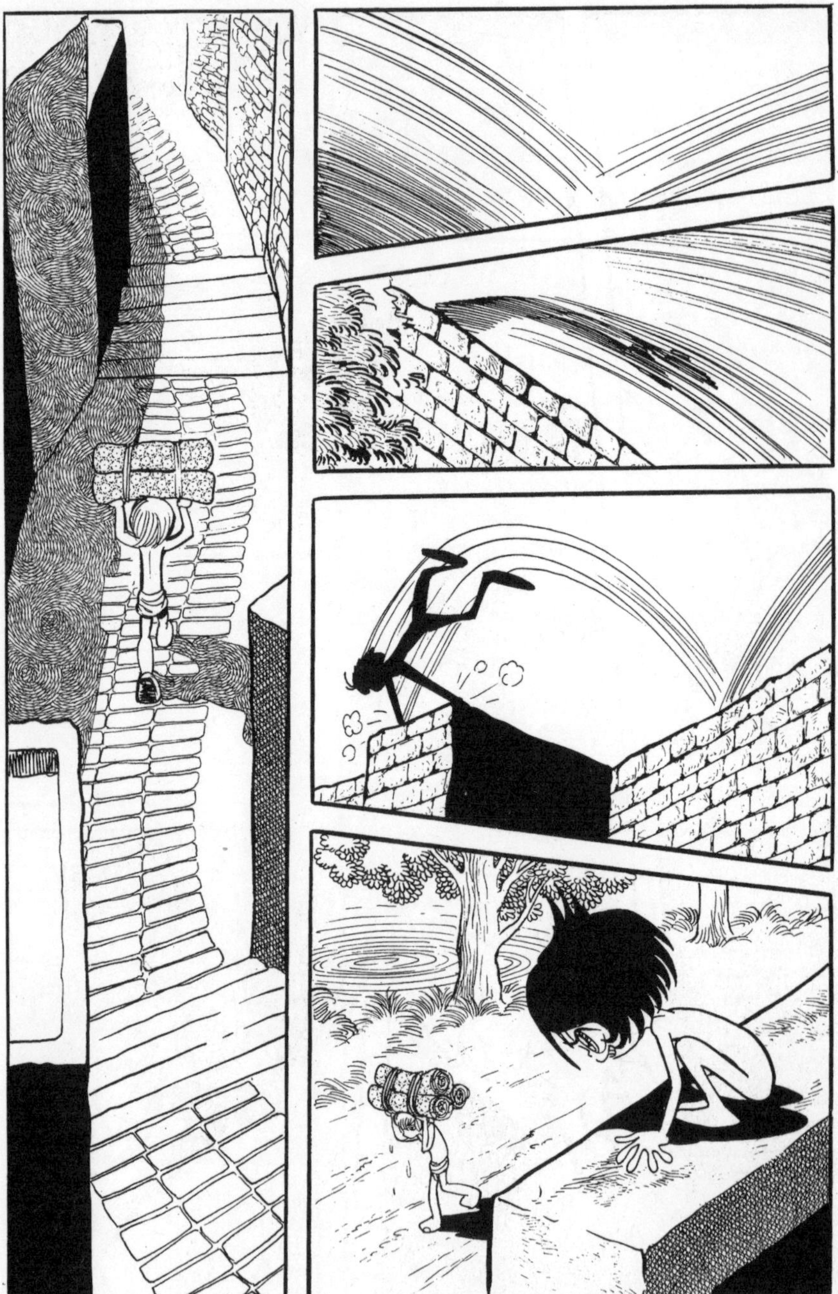

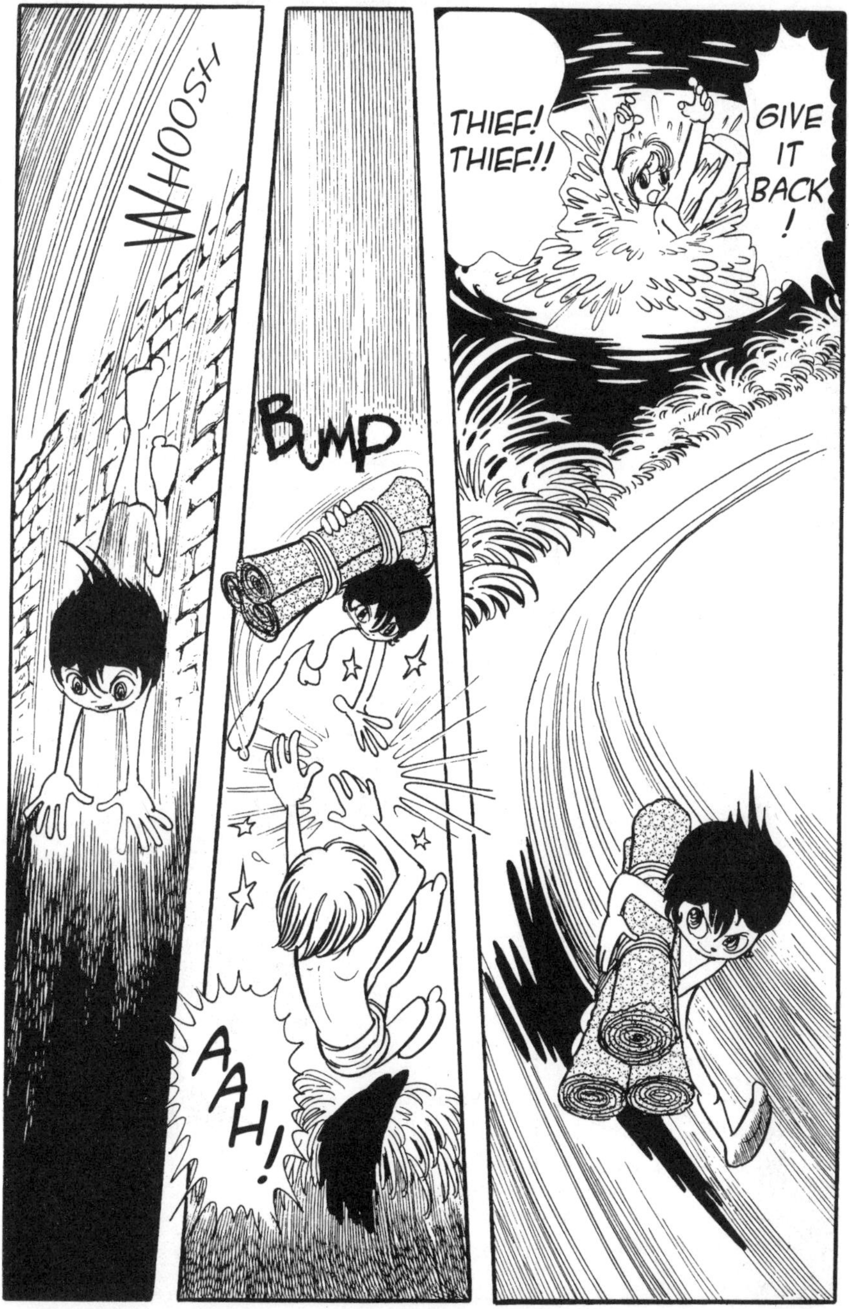
WHOOSH
BUMP
AAH!
THIEF! THIEF!!
GIVE IT BACK!

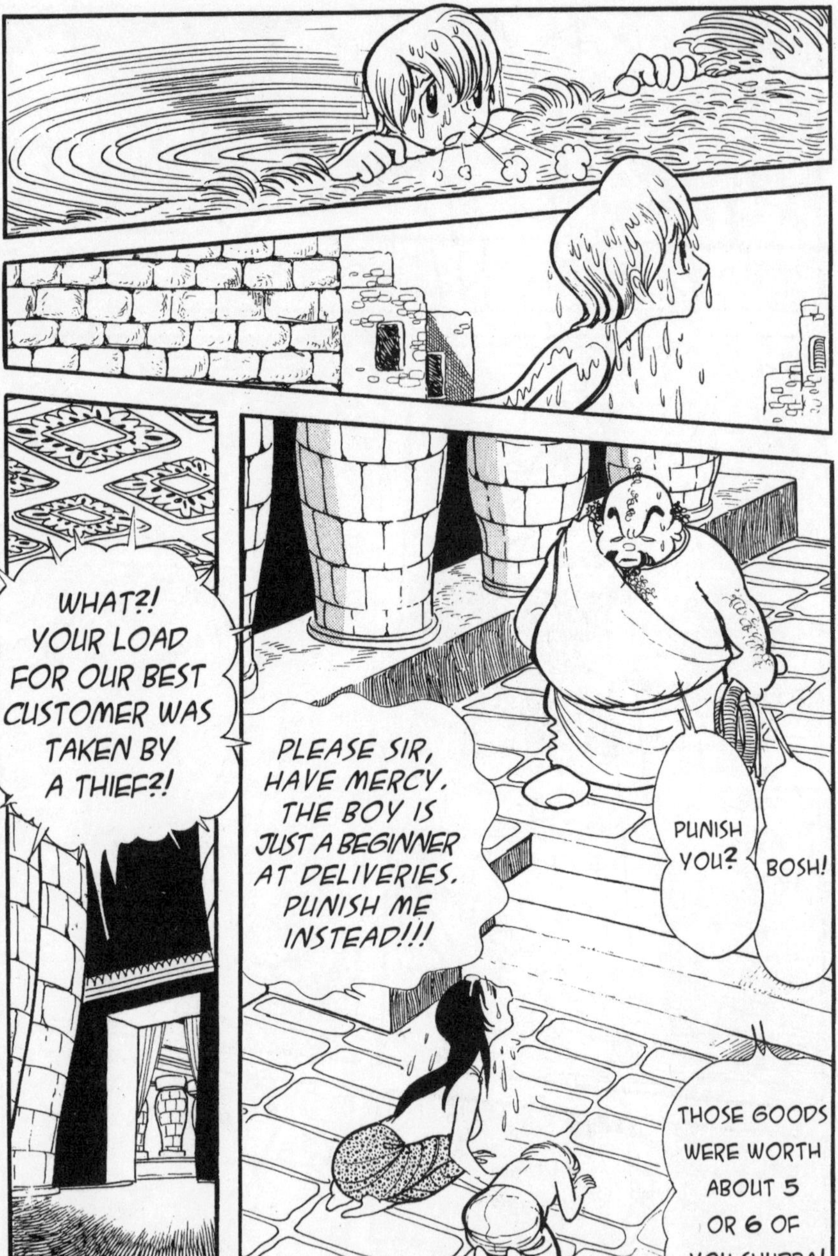
WHAT?! YOUR LOAD FOR OUR BEST CUSTOMER WAS TAKEN BY A THIEF?!
PLEASE SIR, HAVE MERCY. THE BOY IS JUST A BEGINNER AT DELIVERIES. PUNISH ME INSTEAD!!!
PUNISH YOU?
BOSH!
THOSE GOODS WERE WORTH ABOUT 5 OR 6 OF YOU SHUDRA!

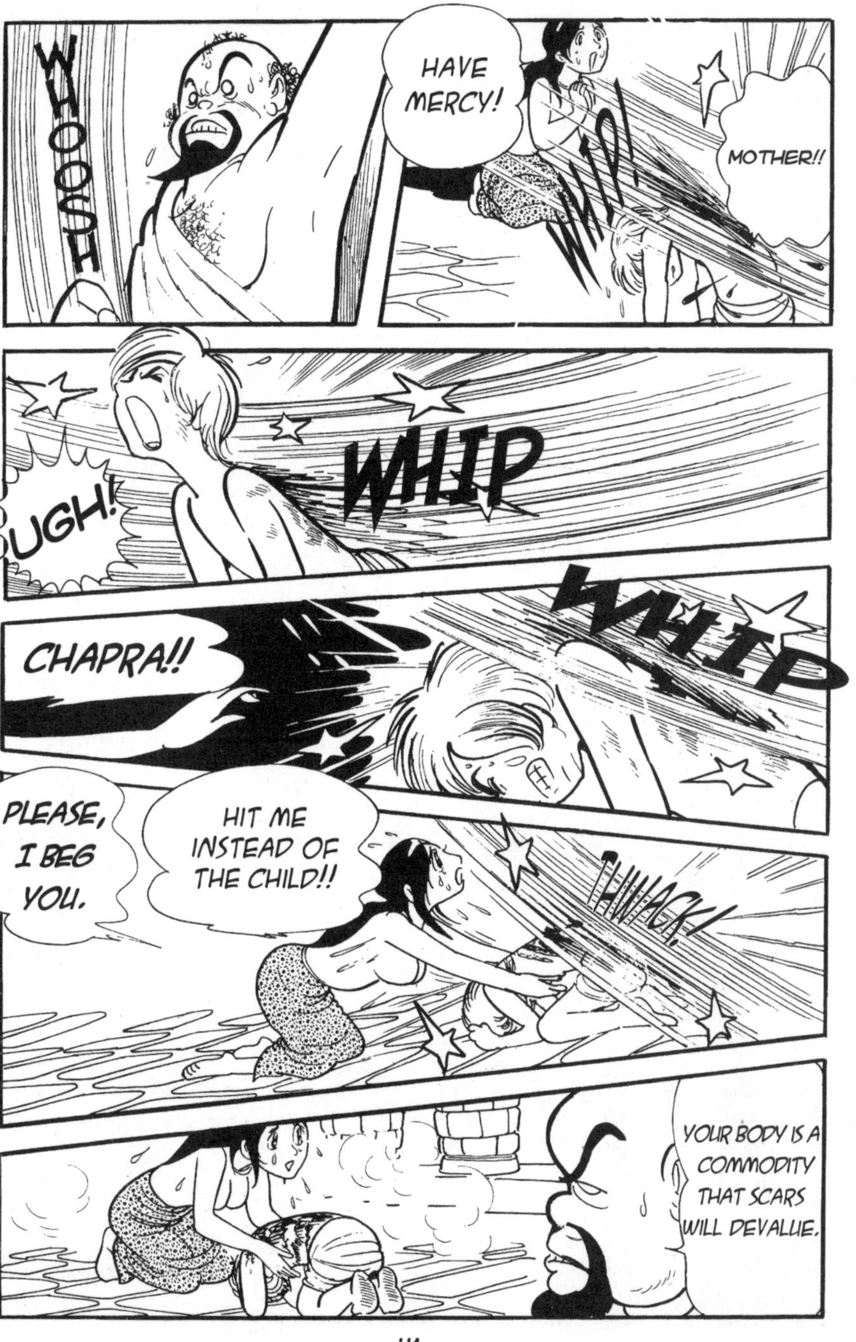
WHOOSH
HAVE MERCY!
WHIP!
MOTHER!!
UGH!
WHIP
CHAPRA!!
WHIP
PLEASE, I BEG YOU.
HIT ME INSTEAD OF THE CHILD!!
THWACK!
YOUR BODY IS A COMMODITY THAT SCARS WILL DEVALUE.

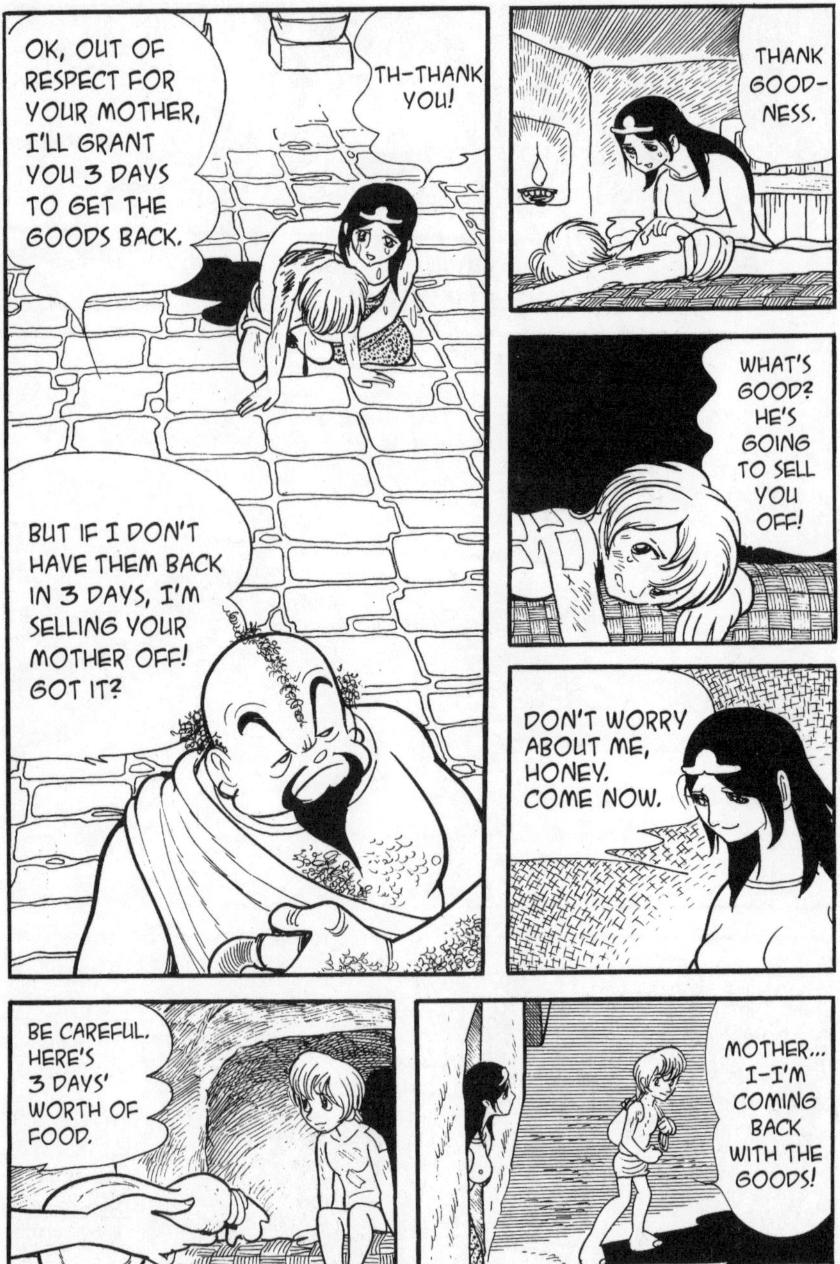

OK, OUT OF RESPECT FOR YOUR MOTHER, I'LL GRANT YOU 3 DAYS TO GET THE GOODS BACK.
TH-THANK YOU!
BUT IF I DON'T HAVE THEM BACK IN 3 DAYS, I'M SELLING YOUR MOTHER OFF! GOT IT?
THANK GOOD-NESS.
WHAT'S GOOD? HE'S GOING TO SELL YOU OFF!
DON'T WORRY ABOUT ME, HONEY. COME NOW.
BE CAREFUL. HERE'S 3 DAYS' WORTH OF FOOD.
MOTHER... I-I'M COMING BACK WITH THE GOODS!

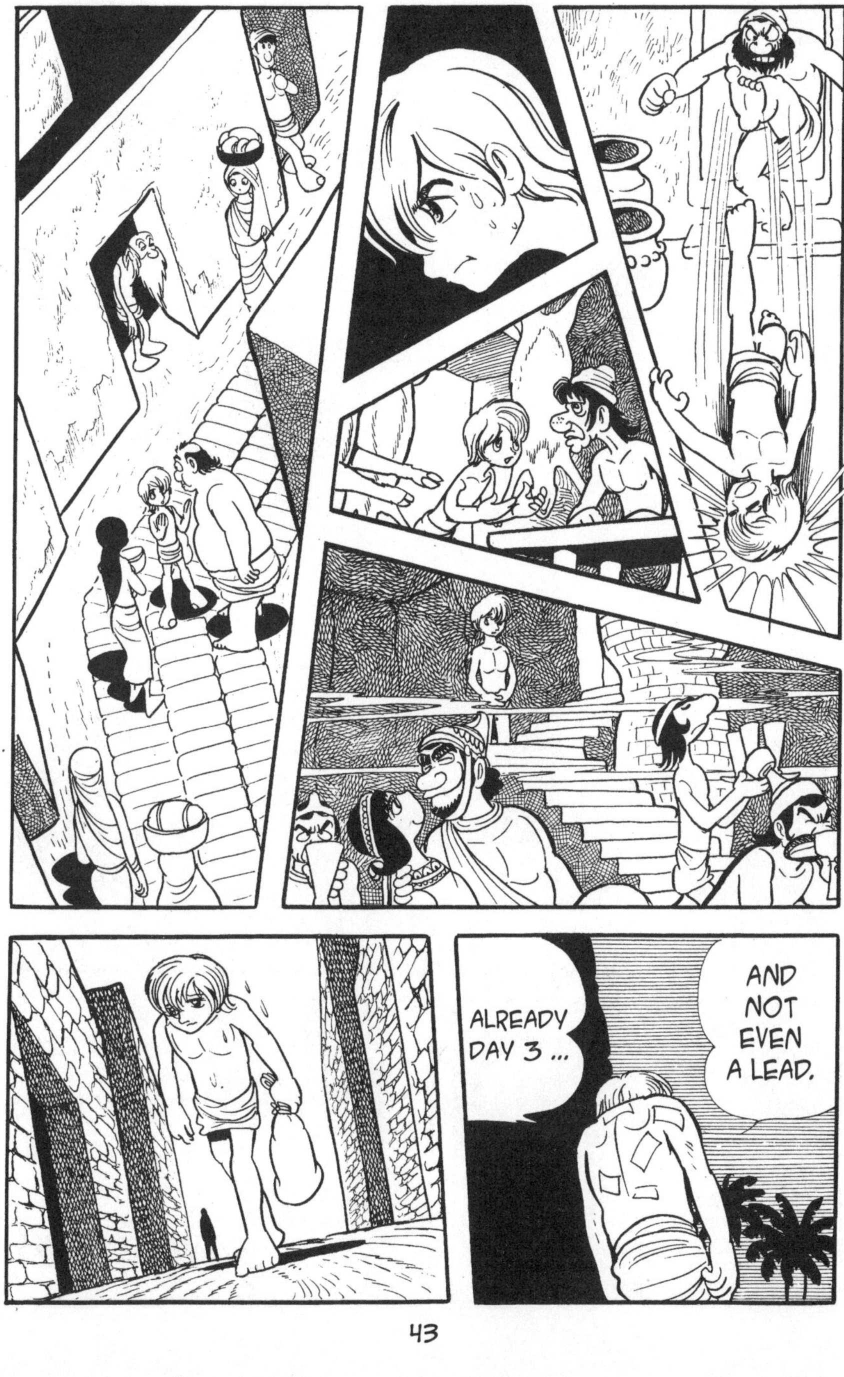
ALREADY DAY 3 ...
AND NOT EVEN A LEAD.

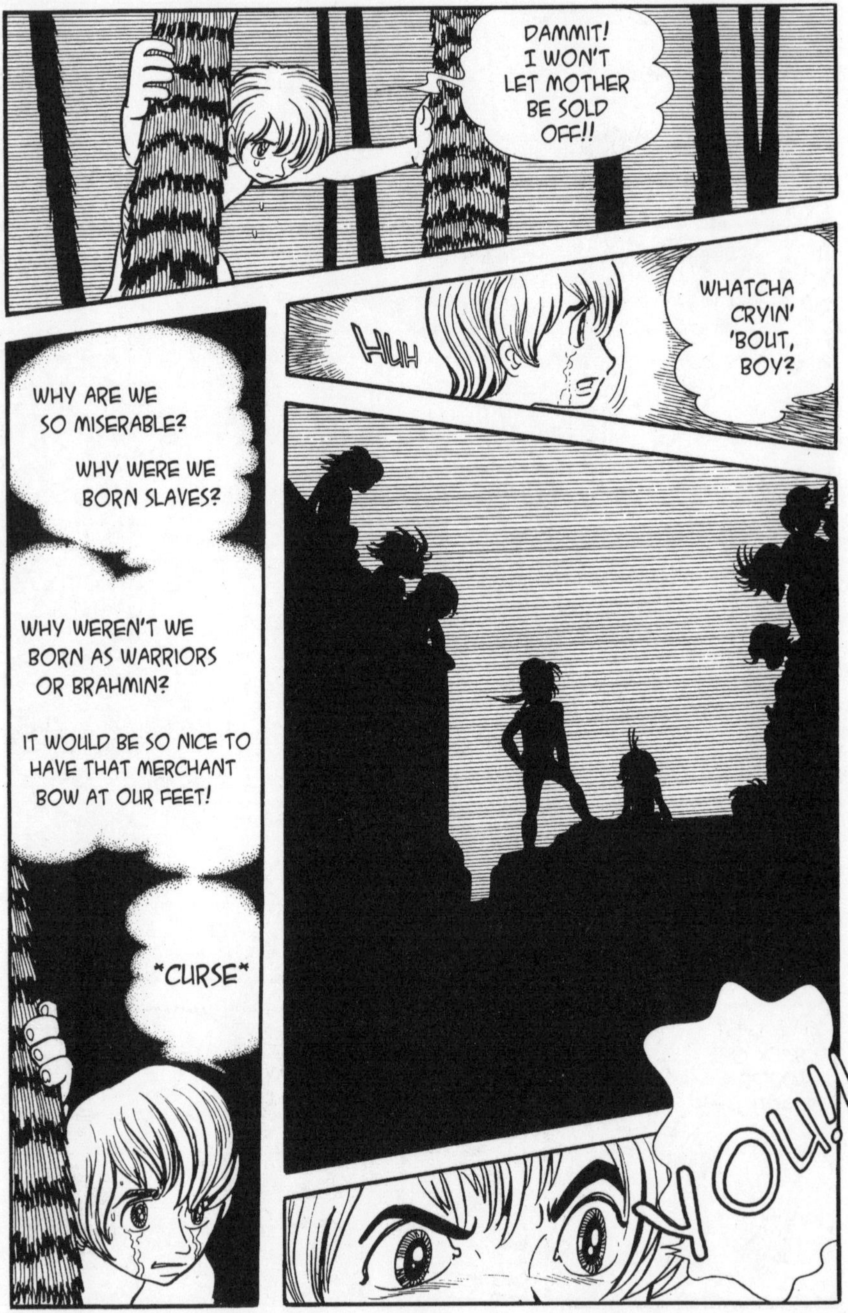
DAMMIT! I WON'T LET MOTHER BE SOLD OFF!!
HUH
WHATCHA CRYIN' 'BOUT, BOY?
WHY ARE WE SO MISERABLE?
WHY WERE WE BORN SLAVES?
WHY WEREN'T WE BORN AS WARRIORS OR BRAHMIN?
IT WOULD BE SO NICE TO HAVE THAT MERCHANT BOW AT OUR FEET!
CURSE
YOU!!

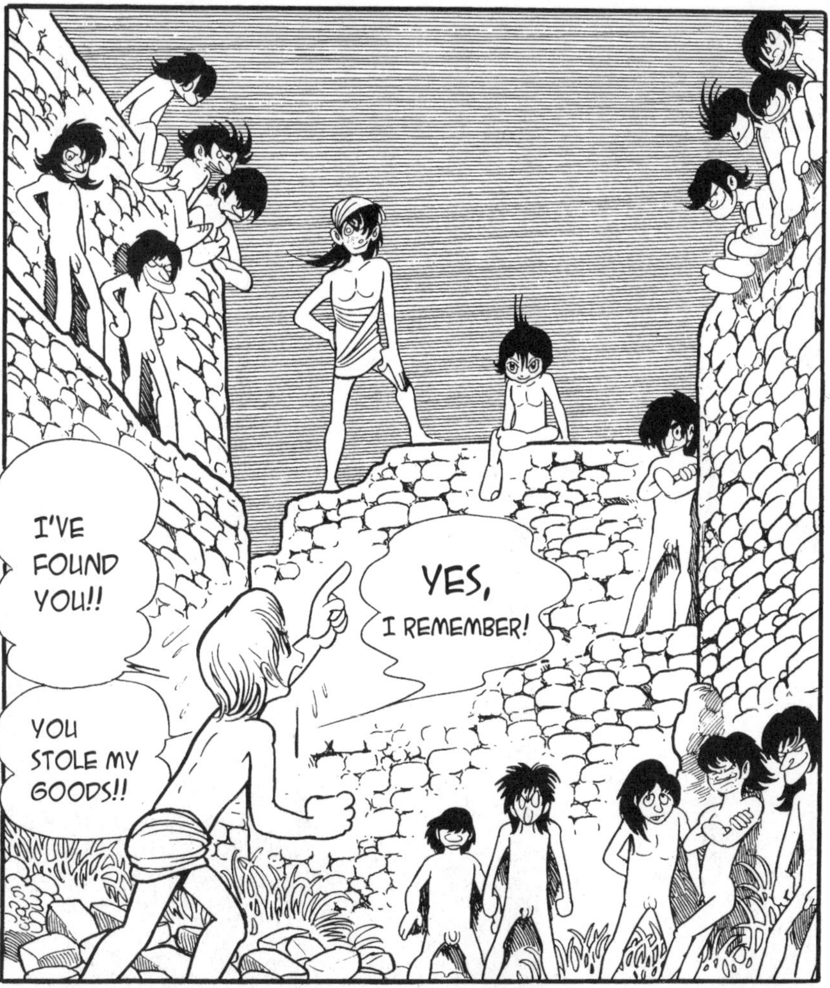
I'VE FOUND YOU!!
YES, I REMEMBER!
YOU STOLE MY GOODS!!

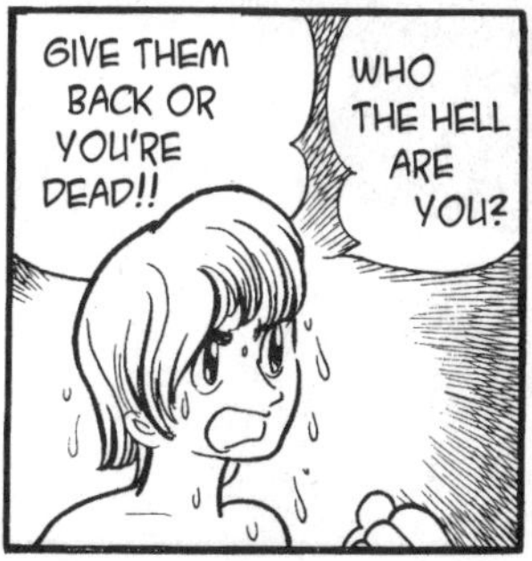
GIVE THEM BACK OR YOU'RE DEAD!!
WHO THE HELL ARE YOU?

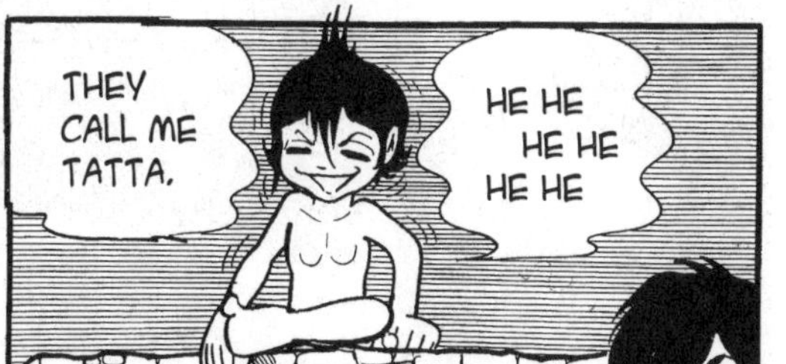
THEY CALL ME TATTA.
HE HE HE HE HE HE

WHAT'S SO FUNNY?! I'VE BEEN LOOKING FOR 3 DAYS...
IF I DON'T BRING THE STUFF BACK MY MOTHER'S GONNA BE SOLD!!

GUFFAW
HA HA HA
HEE HEE HEE

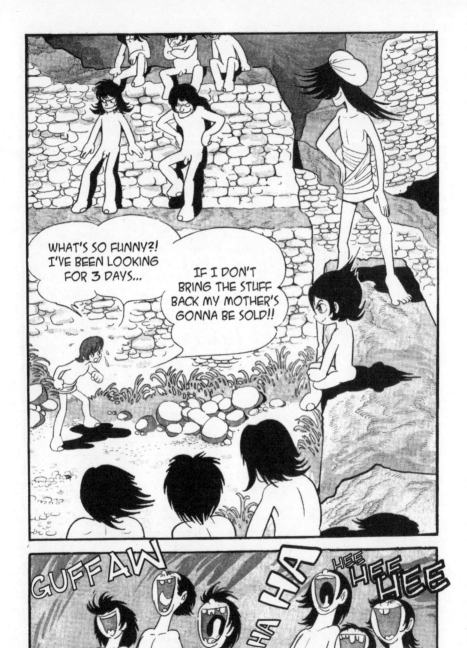

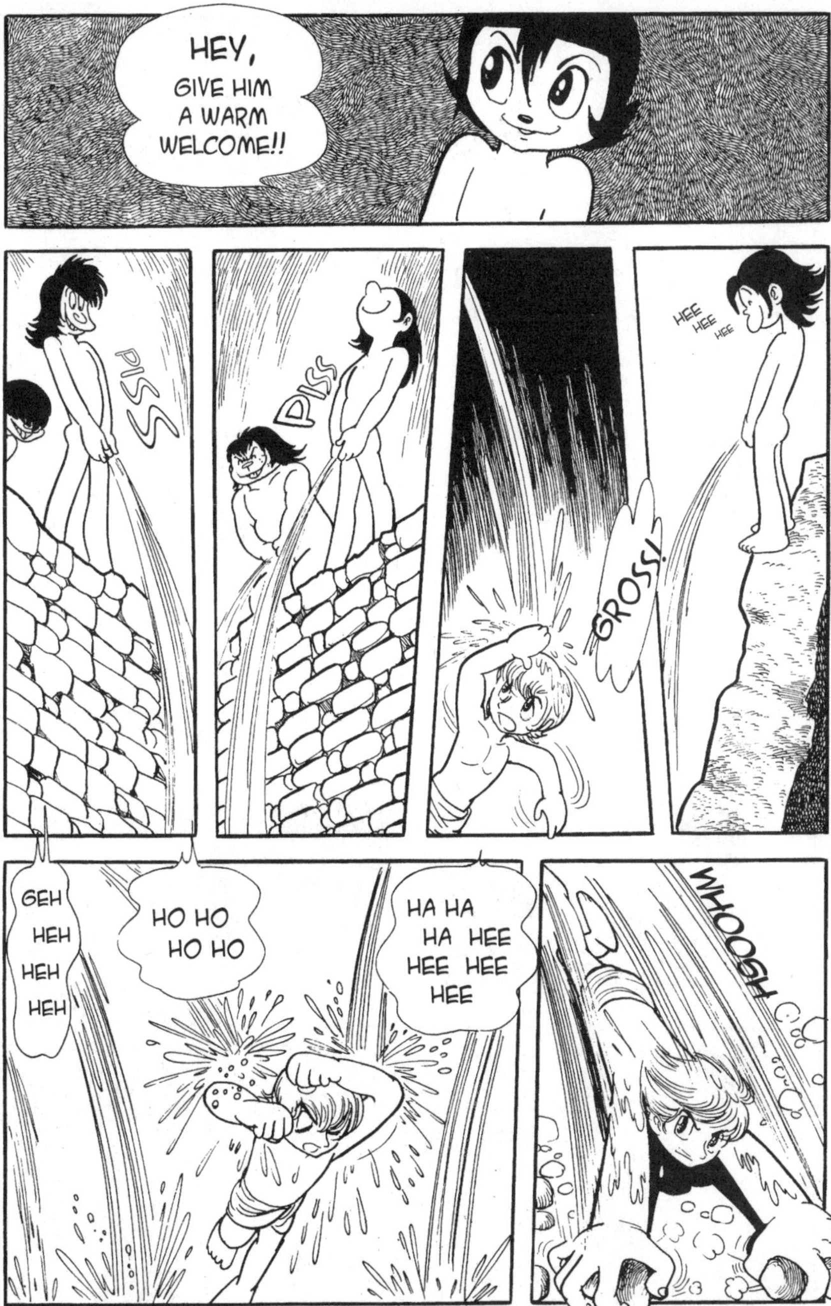
HEY, GIVE HIM A WARM WELCOME!!
PISS
PISS
GROSS!
HEE HEE HEE
GEH HEH HEH HEH
HO HO HO HO
HA HA HA HEE HEE HEE HEE
WHOOGH

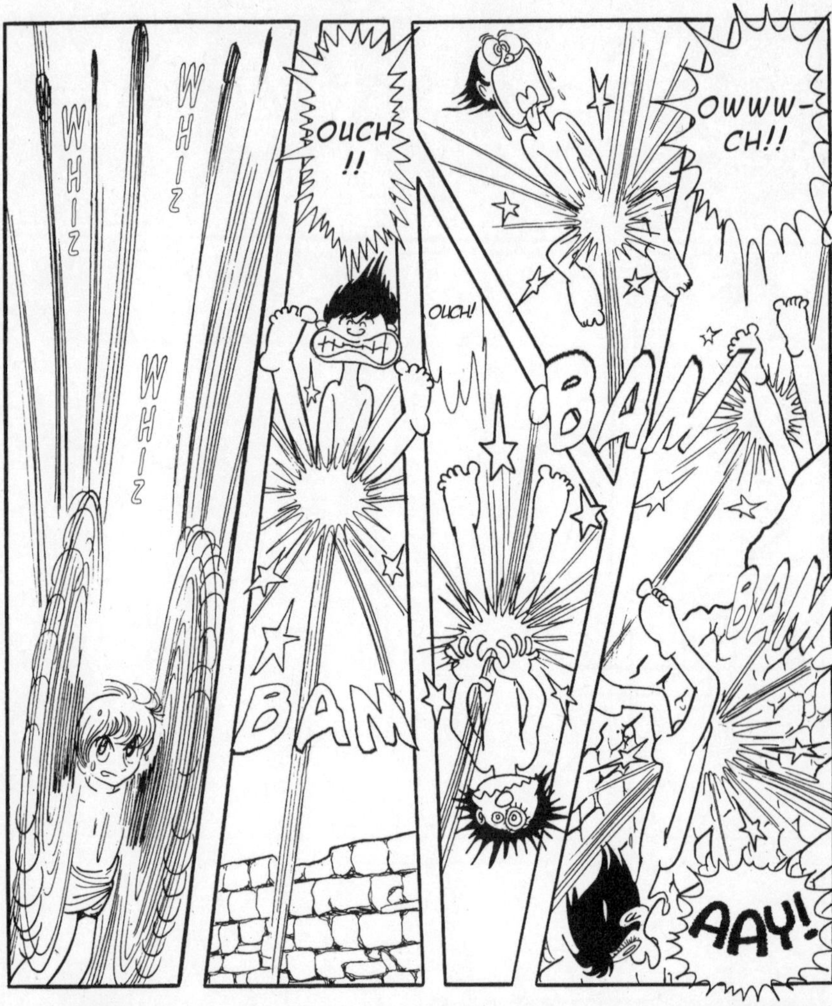
WHIZ
WHIZ
WHIZ
WHIZ
OUCH !!
BAM
OUCH!
OWWW-CH!!
BAM
BAM
AAY!

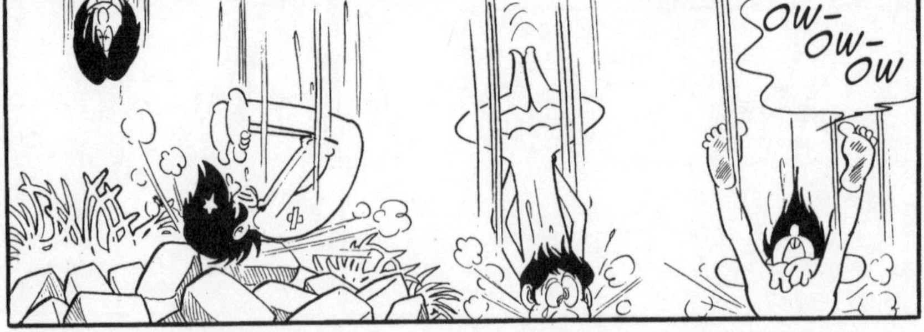
OW-OW-OW

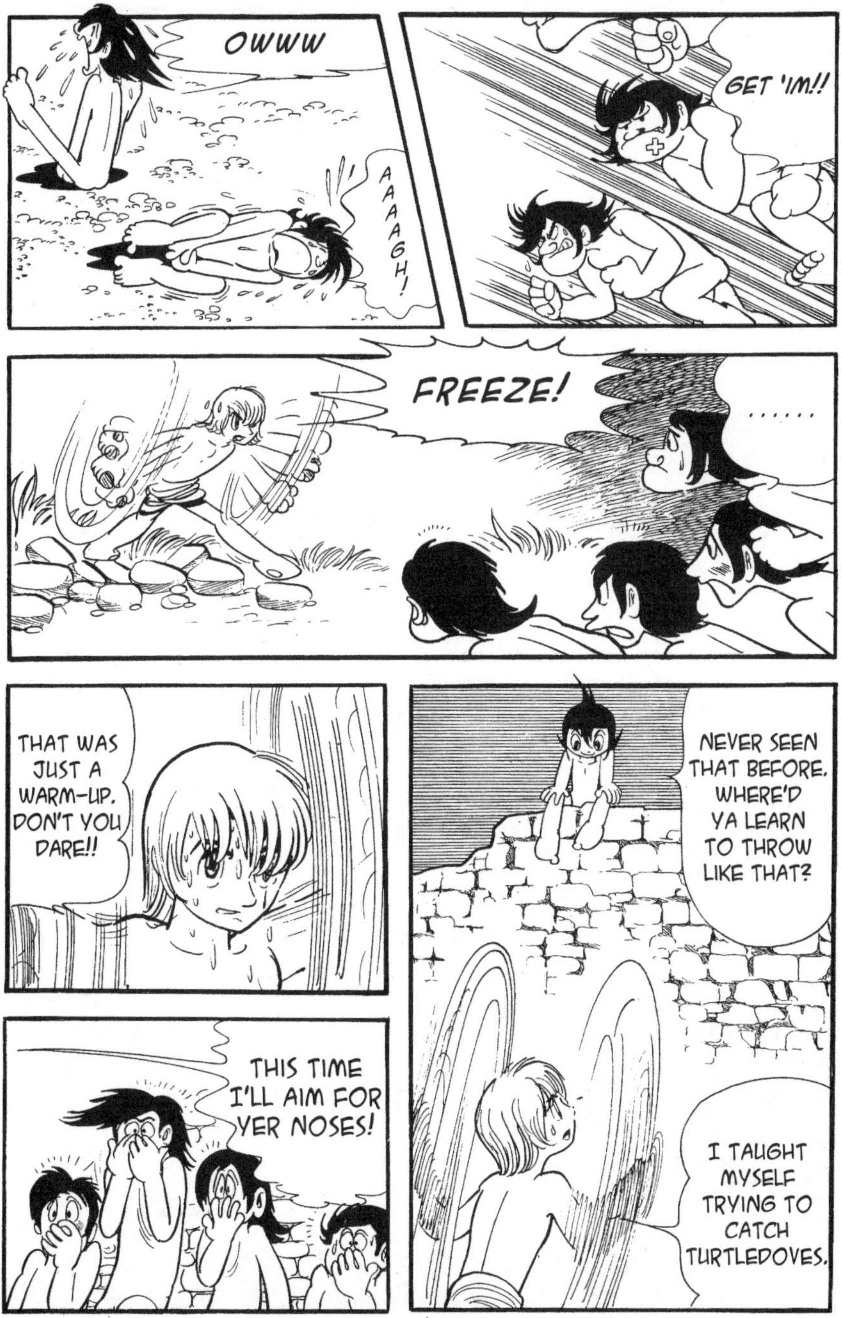
OWWW
AAAAAGH!
GET 'IM!!
FREEZE!
......
THAT WAS JUST A WARM-UP. DON'T YOU DARE!!
NEVER SEEN THAT BEFORE. WHERE'D YA LEARN TO THROW LIKE THAT?
THIS TIME I'LL AIM FOR YER NOSES!
I TAUGHT MYSELF TRYING TO CATCH TURTLEDOVES.

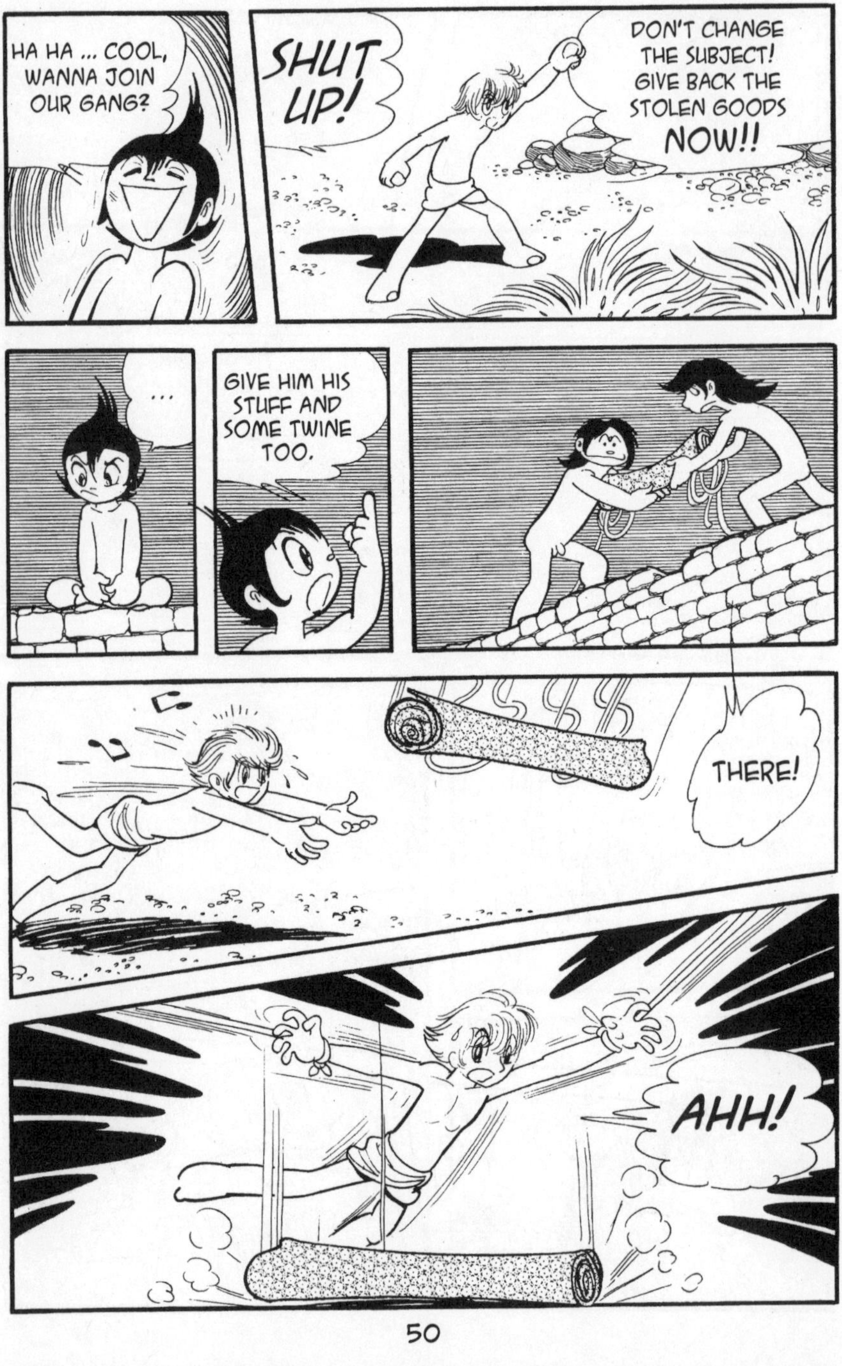
HA HA ... COOL, WANNA JOIN OUR GANG?
SHUT UP!
DON'T CHANGE THE SUBJECT! GIVE BACK THE STOLEN GOODS NOW!!
...
GIVE HIM HIS STUFF AND SOME TWINE TOO.
THERE!
AHH!

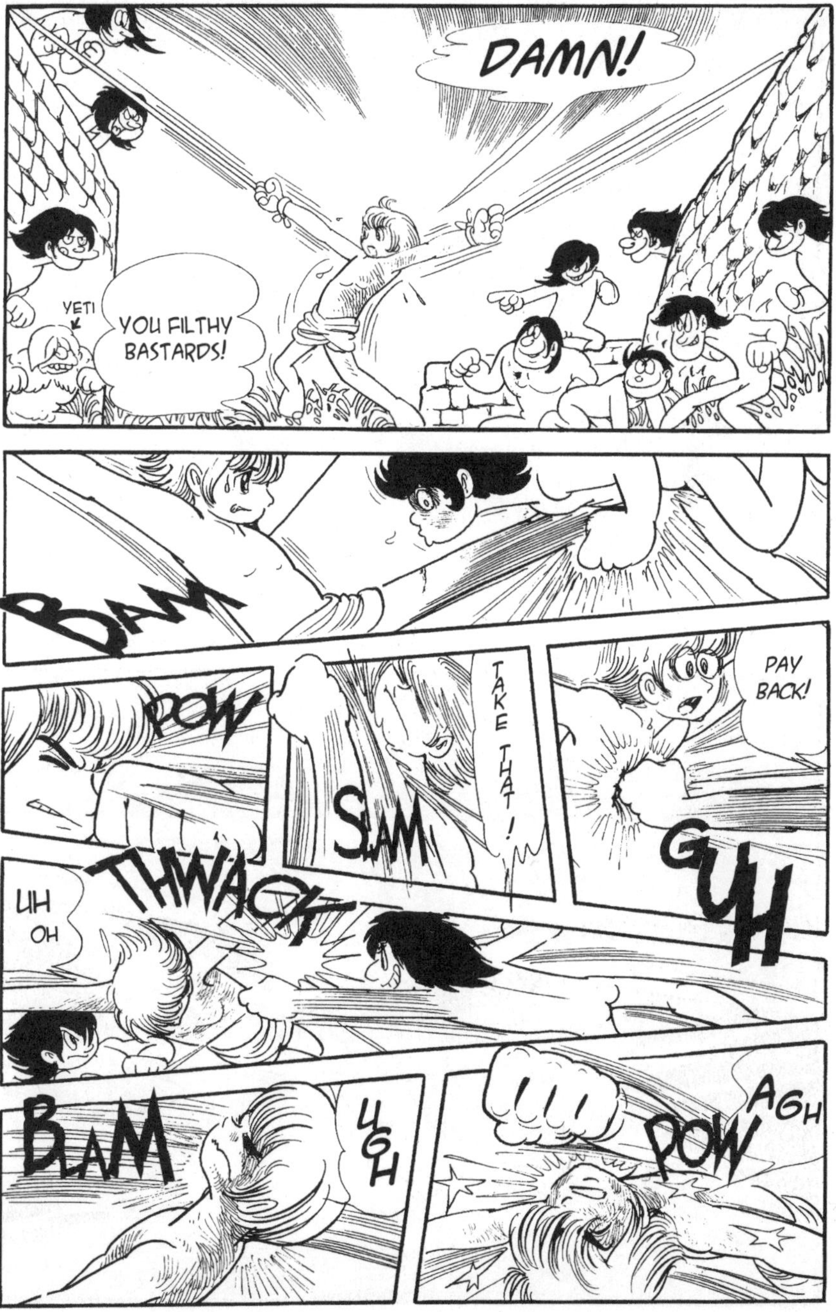
DAMN!
YETI
YOU FILTHY BASTARDS!
BAM
POW
SLAM
TAKE THAT!
PAY BACK!
GUH
UH OH
THWACK
BLAM
UGH
POW
AGH

THAT'LL DO. NO POINT IN KILLIN' HIM.

SHALL WE TOSS HIM OUT?

TAKE HIM TO MY PLACE.

HUH?

WHY NOT HANG 'IM UP IN THE STREET?

DO WHAT I SAY!!

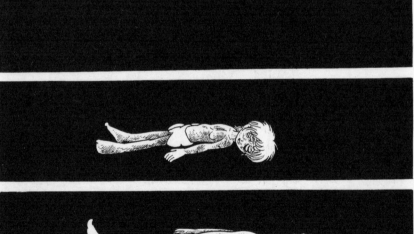

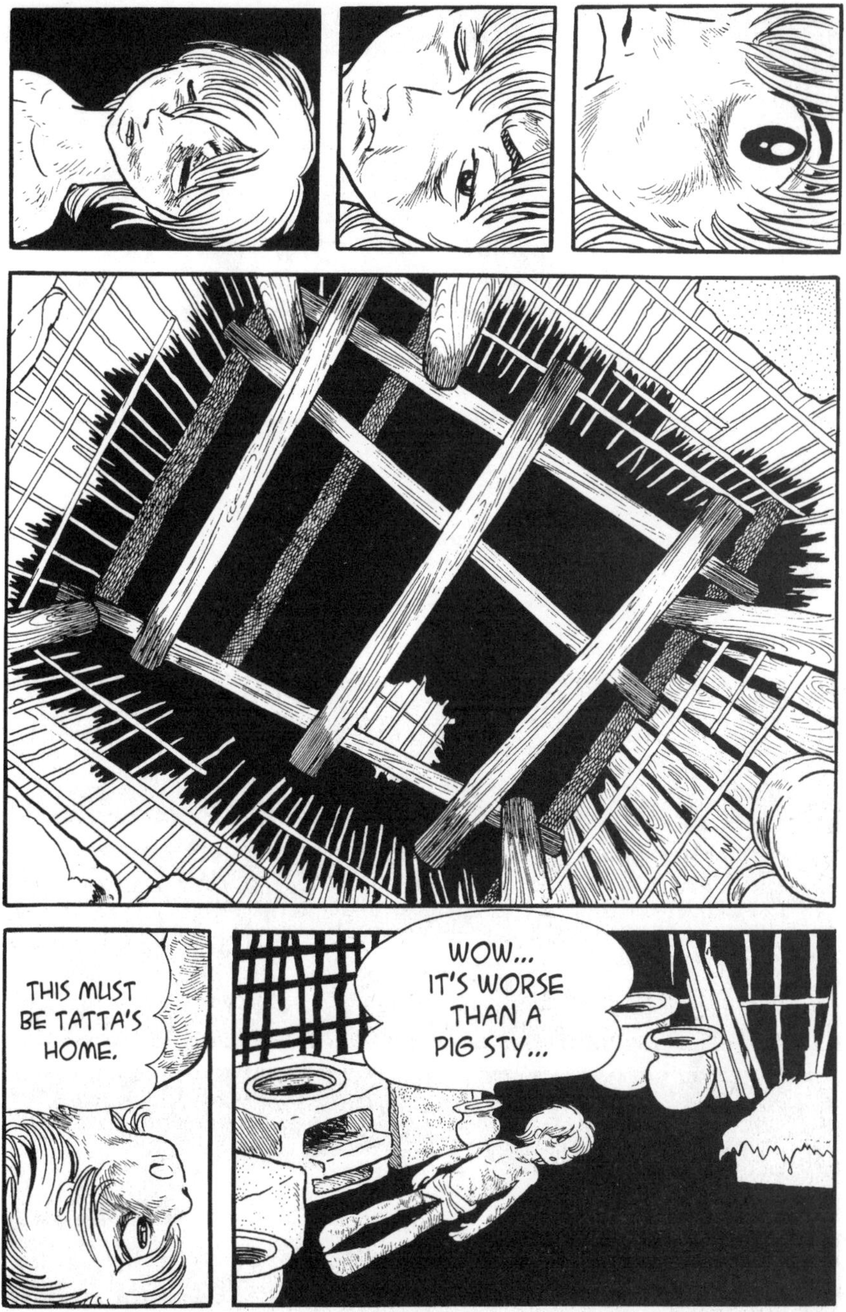
THIS MUST BE TATTA'S HOME.
WOW... IT'S WORSE THAN A PIG STY...

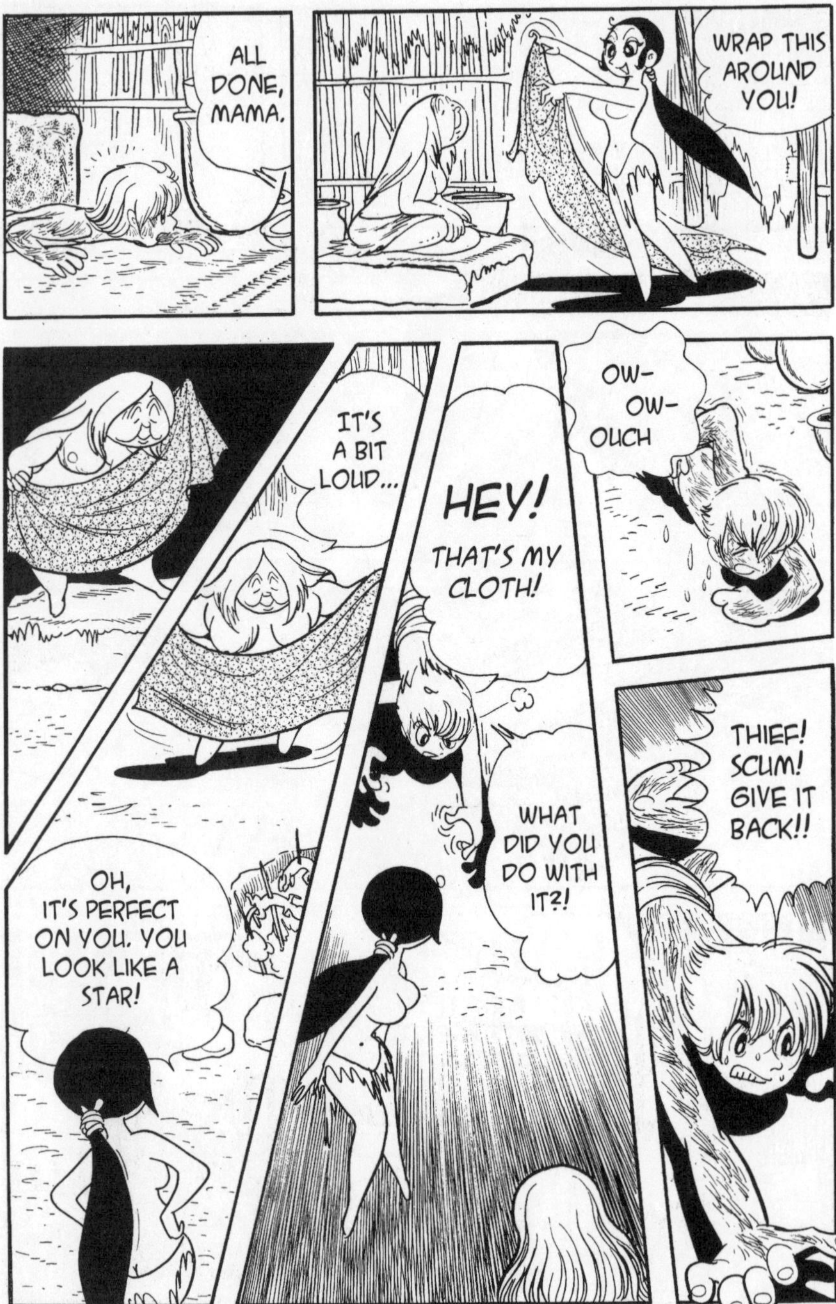

ALL DONE, MAMA.
WRAP THIS AROUND YOU!
IT'S A BIT LOUD...
OH, IT'S PERFECT ON YOU. YOU LOOK LIKE A STAR!
HEY!
THAT'S MY CLOTH!
WHAT DID YOU DO WITH IT?!
OW-OW-OUCH
THIEF! SCUM! GIVE IT BACK!!

NYAA NYAA NYAA. QUIT YOUR WHINING. THIS IS MY HOME.
I GOT THIS CLOTH FROM MY BROTHER; THAT MAKES IT MINE!
NO, IT'S MINE. IT'S NOT FOR BEGGAR WOMEN!
SLAP!
WIPE OFF THAT SORRY LOOK!
LISTEN UP: IN OUR WORLD A BODY'S GOT A RIGHT TO TAKE FROM OTHERS. TOUGH LUCK FOR LOSERS!
YOU JUST WEREN'T CAREFUL ENOUGH!

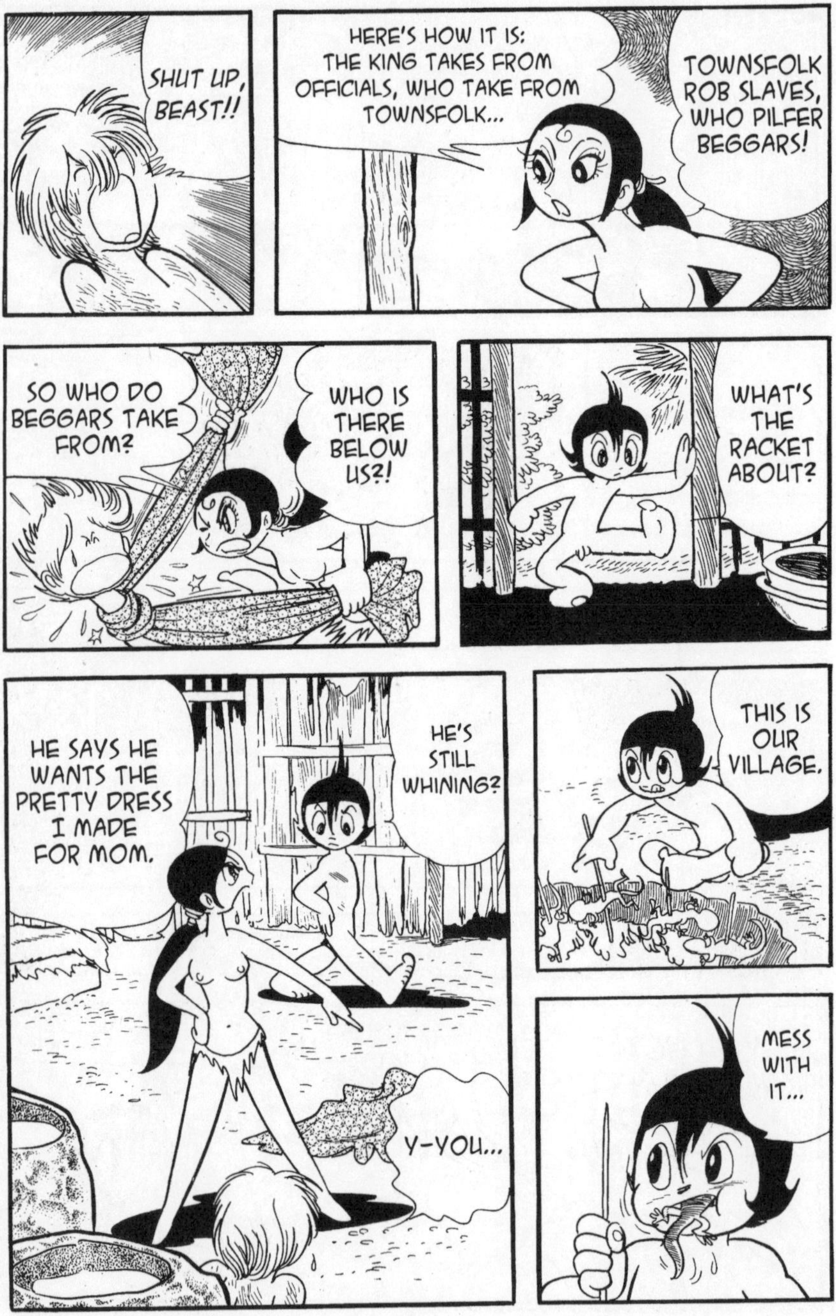
SHUT UP, BEAST!!
HERE'S HOW IT IS: THE KING TAKES FROM OFFICIALS, WHO TAKE FROM TOWNSFOLK...
TOWNSFOLK ROB SLAVES, WHO PILFER BEGGARS!
SO WHO DO BEGGARS TAKE FROM?
WHO IS THERE BELOW US?!
WHAT'S THE RACKET ABOUT?
HE SAYS HE WANTS THE PRETTY DRESS I MADE FOR MOM.
HE'S STILL WHINING?
Y-YOU...
THIS IS OUR VILLAGE.
MESS WITH IT...

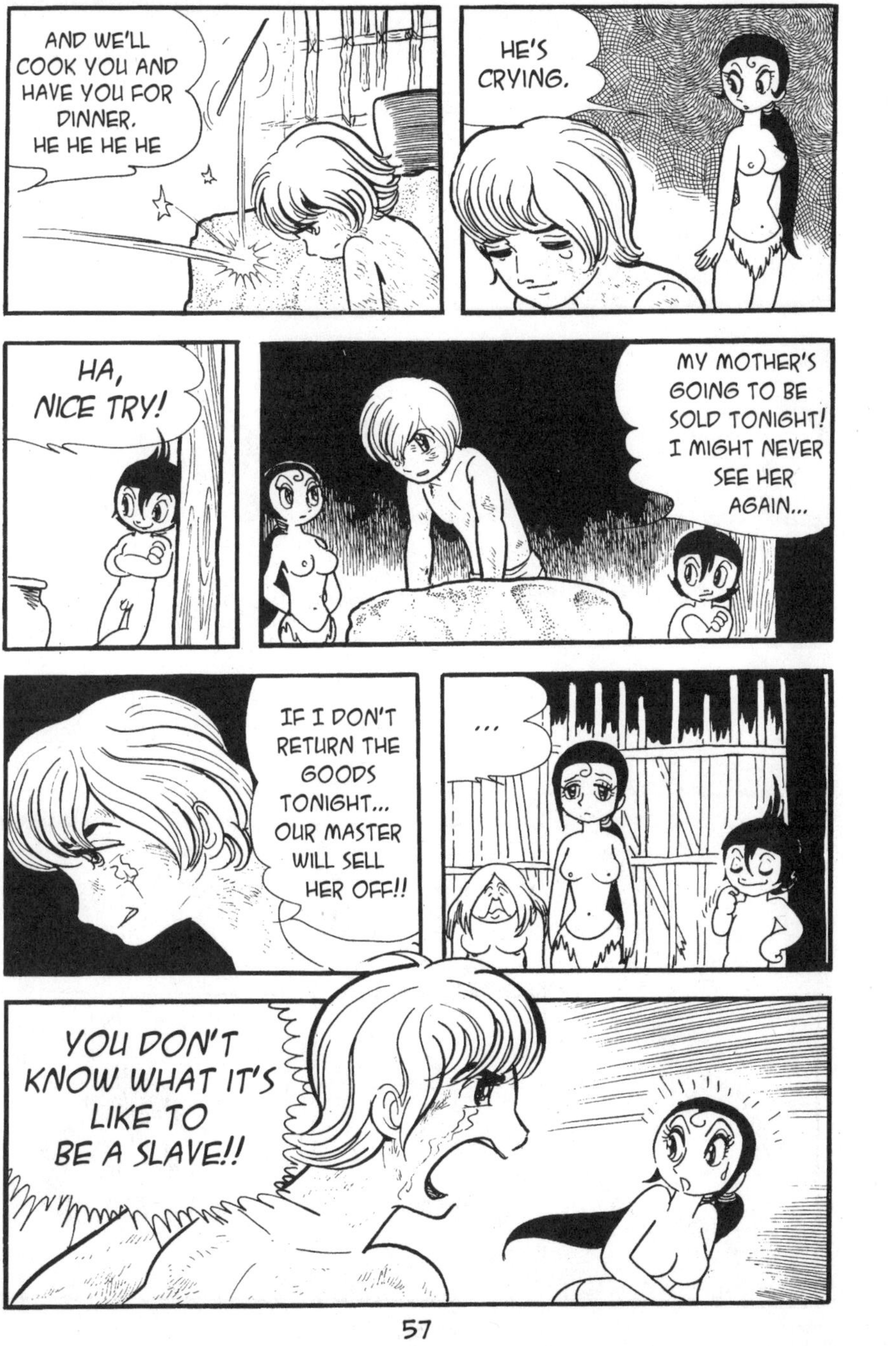
AND WE'LL COOK YOU AND HAVE YOU FOR DINNER. HE HE HE HE
HE'S CRYING.
HA, NICE TRY!
MY MOTHER'S GOING TO BE SOLD TONIGHT! I MIGHT NEVER SEE HER AGAIN...
IF I DON'T RETURN THE GOODS TONIGHT... OUR MASTER WILL SELL HER OFF!!
...
YOU DON'T KNOW WHAT IT'S LIKE TO BE A SLAVE!!

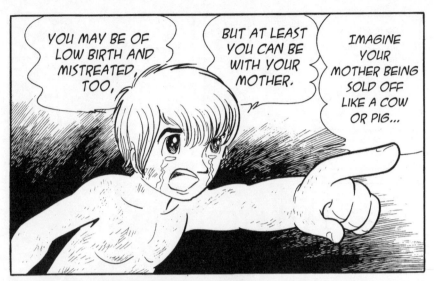

YOU MAY BE OF LOW BIRTH AND MISTREATED, TOO,

BUT AT LEAST YOU CAN BE WITH YOUR MOTHER.

IMAGINE YOUR MOTHER BEING SOLD OFF LIKE A COW OR PIG...

OH NO...

SHOULD WE GO HELP YOUR MOM?

DID YOU SAY "HELP"?

YOU WON'T GIVE BACK WHAT YOU STOLE, BUT YOU'LL HELP HER?!

AND IN RETURN, YOU TWO DON'T EVER HAVE TO GO BACK TO YOUR MASTER.

IT'LL BE A MIRACLE IF WE CAN SAVE HER...

HIGH HIGH

58

CHAPTER TWO

TATTA THE URCHIN

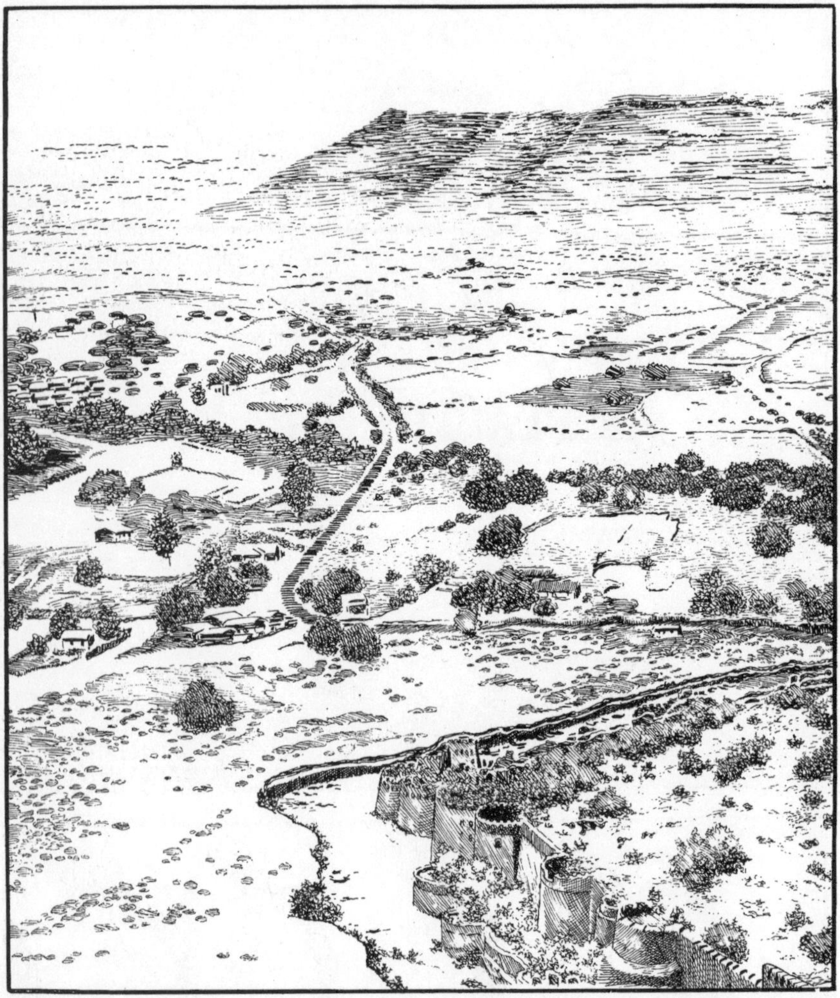

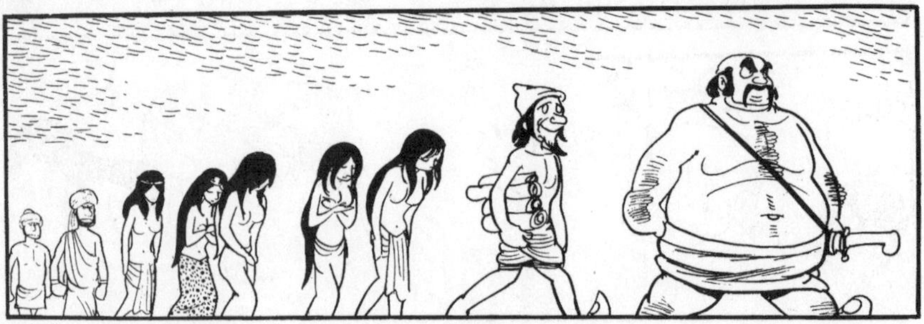

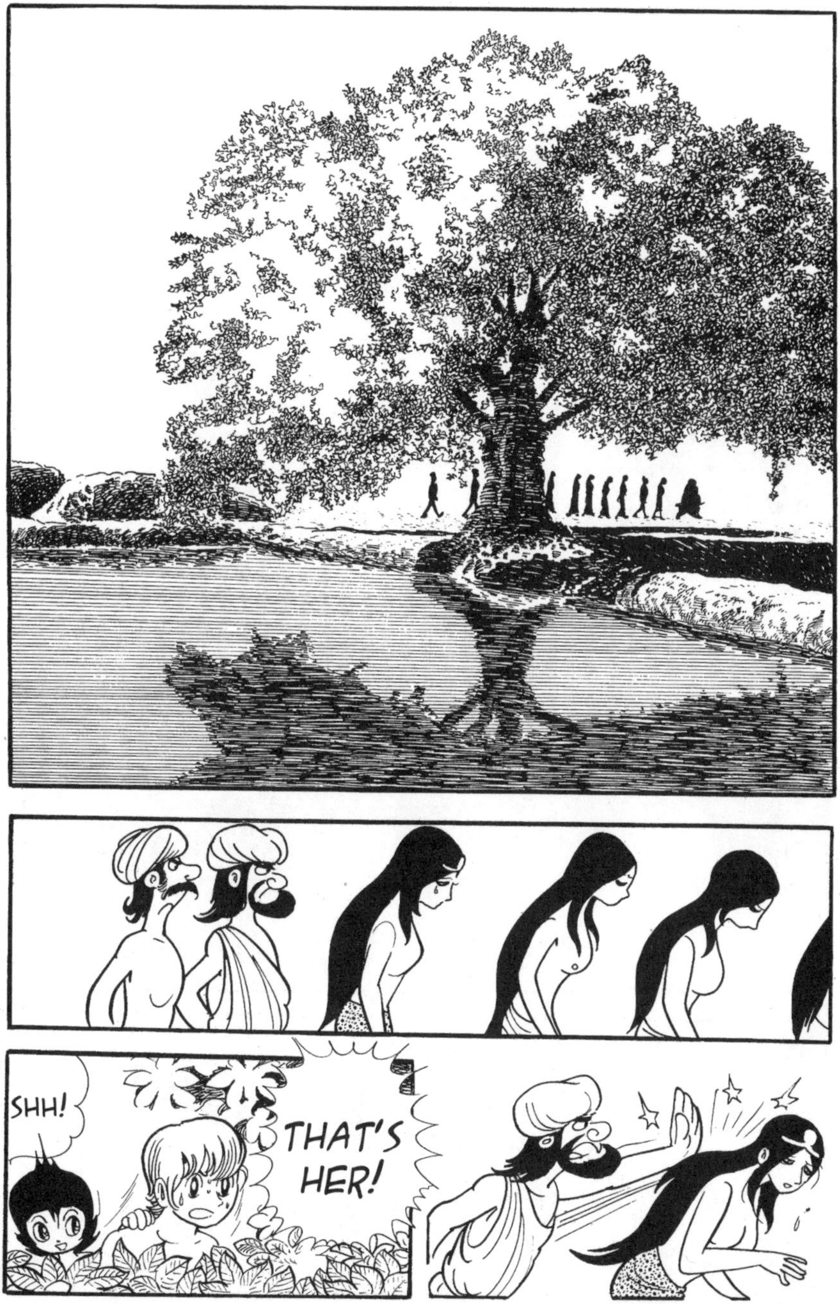
SHH!
THAT'S HER!

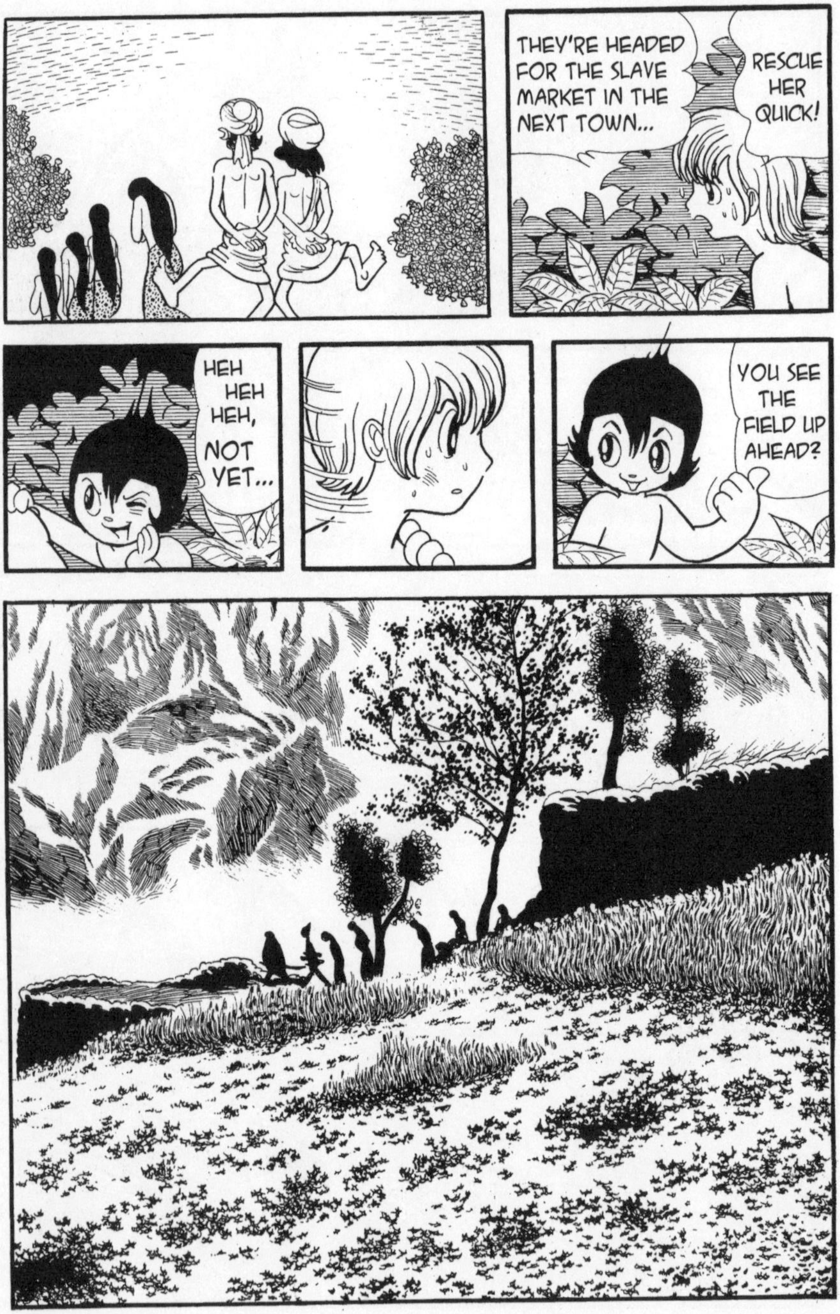
THEY'RE HEADED FOR THE SLAVE MARKET IN THE NEXT TOWN...
RESCUE HER QUICK!
HEH HEH HEH, NOT YET...
YOU SEE THE FIELD UP AHEAD?

CHAPRA, NO MATTER WHAT HAPPENS, STAY HERE AND KEEP STILL.

WH— WHAT'S GONNA HAPPEN?

YOU AREN'T GONNA...

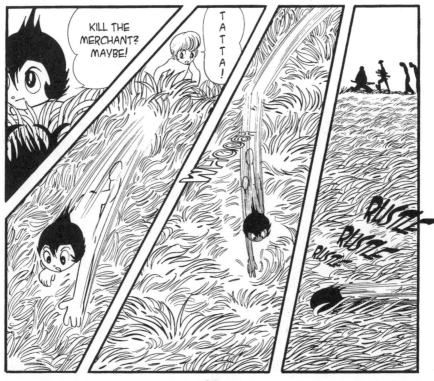

KILL THE MERCHANT? MAYBE!

TATTA!

WHOOSH

RUSTLE
RUSTLE
RUSTLE

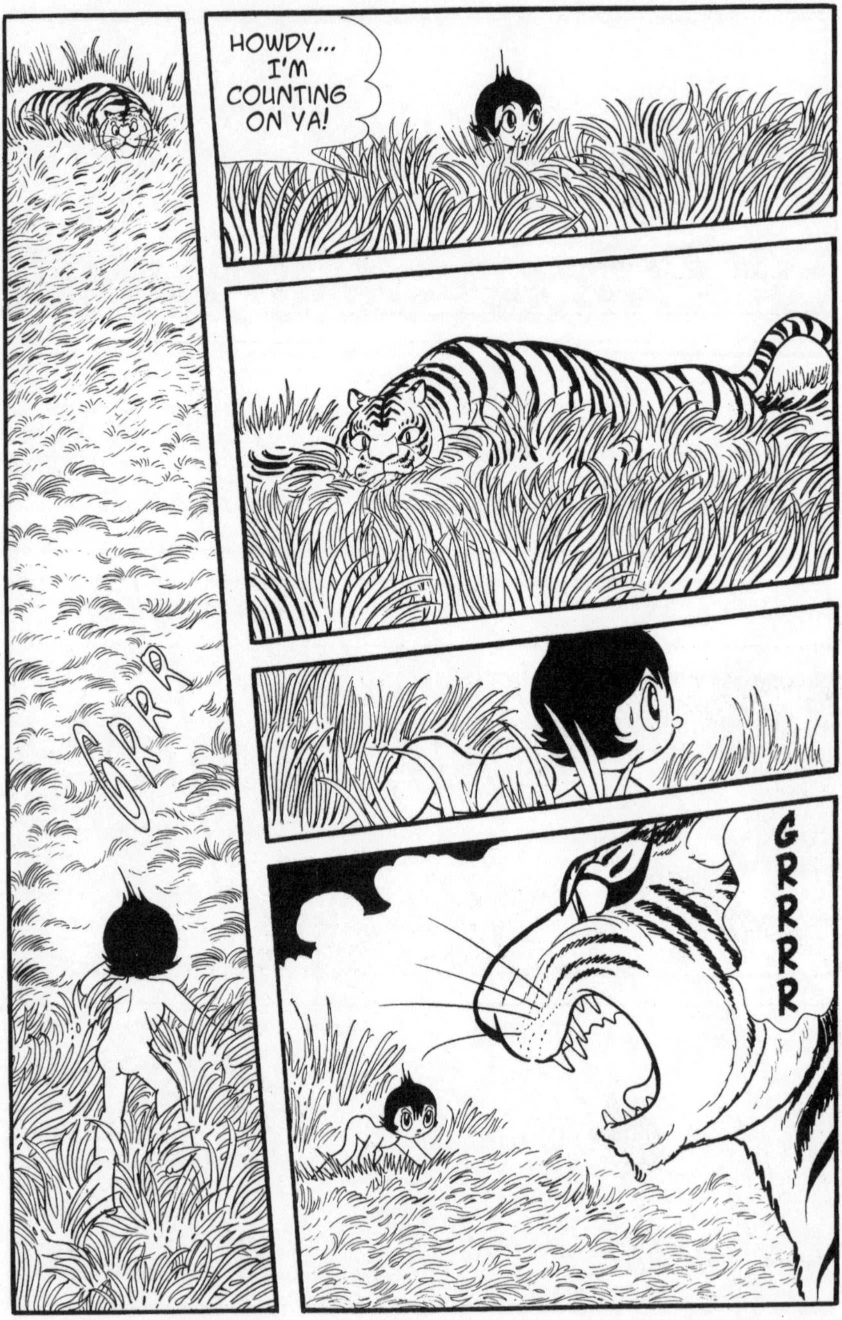
GRRR
HOWDY... I'M COUNTING ON YA!
GRRRR

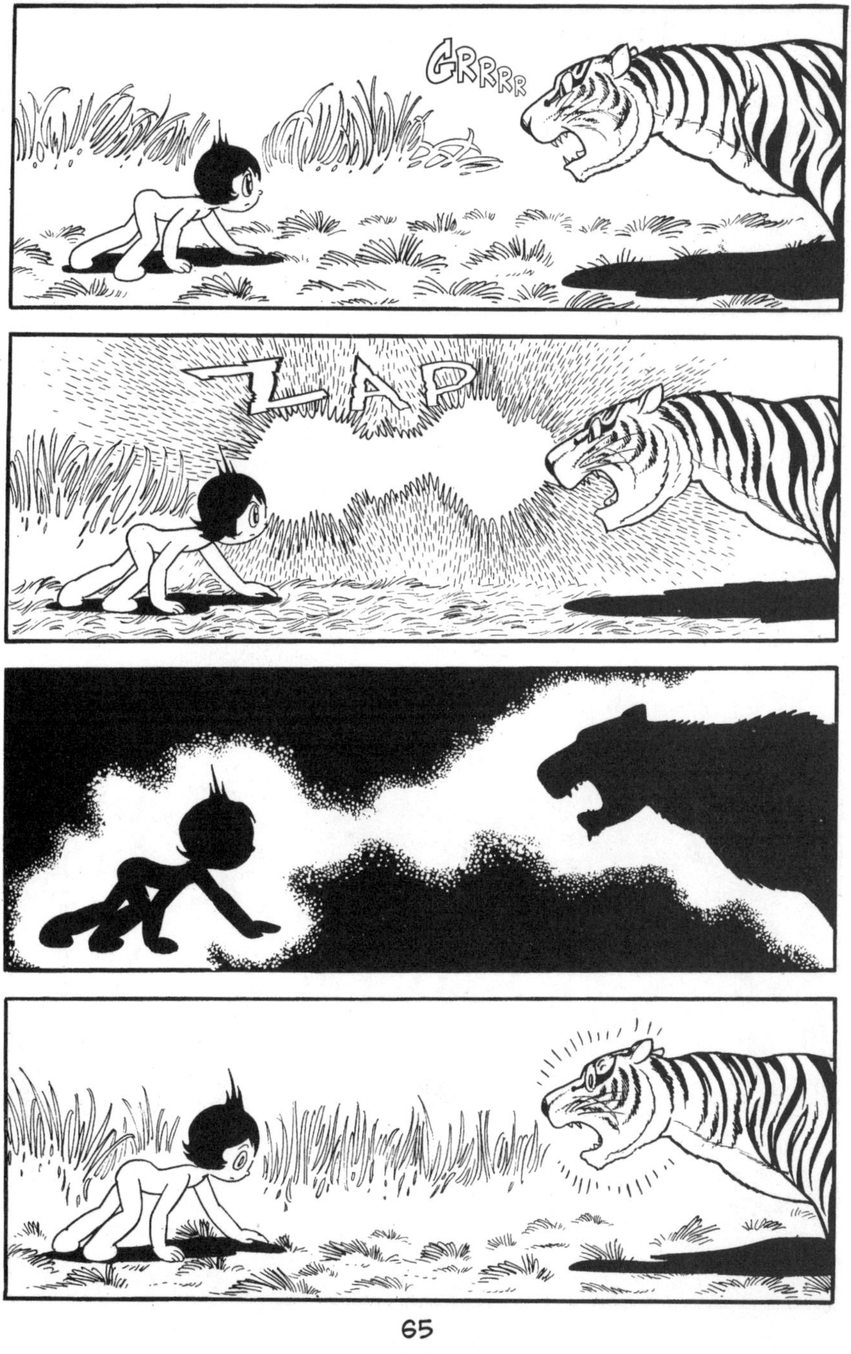
GRRRRR
ZAP

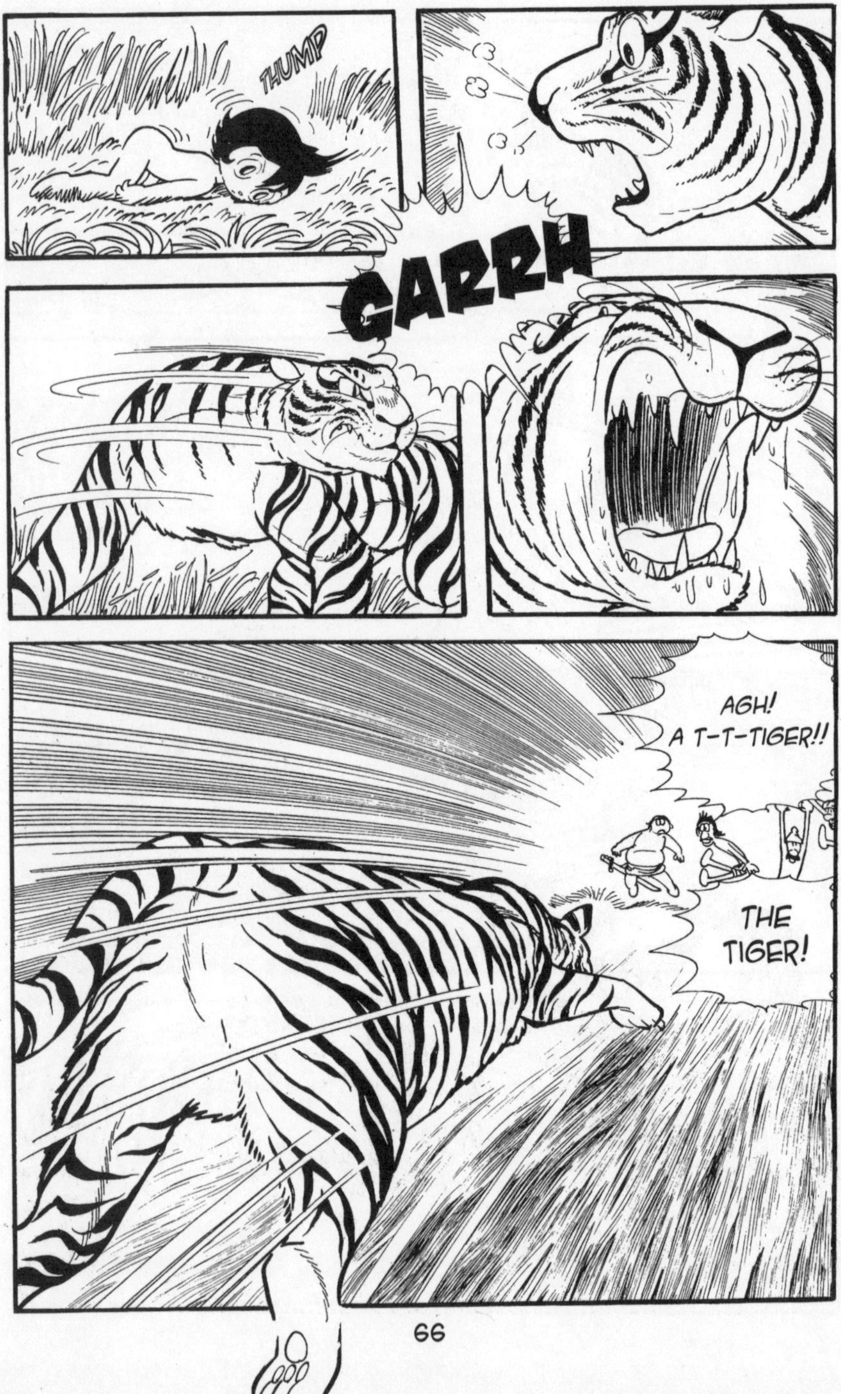
THUMP
GARRH
AGH! A T-T-TIGER!!
THE TIGER!

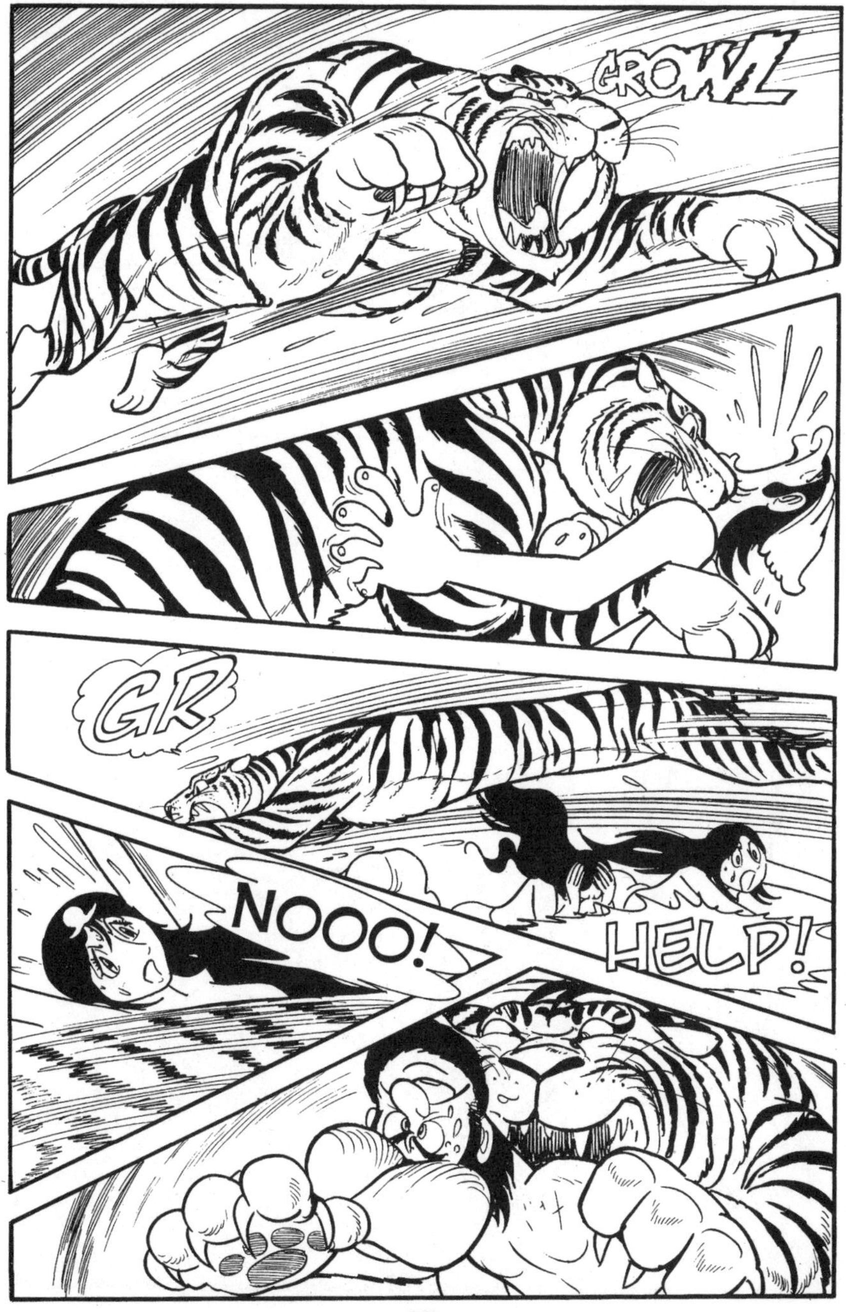
GROWL
GR
NOOO!
HELP!

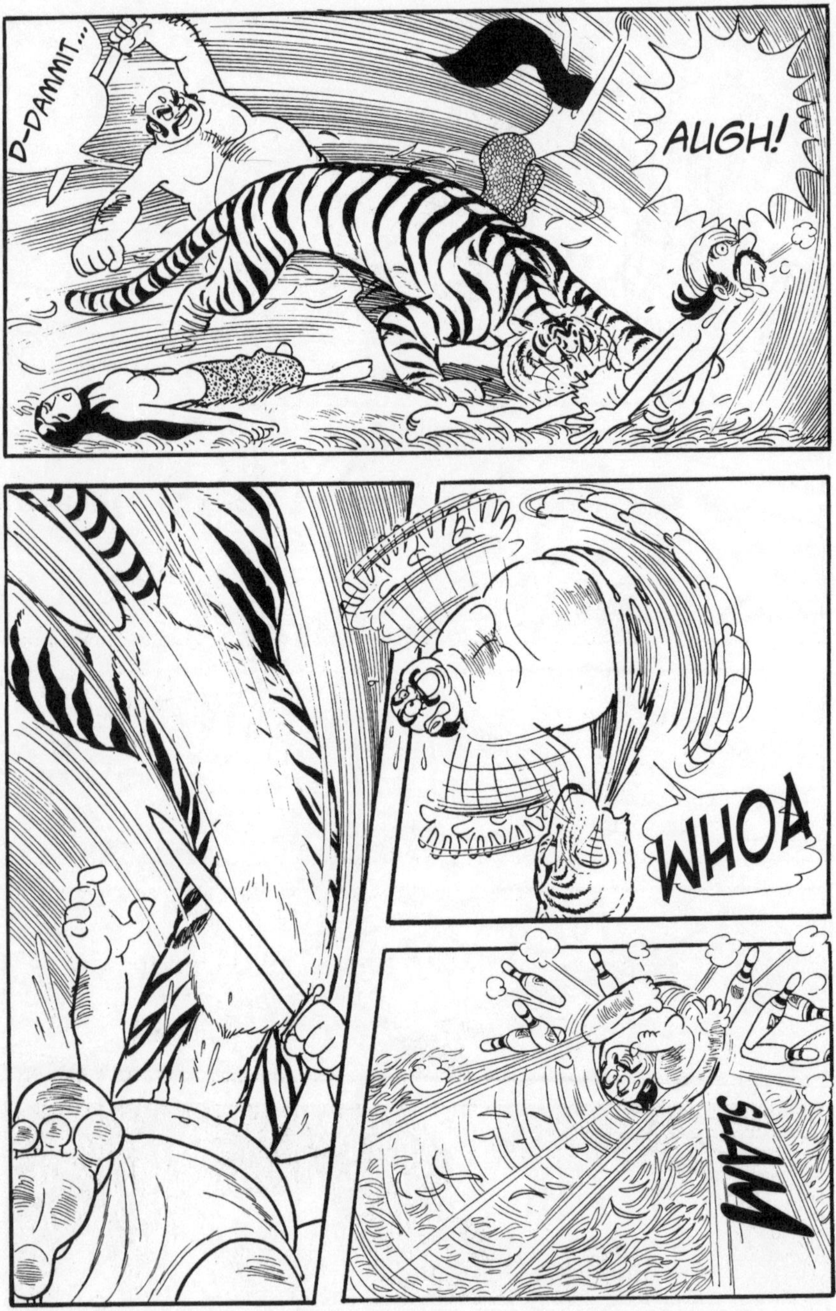
D-DAMMIT...
AUGH!
WHOA
SLAM

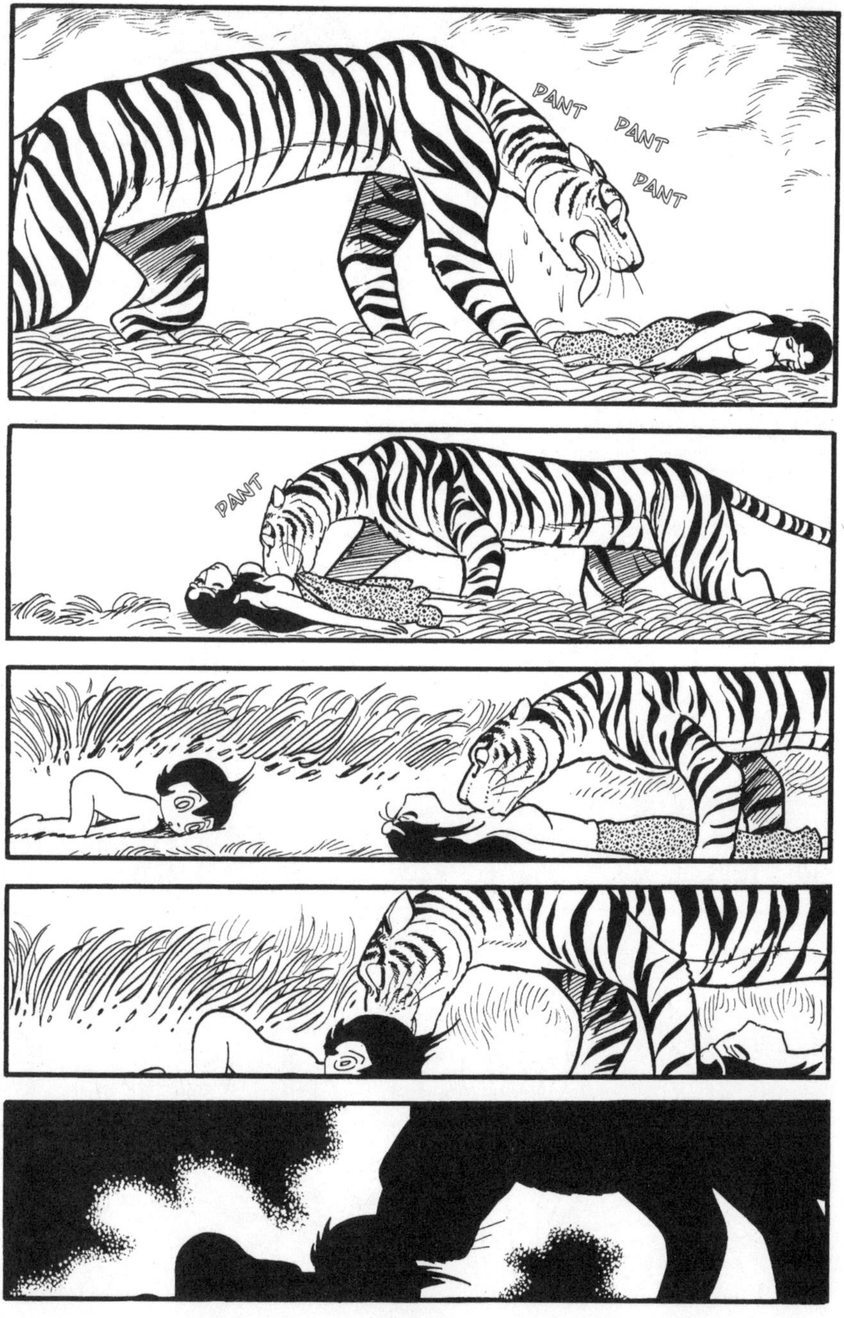
PANT
PANT
PANT
PANT

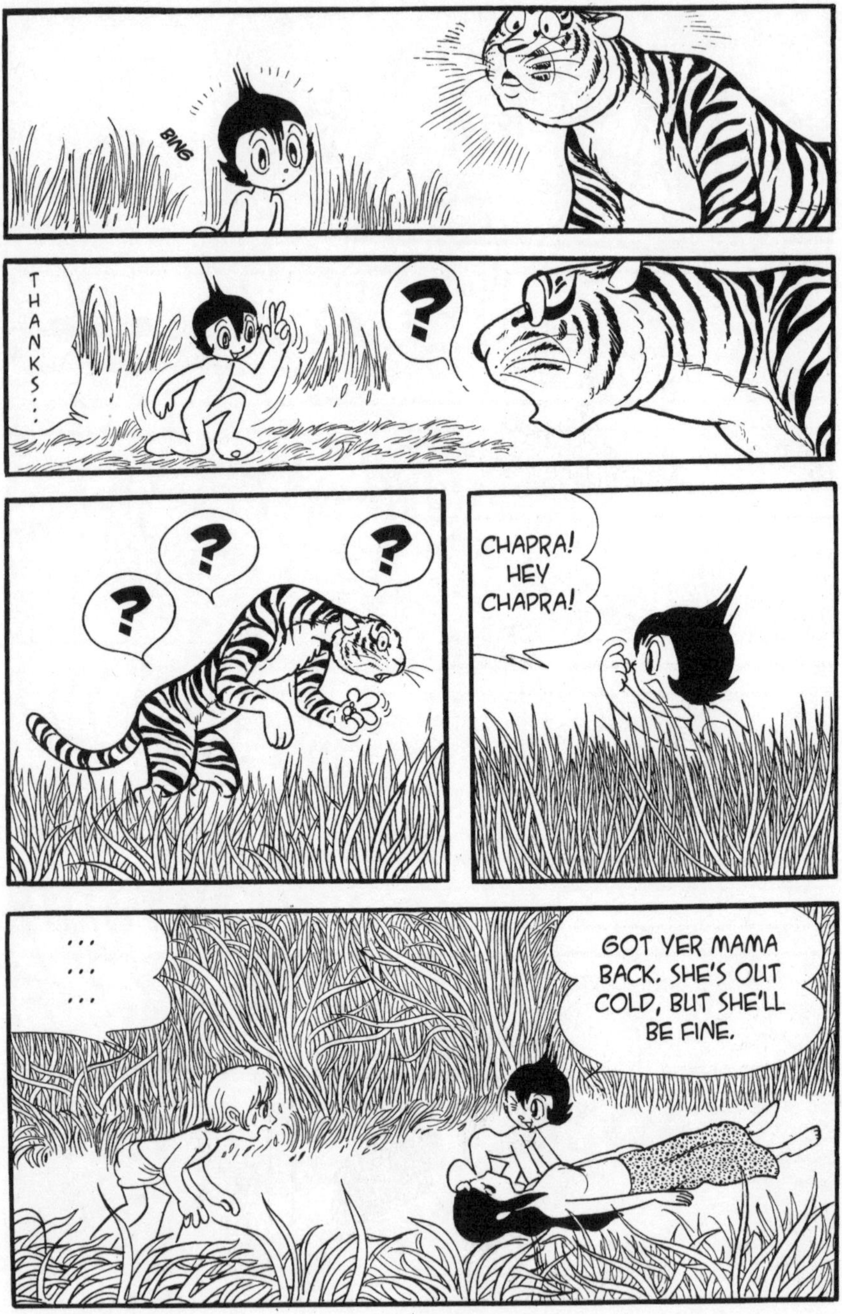
BING
THANKS...
?
?
?
?
CHAPRA! HEY CHAPRA!
...
...
...
GOT YER MAMA BACK. SHE'S OUT COLD, BUT SHE'LL BE FINE.

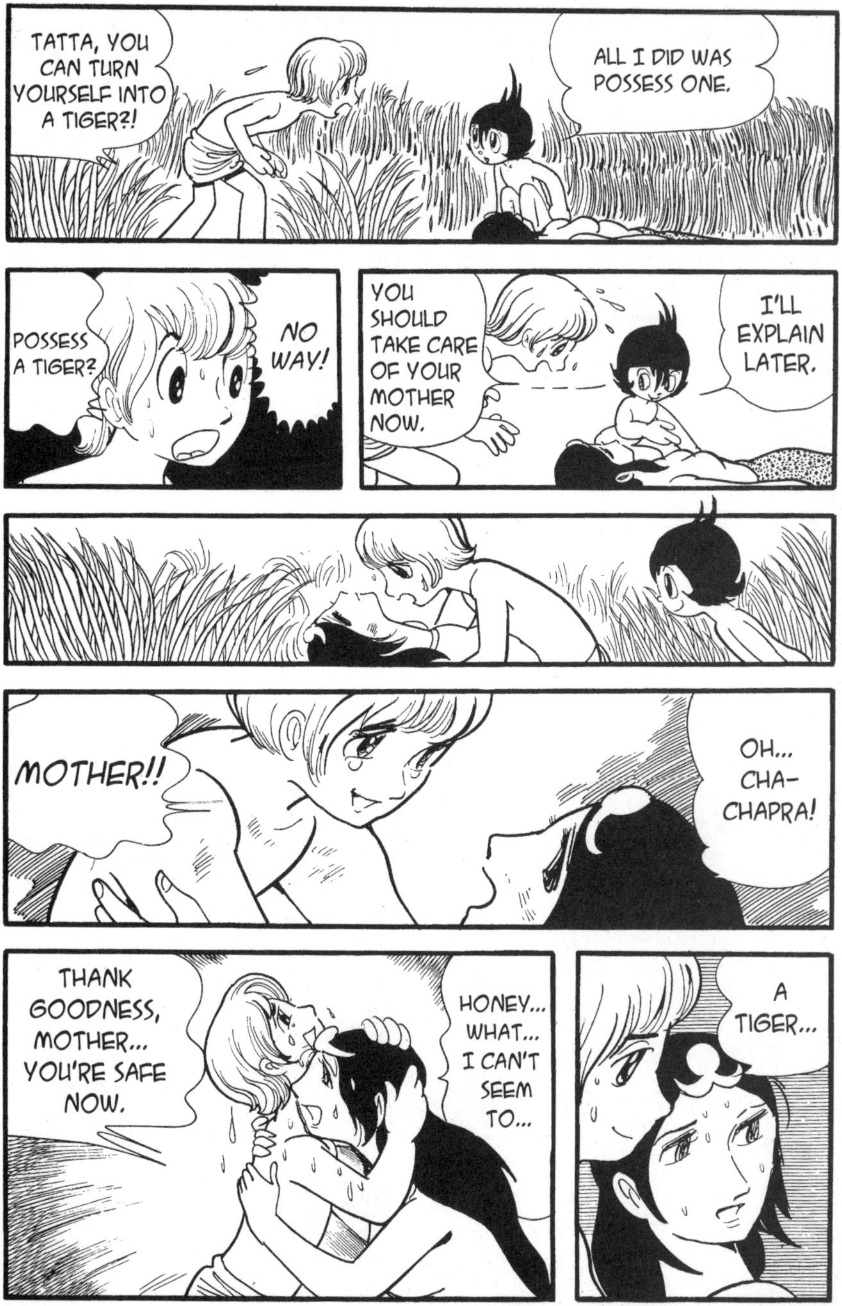
TATTA, YOU CAN TURN YOURSELF INTO A TIGER?!
ALL I DID WAS POSSESS ONE.
POSSESS A TIGER?
NO WAY!
YOU SHOULD TAKE CARE OF YOUR MOTHER NOW.
I'LL EXPLAIN LATER.
MOTHER!!
OH... CHA-CHAPRA!
THANK GOODNESS, MOTHER... YOU'RE SAFE NOW.
HONEY... WHAT... I CAN'T SEEM TO...
A TIGER...

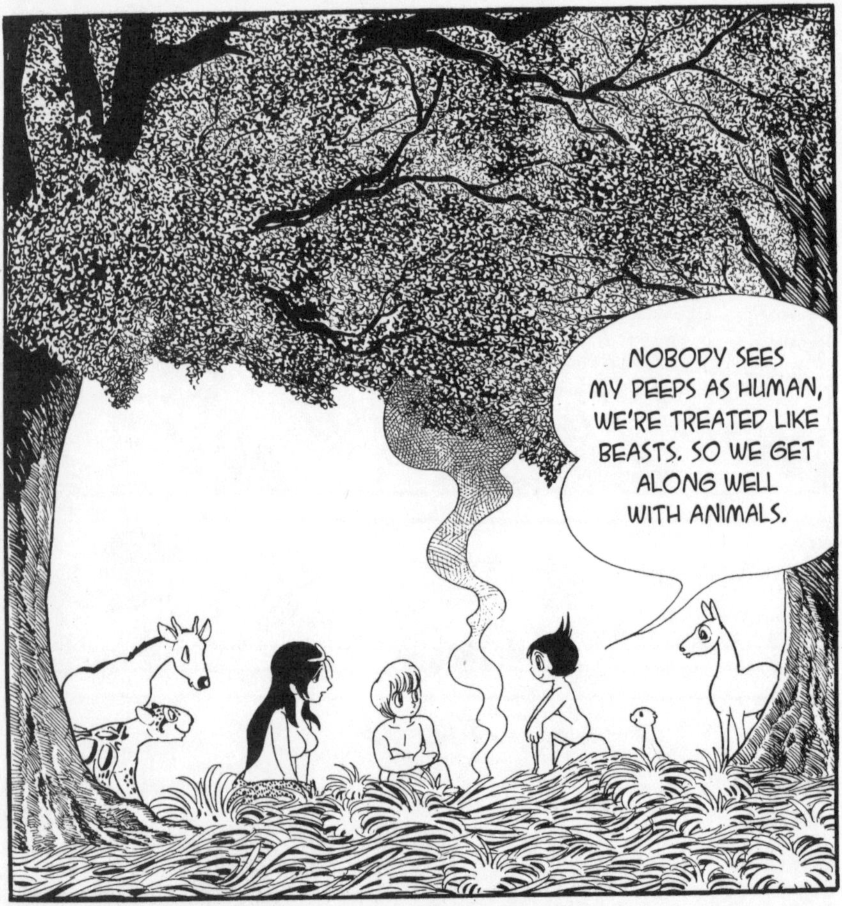
NOBODY SEES MY PEEPS AS HUMAN, WE'RE TREATED LIKE BEASTS. SO WE GET ALONG WELL WITH ANIMALS.

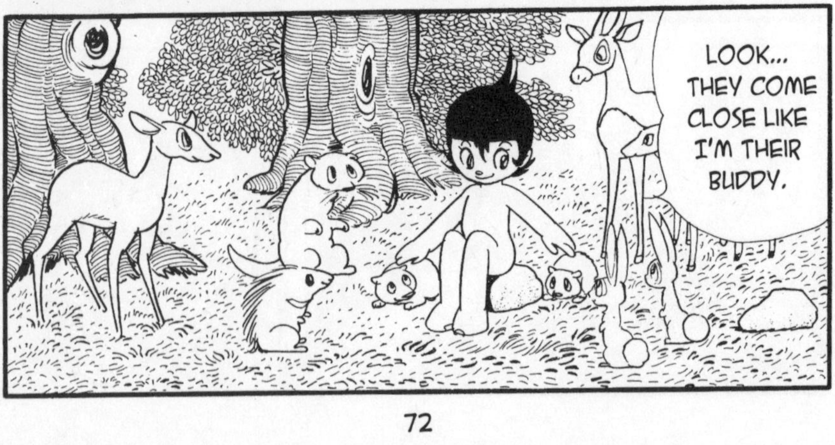
LOOK... THEY COME CLOSE LIKE I'M THEIR BUDDY.

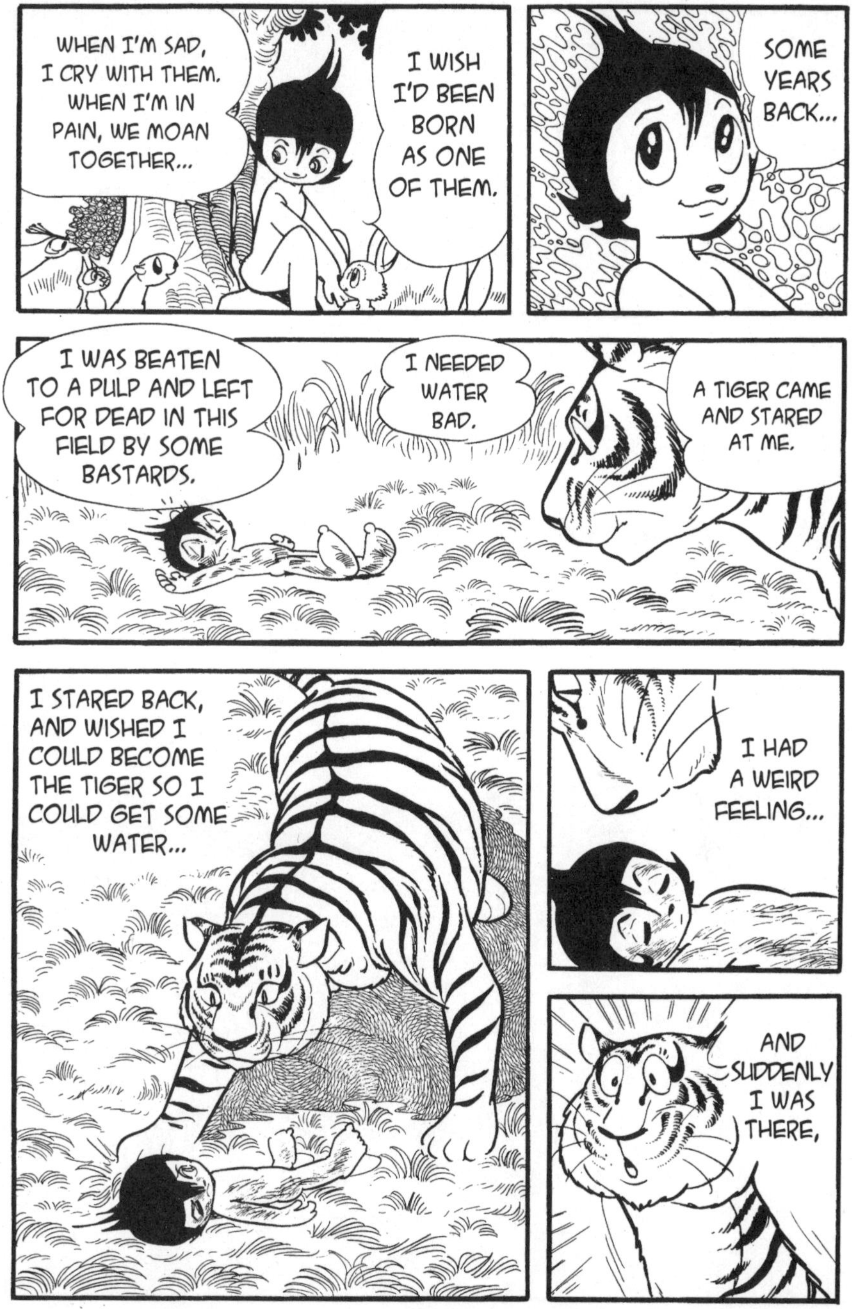
WHEN I'M SAD, I CRY WITH THEM. WHEN I'M IN PAIN, WE MOAN TOGETHER...
I WISH I'D BEEN BORN AS ONE OF THEM.
SOME YEARS BACK...
I WAS BEATEN TO A PULP AND LEFT FOR DEAD IN THIS FIELD BY SOME BASTARDS.
I NEEDED WATER BAD.
A TIGER CAME AND STARED AT ME.
I STARED BACK, AND WISHED I COULD BECOME THE TIGER SO I COULD GET SOME WATER...
I HAD A WEIRD FEELING...
AND SUDDENLY I WAS THERE,

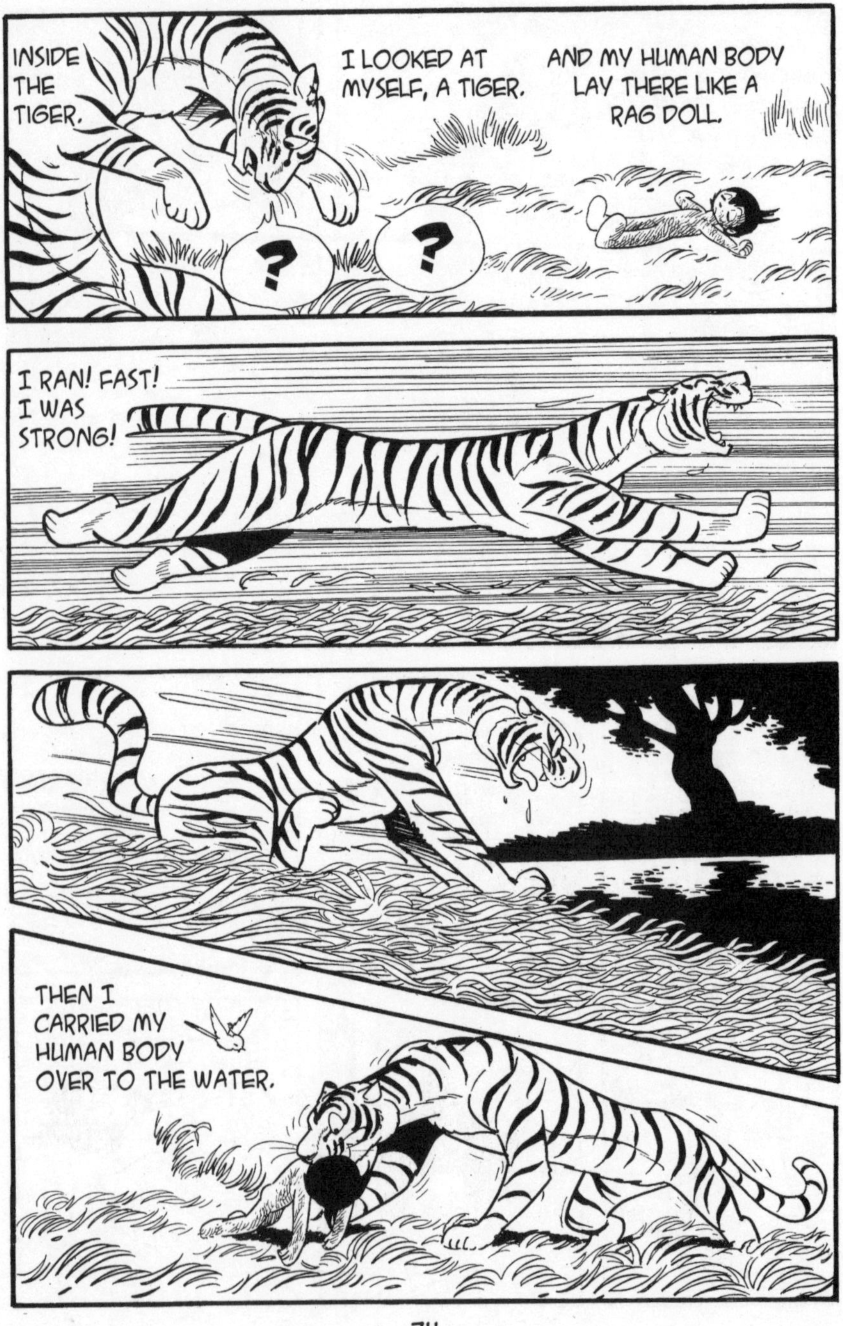

INSIDE THE TIGER.
I LOOKED AT MYSELF, A TIGER.
AND MY HUMAN BODY LAY THERE LIKE A RAG DOLL.
?
?
I RAN! FAST! I WAS STRONG!
THEN I CARRIED MY HUMAN BODY OVER TO THE WATER.

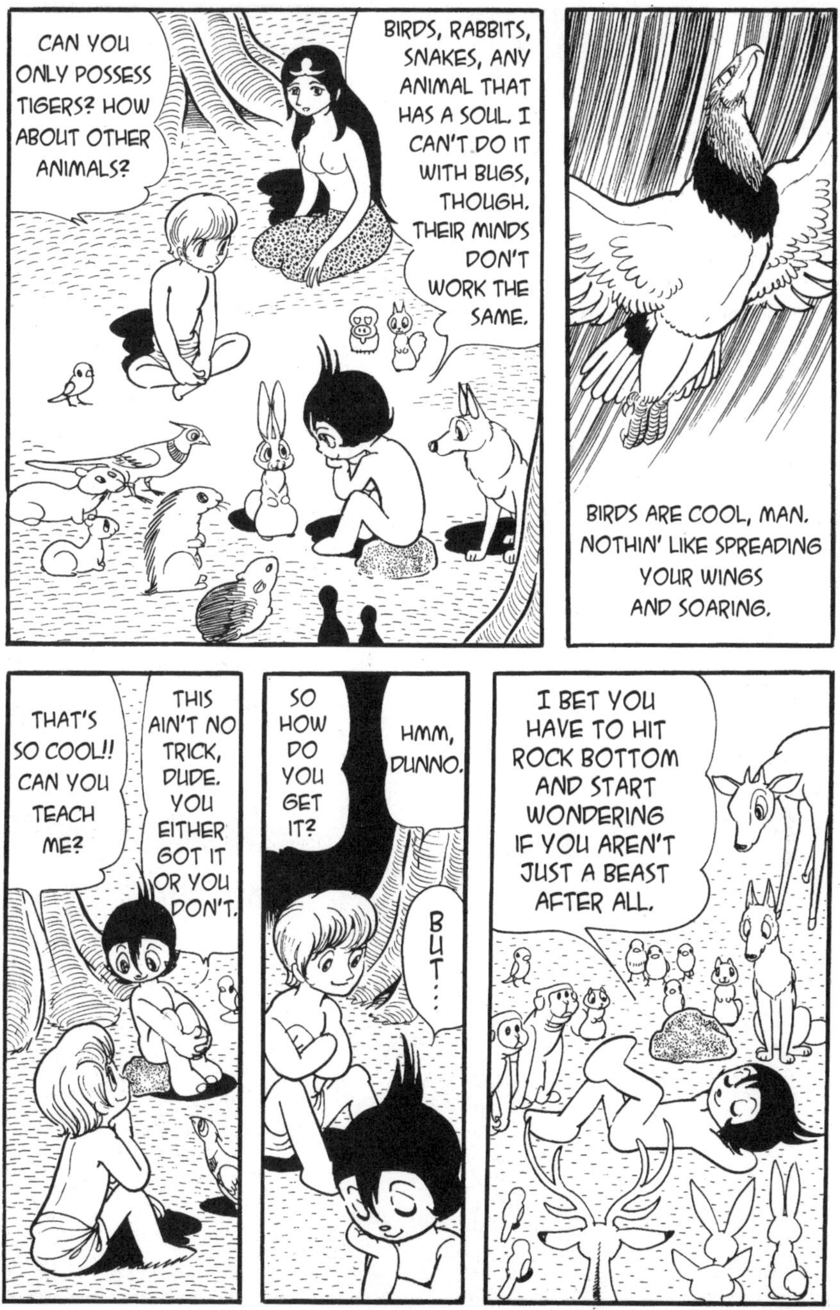
CAN YOU ONLY POSSESS TIGERS? HOW ABOUT OTHER ANIMALS?
BIRDS, RABBITS, SNAKES, ANY ANIMAL THAT HAS A SOUL. I CAN'T DO IT WITH BUGS, THOUGH. THEIR MINDS DON'T WORK THE SAME.
BIRDS ARE COOL, MAN. NOTHIN' LIKE SPREADING YOUR WINGS AND SOARING.
THAT'S SO COOL!! CAN YOU TEACH ME?
THIS AIN'T NO TRICK, DUDE. YOU EITHER GOT IT OR YOU DON'T.
SO HOW DO YOU GET IT?
HMM, DUNNO.
BUT...
I BET YOU HAVE TO HIT ROCK BOTTOM AND START WONDERING IF YOU AREN'T JUST A BEAST AFTER ALL.

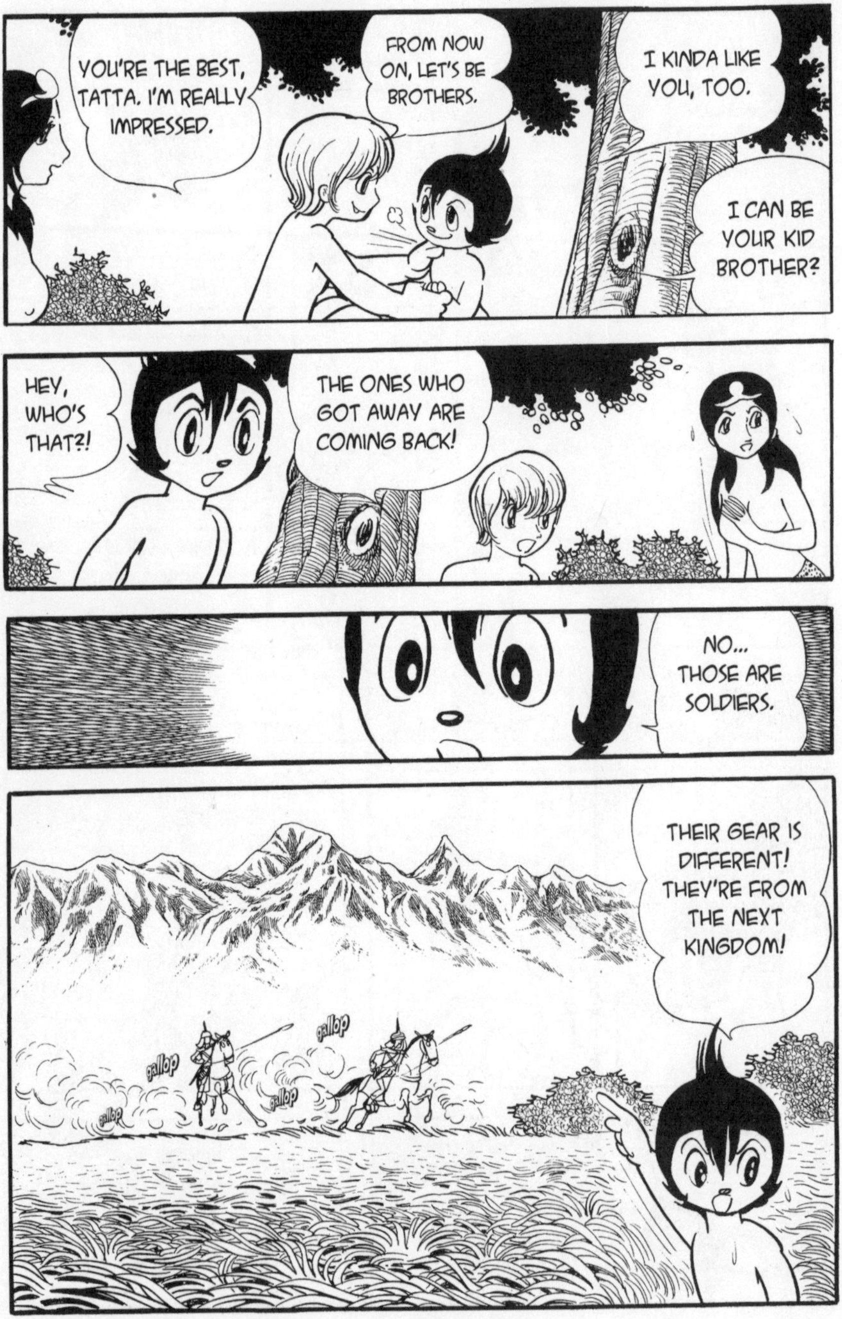
YOU'RE THE BEST, TATTA. I'M REALLY IMPRESSED.
FROM NOW ON, LET'S BE BROTHERS.
I KINDA LIKE YOU, TOO.
I CAN BE YOUR KID BROTHER?
HEY, WHO'S THAT?!
THE ONES WHO GOT AWAY ARE COMING BACK!
NO... THOSE ARE SOLDIERS.
THEIR GEAR IS DIFFERENT! THEY'RE FROM THE NEXT KINGDOM!
gallop
gallop
gallop
gallop

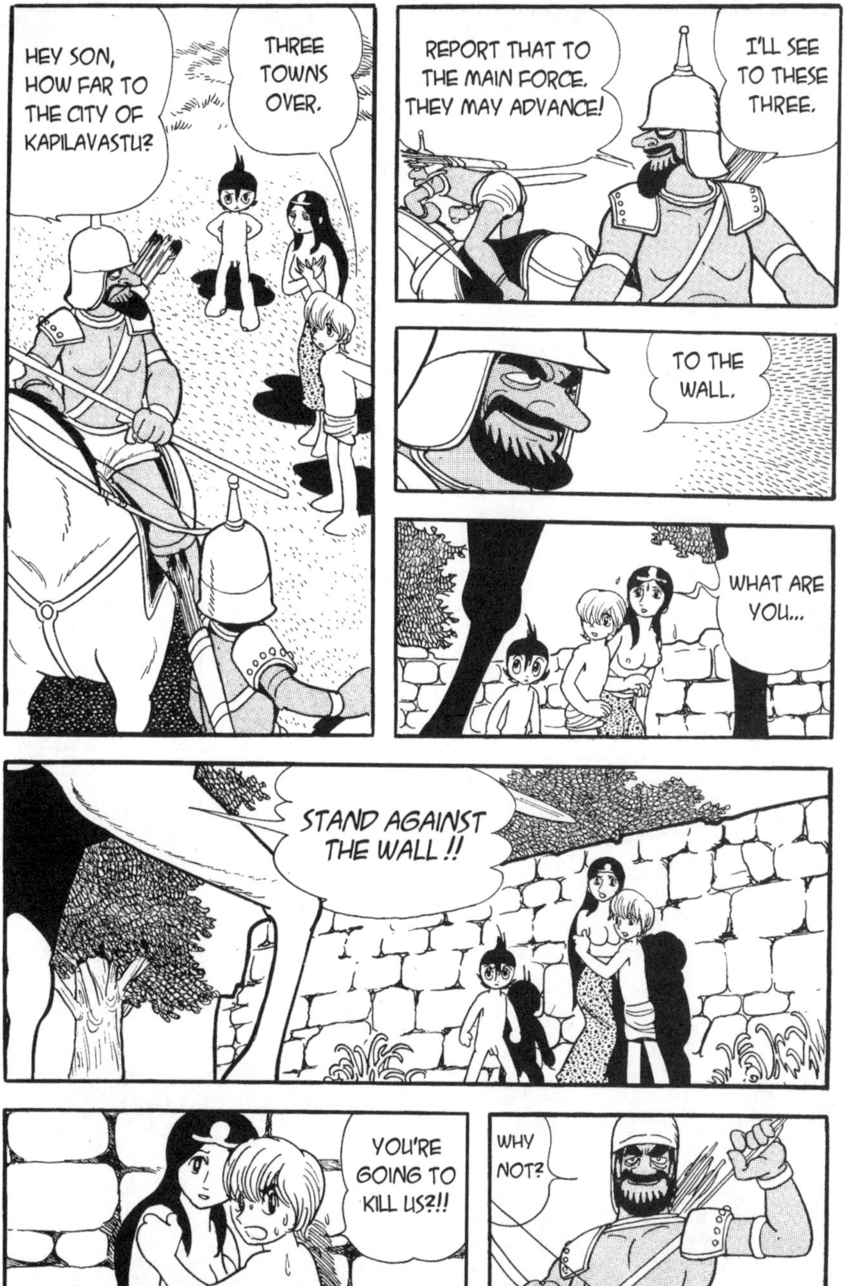
HEY SON, HOW FAR TO THE CITY OF KAPILAVASTU?
THREE TOWNS OVER.
REPORT THAT TO THE MAIN FORCE. THEY MAY ADVANCE!
I'LL SEE TO THESE THREE.
TO THE WALL.
WHAT ARE YOU...
STAND AGAINST THE WALL !!
YOU'RE GOING TO KILL US?!!
WHY NOT?

EASIER THAN KILLING THREE WORMS.

I CAN'T HAVE YOU GO ALERT THE CITY.

WORMS?

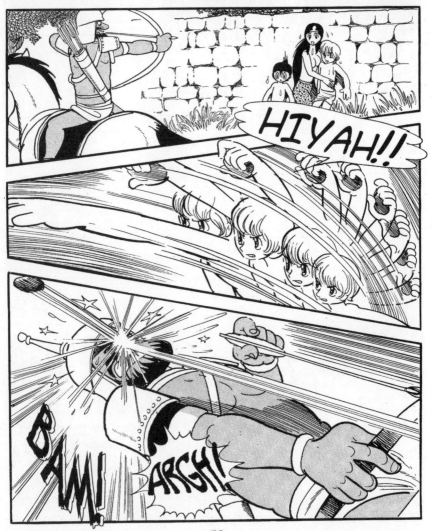

HIYAH!!

BAM!

ARGH!

78

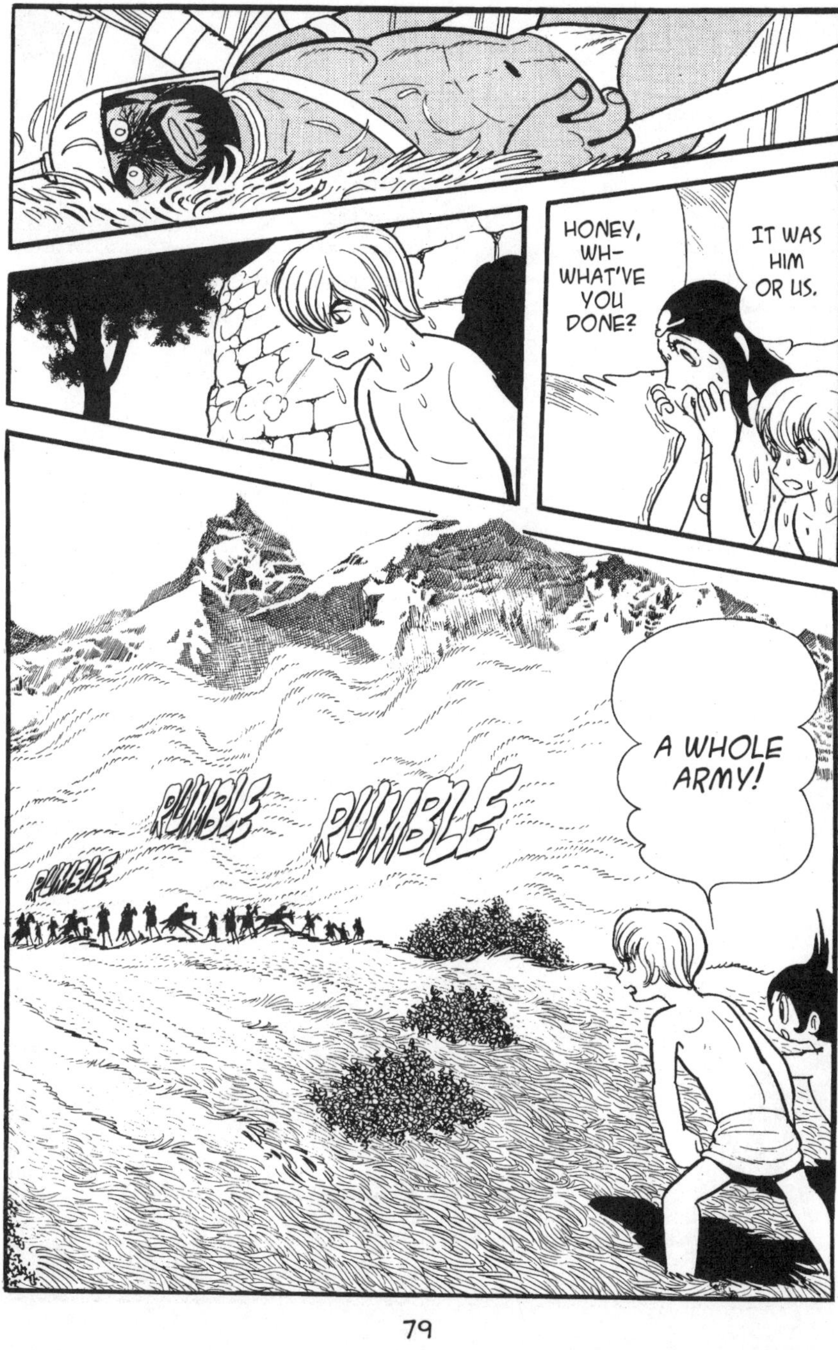
HONEY, WH- WHAT'VE YOU DONE?
IT WAS HIM OR US.
RUMBLE
RUMBLE
RUMBLE
A WHOLE ARMY!

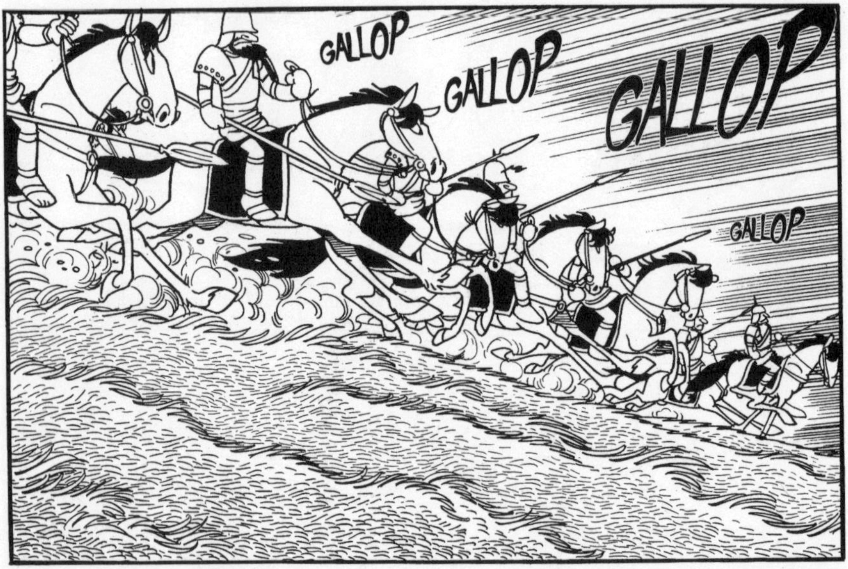
GALLOP
GALLOP
GALLOP
GALLOP
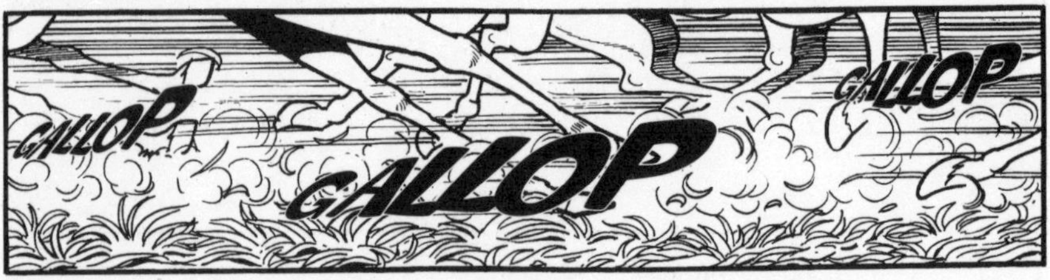
GALLOP
GALLOP
GALLOP
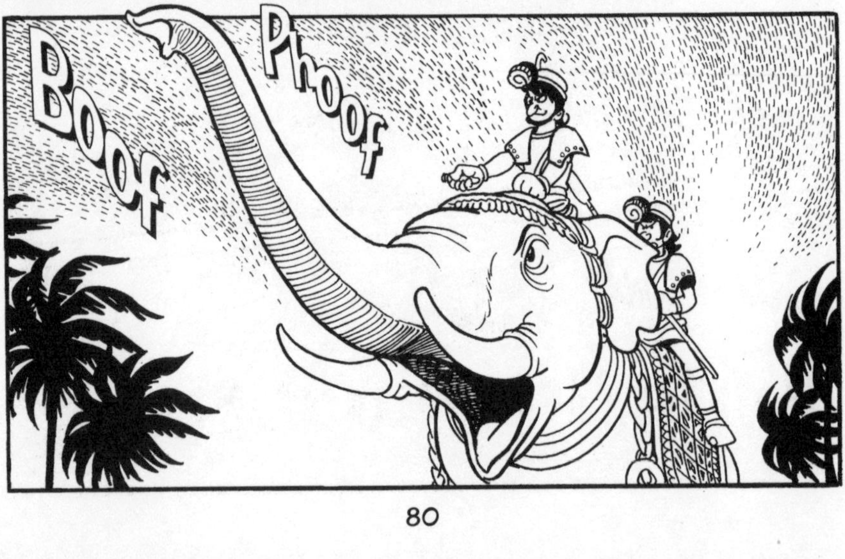
Boof
Phoof

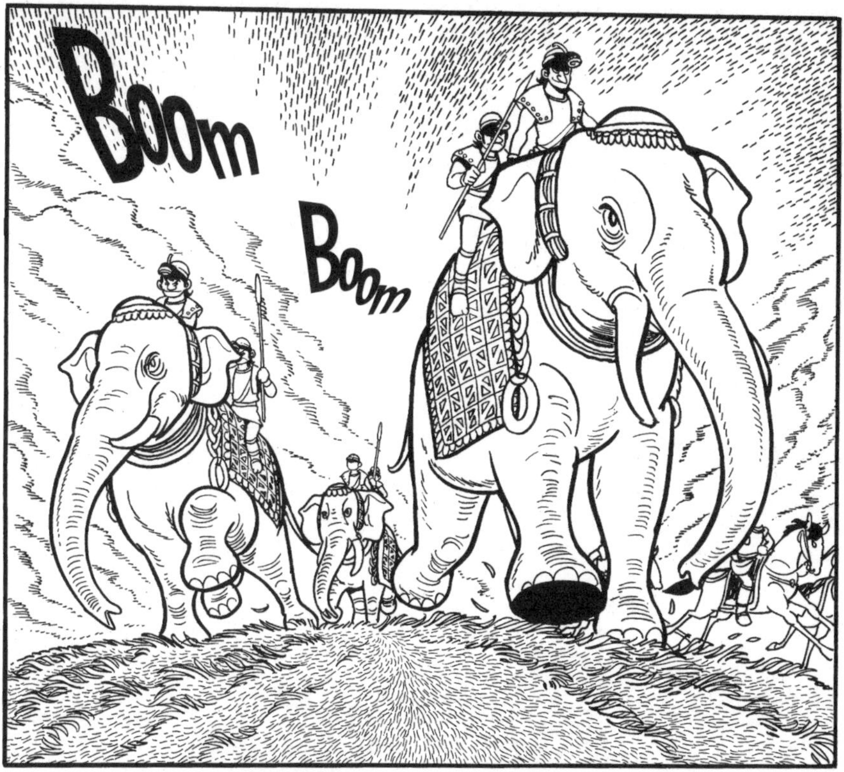
Boom
Boom

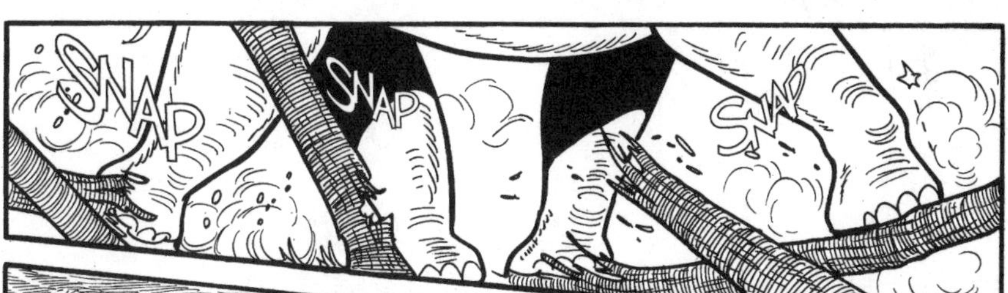
SNAP
SNAP
SNAP

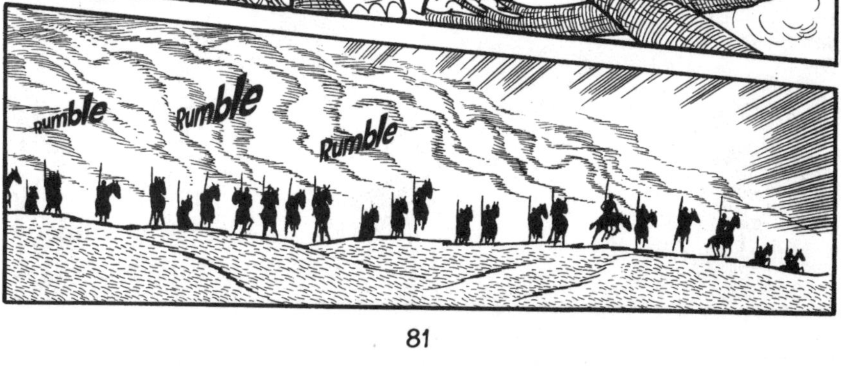
Rumble
Rumble
Rumble

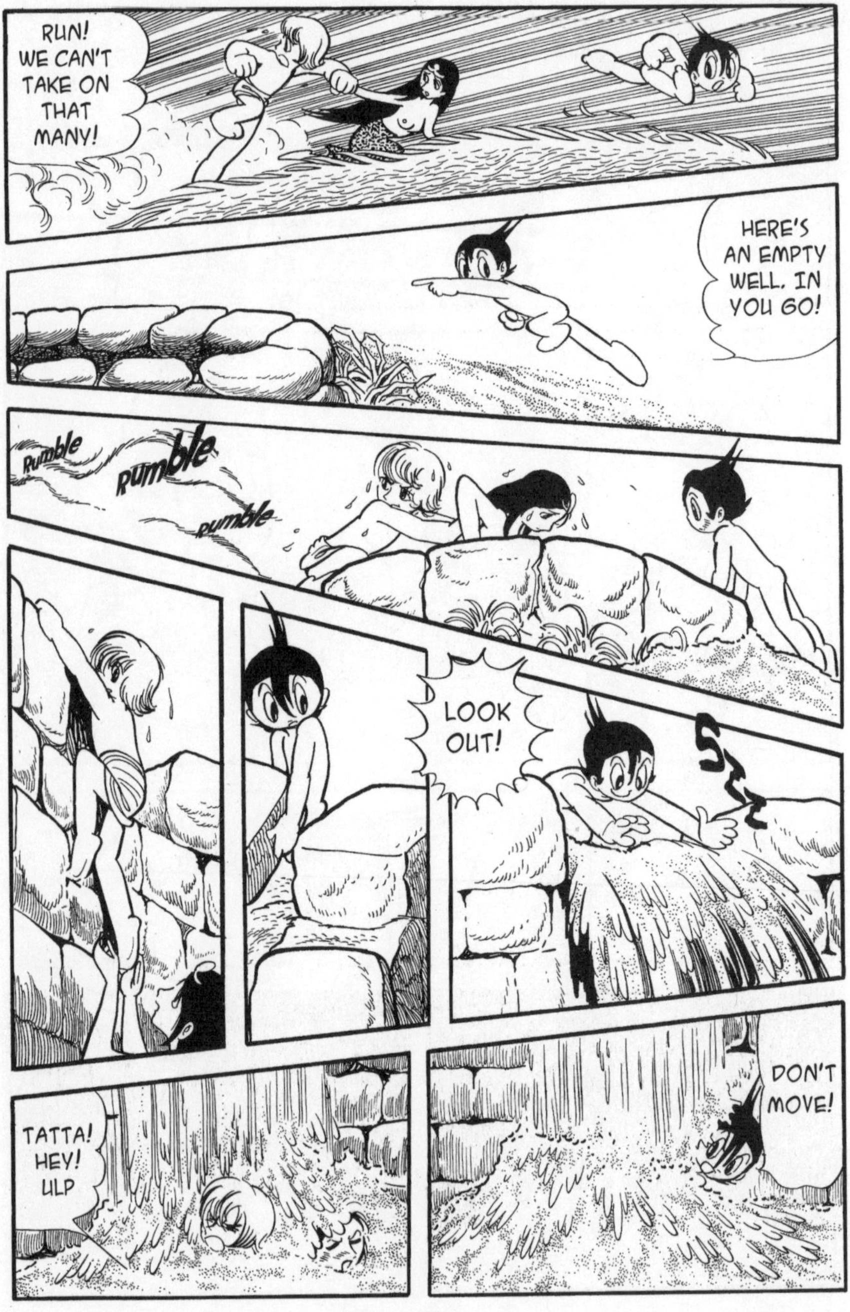
RUN! WE CAN'T TAKE ON THAT MANY!
HERE'S AN EMPTY WELL. IN YOU GO!
Rumble
Rumble
Rumble
LOOK OUT!
TATTA! HEY! ULP
DON'T MOVE!

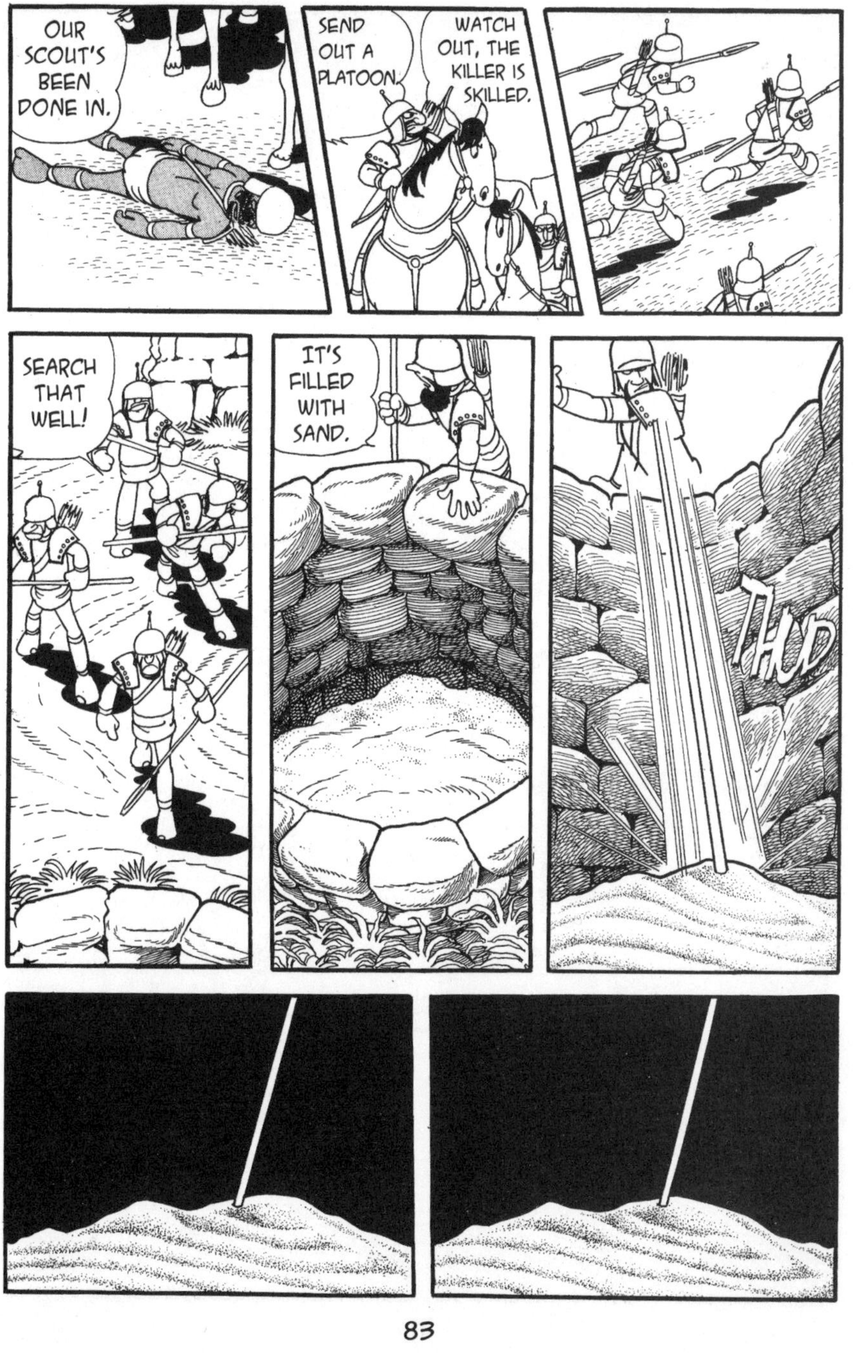
OUR SCOUT'S BEEN DONE IN.
SEND OUT A PLATOON.
WATCH OUT, THE KILLER IS SKILLED.
SEARCH THAT WELL!
IT'S FILLED WITH SAND.
THUD

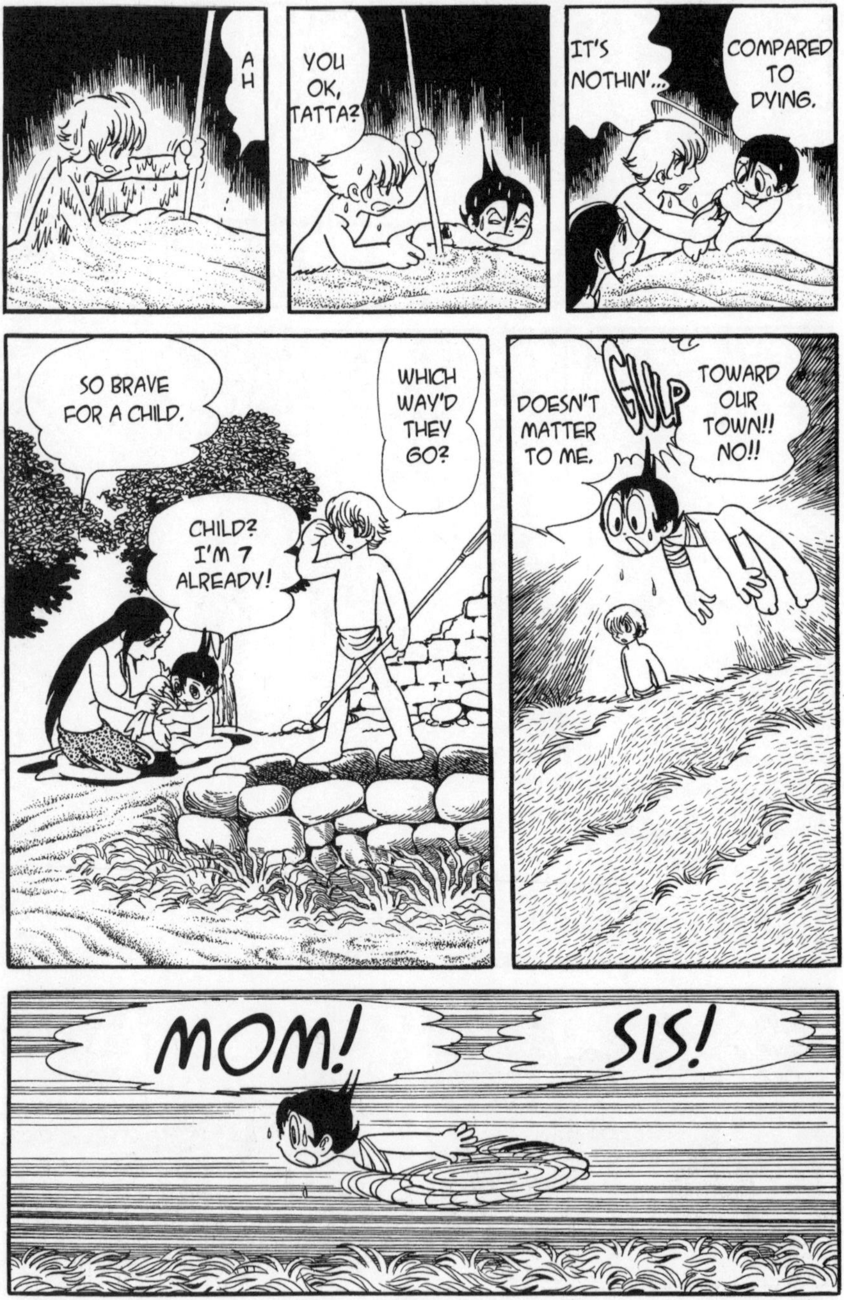
AH
YOU OK, TATTA?
IT'S NOTHIN'...
COMPARED TO DYING.
SO BRAVE FOR A CHILD.
CHILD? I'M 7 ALREADY!
WHICH WAY'D THEY GO?
DOESN'T MATTER TO ME.
GULP
TOWARD OUR TOWN!! NO!!
MOM!
SIS!

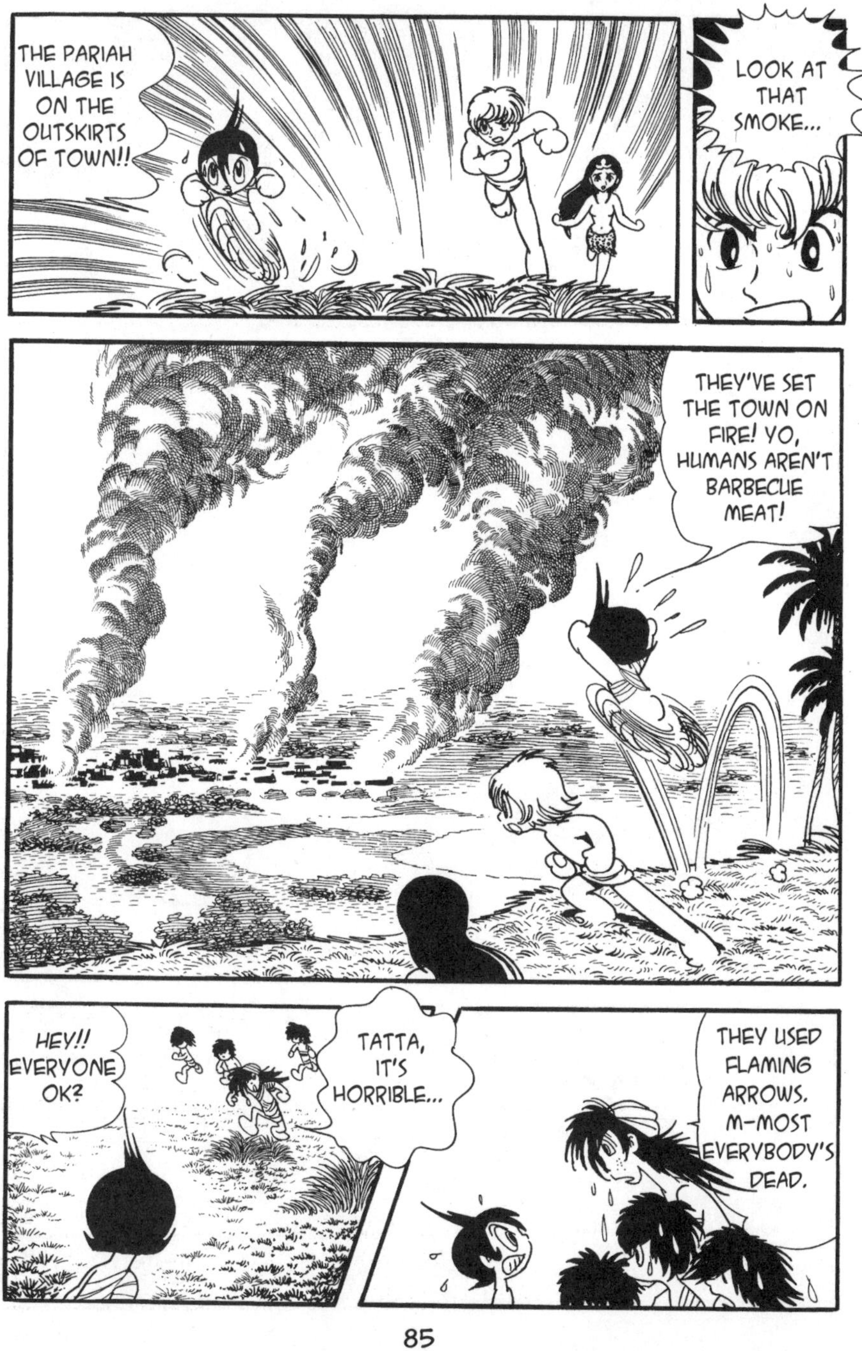
THE PARIAH VILLAGE IS ON THE OUTSKIRTS OF TOWN!!
LOOK AT THAT SMOKE...
THEY'VE SET THE TOWN ON FIRE! YO, HUMANS AREN'T BARBECUE MEAT!
HEY!! EVERYONE OK?
TATTA, IT'S HORRIBLE...
THEY USED FLAMING ARROWS. M-MOST EVERYBODY'S DEAD.

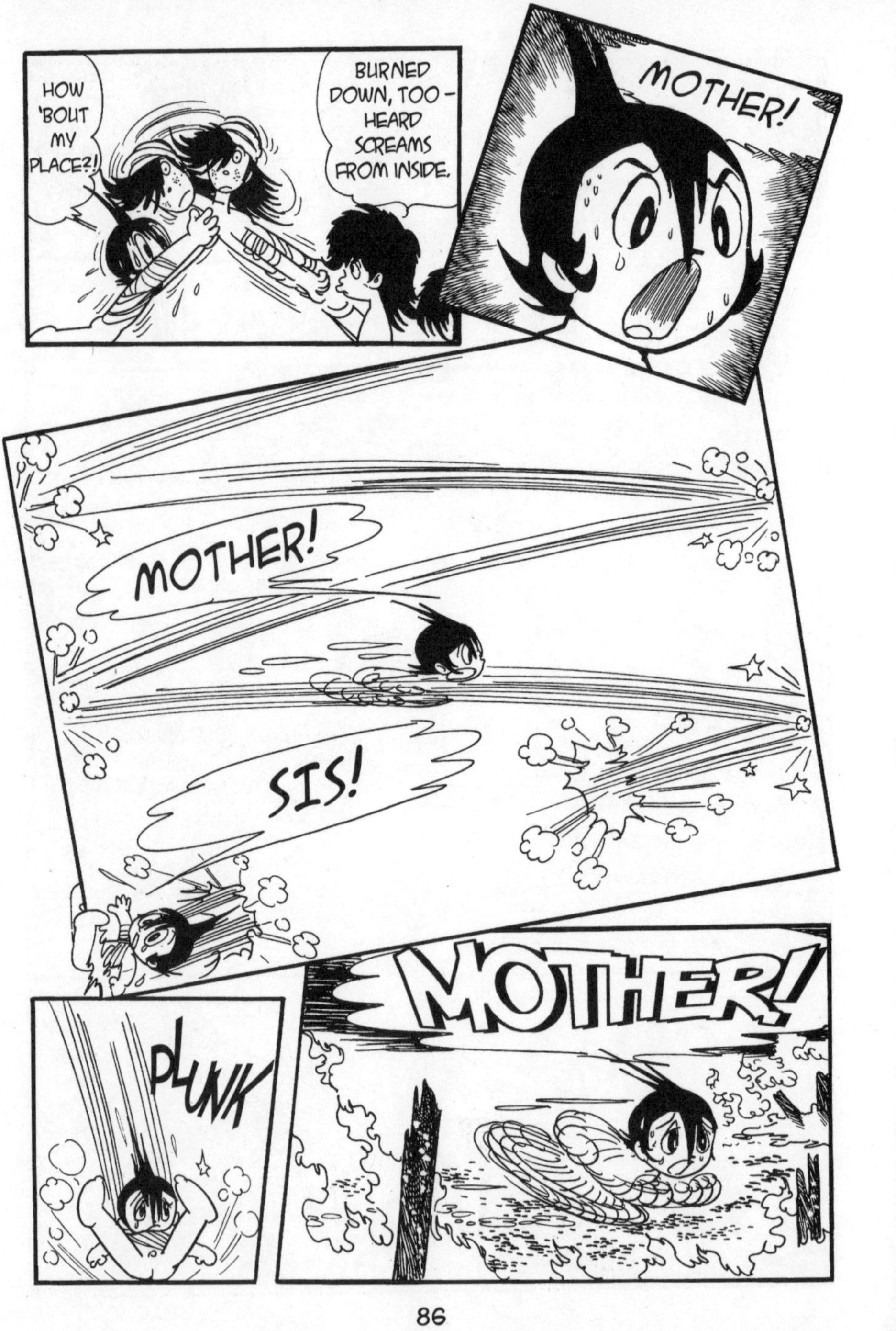
HOW 'BOUT MY PLACE?!
BURNED DOWN, TOO- HEARD SCREAMS FROM INSIDE.
MOTHER!
MOTHER!
SIS!
PLUNK
MOTHER!

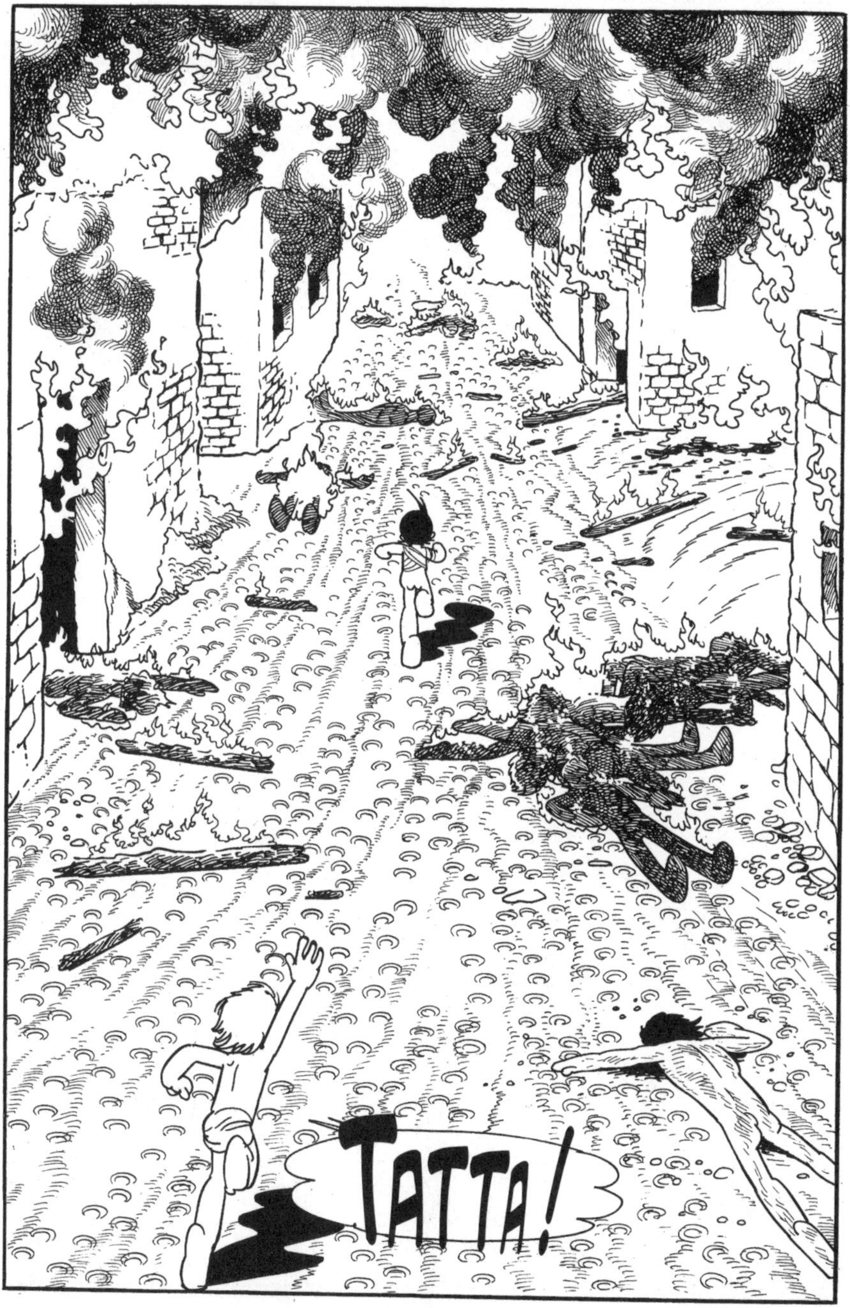
TATTA!

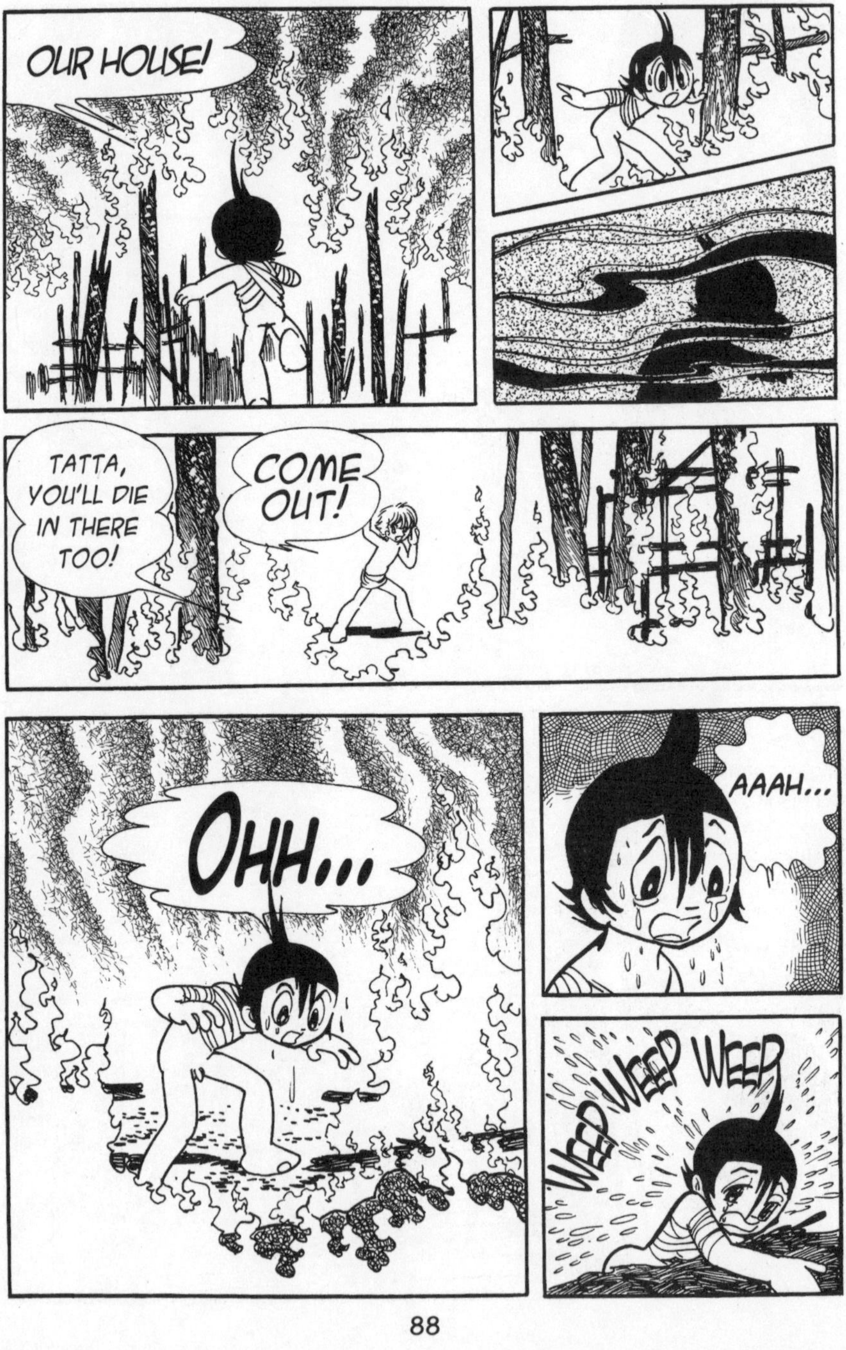
OUR HOUSE!
TATTA, YOU'LL DIE IN THERE TOO!
COME OUT!
OHH...
AAAH...
WEEP WEEP WEEP

KISS KISS

TATTA, I'M SORRY ...

LEAVE ME ALONE!!

HONEY, THERE'S JUST ONE PLACE TO HIDE: BEHIND THE MASTER'S HOUSE IN THE WINE CELLAR. IT'S SAFE FROM THE FIRE AND THE SOLDIERS.

LET'S GO!

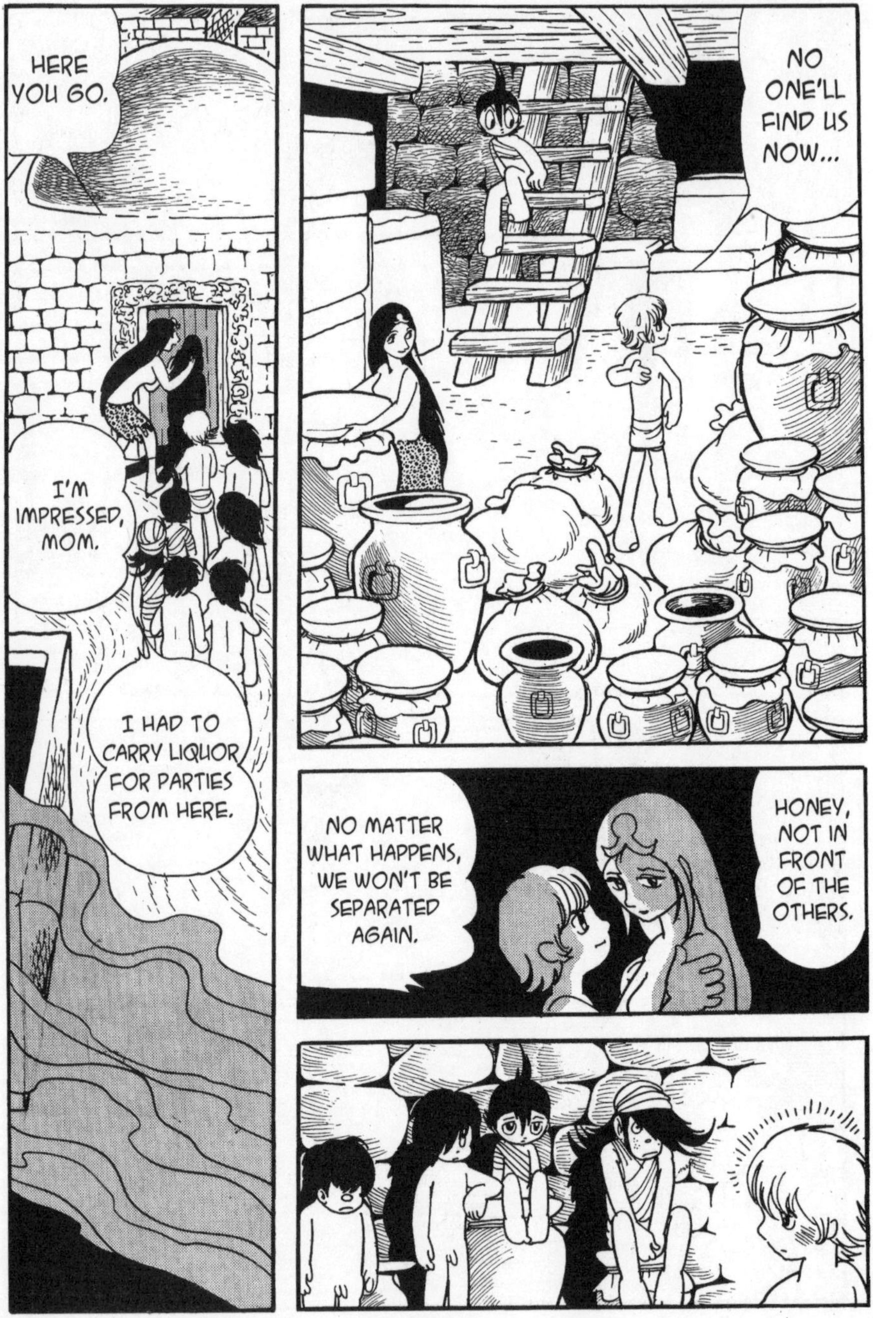
HERE YOU GO.
I'M IMPRESSED, MOM.
I HAD TO CARRY LIQUOR FOR PARTIES FROM HERE.
NO ONE'LL FIND US NOW...
NO MATTER WHAT HAPPENS, WE WON'T BE SEPARATED AGAIN.
HONEY, NOT IN FRONT OF THE OTHERS.

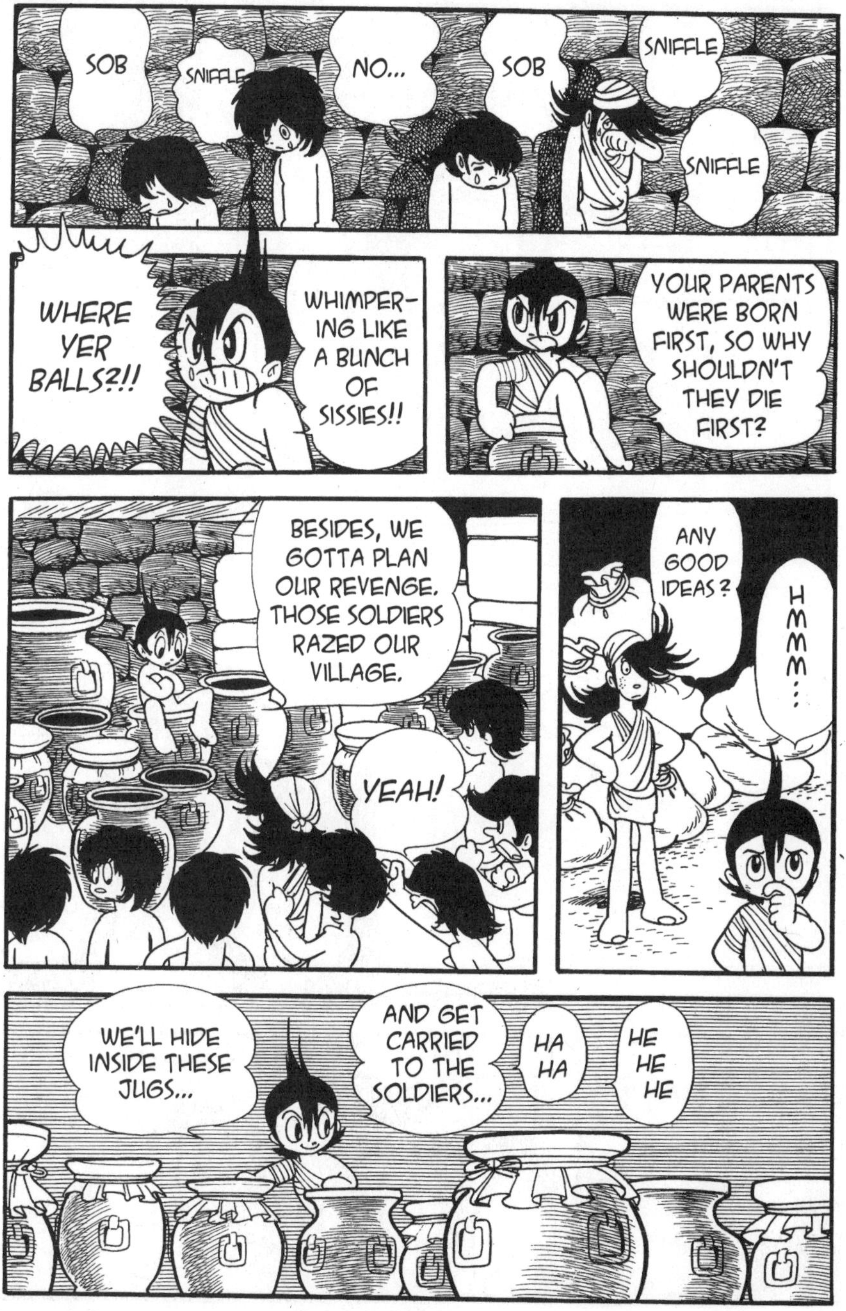
SOB
SNIFFLE
NO...
SOB
SNIFFLE
SNIFFLE
WHERE YER BALLS?!!
WHIMPER-ING LIKE A BUNCH OF SISSIES!!
YOUR PARENTS WERE BORN FIRST, SO WHY SHOULDN'T THEY DIE FIRST?
BESIDES, WE GOTTA PLAN OUR REVENGE. THOSE SOLDIERS RAZED OUR VILLAGE.
YEAH!
ANY GOOD IDEAS?
HMMM...
WE'LL HIDE INSIDE THESE JUGS...
AND GET CARRIED TO THE SOLDIERS...
HA HA
HE HE HE

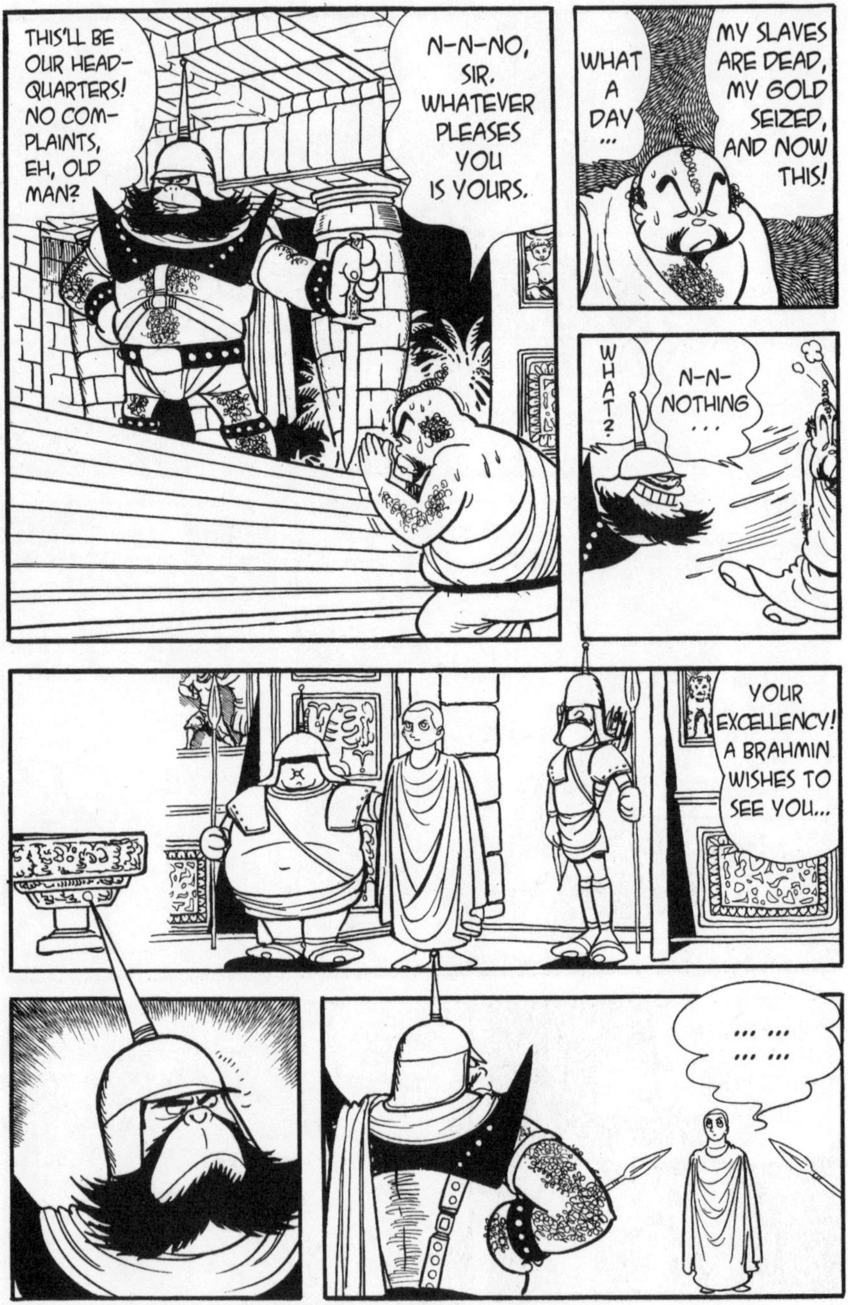
THIS'LL BE OUR HEAD-QUARTERS! NO COM-PLAINTS, EH, OLD MAN?
N-N-NO, SIR. WHATEVER PLEASES YOU IS YOURS.
WHAT A DAY ...
MY SLAVES ARE DEAD, MY GOLD SEIZED, AND NOW THIS!
WHAT?
N-N-NOTHING ...
YOUR EXCELLENCY! A BRAHMIN WISHES TO SEE YOU...
... ...
... ...

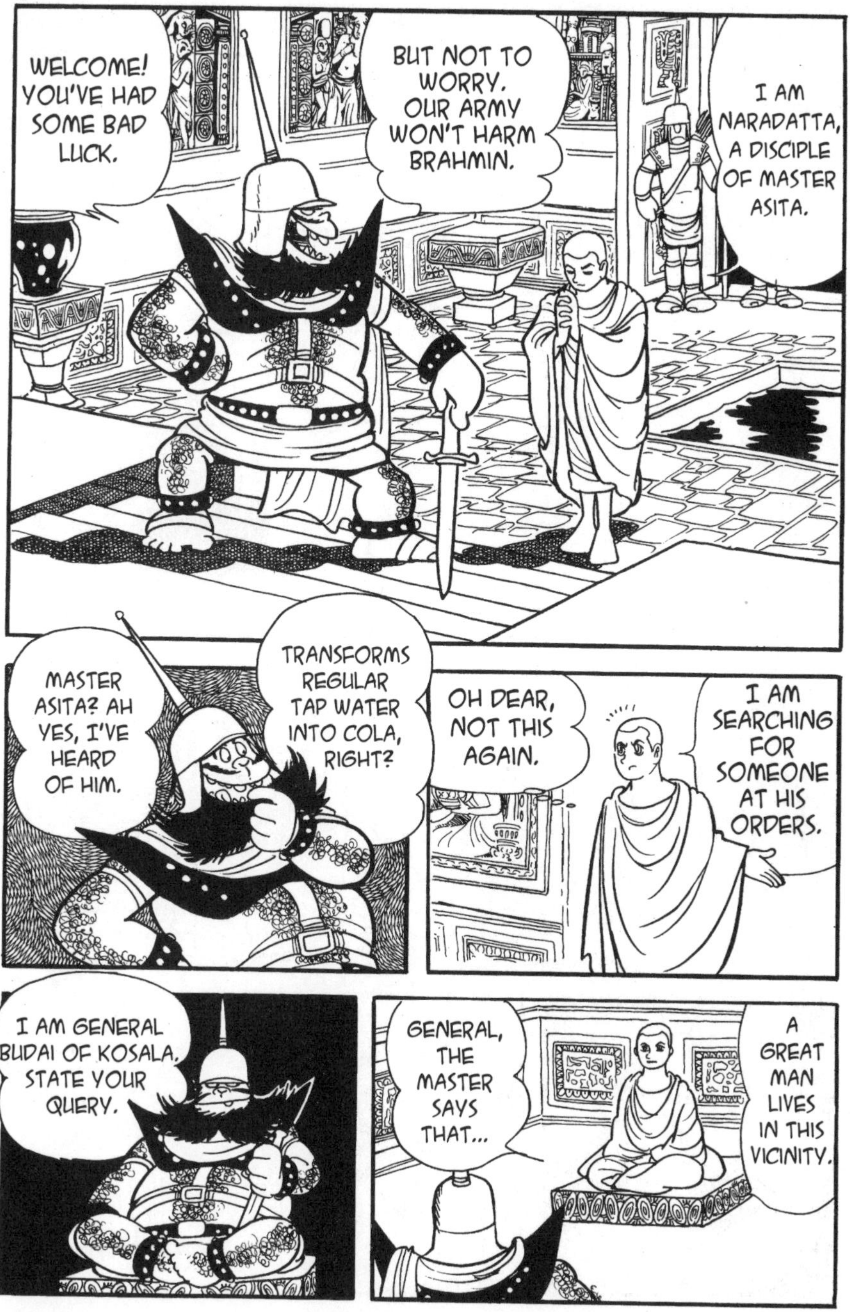
WELCOME! YOU'VE HAD SOME BAD LUCK.
BUT NOT TO WORRY. OUR ARMY WON'T HARM BRAHMIN.
I AM NARADATTA, A DISCIPLE OF MASTER ASITA.
MASTER ASITA? AH YES, I'VE HEARD OF HIM.
TRANSFORMS REGULAR TAP WATER INTO COLA, RIGHT?
OH DEAR, NOT THIS AGAIN.
I AM SEARCHING FOR SOMEONE AT HIS ORDERS.
I AM GENERAL BUDAI OF KOSALA. STATE YOUR QUERY.
GENERAL, THE MASTER SAYS THAT...
A GREAT MAN LIVES IN THIS VICINITY.

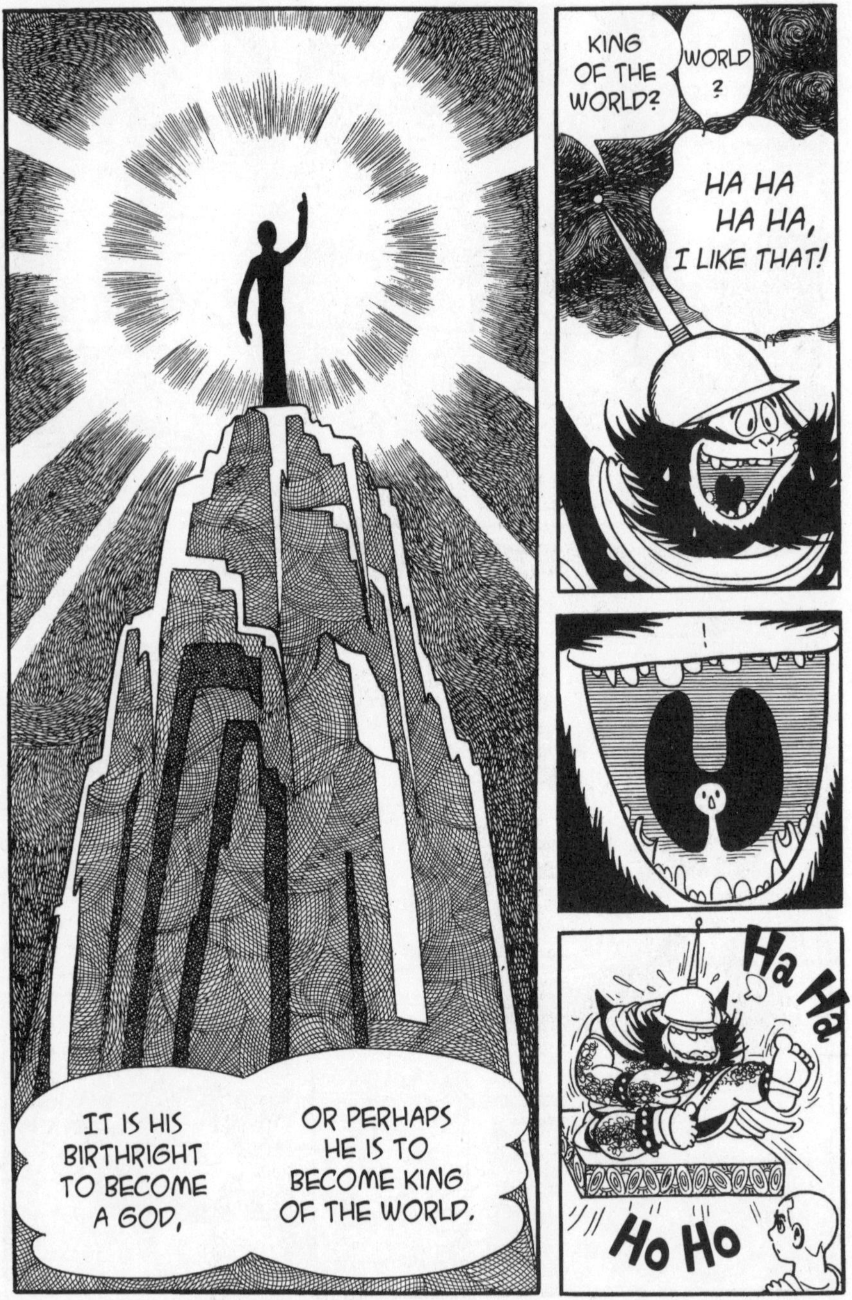
IT IS HIS BIRTHRIGHT TO BECOME A GOD,
OR PERHAPS HE IS TO BECOME KING OF THE WORLD.
KING OF THE WORLD?
WORLD ?
HA HA HA HA, I LIKE THAT!
!
Ha Ha
Ho Ho

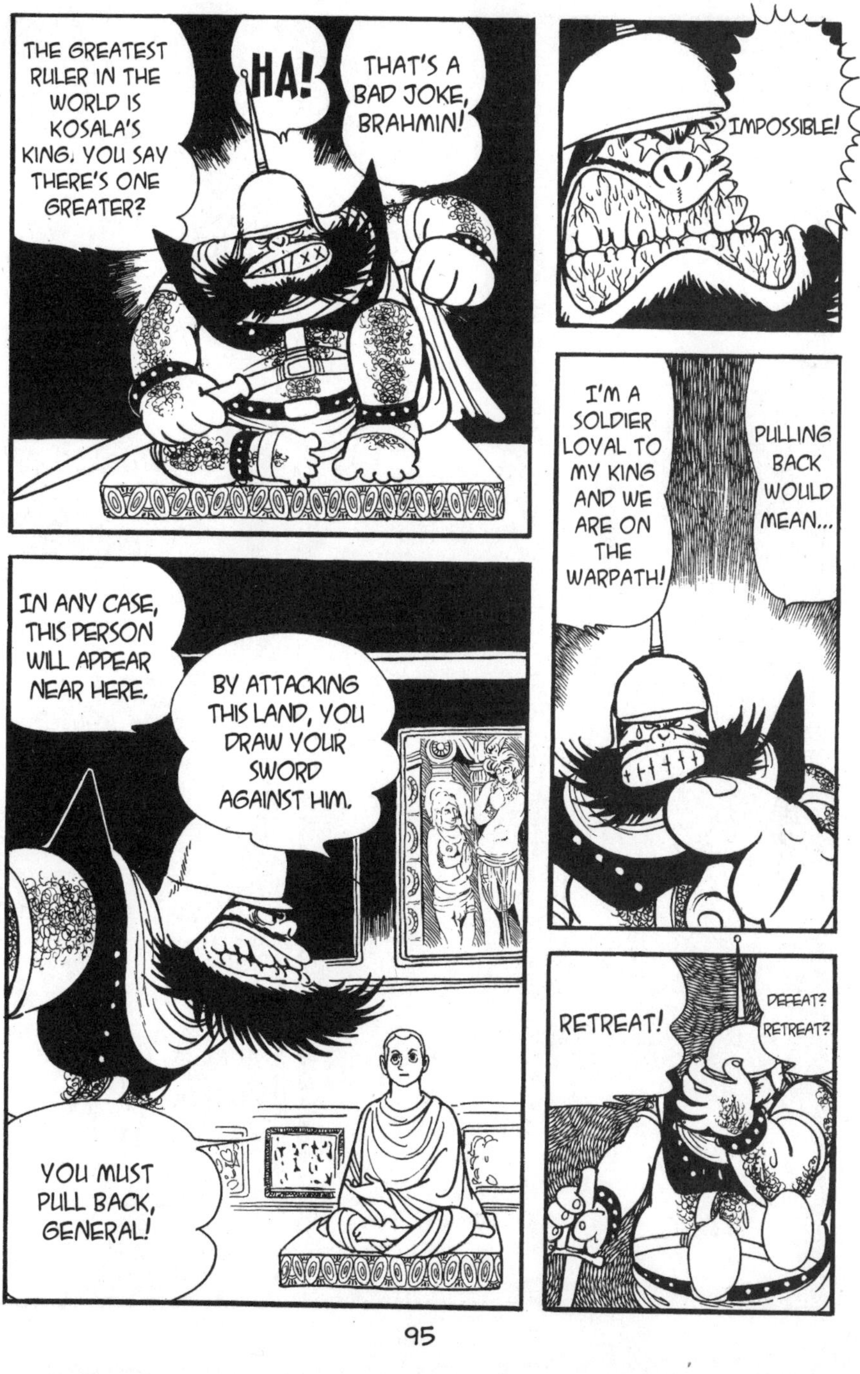
THE GREATEST RULER IN THE WORLD IS KOSALA'S KING. YOU SAY THERE'S ONE GREATER?
HA!
THAT'S A BAD JOKE, BRAHMIN!
IMPOSSIBLE!
IN ANY CASE, THIS PERSON WILL APPEAR NEAR HERE.
BY ATTACKING THIS LAND, YOU DRAW YOUR SWORD AGAINST HIM.
YOU MUST PULL BACK, GENERAL!
I'M A SOLDIER LOYAL TO MY KING AND WE ARE ON THE WARPATH!
PULLING BACK WOULD MEAN...
RETREAT!
DEFEAT? RETREAT?

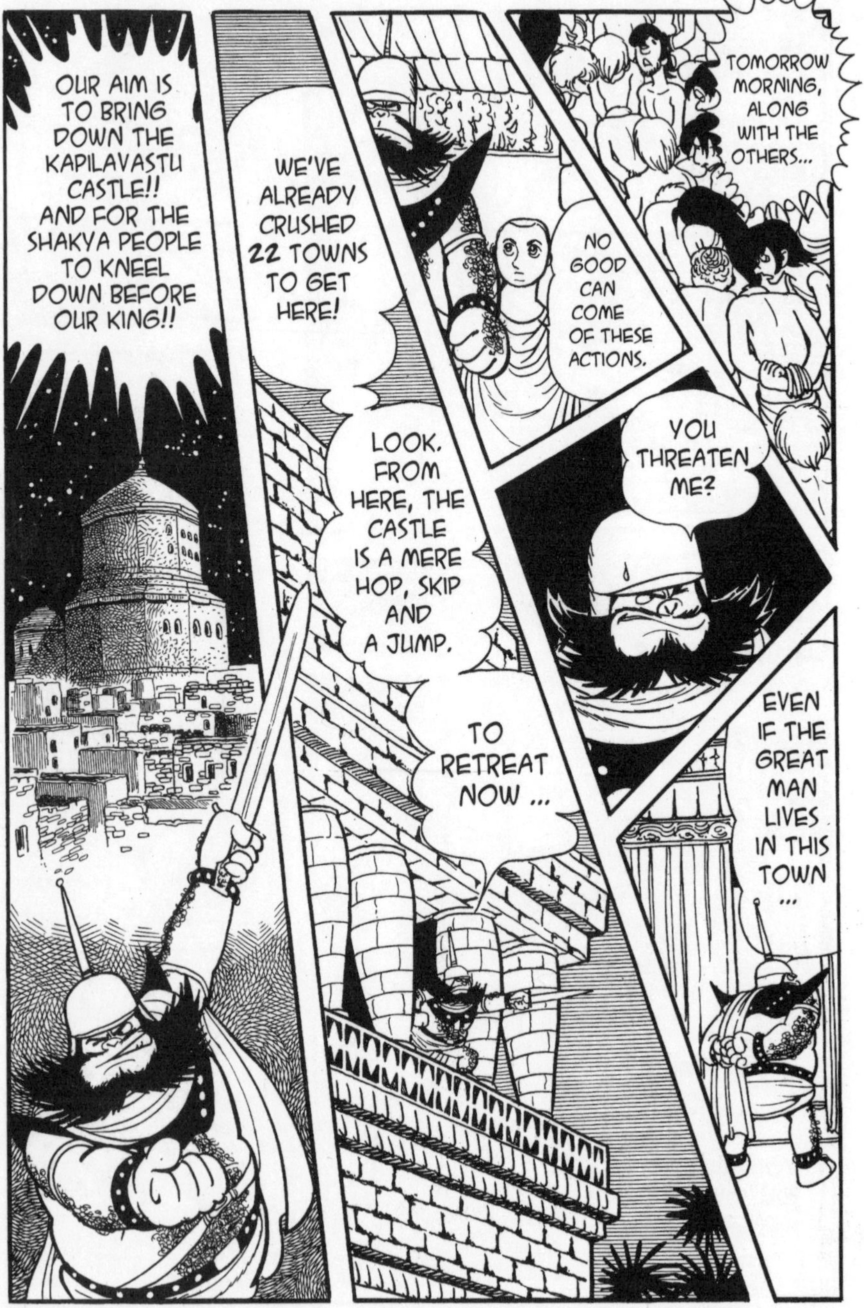
OUR AIM IS TO BRING DOWN THE KAPILAVASTU CASTLE!! AND FOR THE SHAKYA PEOPLE TO KNEEL DOWN BEFORE OUR KING!!
WE'VE ALREADY CRUSHED 22 TOWNS TO GET HERE!
LOOK. FROM HERE, THE CASTLE IS A MERE HOP, SKIP AND A JUMP.
TO RETREAT NOW ...
NO GOOD CAN COME OF THESE ACTIONS.
TOMORROW MORNING, ALONG WITH THE OTHERS...
YOU THREATEN ME?
EVEN IF THE GREAT MAN LIVES IN THIS TOWN ...

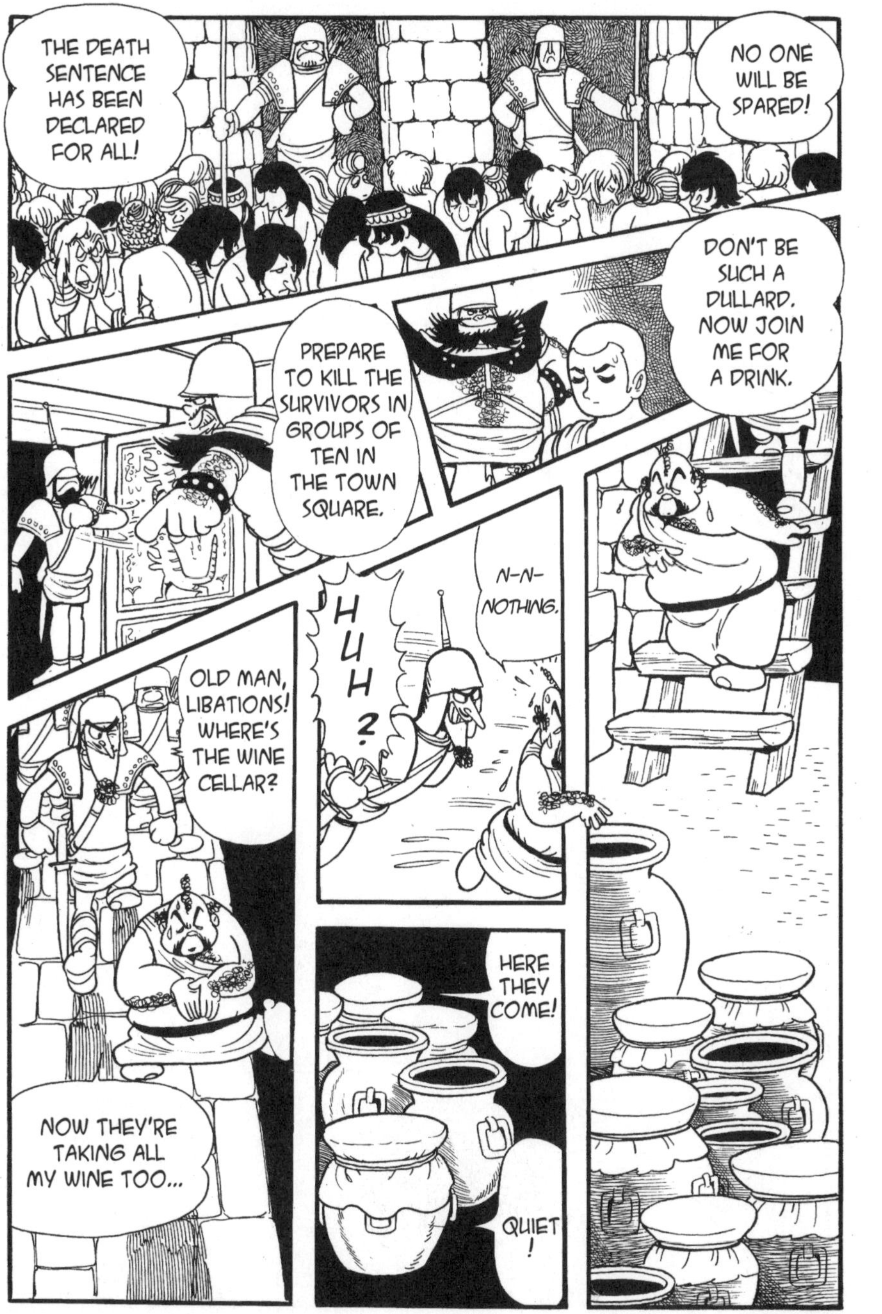
THE DEATH SENTENCE HAS BEEN DECLARED FOR ALL!
NO ONE WILL BE SPARED!
PREPARE TO KILL THE SURVIVORS IN GROUPS OF TEN IN THE TOWN SQUARE.
DON'T BE SUCH A DULLARD. NOW JOIN ME FOR A DRINK.
OLD MAN, LIBATIONS! WHERE'S THE WINE CELLAR?
HUH?
N-N-NOTHING.
NOW THEY'RE TAKING ALL MY WINE TOO...
HERE THEY COME!
QUIET!

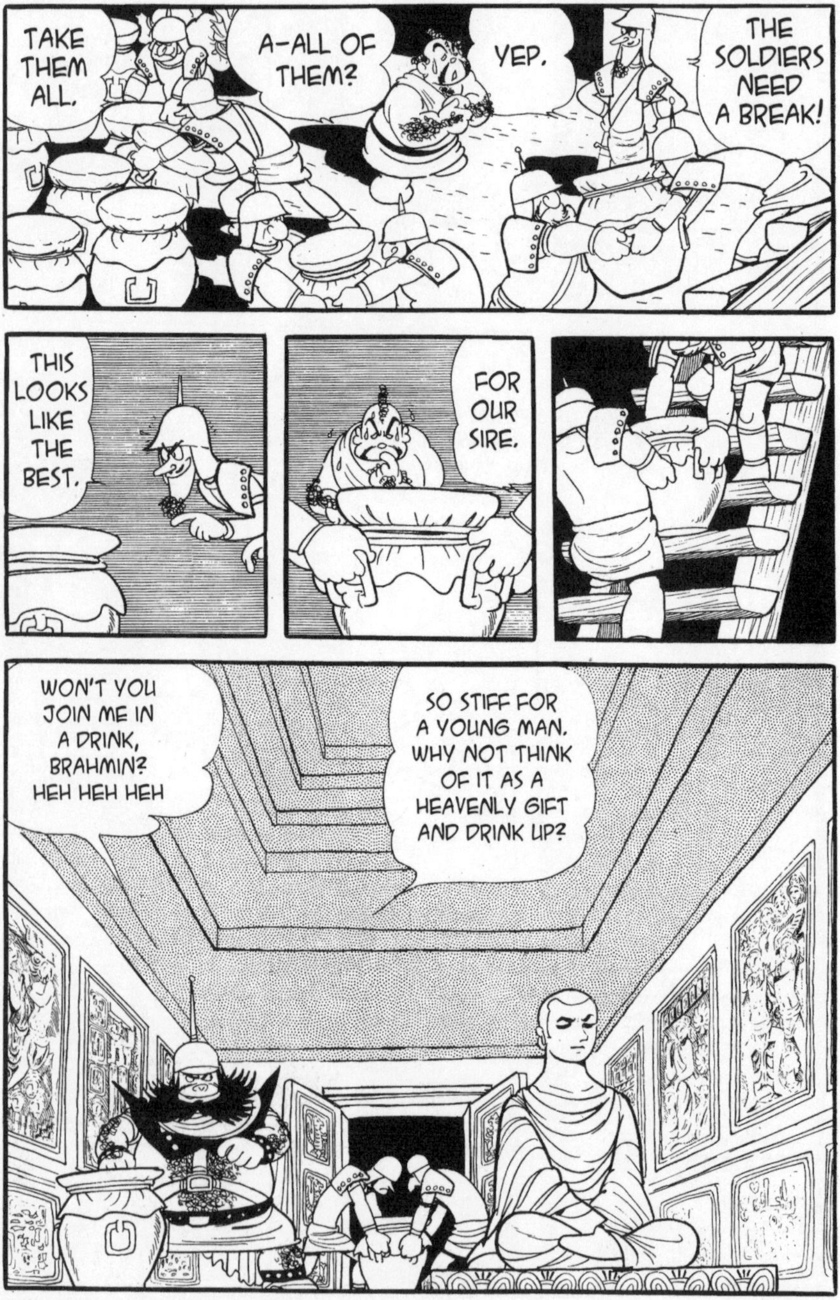
TAKE THEM ALL.
A-ALL OF THEM?
YEP.
THE SOLDIERS NEED A BREAK!
THIS LOOKS LIKE THE BEST.
FOR OUR SIRE.
WON'T YOU JOIN ME IN A DRINK, BRAHMIN? HEH HEH HEH
SO STIFF FOR A YOUNG MAN. WHY NOT THINK OF IT AS A HEAVENLY GIFT AND DRINK UP?

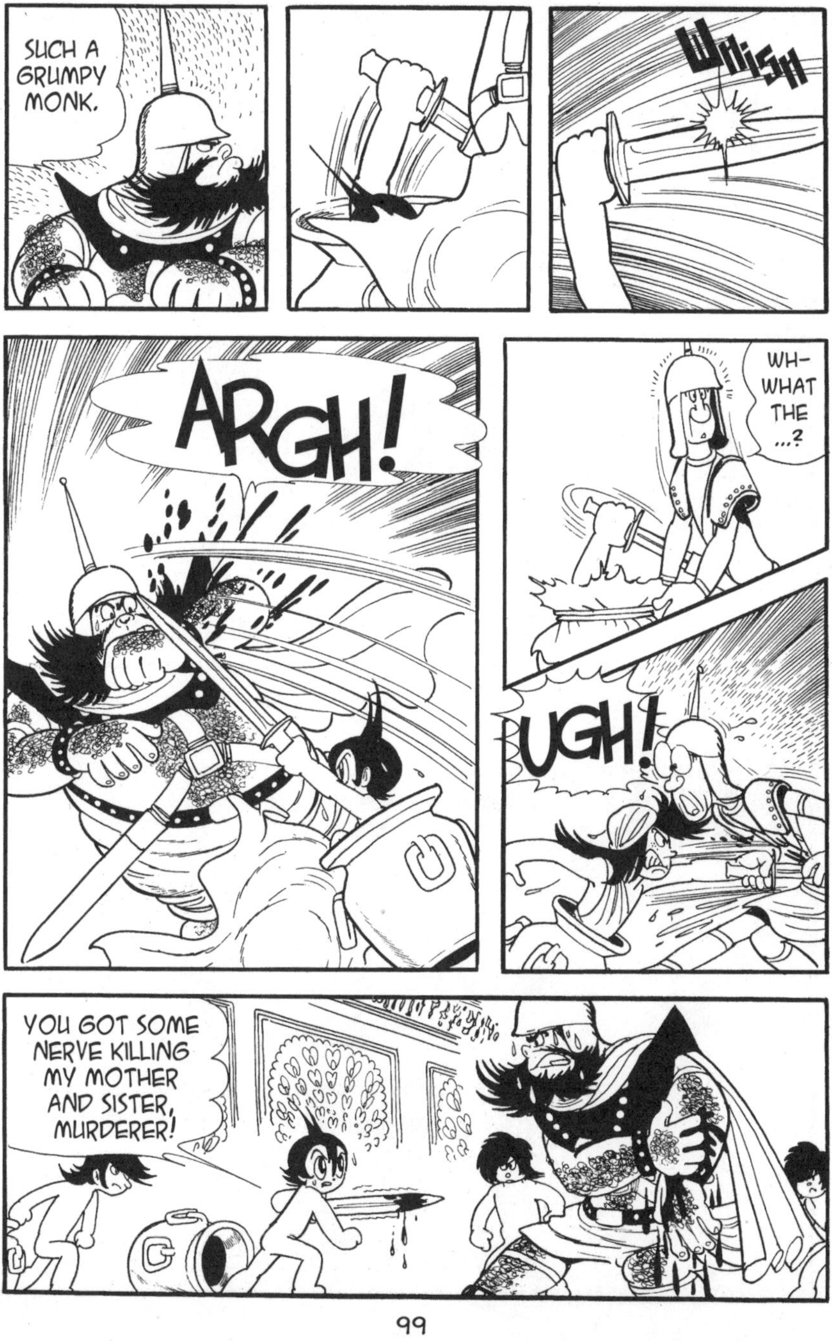
SUCH A GRUMPY MONK.
WHISH
ARGH!
WH- WHAT THE ...?
UGH!
YOU GOT SOME NERVE KILLING MY MOTHER AND SISTER, MURDERER!

HOP

SLAM!

DON'T LET ANYONE THROUGH 'TIL I FINISH OFF THIS BRUTE!

ROGER!

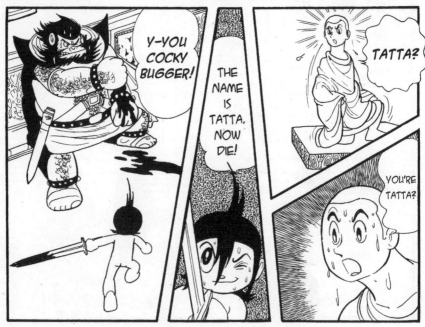

Y-YOU COCKY BUGGER!

THE NAME IS TATTA, NOW DIE!

TATTA?

YOU'RE TATTA?

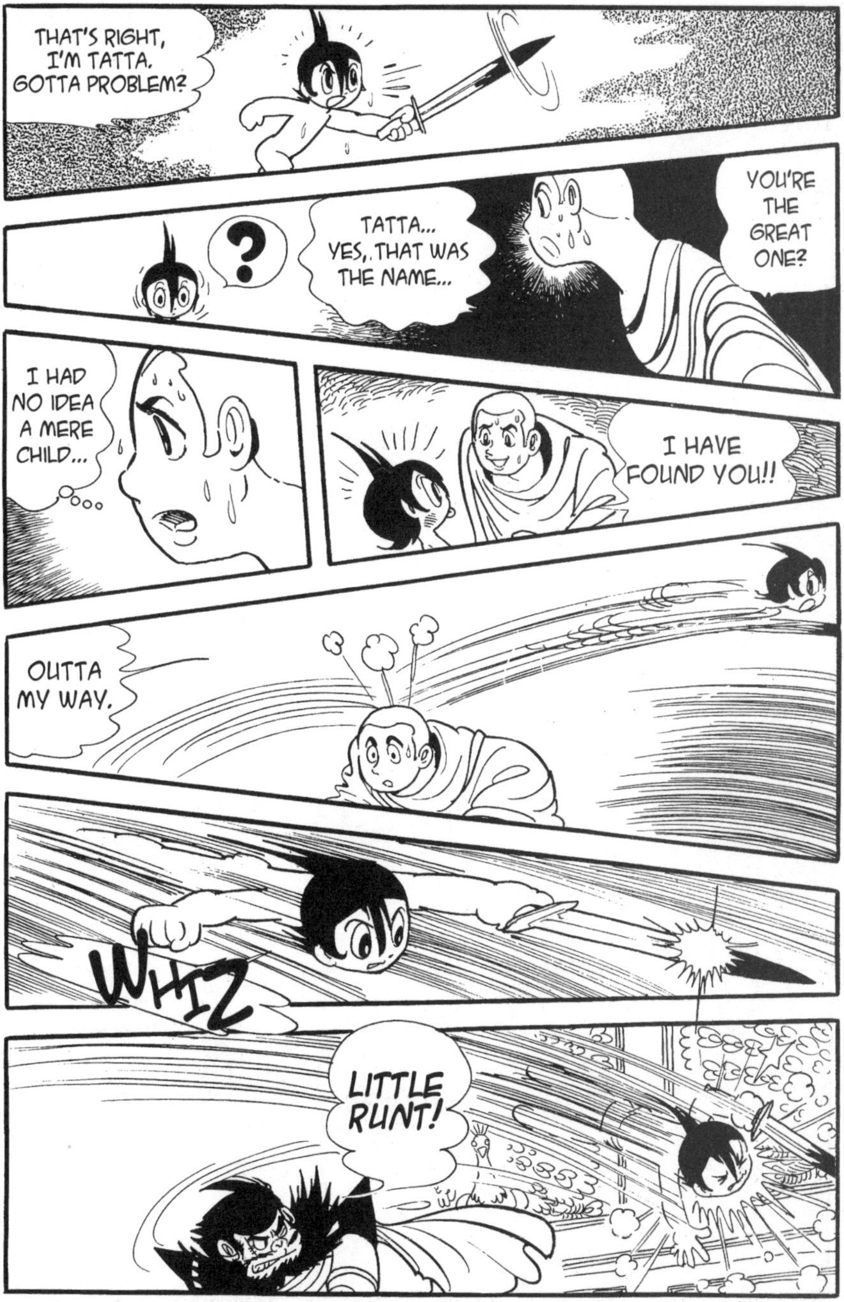
THAT'S RIGHT, I'M TATTA. GOTTA PROBLEM?
?
TATTA... YES,.THAT WAS THE NAME...
YOU'RE THE GREAT ONE?
I HAD NO IDEA A MERE CHILD...
I HAVE FOUND YOU!!
OUTTA MY WAY.
WHIZ
LITTLE RUNT!

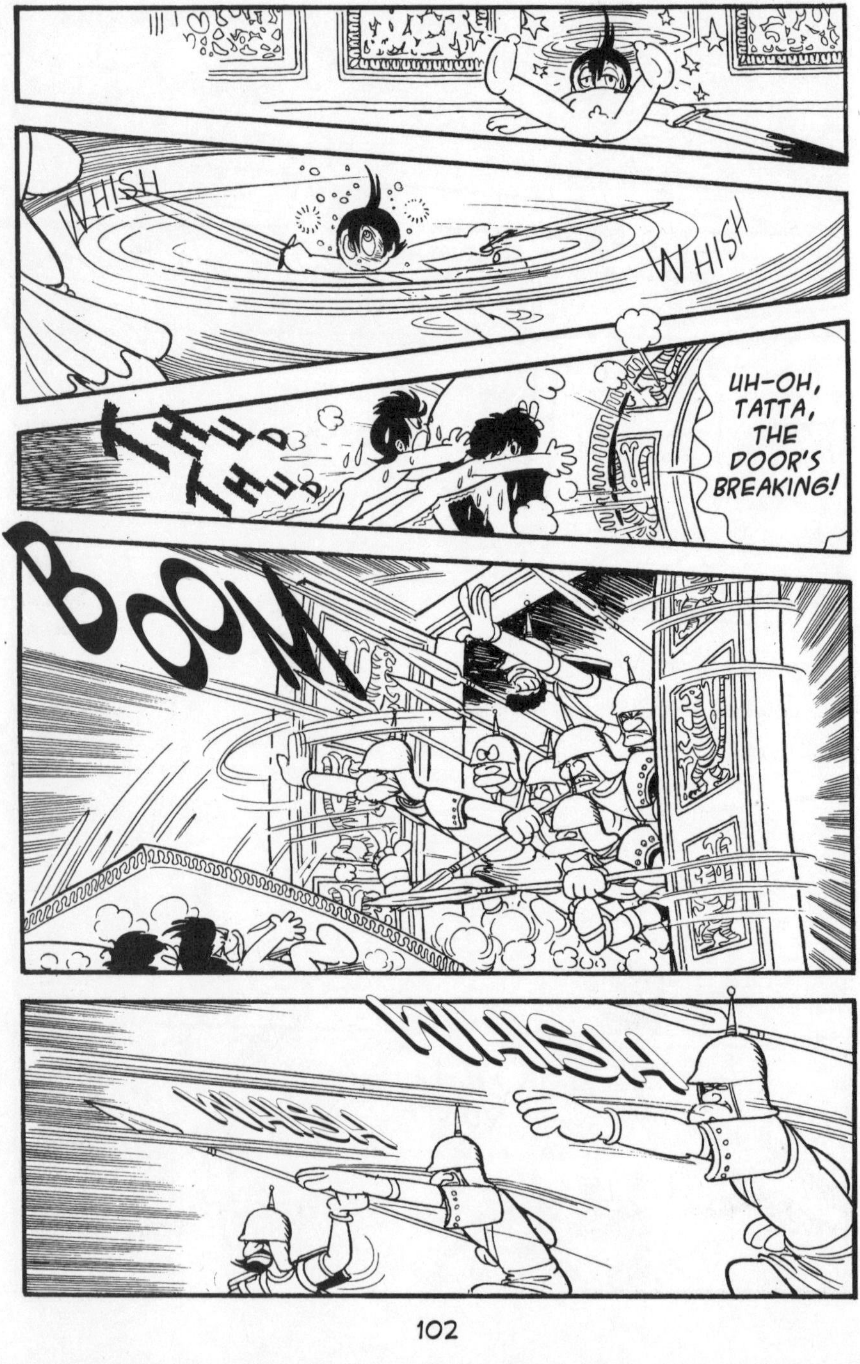
WHISH
WHISH
THUD THUD
UH-OH, TATTA, THE DOOR'S BREAKING!
BOOM
WHSH
WHSH

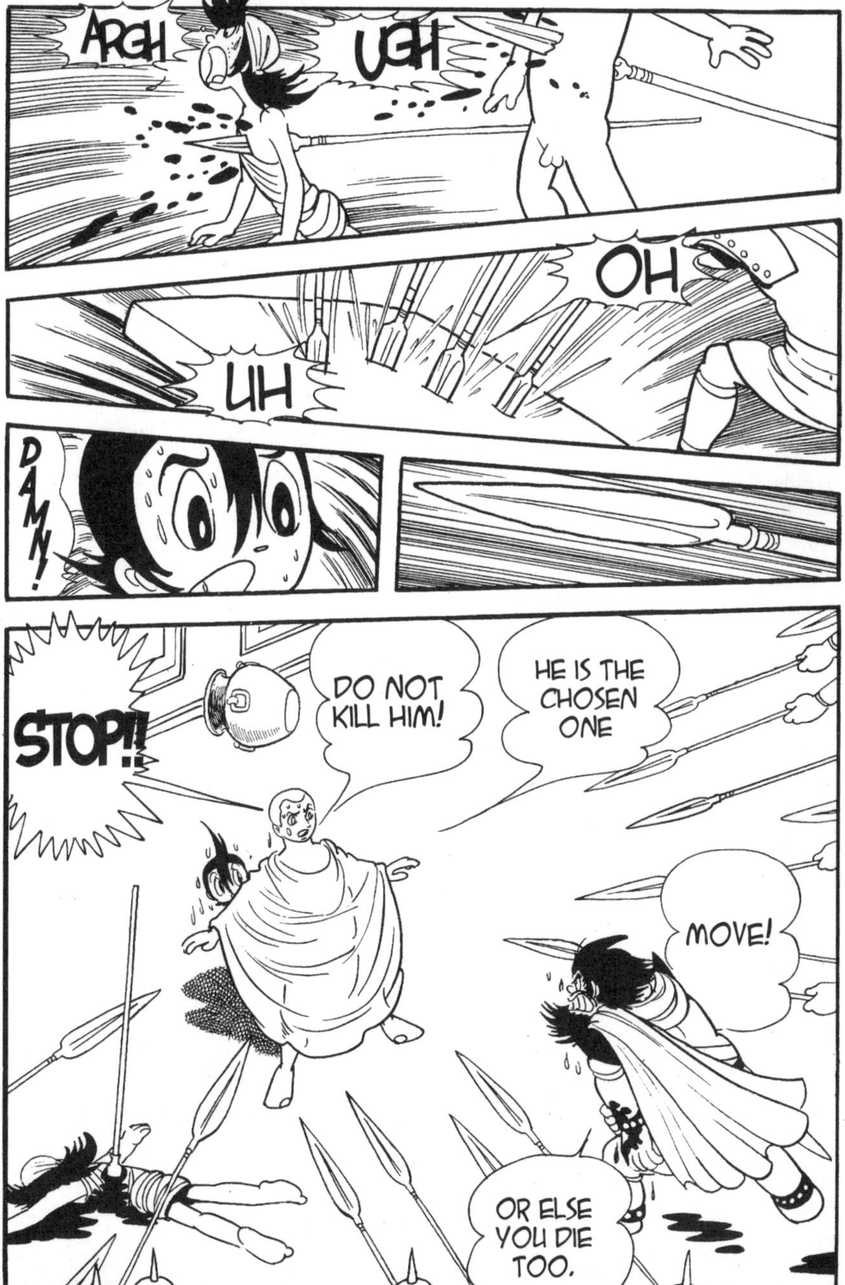
ARGH
UGH
OH
UH
DAMN!
STOP!!
DO NOT KILL HIM!
HE IS THE CHOSEN ONE
MOVE!
OR ELSE YOU DIE TOO.

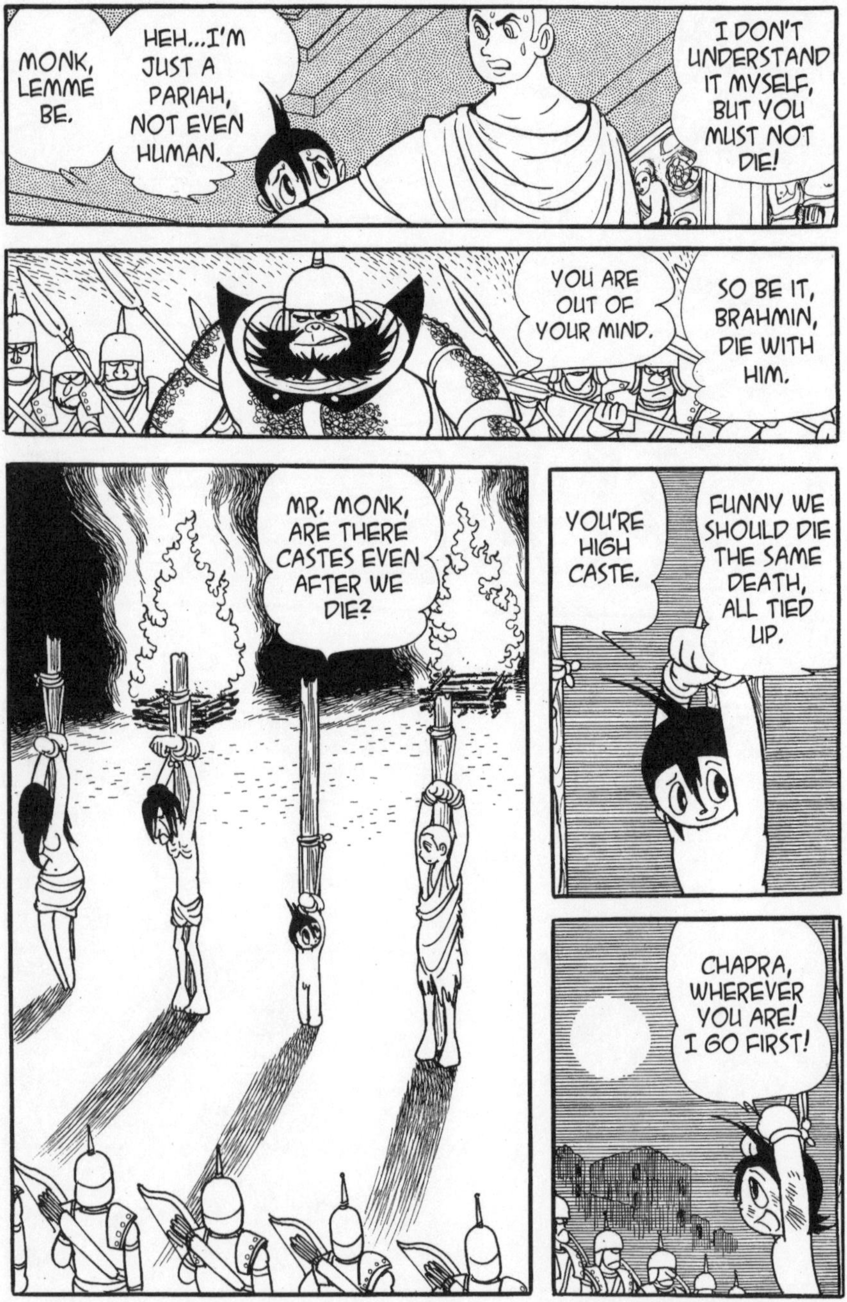
MONK, LEMME BE.
HEH...I'M JUST A PARIAH, NOT EVEN HUMAN.
I DON'T UNDERSTAND IT MYSELF, BUT YOU MUST NOT DIE!
YOU ARE OUT OF YOUR MIND.
SO BE IT, BRAHMIN, DIE WITH HIM.
MR. MONK, ARE THERE CASTES EVEN AFTER WE DIE?
YOU'RE HIGH CASTE.
FUNNY WE SHOULD DIE THE SAME DEATH, ALL TIED UP.
CHAPRA, WHEREVER YOU ARE! I GO FIRST!

CHAPTER THREE

GENERAL BUDAI

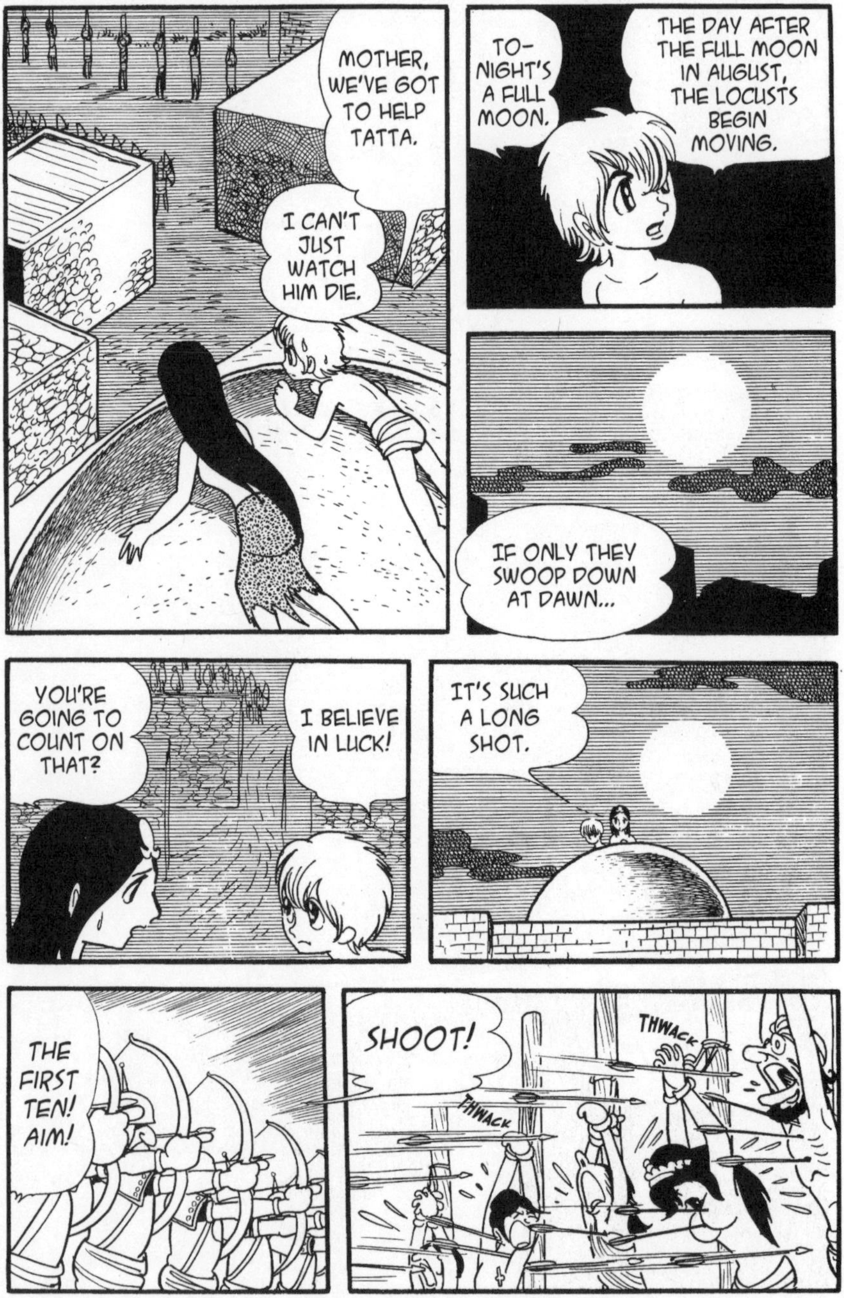
MOTHER, WE'VE GOT TO HELP TATTA.
I CAN'T JUST WATCH HIM DIE.
TO-NIGHT'S A FULL MOON.
THE DAY AFTER THE FULL MOON IN AUGUST, THE LOCUSTS BEGIN MOVING.
IF ONLY THEY SWOOP DOWN AT DAWN...
YOU'RE GOING TO COUNT ON THAT?
I BELIEVE IN LUCK!
IT'S SUCH A LONG SHOT.
THE FIRST TEN! AIM!
SHOOT!
THWACK
THWACK

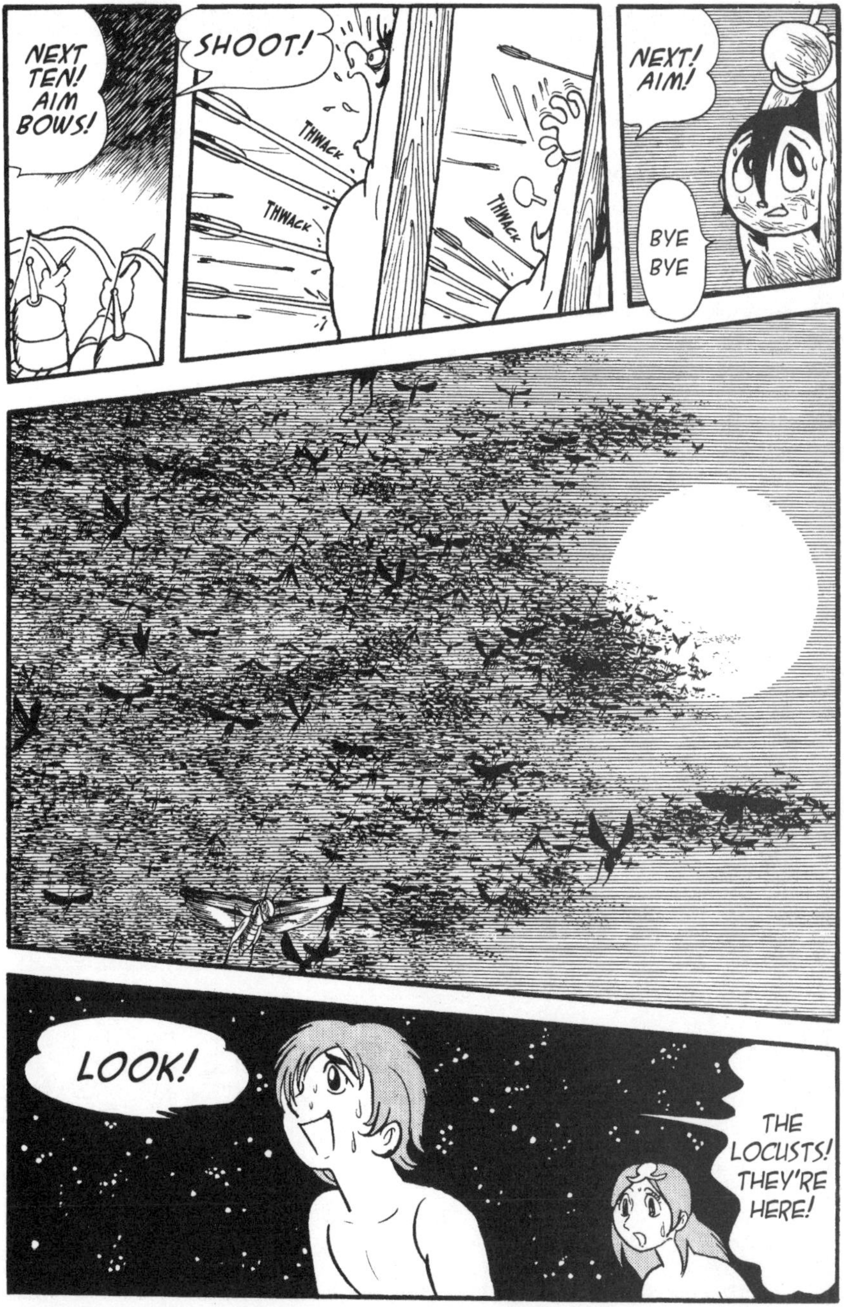
NEXT TEN! AIM BOWS!
SHOOT!
THWACK
THWACK
THWACK
NEXT! AIM!
BYE BYE
LOOK!
THE LOCUSTS! THEY'RE HERE!

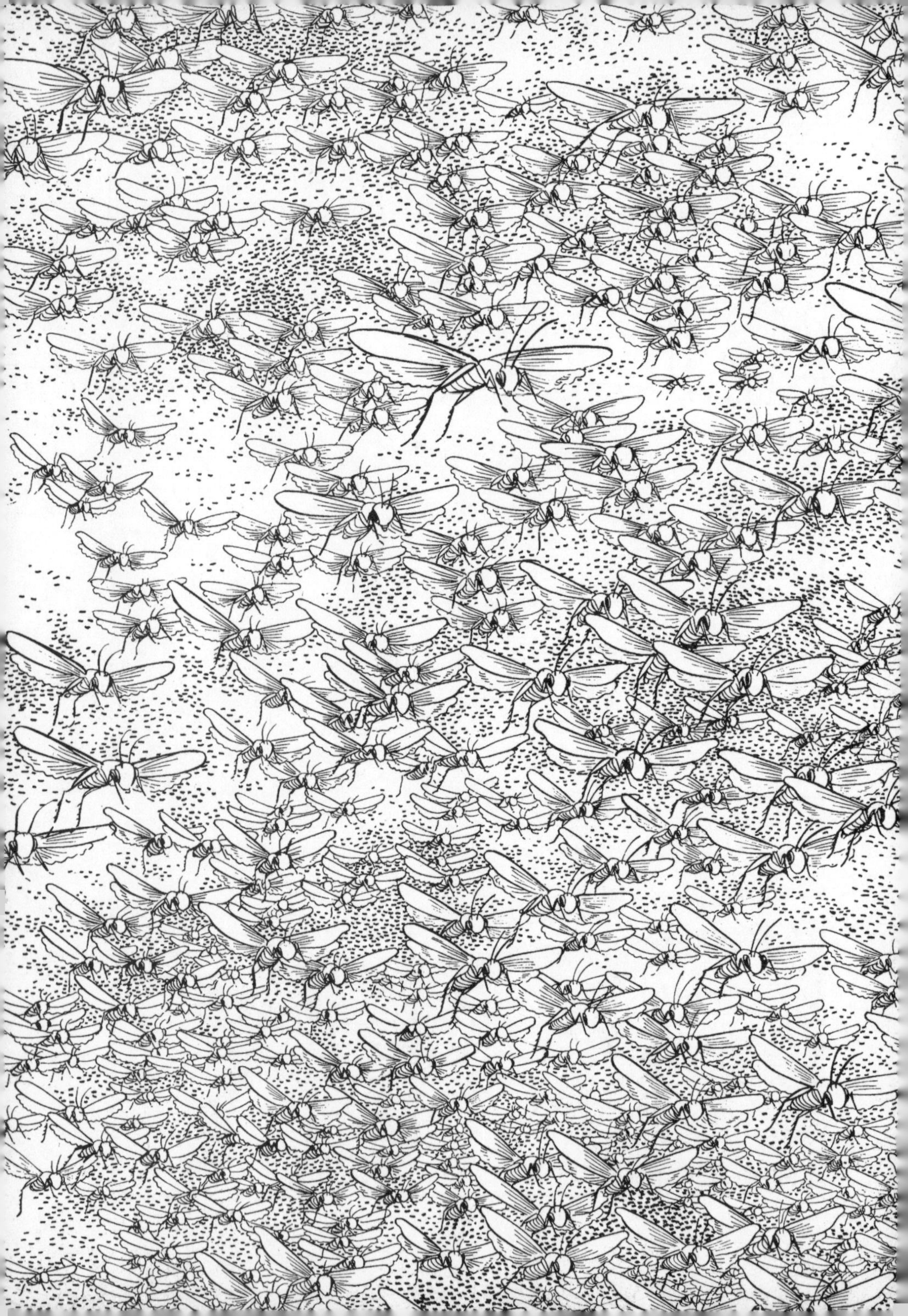

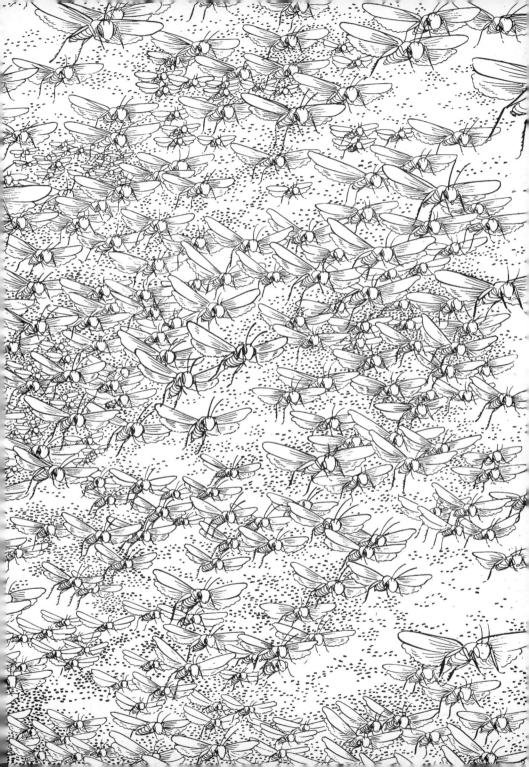

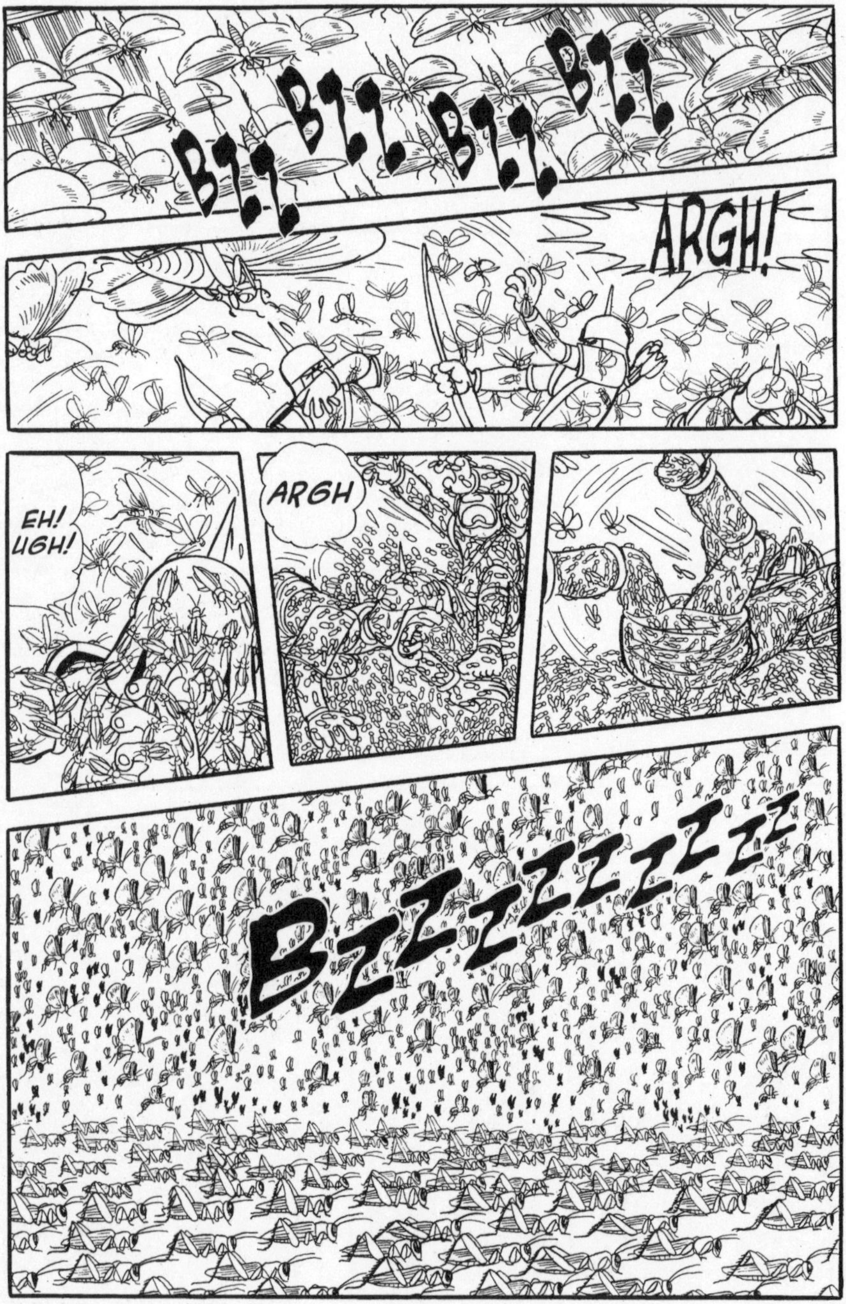
BZZ BZZ BZZ BZZ
ARGH!
EH! UGH!
ARGH
BZZZZZZZZZZ

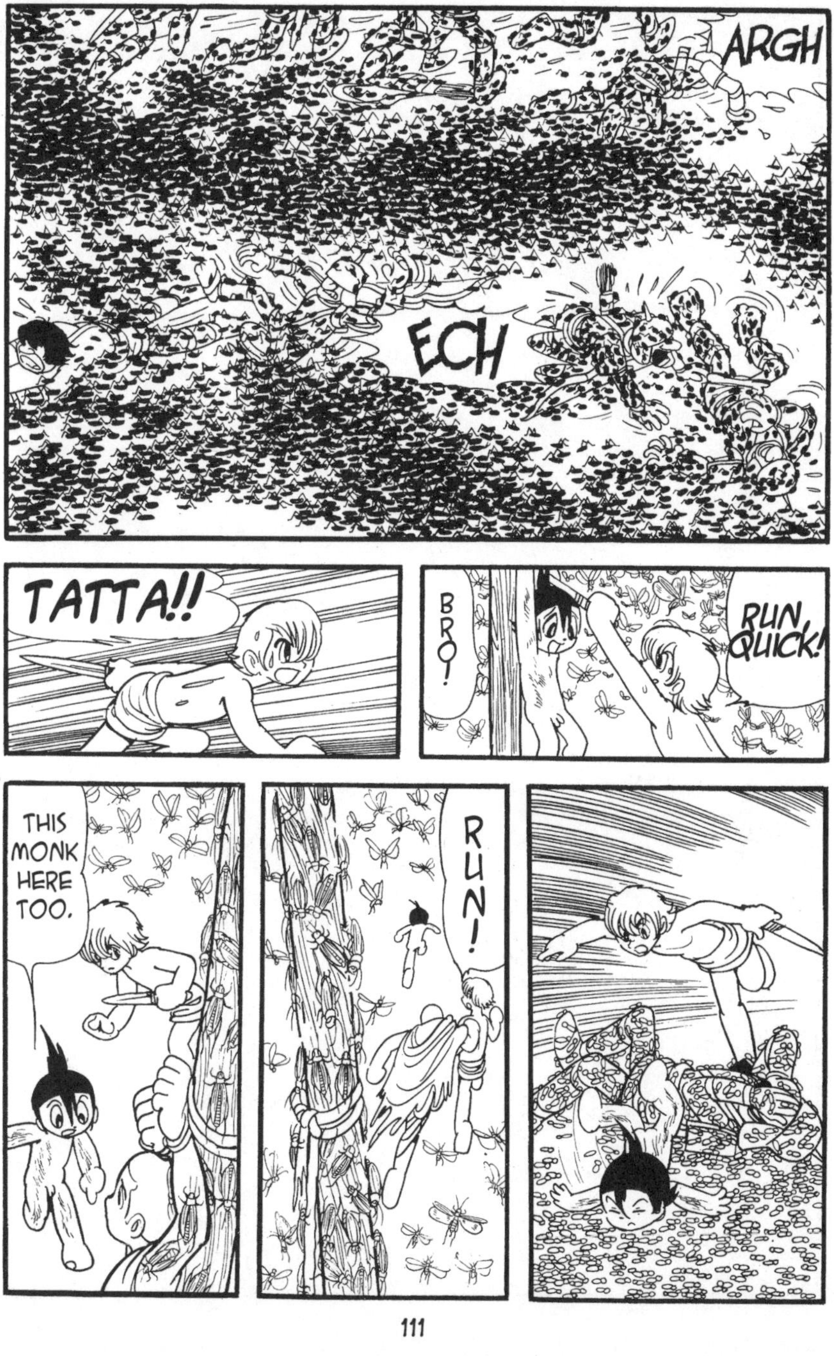
ARGH
ECH
TATTA!!
BRO!
RUN QUICK!
THIS MONK HERE TOO.
RUN!

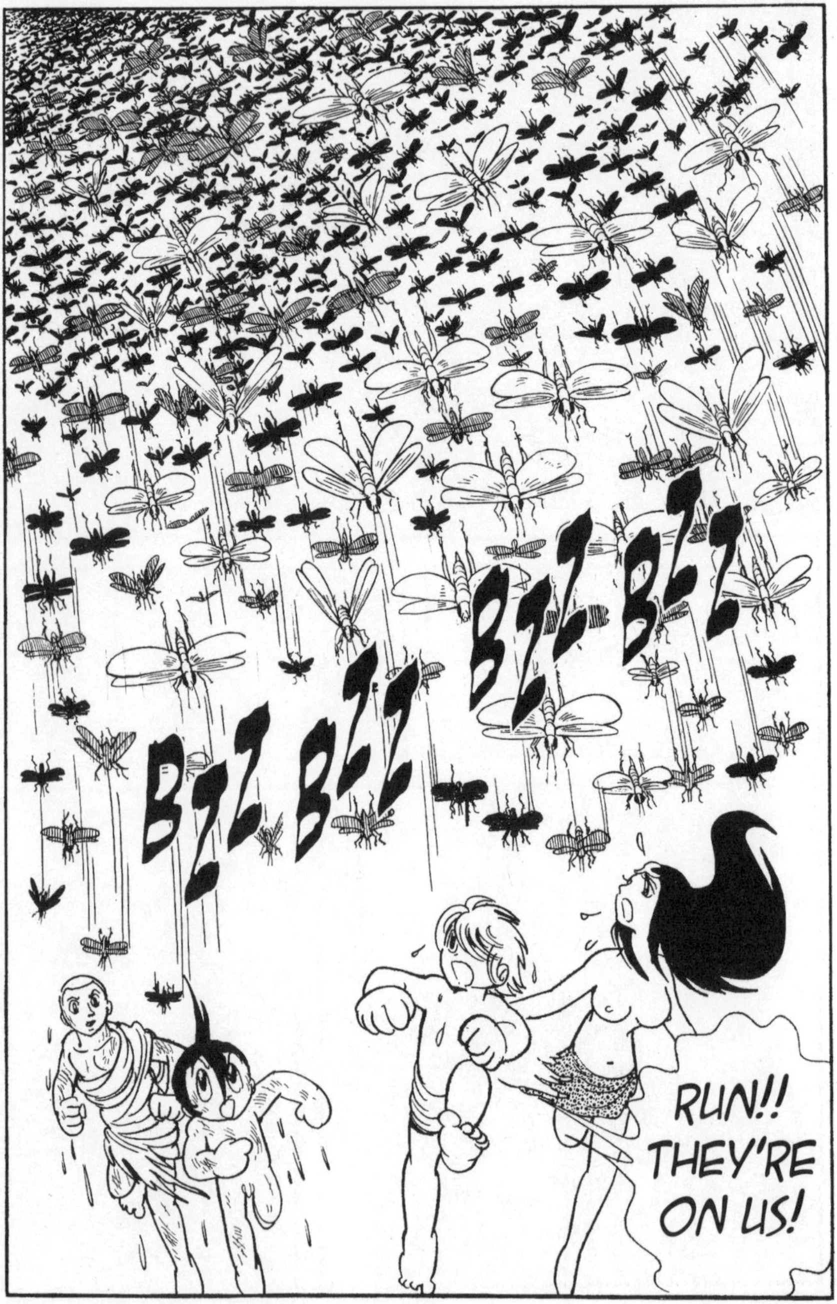
BZZ BZZ
BZZ BZZ
RUN!! THEY'RE ON US!

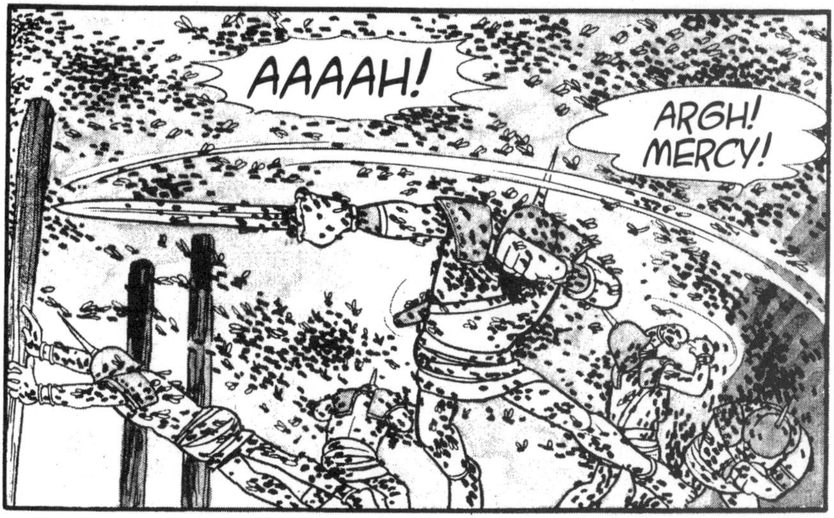
AAAAH!
ARGH! MERCY!
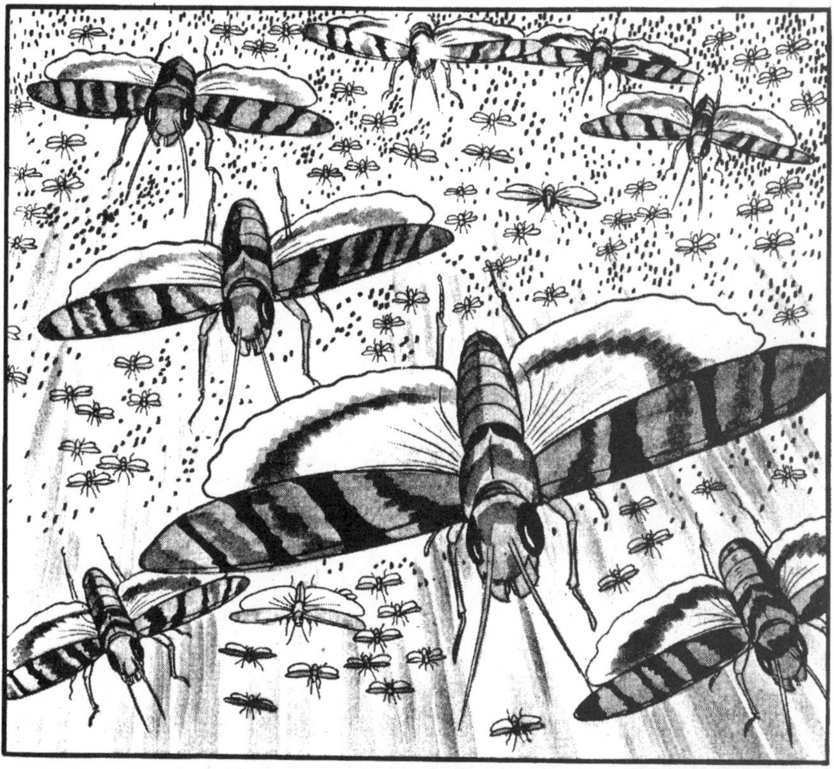

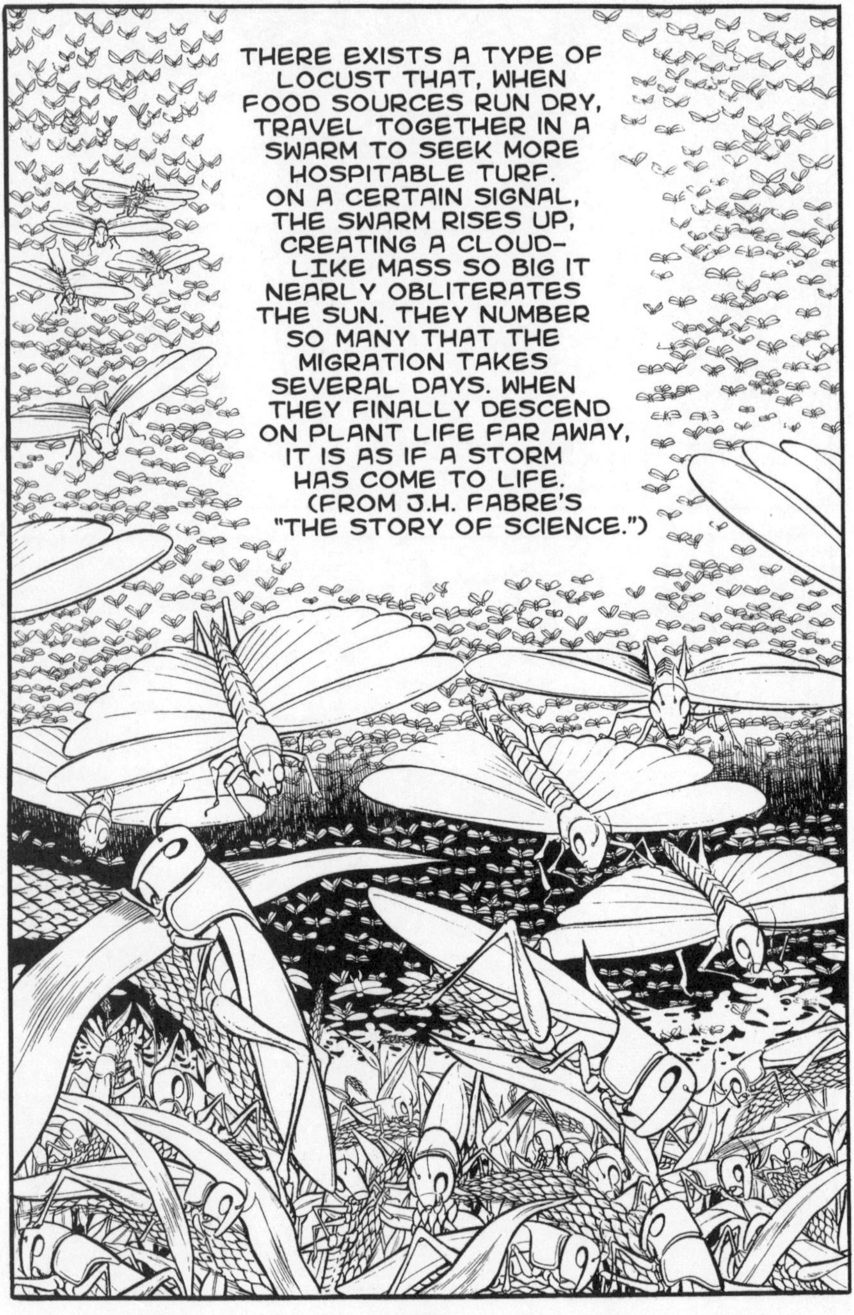
THERE EXISTS A TYPE OF LOCUST THAT, WHEN FOOD SOURCES RUN DRY, TRAVEL TOGETHER IN A SWARM TO SEEK MORE HOSPITABLE TURF. ON A CERTAIN SIGNAL, THE SWARM RISES UP, CREATING A CLOUD-LIKE MASS SO BIG IT NEARLY OBLITERATES THE SUN. THEY NUMBER SO MANY THAT THE MIGRATION TAKES SEVERAL DAYS. WHEN THEY FINALLY DESCEND ON PLANT LIFE FAR AWAY, IT IS AS IF A STORM HAS COME TO LIFE. (FROM J.H. FABRE'S "THE STORY OF SCIENCE.")

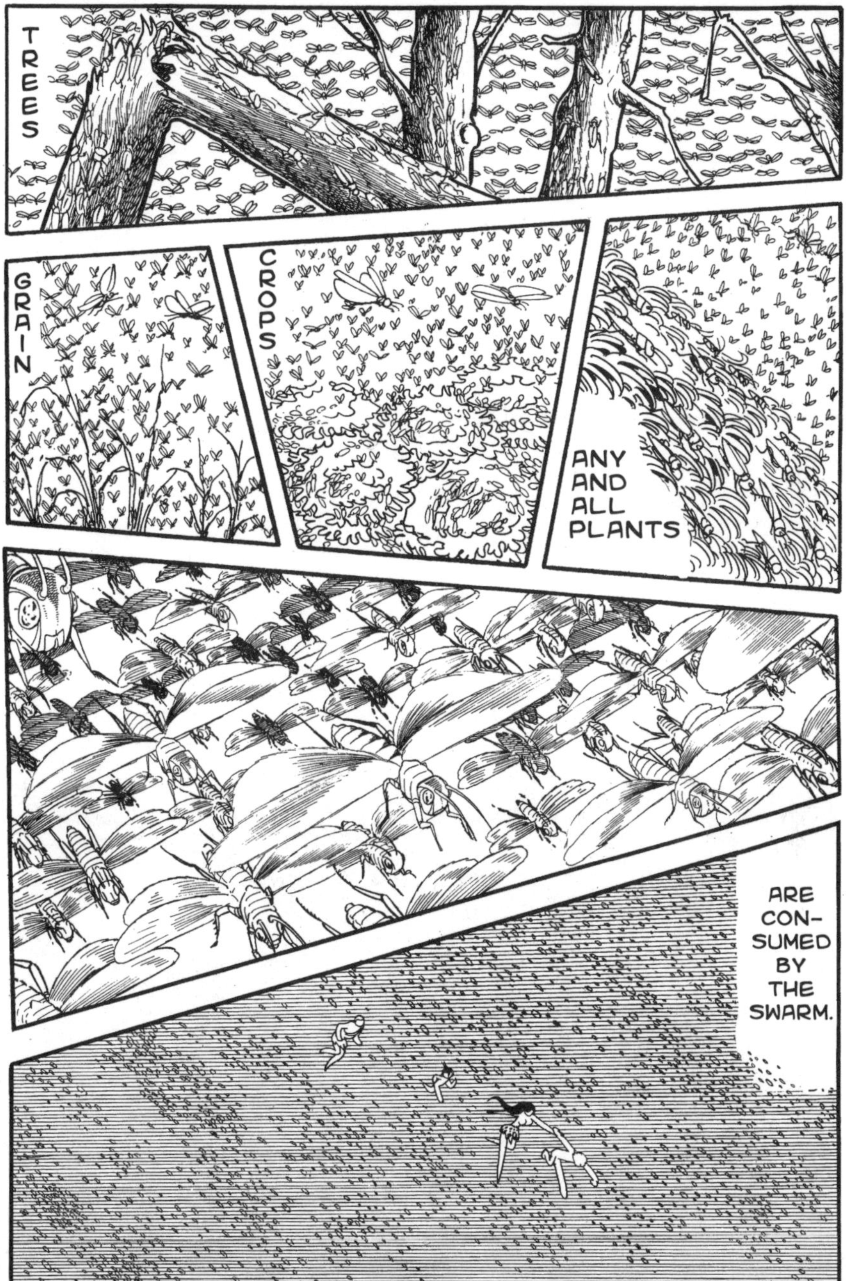
TREES
GRAIN
CROPS
ANY AND ALL PLANTS
ARE CON-SUMED BY THE SWARM.

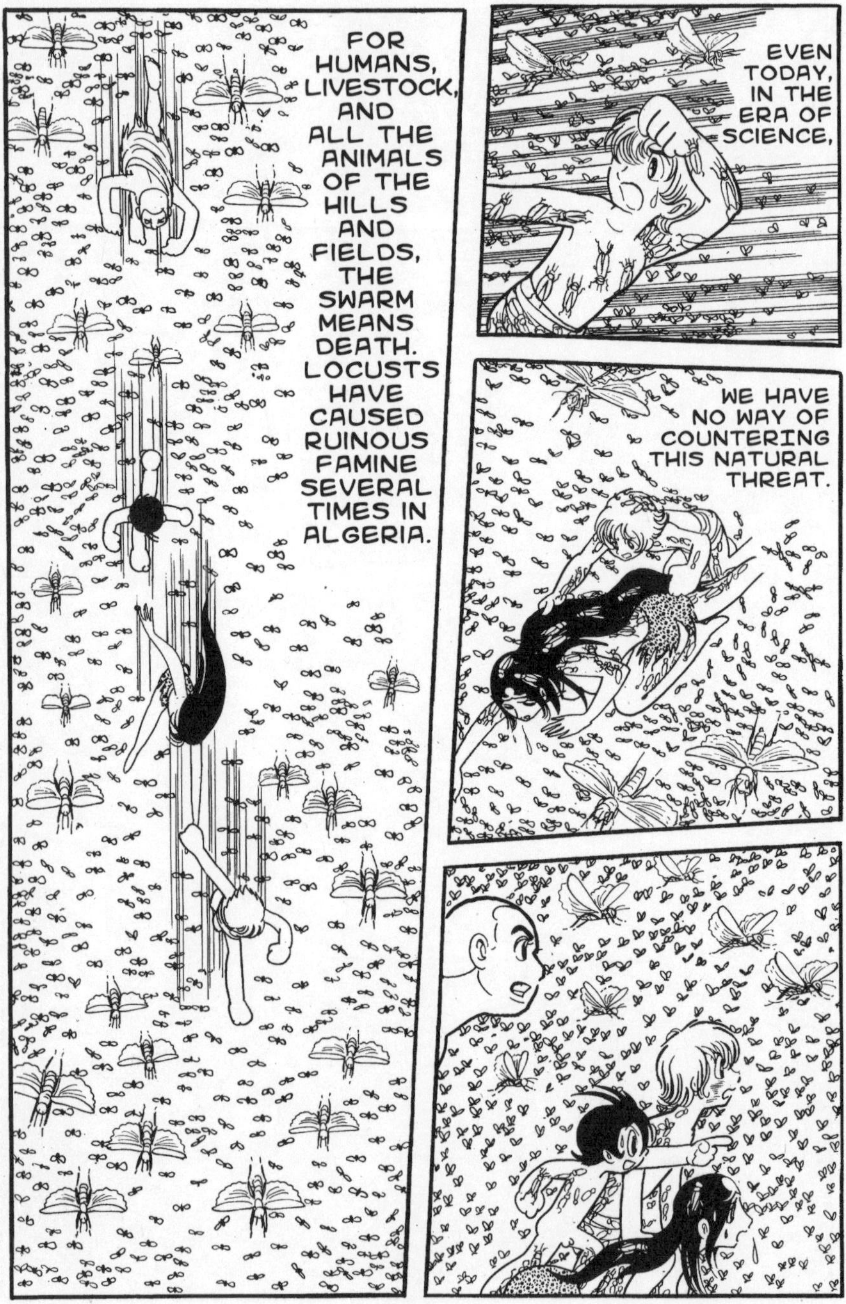
FOR HUMANS, LIVESTOCK, AND ALL THE ANIMALS OF THE HILLS AND FIELDS, THE SWARM MEANS DEATH. LOCUSTS HAVE CAUSED RUINOUS FAMINE SEVERAL TIMES IN ALGERIA.
EVEN TODAY, IN THE ERA OF SCIENCE,
WE HAVE NO WAY OF COUNTERING THIS NATURAL THREAT.

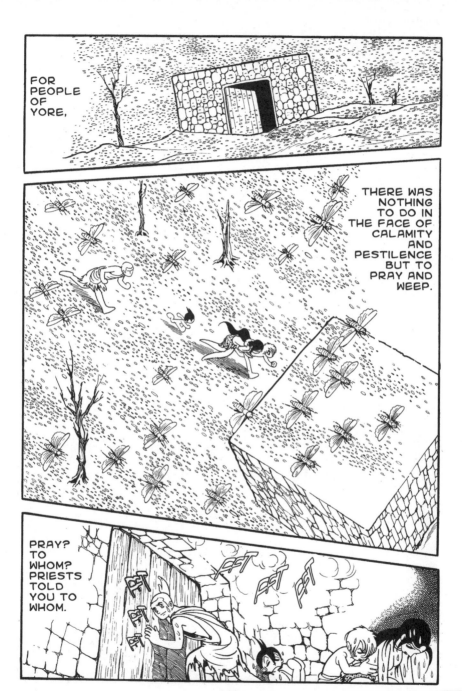

FOR PEOPLE OF YORE,

THERE WAS NOTHING TO DO IN THE FACE OF CALAMITY AND PESTILENCE BUT TO PRAY AND WEEP.

PRAY? TO WHOM? PRIESTS TOLD YOU TO WHOM.

MONKS AND PRIESTS EXPLAINED THAT NATURE'S MYSTERIES AND TERRIFYING POWER WERE THE WORK OF GODS. THEY TAUGHT PEOPLE TO CELEBRATE, SERVE AND PRAY TO THESE GODS.

BUT DID THAT HELP THEM ESCAPE MISFORTUNE?

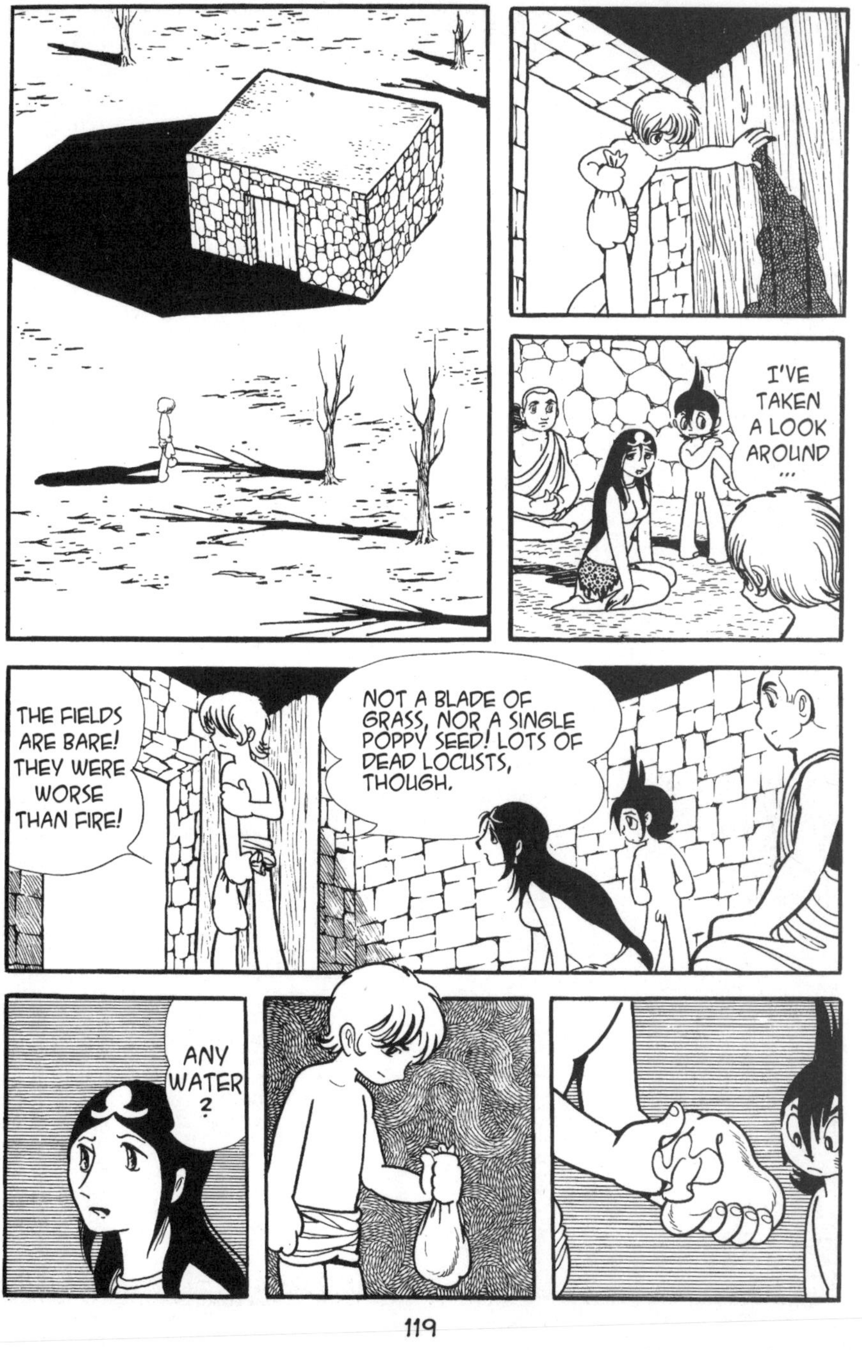
I'VE TAKEN A LOOK AROUND ...
THE FIELDS ARE BARE! THEY WERE WORSE THAN FIRE!
NOT A BLADE OF GRASS, NOR A SINGLE POPPY SEED! LOTS OF DEAD LOCUSTS, THOUGH.
ANY WATER ?

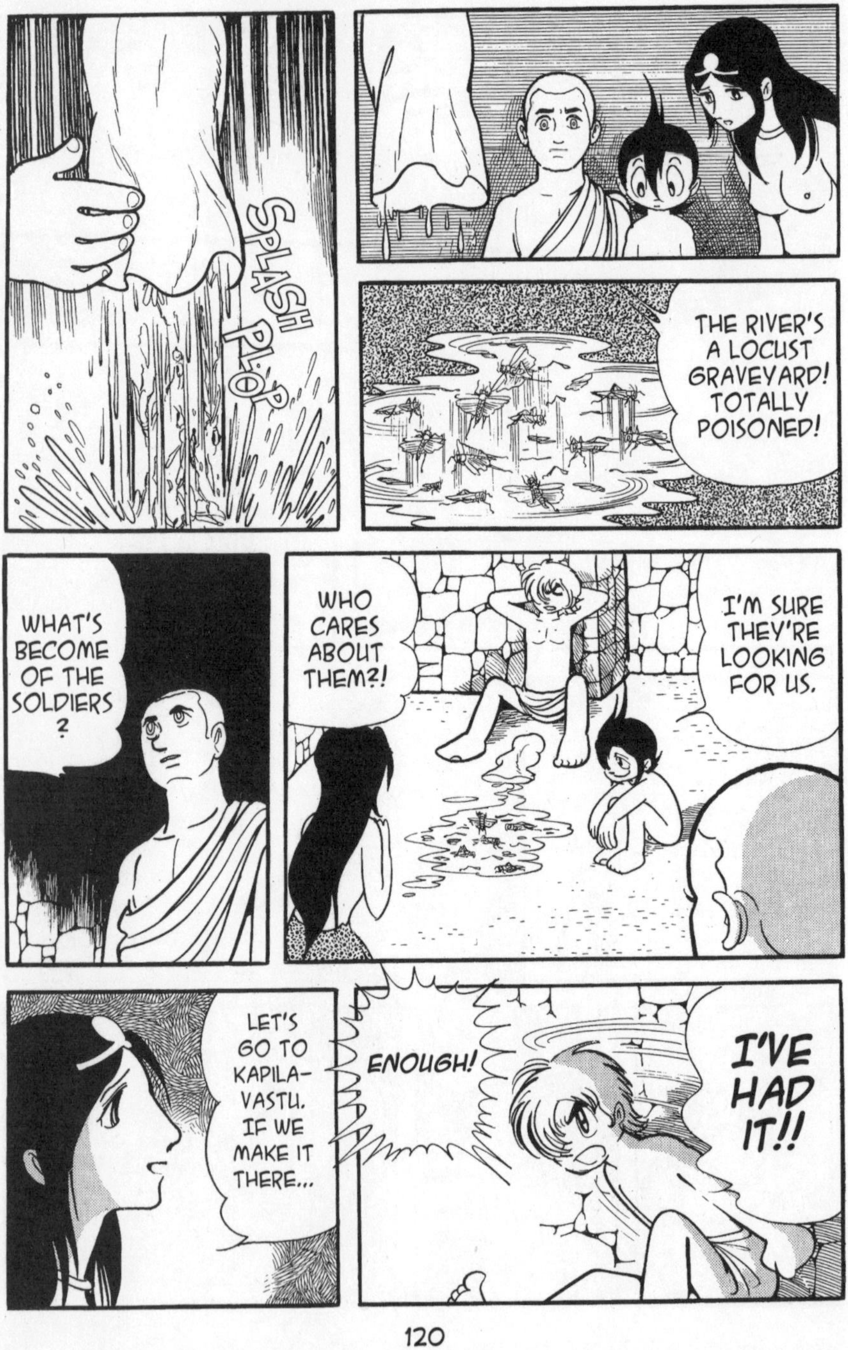
SPLASH
PLOP
THE RIVER'S A LOCUST GRAVEYARD! TOTALLY POISONED!
WHAT'S BECOME OF THE SOLDIERS?
WHO CARES ABOUT THEM?!
I'M SURE THEY'RE LOOKING FOR US.
LET'S GO TO KAPILA-VASTU. IF WE MAKE IT THERE...
ENOUGH!
I'VE HAD IT!!

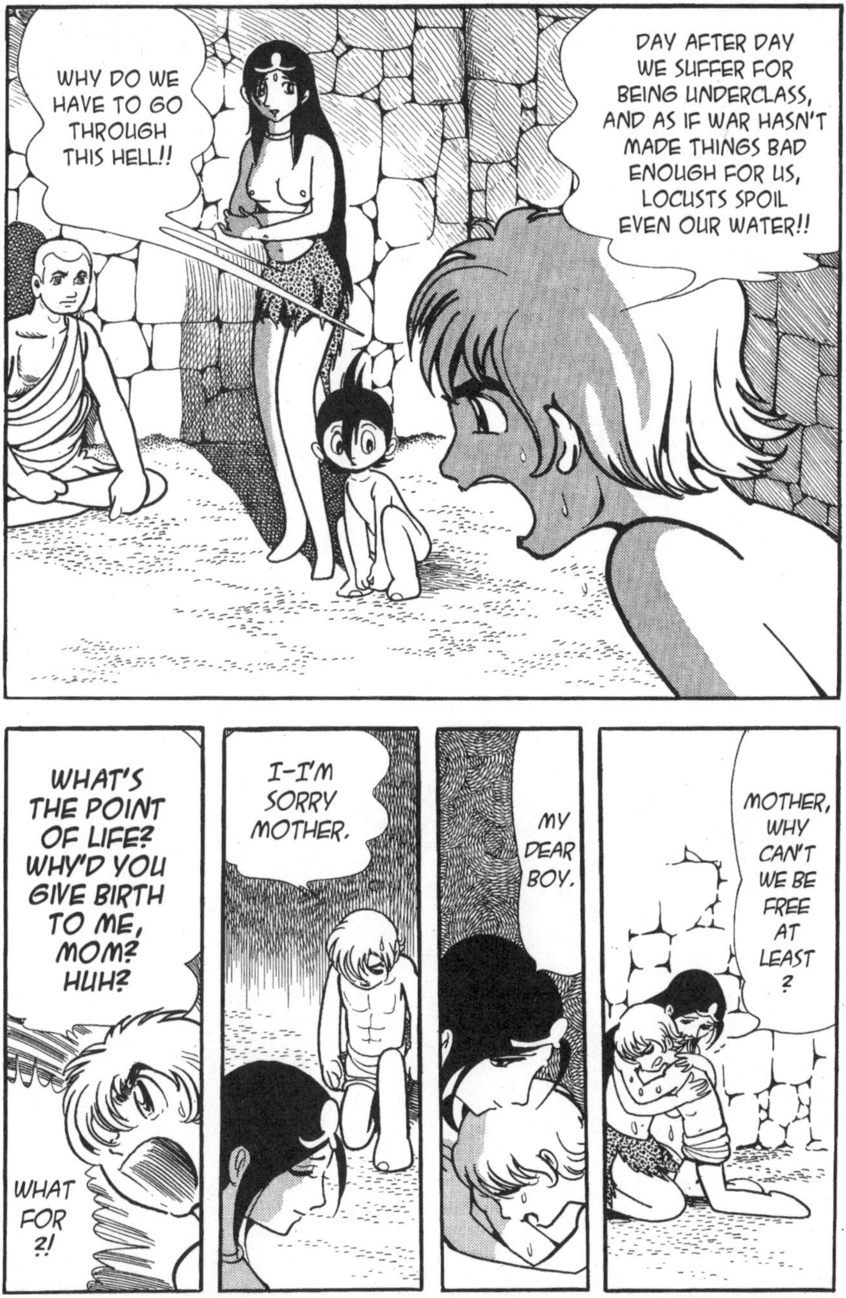
WHY DO WE HAVE TO GO THROUGH THIS HELL!!
DAY AFTER DAY WE SUFFER FOR BEING UNDERCLASS, AND AS IF WAR HASN'T MADE THINGS BAD ENOUGH FOR US, LOCUSTS SPOIL EVEN OUR WATER!!
WHAT'S THE POINT OF LIFE? WHY'D YOU GIVE BIRTH TO ME, MOM? HUH?
WHAT FOR ?!
I-I'M SORRY MOTHER.
MY DEAR BOY.
MOTHER, WHY CAN'T WE BE FREE AT LEAST ?

I KNOW.

I'M GOING TO HIDE THAT I'M A SLAVE.

I'LL MOVE UP IN THE WORLD.

BUT YOU CAN'T.

A SLAVE IS A SLAVE. NO MATTER WHERE YOU GO, THAT'LL NEVER CHANGE.

WHY? WHAT IF I DON'T TELL ANYONE?

LOOK AT YOUR FOOT.

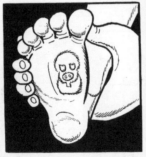

THAT BRAND CAN'T BE ERASED. THEY'LL KNOW.

RATS!!

STAMP

STAMP

I'LL CUT OFF MY FOOT THEN!!

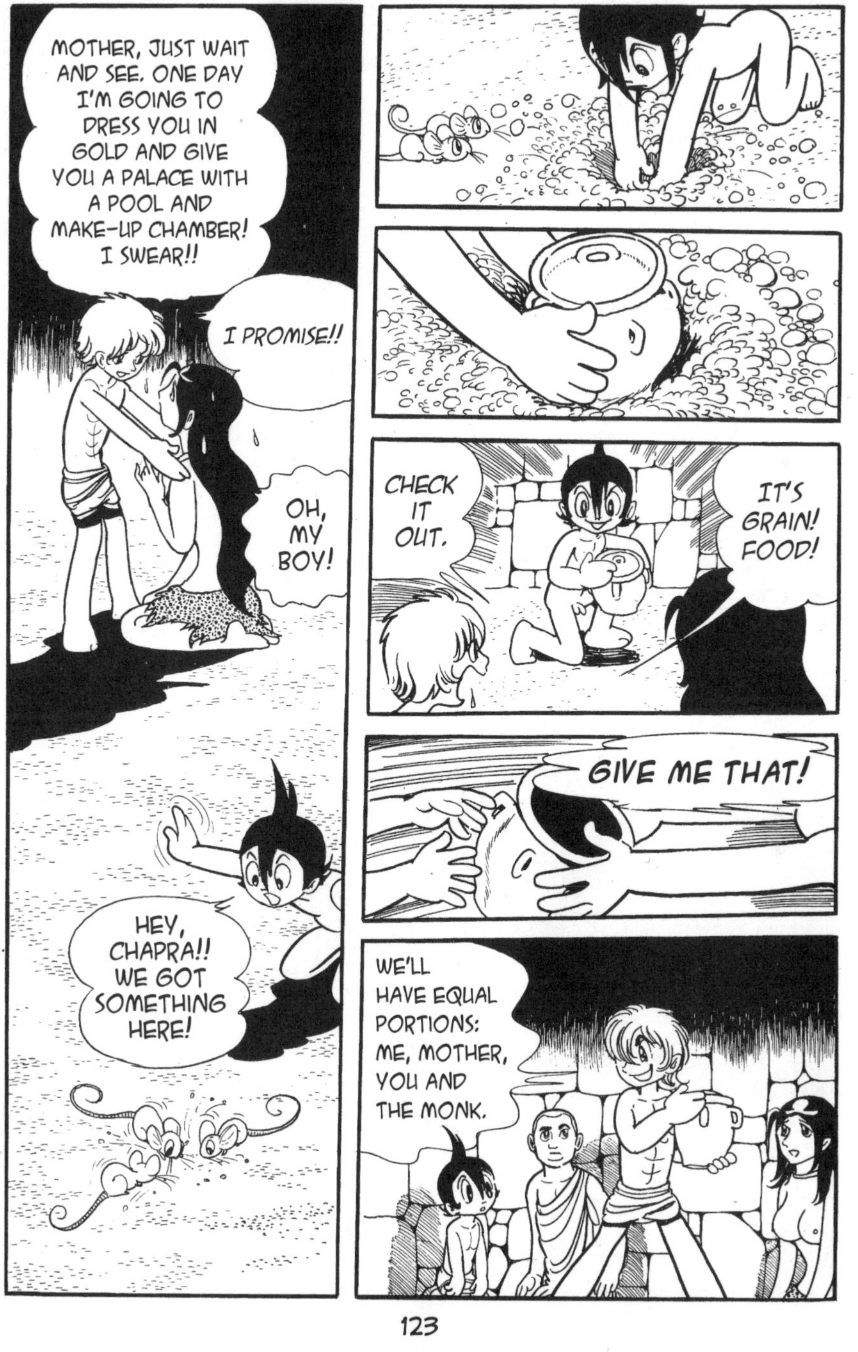
MOTHER, JUST WAIT AND SEE. ONE DAY I'M GOING TO DRESS YOU IN GOLD AND GIVE YOU A PALACE WITH A POOL AND MAKE-UP CHAMBER! I SWEAR!!
I PROMISE!!
OH, MY BOY!
HEY, CHAPRA!! WE GOT SOMETHING HERE!
CHECK IT OUT.
IT'S GRAIN! FOOD!
GIVE ME THAT!
WE'LL HAVE EQUAL PORTIONS: ME, MOTHER, YOU AND THE MONK.

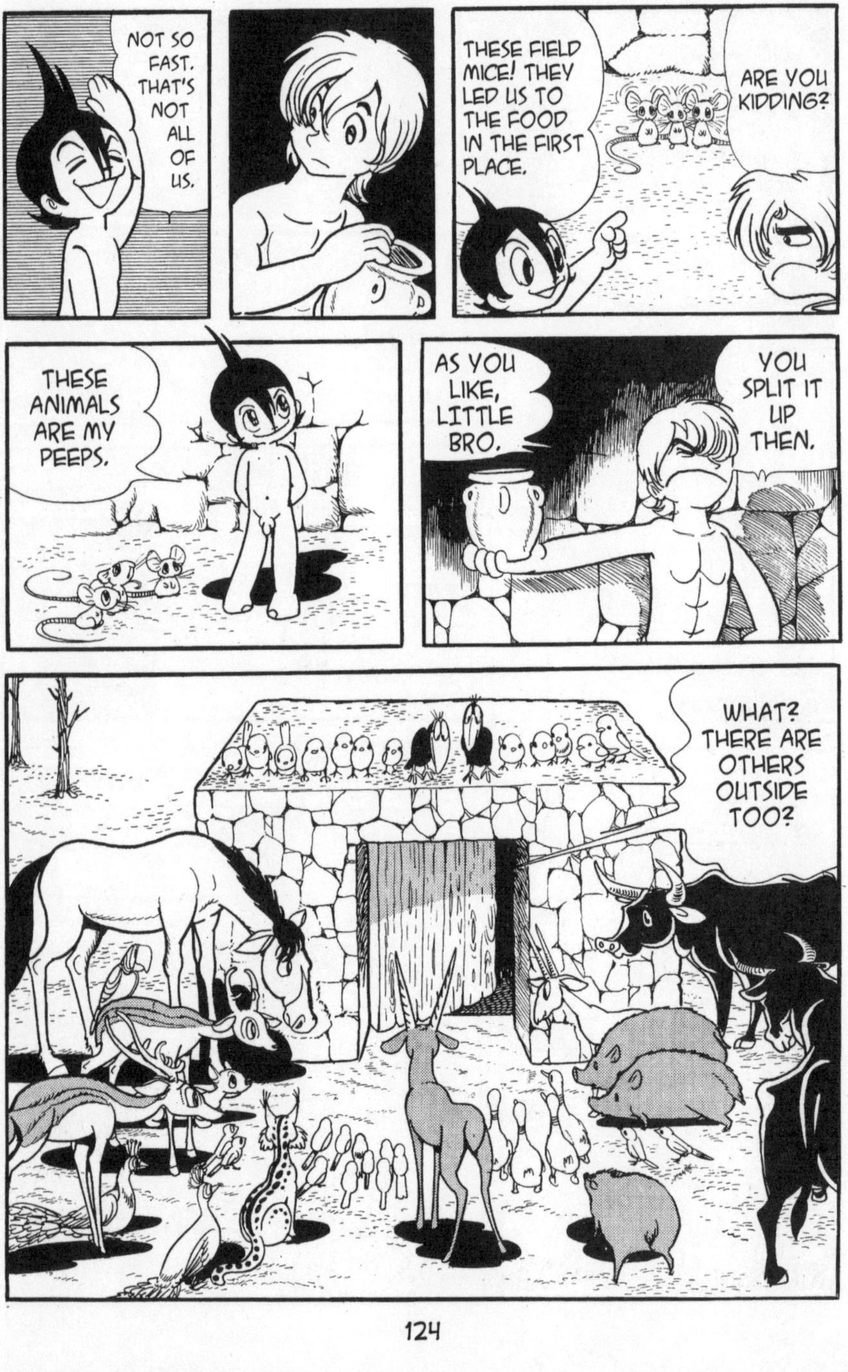
NOT SO FAST. THAT'S NOT ALL OF US.
THESE FIELD MICE! THEY LED US TO THE FOOD IN THE FIRST PLACE.
ARE YOU KIDDING?
THESE ANIMALS ARE MY PEEPS.
AS YOU LIKE, LITTLE BRO.
YOU SPLIT IT UP THEN.
WHAT? THERE ARE OTHERS OUTSIDE TOO?

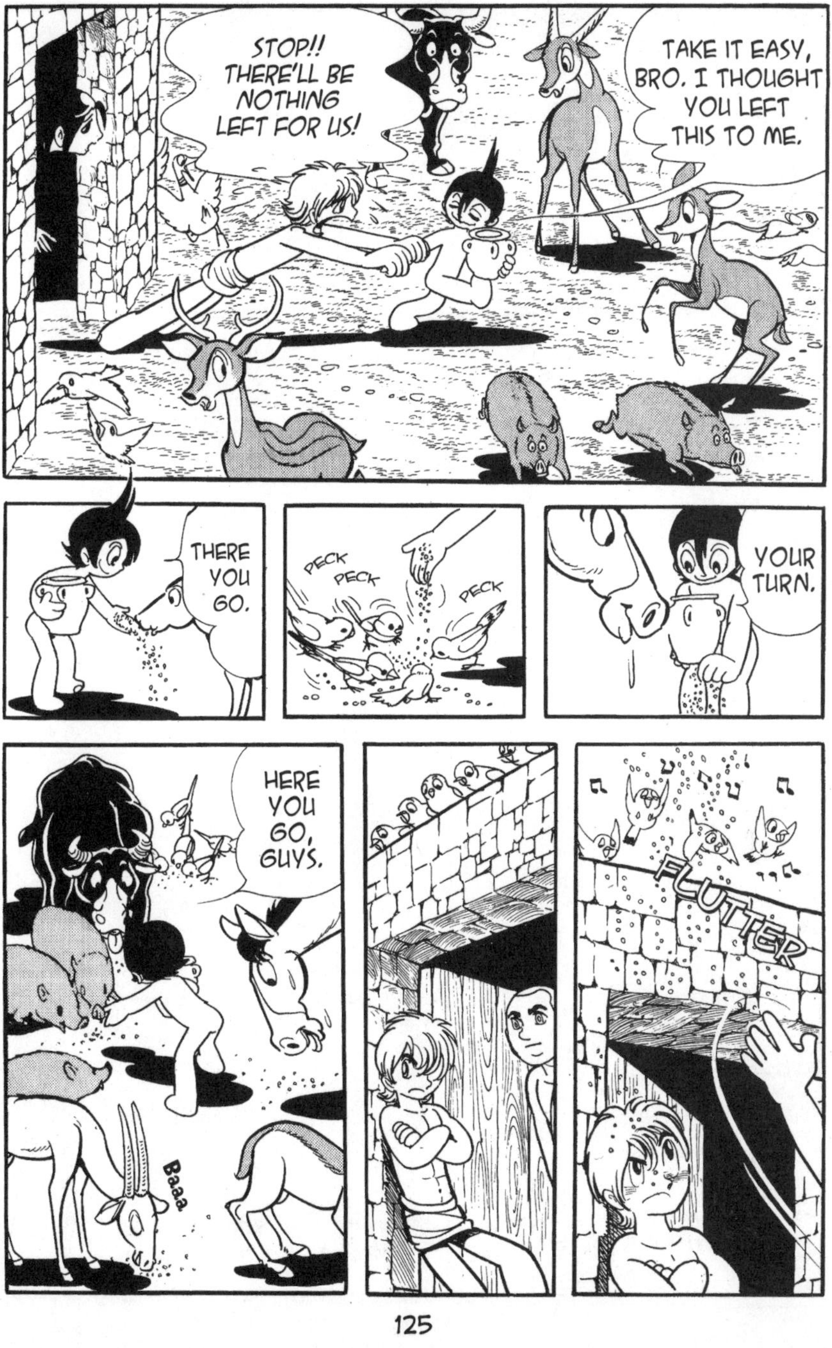
STOP!! THERE'LL BE NOTHING LEFT FOR US!
TAKE IT EASY, BRO. I THOUGHT YOU LEFT THIS TO ME.
THERE YOU GO.
PECK PECK
PECK
YOUR TURN.
HERE YOU GO, GUYS.
Baaa
FLUTTER

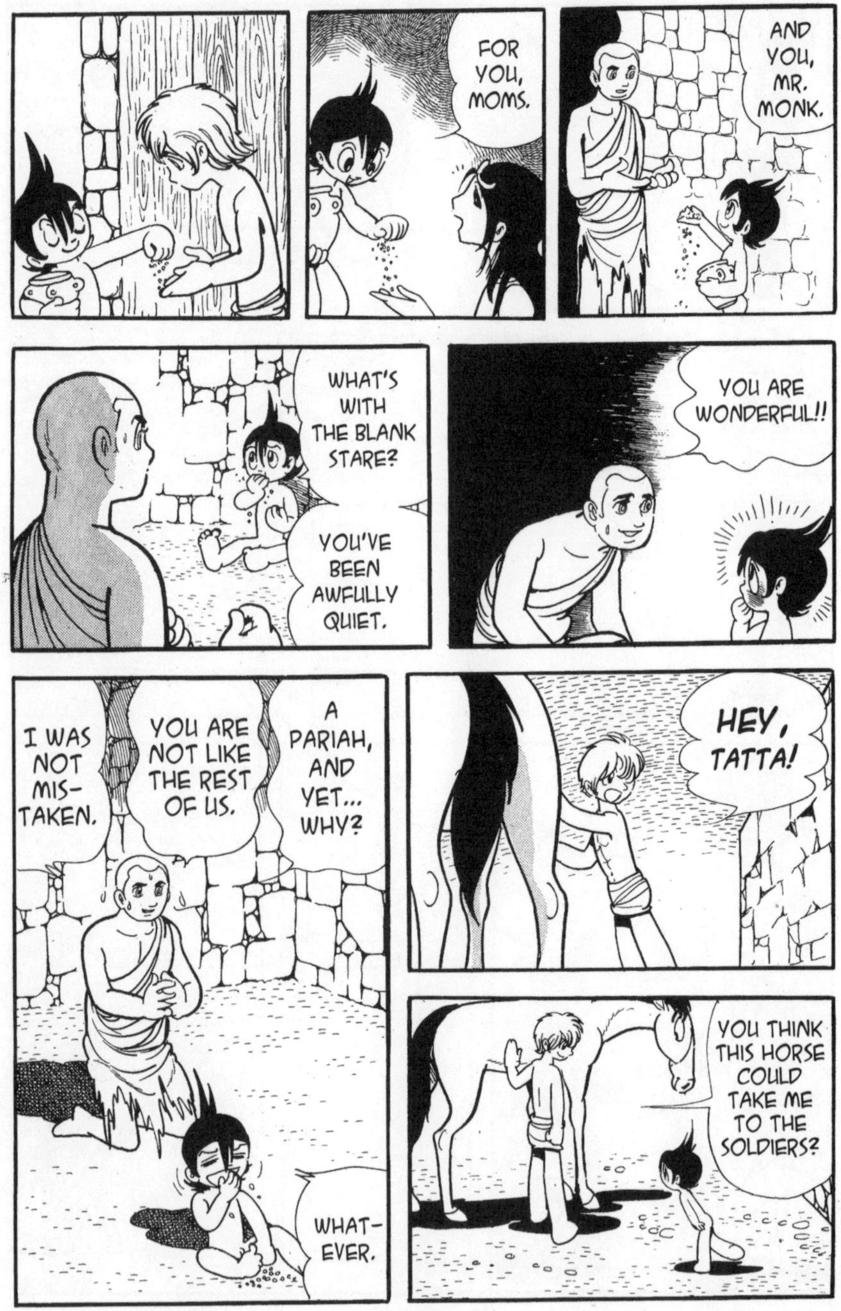
FOR YOU, MOMS.
AND YOU, MR. MONK.
WHAT'S WITH THE BLANK STARE?
YOU'VE BEEN AWFULLY QUIET.
YOU ARE WONDERFUL!!
I WAS NOT MIS-TAKEN.
YOU ARE NOT LIKE THE REST OF US.
A PARIAH, AND YET... WHY?
WHAT-EVER.
HEY, TATTA!
YOU THINK THIS HORSE COULD TAKE ME TO THE SOLDIERS?

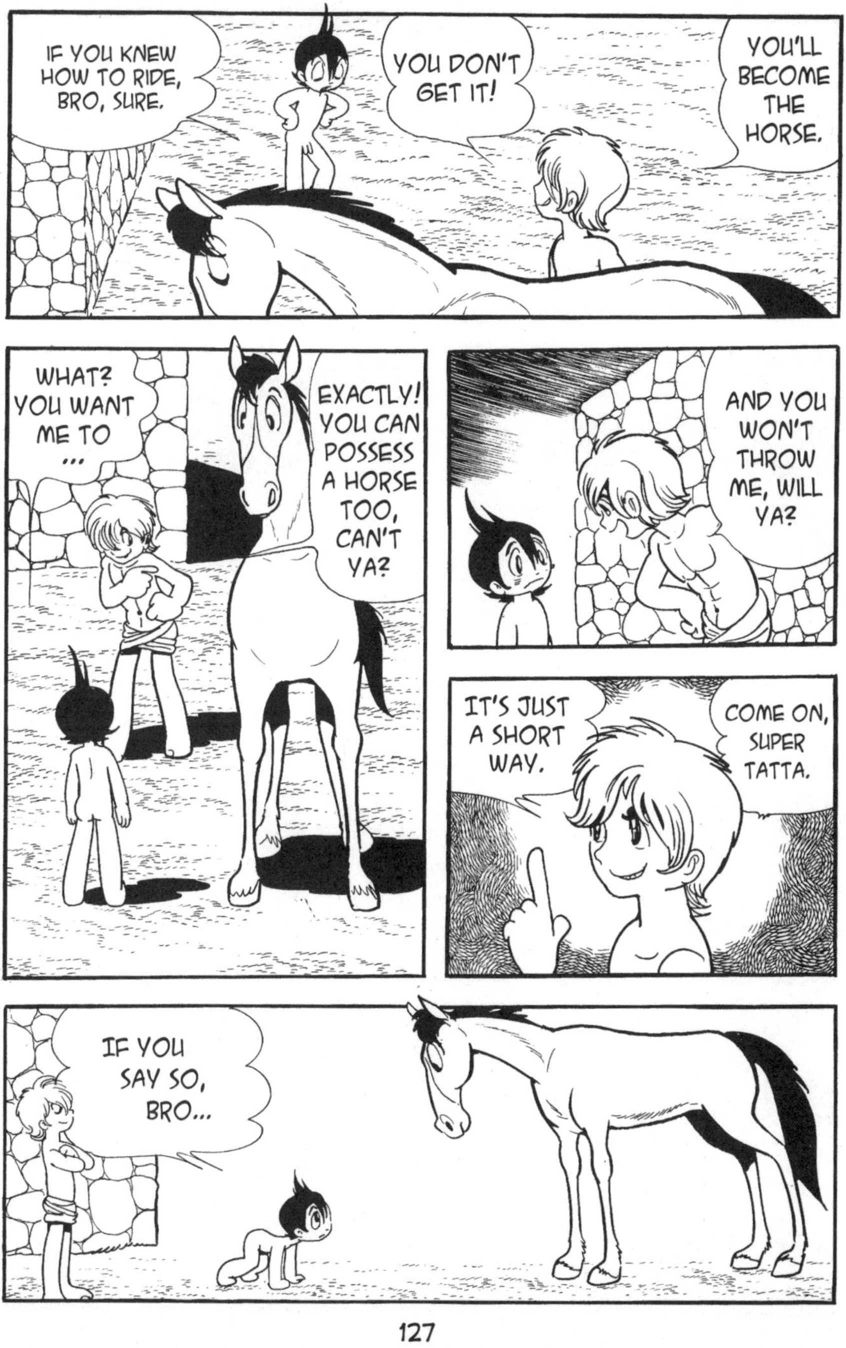
IF YOU KNEW HOW TO RIDE, BRO, SURE.
YOU DON'T GET IT!
YOU'LL BECOME THE HORSE.
WHAT? YOU WANT ME TO ...
EXACTLY! YOU CAN POSSESS A HORSE TOO, CAN'T YA?
AND YOU WON'T THROW ME, WILL YA?
IT'S JUST A SHORT WAY.
COME ON, SUPER TATTA.
IF YOU SAY SO, BRO...

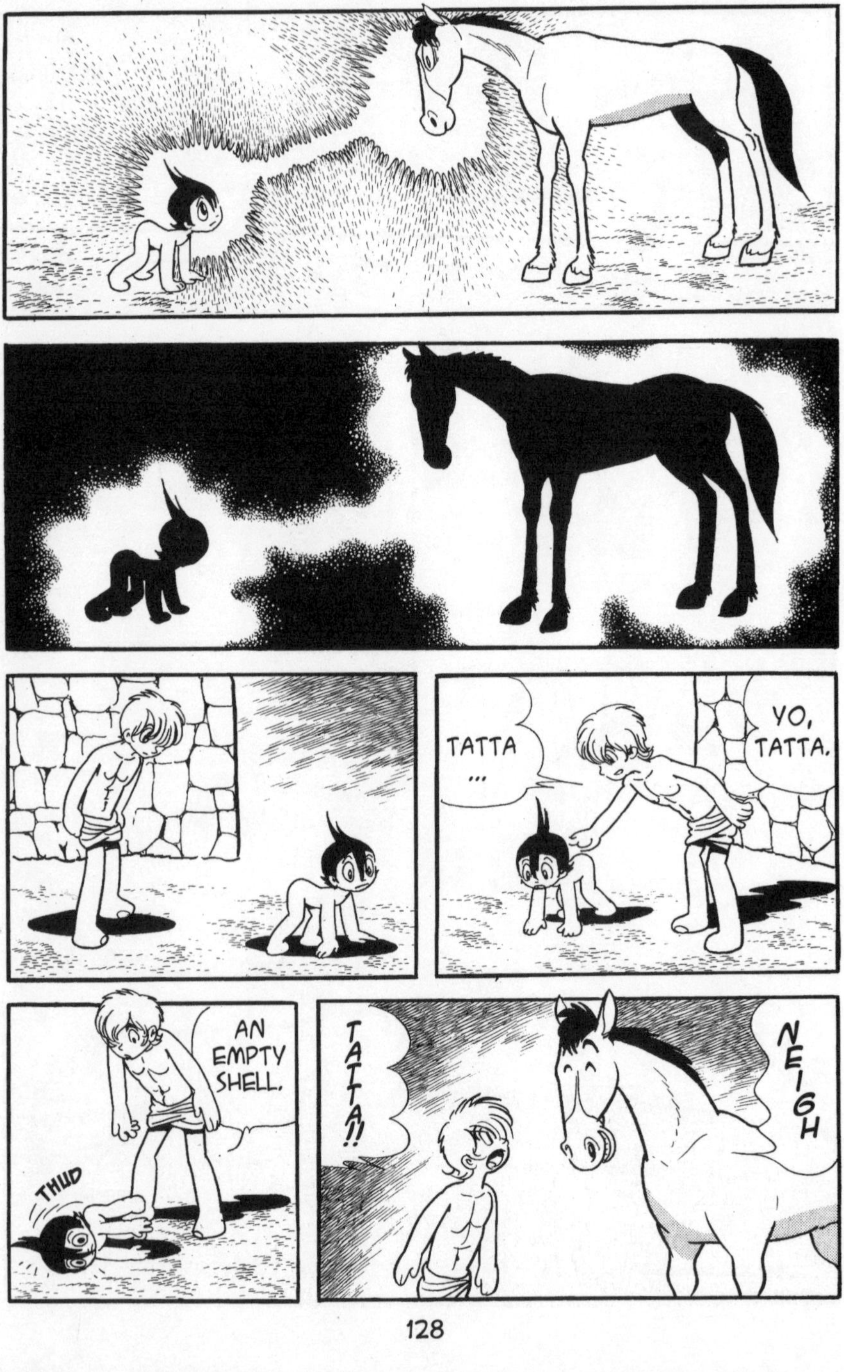

TATTA ...
YO, TATTA.
AN EMPTY SHELL.
THUD
TATTA!!
NEIGH

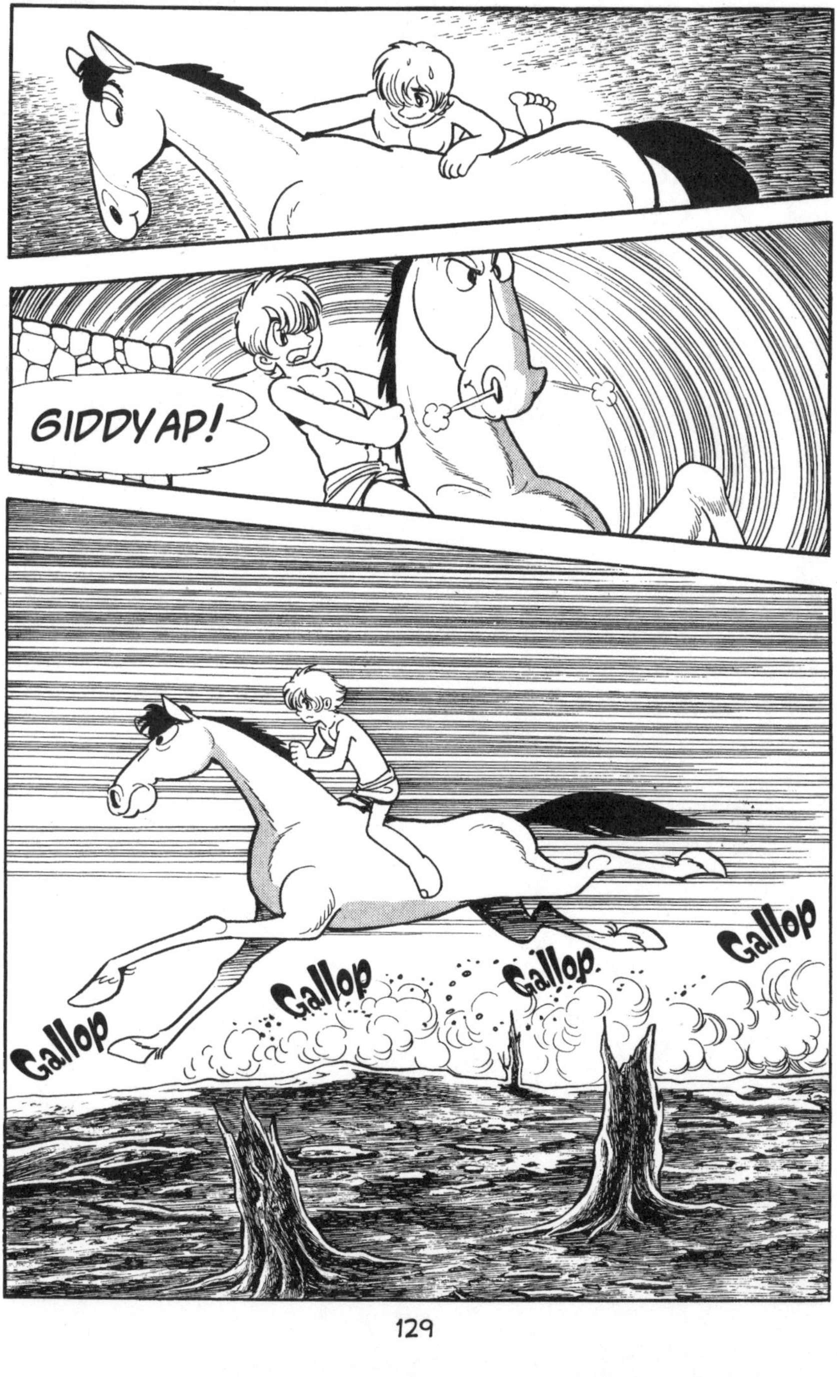
GIDDYAP!
Gallop
Gallop
Gallop
Gallop

YOUR SON JUST TOOK OFF ON HORSEBACK.

WHAT?

TATTA! OH DEAR...

WAKE UP!

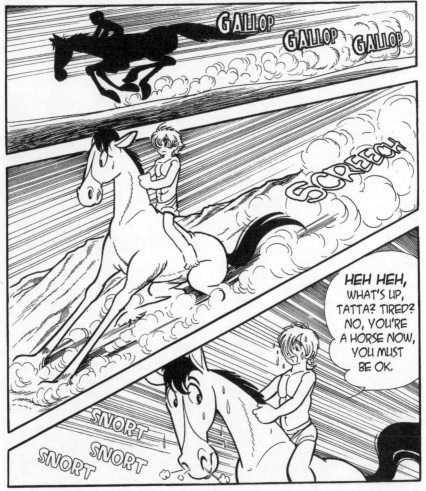

GALLOP

GALLOP

GALLOP

SCREECH

HEH HEH, WHAT'S UP, TATTA? TIRED? NO, YOU'RE A HORSE NOW, YOU MUST BE OK.

SNORT

SNORT

SNORT

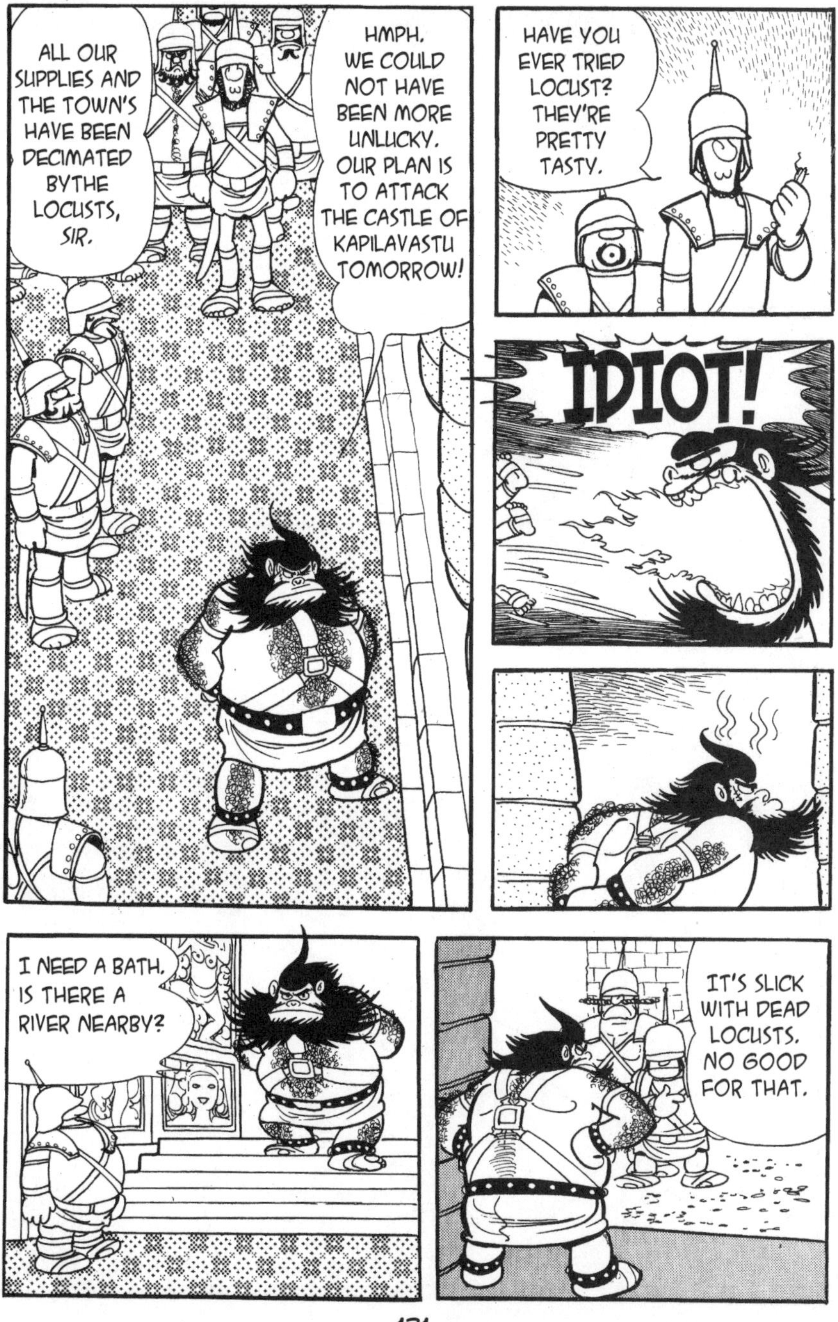
ALL OUR SUPPLIES AND THE TOWN'S HAVE BEEN DECIMATED BYTHE LOCUSTS, SIR.
HMPH. WE COULD NOT HAVE BEEN MORE UNLUCKY. OUR PLAN IS TO ATTACK THE CASTLE OF KAPILAVASTU TOMORROW!
HAVE YOU EVER TRIED LOCUST? THEY'RE PRETTY TASTY.
IDIOT!
I NEED A BATH. IS THERE A RIVER NEARBY?
IT'S SLICK WITH DEAD LOCUSTS. NO GOOD FOR THAT.

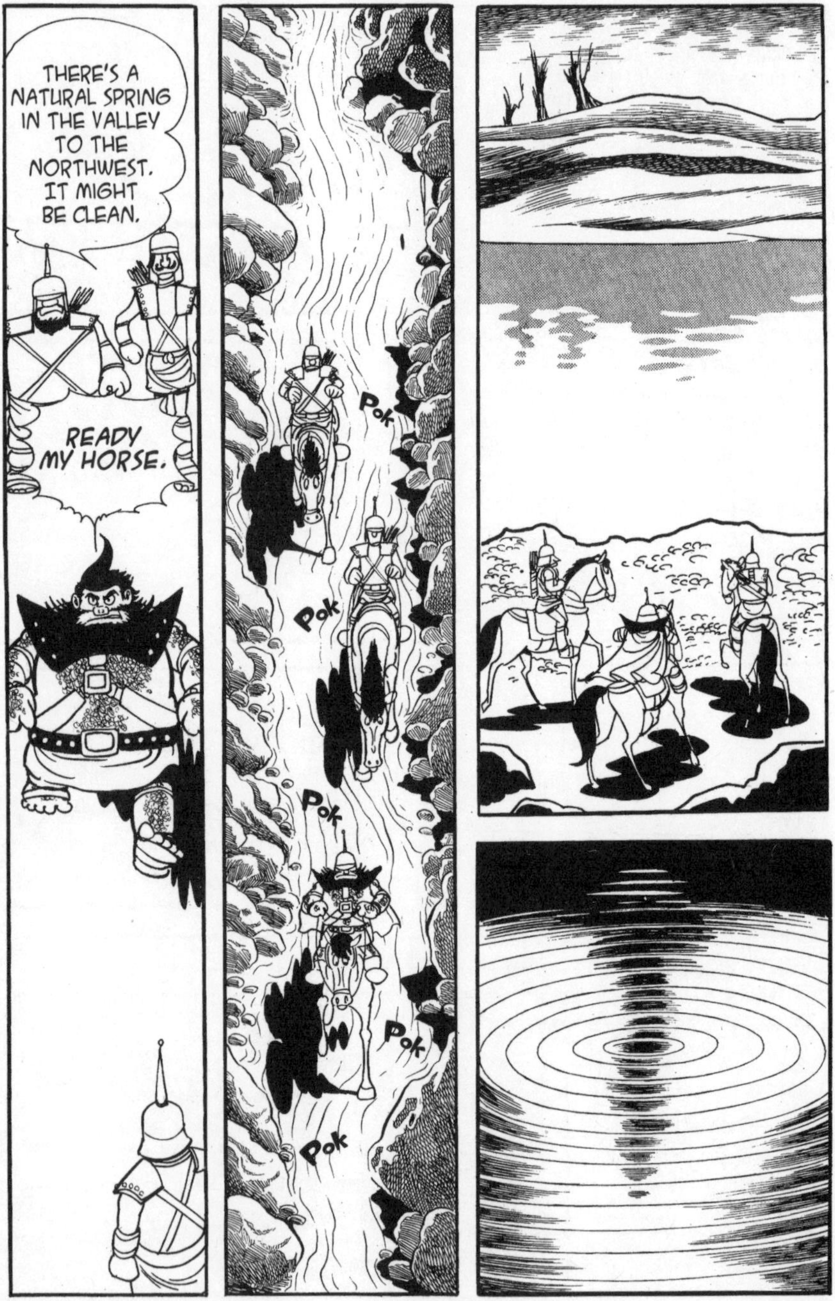
THERE'S A NATURAL SPRING IN THE VALLEY TO THE NORTHWEST. IT MIGHT BE CLEAN.
READY MY HORSE.
Pok
Pok
Pok
Pok
Pok

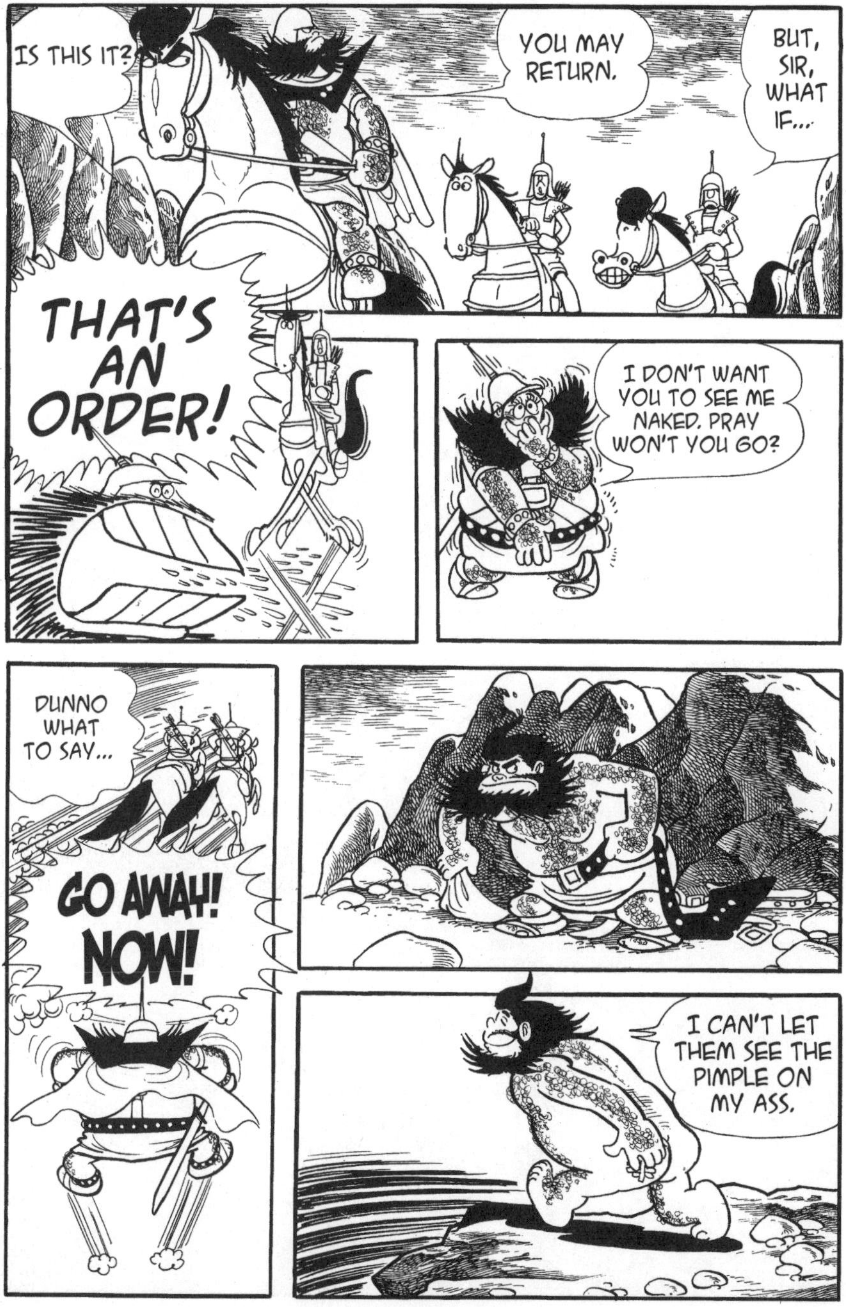
IS THIS IT?
YOU MAY RETURN.
BUT, SIR, WHAT IF...
THAT'S AN ORDER!
I DON'T WANT YOU TO SEE ME NAKED. PRAY WON'T YOU GO?
DUNNO WHAT TO SAY...
GO AWAY! NOW!
I CAN'T LET THEM SEE THE PIMPLE ON MY ASS.

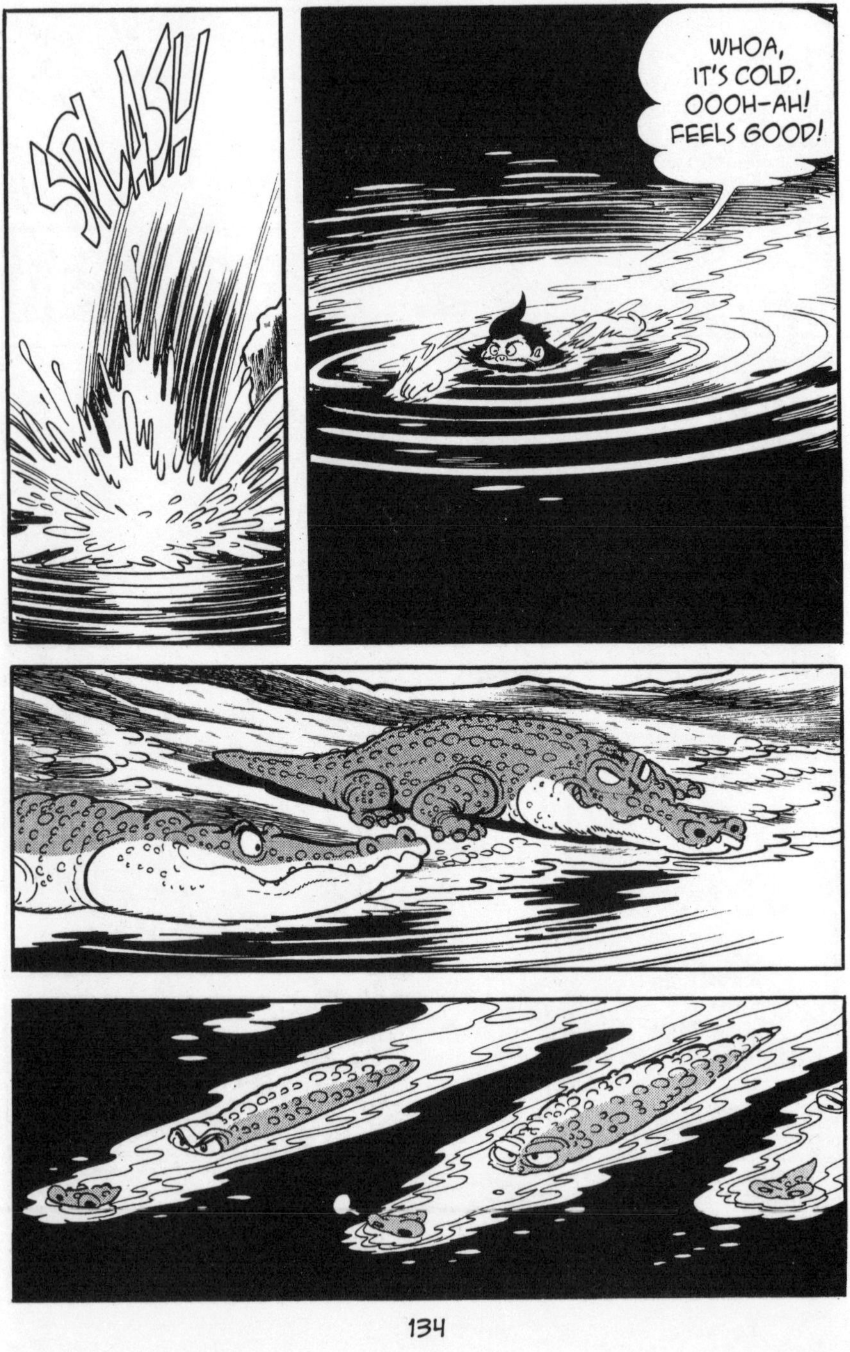
SPLASH
WHOA, IT'S COLD. OOOH-AH! FEELS GOOD!

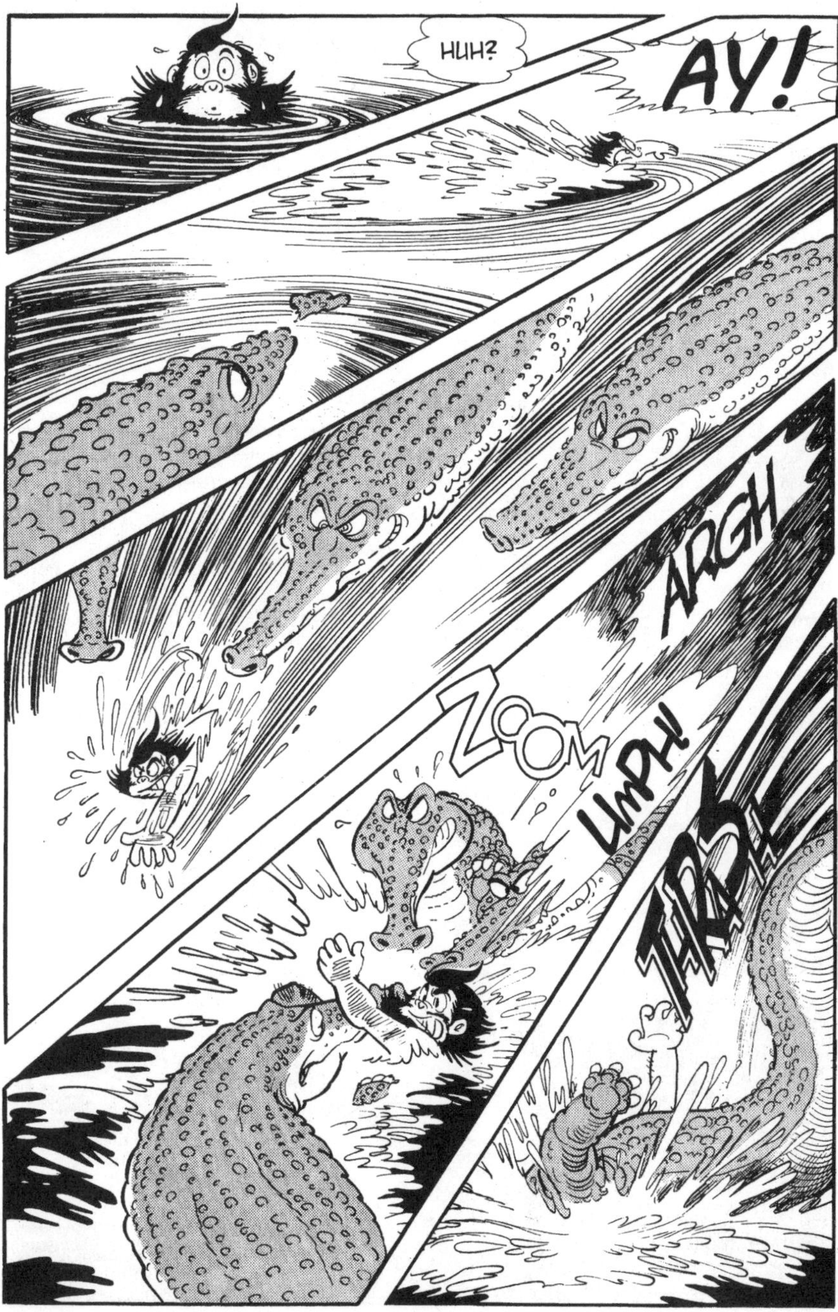
HUH?
AY!
ARGH
ZOOM
UMPH!
THRASH!

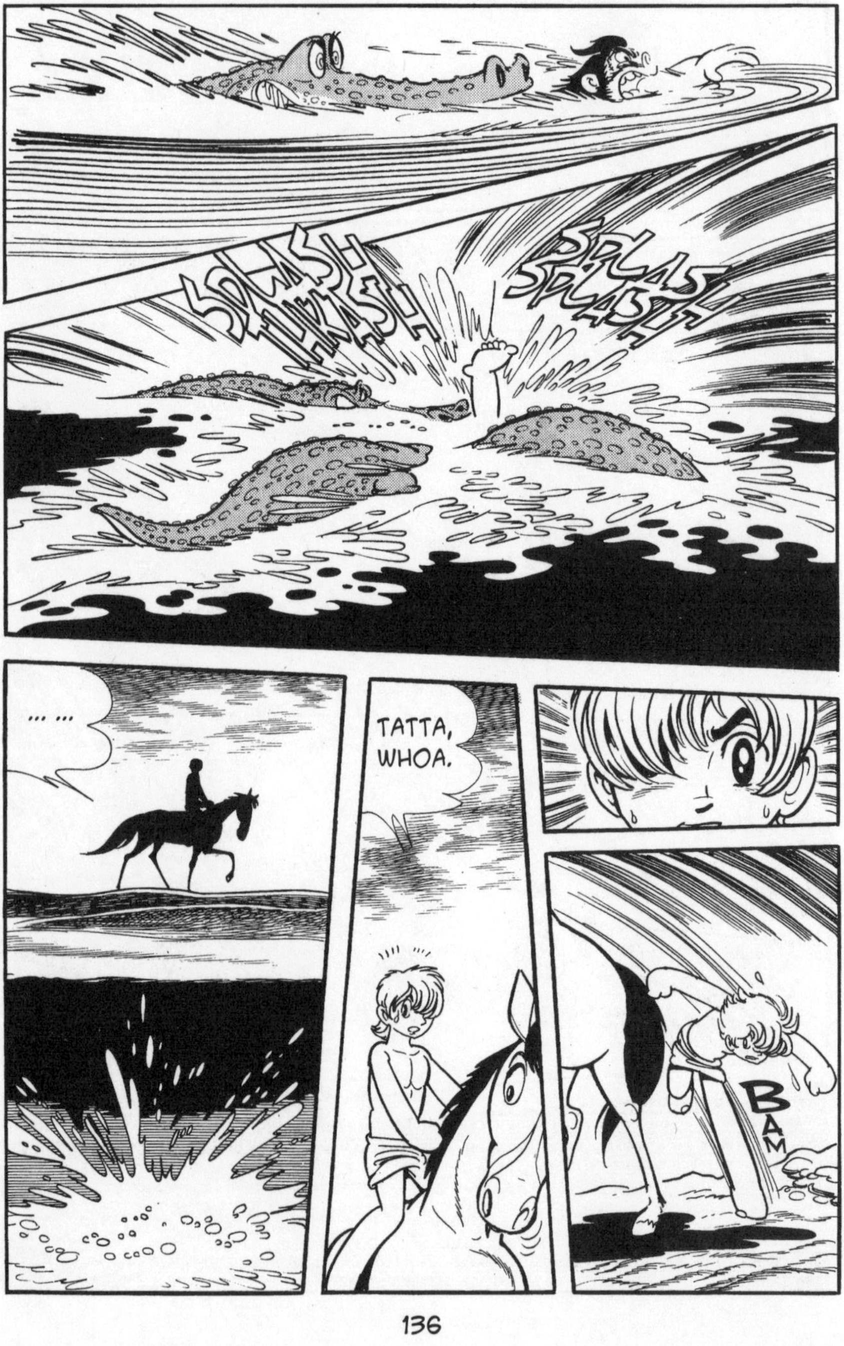
SPLASH
SPLASH
SPLASH
SPLASH
... ...
TATTA, WHOA.
BAM

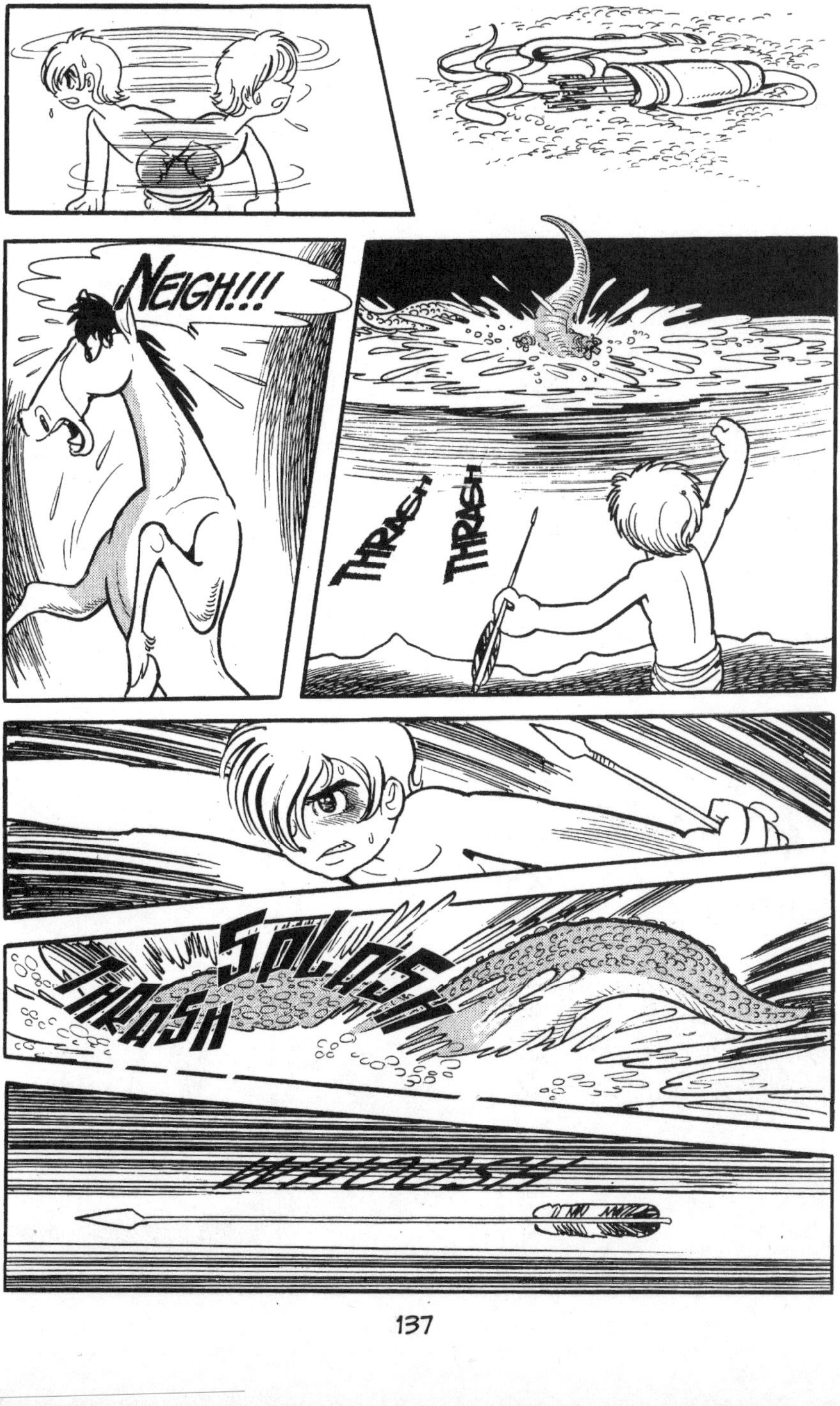
NEIGH!!!
THRASH
THRASH
THRASH
SPLASH
WHOOSH

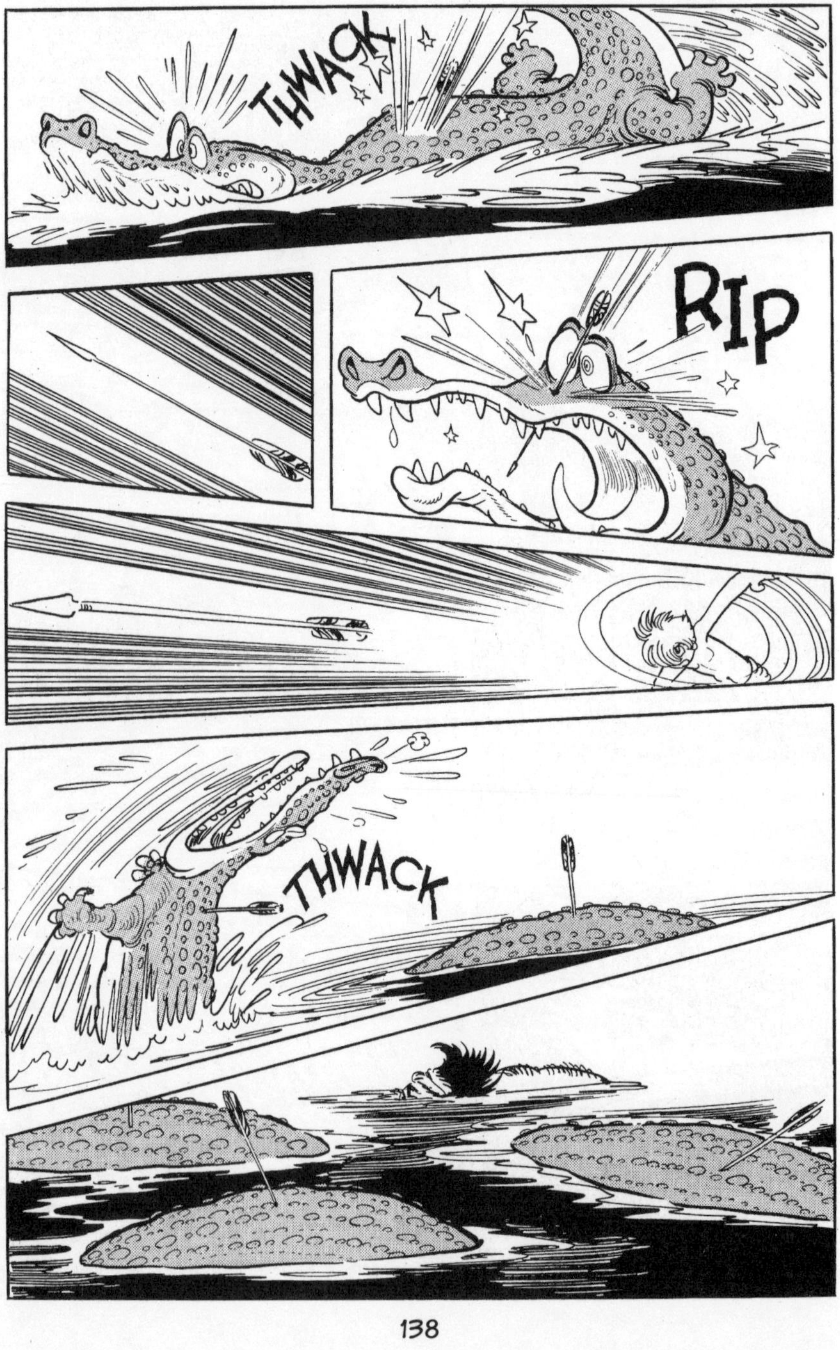
THWACK
RIP
THWACK

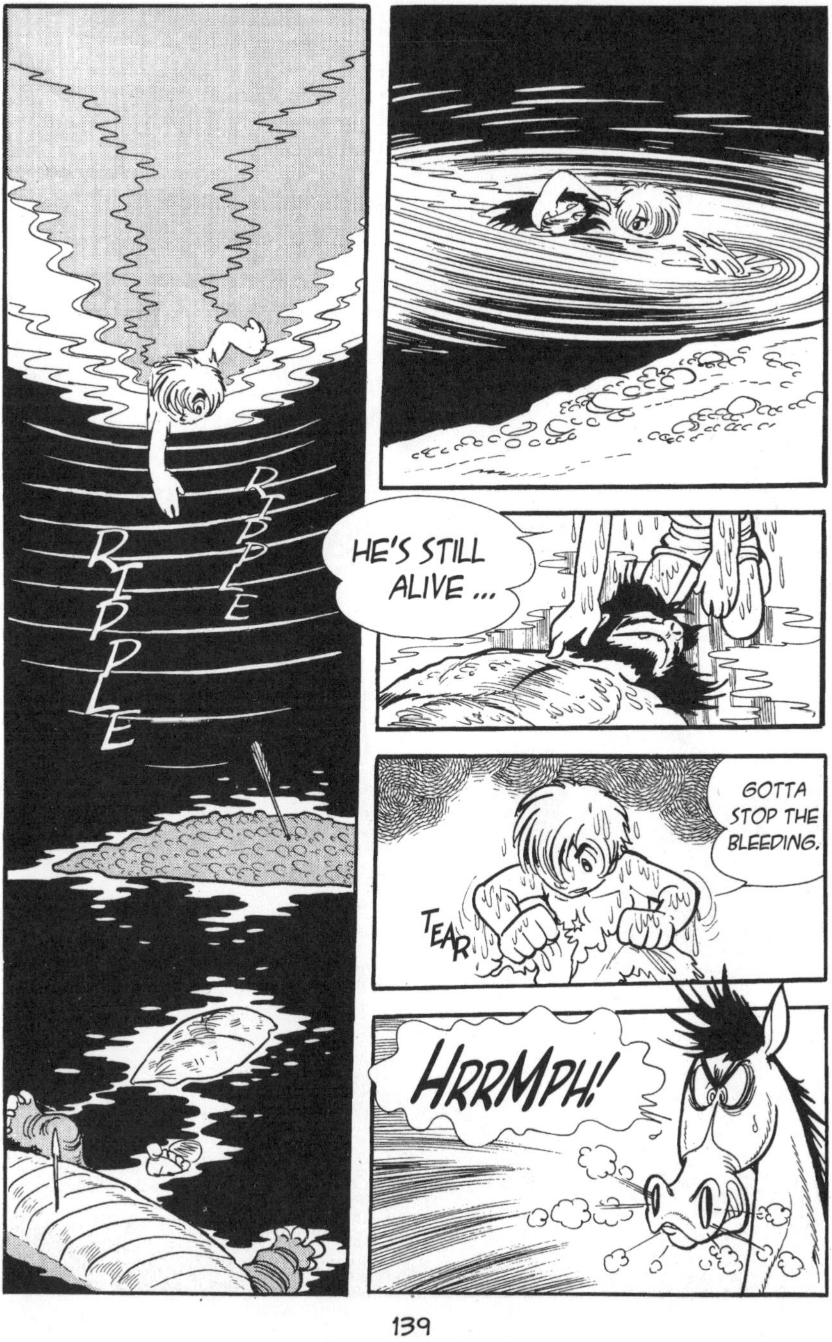
RIPPLE
RIPPLE
HE'S STILL ALIVE ...
GOTTA STOP THE BLEEDING.
TEAR
HRRMPH!

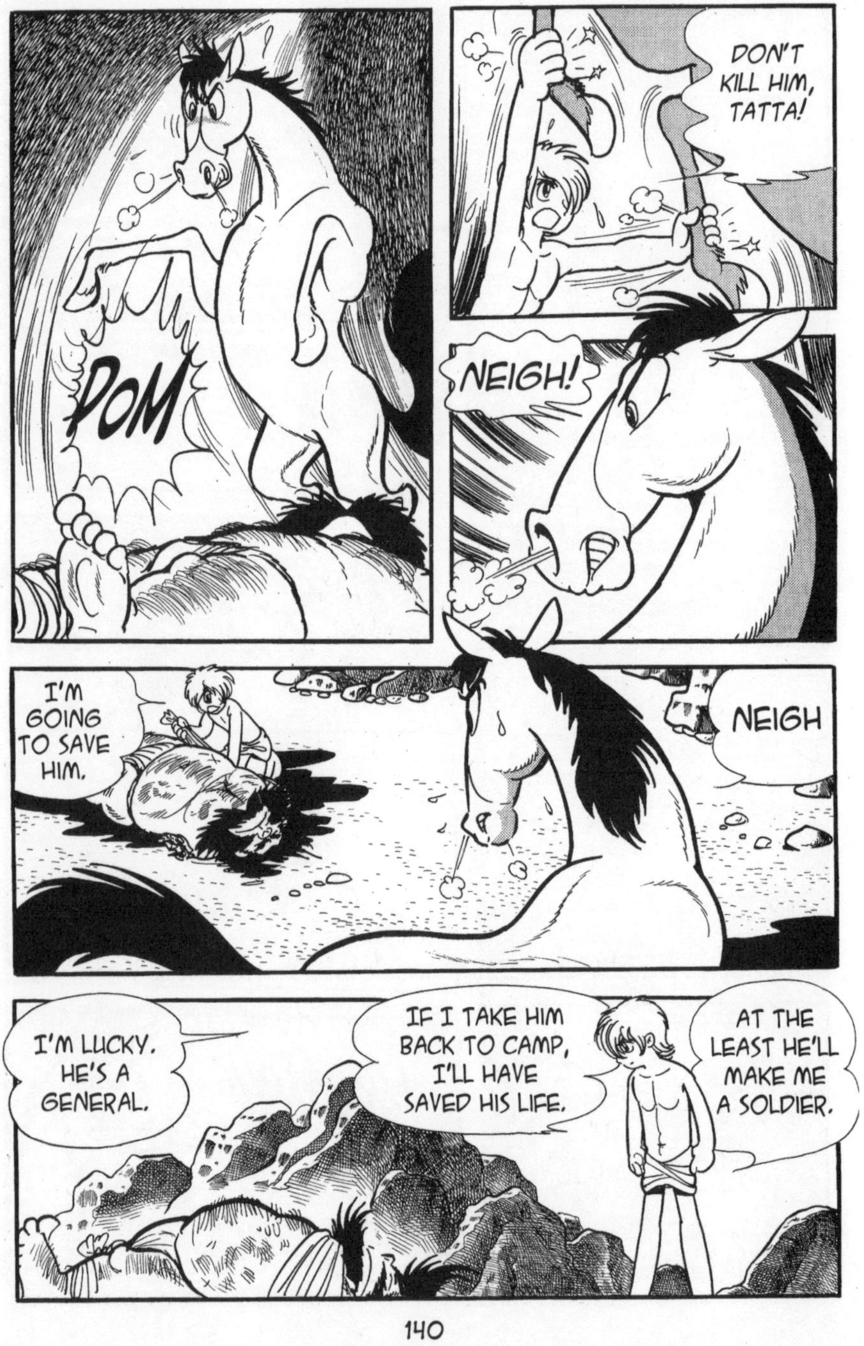
POM
DON'T KILL HIM, TATTA!
NEIGH!
I'M GOING TO SAVE HIM.
NEIGH
I'M LUCKY. HE'S A GENERAL.
IF I TAKE HIM BACK TO CAMP, I'LL HAVE SAVED HIS LIFE.
AT THE LEAST HE'LL MAKE ME A SOLDIER.

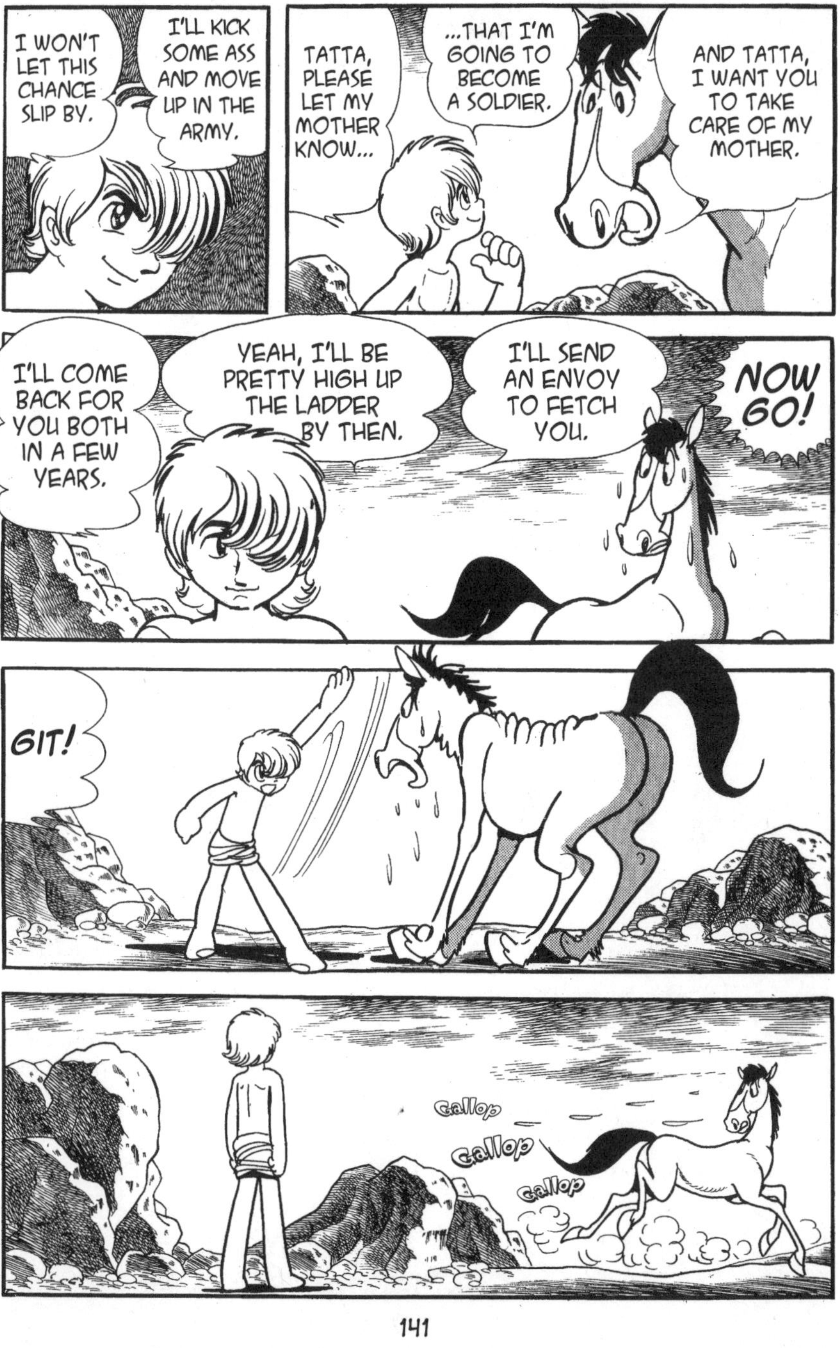
I WON'T LET THIS CHANCE SLIP BY.
I'LL KICK SOME ASS AND MOVE UP IN THE ARMY.
TATTA, PLEASE LET MY MOTHER KNOW...
...THAT I'M GOING TO BECOME A SOLDIER.
AND TATTA, I WANT YOU TO TAKE CARE OF MY MOTHER.
I'LL COME BACK FOR YOU BOTH IN A FEW YEARS.
YEAH, I'LL BE PRETTY HIGH UP THE LADDER BY THEN.
I'LL SEND AN ENVOY TO FETCH YOU.
NOW GO!
GIT!
Gallop
Gallop
Gallop

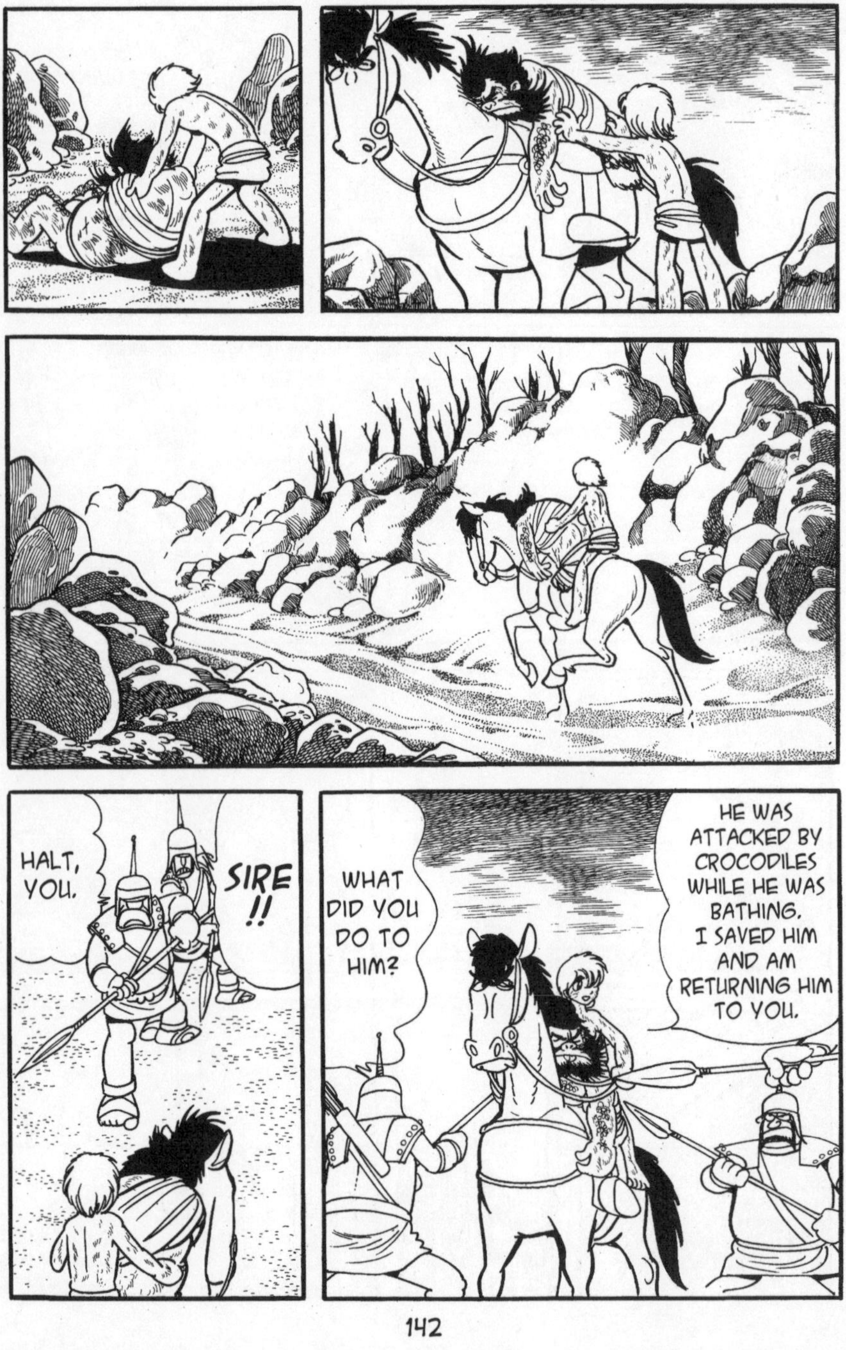
HALT, YOU.
SIRE !!
WHAT DID YOU DO TO HIM?
HE WAS ATTACKED BY CROCODILES WHILE HE WAS BATHING. I SAVED HIM AND AM RETURNING HIM TO YOU.

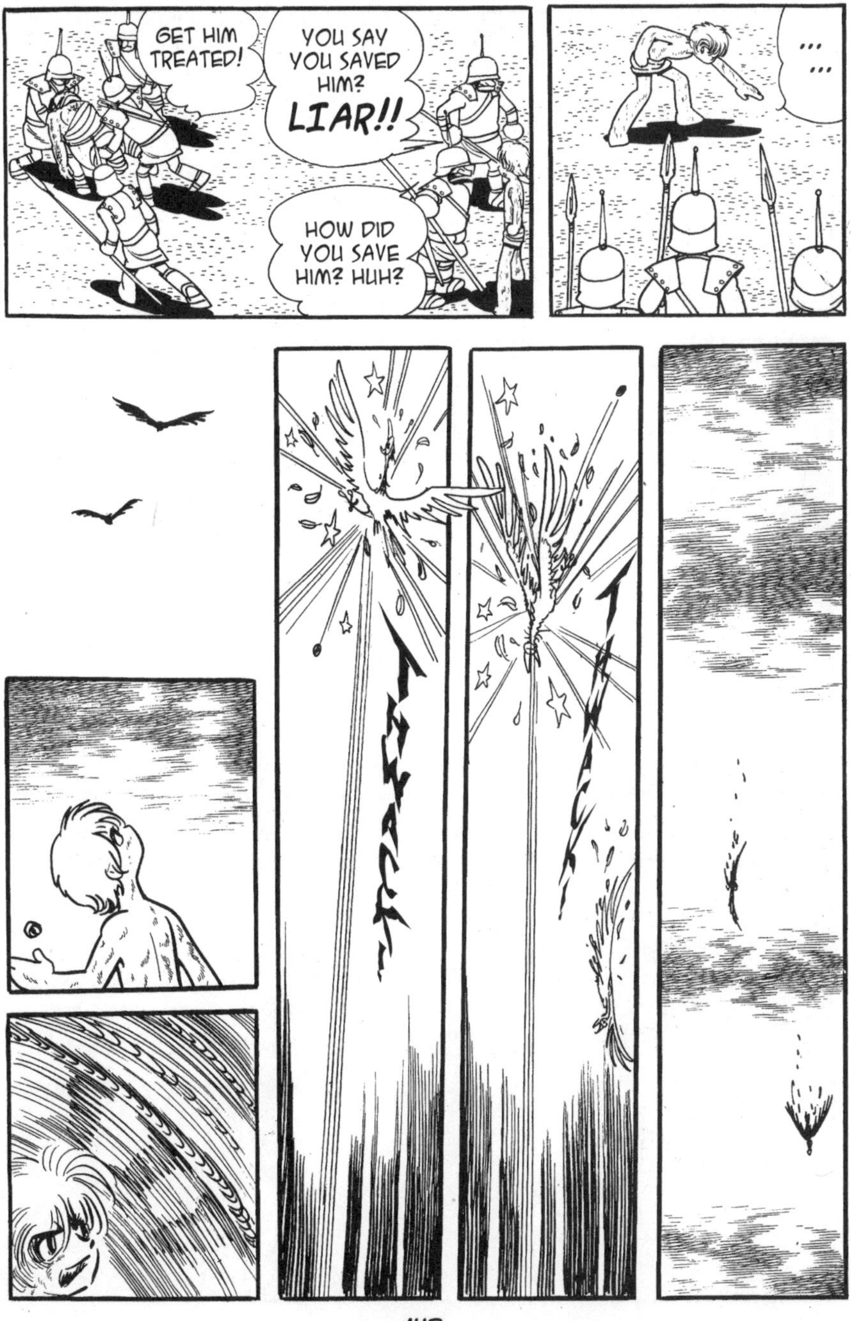
GET HIM TREATED!
YOU SAY YOU SAVED HIM? LIAR!!
HOW DID YOU SAVE HIM? HUH?
... ...
THWACK
THWACK

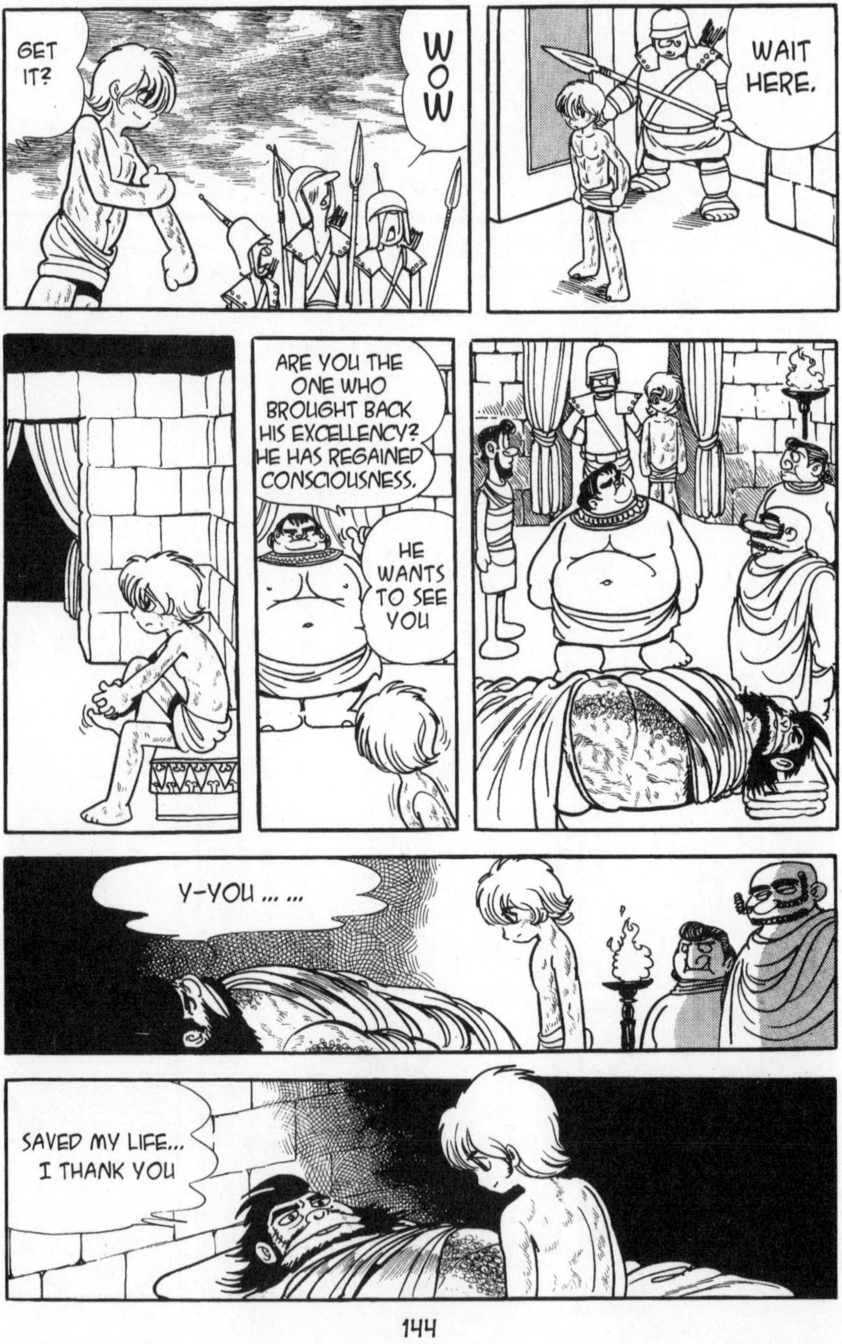
GET IT?
WOW
WAIT HERE.
ARE YOU THE ONE WHO BROUGHT BACK HIS EXCELLENCY? HE HAS REGAINED CONSCIOUSNESS.
HE WANTS TO SEE YOU
Y-YOU ... ...
SAVED MY LIFE... I THANK YOU

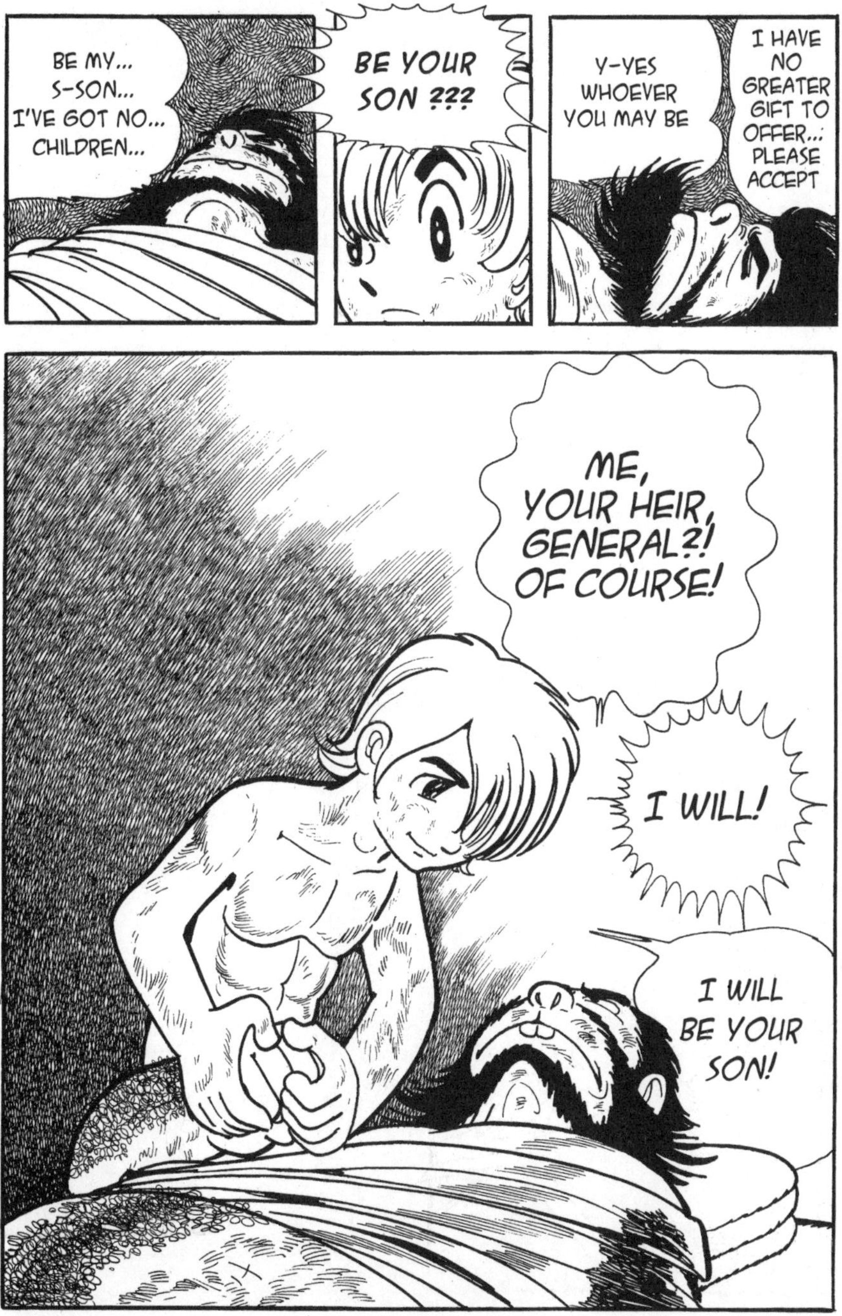
BE MY... S-SON... I'VE GOT NO... CHILDREN...
BE YOUR SON ???
Y-YES WHOEVER YOU MAY BE
I HAVE NO GREATER GIFT TO OFFER...: PLEASE ACCEPT
ME, YOUR HEIR, GENERAL?! OF COURSE!
I WILL!
I WILL BE YOUR SON!

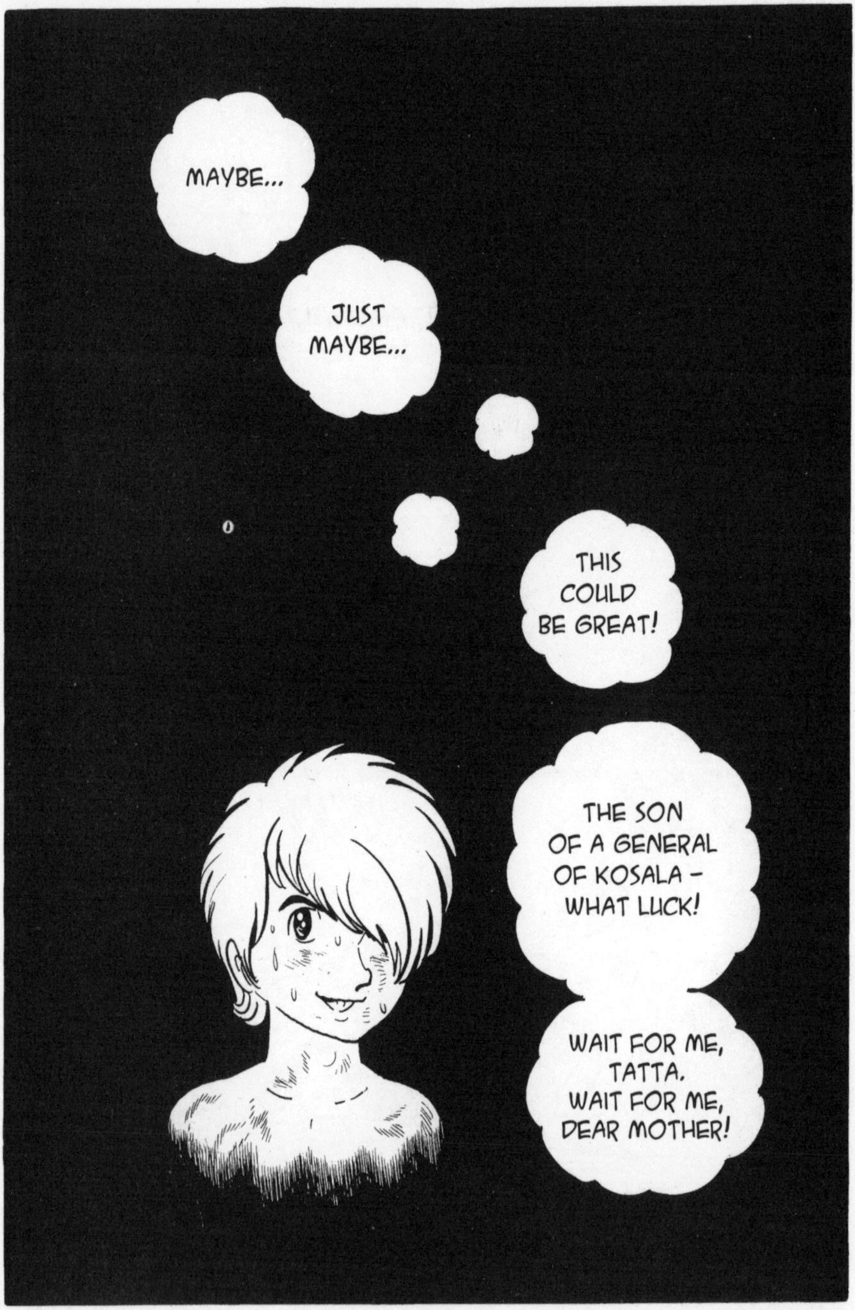
MAYBE...
JUST MAYBE...
THIS COULD BE GREAT!
THE SON OF A GENERAL OF KOSALA - WHAT LUCK!
WAIT FOR ME, TATTA. WAIT FOR ME, DEAR MOTHER!

CHAPTER FOUR

THE ANNOUNCEMENT

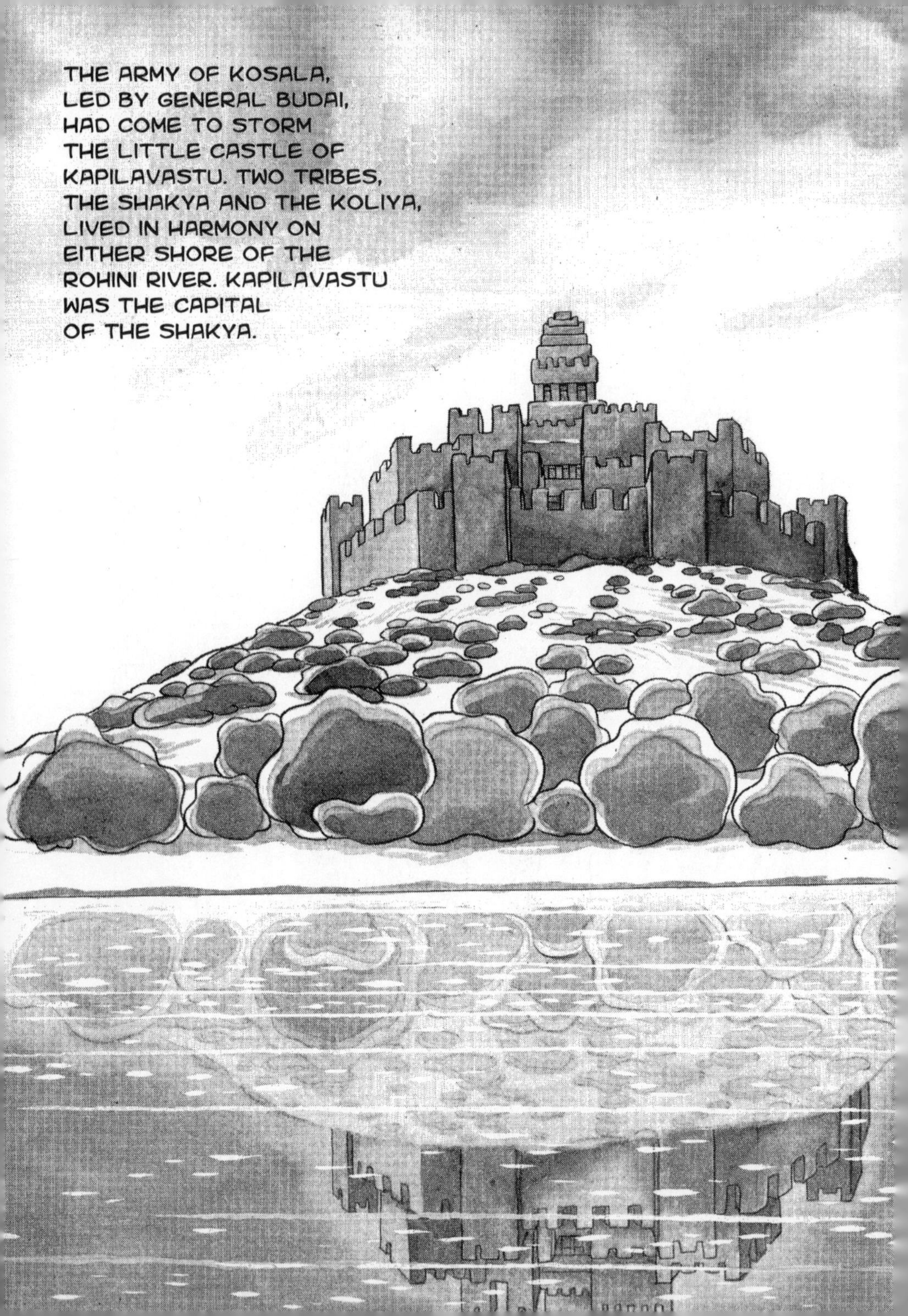
THE ARMY OF KOSALA, LED BY GENERAL BUDAI, HAD COME TO STORM THE LITTLE CASTLE OF KAPILAVASTU. TWO TRIBES, THE SHAKYA AND THE KOLIYA, LIVED IN HARMONY ON EITHER SHORE OF THE ROHINI RIVER. KAPILAVASTU WAS THE CAPITAL OF THE SHAKYA.

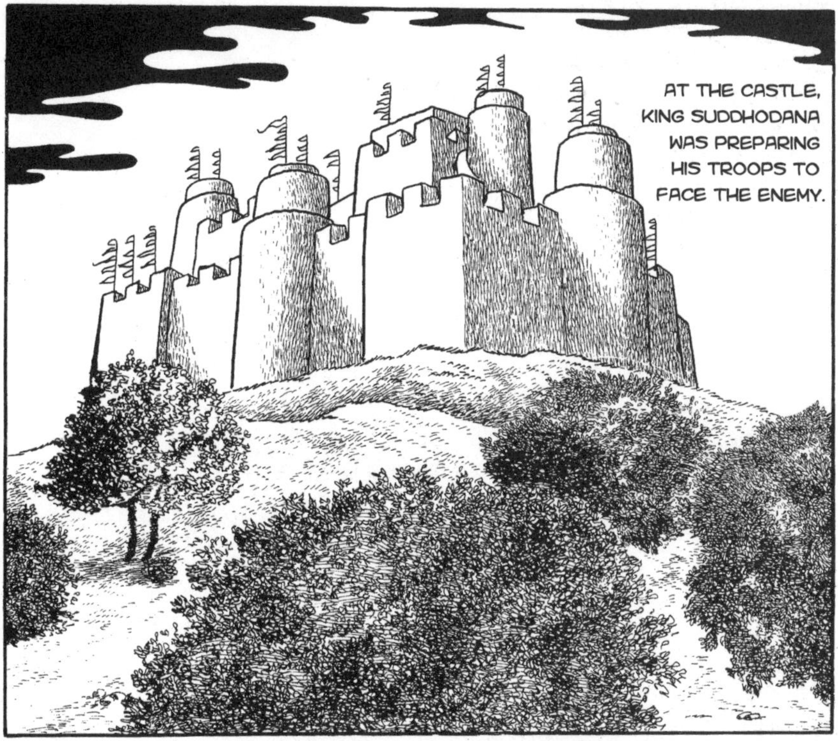
AT THE CASTLE, KING SUDDHODANA WAS PREPARING HIS TROOPS TO FACE THE ENEMY.
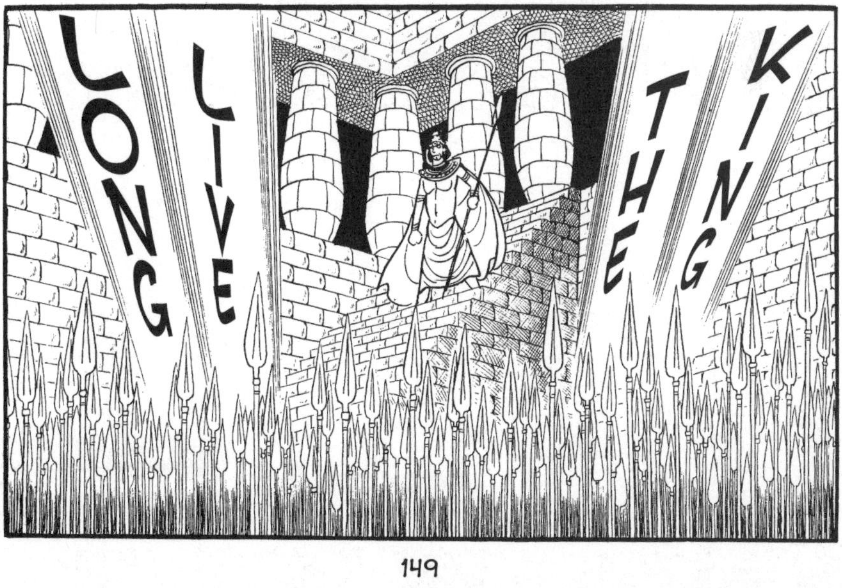
LONG LIVE THE KING

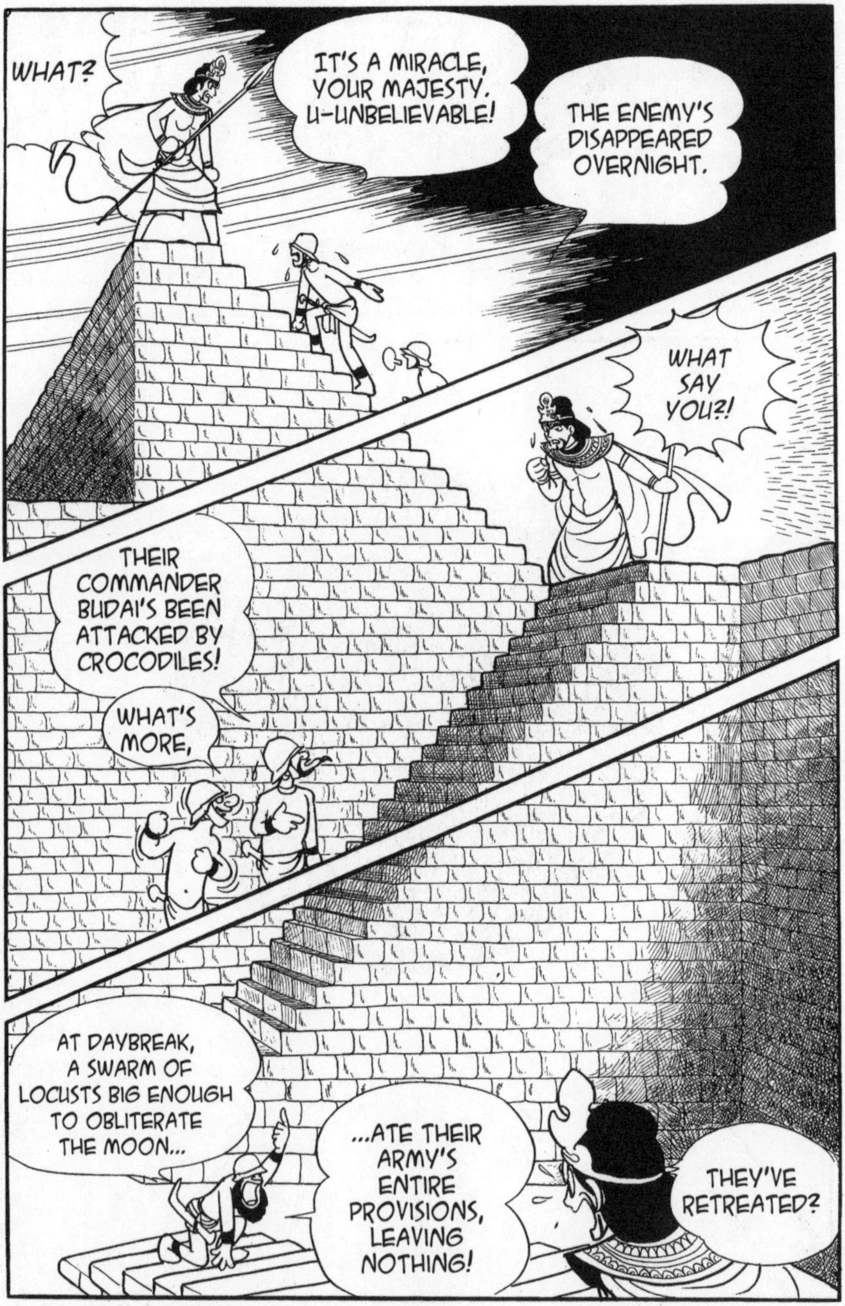
WHAT?
IT'S A MIRACLE, YOUR MAJESTY. U-UNBELIEVABLE!
THE ENEMY'S DISAPPEARED OVERNIGHT.
WHAT SAY YOU?!
THEIR COMMANDER BUDAI'S BEEN ATTACKED BY CROCODILES!
WHAT'S MORE,
AT DAYBREAK, A SWARM OF LOCUSTS BIG ENOUGH TO OBLITERATE THE MOON...
...ATE THEIR ARMY'S ENTIRE PROVISIONS, LEAVING NOTHING!
THEY'VE RETREATED?

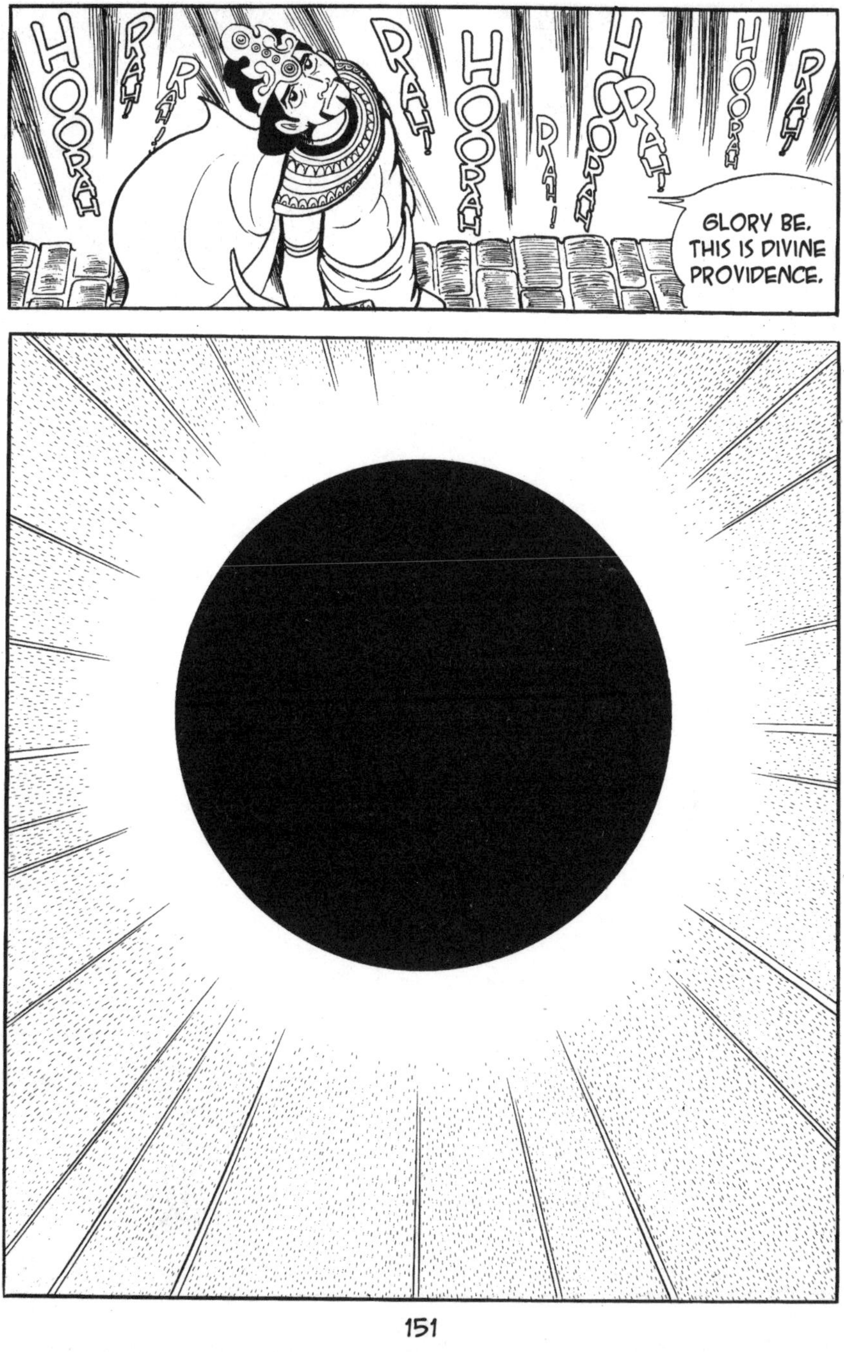
HOORAH
RAH!
RAH!
RAH!
HOORAH
RAH!
HOORAH
RAH!
HOORAH
RAH!
GLORY BE. THIS IS DIVINE PROVIDENCE.

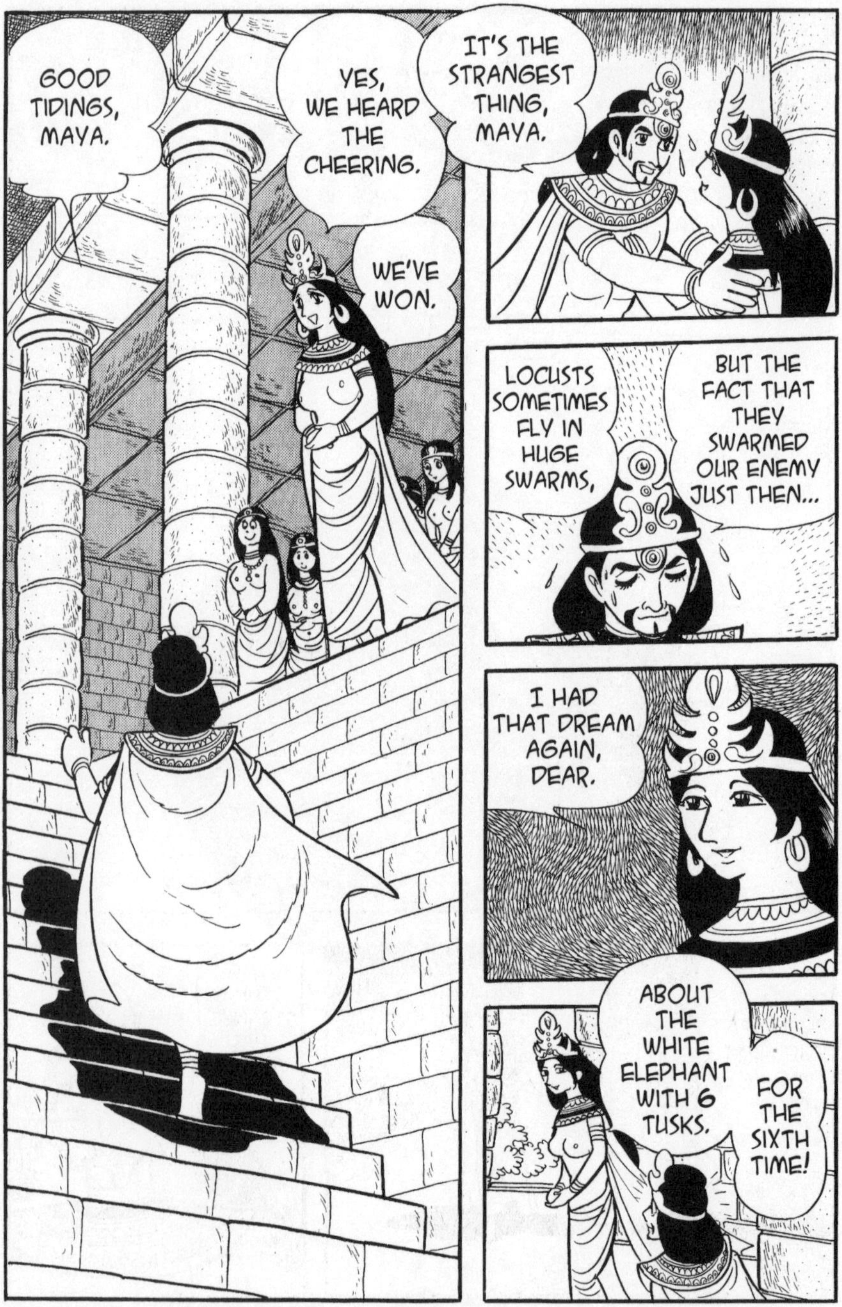
GOOD TIDINGS, MAYA.
YES, WE HEARD THE CHEERING.
WE'VE WON.
IT'S THE STRANGEST THING, MAYA.
LOCUSTS SOMETIMES FLY IN HUGE SWARMS,
BUT THE FACT THAT THEY SWARMED OUR ENEMY JUST THEN...
I HAD THAT DREAM AGAIN, DEAR.
ABOUT THE WHITE ELEPHANT WITH 6 TUSKS.
FOR THE SIXTH TIME!

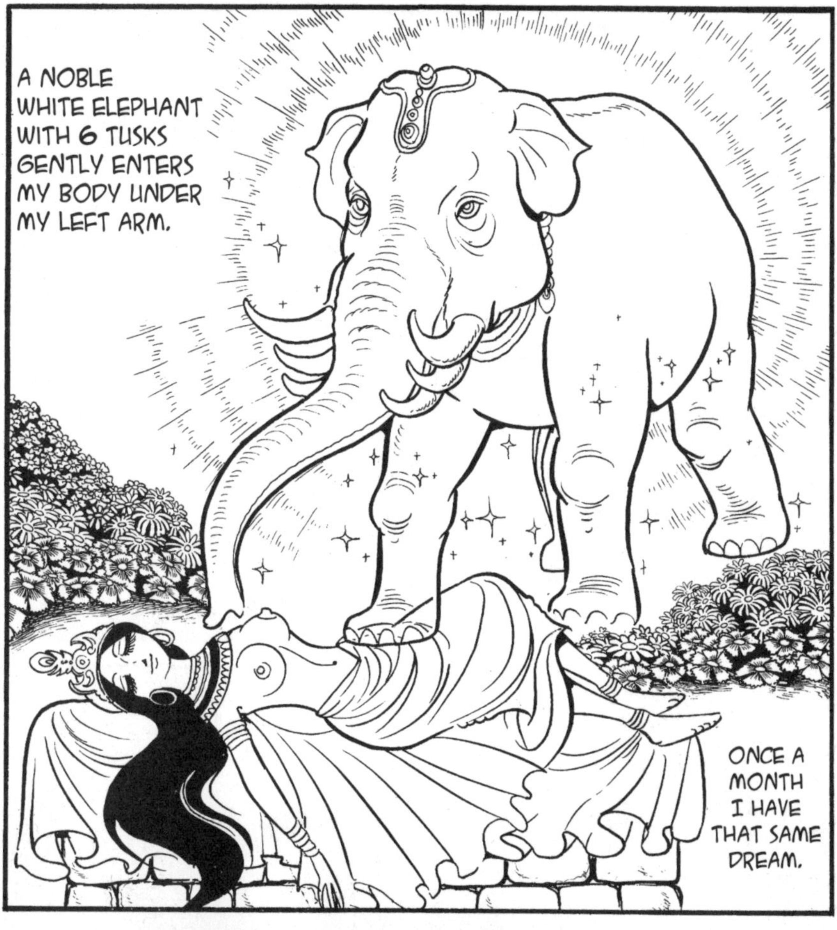
A NOBLE WHITE ELEPHANT WITH 6 TUSKS GENTLY ENTERS MY BODY UNDER MY LEFT ARM.
ONCE A MONTH I HAVE THAT SAME DREAM.

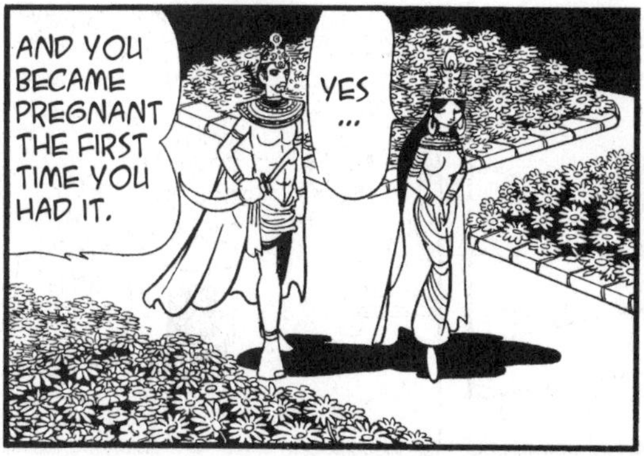
AND YOU BECAME PREGNANT THE FIRST TIME YOU HAD IT.
YES ...

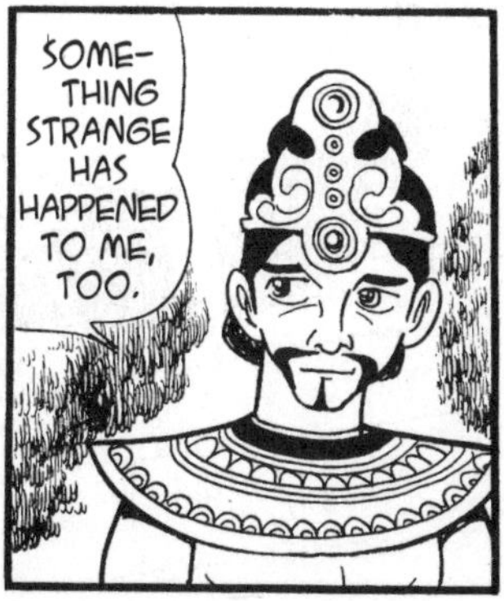
SOME-THING STRANGE HAS HAPPENED TO ME, TOO.

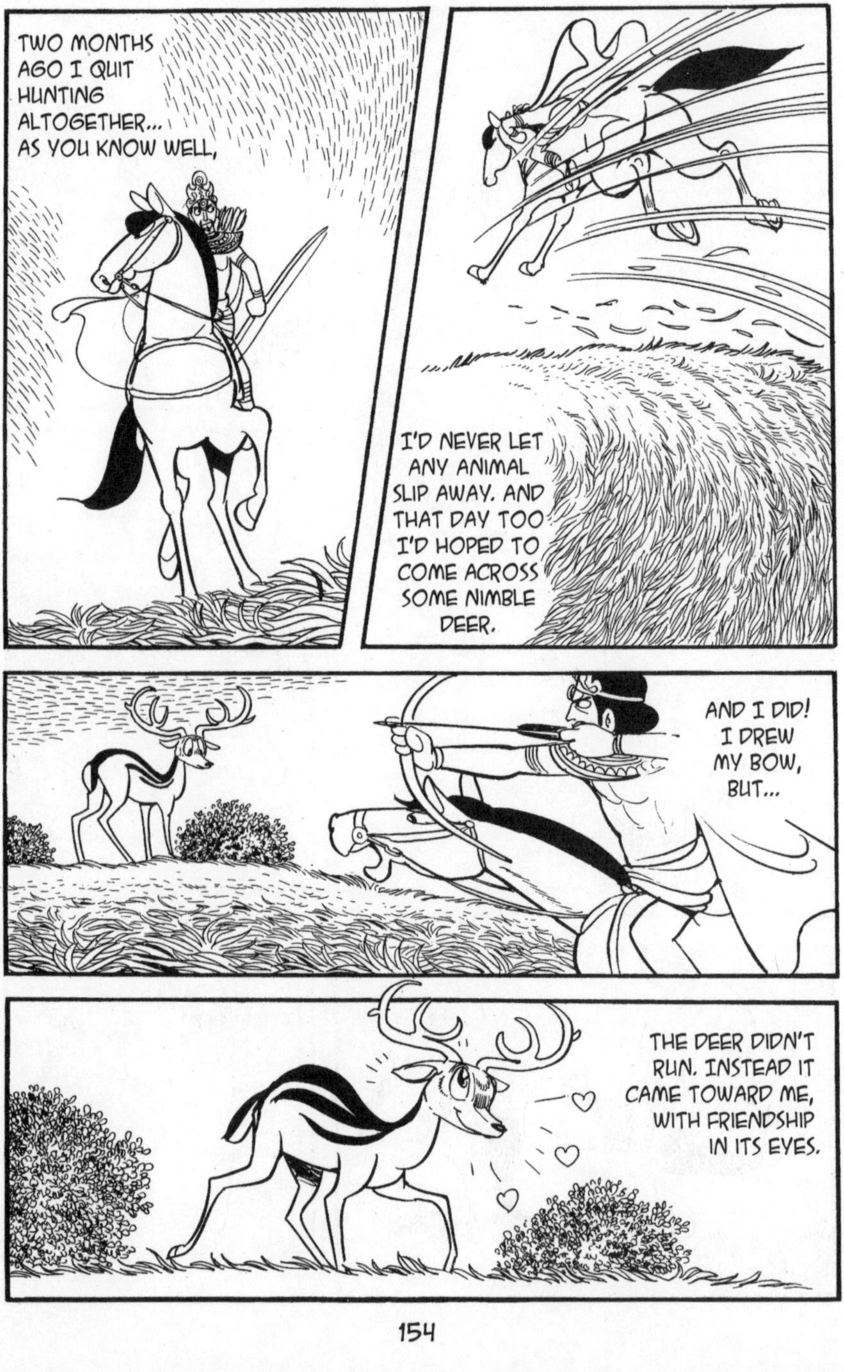
TWO MONTHS AGO I QUIT HUNTING ALTOGETHER... AS YOU KNOW WELL,
I'D NEVER LET ANY ANIMAL SLIP AWAY. AND THAT DAY TOO I'D HOPED TO COME ACROSS SOME NIMBLE DEER.
AND I DID! I DREW MY BOW, BUT...
THE DEER DIDN'T RUN. INSTEAD IT CAME TOWARD ME, WITH FRIENDSHIP IN ITS EYES.

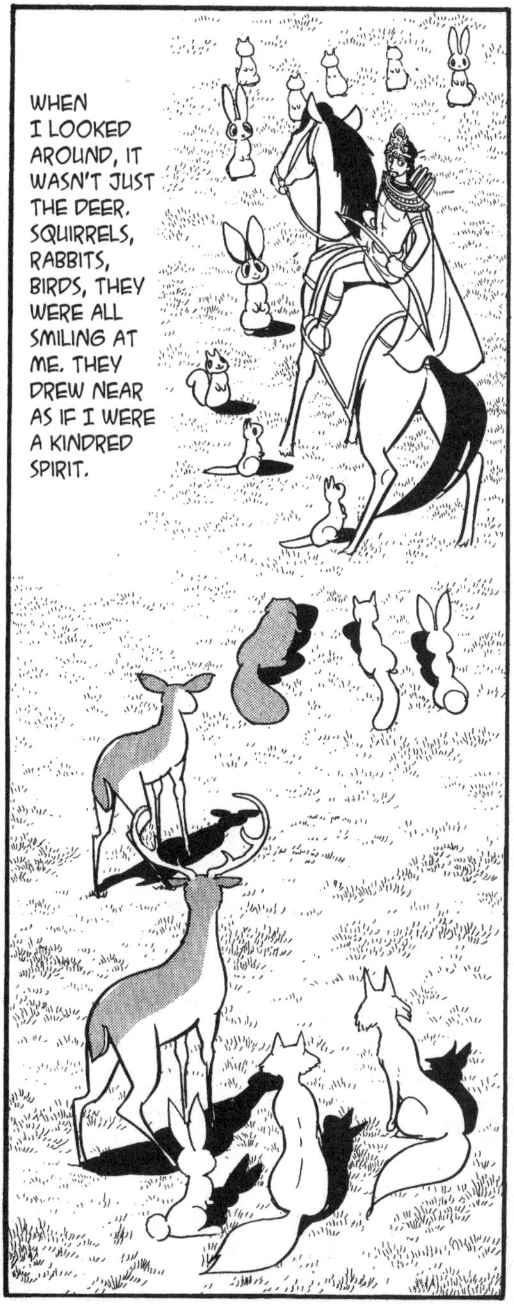
WHEN I LOOKED AROUND, IT WASN'T JUST THE DEER. SQUIRRELS, RABBITS, BIRDS, THEY WERE ALL SMILING AT ME. THEY DREW NEAR AS IF I WERE A KINDRED SPIRIT.

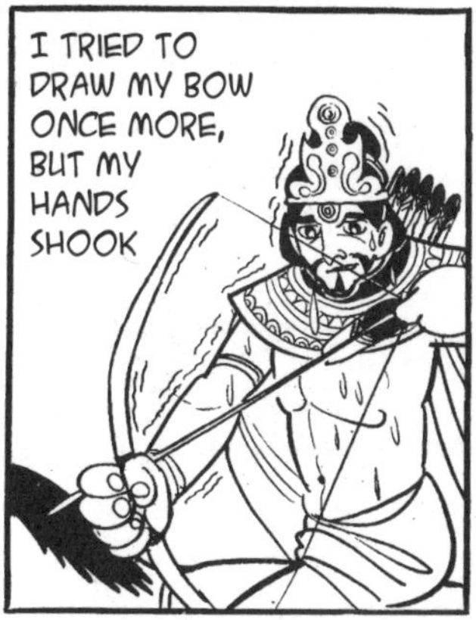
I TRIED TO DRAW MY BOW ONCE MORE, BUT MY HANDS SHOOK

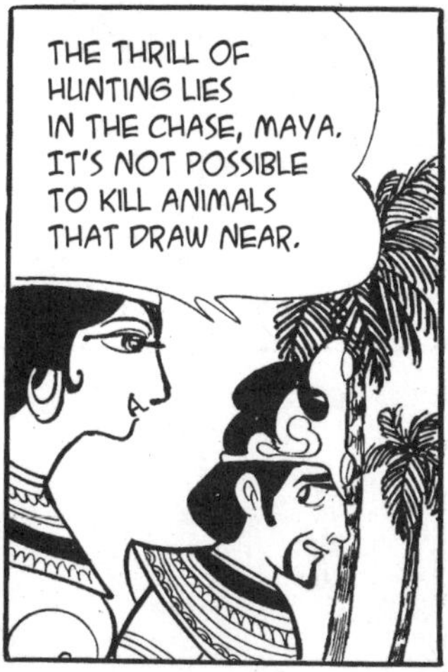
THE THRILL OF HUNTING LIES IN THE CHASE, MAYA. IT'S NOT POSSIBLE TO KILL ANIMALS THAT DRAW NEAR.

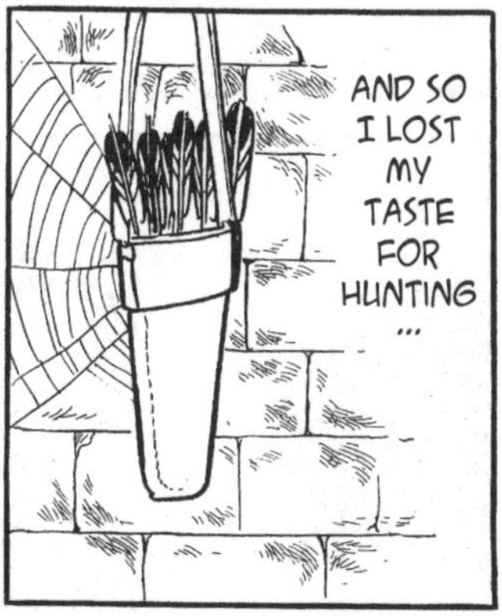
AND SO I LOST MY TASTE FOR HUNTING ...

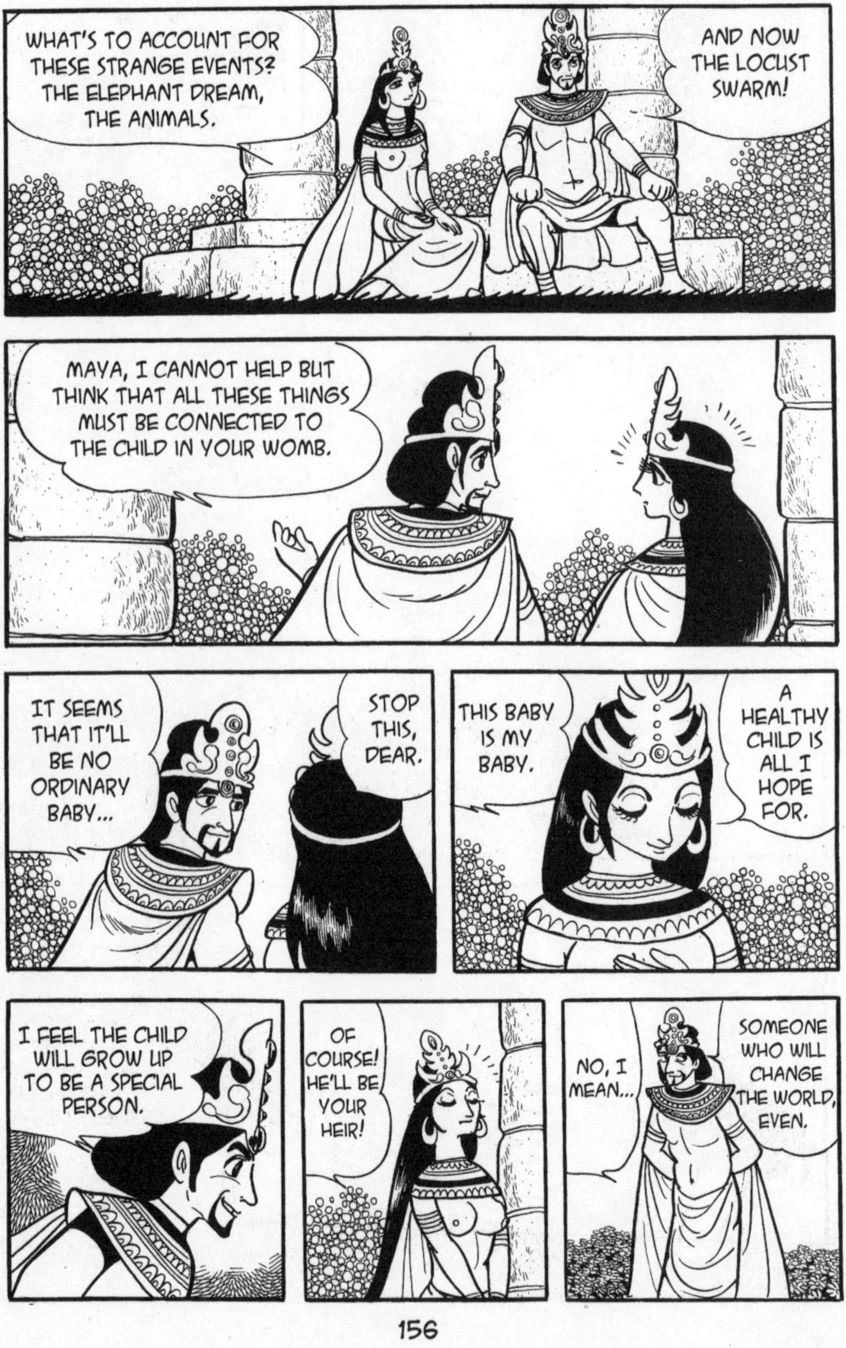
WHAT'S TO ACCOUNT FOR THESE STRANGE EVENTS? THE ELEPHANT DREAM, THE ANIMALS.
AND NOW THE LOCUST SWARM!
MAYA, I CANNOT HELP BUT THINK THAT ALL THESE THINGS MUST BE CONNECTED TO THE CHILD IN YOUR WOMB.
IT SEEMS THAT IT'LL BE NO ORDINARY BABY...
STOP THIS, DEAR.
THIS BABY IS MY BABY.
A HEALTHY CHILD IS ALL I HOPE FOR.
I FEEL THE CHILD WILL GROW UP TO BE A SPECIAL PERSON.
OF COURSE! HE'LL BE YOUR HEIR!
NO, I MEAN...
SOMEONE WHO WILL CHANGE THE WORLD, EVEN.

I FEEL IT IN MY BONES.

MAYA, TAKE CARE OF YOURSELF.

IT'S STILL 4 MONTHS AWAY.

RIGHT DURING THE DRY SEASON ...

FROM MARCH TO MAY, THE "SEASON OF DEATH" COMES TO INDIA. THE TEMPERATURE RISES ABOVE 110 DEGREES, AND EVERYTHING BECOMES PARCHED.

WHOOSH

WHOOSH

WHOOSH

SANDSTORMS AND TORNADOES SWIRL, GRASS AND TREES WILT, RIVERS RUN DRY, AND THEN COME THE EPIDEMICS, ALL IN THE 110-PLUS DEGREE HEAT.

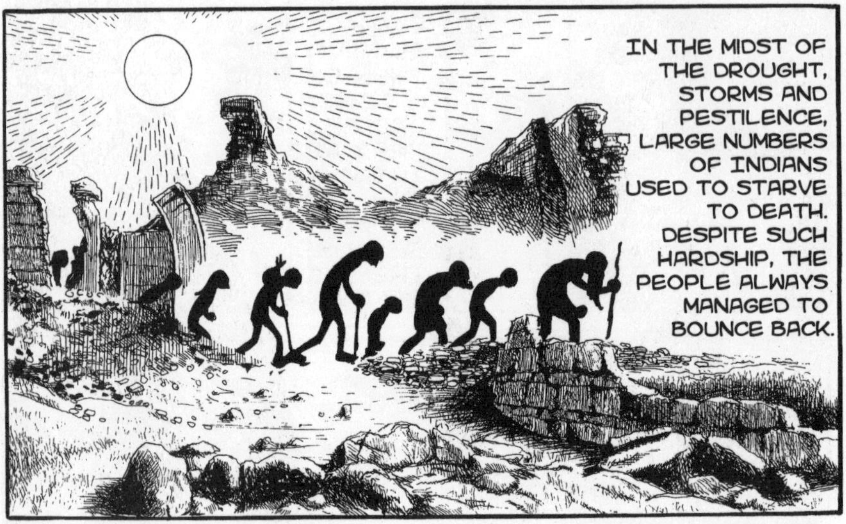
IN THE MIDST OF THE DROUGHT, STORMS AND PESTILENCE, LARGE NUMBERS OF INDIANS USED TO STARVE TO DEATH. DESPITE SUCH HARDSHIP, THE PEOPLE ALWAYS MANAGED TO BOUNCE BACK.

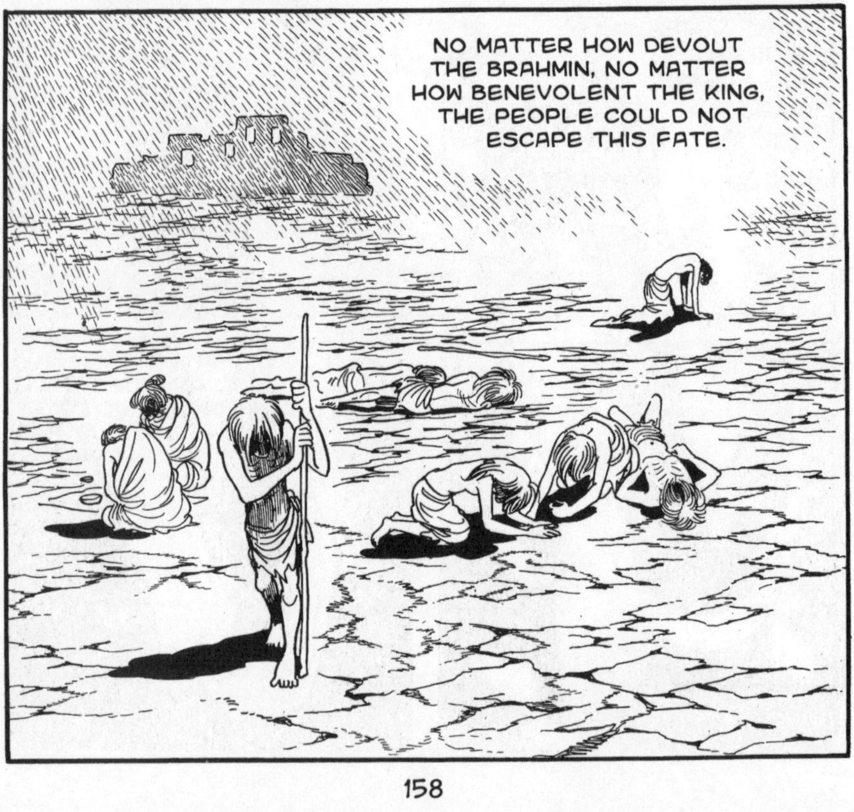
NO MATTER HOW DEVOUT THE BRAHMIN, NO MATTER HOW BENEVOLENT THE KING, THE PEOPLE COULD NOT ESCAPE THIS FATE.

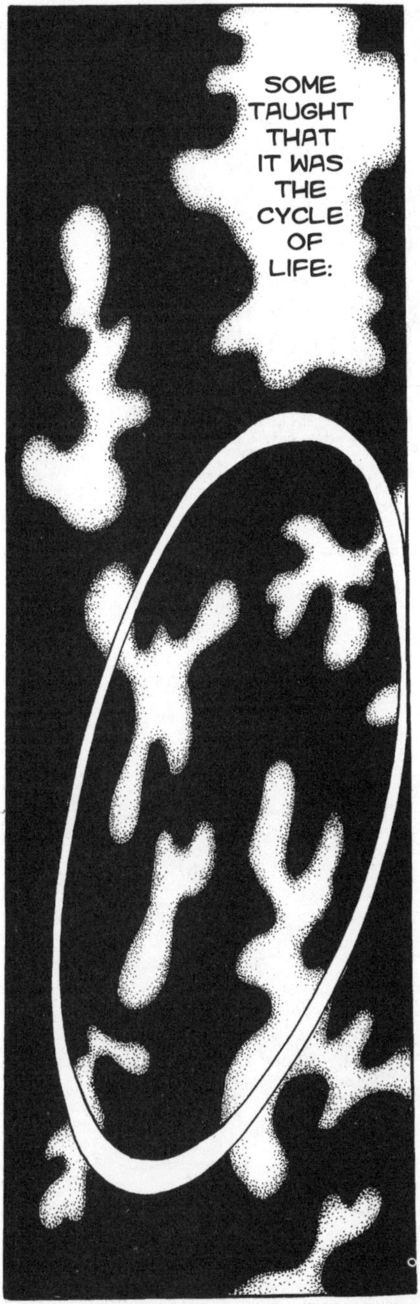
SOME TAUGHT THAT IT WAS THE CYCLE OF LIFE:

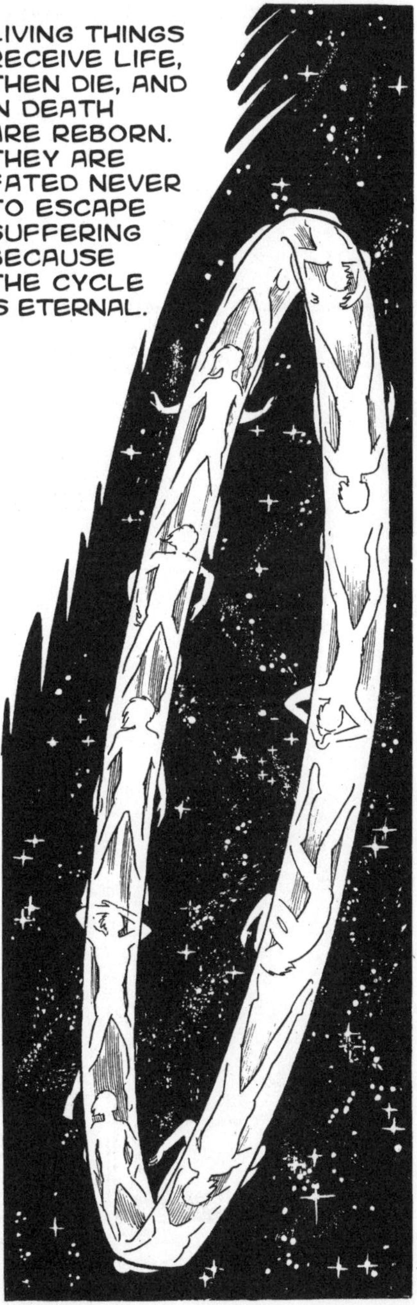
LIVING THINGS RECEIVE LIFE, THEN DIE, AND IN DEATH ARE REBORN. THEY ARE FATED NEVER TO ESCAPE SUFFERING BECAUSE THE CYCLE IS ETERNAL.

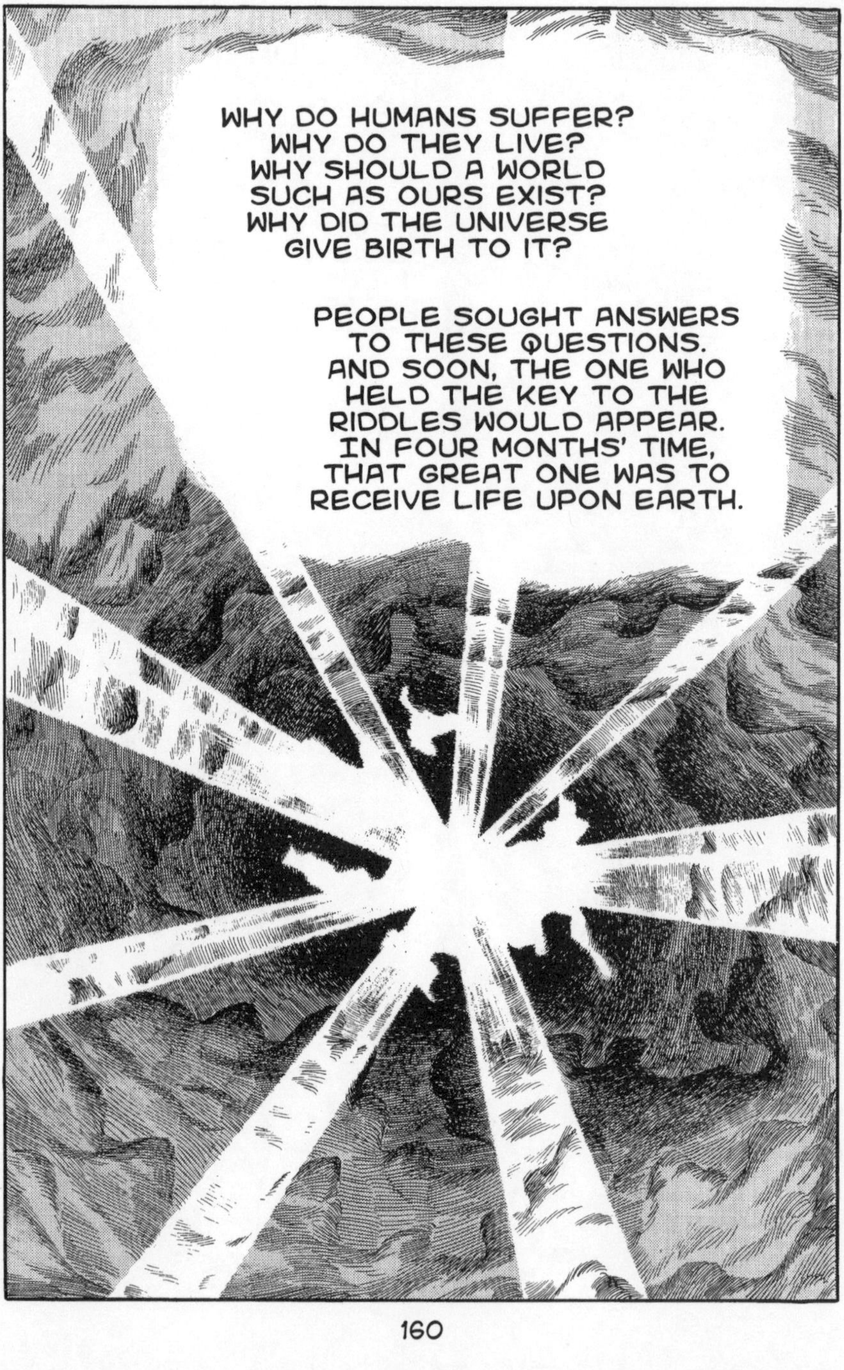
WHY DO HUMANS SUFFER?
WHY DO THEY LIVE?
WHY SHOULD A WORLD
SUCH AS OURS EXIST?
WHY DID THE UNIVERSE
GIVE BIRTH TO IT?
PEOPLE SOUGHT ANSWERS
TO THESE QUESTIONS.
AND SOON, THE ONE WHO
HELD THE KEY TO THE
RIDDLES WOULD APPEAR.
IN FOUR MONTHS' TIME,
THAT GREAT ONE WAS TO
RECEIVE LIFE UPON EARTH.

CHAPTER FIVE

CHAPRA

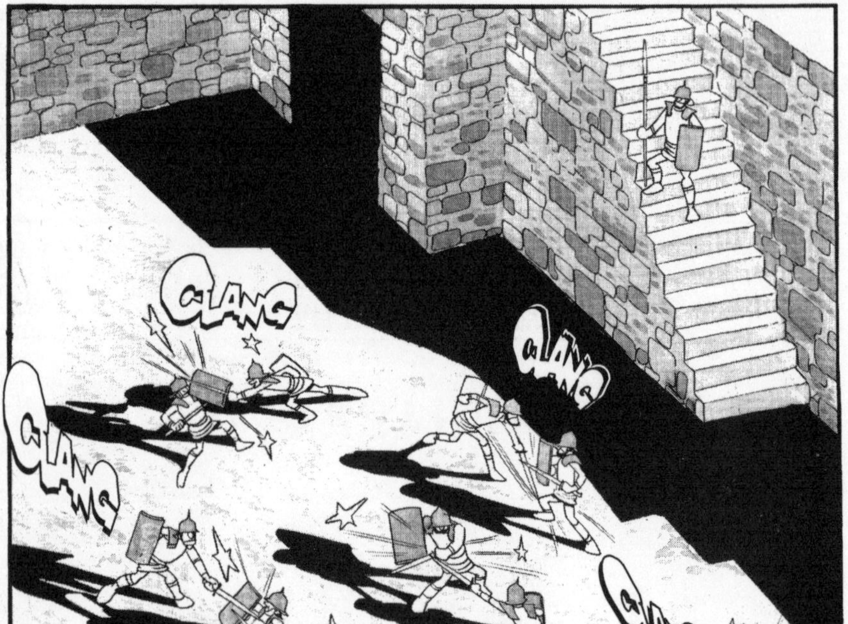
CLANG
CLANG
CLANG
CLANG
CLANG
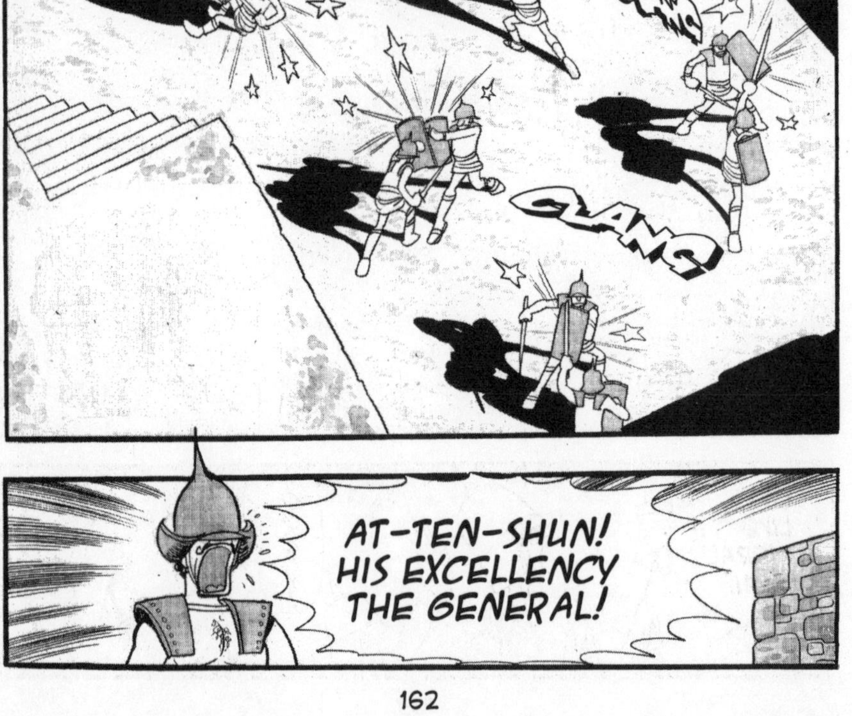
AT-TEN-SHUN!
HIS EXCELLENCY
THE GENERAL!

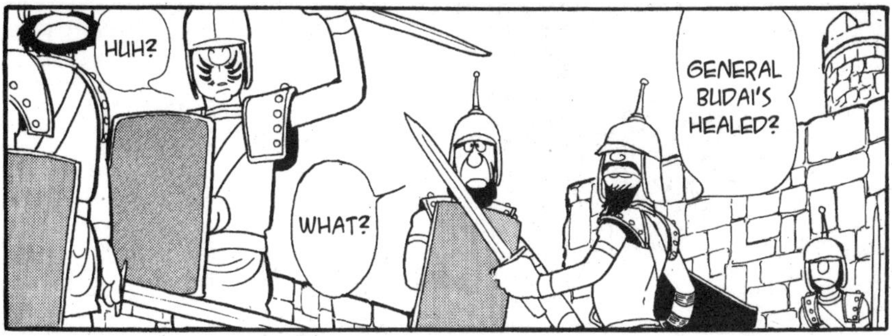
HUH?
WHAT?
GENERAL BUDAI'S HEALED?

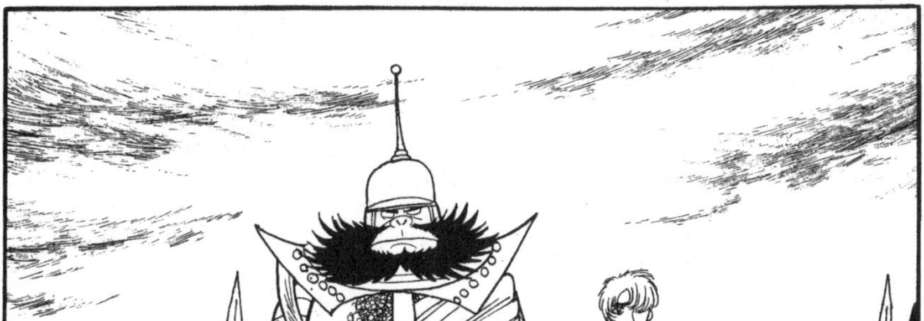

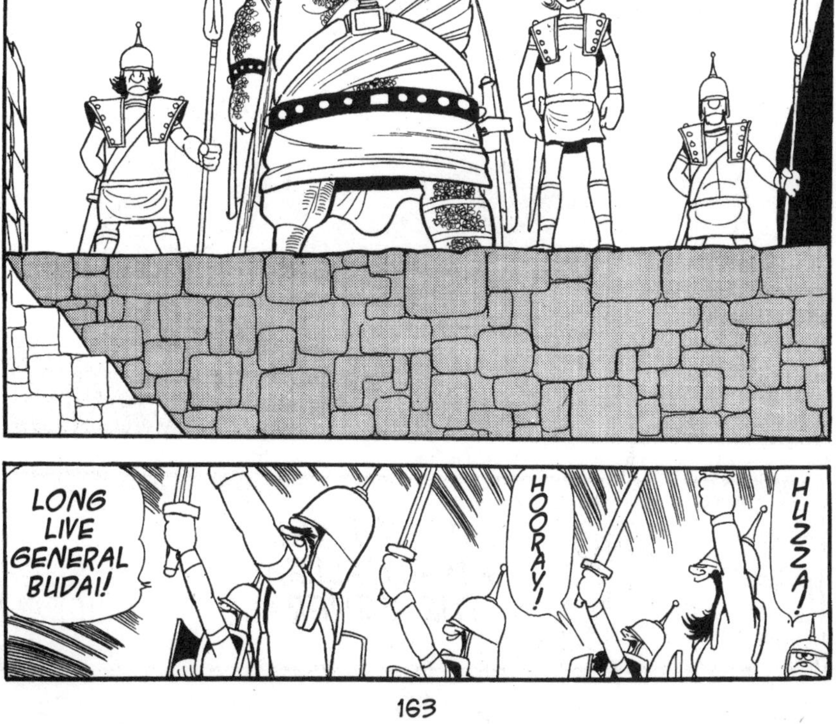
LONG LIVE GENERAL BUDAI!
HOORAY!
HUZZA!

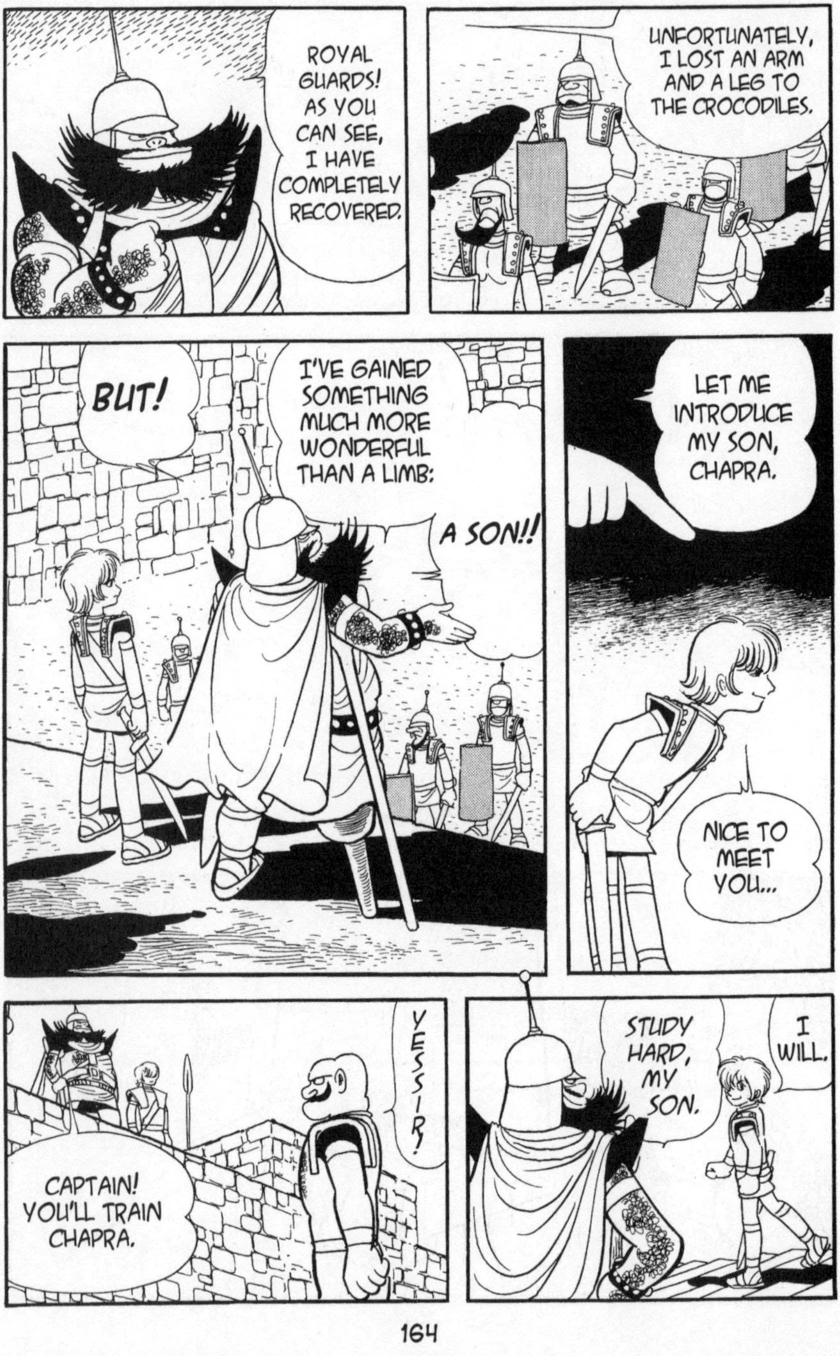
ROYAL GUARDS! AS YOU CAN SEE, I HAVE COMPLETELY RECOVERED.
UNFORTUNATELY, I LOST AN ARM AND A LEG TO THE CROCODILES.
BUT!
I'VE GAINED SOMETHING MUCH MORE WONDERFUL THAN A LIMB:
A SON!!
LET ME INTRODUCE MY SON, CHAPRA.
NICE TO MEET YOU...
YESSIR!
CAPTAIN! YOU'LL TRAIN CHAPRA.
STUDY HARD, MY SON.
I WILL.

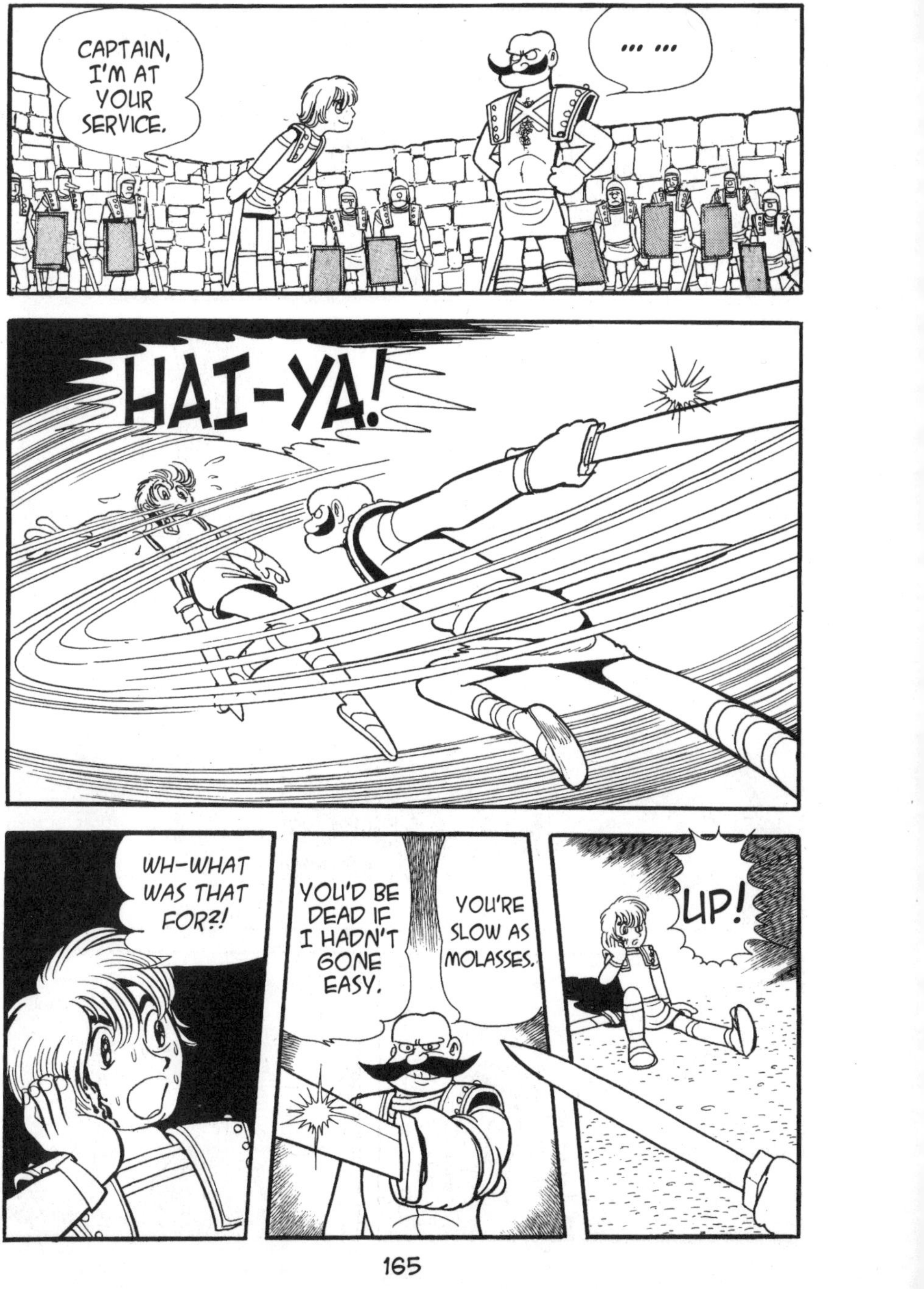
CAPTAIN, I'M AT YOUR SERVICE.
... ...
HAI-YA!
WH-WHAT WAS THAT FOR?!
YOU'D BE DEAD IF I HADN'T GONE EASY.
YOU'RE SLOW AS MOLASSES.
UP!

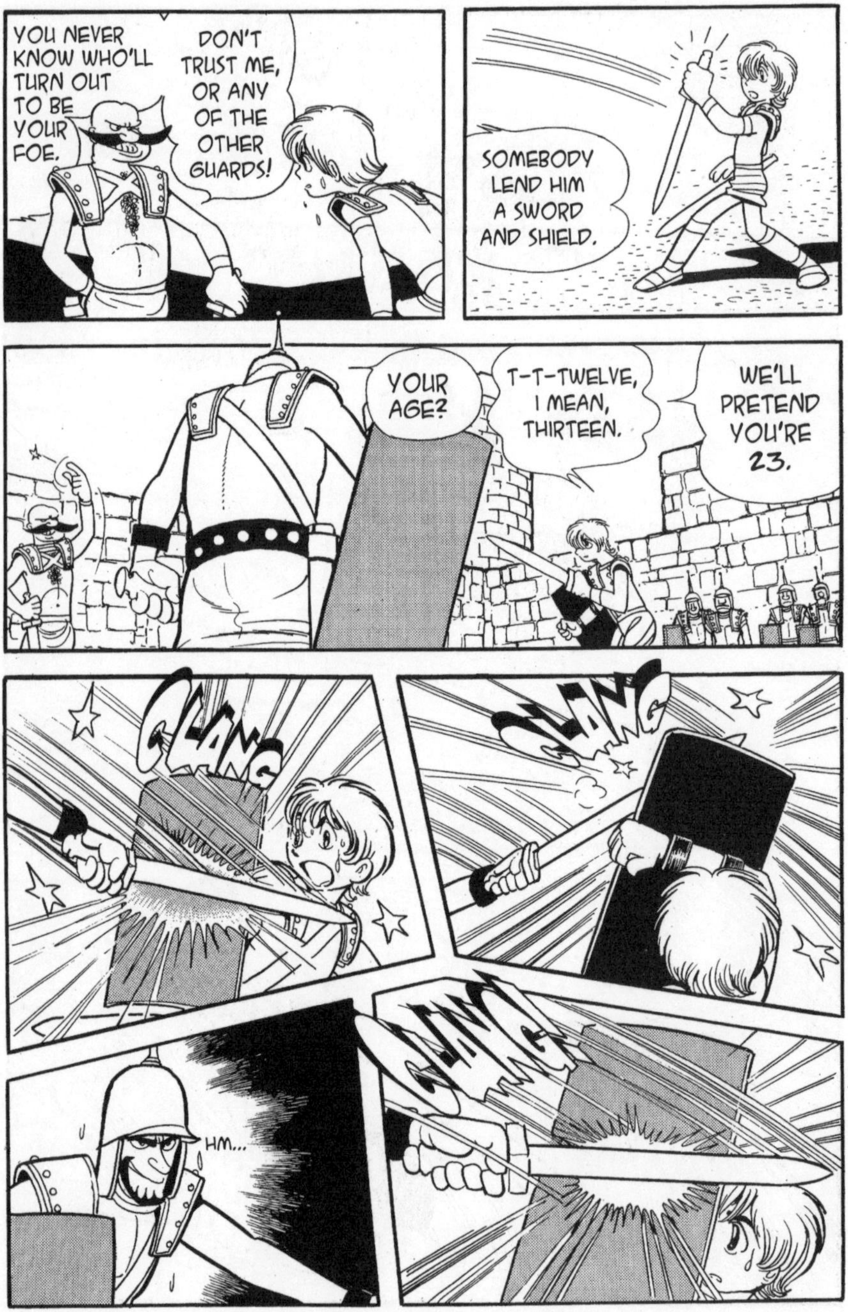
YOU NEVER KNOW WHO'LL TURN OUT TO BE YOUR FOE.
DON'T TRUST ME, OR ANY OF THE OTHER GUARDS!
SOMEBODY LEND HIM A SWORD AND SHIELD.
YOUR AGE?
T-T-TWELVE, I MEAN, THIRTEEN.
WE'LL PRETEND YOU'RE 23.
CLANG
CLANG
HM...
CLANG

BAM
GONG
CLANG
BANG

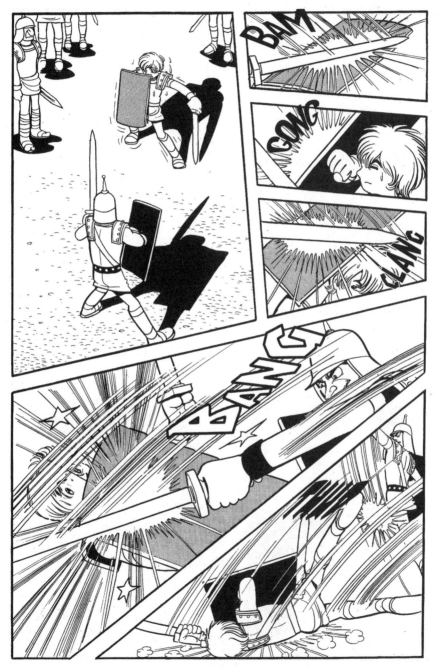

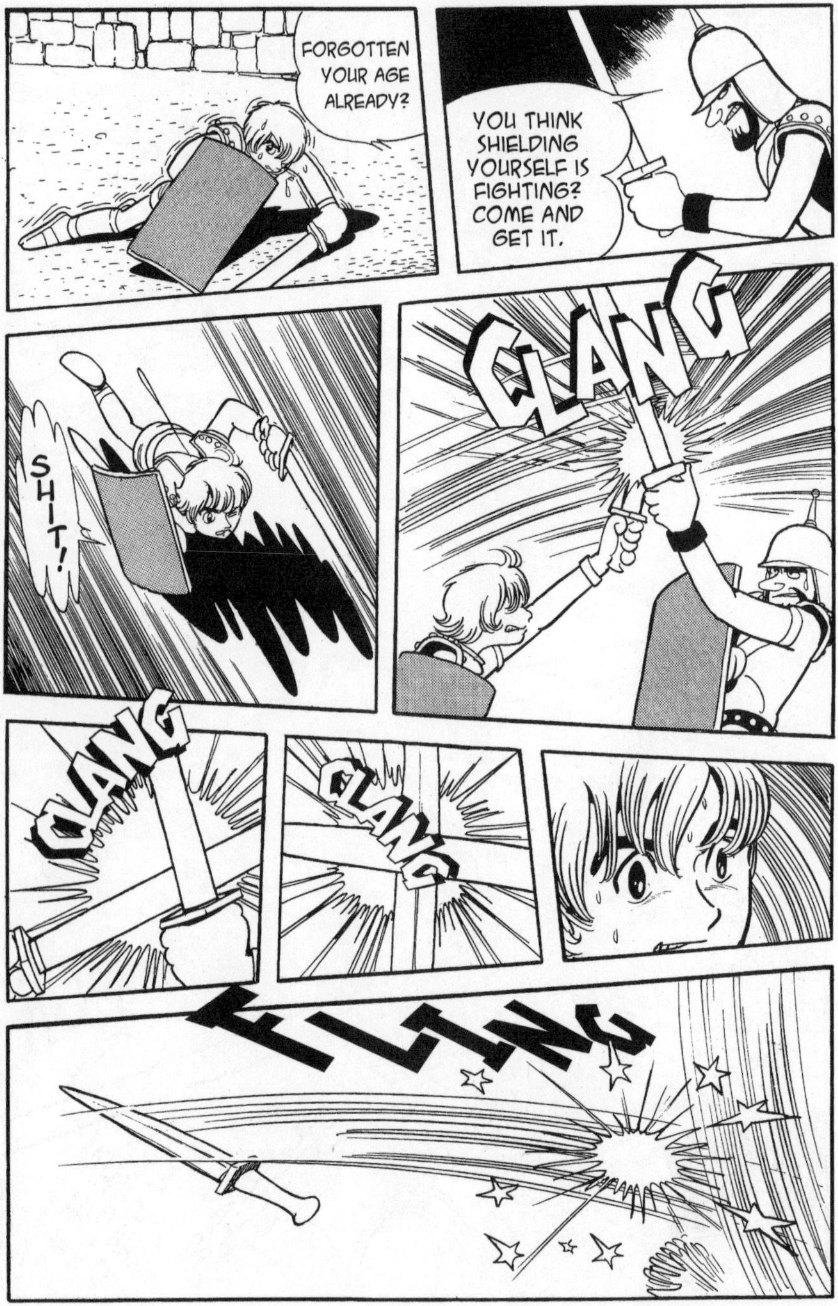
FORGOTTEN YOUR AGE ALREADY?
YOU THINK SHIELDING YOURSELF IS FIGHTING? COME AND GET IT.
SHIT!!
CLANG
CLANG
CLANG
FLING

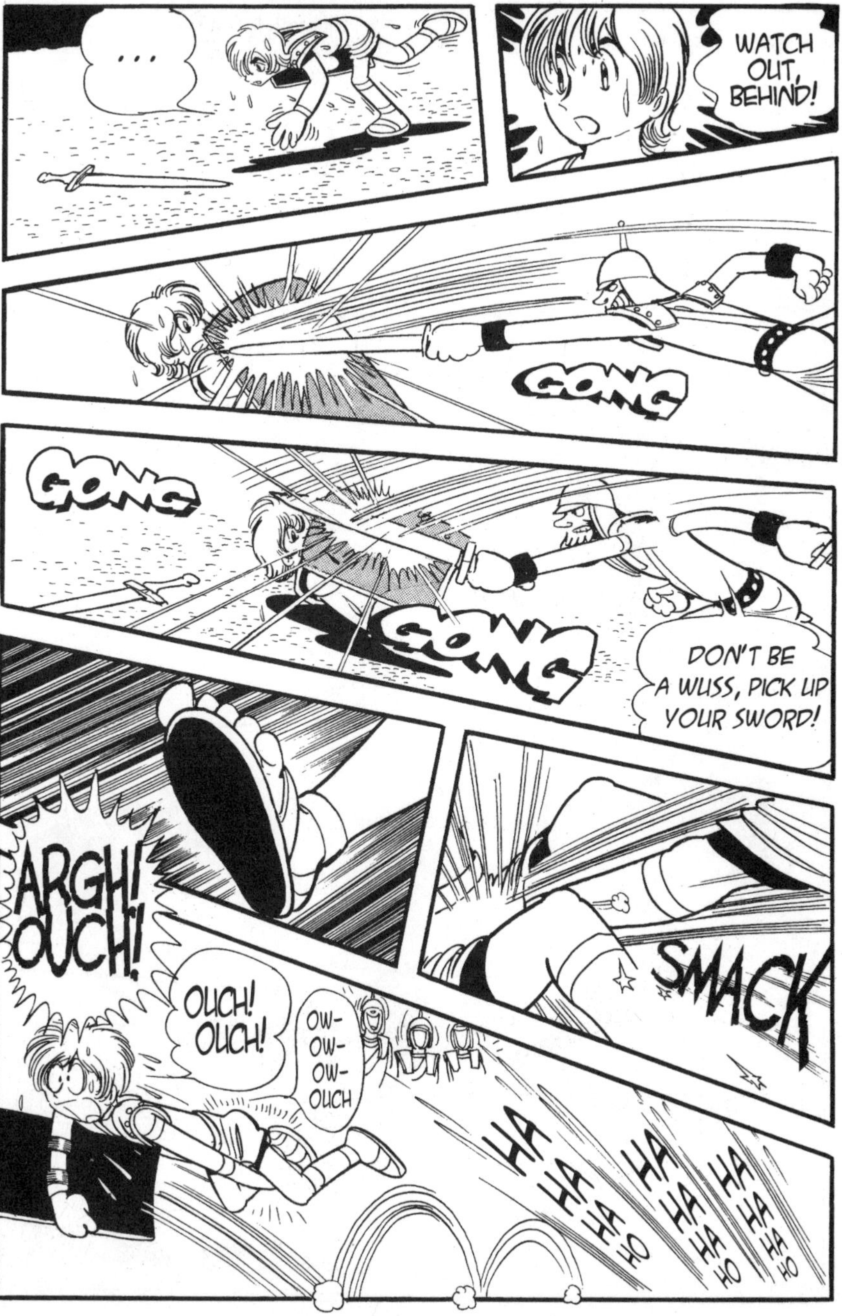
...
WATCH OUT, BEHIND!
GONG
GONG
GONG
DON'T BE A WUSS, PICK UP YOUR SWORD!
ARGH! OUCH!
SMACK
OUCH! OUCH!
OW-OW-OW-OUCH
HA HA HA HO
HA HA HA HA HA HO
HA HA HA HA HO

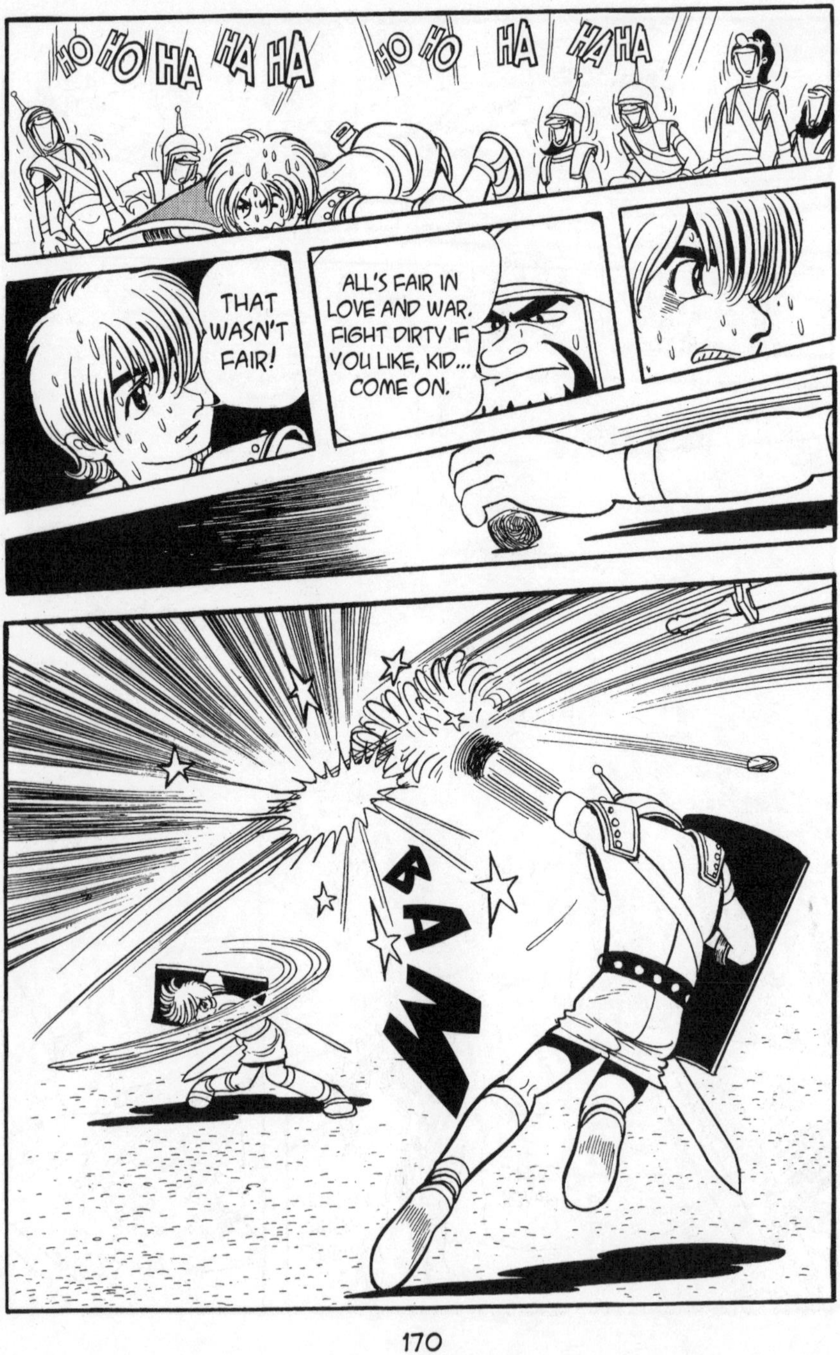
HO HO HA HA HA
HO HO HA HA HA
THAT WASN'T FAIR!
ALL'S FAIR IN LOVE AND WAR. FIGHT DIRTY IF YOU LIKE, KID... COME ON.
BAM

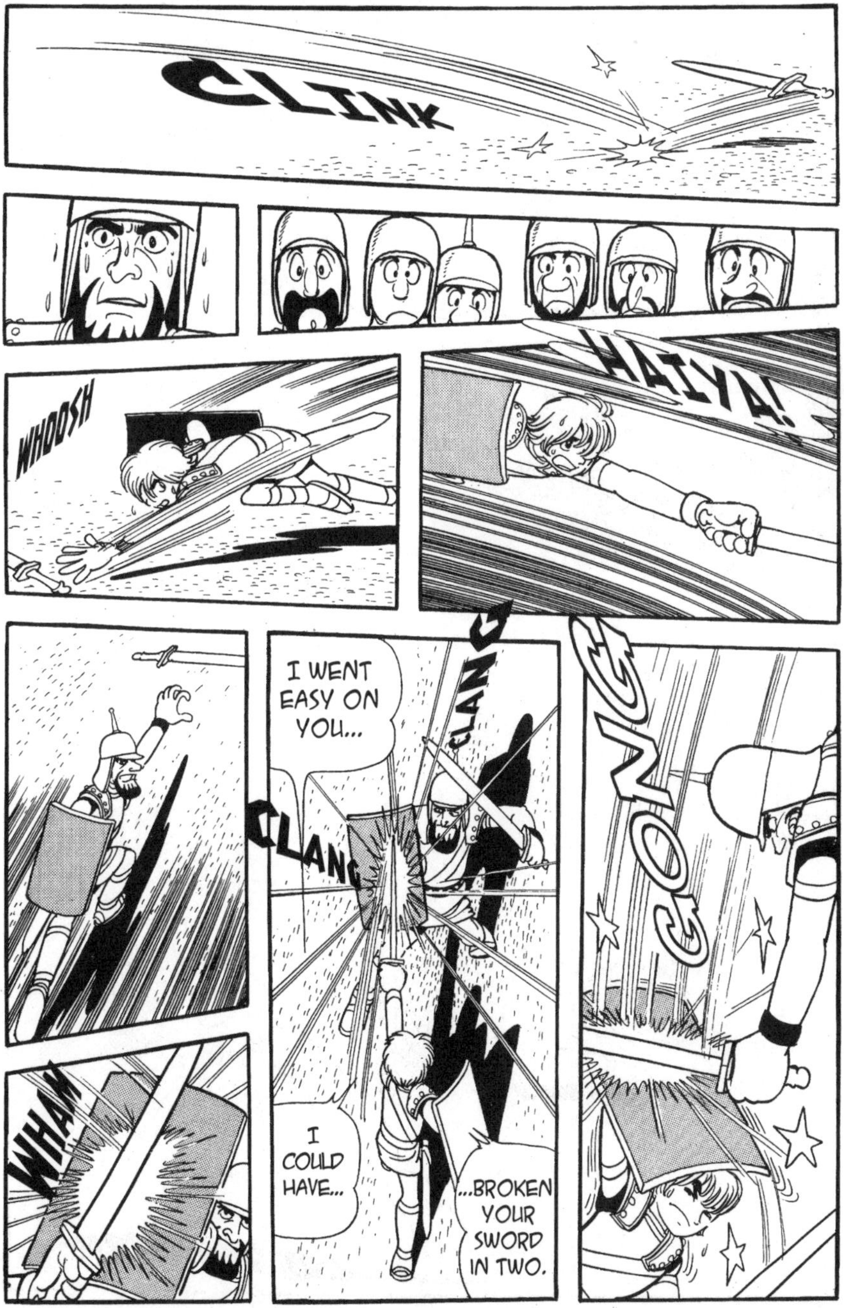
CLINK
WHOOSH
HAIYA!
WHAM
I WENT EASY ON YOU...
CLANG
CLANG
I COULD HAVE...
...BROKEN YOUR SWORD IN TWO.
GONG

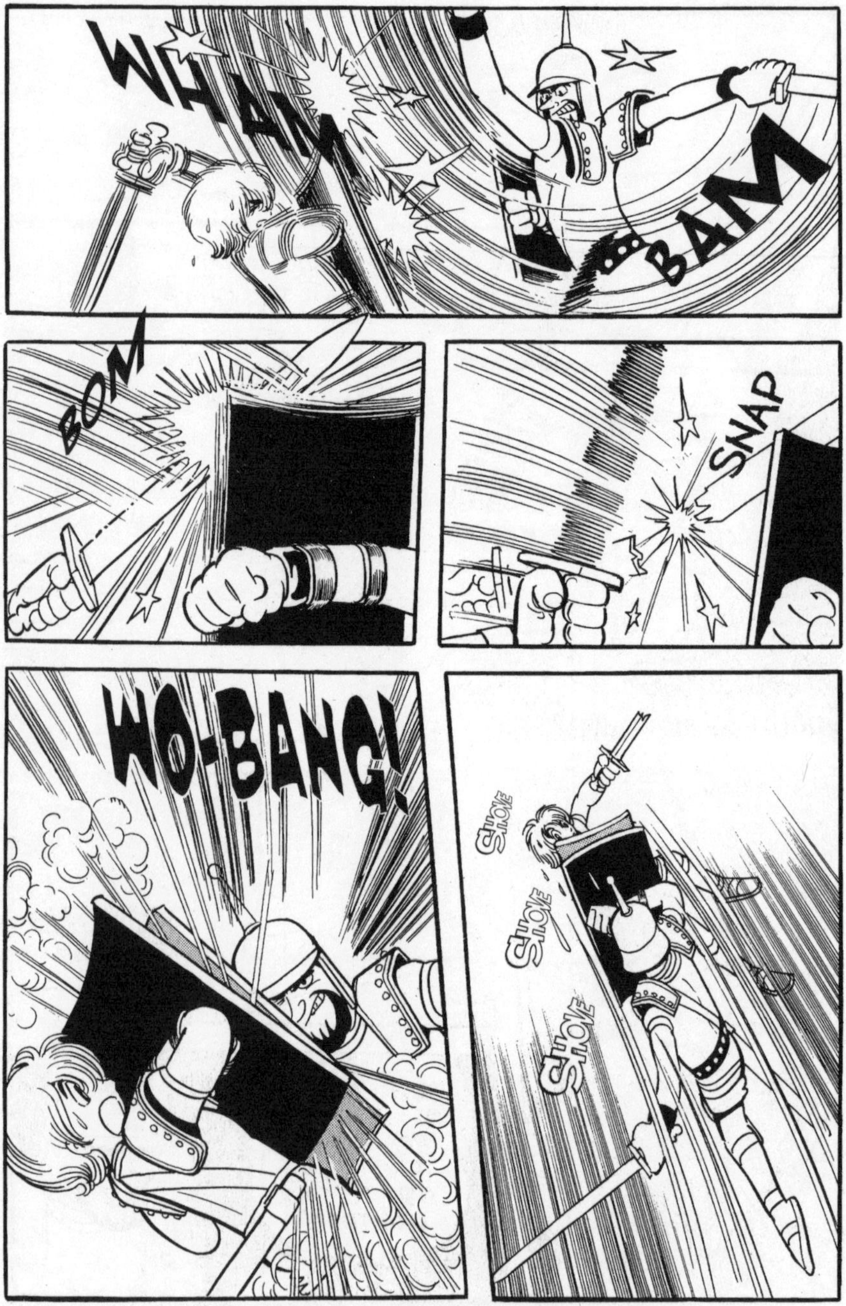
WHAM
BAM
BOM
SNAP
WO-BANG!
SHOVE
SHOVE
SHOVE
SHOVE

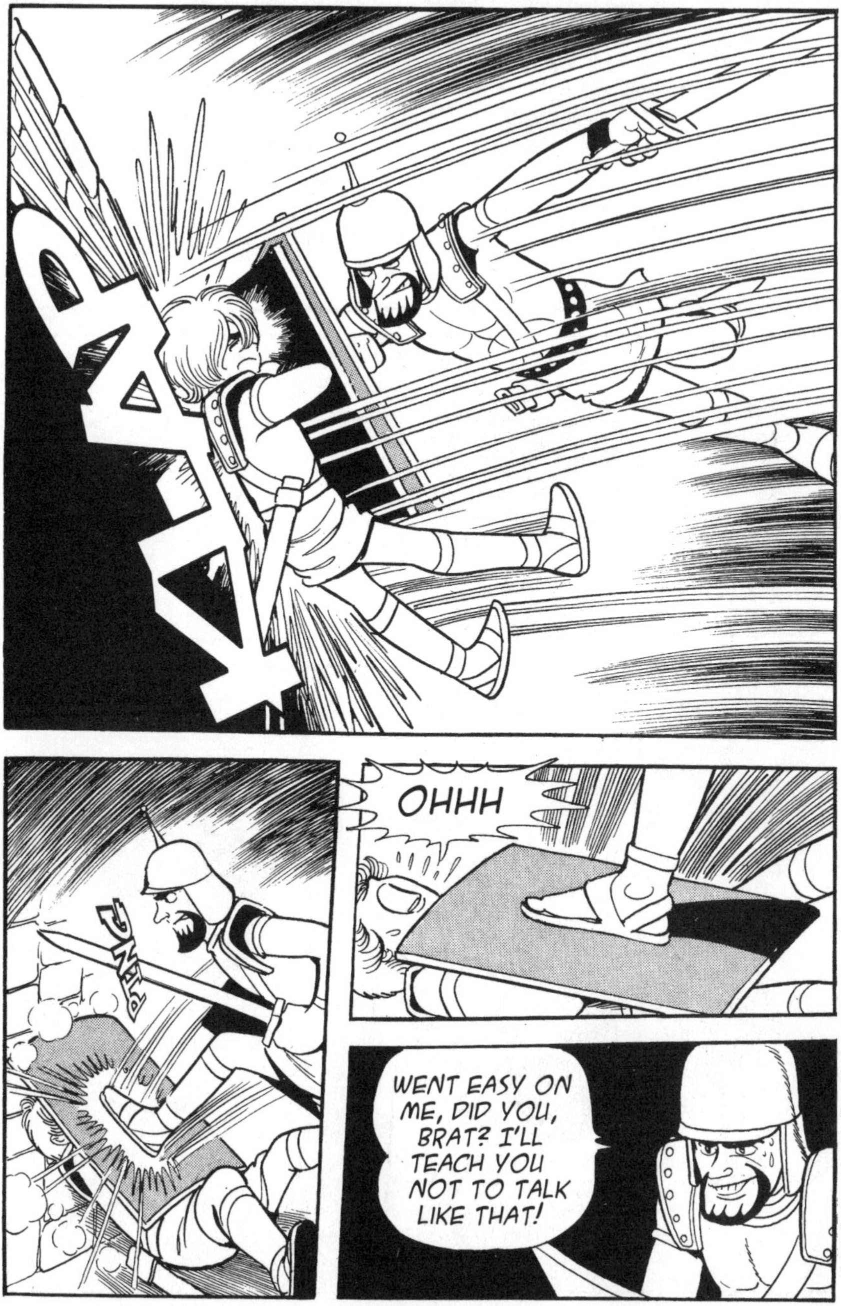
OHHH
WENT EASY ON ME, DID YOU, BRAT? I'LL TEACH YOU NOT TO TALK LIKE THAT!

SQUISH!
UGH...
THAT'S ALL FOR TODAY.
ONE OF YOU, MAKE SURE HE'S BREATHING.
GUFFAW
GUFFAW
HA HA HA

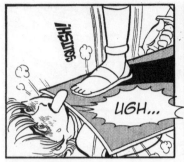

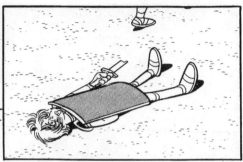

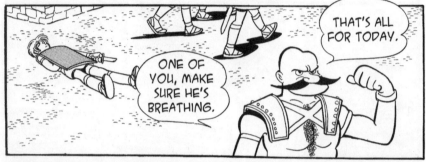

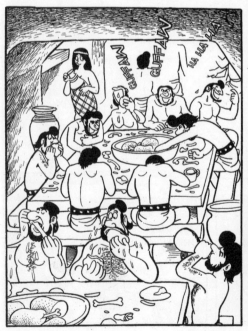

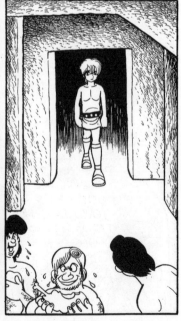

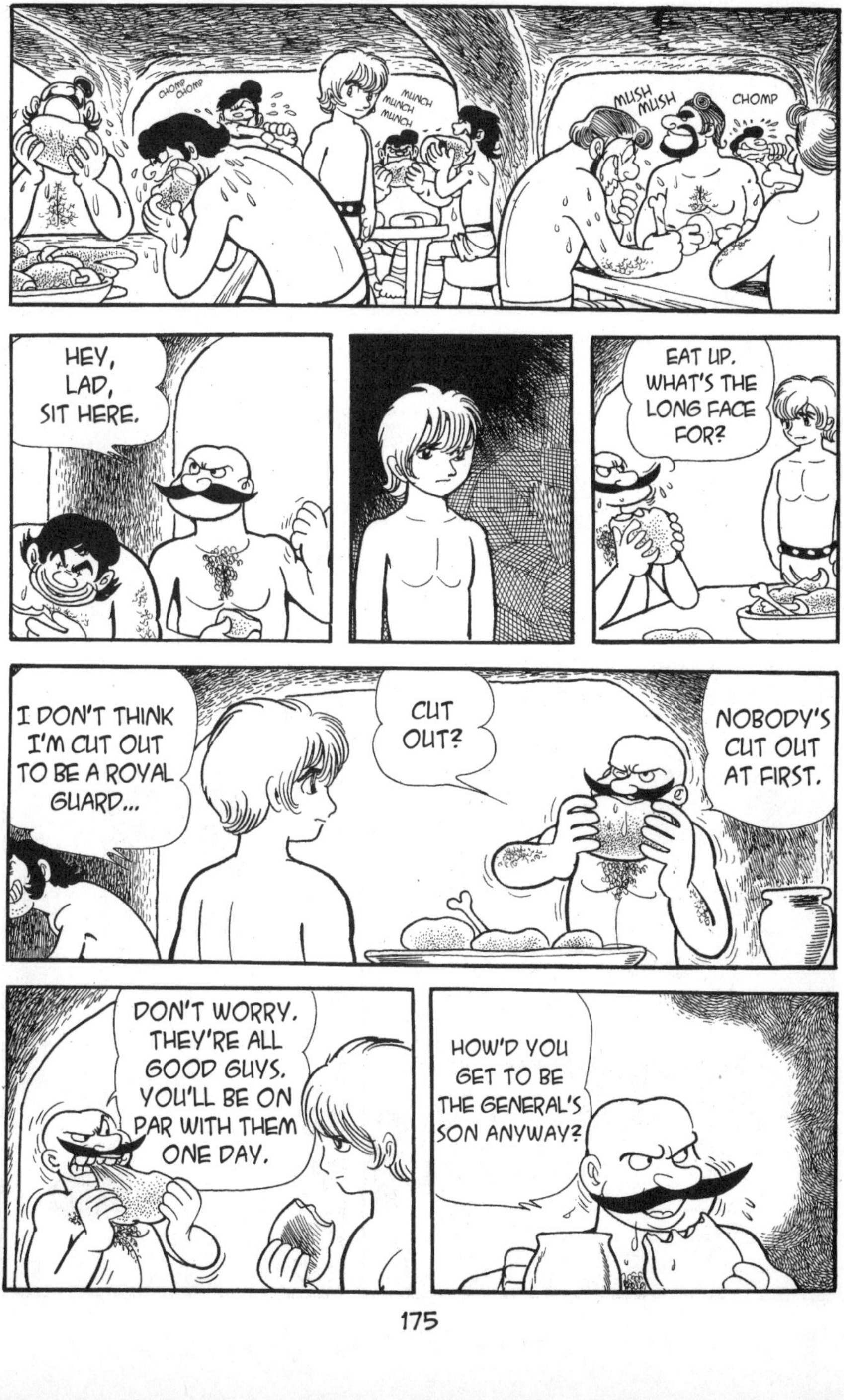
CHOMP CHOMP
MUNCH MUNCH MUNCH
MUSH MUSH
CHOMP
HEY, LAD, SIT HERE.
EAT UP. WHAT'S THE LONG FACE FOR?
I DON'T THINK I'M CUT OUT TO BE A ROYAL GUARD...
CUT OUT?
NOBODY'S CUT OUT AT FIRST.
DON'T WORRY. THEY'RE ALL GOOD GUYS. YOU'LL BE ON PAR WITH THEM ONE DAY.
HOW'D YOU GET TO BE THE GENERAL'S SON ANYWAY?

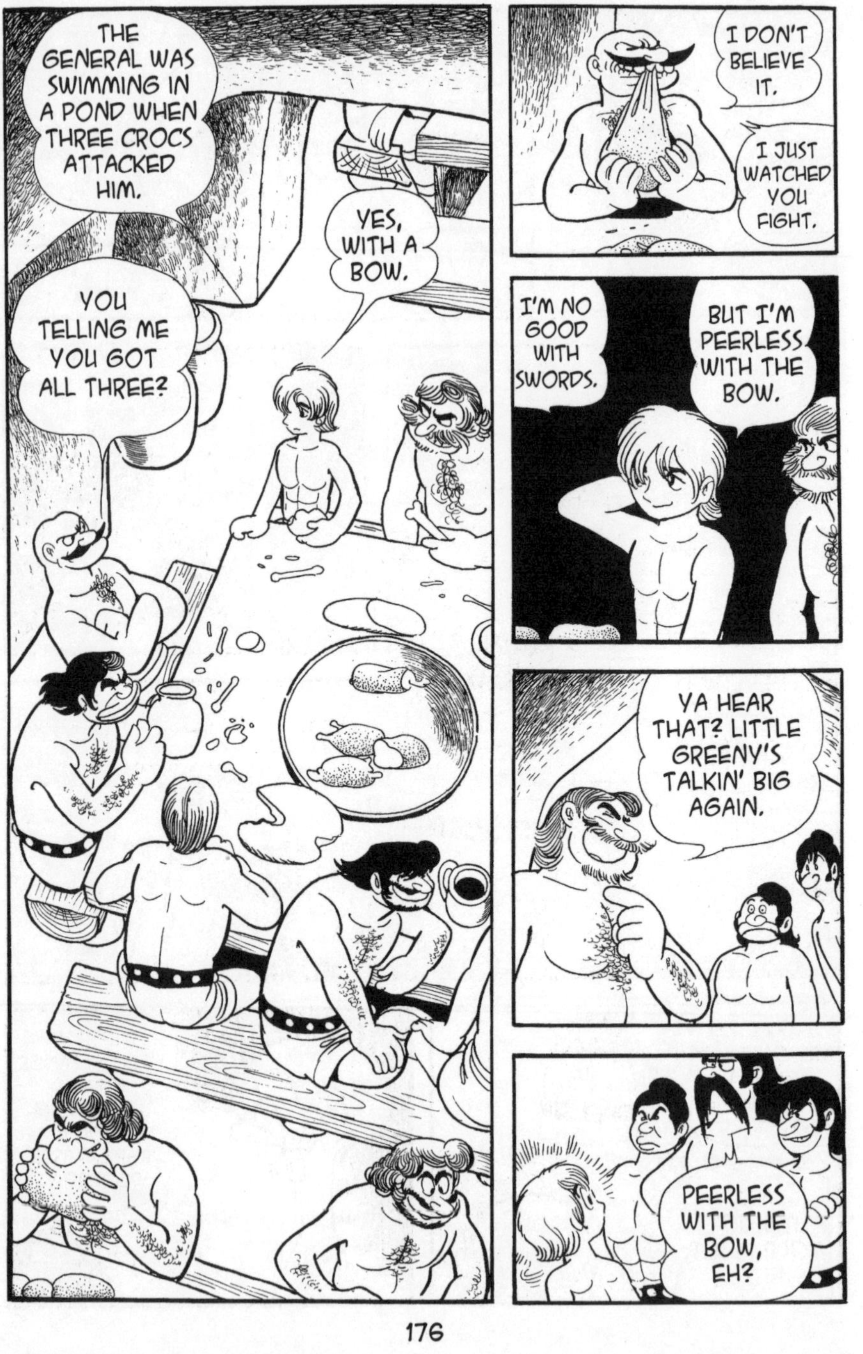
THE GENERAL WAS SWIMMING IN A POND WHEN THREE CROCS ATTACKED HIM.
YES, WITH A BOW.
YOU TELLING ME YOU GOT ALL THREE?
I DON'T BELIEVE IT.
I JUST WATCHED YOU FIGHT.
I'M NO GOOD WITH SWORDS.
BUT I'M PEERLESS WITH THE BOW.
YA HEAR THAT? LITTLE GREENY'S TALKIN' BIG AGAIN.
PEERLESS WITH THE BOW, EH?

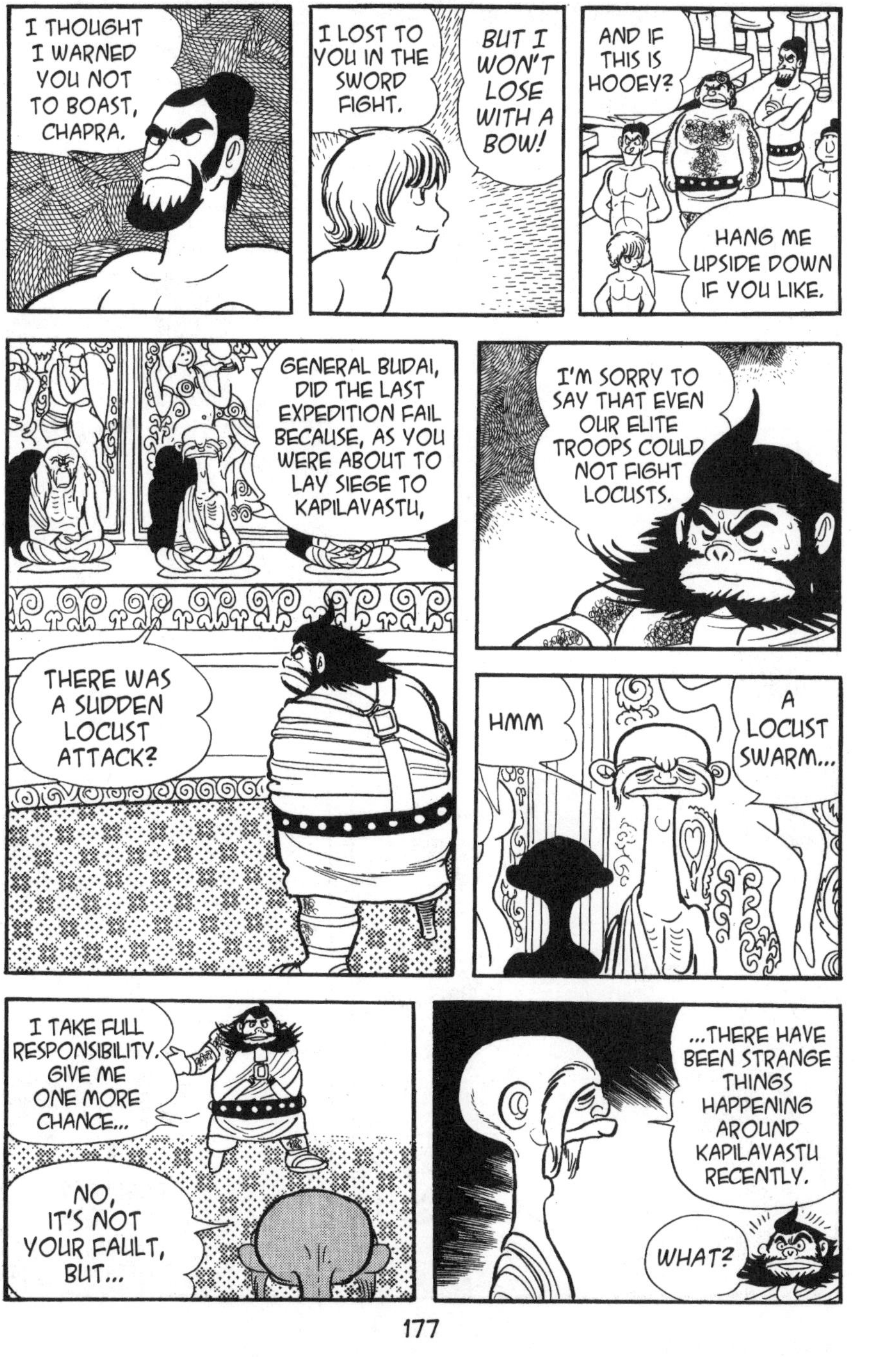
I THOUGHT I WARNED YOU NOT TO BOAST, CHAPRA.
I LOST TO YOU IN THE SWORD FIGHT.
BUT I WON'T LOSE WITH A BOW!
AND IF THIS IS HOOEY?
HANG ME UPSIDE DOWN IF YOU LIKE.
GENERAL BUDAI, DID THE LAST EXPEDITION FAIL BECAUSE, AS YOU WERE ABOUT TO LAY SIEGE TO KAPILAVASTU,
THERE WAS A SUDDEN LOCUST ATTACK?
I'M SORRY TO SAY THAT EVEN OUR ELITE TROOPS COULD NOT FIGHT LOCUSTS.
HMM
A LOCUST SWARM...
I TAKE FULL RESPONSIBILITY. GIVE ME ONE MORE CHANCE...
NO, IT'S NOT YOUR FAULT, BUT...
...THERE HAVE BEEN STRANGE THINGS HAPPENING AROUND KAPILAVASTU RECENTLY.
WHAT?

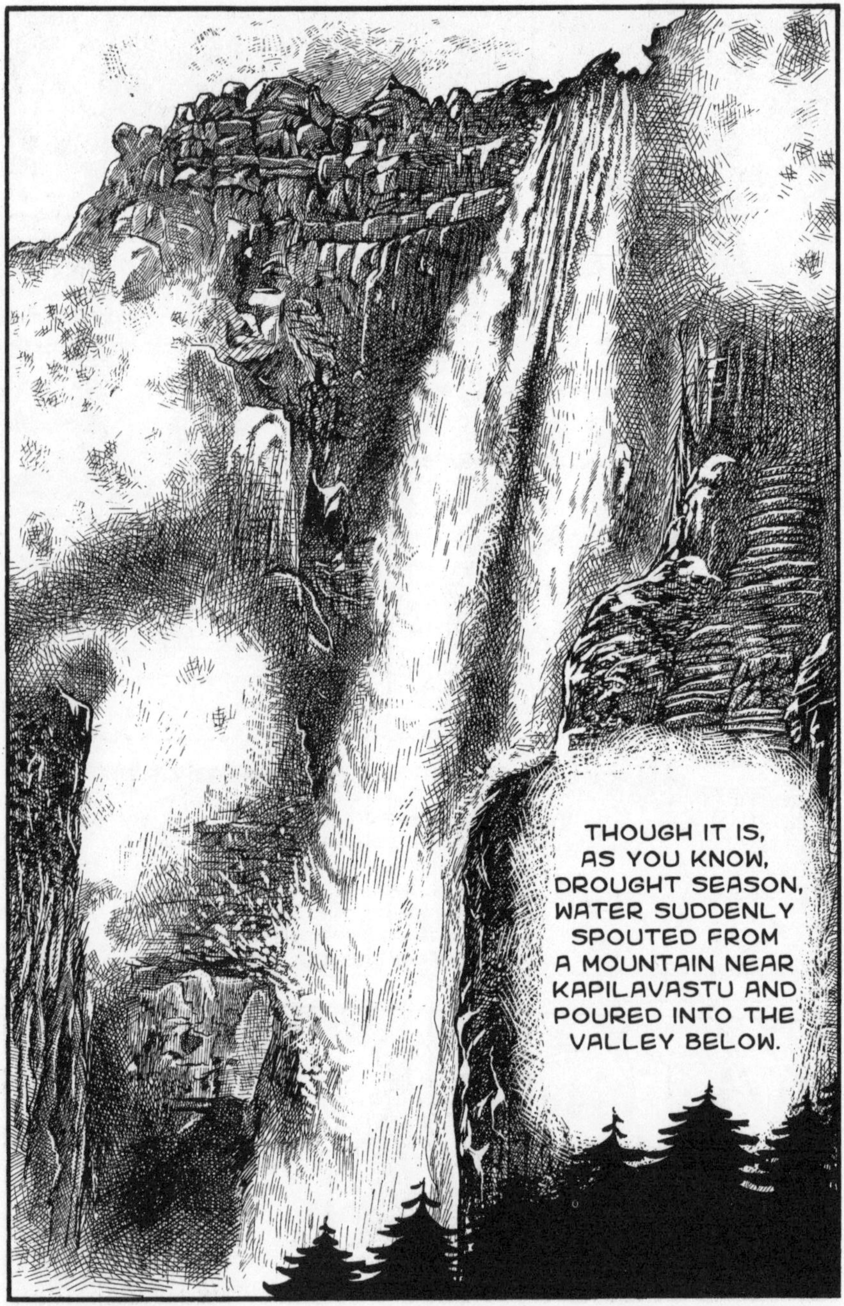
THOUGH IT IS,
AS YOU KNOW,
DROUGHT SEASON,
WATER SUDDENLY
SPOUTED FROM
A MOUNTAIN NEAR
KAPILAVASTU AND
POURED INTO THE
VALLEY BELOW.

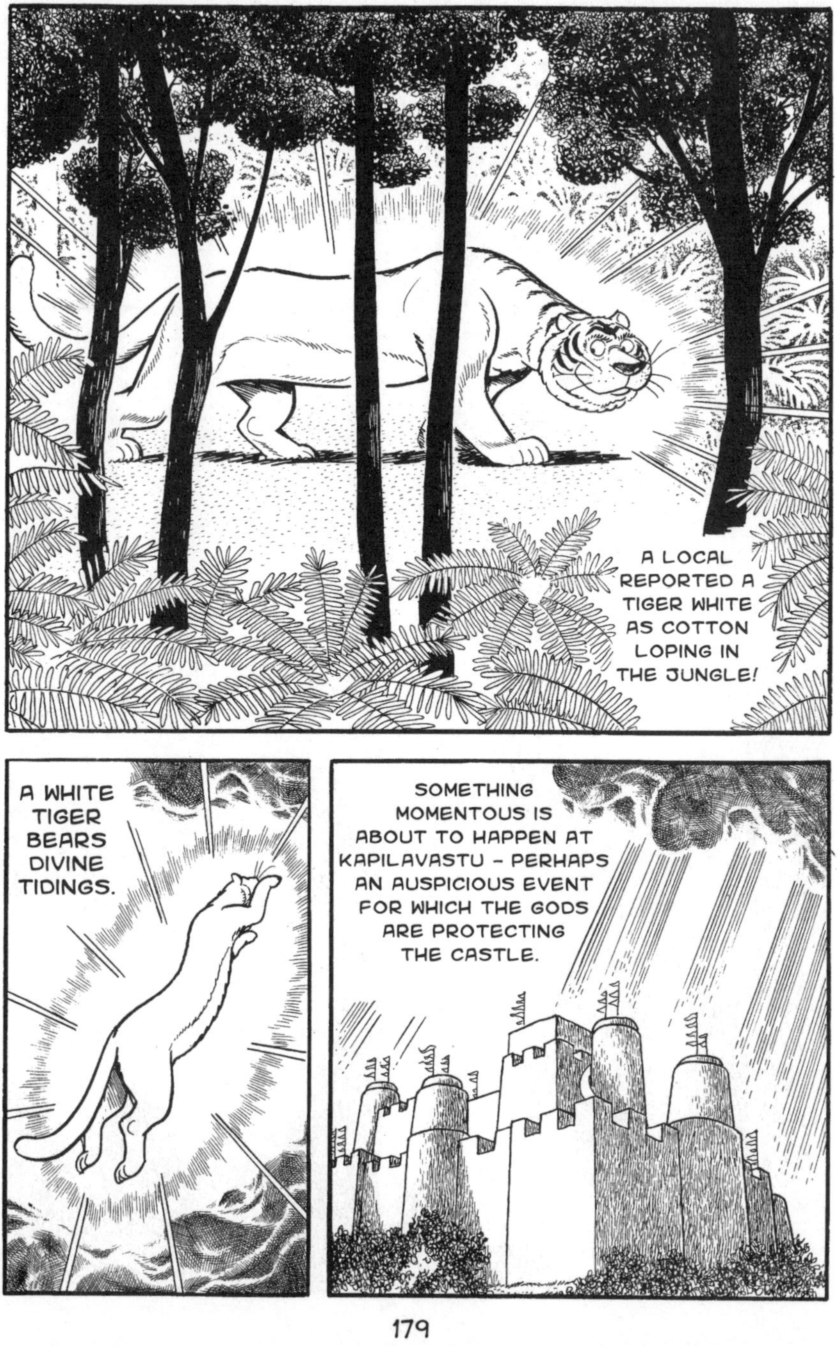
A LOCAL REPORTED A TIGER WHITE AS COTTON LOPING IN THE JUNGLE!
A WHITE TIGER BEARS DIVINE TIDINGS.
SOMETHING MOMENTOUS IS ABOUT TO HAPPEN AT KAPILAVASTU - PERHAPS AN AUSPICIOUS EVENT FOR WHICH THE GODS ARE PROTECTING THE CASTLE.

FOR NOW, THE KING HAS DECREED THAT ALL ATTACKS ON KAPILAVASTU BE HALTED.

WHAT IN THE—

OUR MIGHTY KOSALA...

BOWING TO PUNY KAPILAVASTU? WE WILL BE THE LAUGHING-STOCK OF THE WORLD!

KING'S ORDERS.

I SEE. I AM OF NO USE IN TIMES OF PEACE.

IF THE WAR IS OVER, YOU HAVE NO NEED FOR ME.

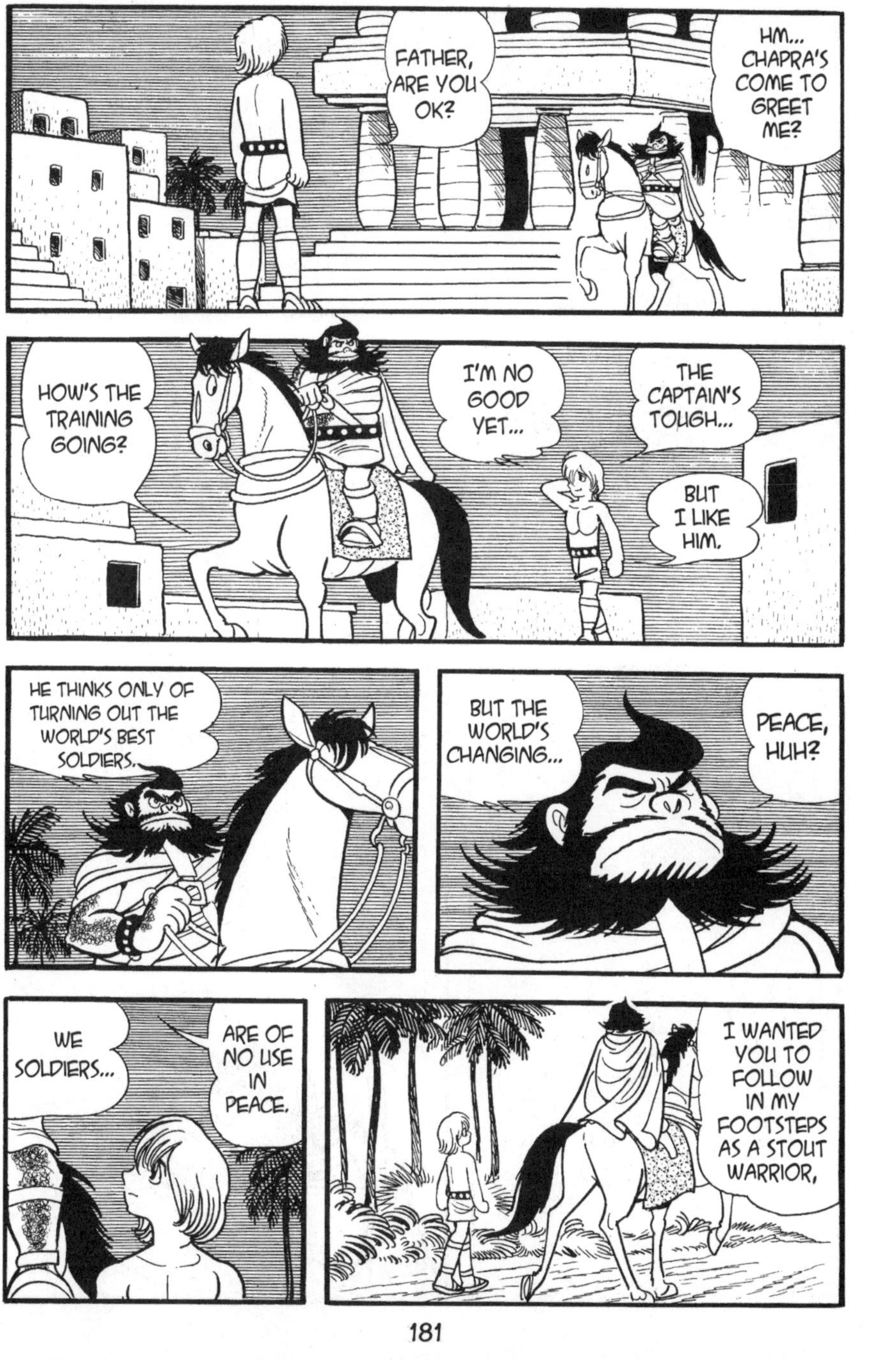
FATHER, ARE YOU OK?
HM... CHAPRA'S COME TO GREET ME?
HOW'S THE TRAINING GOING?
I'M NO GOOD YET...
THE CAPTAIN'S TOUGH...
BUT I LIKE HIM.
HE THINKS ONLY OF TURNING OUT THE WORLD'S BEST SOLDIERS.
BUT THE WORLD'S CHANGING...
PEACE, HUH?
WE SOLDIERS...
ARE OF NO USE IN PEACE.
I WANTED YOU TO FOLLOW IN MY FOOTSTEPS AS A STOUT WARRIOR,

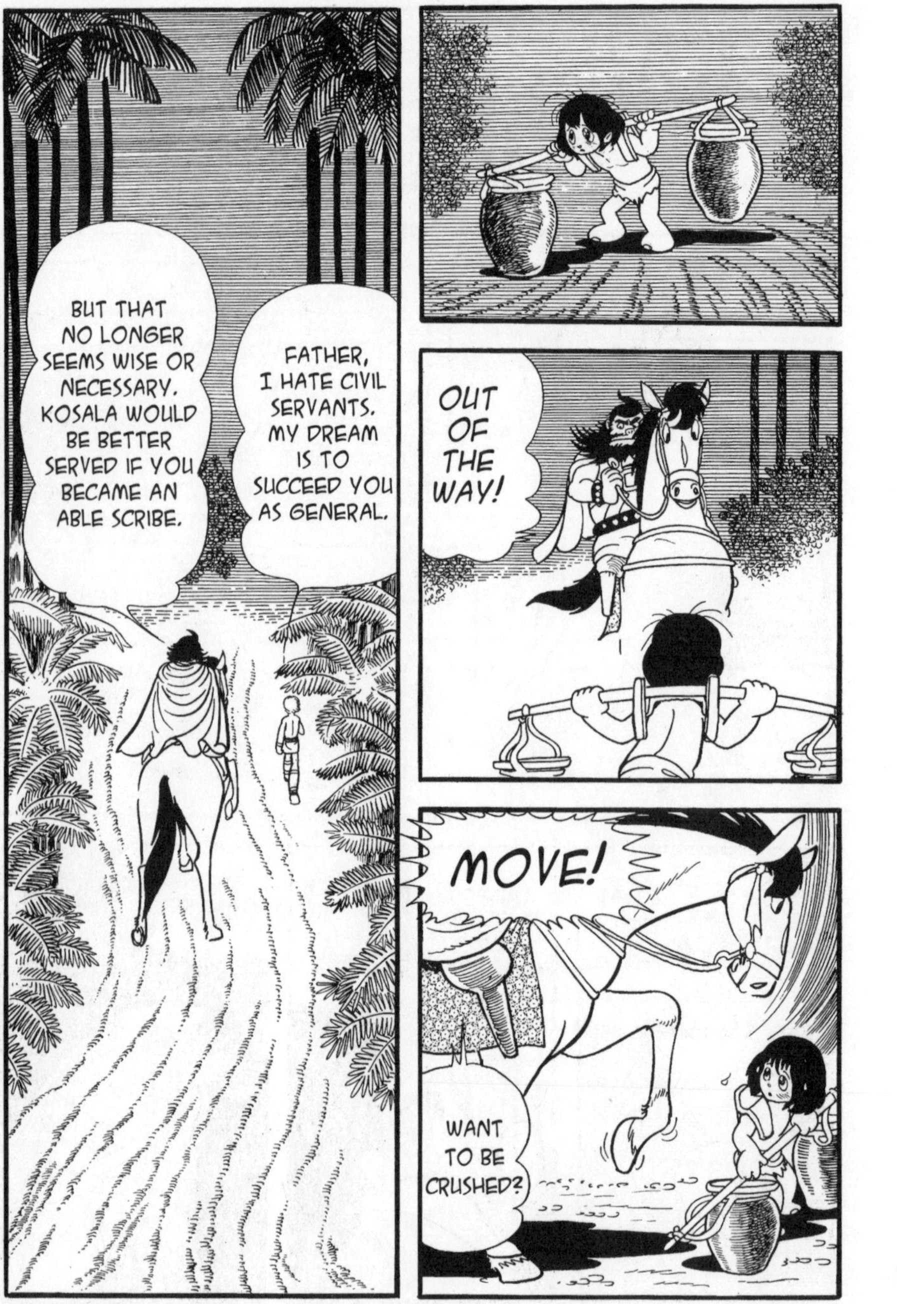
BUT THAT NO LONGER SEEMS WISE OR NECESSARY. KOSALA WOULD BE BETTER SERVED IF YOU BECAME AN ABLE SCRIBE.
FATHER, I HATE CIVIL SERVANTS. MY DREAM IS TO SUCCEED YOU AS GENERAL.
OUT OF THE WAY!
MOVE!
WANT TO BE CRUSHED?

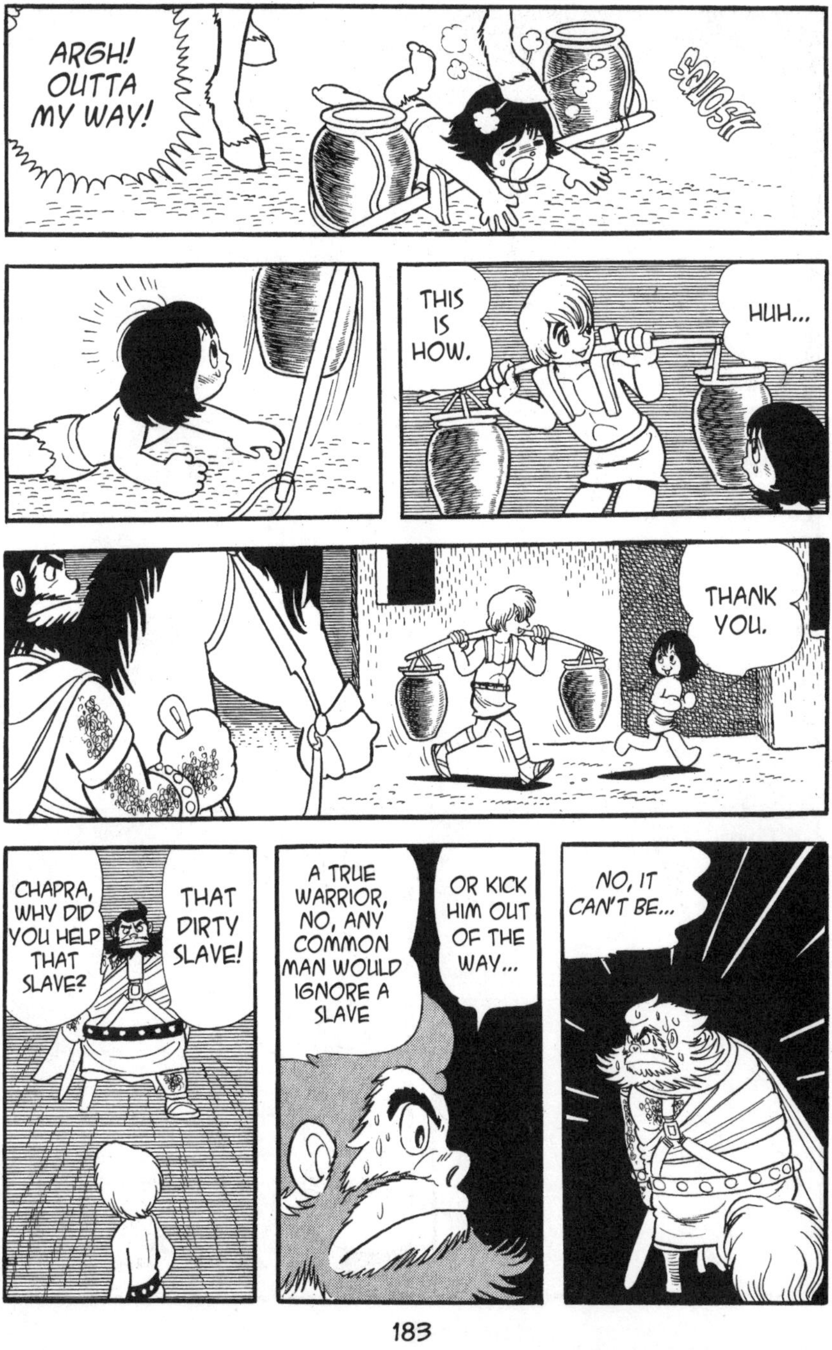
ARGH! OUTTA MY WAY!
SPLOSH!!
THIS IS HOW.
HUH...
THANK YOU.
CHAPRA, WHY DID YOU HELP THAT SLAVE?
THAT DIRTY SLAVE!
A TRUE WARRIOR, NO, ANY COMMON MAN WOULD IGNORE A SLAVE
OR KICK HIM OUT OF THE WAY...
NO, IT CAN'T BE...

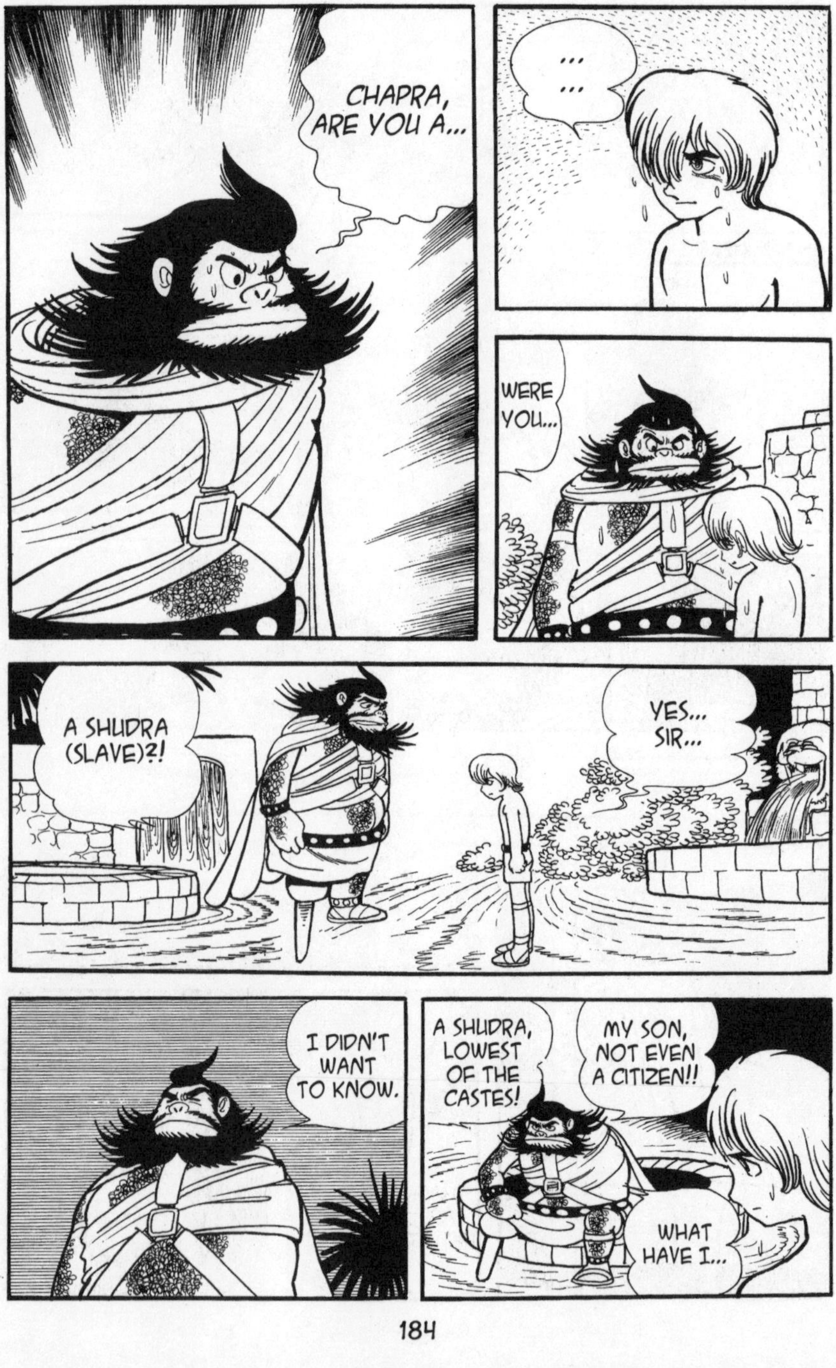
CHAPRA, ARE YOU A...
...
...
WERE YOU...
A SHUDRA (SLAVE)?!
YES... SIR...
I DIDN'T WANT TO KNOW.
A SHUDRA, LOWEST OF THE CASTES!
MY SON, NOT EVEN A CITIZEN!!
WHAT HAVE I...

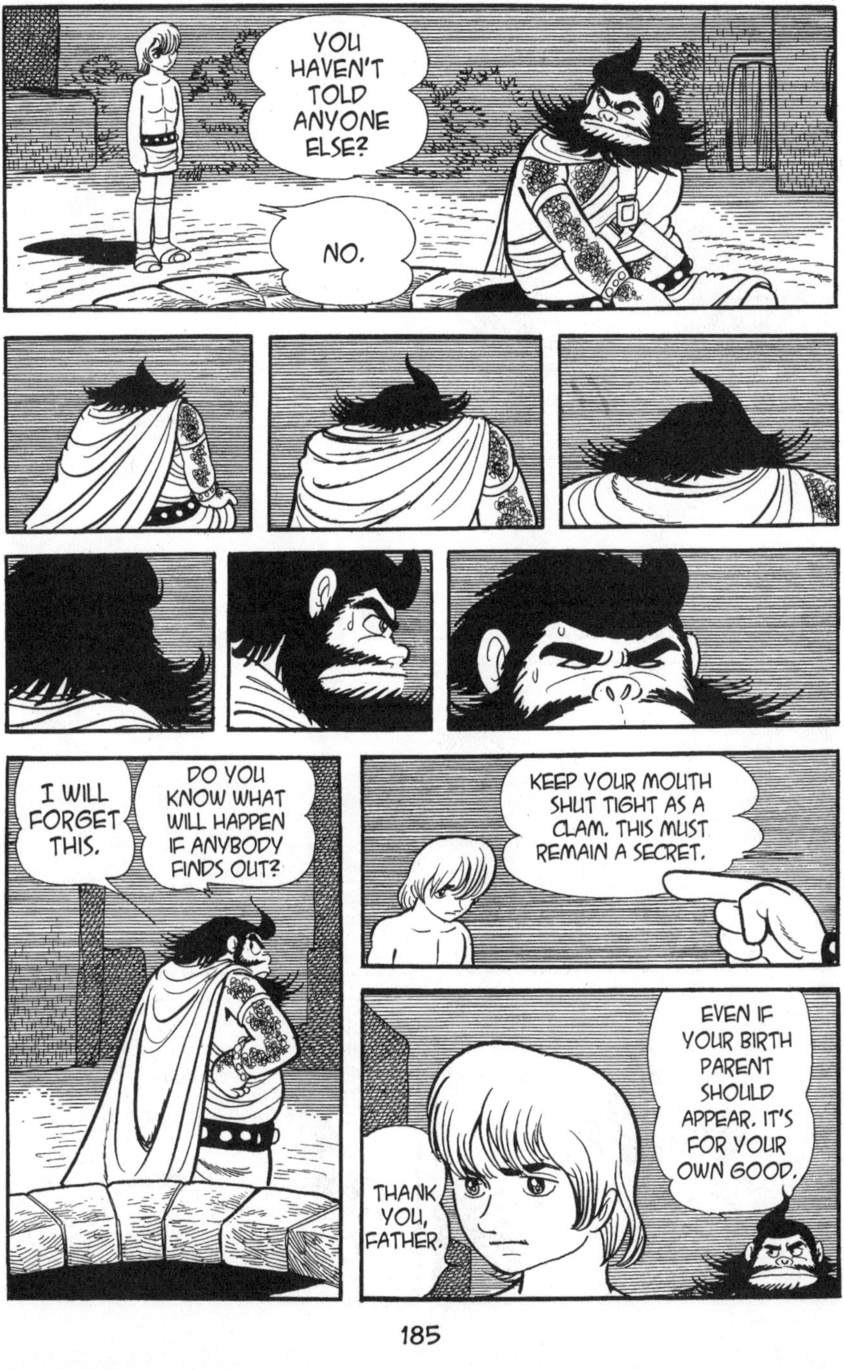
YOU HAVEN'T TOLD ANYONE ELSE?
NO.
I WILL FORGET THIS.
DO YOU KNOW WHAT WILL HAPPEN IF ANYBODY FINDS OUT?
KEEP YOUR MOUTH SHUT TIGHT AS A CLAM. THIS MUST REMAIN A SECRET.
EVEN IF YOUR BIRTH PARENT SHOULD APPEAR. IT'S FOR YOUR OWN GOOD.
THANK YOU, FATHER.

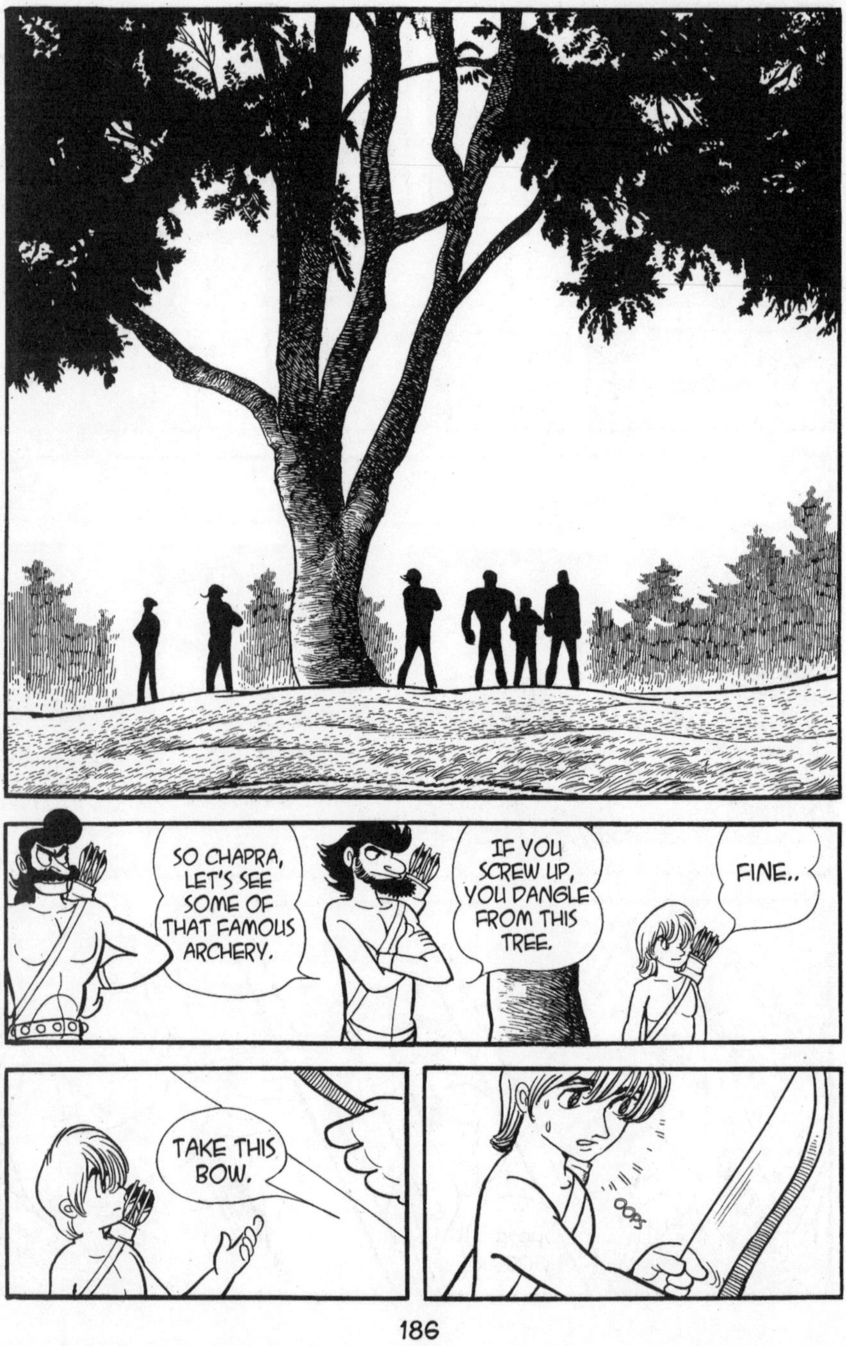
SO CHAPRA, LET'S SEE SOME OF THAT FAMOUS ARCHERY.
IF YOU SCREW UP, YOU DANGLE FROM THIS TREE.
FINE..
TAKE THIS BOW.
OOPS

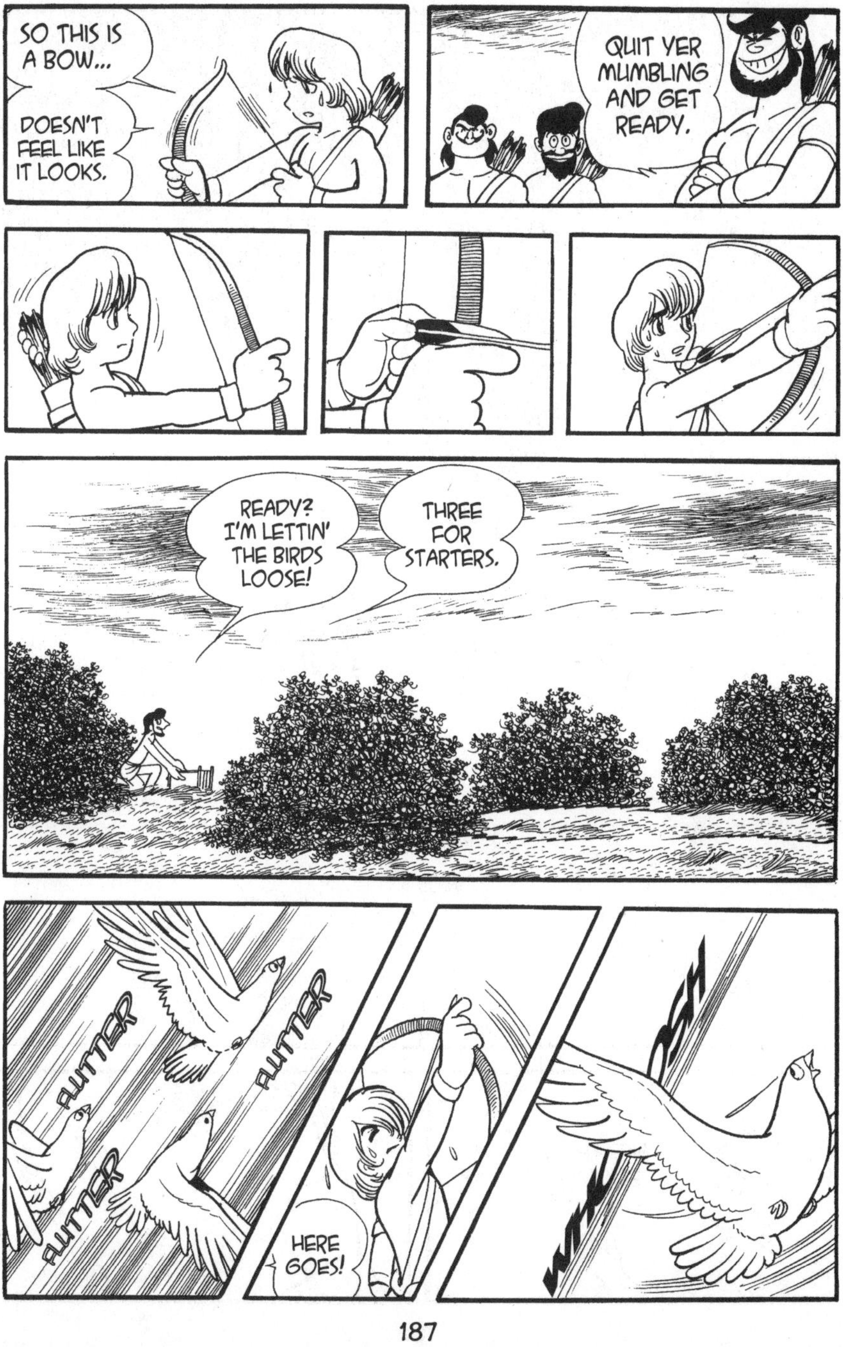
SO THIS IS A BOW...
DOESN'T FEEL LIKE IT LOOKS.
QUIT YER MUMBLING AND GET READY.
READY? I'M LETTIN' THE BIRDS LOOSE!
THREE FOR STARTERS.
FLUTTER
FLUTTER
FLUTTER
FLUTTER
HERE GOES!
WHOOSH

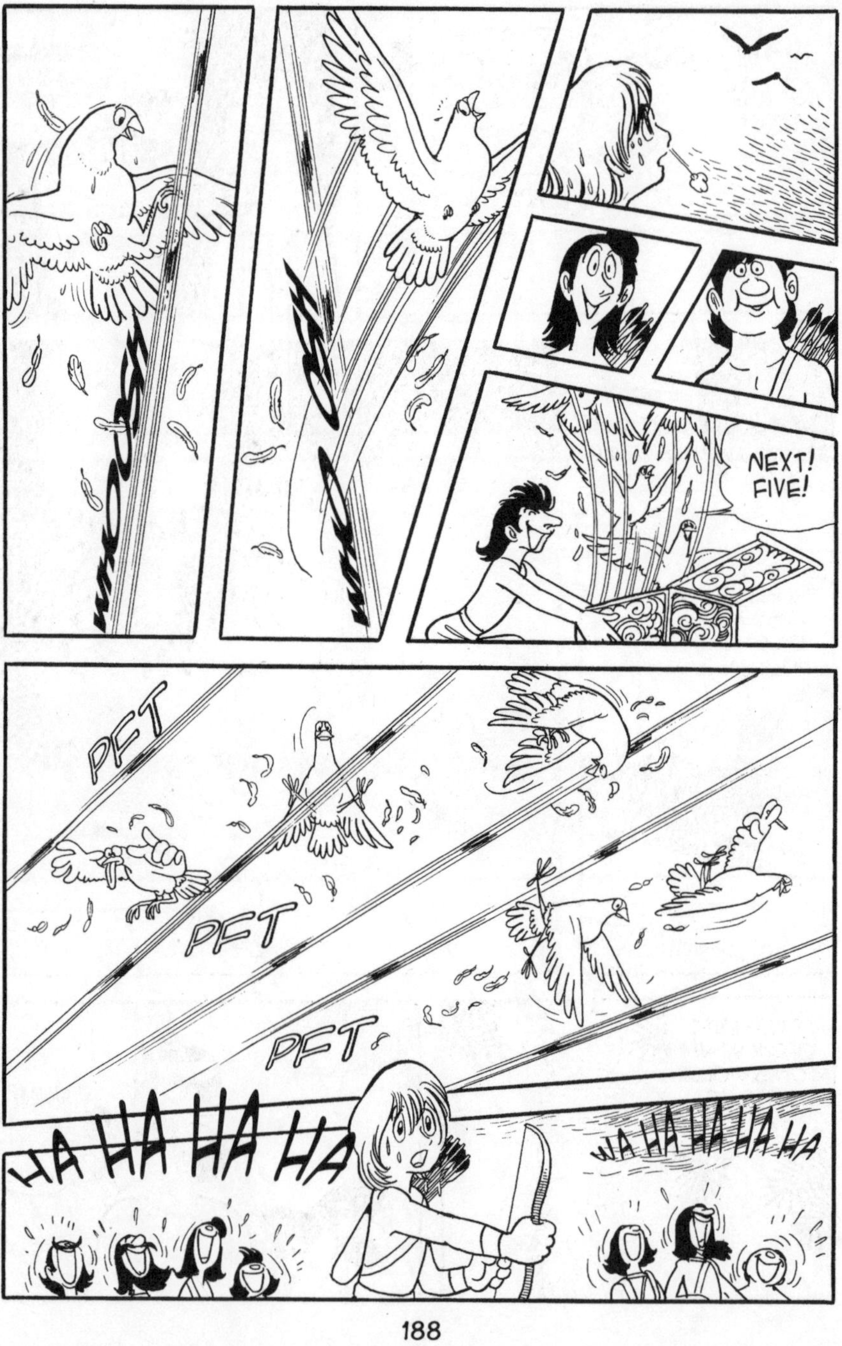
WHOOSH
WHOOSH
NEXT! FIVE!
PFT
PFT
PFT
HA HA HA HA
HA HA HA HA HA

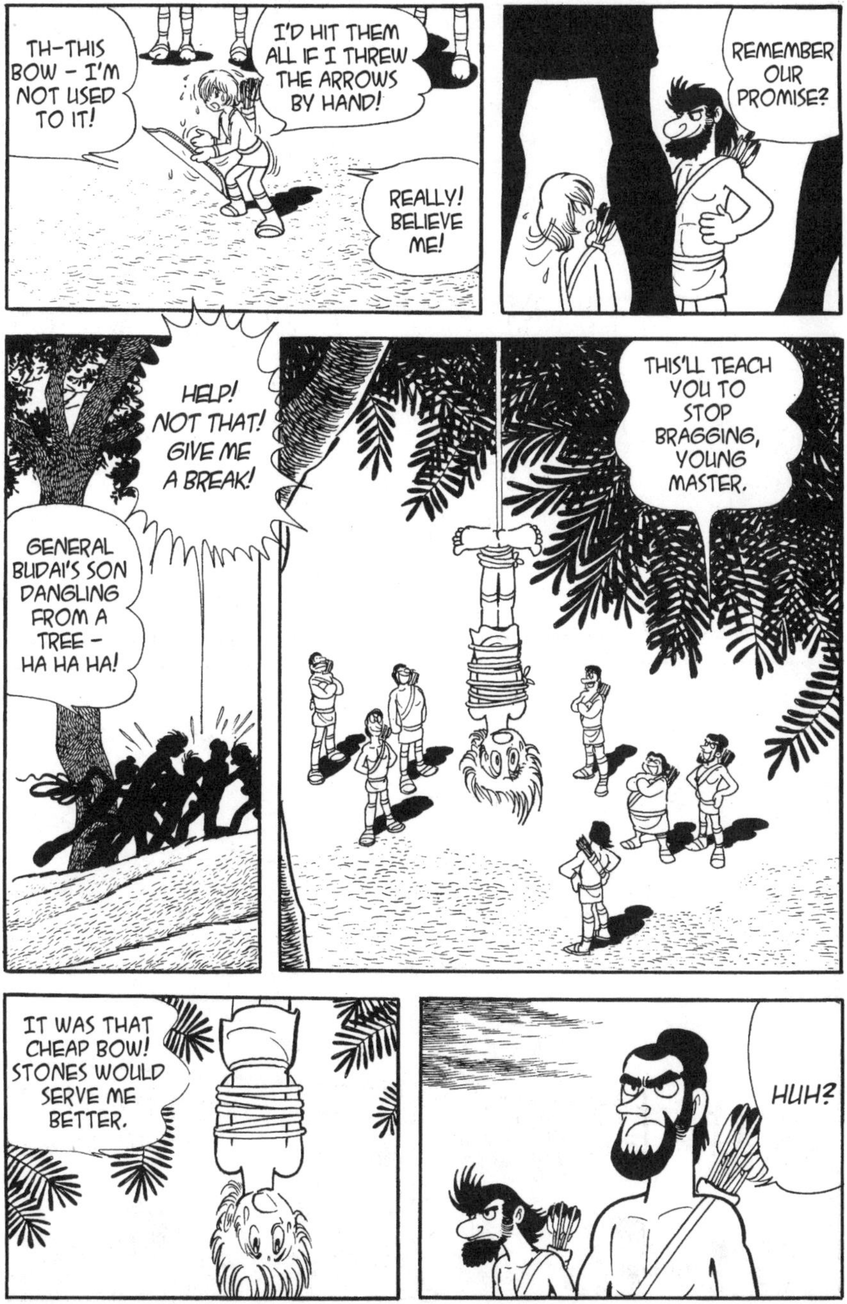
TH-THIS BOW - I'M NOT USED TO IT!
I'D HIT THEM ALL IF I THREW THE ARROWS BY HAND!
REALLY! BELIEVE ME!
REMEMBER OUR PROMISE?
HELP! NOT THAT! GIVE ME A BREAK!
GENERAL BUDAI'S SON DANGLING FROM A TREE - HA HA HA!
THIS'LL TEACH YOU TO STOP BRAGGING, YOUNG MASTER.
IT WAS THAT CHEAP BOW! STONES WOULD SERVE ME BETTER.
HUH?

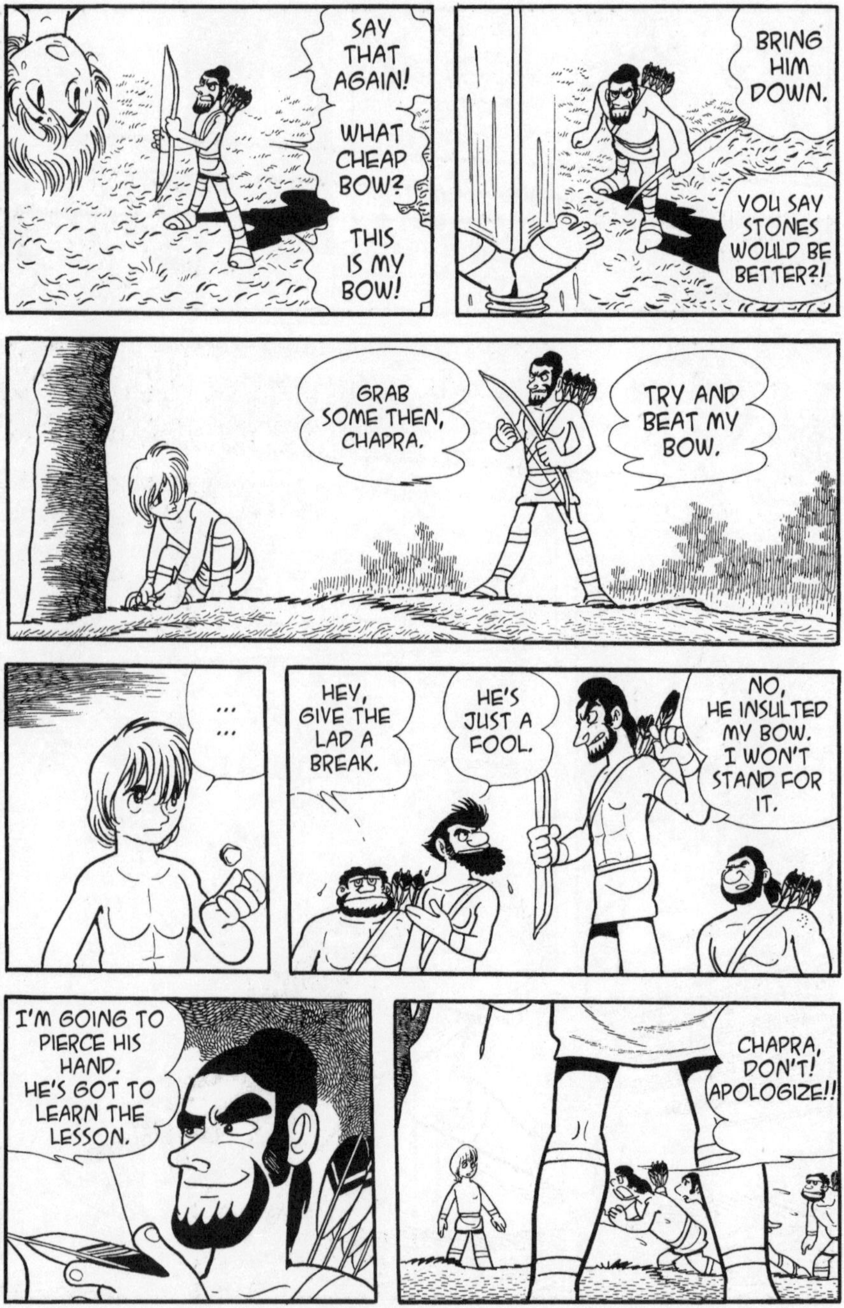
SAY THAT AGAIN!
WHAT CHEAP BOW?
THIS IS MY BOW!
BRING HIM DOWN.
YOU SAY STONES WOULD BE BETTER?!
GRAB SOME THEN, CHAPRA.
TRY AND BEAT MY BOW.
... ...
HEY, GIVE THE LAD A BREAK.
HE'S JUST A FOOL.
NO, HE INSULTED MY BOW. I WON'T STAND FOR IT.
I'M GOING TO PIERCE HIS HAND. HE'S GOT TO LEARN THE LESSON.
CHAPRA, DON'T! APOLOGIZE!!

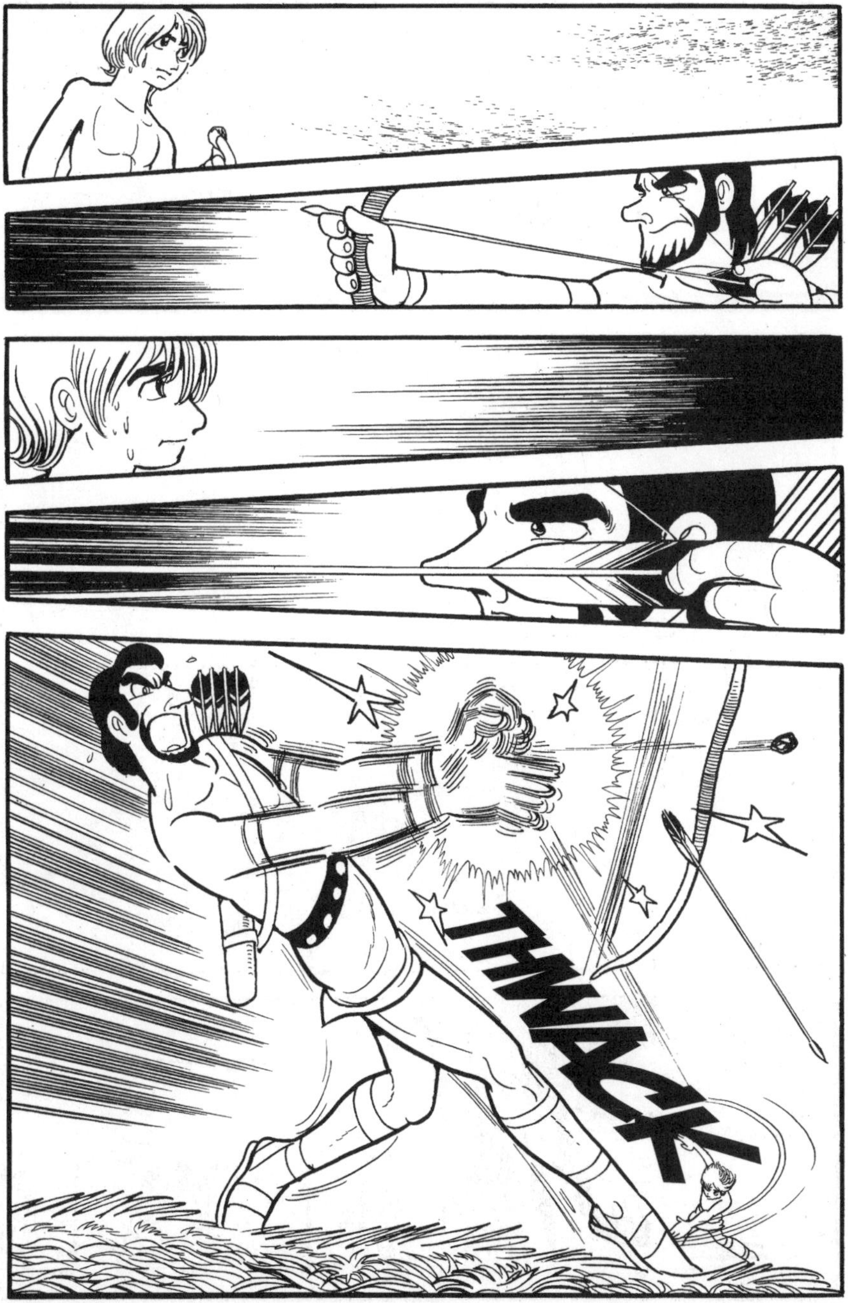
THWACK

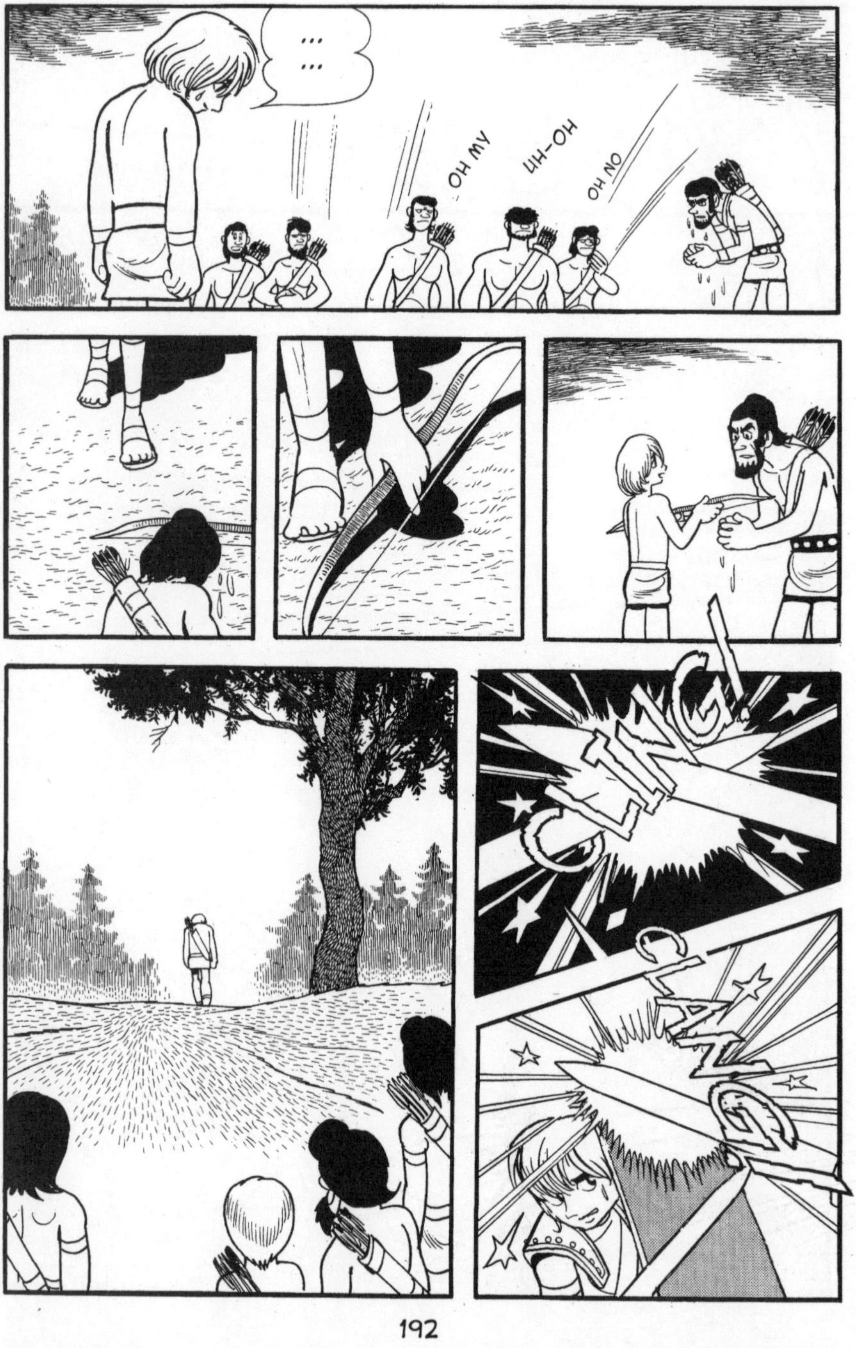
...
...
OH MY
UH-OH
OH NO
CLING
CLANG

CHAPRA!! YOU AREN'T USING YOUR SHIELD ENOUGH!

HAVE YOU FORGOTTEN YOUR LESSONS?!

WHAT ARE YOU HIDING UNDER THAT SHIELD?

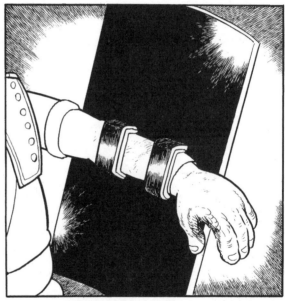

SHOW ME!

WHAT'S WRONG WITH YOUR SKIN?

CAPTAIN, HE'S BEEN PRACTICING ARCHERY SEVEN HOURS A NIGHT.

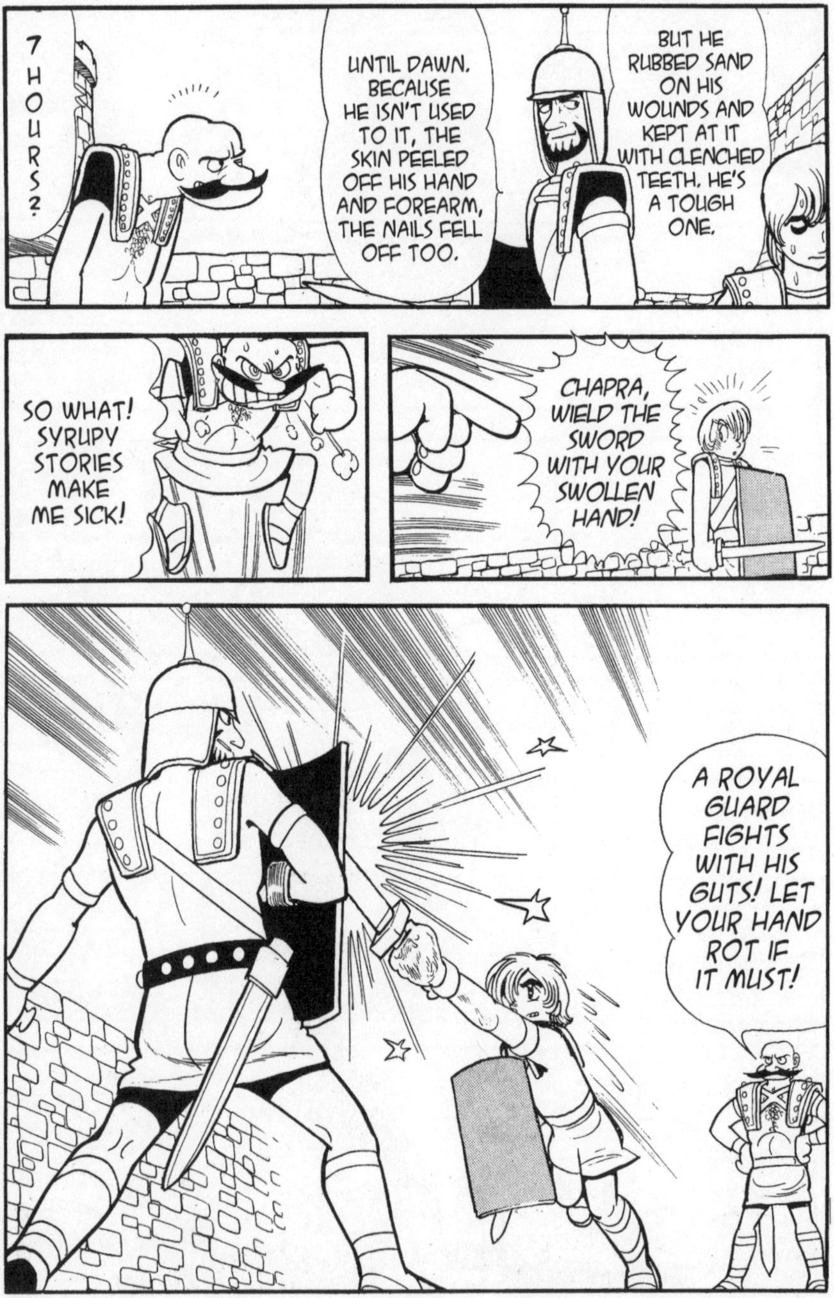
7 HOURS?
UNTIL DAWN. BECAUSE HE ISN'T USED TO IT, THE SKIN PEELED OFF HIS HAND AND FOREARM, THE NAILS FELL OFF TOO.
BUT HE RUBBED SAND ON HIS WOUNDS AND KEPT AT IT WITH CLENCHED TEETH. HE'S A TOUGH ONE.
SO WHAT! SYRUPY STORIES MAKE ME SICK!
CHAPRA, WIELD THE SWORD WITH YOUR SWOLLEN HAND!
A ROYAL GUARD FIGHTS WITH HIS GUTS! LET YOUR HAND ROT IF IT MUST!

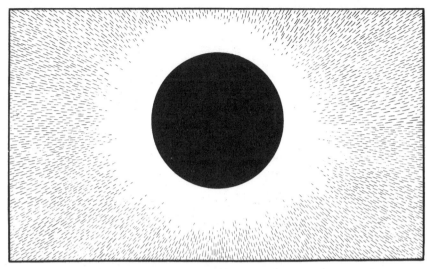

MOMS, STOP! IF WE GO ANY FURTHER WE'LL KEEL OVER AND DIE.

NO, I'M HANGING ON UNTIL I SEE MY CHAPRA AGAIN.

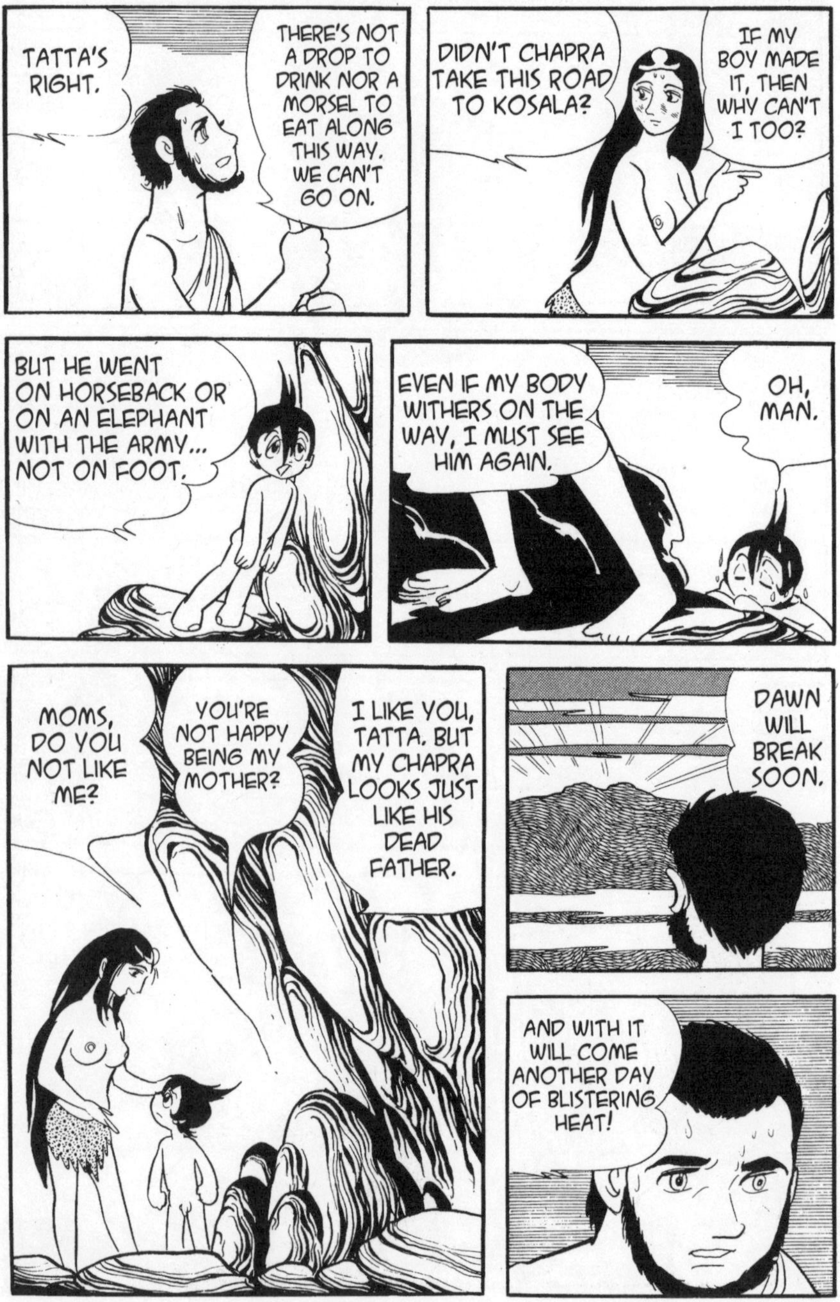
TATTA'S RIGHT.
THERE'S NOT A DROP TO DRINK NOR A MORSEL TO EAT ALONG THIS WAY. WE CAN'T GO ON.
DIDN'T CHAPRA TAKE THIS ROAD TO KOSALA?
IF MY BOY MADE IT, THEN WHY CAN'T I TOO?
BUT HE WENT ON HORSEBACK OR ON AN ELEPHANT WITH THE ARMY... NOT ON FOOT.
EVEN IF MY BODY WITHERS ON THE WAY, I MUST SEE HIM AGAIN.
OH, MAN.
MOMS, DO YOU NOT LIKE ME?
YOU'RE NOT HAPPY BEING MY MOTHER?
I LIKE YOU, TATTA. BUT MY CHAPRA LOOKS JUST LIKE HIS DEAD FATHER.
DAWN WILL BREAK SOON.
AND WITH IT WILL COME ANOTHER DAY OF BLISTERING HEAT!

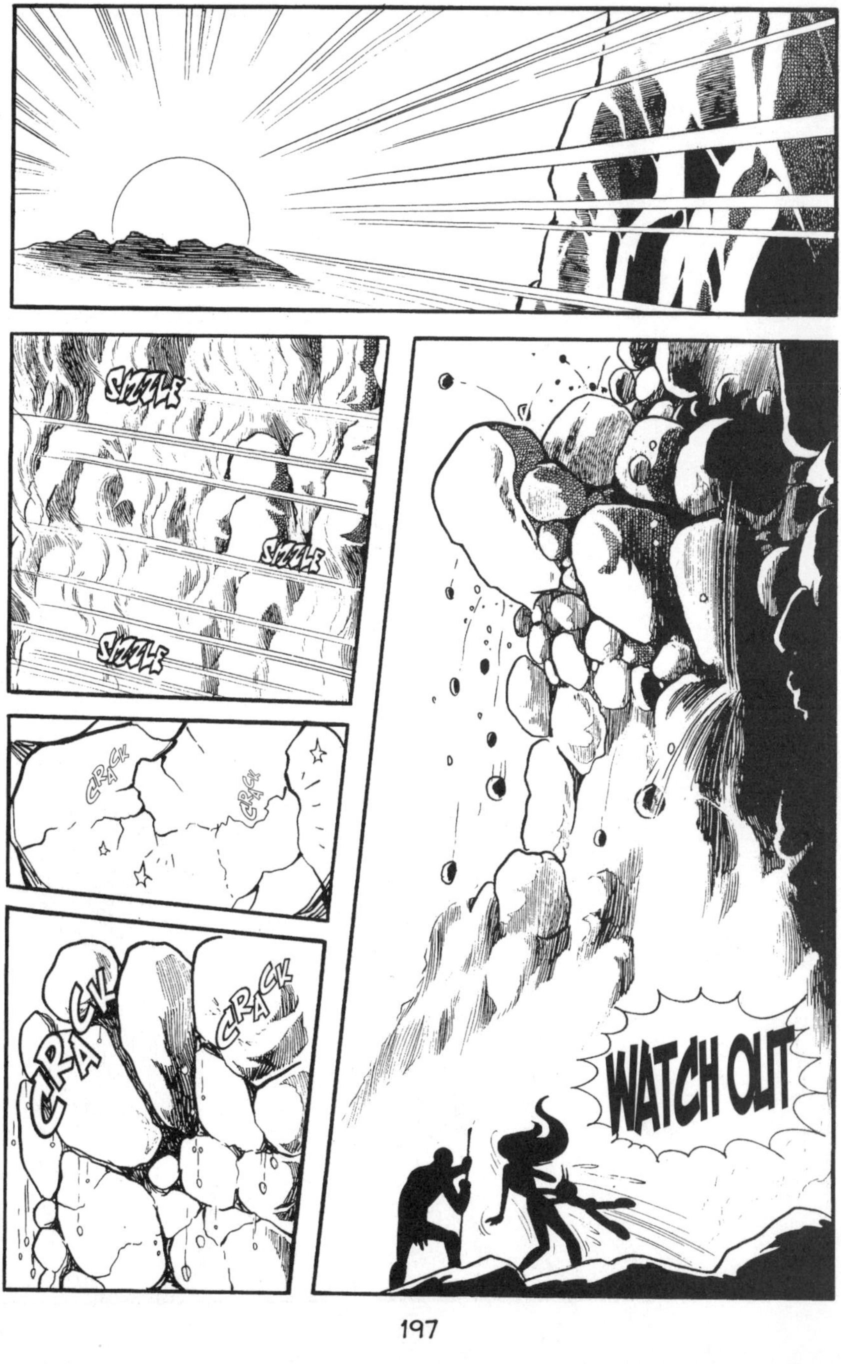
SIZZLE
SIZZLE
SIZZLE
CRACK
CRACK
CRACK
CRACK
WATCH OUT

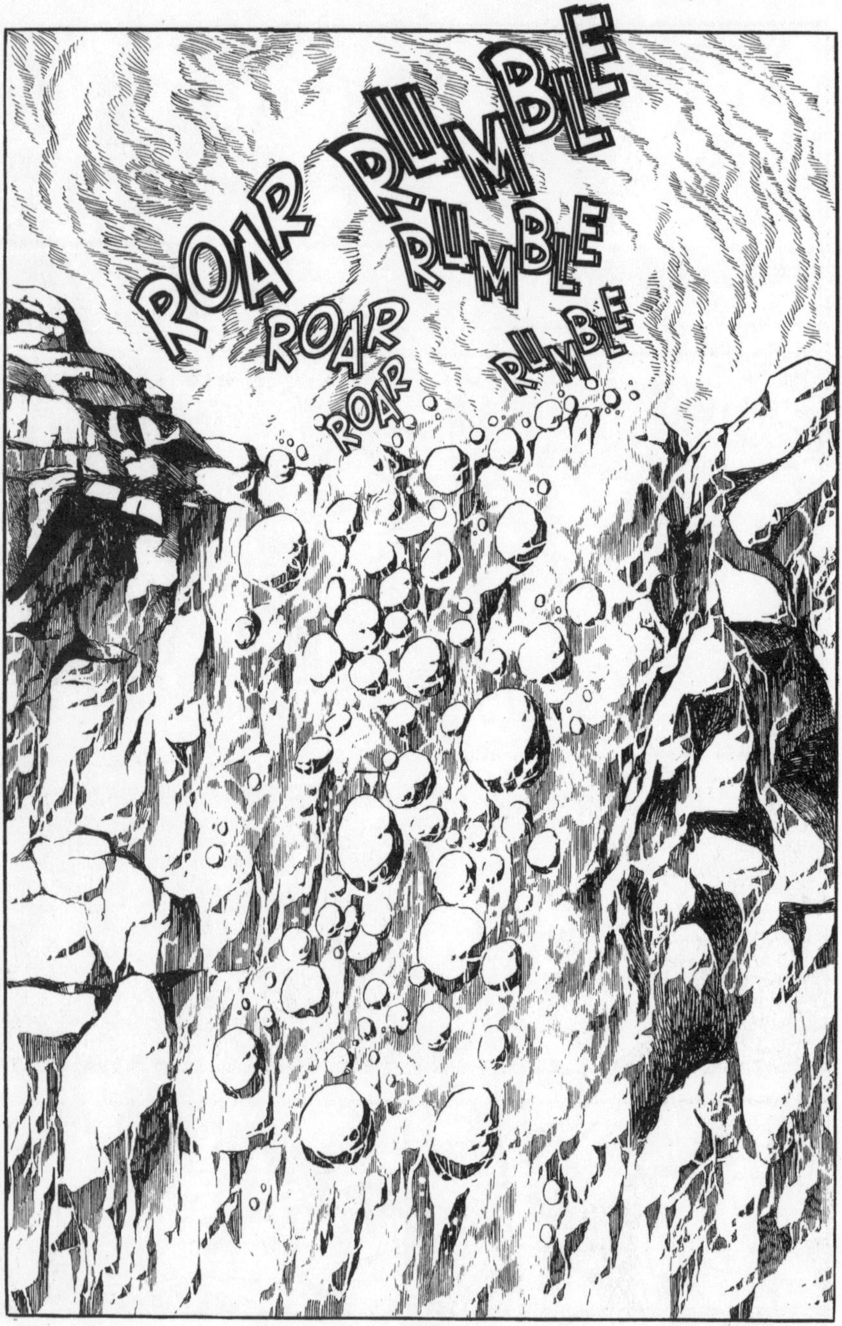
ROAR RUMBLE
RUMBLE
ROAR
ROAR
RUMBLE

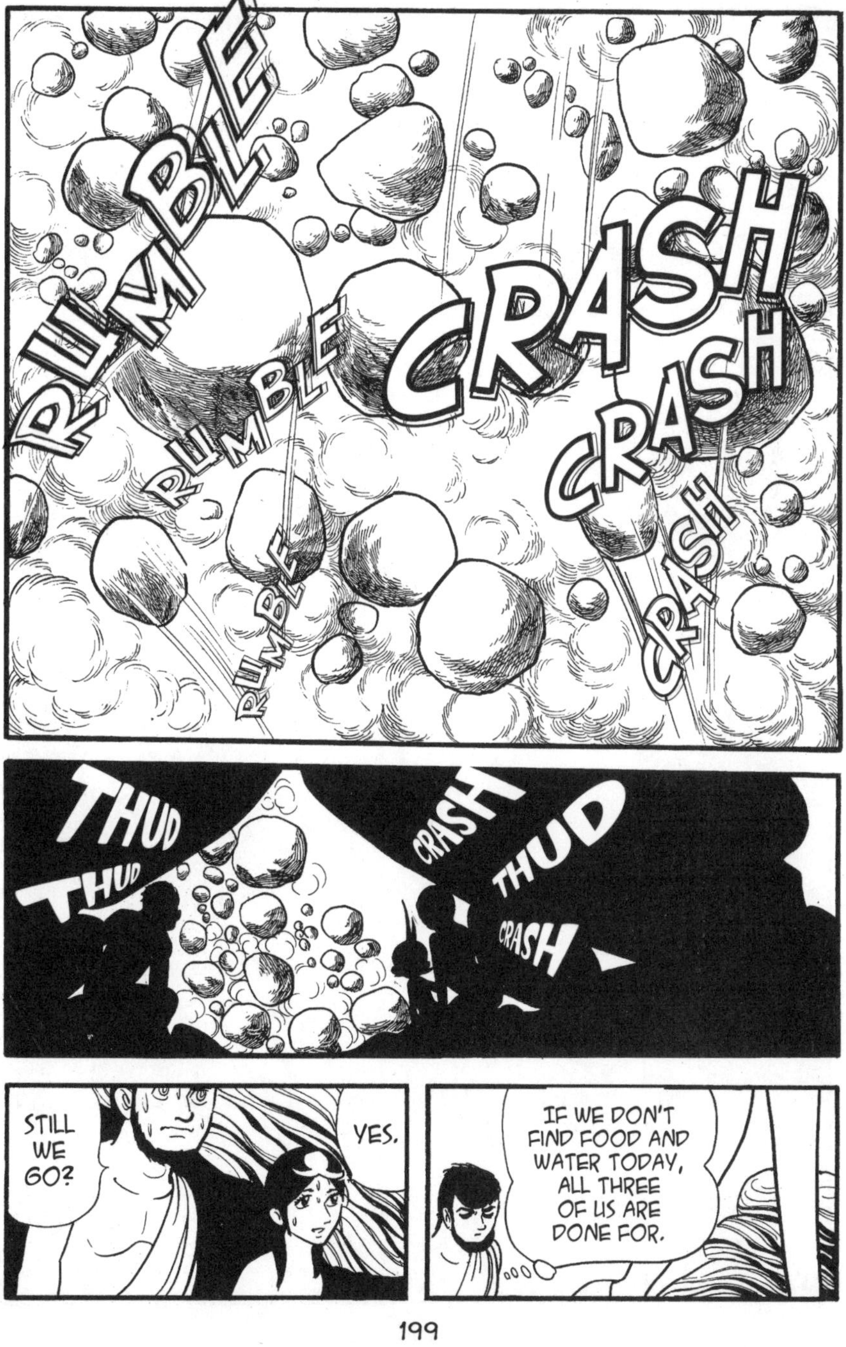
RUMBLE
RUMBLE
RUMBLE
CRASH
CRASH
CRASH
THUD
THUD
CRASH
THUD
CRASH
STILL WE GO?
YES.
IF WE DON'T FIND FOOD AND WATER TODAY, ALL THREE OF US ARE DONE FOR.

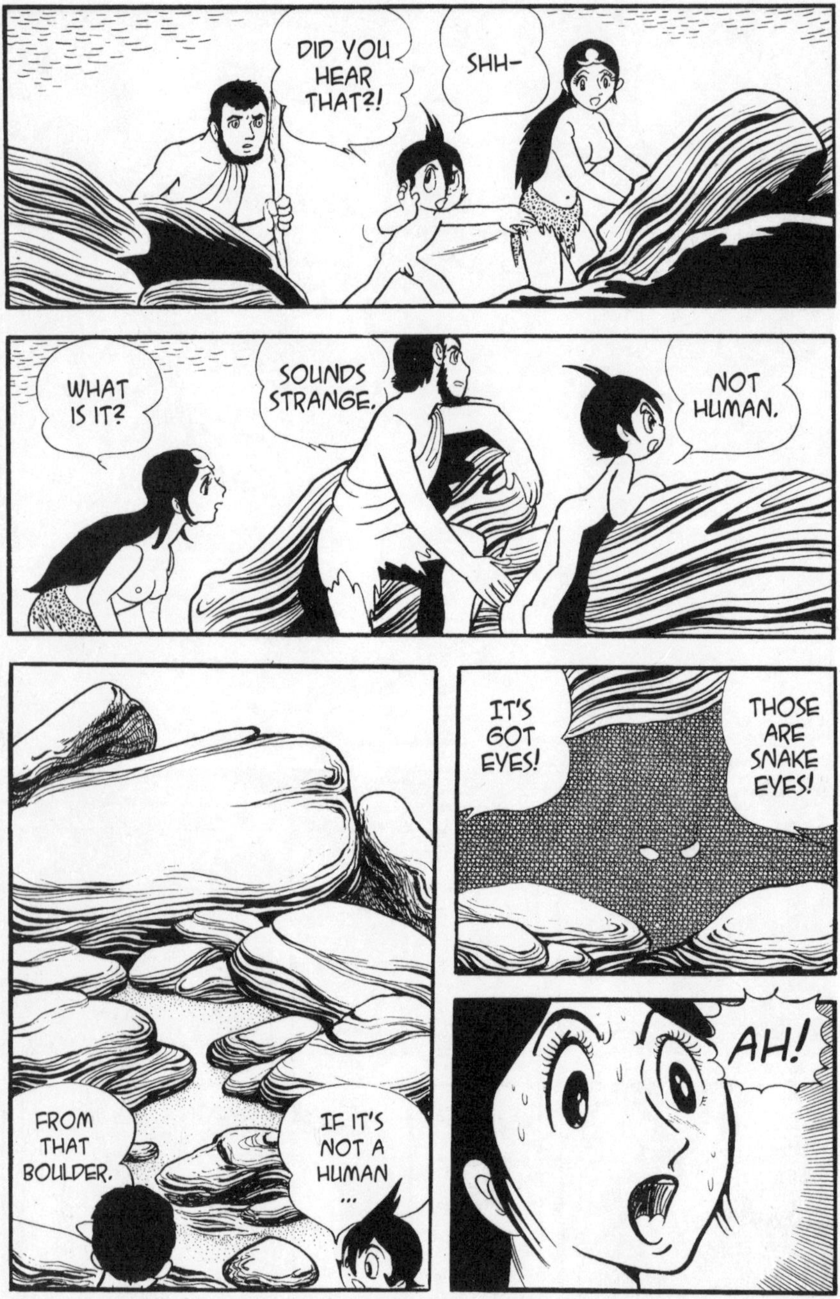
DID YOU HEAR THAT?!
SHH-
WHAT IS IT?
SOUNDS STRANGE.
NOT HUMAN.
FROM THAT BOULDER.
IF IT'S NOT A HUMAN ...
IT'S GOT EYES!
THOSE ARE SNAKE EYES!
AH!

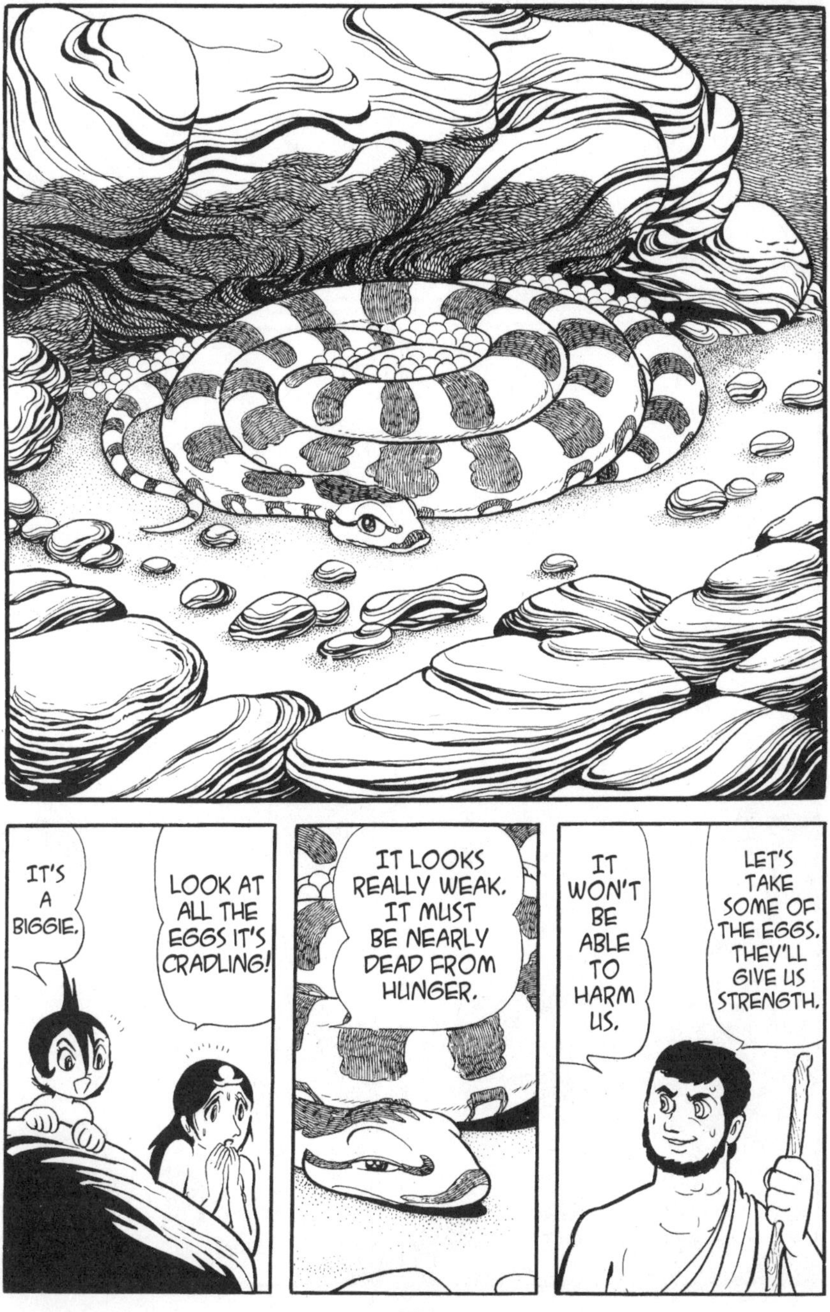
IT'S A BIGGIE.
LOOK AT ALL THE EGGS IT'S CRADLING!
IT LOOKS REALLY WEAK. IT MUST BE NEARLY DEAD FROM HUNGER.
IT WON'T BE ABLE TO HARM US.
LET'S TAKE SOME OF THE EGGS. THEY'LL GIVE US STRENGTH.

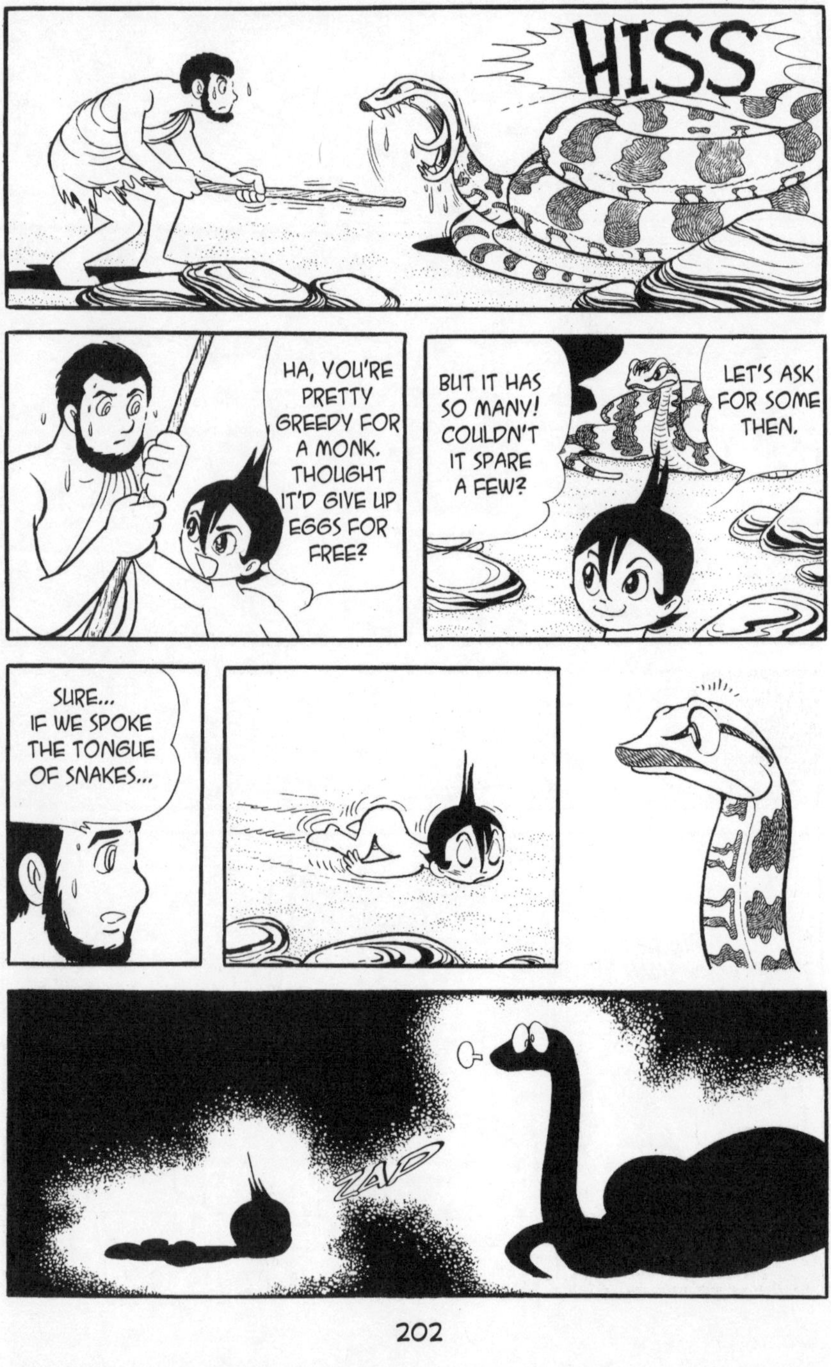
HISS
HA, YOU'RE PRETTY GREEDY FOR A MONK. THOUGHT IT'D GIVE UP EGGS FOR FREE?
BUT IT HAS SO MANY! COULDN'T IT SPARE A FEW?
LET'S ASK FOR SOME THEN.
SURE... IF WE SPOKE THE TONGUE OF SNAKES...
ZAP

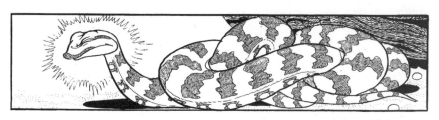

I ENTERED THE SNAKE'S MIND AND ASKED.

IT'LL GIVE US SOME, BUT IN RETURN

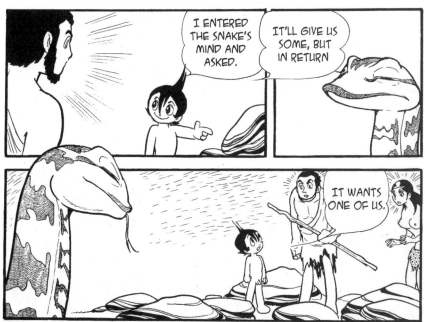

IT WANTS ONE OF US.

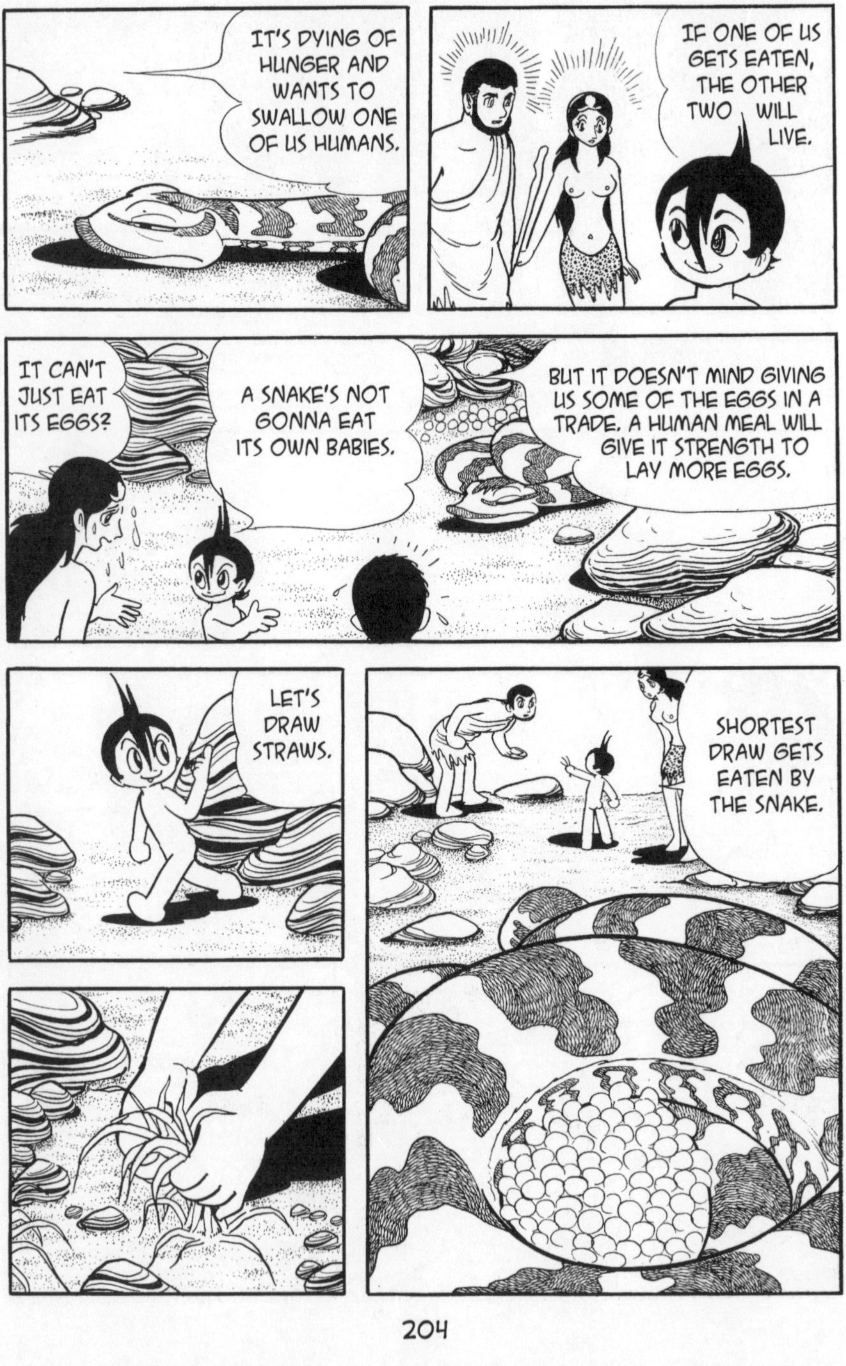
IT'S DYING OF HUNGER AND WANTS TO SWALLOW ONE OF US HUMANS.
IF ONE OF US GETS EATEN, THE OTHER TWO WILL LIVE.
IT CAN'T JUST EAT ITS EGGS?
A SNAKE'S NOT GONNA EAT ITS OWN BABIES.
BUT IT DOESN'T MIND GIVING US SOME OF THE EGGS IN A TRADE. A HUMAN MEAL WILL GIVE IT STRENGTH TO LAY MORE EGGS.
LET'S DRAW STRAWS.
SHORTEST DRAW GETS EATEN BY THE SNAKE.

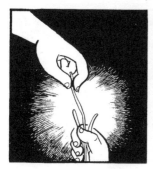

HA HA HA, MINE'S THE SHORTEST!

TATTA!! THAT WAS RIGGED!

WELL, I'M THE BEST CHOICE. MOTHER'S SEARCHING FOR CHAPRA, AND IT WOULDN'T BE COOL FOR A MONK TO GET EATEN BY A SNAKE!

BYE-BYE NOW... TAKE CARE, MOMS.

SAY HI TO BRO WHEN YOU SEE HIM.

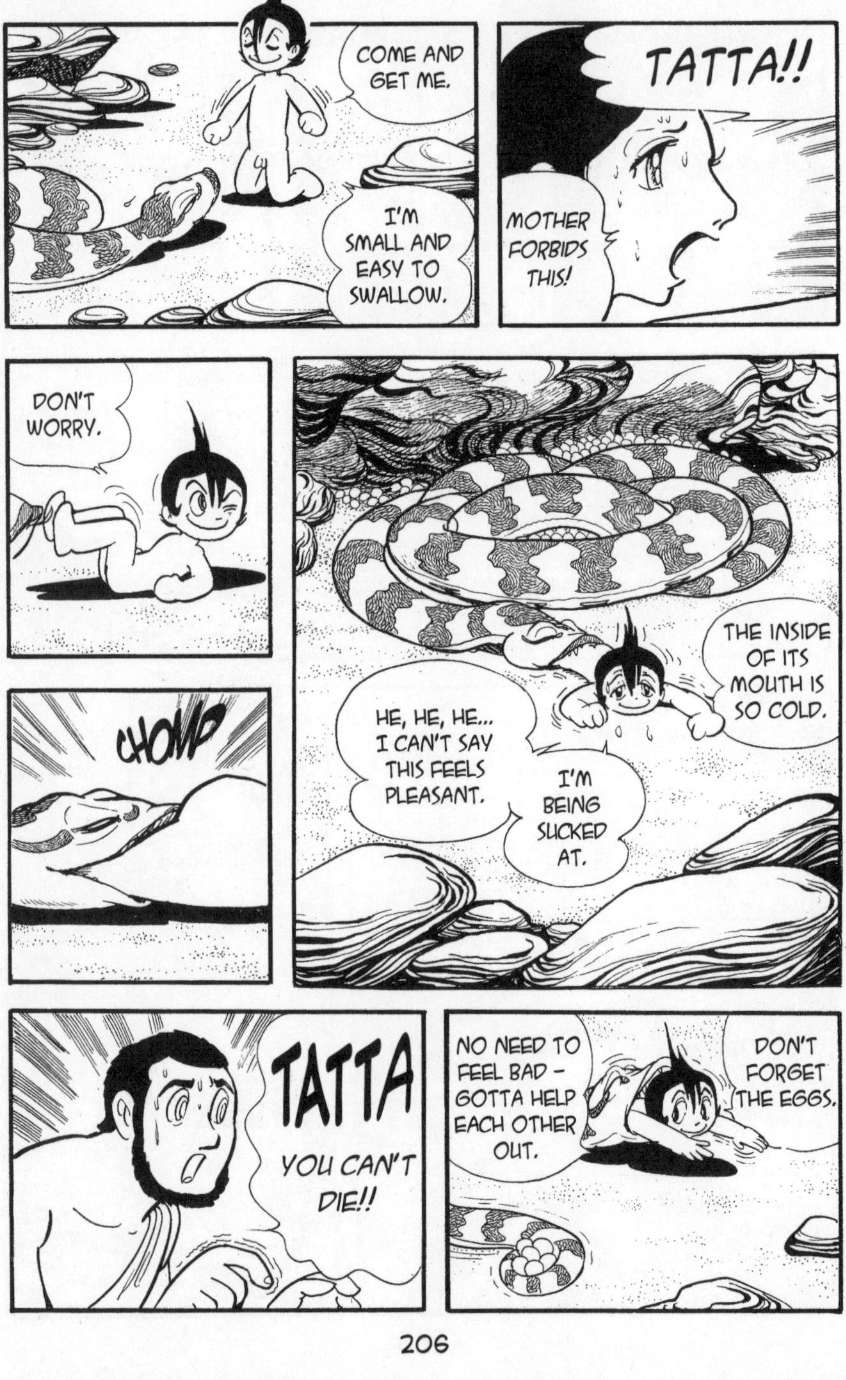
COME AND GET ME.
I'M SMALL AND EASY TO SWALLOW.
TATTA!!
MOTHER FORBIDS THIS!
DON'T WORRY.
CHOMP
THE INSIDE OF ITS MOUTH IS SO COLD.
HE, HE, HE... I CAN'T SAY THIS FEELS PLEASANT.
I'M BEING SUCKED AT.
TATTA
YOU CAN'T DIE!!
DON'T FORGET THE EGGS.
NO NEED TO FEEL BAD - GOTTA HELP EACH OTHER OUT.

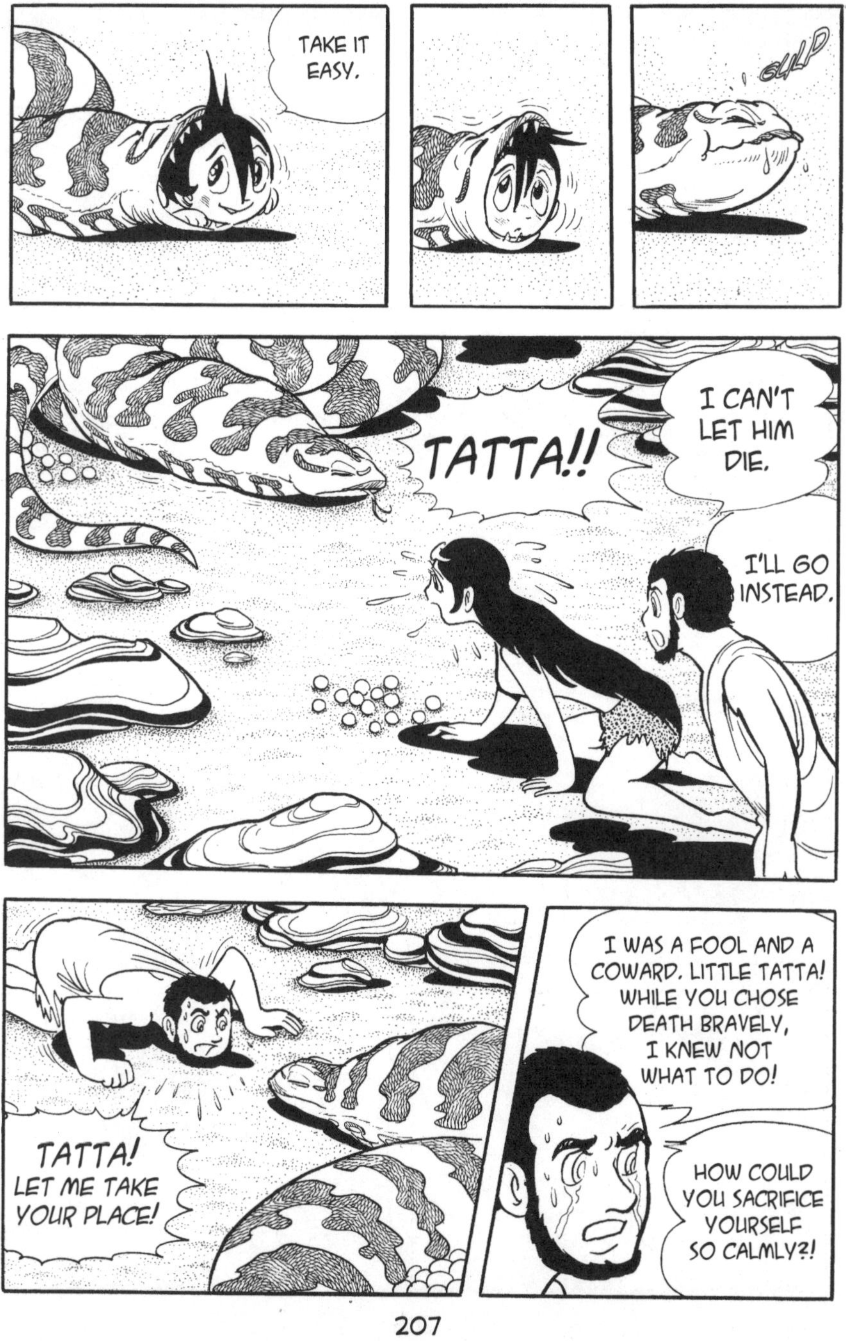
TAKE IT EASY.
GULP
TATTA!!
I CAN'T LET HIM DIE.
I'LL GO INSTEAD.
TATTA! LET ME TAKE YOUR PLACE!
I WAS A FOOL AND A COWARD. LITTLE TATTA! WHILE YOU CHOSE DEATH BRAVELY, I KNEW NOT WHAT TO DO!
HOW COULD YOU SACRIFICE YOURSELF SO CALMLY?!

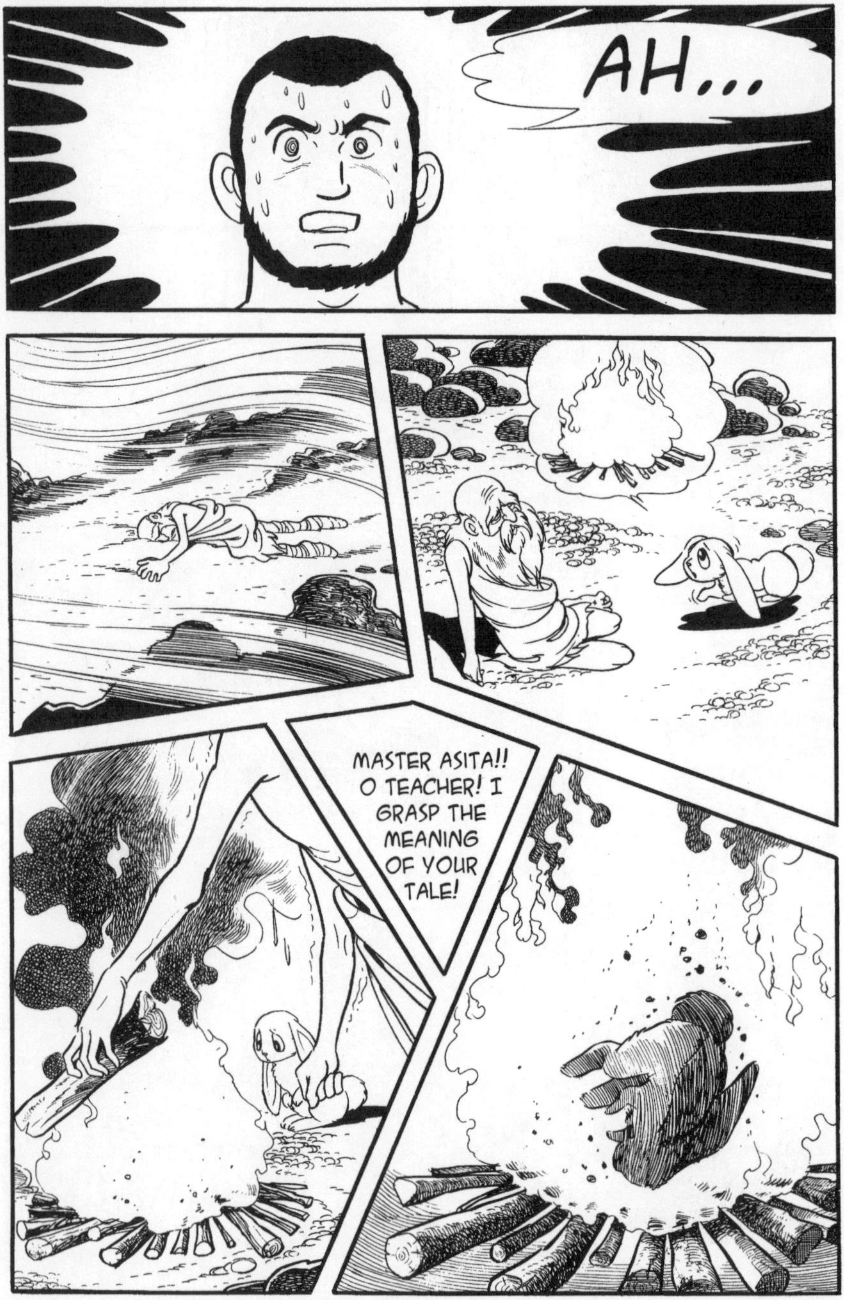
AH...
MASTER ASITA!! O TEACHER! I GRASP THE MEANING OF YOUR TALE!

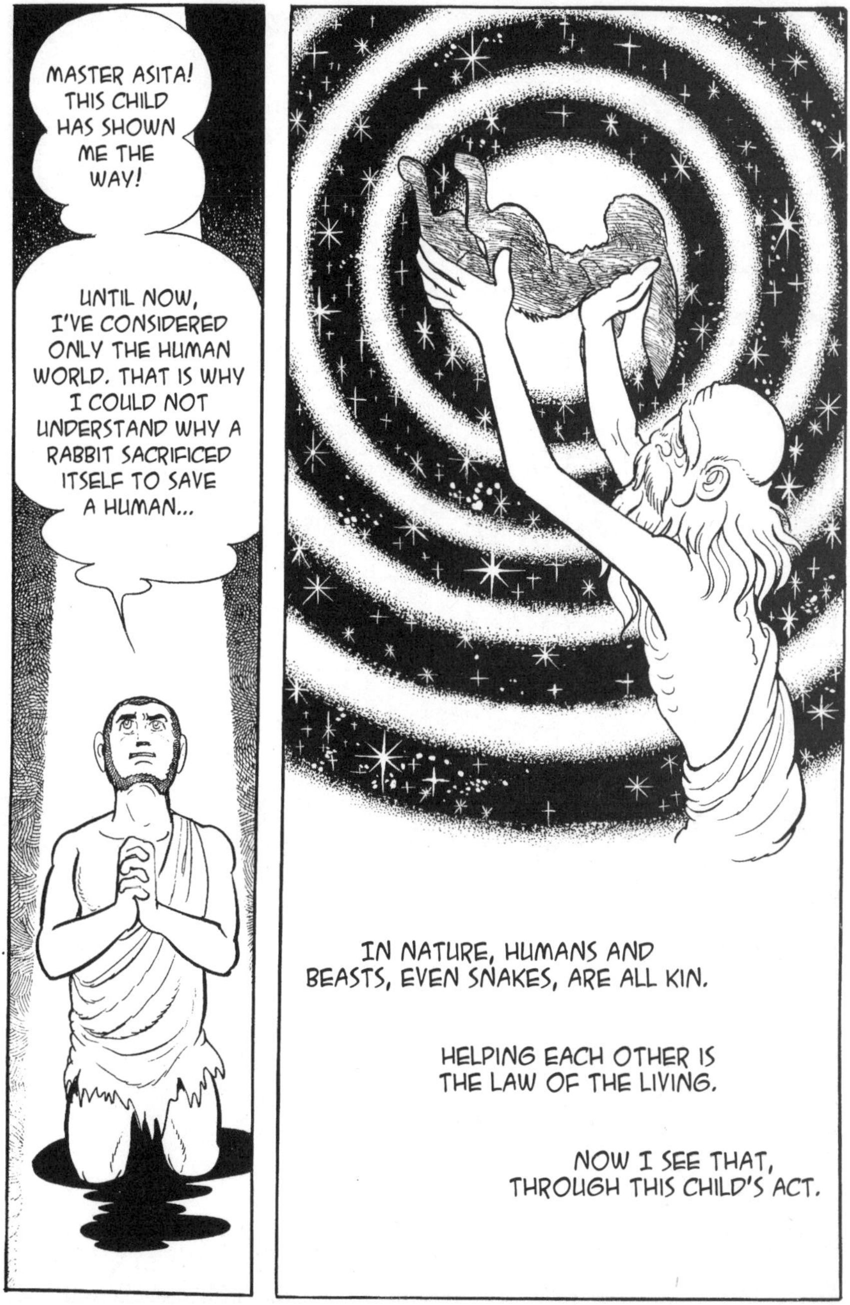
MASTER ASITA! THIS CHILD HAS SHOWN ME THE WAY!
UNTIL NOW, I'VE CONSIDERED ONLY THE HUMAN WORLD. THAT IS WHY I COULD NOT UNDERSTAND WHY A RABBIT SACRIFICED ITSELF TO SAVE A HUMAN...
IN NATURE, HUMANS AND BEASTS, EVEN SNAKES, ARE ALL KIN.
HELPING EACH OTHER IS THE LAW OF THE LIVING.
NOW I SEE THAT, THROUGH THIS CHILD'S ACT.

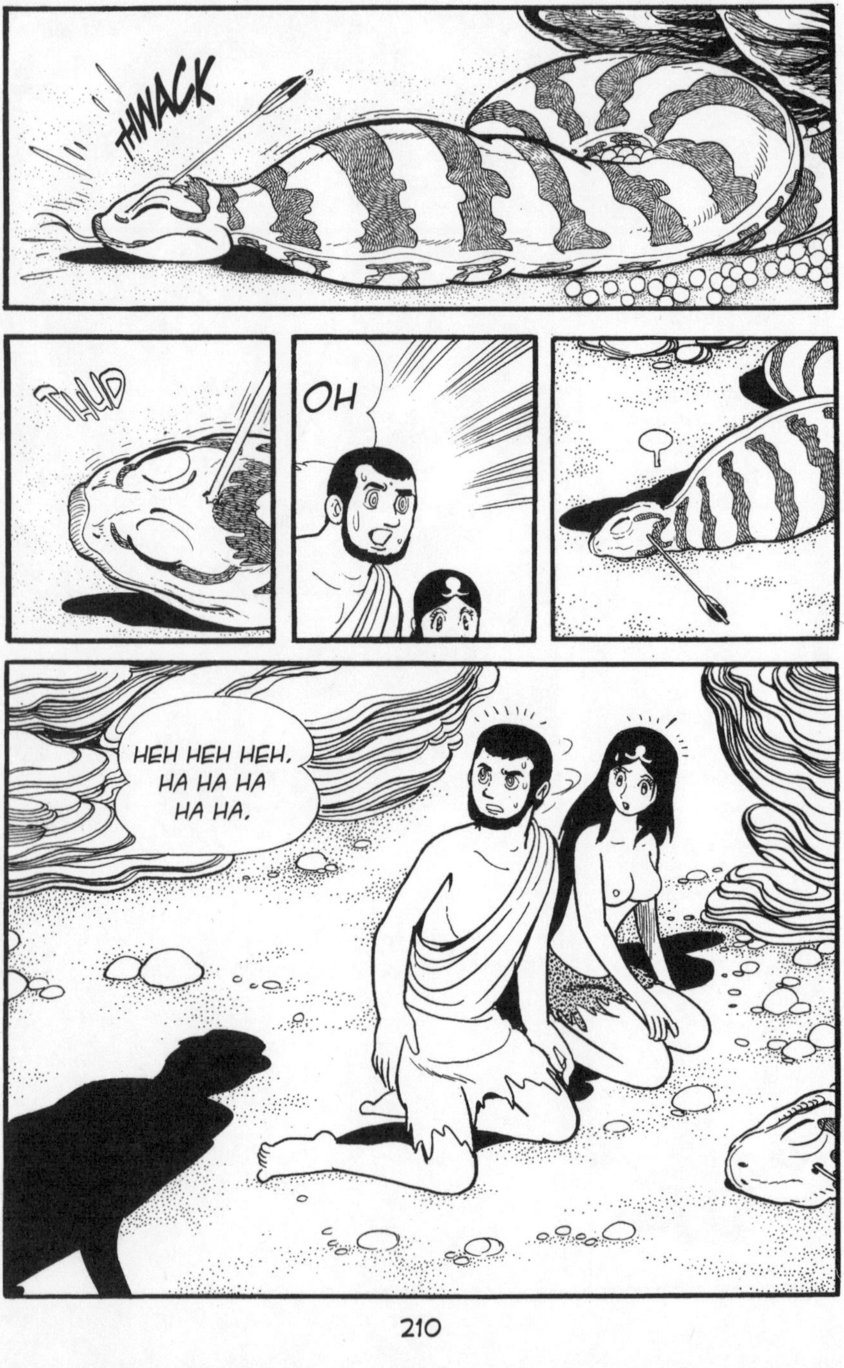
THWACK
THUD
OH
HEH HEH HEH, HA HA HA HA HA.

CHAPTER SIX

THE KING'S CUP

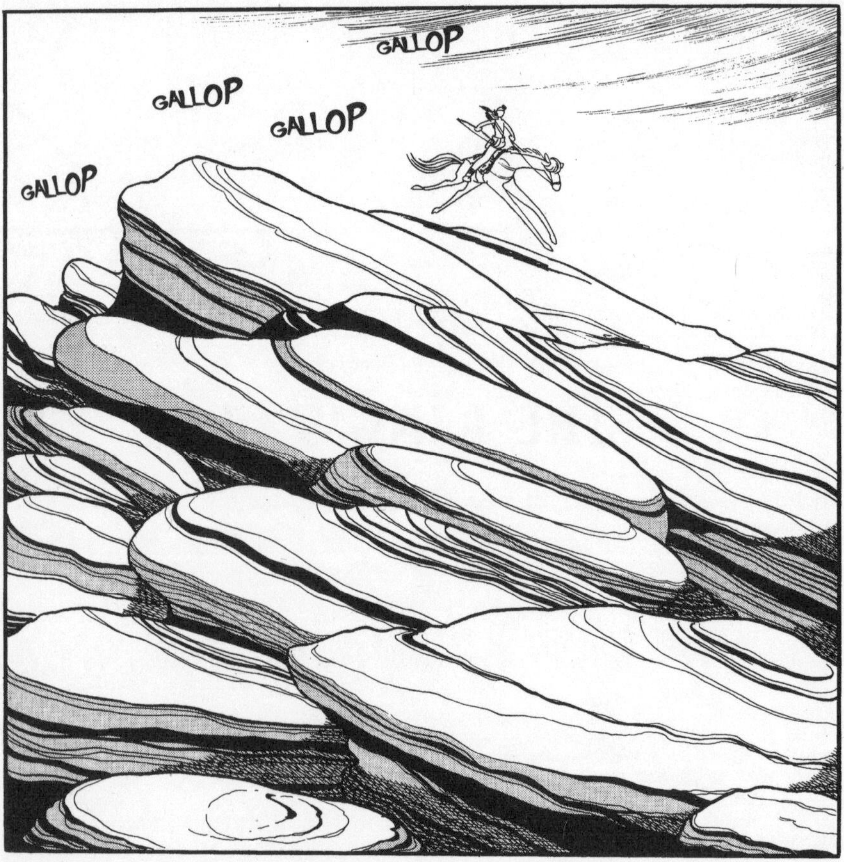
GALLOP
GALLOP
GALLOP
GALLOP

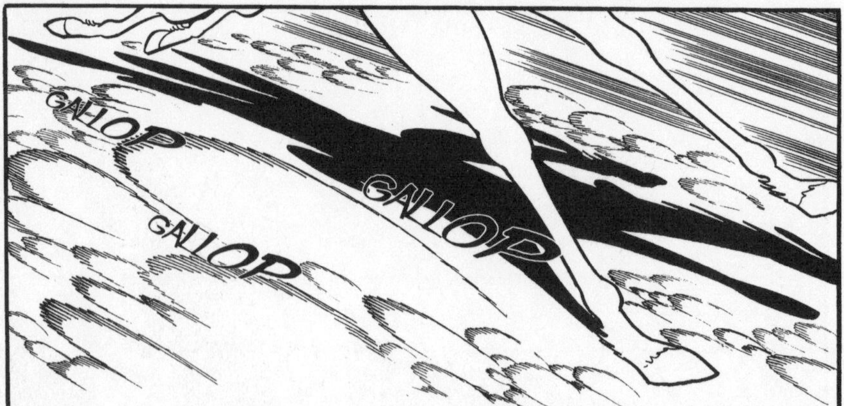
GALLOP
GALLOP
GALLOP

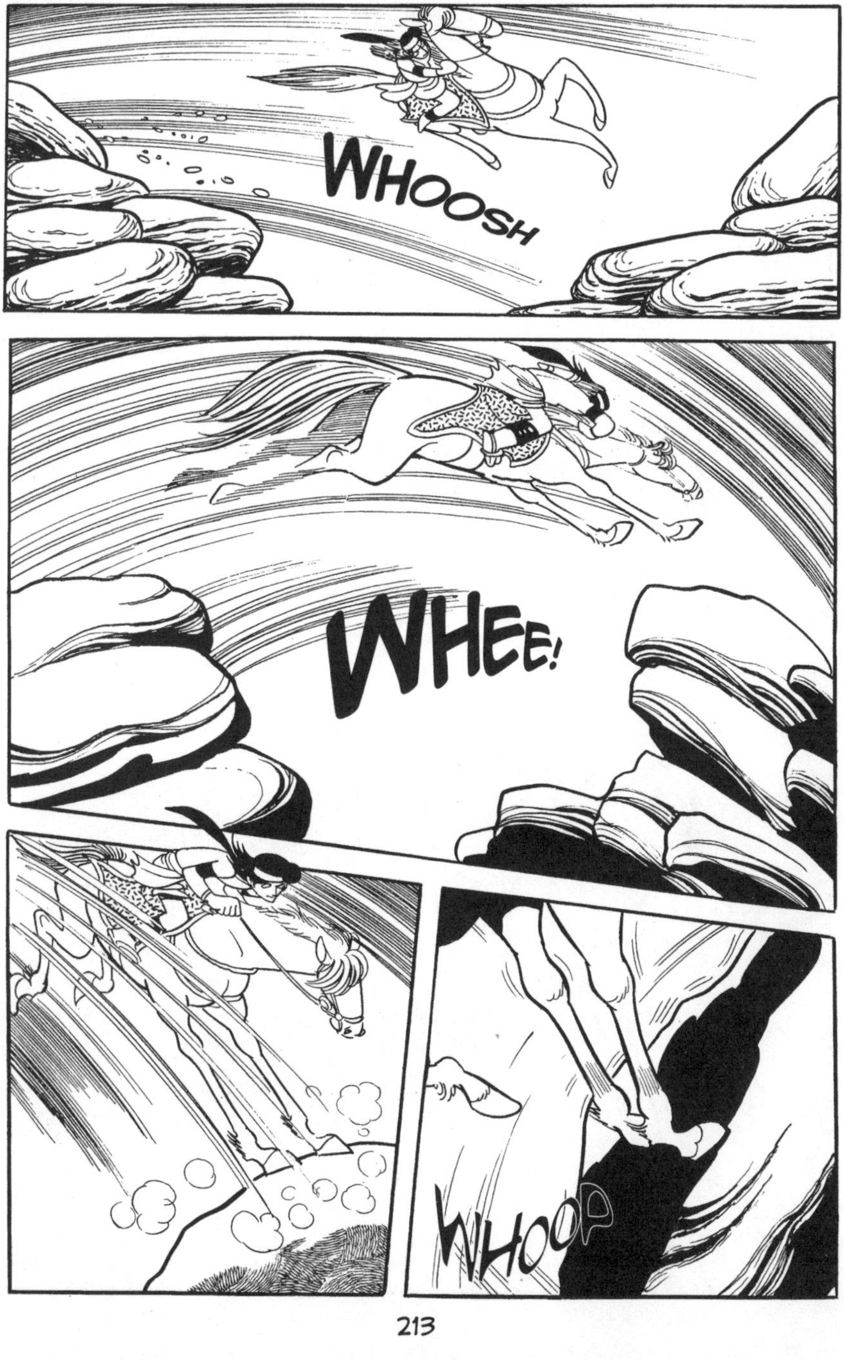
WHOOSH
WHEE!
WHOOP

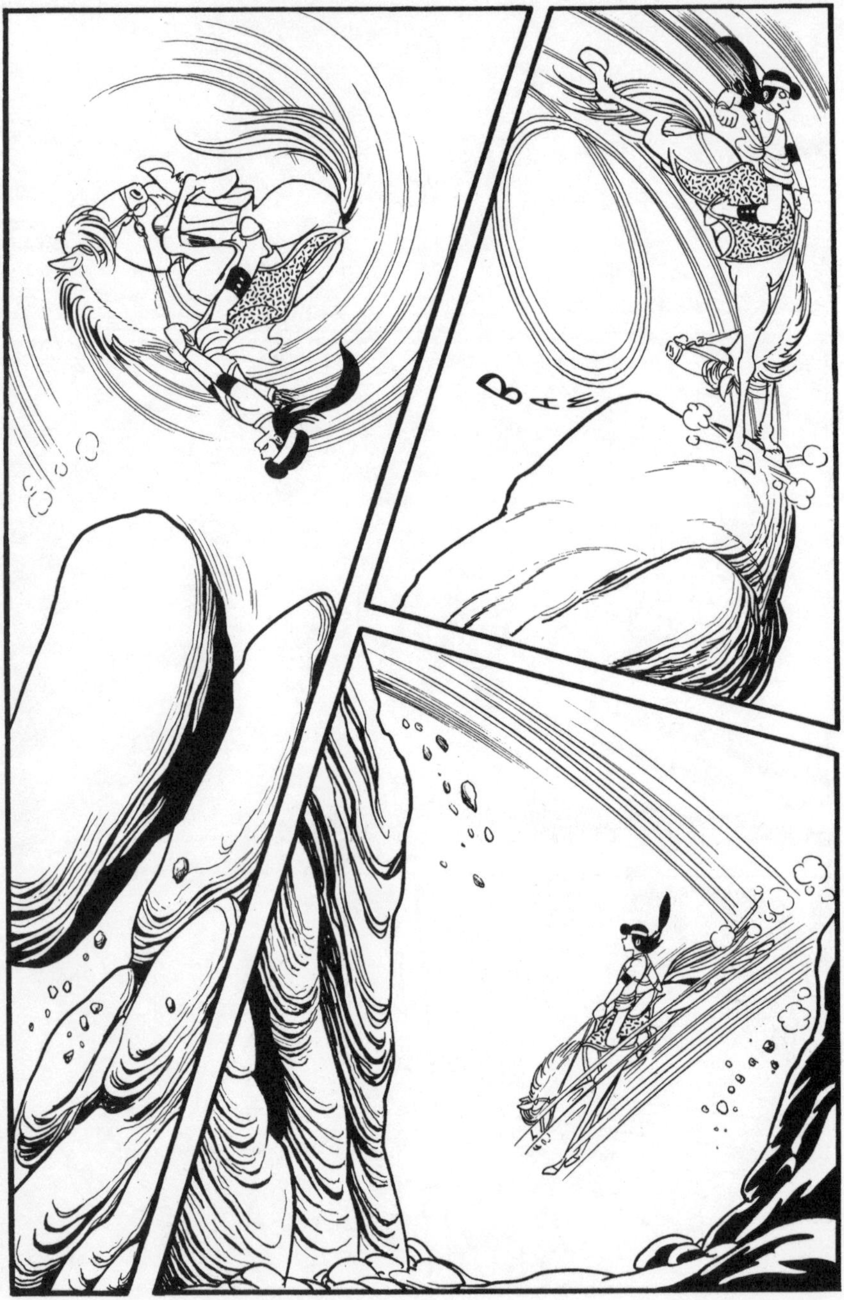
BAM

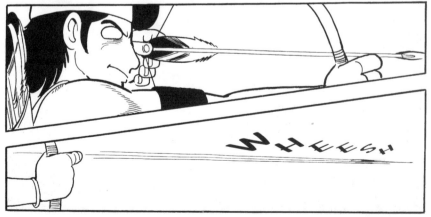

WHEESH

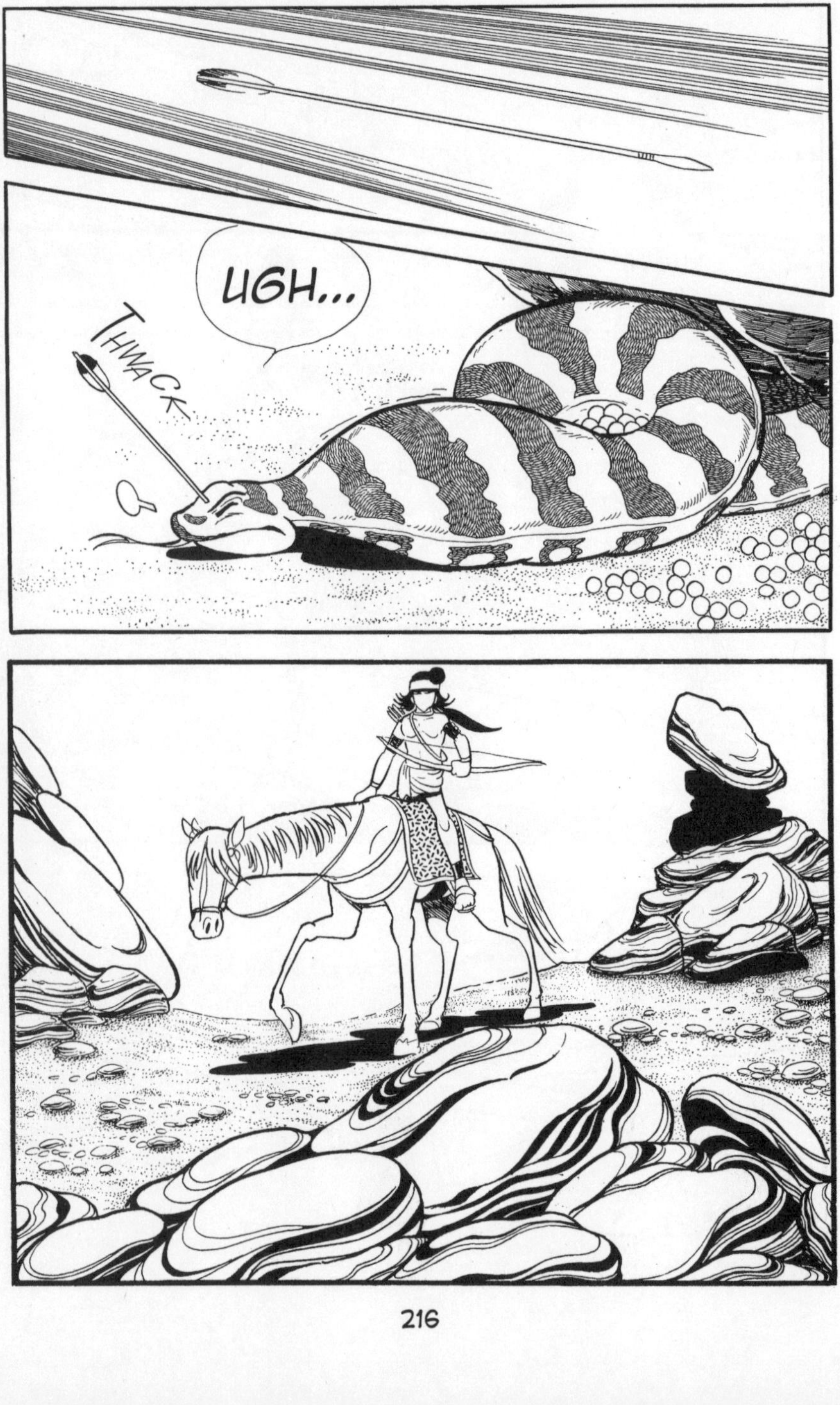
UGH...
THWACK

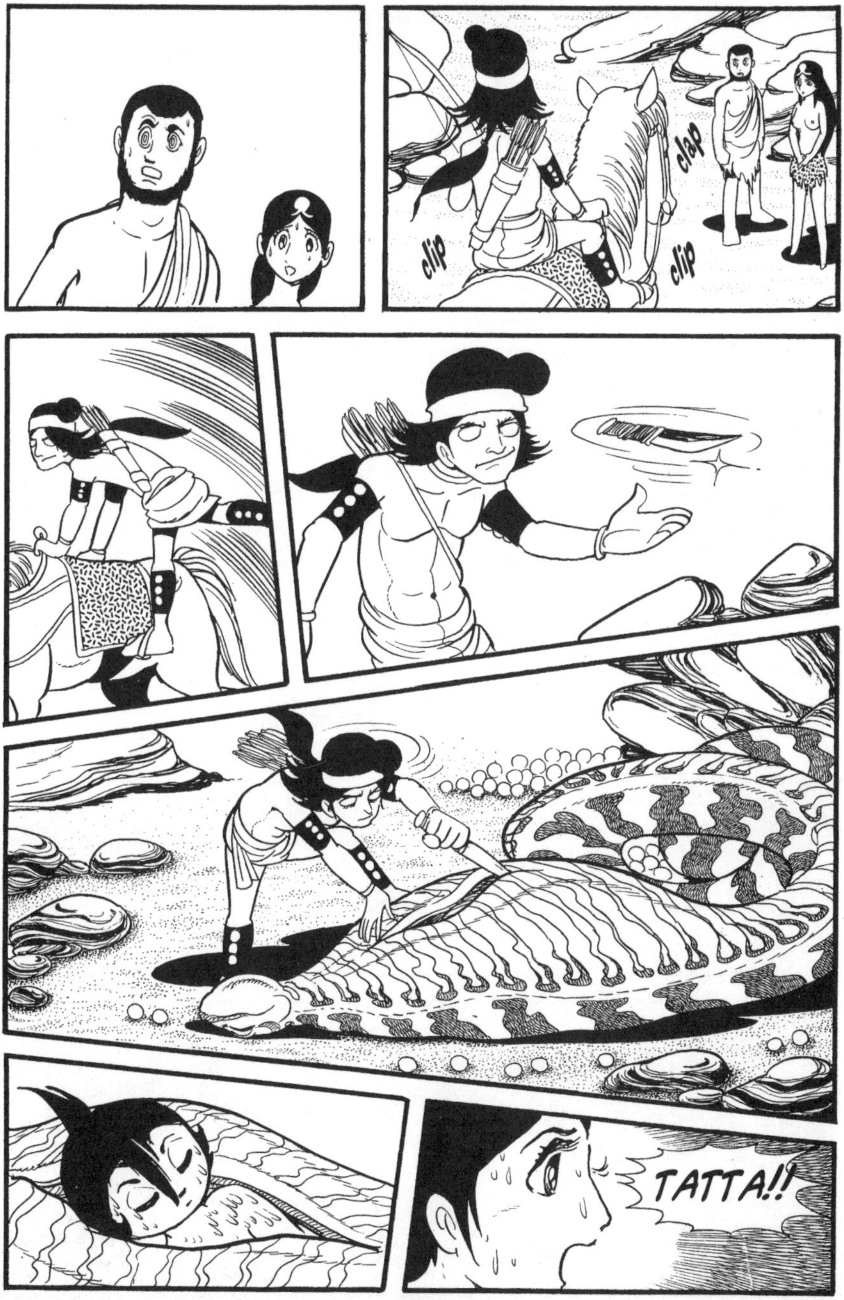
clip
clap
clip
TATTA!!

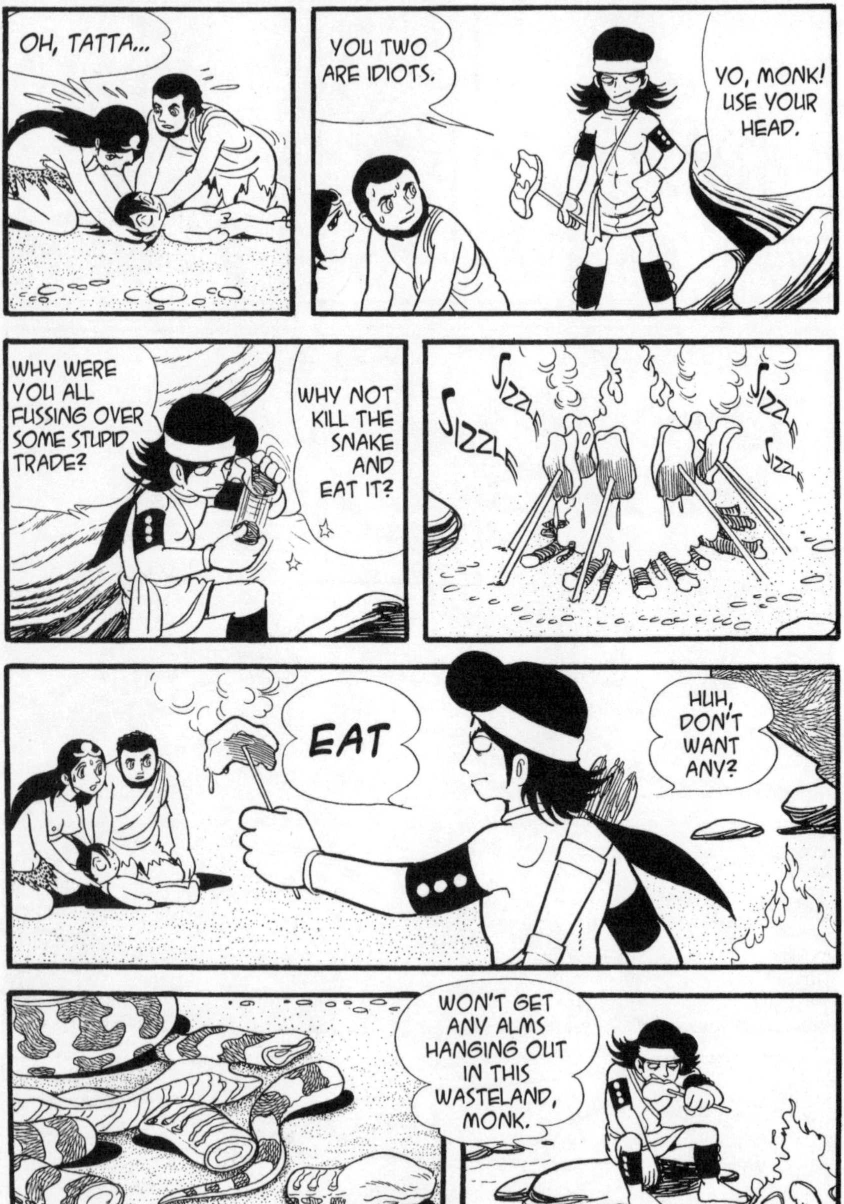

OH, TATTA...
YOU TWO ARE IDIOTS.
YO, MONK! USE YOUR HEAD.
WHY WERE YOU ALL FUSSING OVER SOME STUPID TRADE?
WHY NOT KILL THE SNAKE AND EAT IT?
SIZZLE
SIZZLE
SIZZLE
SIZZLE
EAT
HUH, DON'T WANT ANY?
WON'T GET ANY ALMS HANGING OUT IN THIS WASTELAND, MONK.

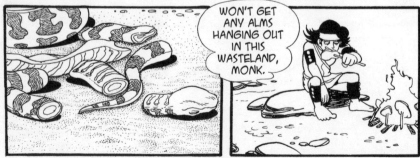

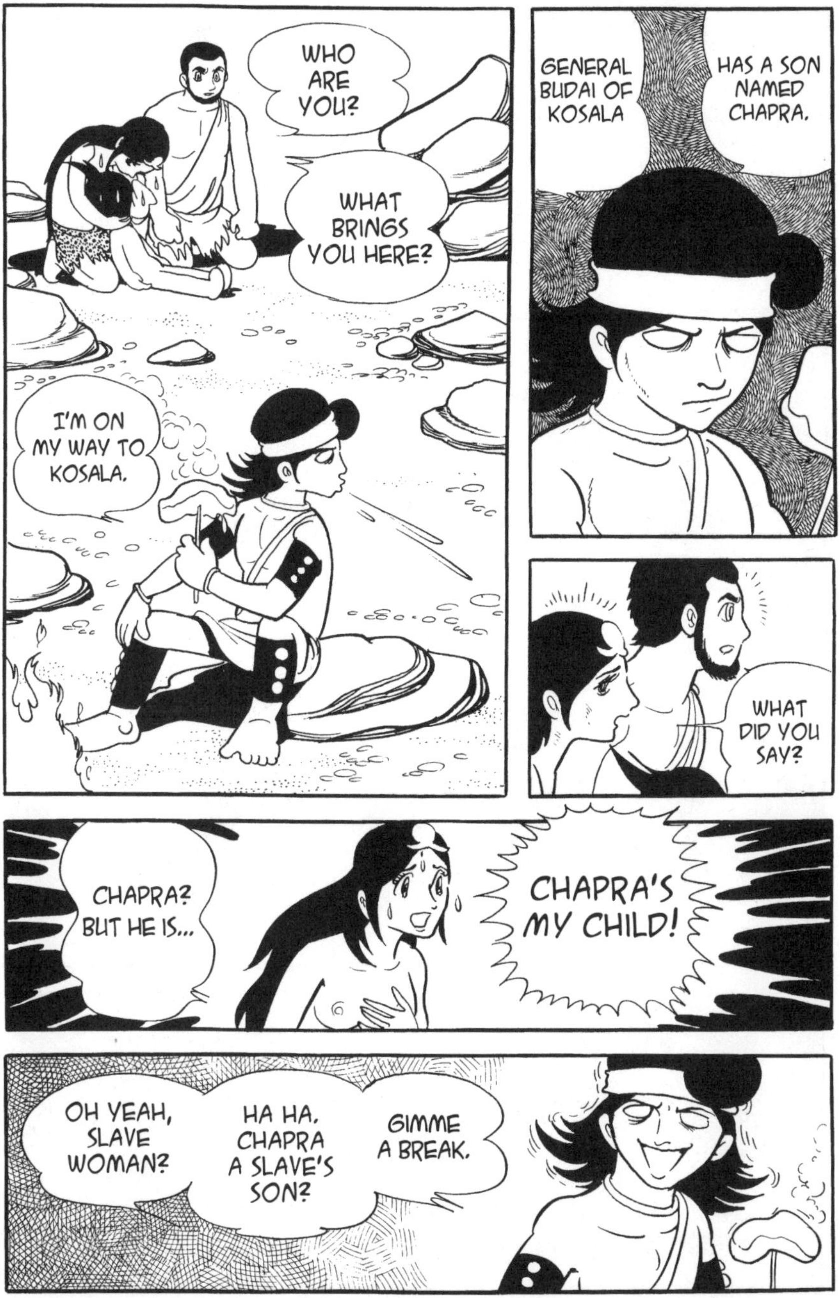
WHO ARE YOU?
WHAT BRINGS YOU HERE?
I'M ON MY WAY TO KOSALA.
GENERAL BUDAI OF KOSALA
HAS A SON NAMED CHAPRA.
WHAT DID YOU SAY?
CHAPRA? BUT HE IS...
CHAPRA'S MY CHILD!
OH YEAH, SLAVE WOMAN?
HA HA. CHAPRA A SLAVE'S SON?
GIMME A BREAK.

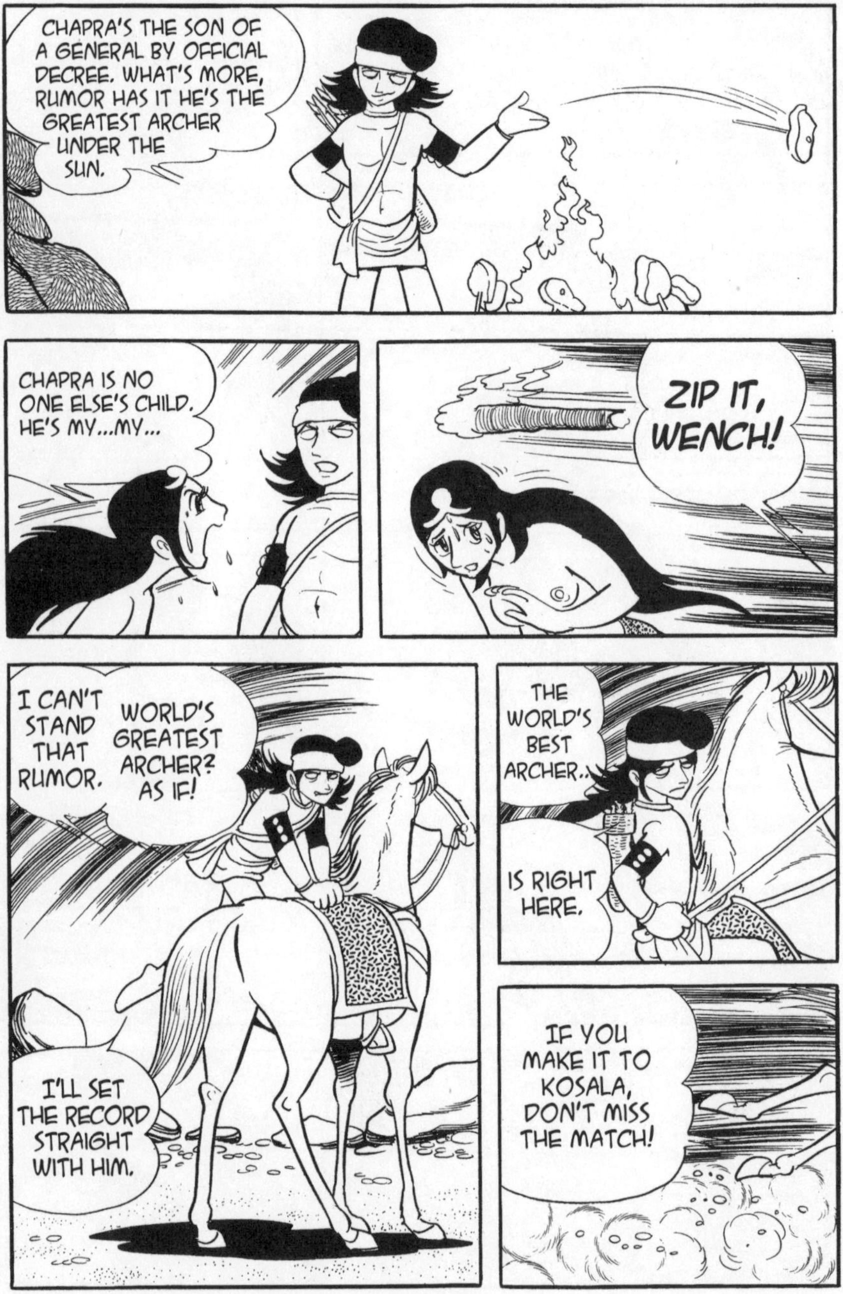
CHAPRA'S THE SON OF A GENERAL BY OFFICIAL DECREE. WHAT'S MORE, RUMOR HAS IT HE'S THE GREATEST ARCHER UNDER THE SUN.
CHAPRA IS NO ONE ELSE'S CHILD. HE'S MY...MY...
ZIP IT, WENCH!
I CAN'T STAND THAT RUMOR.
WORLD'S GREATEST ARCHER? AS IF!
I'LL SET THE RECORD STRAIGHT WITH HIM.
THE WORLD'S BEST ARCHER...
IS RIGHT HERE.
IF YOU MAKE IT TO KOSALA, DON'T MISS THE MATCH!

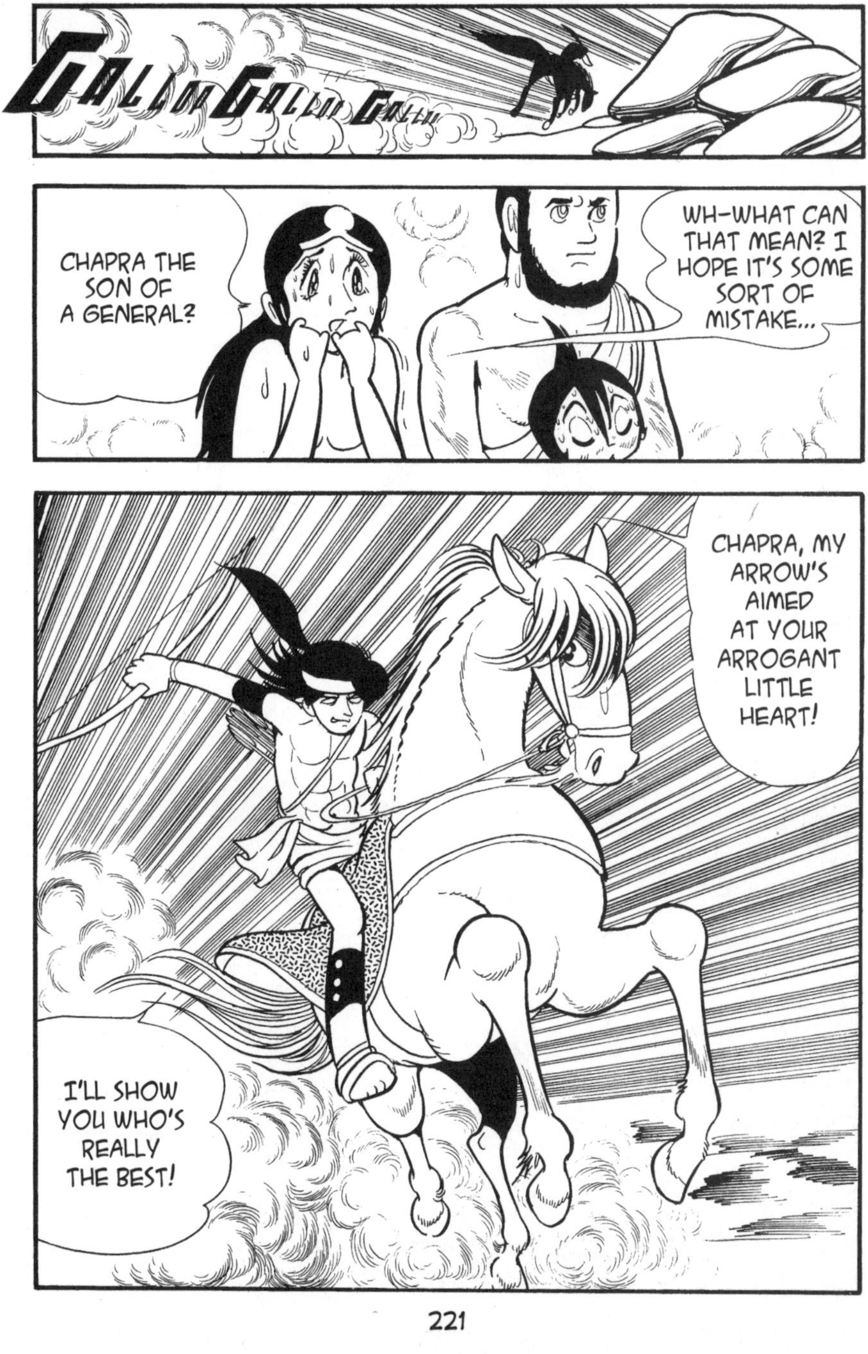
GALLOP GALLOP GALLL
CHAPRA THE SON OF A GENERAL?
WH-WHAT CAN THAT MEAN? I HOPE IT'S SOME SORT OF MISTAKE...
CHAPRA, MY ARROW'S AIMED AT YOUR ARROGANT LITTLE HEART!
I'LL SHOW YOU WHO'S REALLY THE BEST!

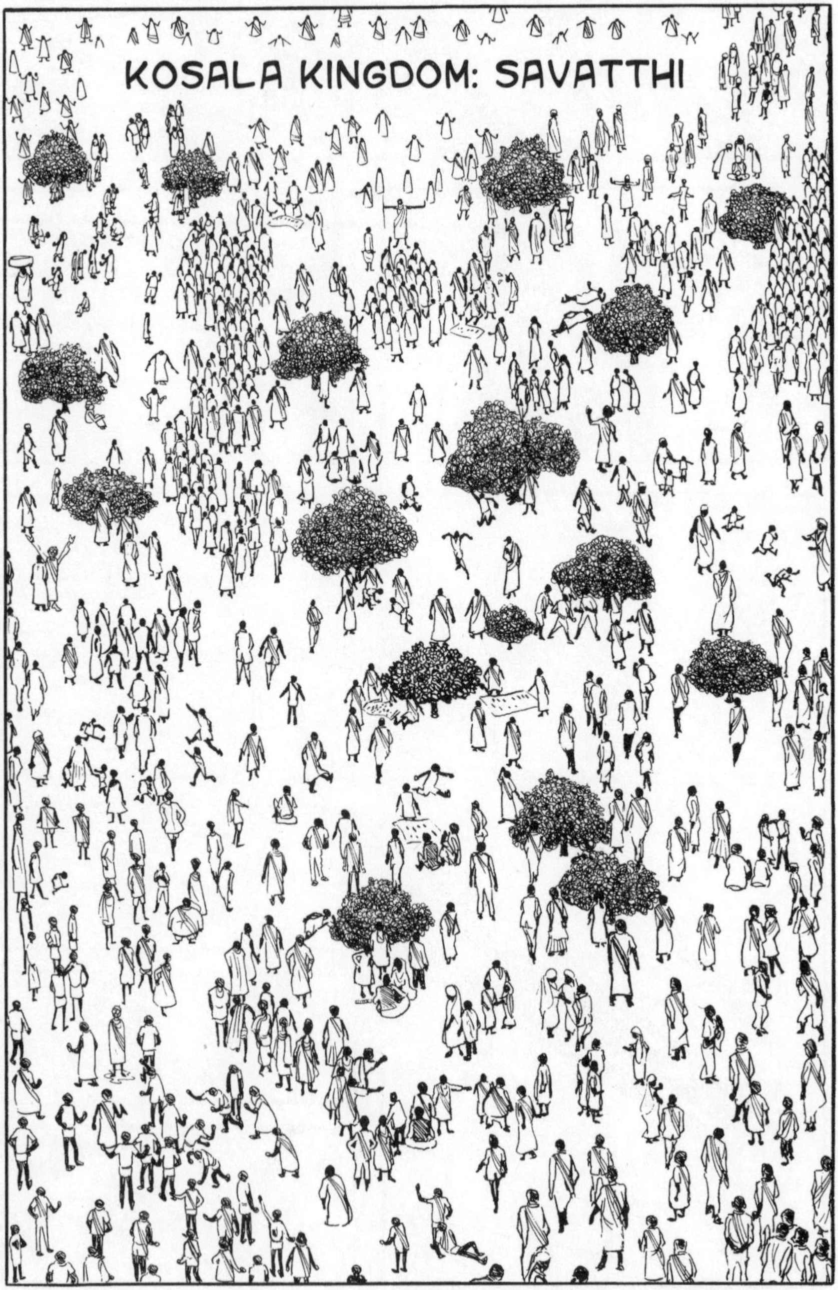
KOSALA KINGDOM: SAVATTHI

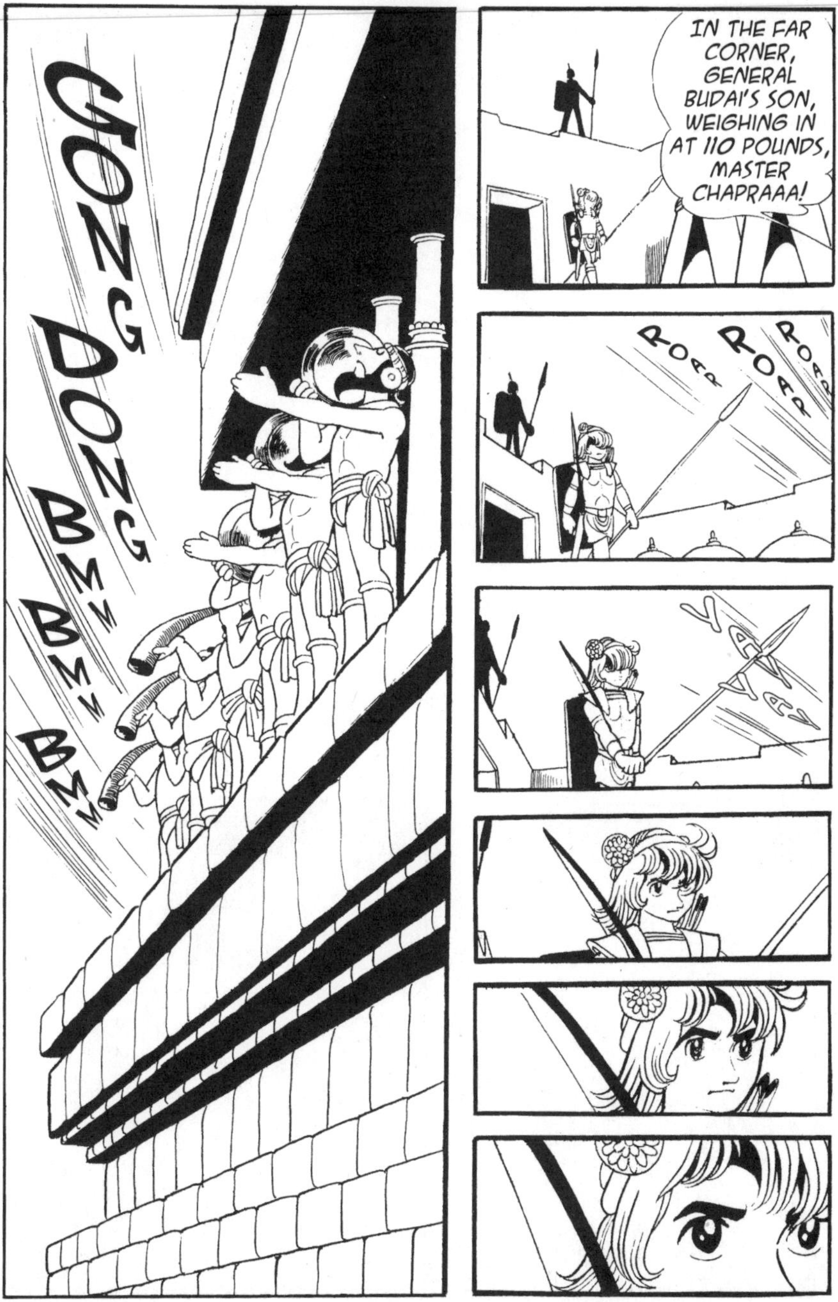
GONG DONG
BMM BMM BMM
IN THE FAR CORNER, GENERAL BUDAI'S SON, WEIGHING IN AT 110 POUNDS, MASTER CHAPRAAA!
ROAR ROAR ROAR
YAY YAY

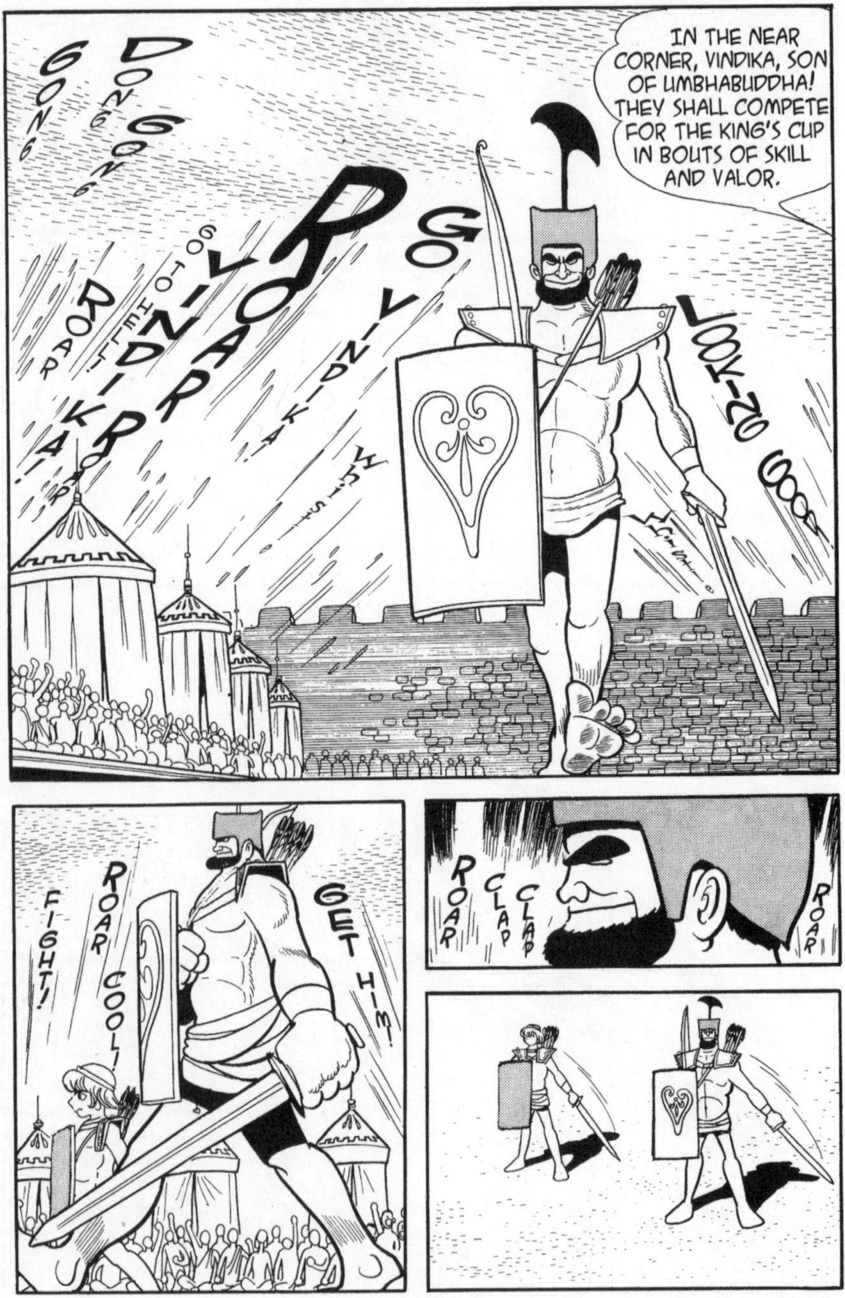
IN THE NEAR CORNER, VINDIKA, SON OF UMBHABUDDHA! THEY SHALL COMPETE FOR THE KING'S CUP IN BOUTS OF SKILL AND VALOR.
GONG
DONG GONG GONG
ROAR
VINDIKA!
ROAR
GO TO HELL!
ROAR
GO VINDIKA!
LOOKING GOOD!
FIGHT!
ROAR
COOL!
GET HIM!
ROAR
CLAP
CLAP
ROAR

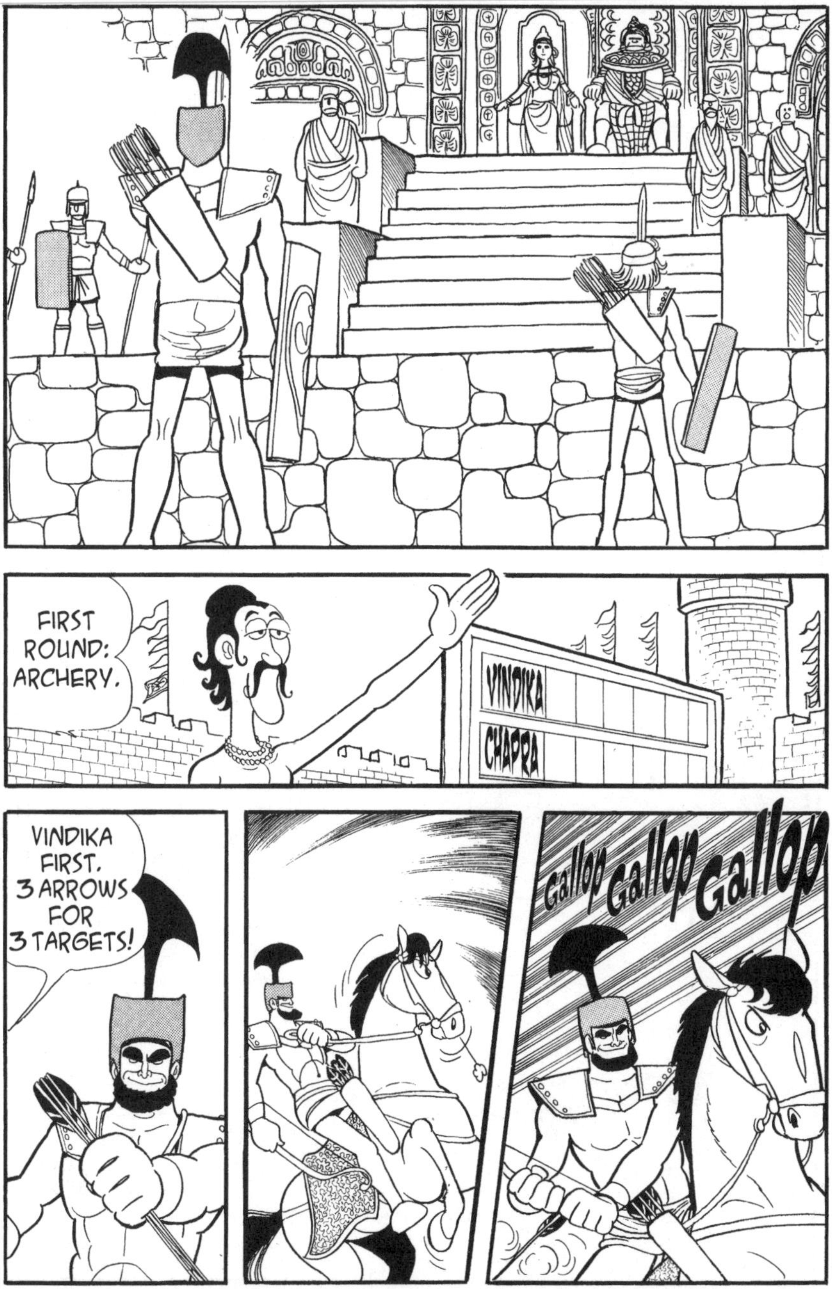
FIRST ROUND: ARCHERY.
VINDIKA
CHAPRA
VINDIKA FIRST. 3 ARROWS FOR 3 TARGETS!
Gallop Gallop Gallop

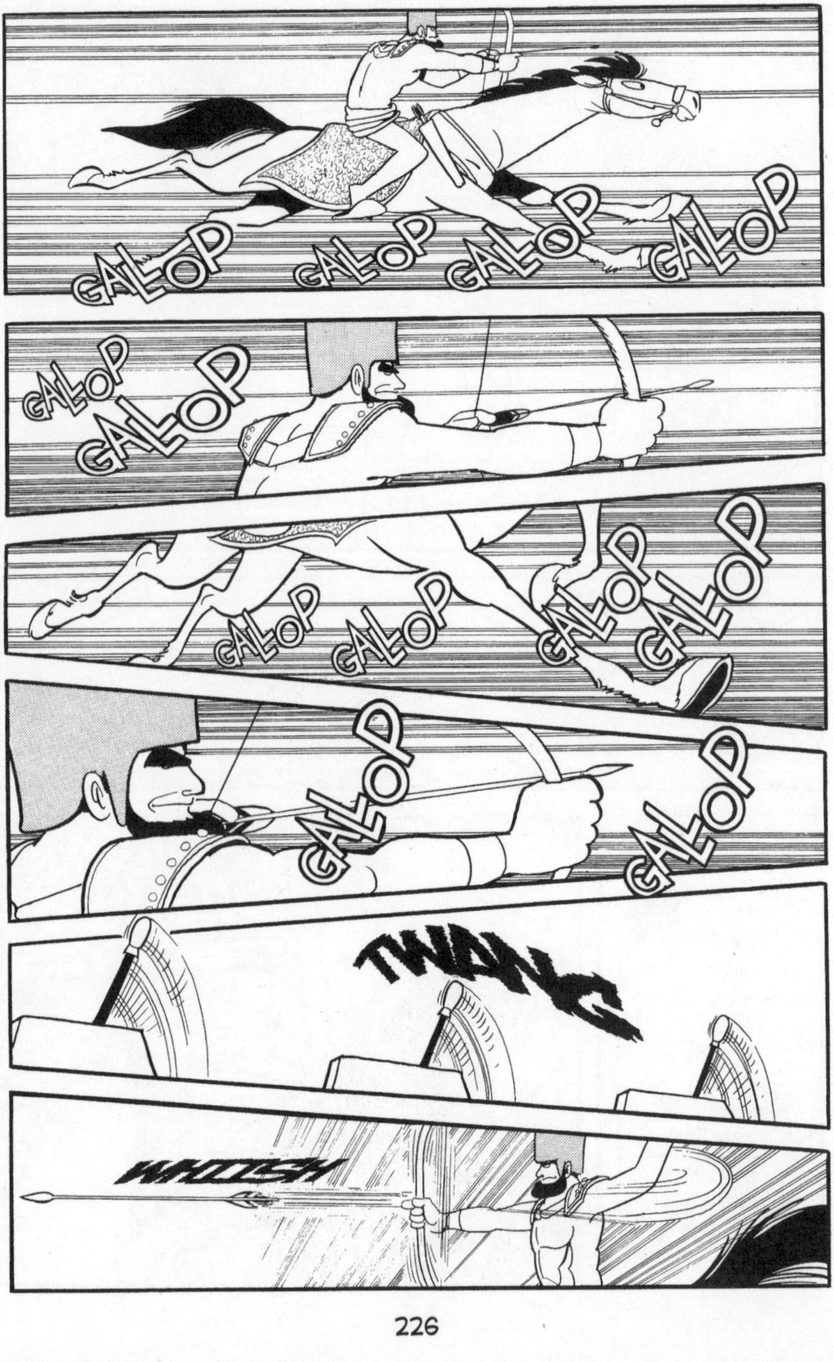
GALOP
GALOP
GALOP
GALOP
GALOP
GALOP
GALOP
GALOP
GALOP
GALOP
GALOP
GALOP
TWANG
WHOOSH

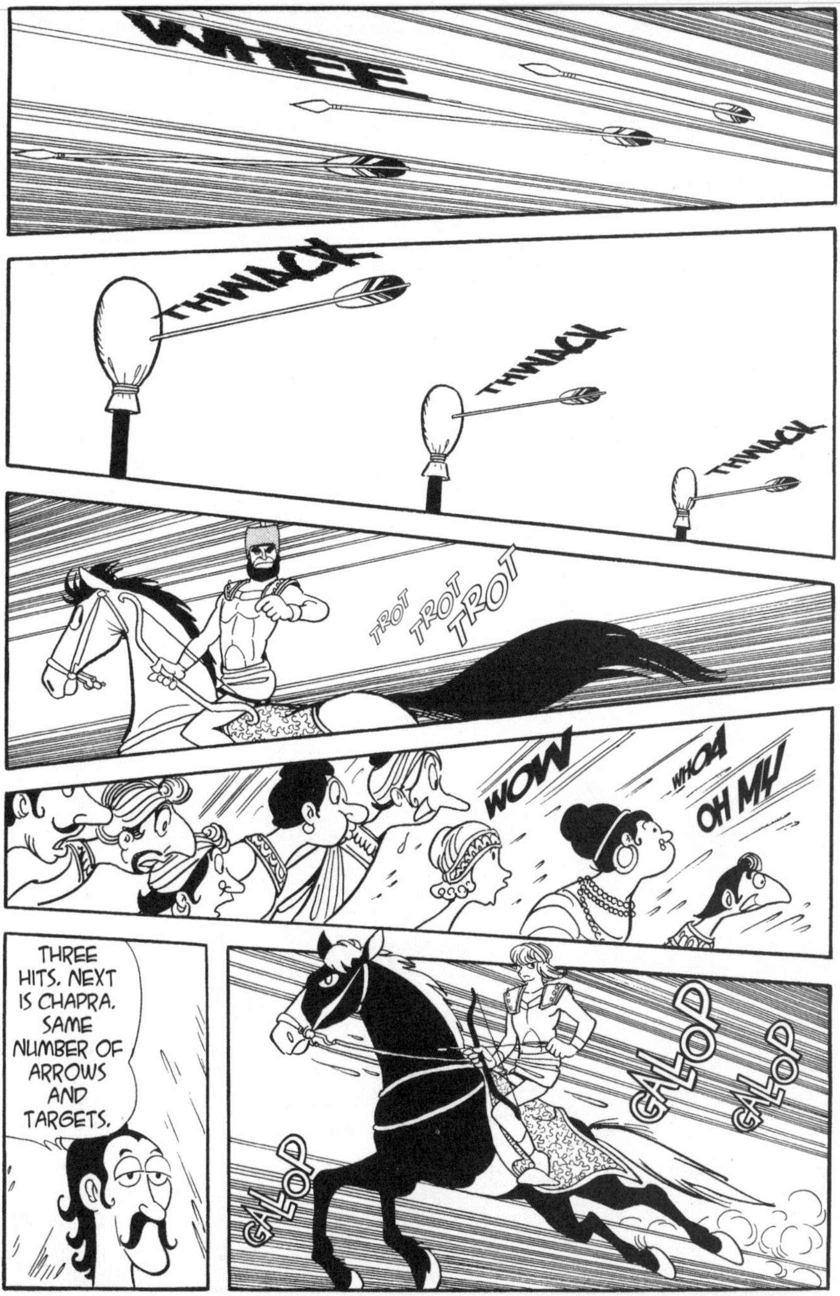
WHEE
THWACK
THWACK
THWACK
TROT TROT TROT
WOW
WHOA
OH MY
THREE HITS. NEXT IS CHAPRA. SAME NUMBER OF ARROWS AND TARGETS.
GALLOP
GALLOP
GALLOP
GALLOP

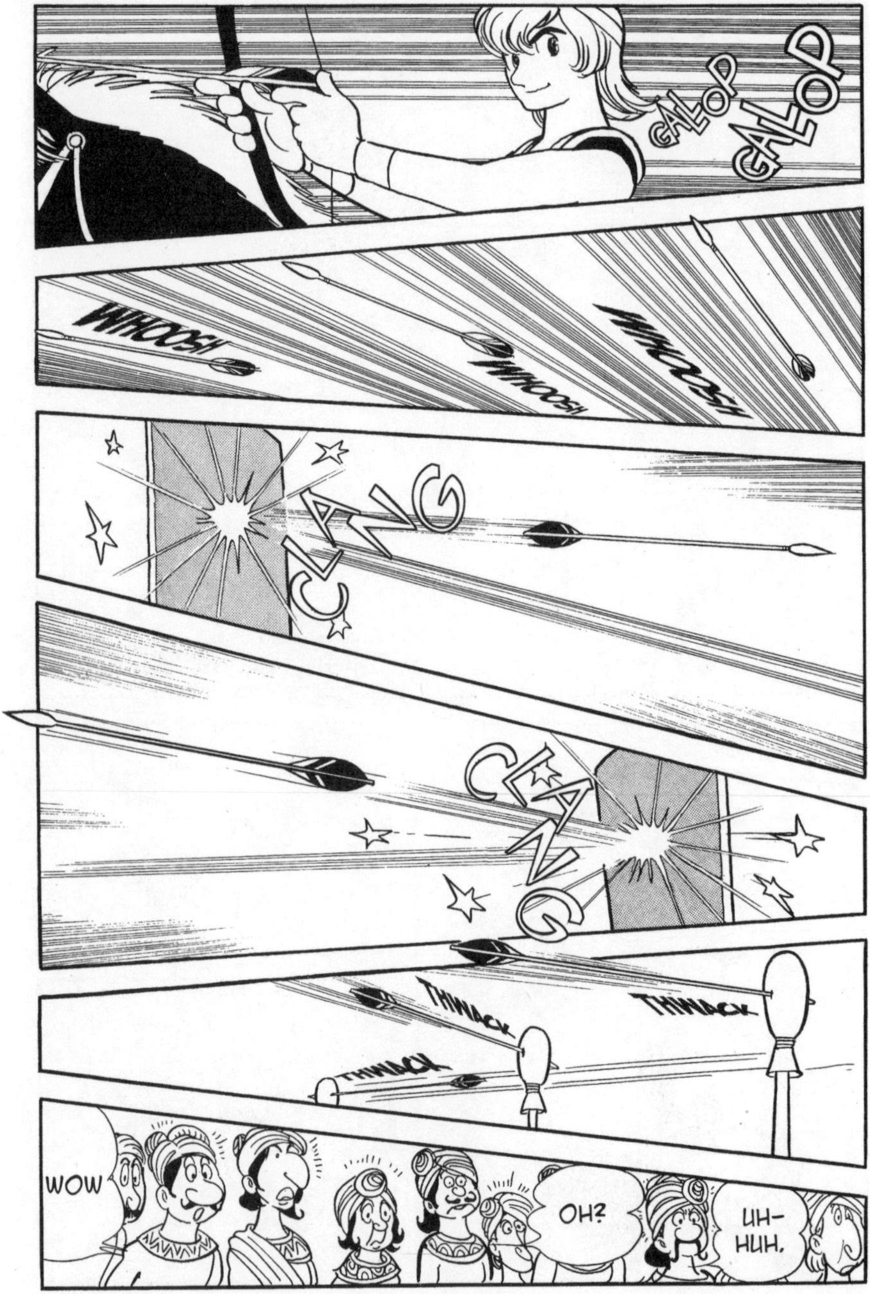
GALOP
GALOP
WHOOSH
WHOOSH
WHOOSH
CLANG
CLANG
THWACK
THWACK
THWACK
WOW
OH?
UH-HUH.

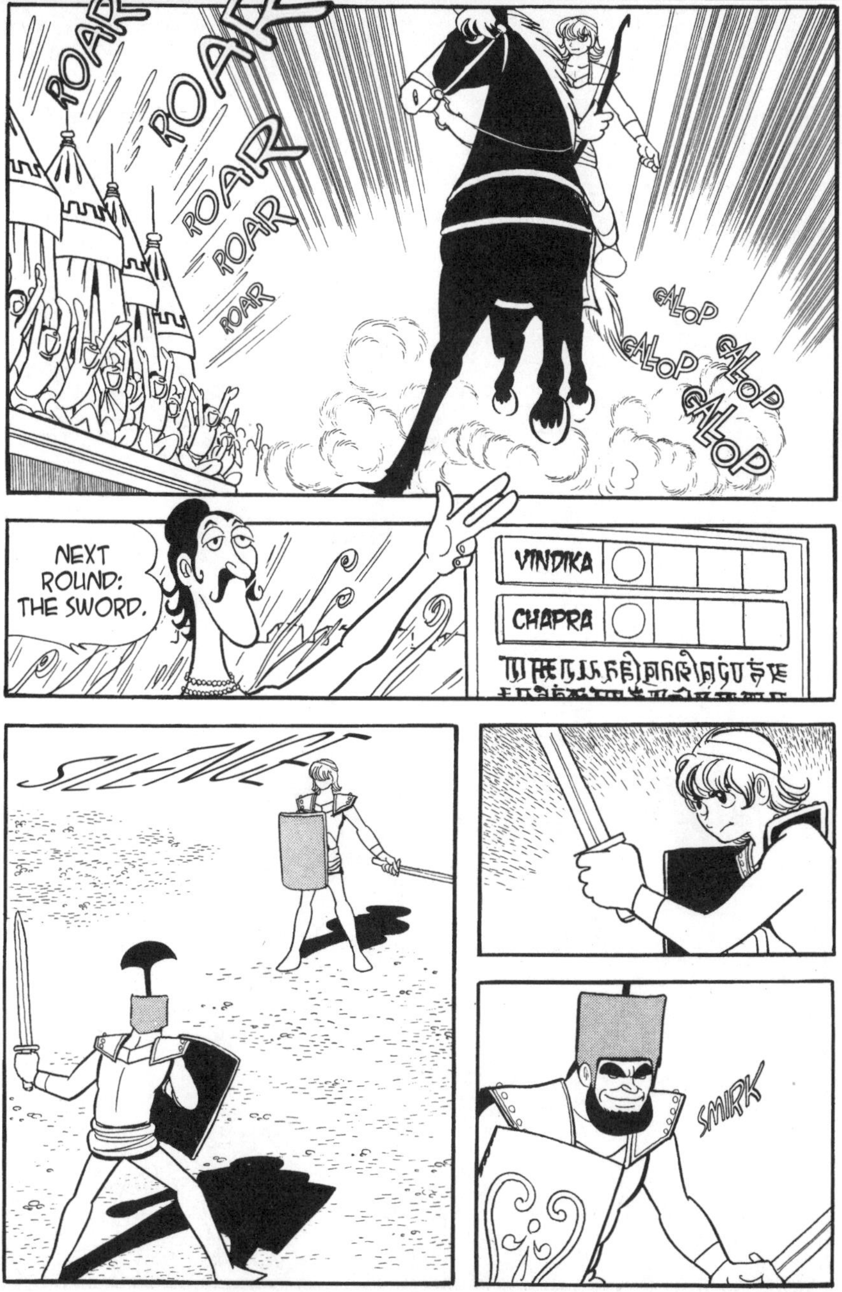
ROAR
ROAR
ROAR
ROAR
ROAR
ROAR
GALLOP
GALLOP
GALLOP
GALLOP
NEXT ROUND: THE SWORD.
VINDIKA
CHAPRA
SILENCE
SMIRK

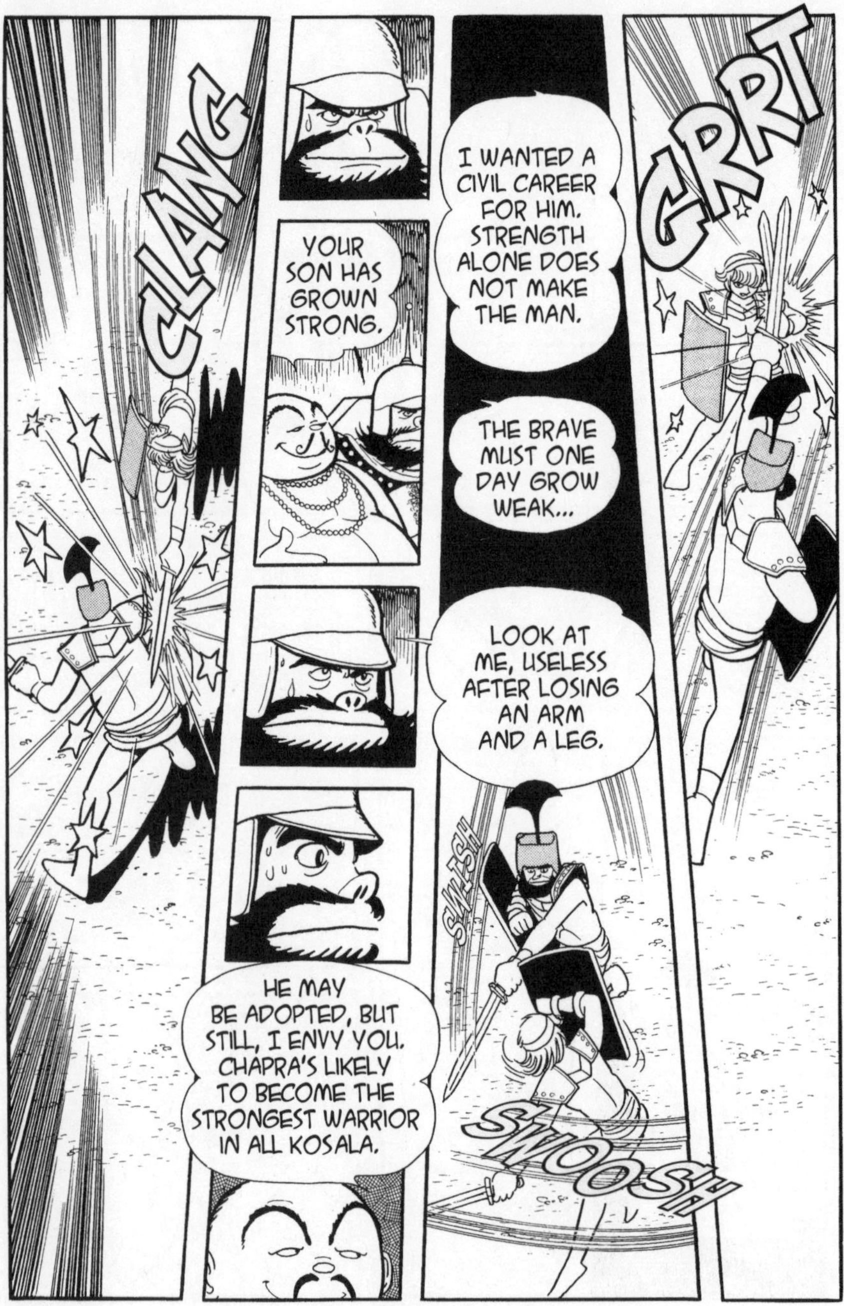
CLANG
YOUR SON HAS GROWN STRONG.
HE MAY BE ADOPTED, BUT STILL, I ENVY YOU. CHAPRA'S LIKELY TO BECOME THE STRONGEST WARRIOR IN ALL KOSALA.
I WANTED A CIVIL CAREER FOR HIM. STRENGTH ALONE DOES NOT MAKE THE MAN.
THE BRAVE MUST ONE DAY GROW WEAK...
LOOK AT ME, USELESS AFTER LOSING AN ARM AND A LEG.
SWISH
SWOOSH
GRRT

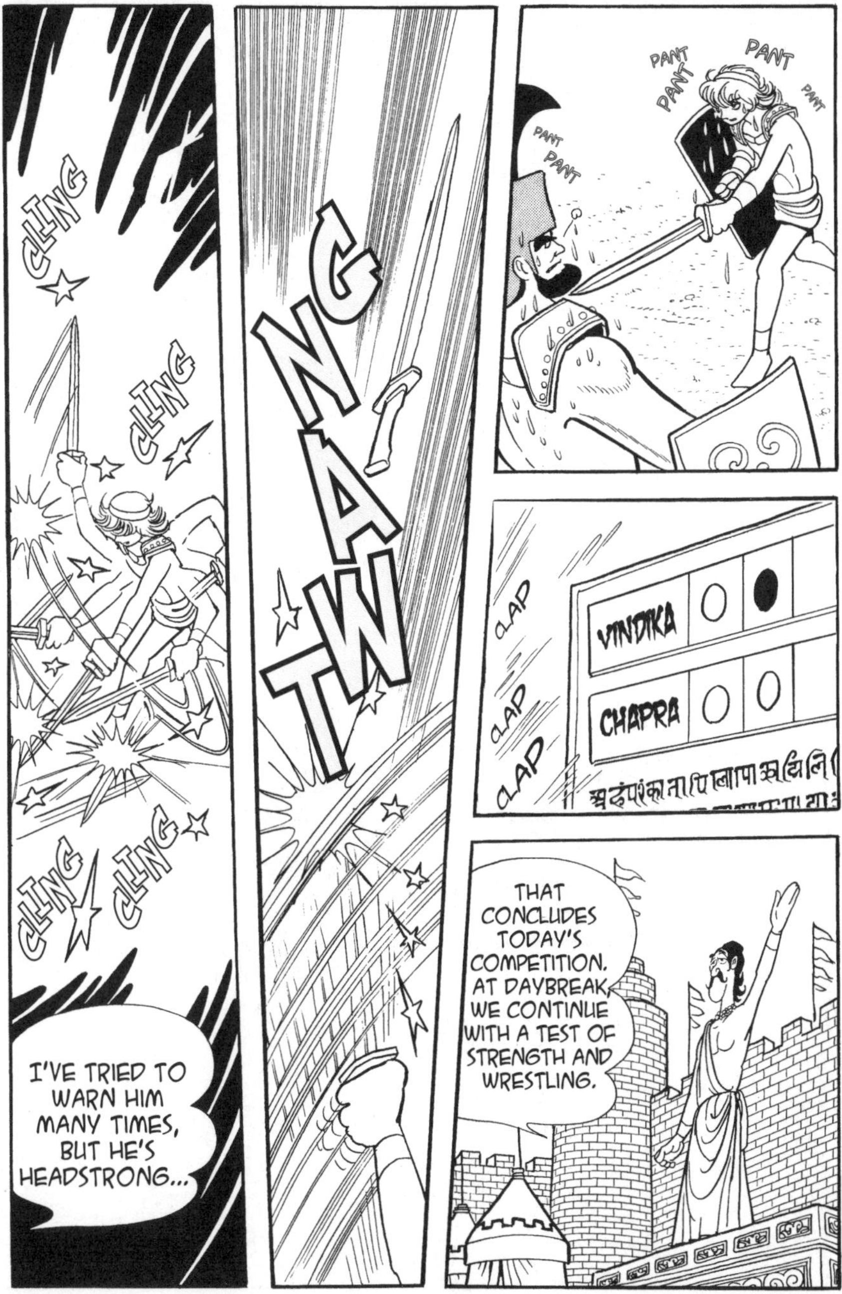
CLING
CLING
CLING
CLING
I'VE TRIED TO WARN HIM MANY TIMES, BUT HE'S HEADSTRONG...
TWANG
PANT PANT PANT PANT
PANT PANT PANT
VINDIKA
CHAPRA
CLAP CLAP CLAP
THAT CONCLUDES TODAY'S COMPETITION. AT DAYBREAK, WE CONTINUE WITH A TEST OF STRENGTH AND WRESTLING.

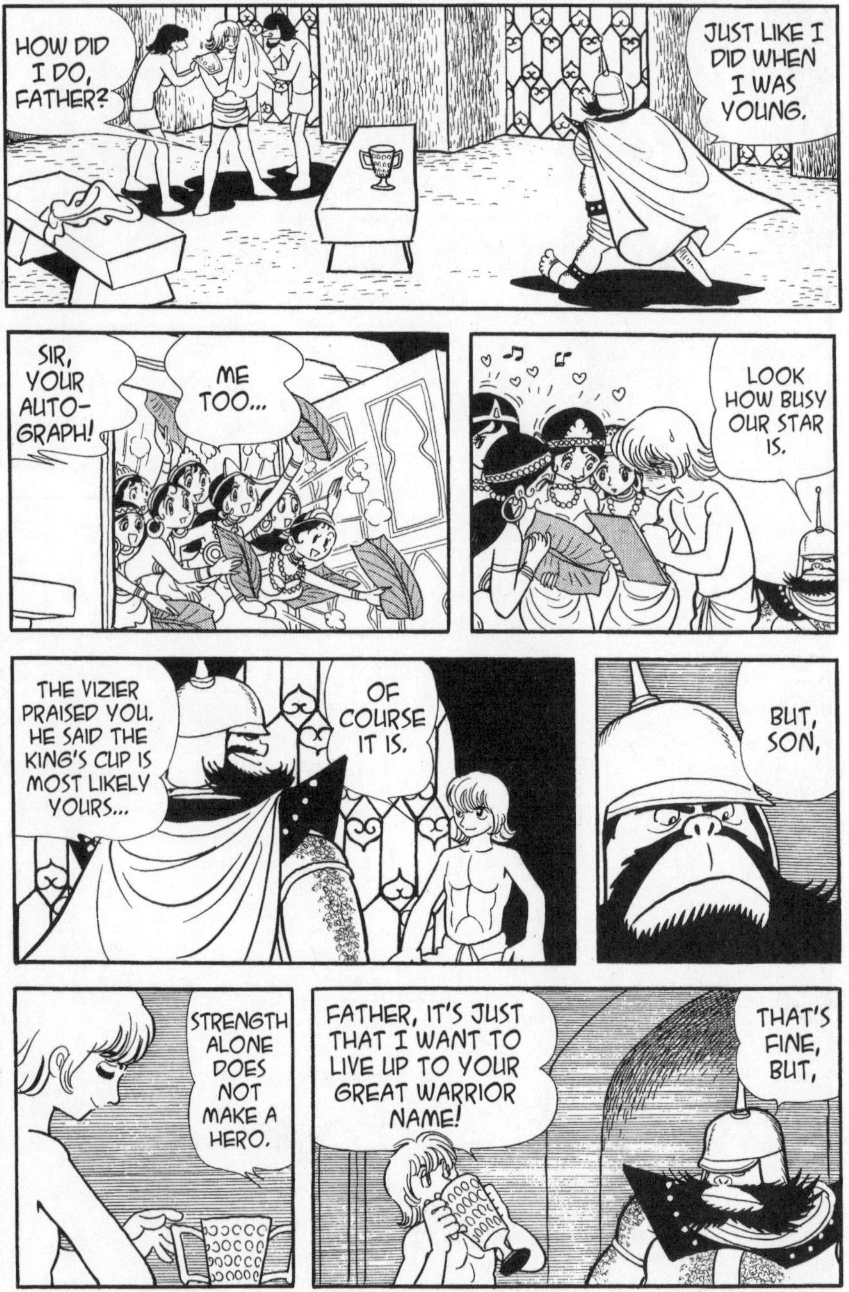
HOW DID I DO, FATHER?
JUST LIKE I DID WHEN I WAS YOUNG.
SIR, YOUR AUTO-GRAPH!
ME TOO...
LOOK HOW BUSY OUR STAR IS.
THE VIZIER PRAISED YOU. HE SAID THE KING'S CUP IS MOST LIKELY YOURS...
OF COURSE IT IS.
BUT, SON,
STRENGTH ALONE DOES NOT MAKE A HERO.
FATHER, IT'S JUST THAT I WANT TO LIVE UP TO YOUR GREAT WARRIOR NAME!
THAT'S FINE, BUT,

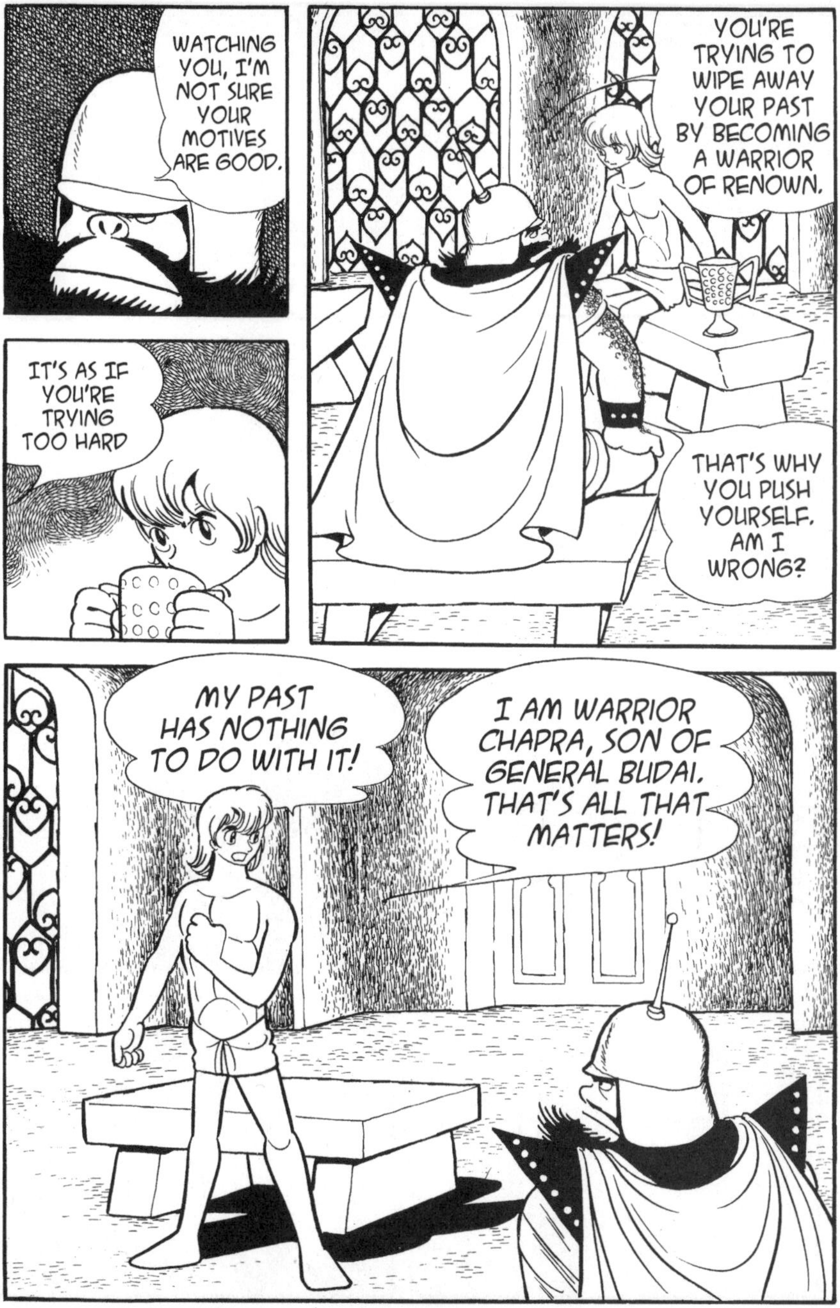
WATCHING YOU, I'M NOT SURE YOUR MOTIVES ARE GOOD.
YOU'RE TRYING TO WIPE AWAY YOUR PAST BY BECOMING A WARRIOR OF RENOWN.
IT'S AS IF YOU'RE TRYING TOO HARD
THAT'S WHY YOU PUSH YOURSELF. AM I WRONG?
MY PAST HAS NOTHING TO DO WITH IT!
I AM WARRIOR CHAPRA, SON OF GENERAL BUDAI. THAT'S ALL THAT MATTERS!

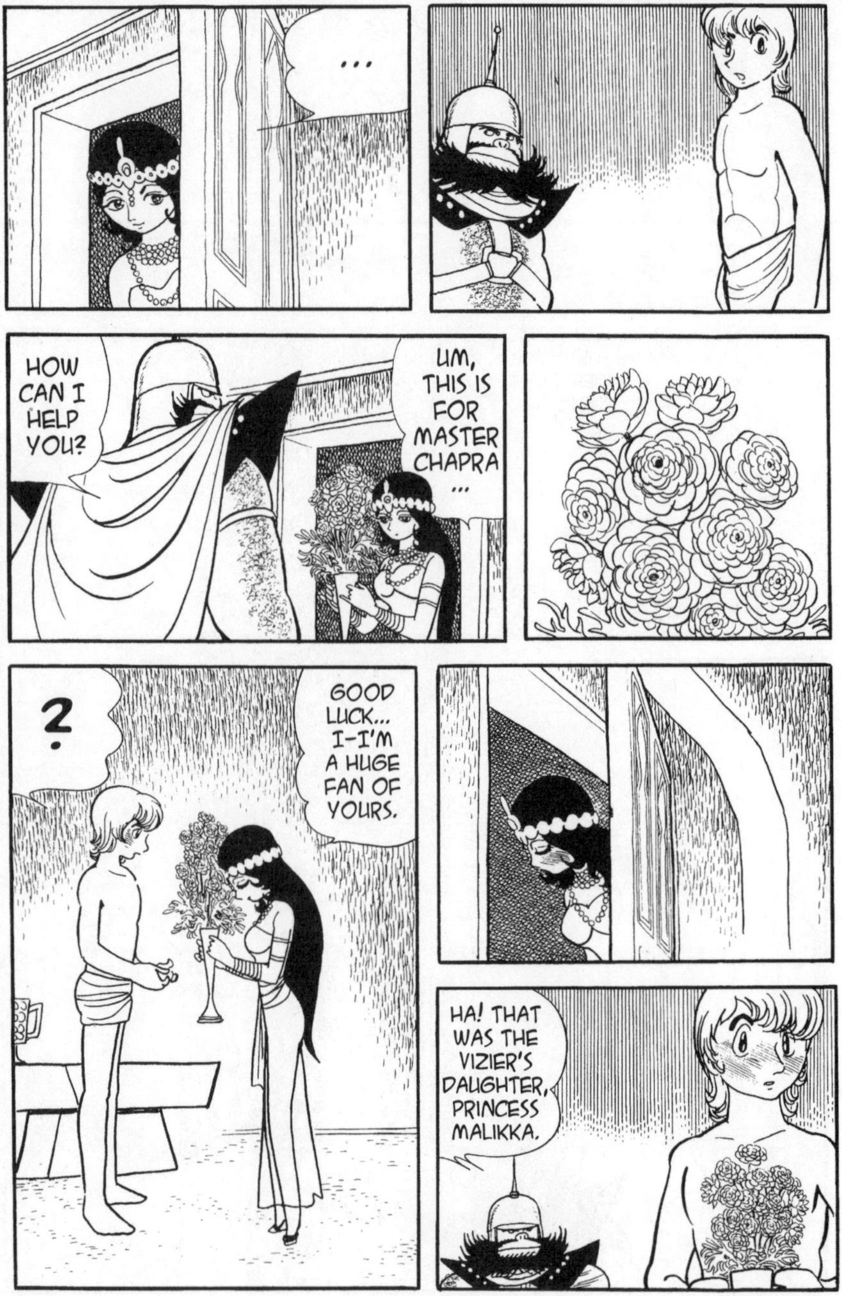
...
HOW CAN I HELP YOU?
UM, THIS IS FOR MASTER CHAPRA ...
?
GOOD LUCK... I-I'M A HUGE FAN OF YOURS.
HA! THAT WAS THE VIZIER'S DAUGHTER, PRINCESS MALIKKA.

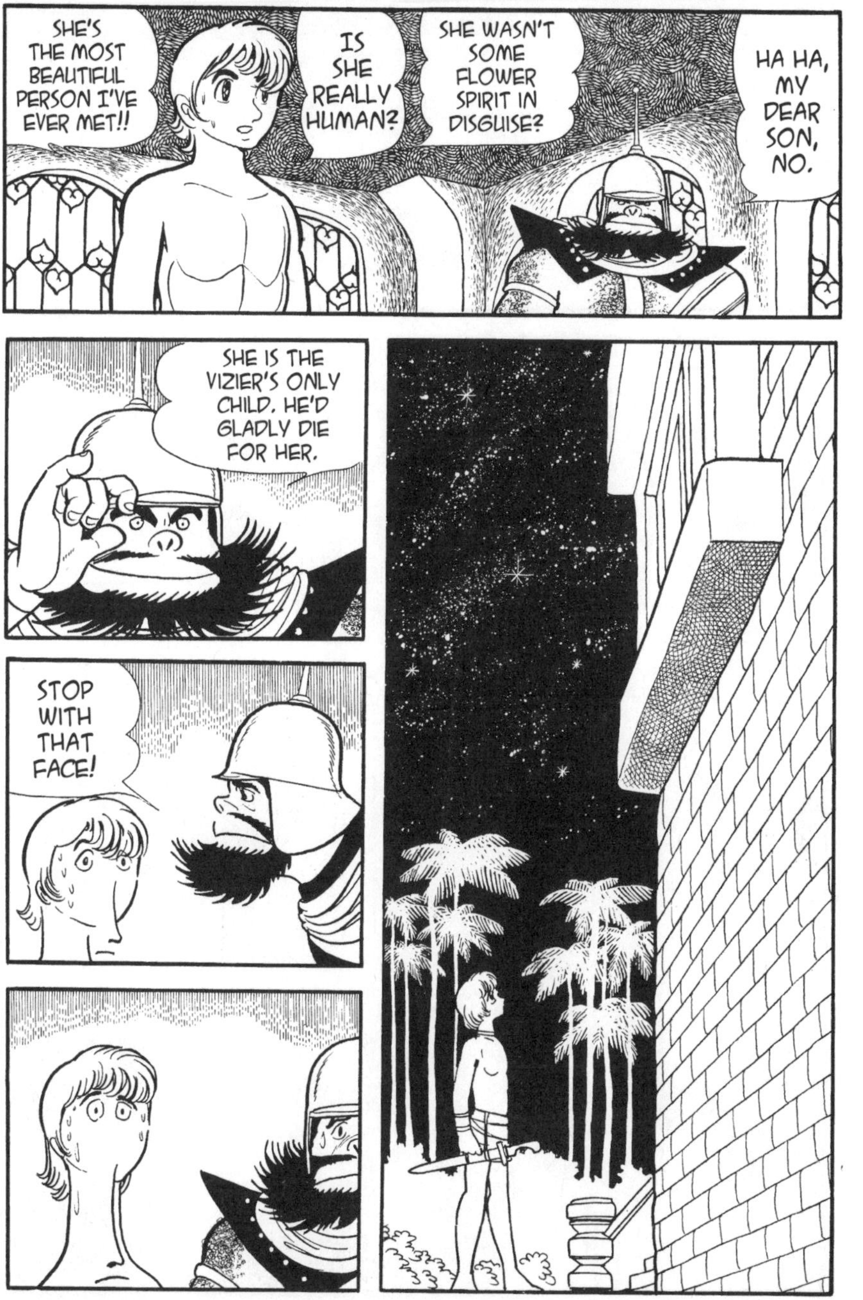
SHE'S THE MOST BEAUTIFUL PERSON I'VE EVER MET!!
IS SHE REALLY HUMAN?
SHE WASN'T SOME FLOWER SPIRIT IN DISGUISE?
HA HA, MY DEAR SON, NO.
SHE IS THE VIZIER'S ONLY CHILD. HE'D GLADLY DIE FOR HER.
STOP WITH THAT FACE!

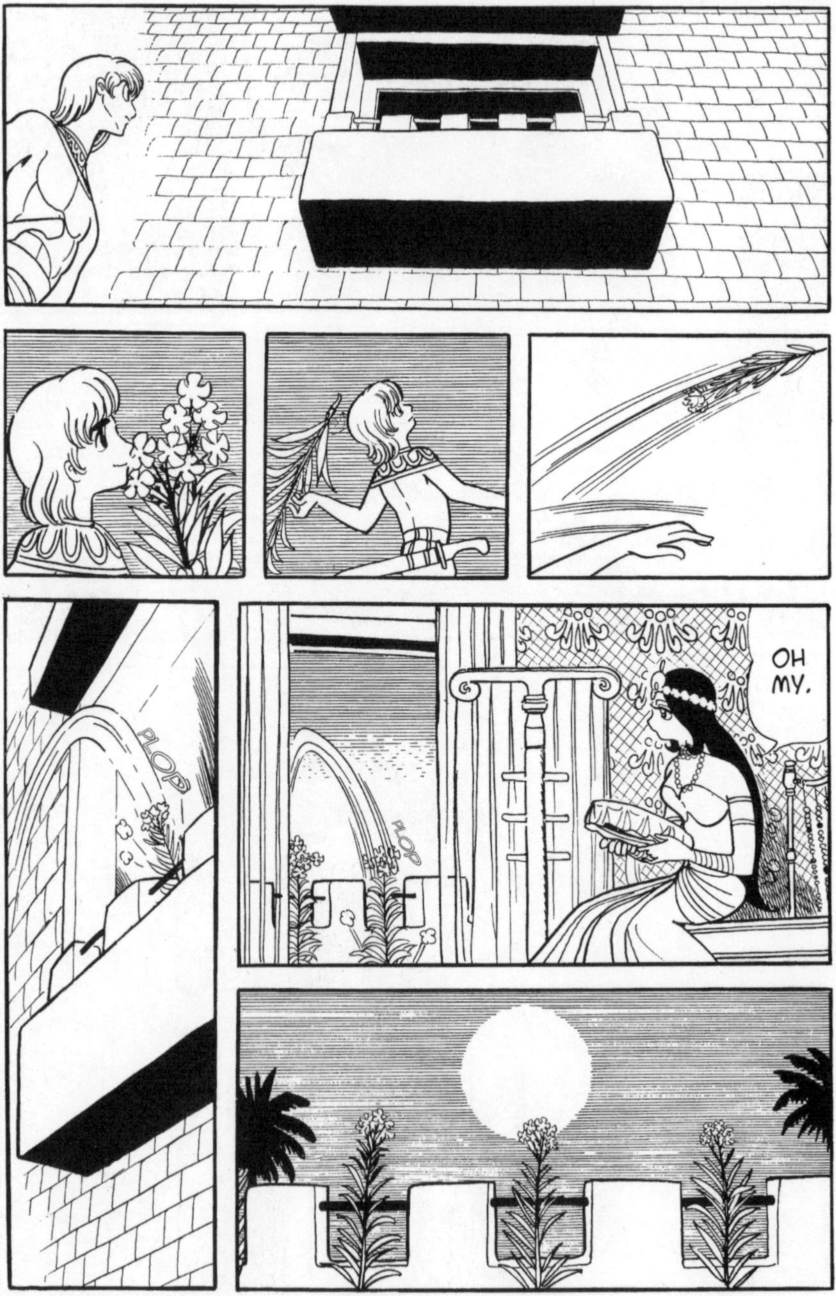
PLOP
PLOP
OH MY.

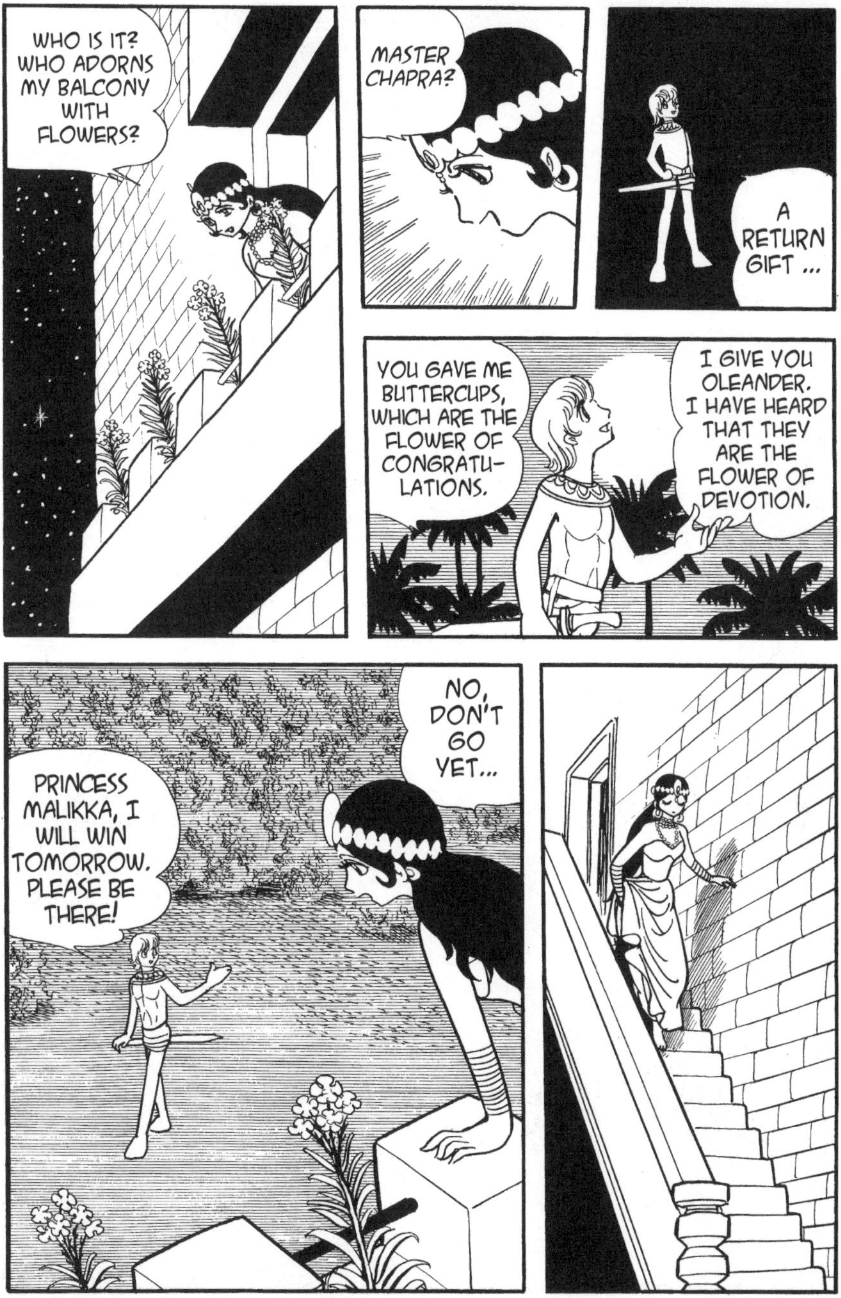
WHO IS IT? WHO ADORNS MY BALCONY WITH FLOWERS?
MASTER CHAPRA?
A RETURN GIFT ...
YOU GAVE ME BUTTERCUPS, WHICH ARE THE FLOWER OF CONGRATU-LATIONS.
I GIVE YOU OLEANDER. I HAVE HEARD THAT THEY ARE THE FLOWER OF DEVOTION.
PRINCESS MALIKKA, I WILL WIN TOMORROW. PLEASE BE THERE!
NO, DON'T GO YET...

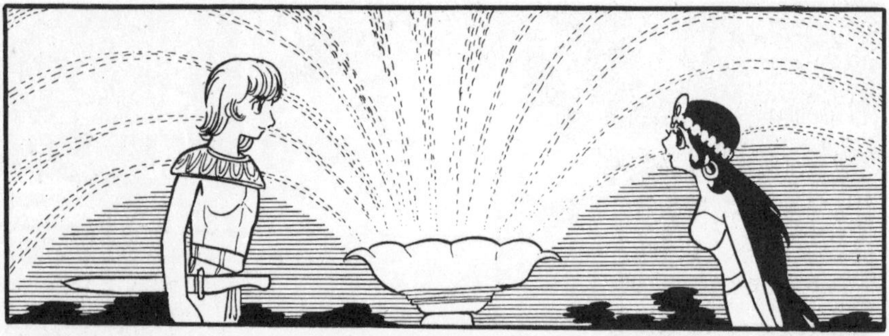
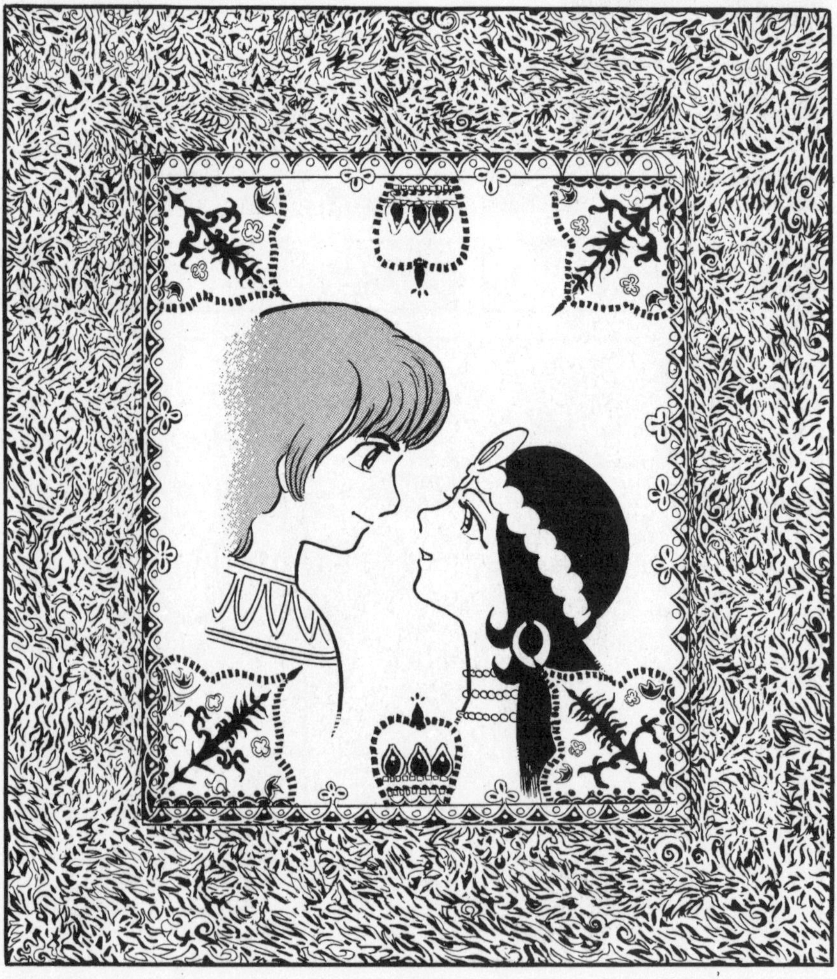

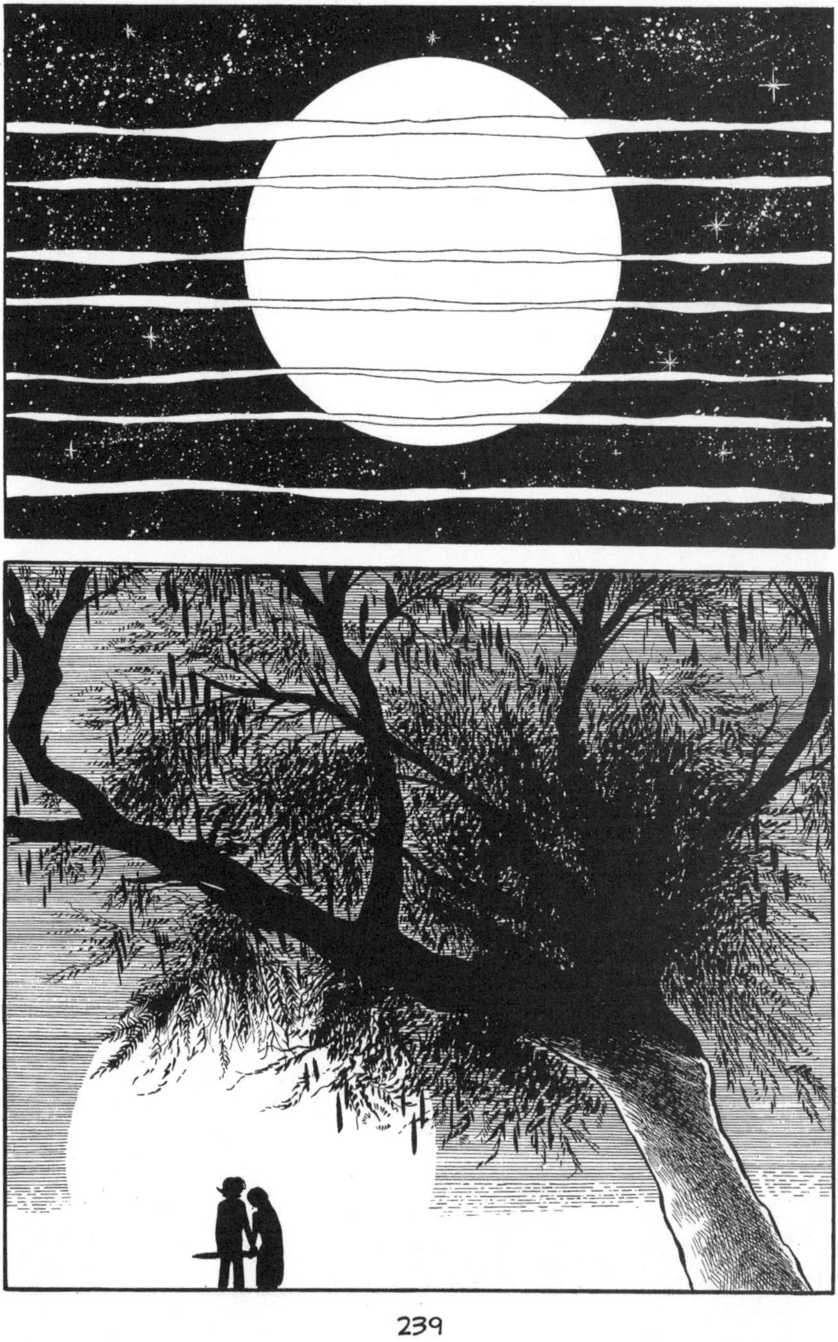

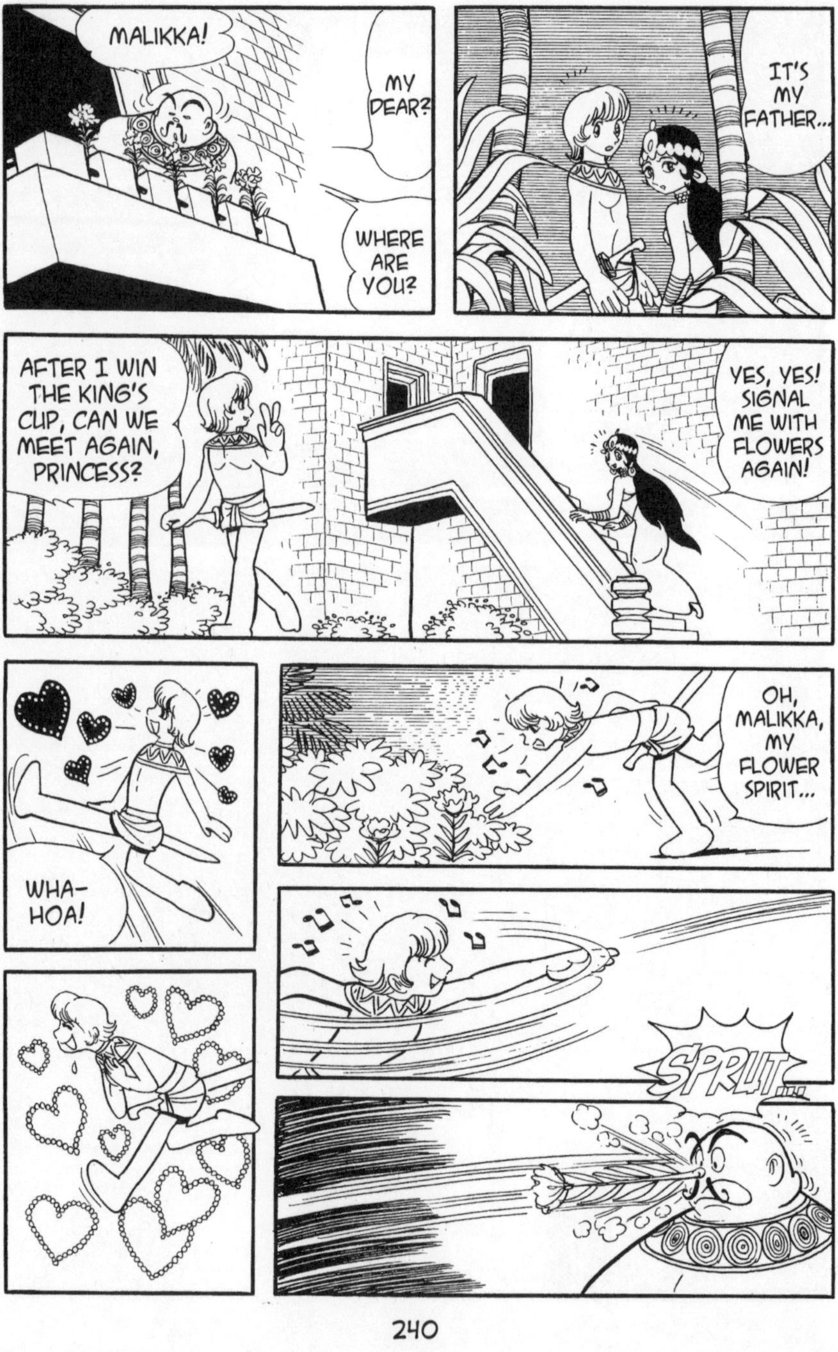
MALIKKA!
MY DEAR?
WHERE ARE YOU?
IT'S MY FATHER...
AFTER I WIN THE KING'S CUP, CAN WE MEET AGAIN, PRINCESS?
YES, YES! SIGNAL ME WITH FLOWERS AGAIN!
WHA-HOA!
OH, MALIKKA, MY FLOWER SPIRIT...
SPRUT...

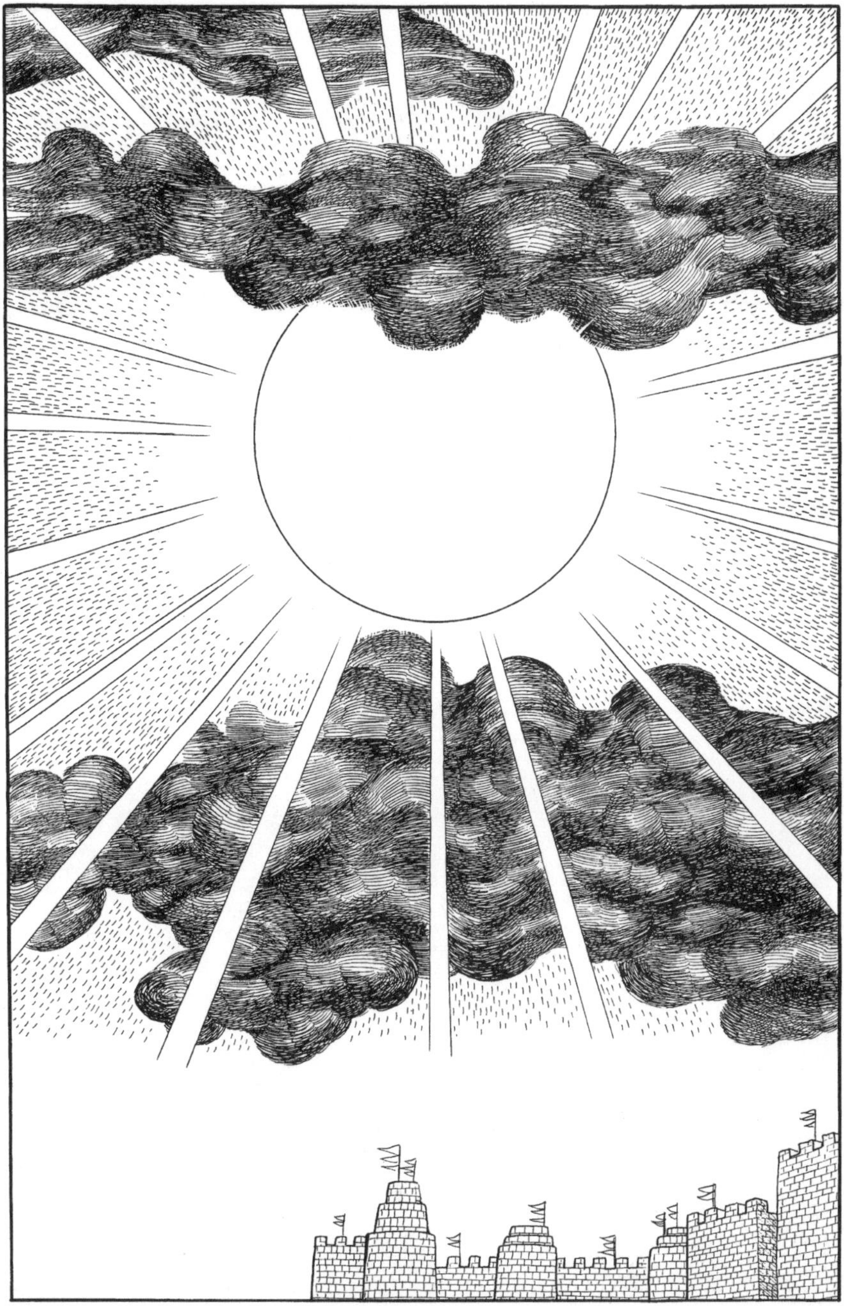

GONG DONG
ARGH
ARGH
ROAR
ROAR
ROAR
ROAR
ZIM
ZIM
ROAR
ROAR
ROAR
ROAR
VINDIKA HAS WON THE TEST OF STRENGTH.

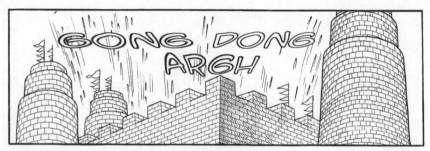

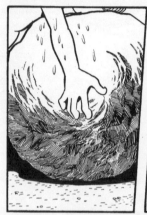

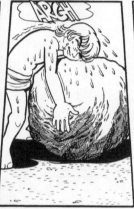

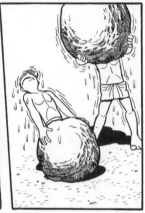

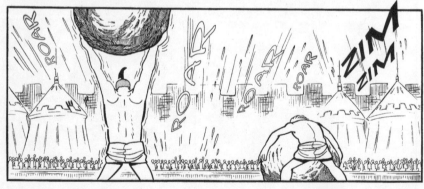

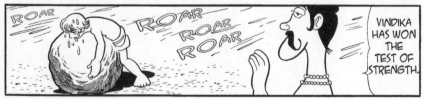

NO!! I'VE GOT TO WIN!!

THE LAST ROUND IS WRESTLING. CONTESTANTS, ENTER THE RING.

COME ON, CHAPRA!

GO CHAPRA!

ROAR ROAR

GO VINDKA!

NOW

HUP

HANG IN THERE, CHAPRA!!

THE KING'S CUP IS WITHIN REACH!

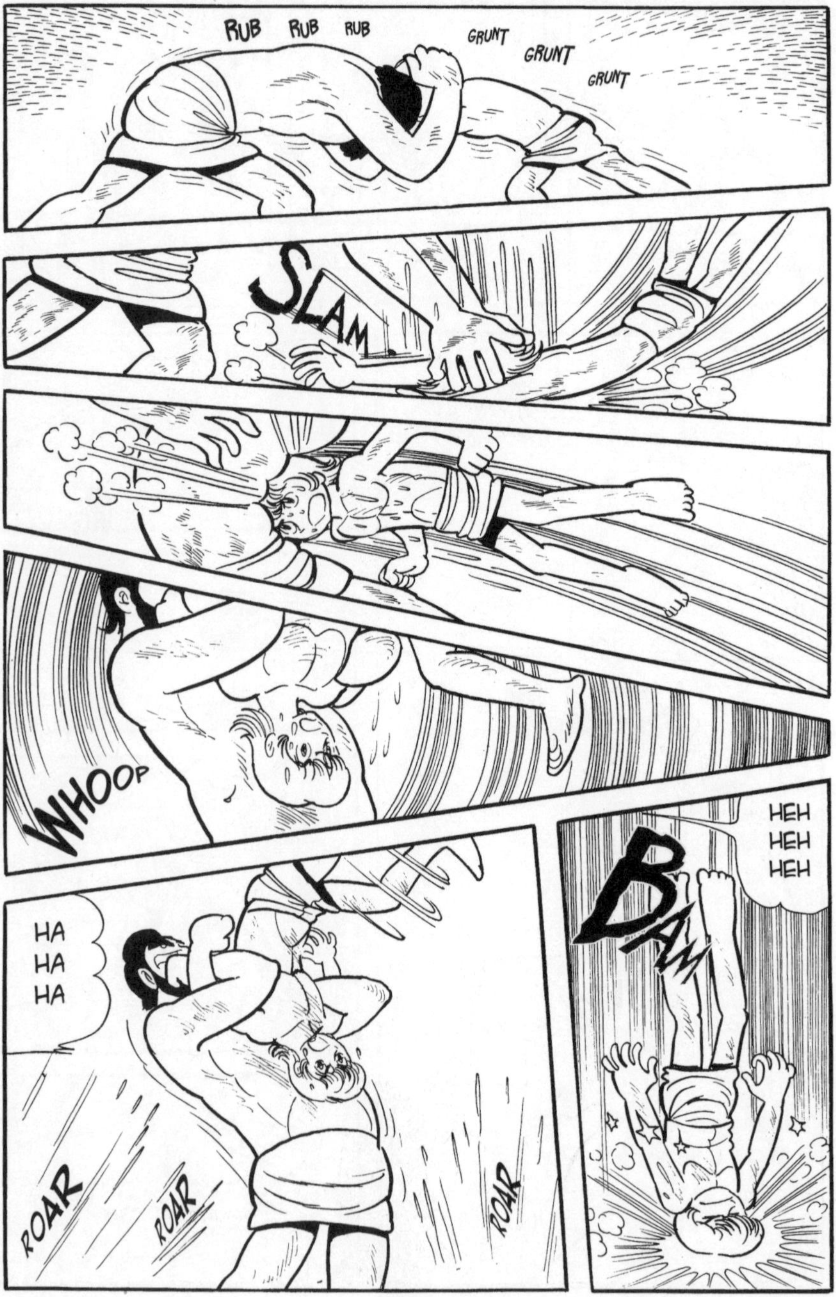
RUB RUB RUB
GRUNT GRUNT GRUNT
SLAM
WHOOP
HA
HA
HA
ROAR ROAR ROAR
BAM
HEH
HEH
HEH

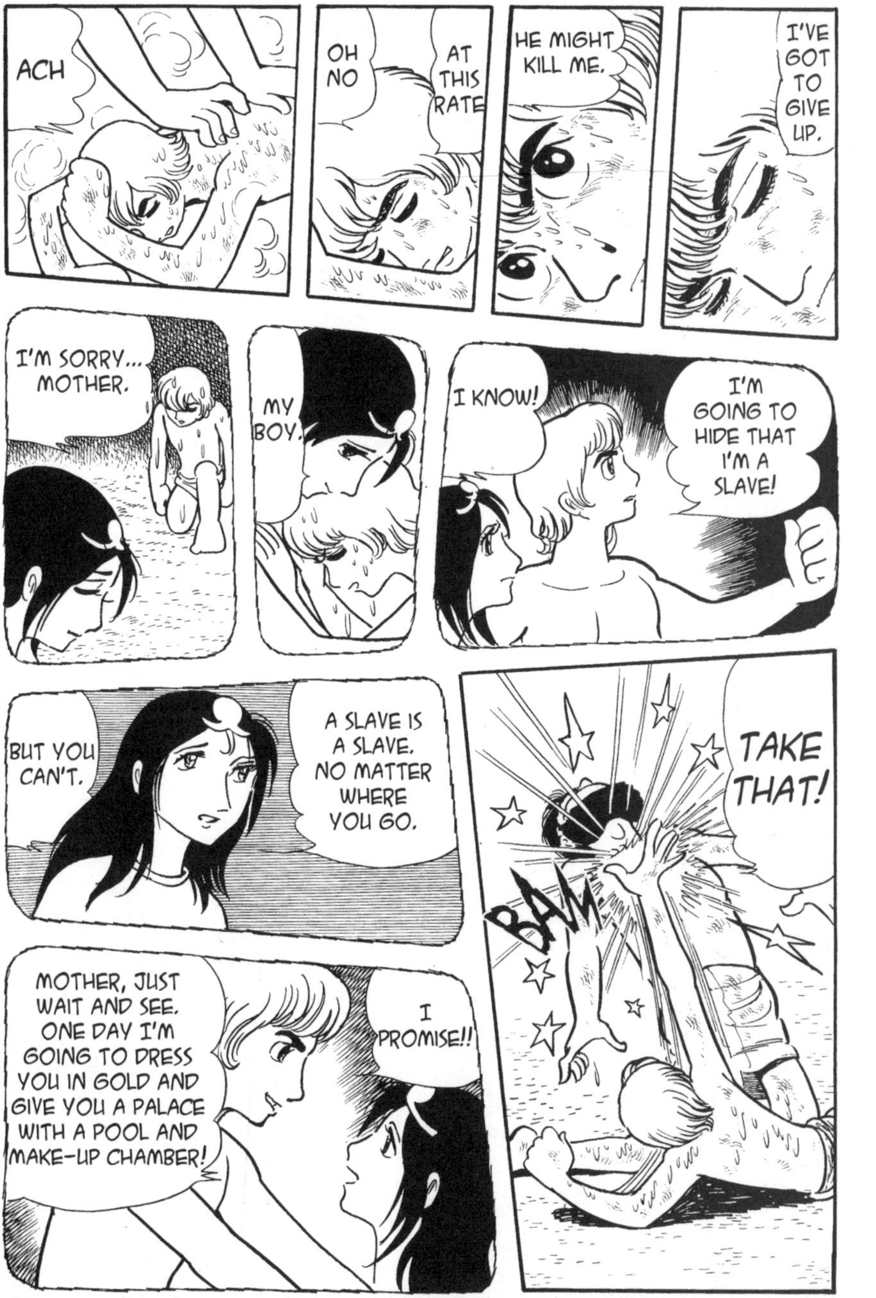
ACH
OH NO
AT THIS RATE
HE MIGHT KILL ME.
I'VE GOT TO GIVE UP.
I'M SORRY... MOTHER.
MY BOY.
I KNOW!
I'M GOING TO HIDE THAT I'M A SLAVE!
BUT YOU CAN'T.
A SLAVE IS A SLAVE. NO MATTER WHERE YOU GO.
MOTHER, JUST WAIT AND SEE. ONE DAY I'M GOING TO DRESS YOU IN GOLD AND GIVE YOU A PALACE WITH A POOL AND MAKE-UP CHAMBER!
I PROMISE!!
TAKE THAT!
BAM

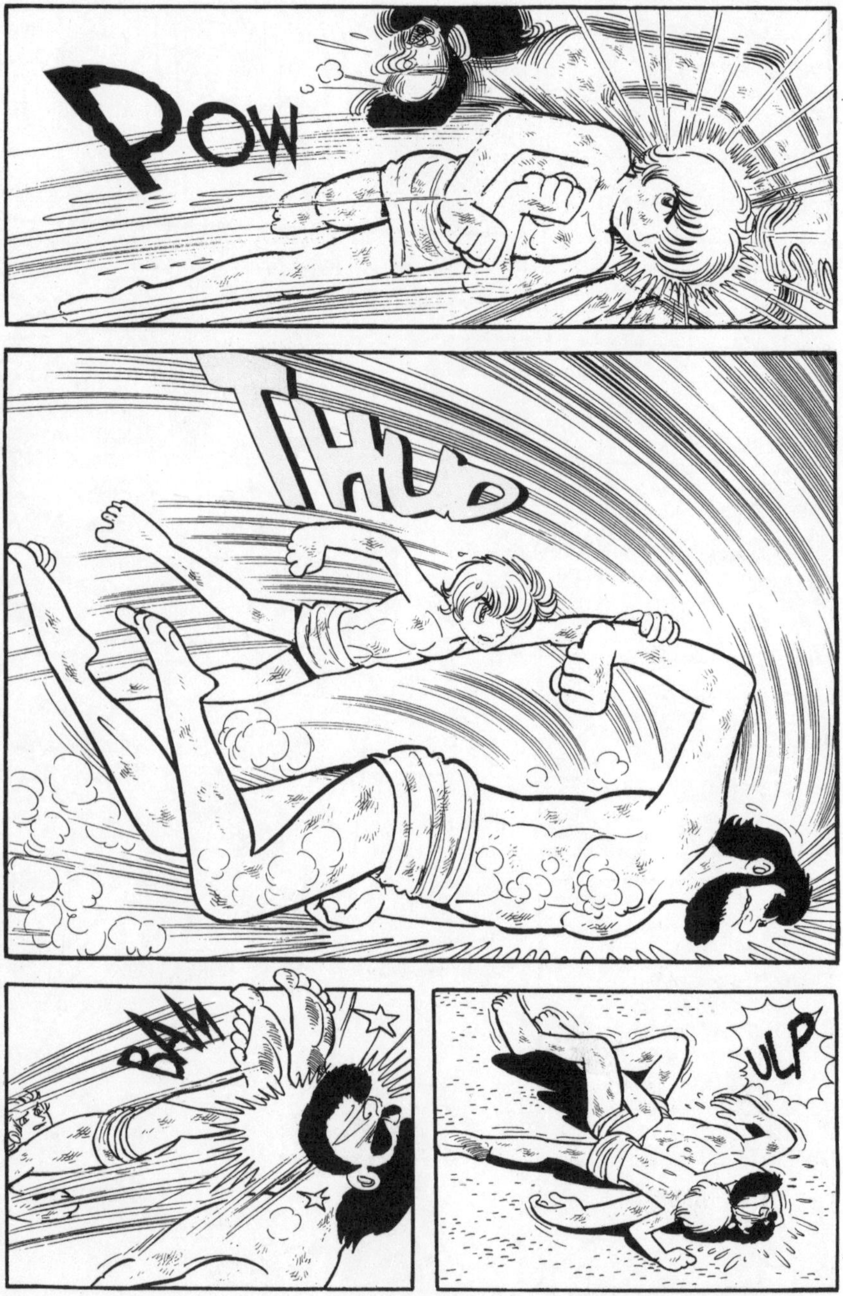
POW
THUD
BAM
ULP

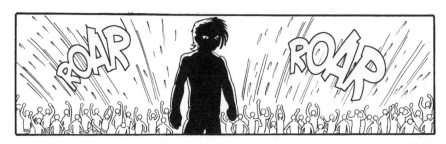

ROAR
ROAR
CHAPRA!
YOU DID IT, MY SON! WHAT A COMEBACK!
VINDIKA: 2 POINTS. CHAPRA: 3 POINTS.
THE WINNER IS CHAPRA.
RIGHT THIS WAY...
MASTER CHAPRA, SON OF BUDAI, WE BESTOW UPON YOU THE TITLE OF CHAMPION IN RECOGNITION OF YOUR SKILL AND VALOR, SECOND TO NONE IN ALL OF KOSALA. ACCEPT THIS CUP FROM THE KING.

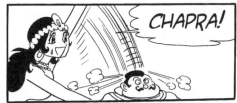

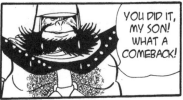

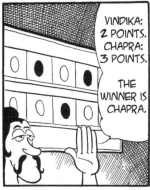

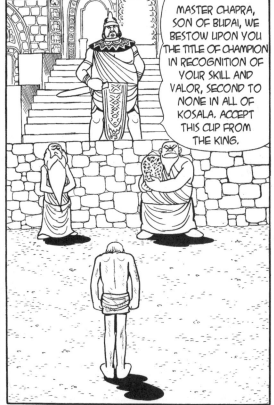

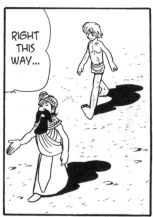

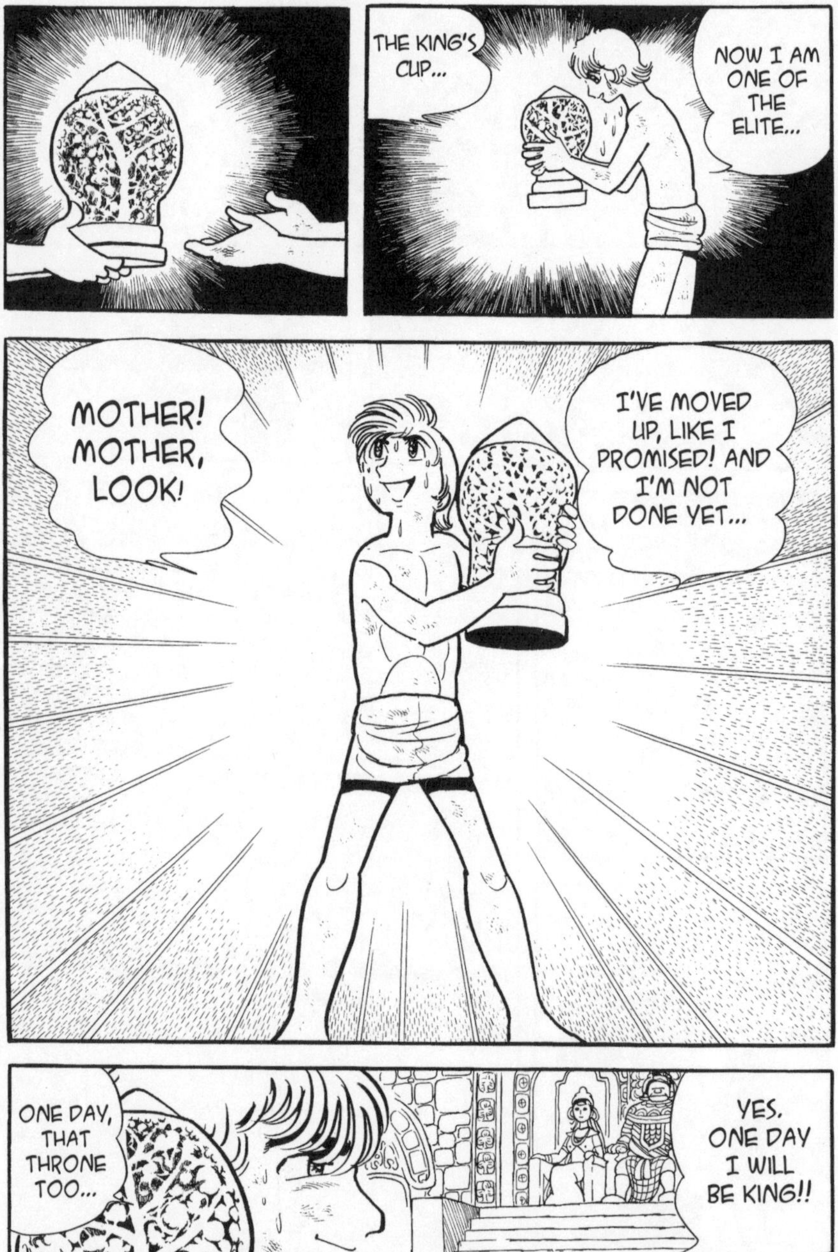
THE KING'S CUP...
NOW I AM ONE OF THE ELITE...
MOTHER! MOTHER, LOOK!
I'VE MOVED UP, LIKE I PROMISED! AND I'M NOT DONE YET...
ONE DAY, THAT THRONE TOO...
YES. ONE DAY I WILL BE KING!!

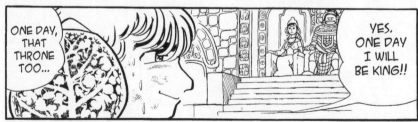

CHAPTER SEVEN

THE BIRTH

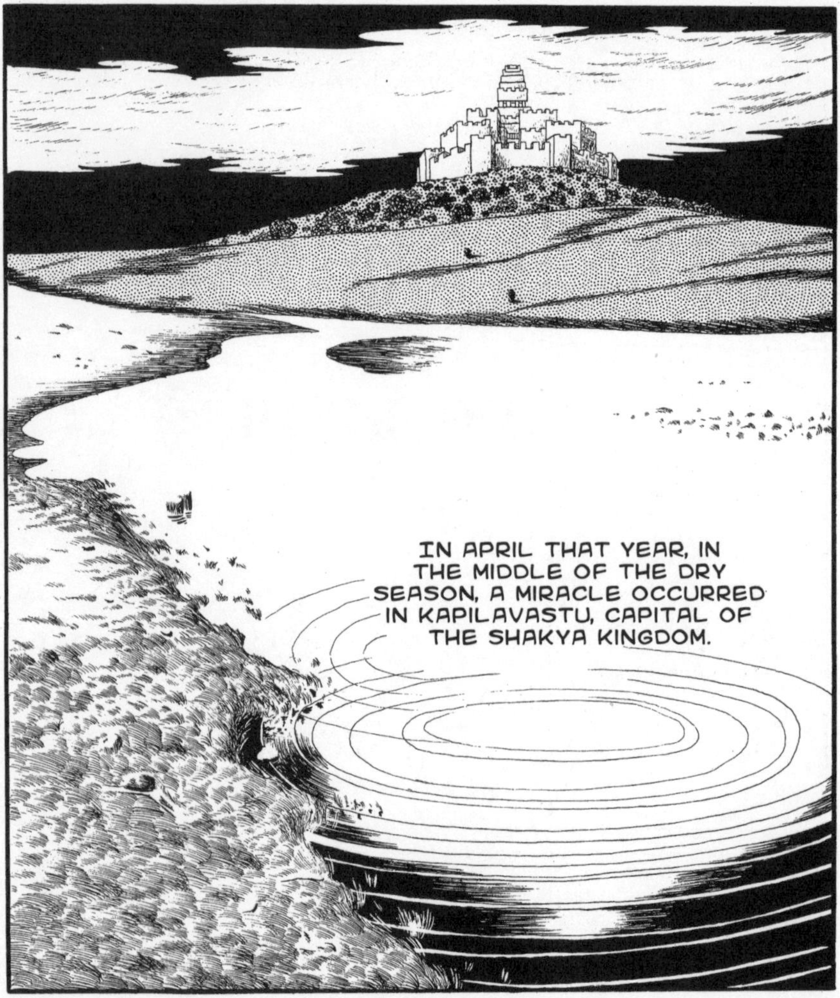
IN APRIL THAT YEAR, IN THE MIDDLE OF THE DRY SEASON, A MIRACLE OCCURRED IN KAPILAVASTU, CAPITAL OF THE SHAKYA KINGDOM.

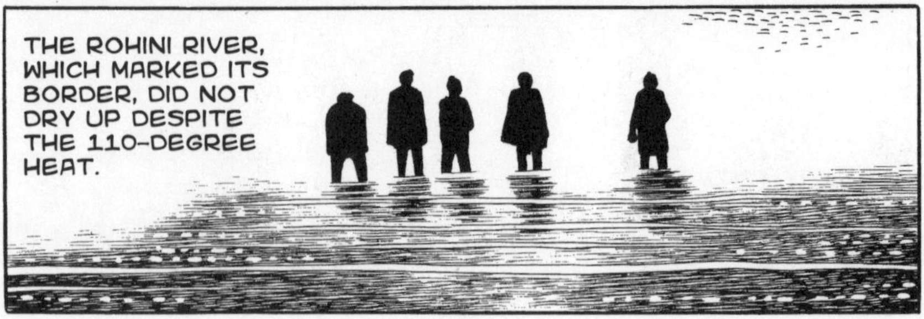
THE ROHINI RIVER, WHICH MARKED ITS BORDER, DID NOT DRY UP DESPITE THE 110-DEGREE HEAT.

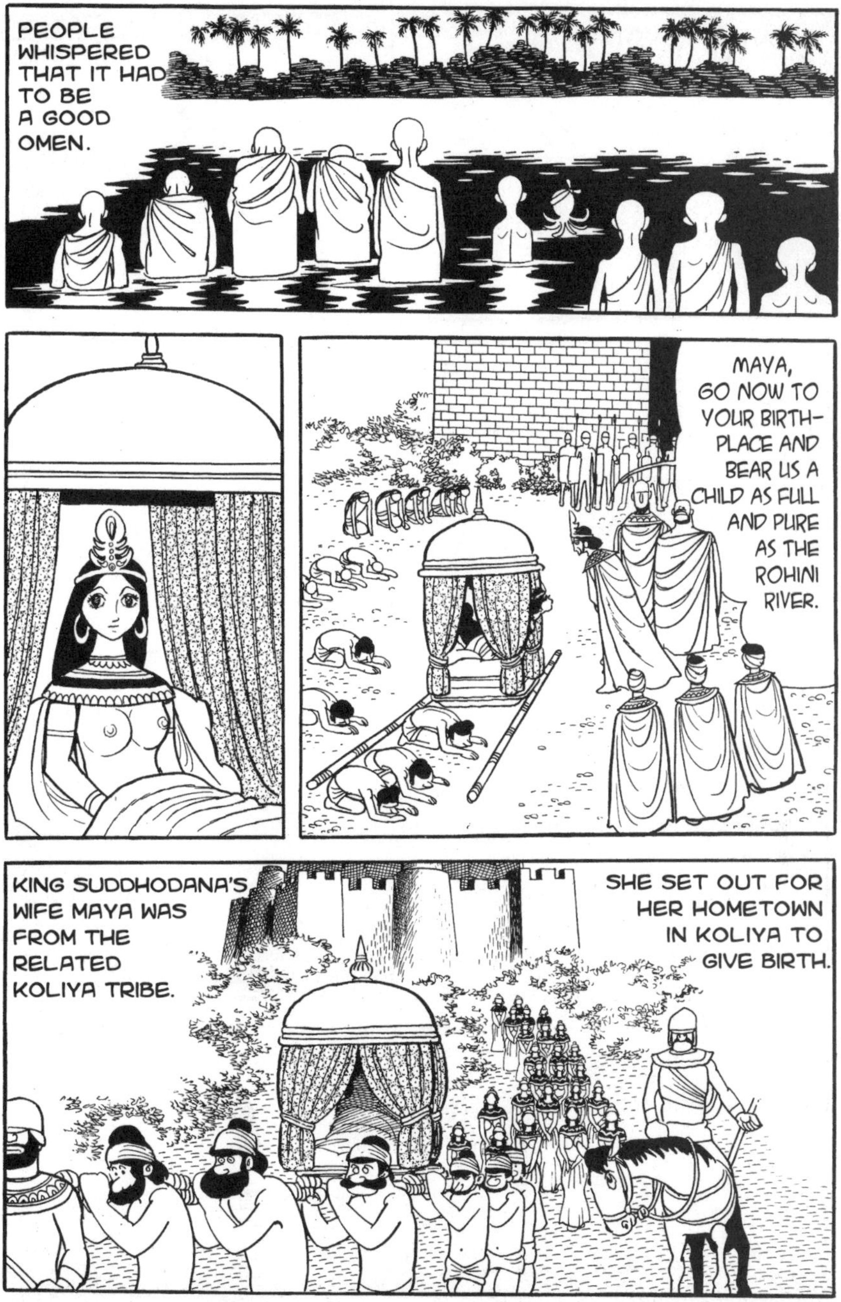

PEOPLE WHISPERED THAT IT HAD TO BE A GOOD OMEN.
MAYA, GO NOW TO YOUR BIRTH-PLACE AND BEAR US A CHILD AS FULL AND PURE AS THE ROHINI RIVER.
KING SUDDHODANA'S WIFE MAYA WAS FROM THE RELATED KOLIYA TRIBE.
SHE SET OUT FOR HER HOMETOWN IN KOLIYA TO GIVE BIRTH.

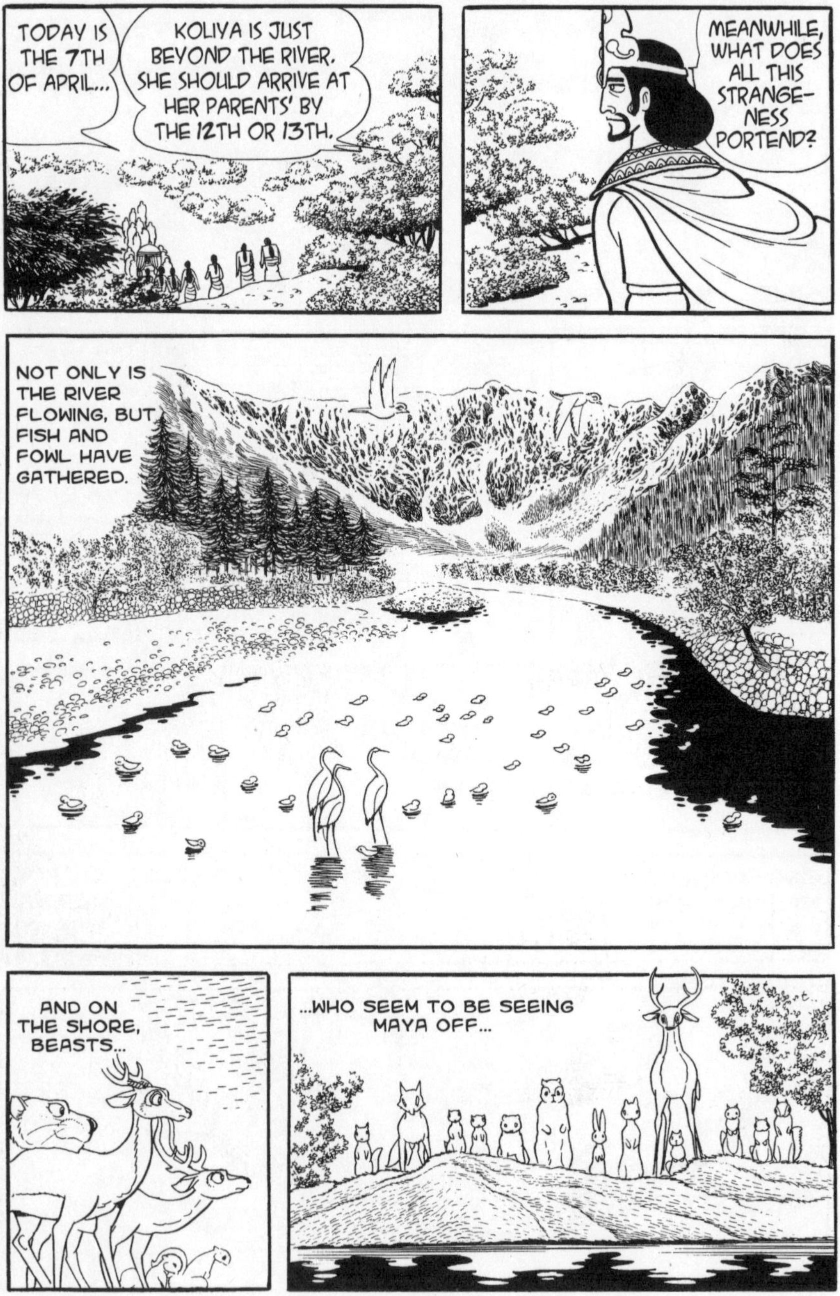
TODAY IS THE 7TH OF APRIL...
KOLIYA IS JUST BEYOND THE RIVER. SHE SHOULD ARRIVE AT HER PARENTS' BY THE 12TH OR 13TH.
MEANWHILE, WHAT DOES ALL THIS STRANGE-NESS PORTEND?
NOT ONLY IS THE RIVER FLOWING, BUT FISH AND FOWL HAVE GATHERED.
AND ON THE SHORE, BEASTS...
...WHO SEEM TO BE SEEING MAYA OFF...

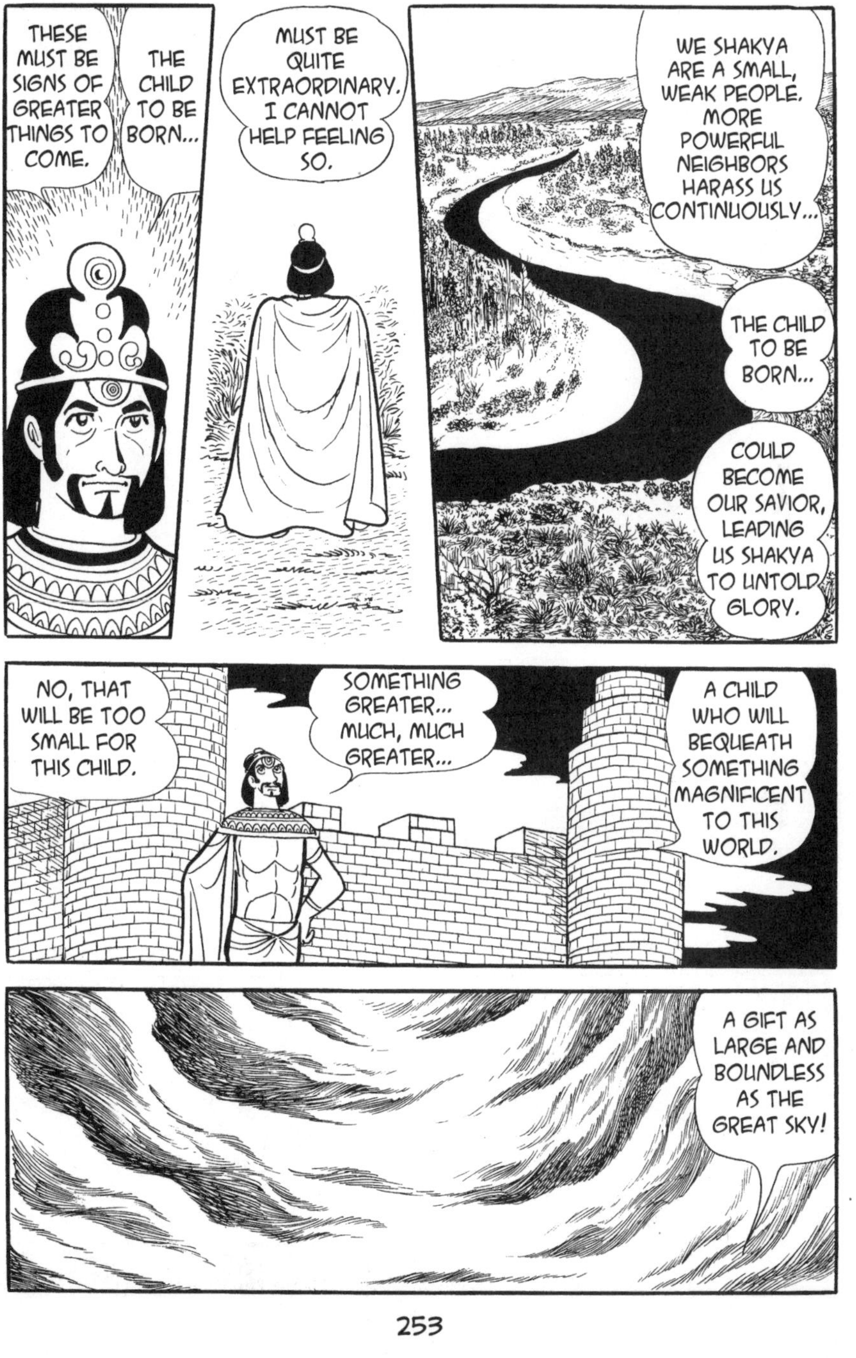
THESE MUST BE SIGNS OF GREATER THINGS TO COME.
THE CHILD TO BE BORN...
MUST BE QUITE EXTRAORDINARY. I CANNOT HELP FEELING SO.
WE SHAKYA ARE A SMALL, WEAK PEOPLE. MORE POWERFUL NEIGHBORS HARASS US CONTINUOUSLY...
THE CHILD TO BE BORN...
COULD BECOME OUR SAVIOR, LEADING US SHAKYA TO UNTOLD GLORY.
NO, THAT WILL BE TOO SMALL FOR THIS CHILD.
SOMETHING GREATER... MUCH, MUCH GREATER...
A CHILD WHO WILL BEQUEATH SOMETHING MAGNIFICENT TO THIS WORLD.
A GIFT AS LARGE AND BOUNDLESS AS THE GREAT SKY!

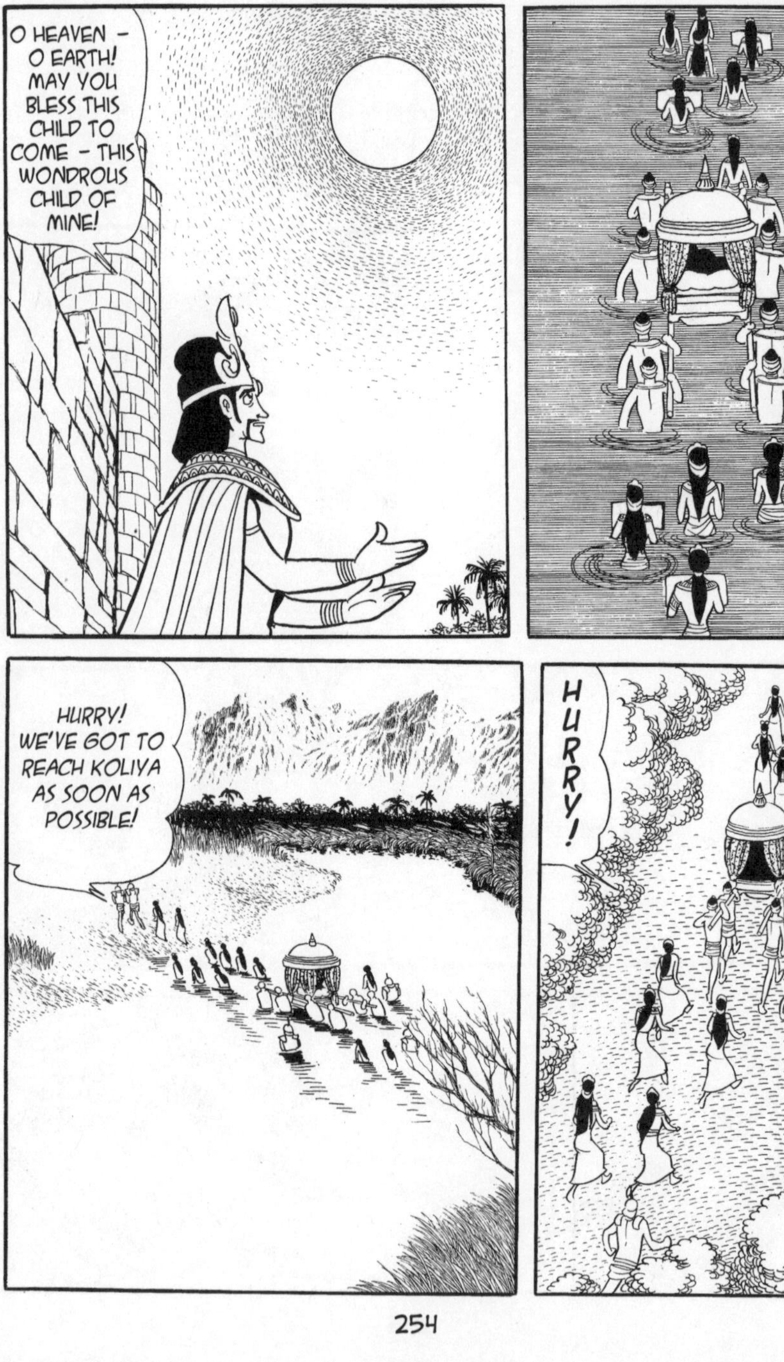
O HEAVEN - O EARTH! MAY YOU BLESS THIS CHILD TO COME - THIS WONDROUS CHILD OF MINE!
HURRY! WE'VE GOT TO REACH KOLIYA AS SOON AS POSSIBLE!
HURRY!

OH...
UH...
AHHH...

MY LADY!

SHE IS HAVING CONTRACTIONS!

WHAT? BUT WE'VE ONLY JUST CROSSED THE RIVER!

WE'RE NOT THERE YET?

WE ARE NOT TOO FAR, MY LADY.

OH! OOO, OH...

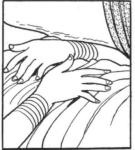

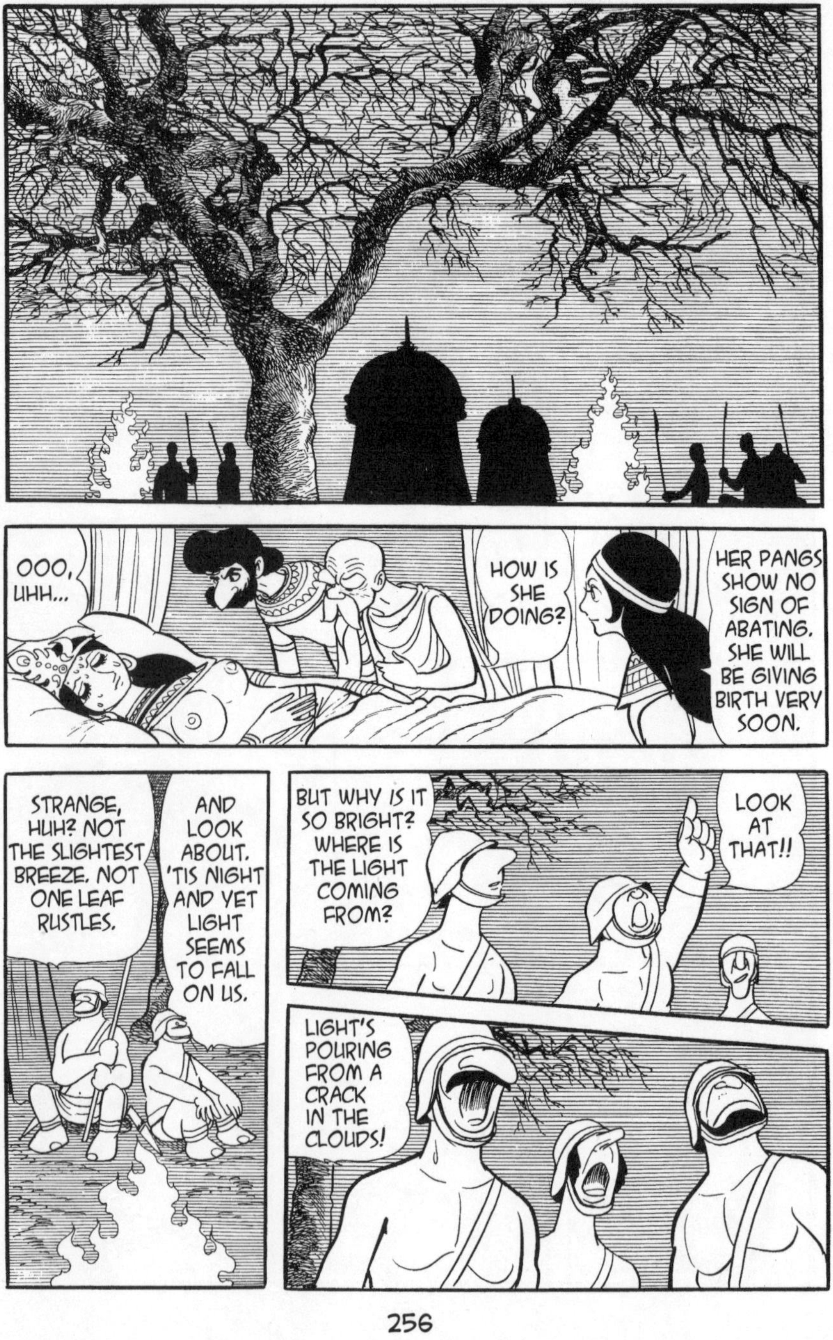
OOO, UHH...
HOW IS SHE DOING?
HER PANGS SHOW NO SIGN OF ABATING. SHE WILL BE GIVING BIRTH VERY SOON.
STRANGE, HUH? NOT THE SLIGHTEST BREEZE. NOT ONE LEAF RUSTLES.
AND LOOK ABOUT. 'TIS NIGHT AND YET LIGHT SEEMS TO FALL ON US.
BUT WHY IS IT SO BRIGHT? WHERE IS THE LIGHT COMING FROM?
LOOK AT THAT!!
LIGHT'S POURING FROM A CRACK IN THE CLOUDS!

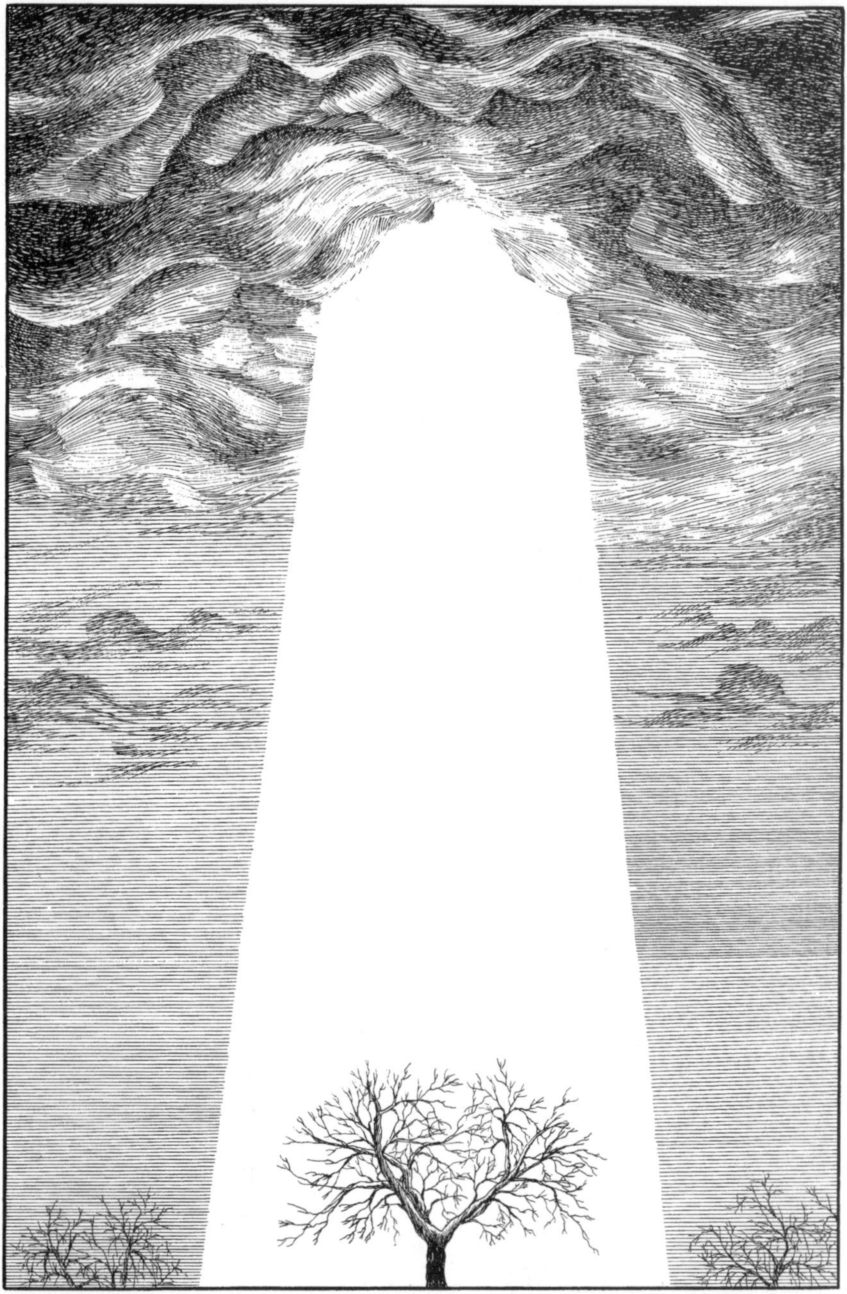

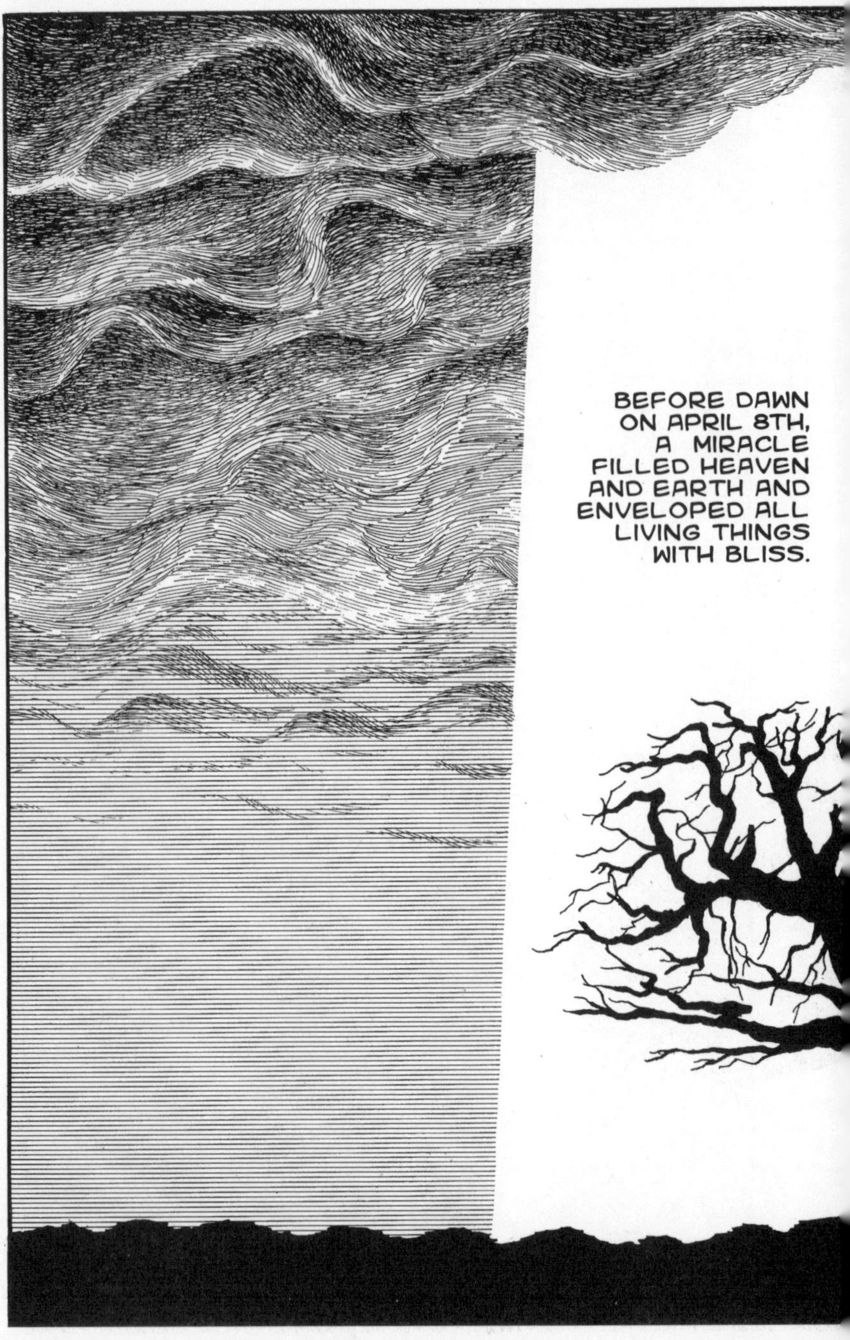
BEFORE DAWN ON APRIL 8TH, A MIRACLE FILLED HEAVEN AND EARTH AND ENVELOPED ALL LIVING THINGS WITH BLISS.

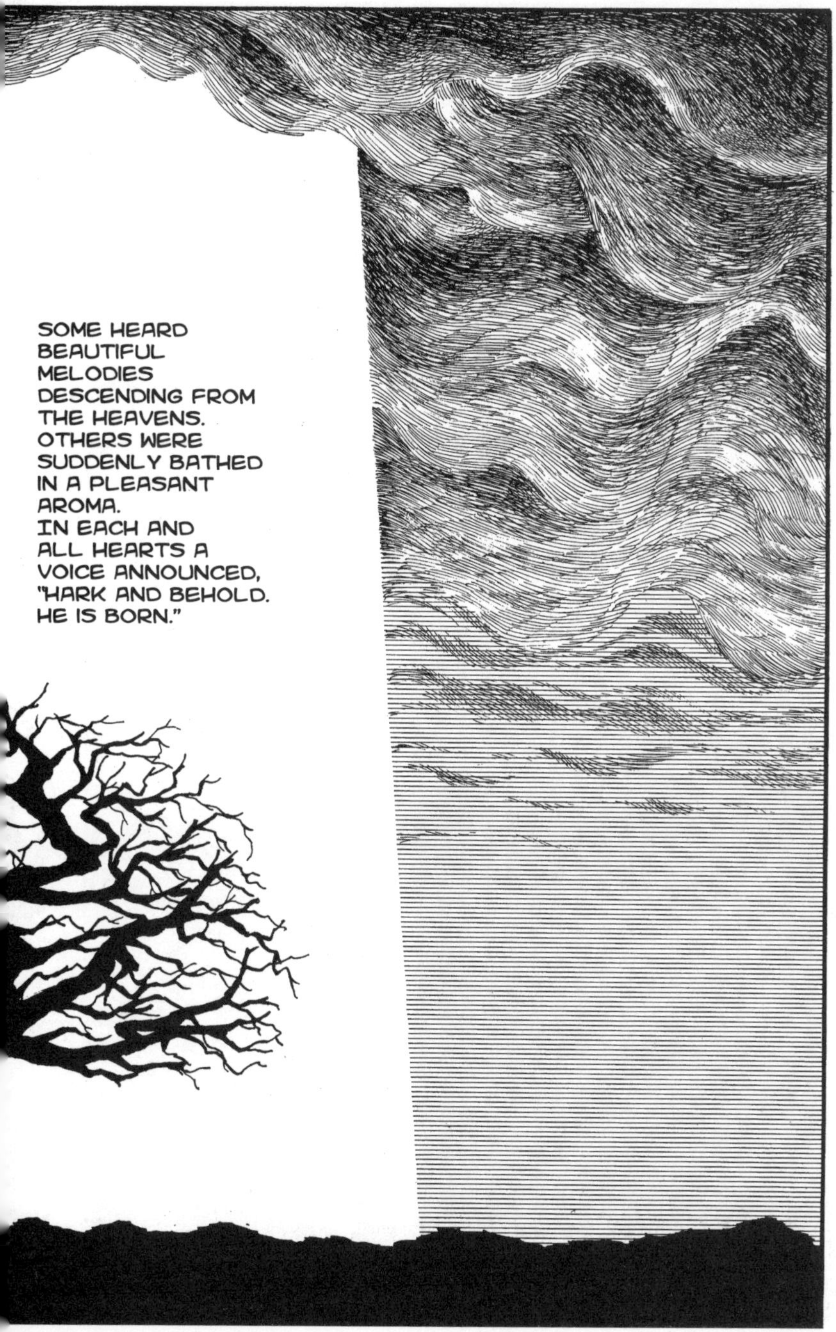
SOME HEARD BEAUTIFUL MELODIES DESCENDING FROM THE HEAVENS. OTHERS WERE SUDDENLY BATHED IN A PLEASANT AROMA. IN EACH AND ALL HEARTS A VOICE ANNOUNCED, "HARK AND BEHOLD. HE IS BORN."

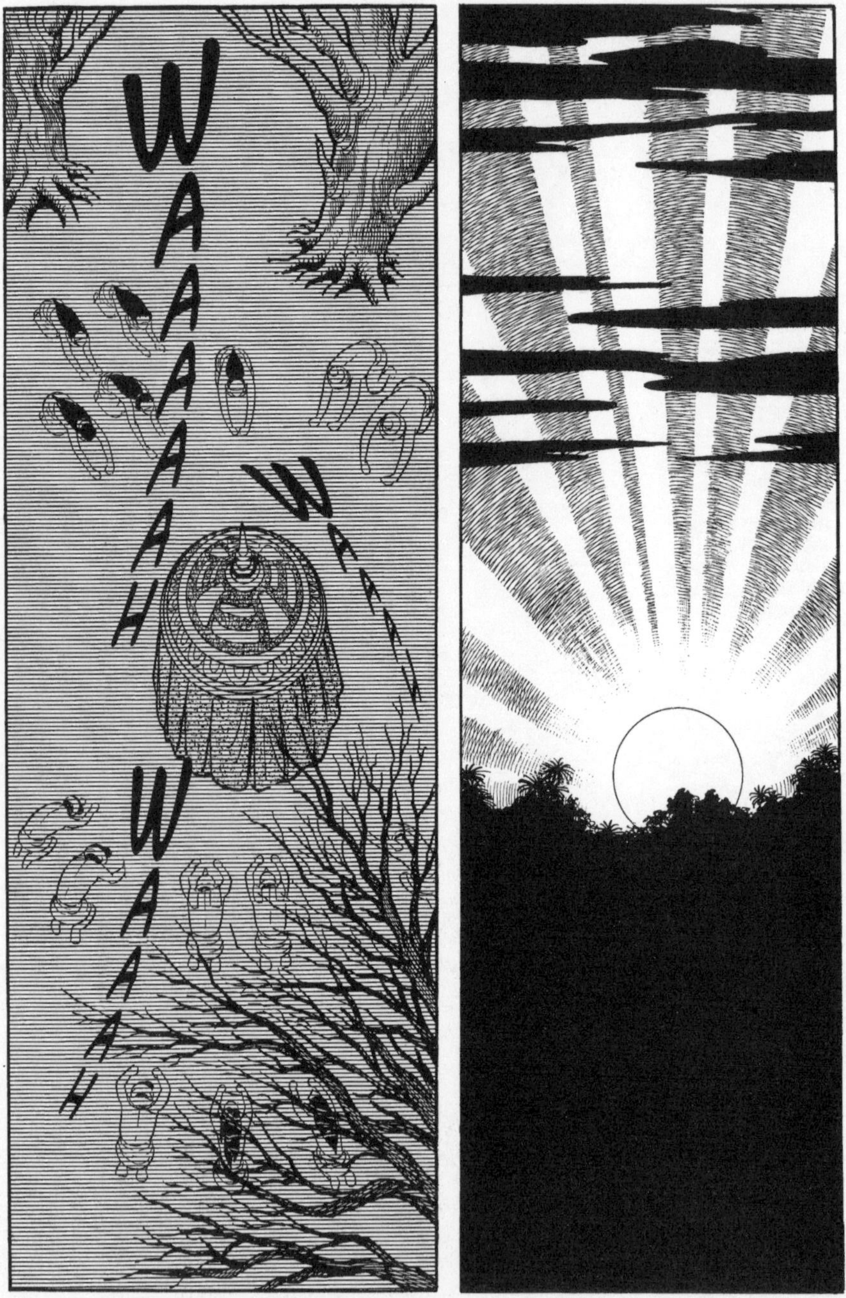
WAAAAAAH
WAAAAAA
WAAAAH

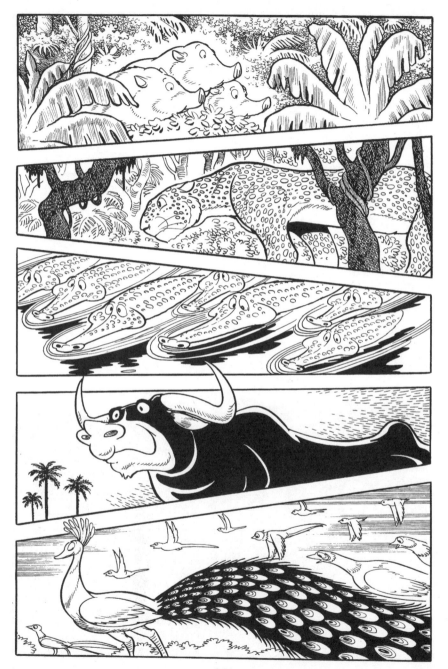

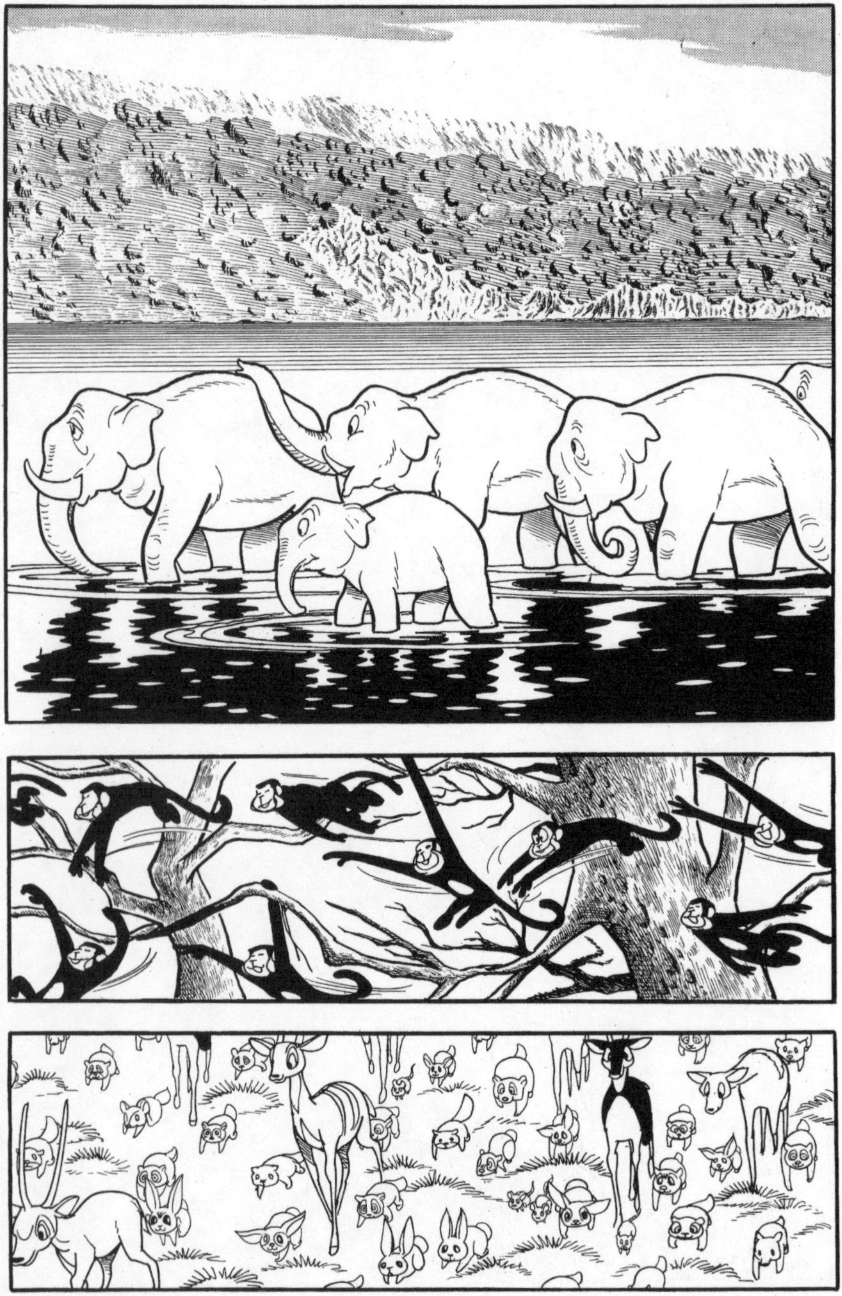

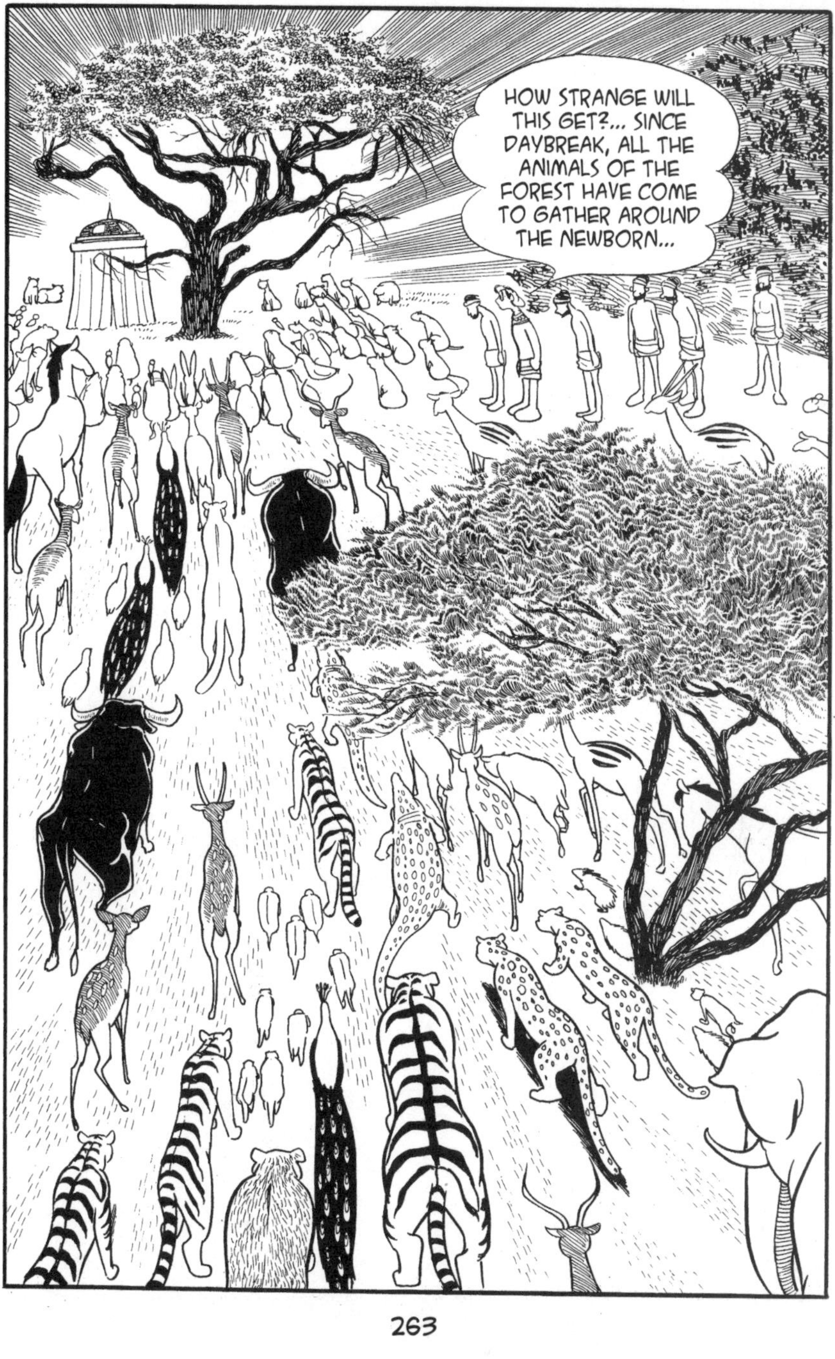
HOW STRANGE WILL THIS GET?... SINCE DAYBREAK, ALL THE ANIMALS OF THE FOREST HAVE COME TO GATHER AROUND THE NEWBORN...

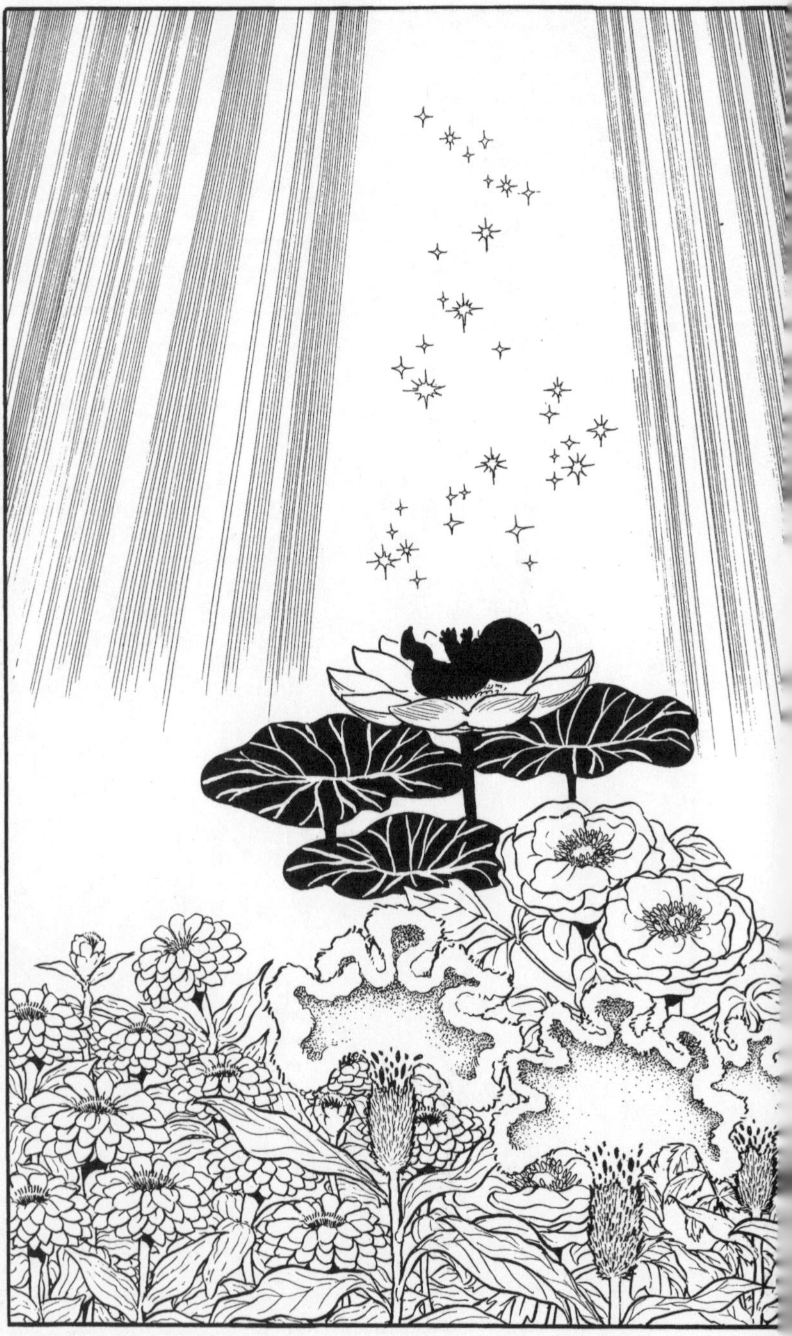

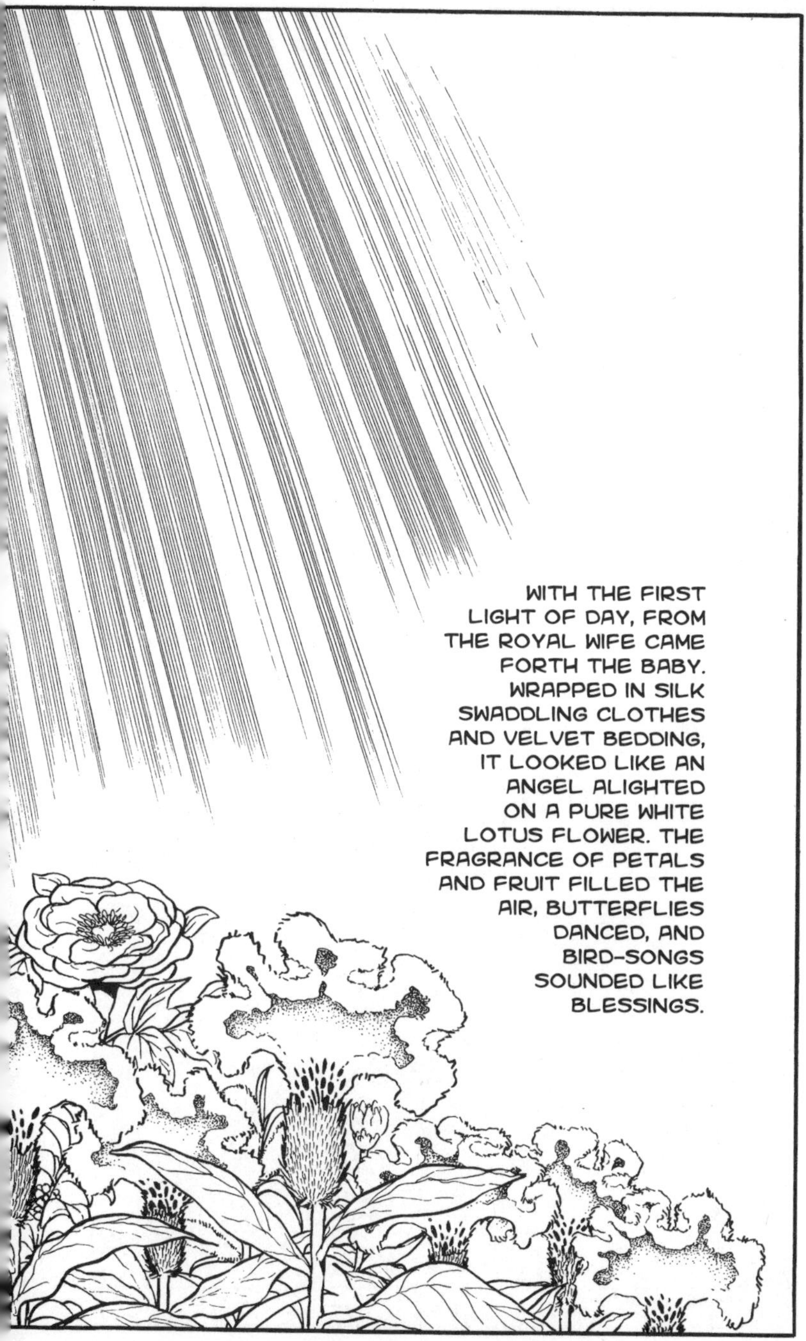
WITH THE FIRST LIGHT OF DAY, FROM THE ROYAL WIFE CAME FORTH THE BABY. WRAPPED IN SILK SWADDLING CLOTHES AND VELVET BEDDING, IT LOOKED LIKE AN ANGEL ALIGHTED ON A PURE WHITE LOTUS FLOWER. THE FRAGRANCE OF PETALS AND FRUIT FILLED THE AIR, BUTTERFLIES DANCED, AND BIRD-SONGS SOUNDED LIKE BLESSINGS.

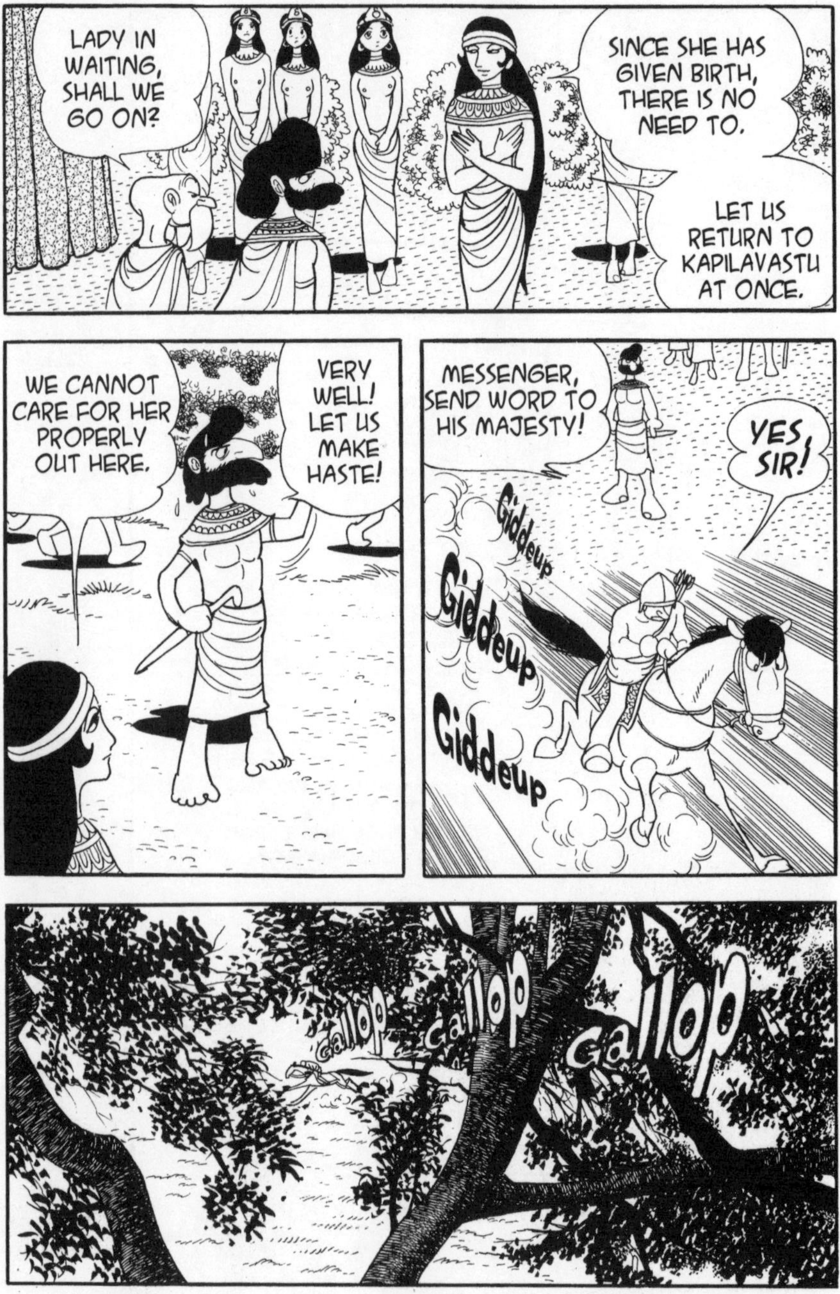
LADY IN WAITING, SHALL WE GO ON?
SINCE SHE HAS GIVEN BIRTH, THERE IS NO NEED TO.
LET US RETURN TO KAPILAVASTU AT ONCE.
WE CANNOT CARE FOR HER PROPERLY OUT HERE.
VERY WELL! LET US MAKE HASTE!
MESSENGER, SEND WORD TO HIS MAJESTY!
YES, SIR!
Giddeup
Giddeup
Giddeup
Giddeup
gallop
gallop
gallop

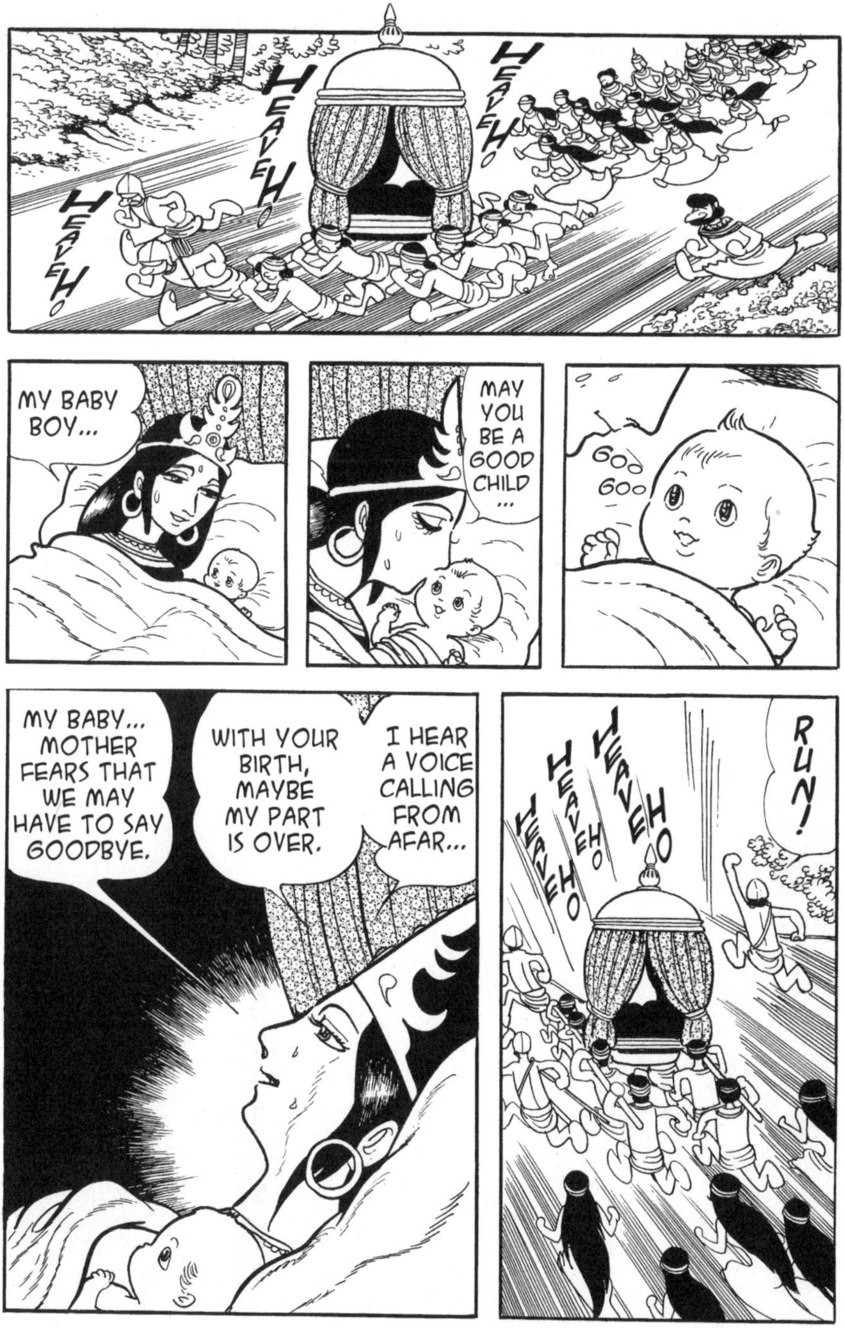
HEAVE HO
HEAVE HO
HEAVE HO
MY BABY BOY...
MAY YOU BE A GOOD CHILD...
GOO GOO
MY BABY... MOTHER FEARS THAT WE MAY HAVE TO SAY GOODBYE.
WITH YOUR BIRTH, MAYBE MY PART IS OVER.
I HEAR A VOICE CALLING FROM AFAR...
RUN!
HEAVE HO
HEAVE HO
HEAVE HO

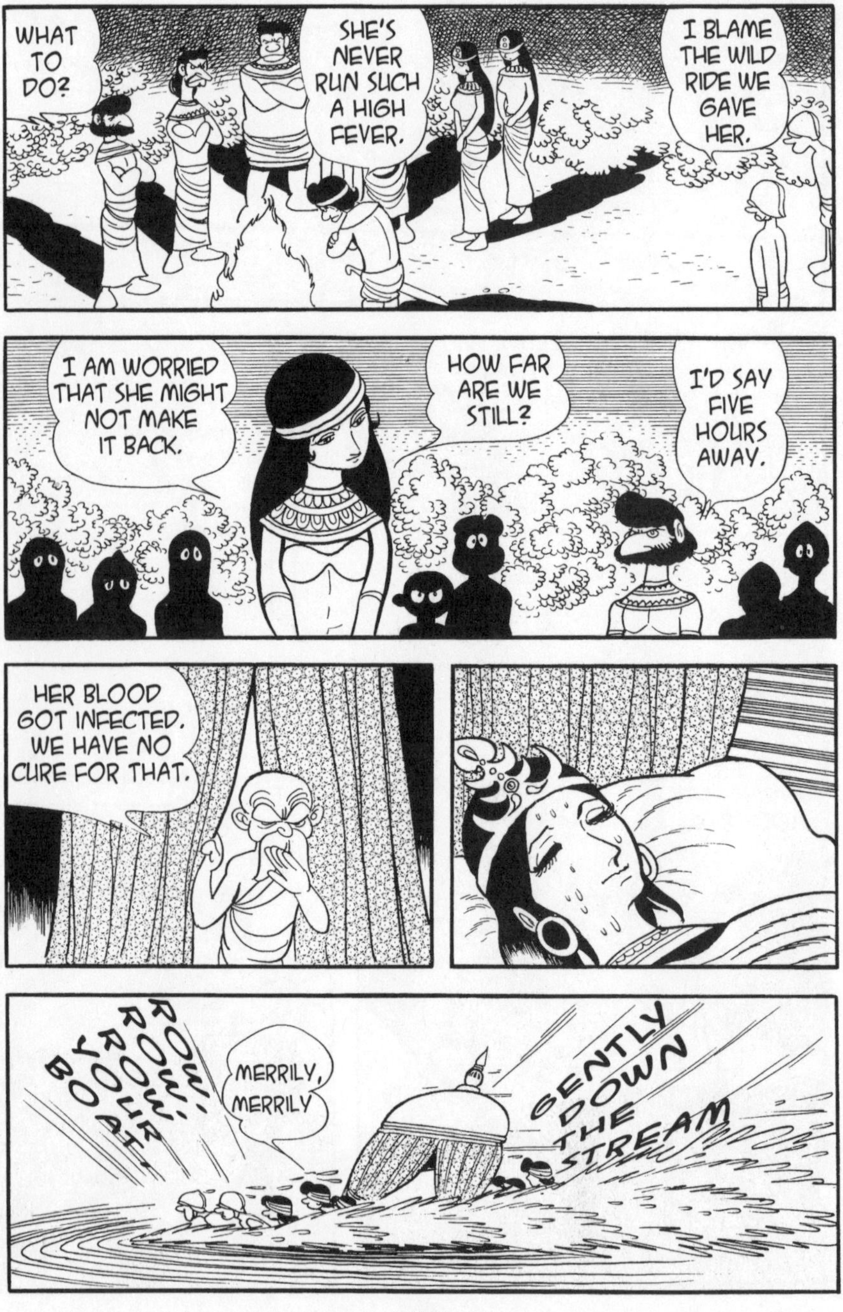
WHAT TO DO?
SHE'S NEVER RUN SUCH A HIGH FEVER.
I BLAME THE WILD RIDE WE GAVE HER.
I AM WORRIED THAT SHE MIGHT NOT MAKE IT BACK.
HOW FAR ARE WE STILL?
I'D SAY FIVE HOURS AWAY.
HER BLOOD GOT INFECTED. WE HAVE NO CURE FOR THAT.
ROW, ROW, ROW YOUR BOAT
MERRILY, MERRILY
GENTLY DOWN THE STREAM

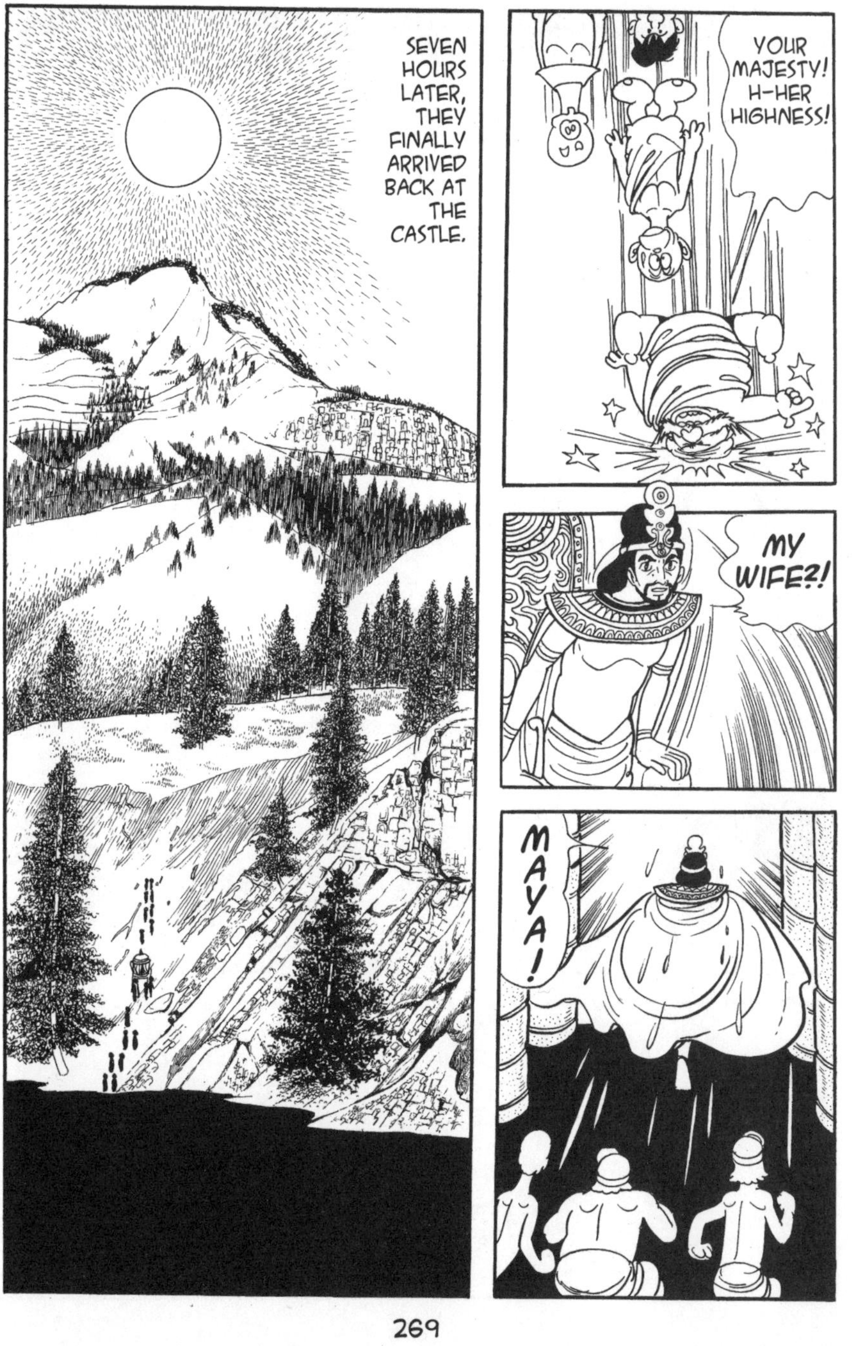
SEVEN HOURS LATER, THEY FINALLY ARRIVED BACK AT THE CASTLE.
YOUR MAJESTY! H-HER HIGHNESS!
MY WIFE?!
MAYA!

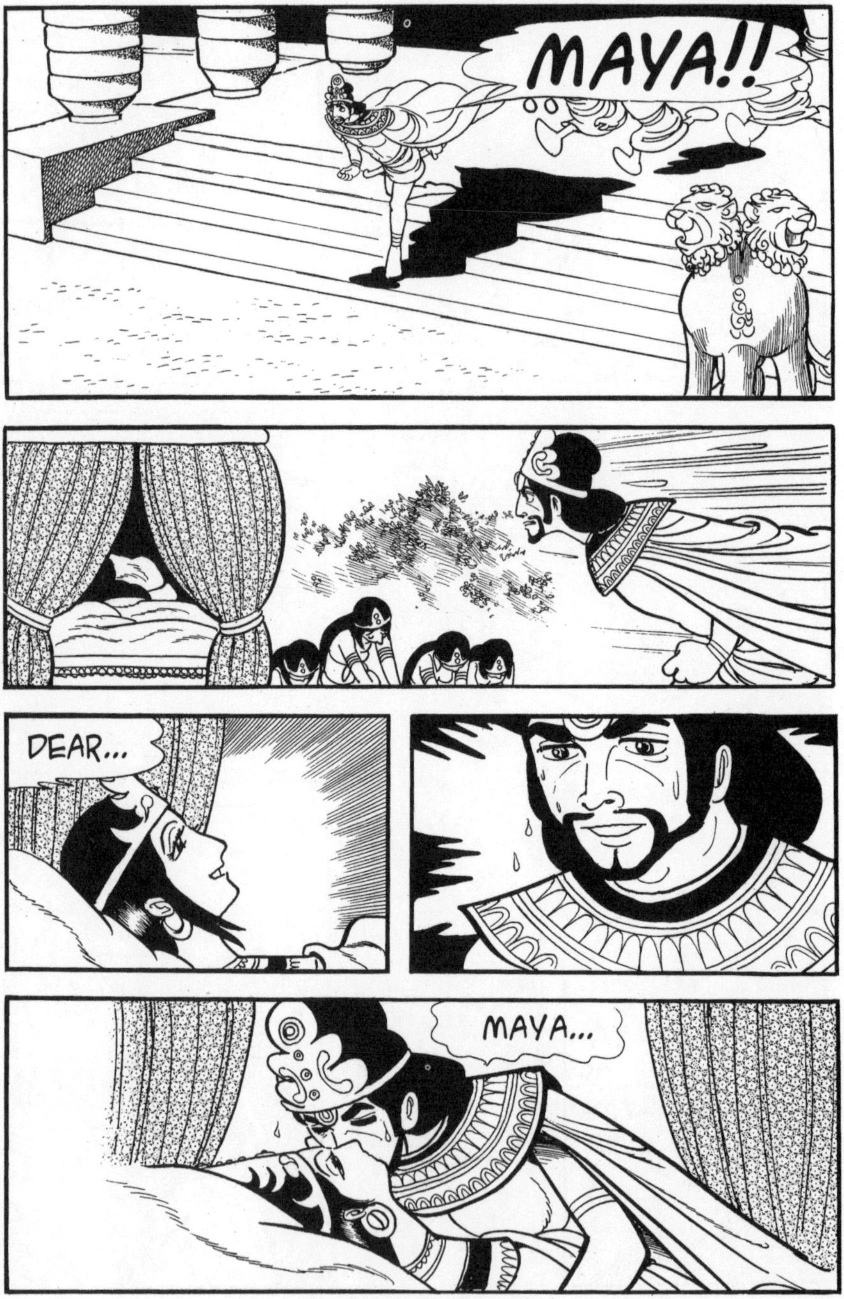
MAYA!!
DEAR...
MAYA...

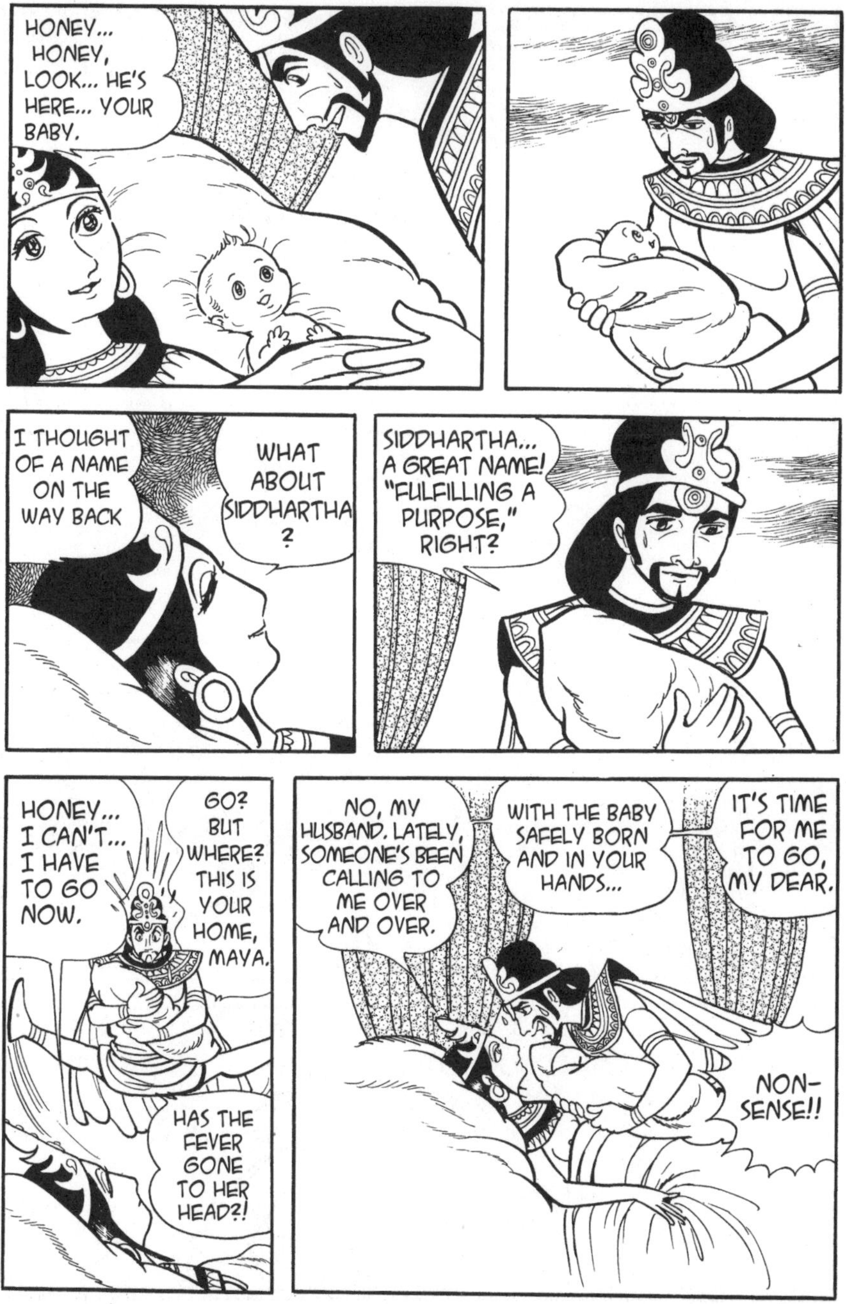
HONEY... HONEY, LOOK... HE'S HERE... YOUR BABY.
I THOUGHT OF A NAME ON THE WAY BACK
WHAT ABOUT SIDDHARTHA ?
SIDDHARTHA... A GREAT NAME! "FULFILLING A PURPOSE," RIGHT?
HONEY... I CAN'T... I HAVE TO GO NOW.
GO? BUT WHERE? THIS IS YOUR HOME, MAYA.
HAS THE FEVER GONE TO HER HEAD?!
NO, MY HUSBAND. LATELY, SOMEONE'S BEEN CALLING TO ME OVER AND OVER.
WITH THE BABY SAFELY BORN AND IN YOUR HANDS...
IT'S TIME FOR ME TO GO, MY DEAR.
NON-SENSE!!

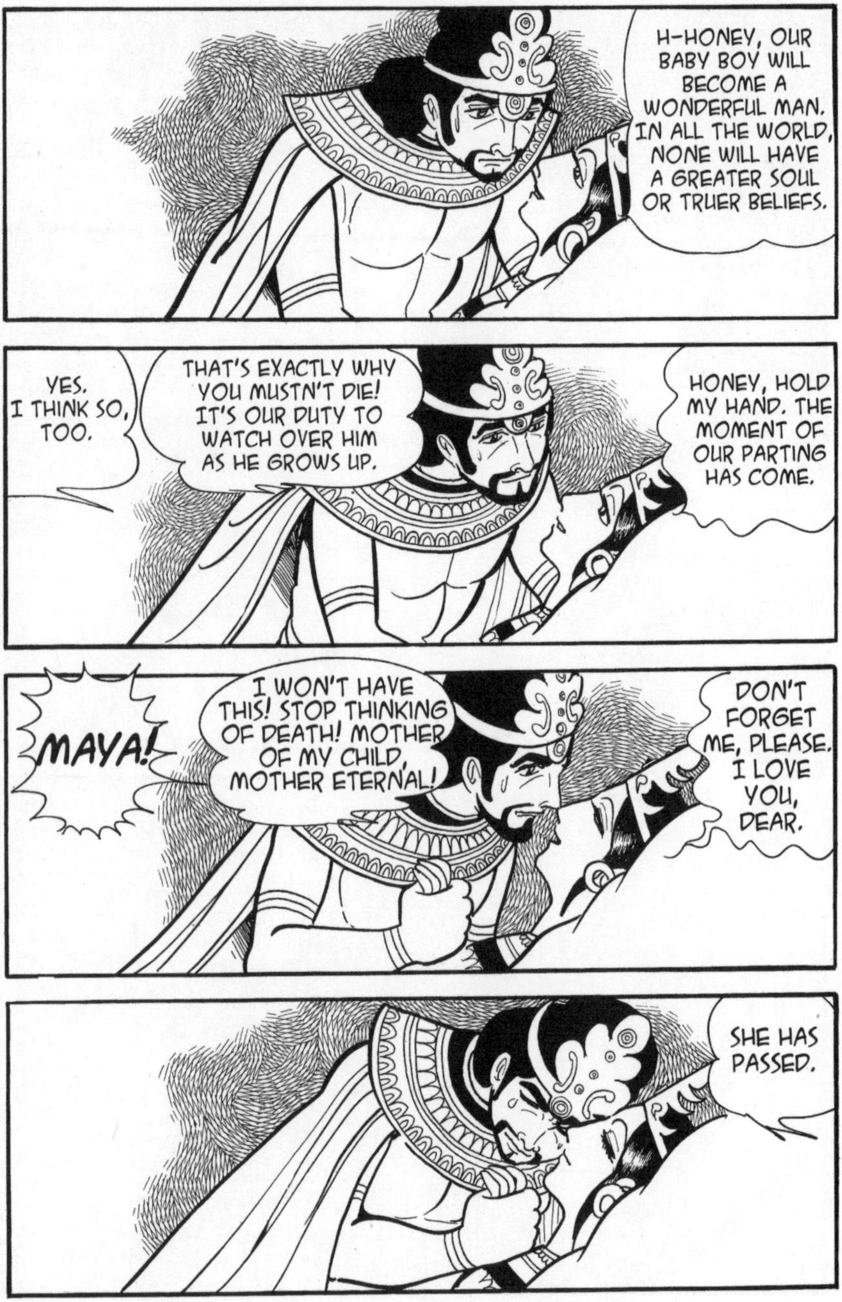
H-HONEY, OUR BABY BOY WILL BECOME A WONDERFUL MAN. IN ALL THE WORLD, NONE WILL HAVE A GREATER SOUL OR TRUER BELIEFS.
YES. I THINK SO, TOO.
THAT'S EXACTLY WHY YOU MUSTN'T DIE! IT'S OUR DUTY TO WATCH OVER HIM AS HE GROWS UP.
HONEY, HOLD MY HAND. THE MOMENT OF OUR PARTING HAS COME.
MAYA!
I WON'T HAVE THIS! STOP THINKING OF DEATH! MOTHER OF MY CHILD, MOTHER ETERNAL!
DON'T FORGET ME, PLEASE. I LOVE YOU, DEAR.
SHE HAS PASSED.

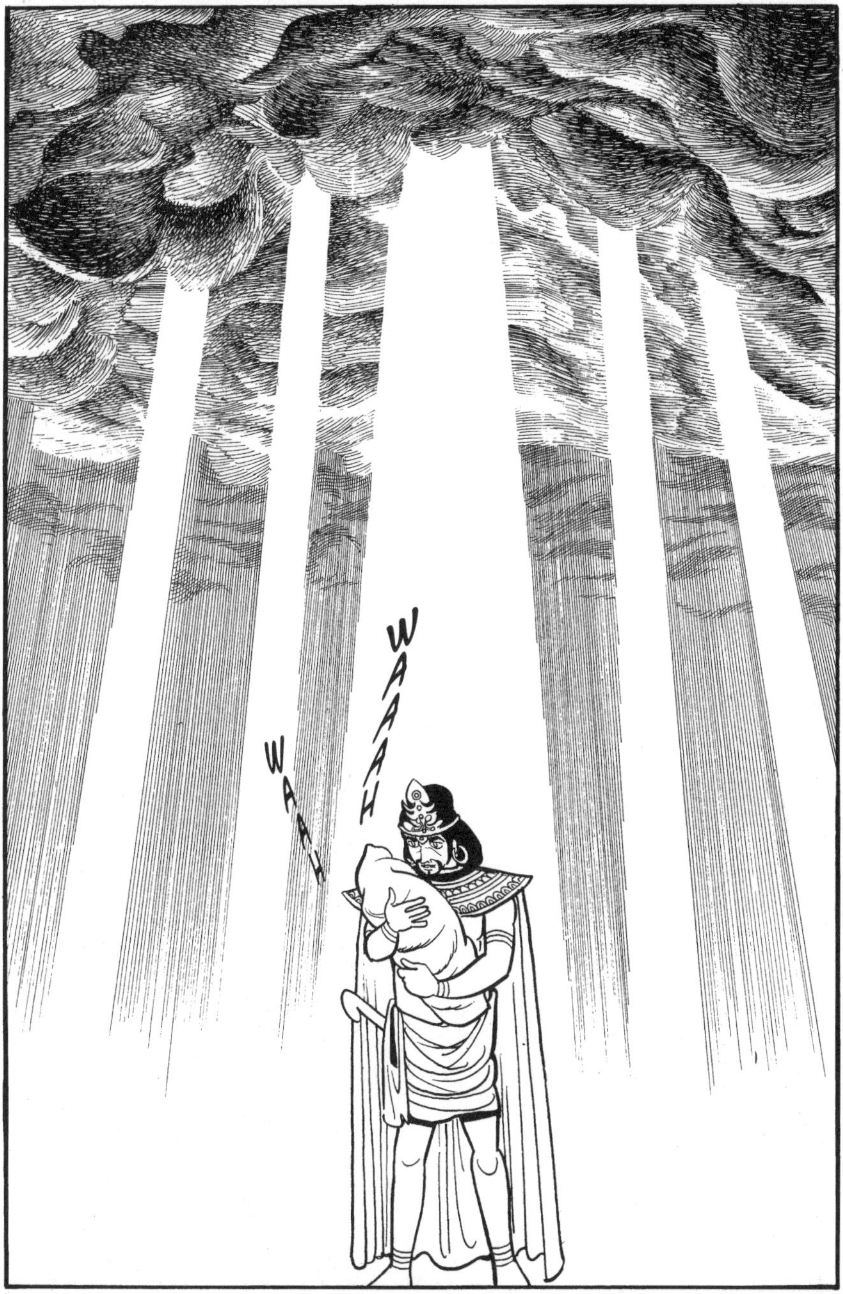
WAAAAH
WAAAH

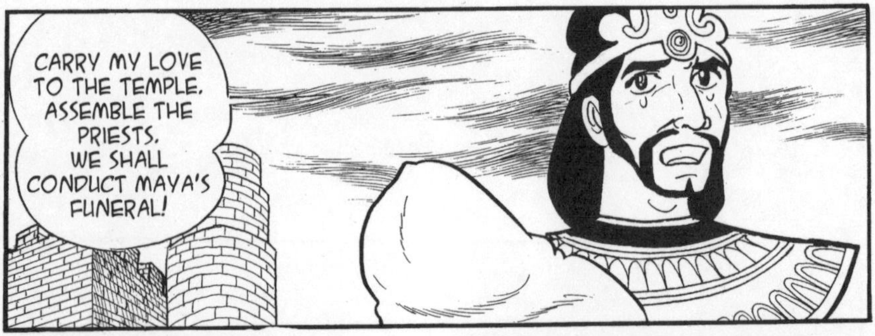
CARRY MY LOVE TO THE TEMPLE. ASSEMBLE THE PRIESTS. WE SHALL CONDUCT MAYA'S FUNERAL!

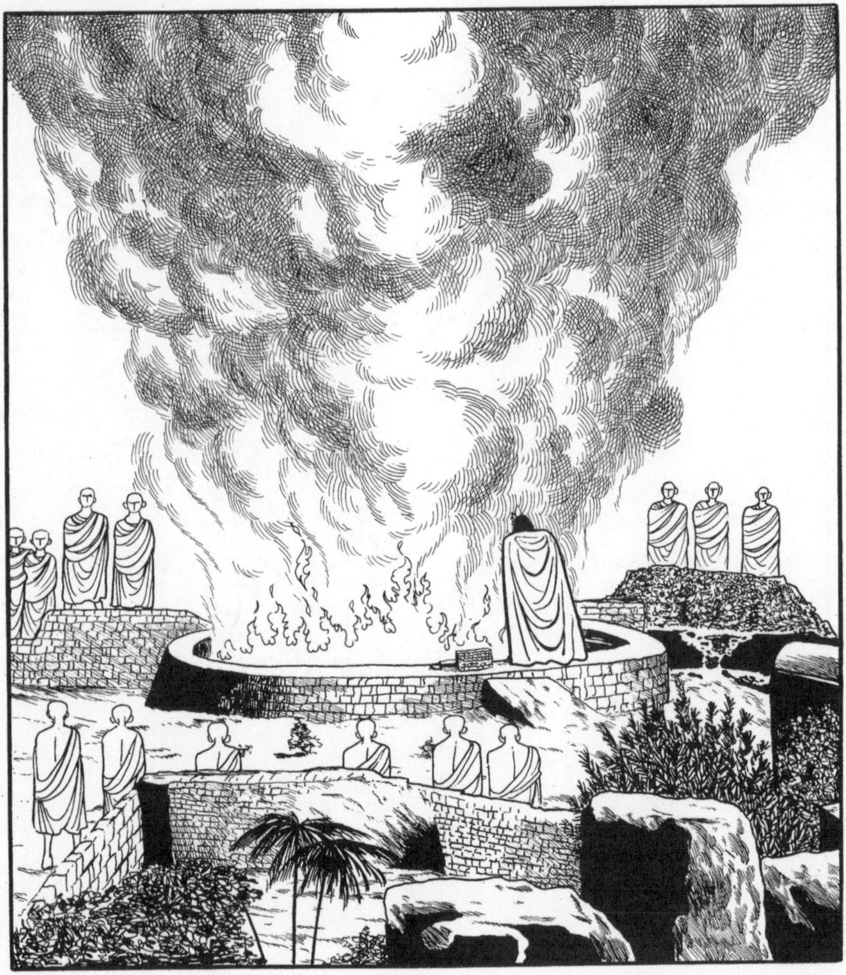

CHAPTER EIGHT

THE CONTEST

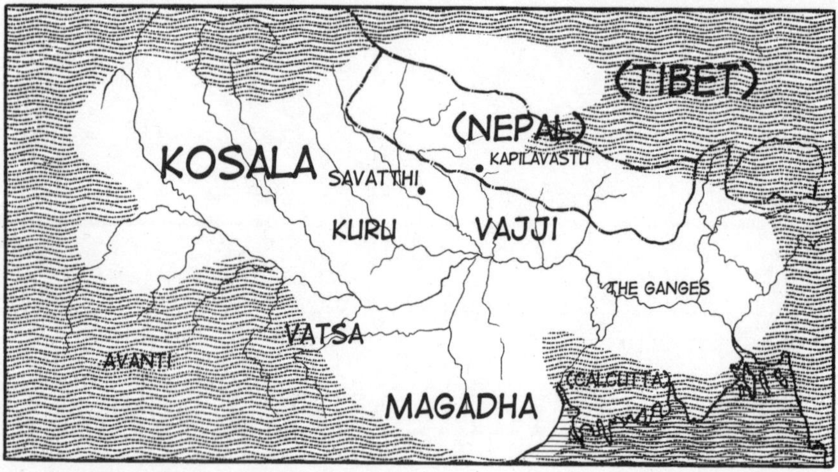
(TIBET)
(NEPAL)
KOSALA
SAVATTHI
KAPILAVASTU
KURU
VAJJI
THE GANGES
VATSA
AVANTI
(CALCUTTA)
MAGADHA

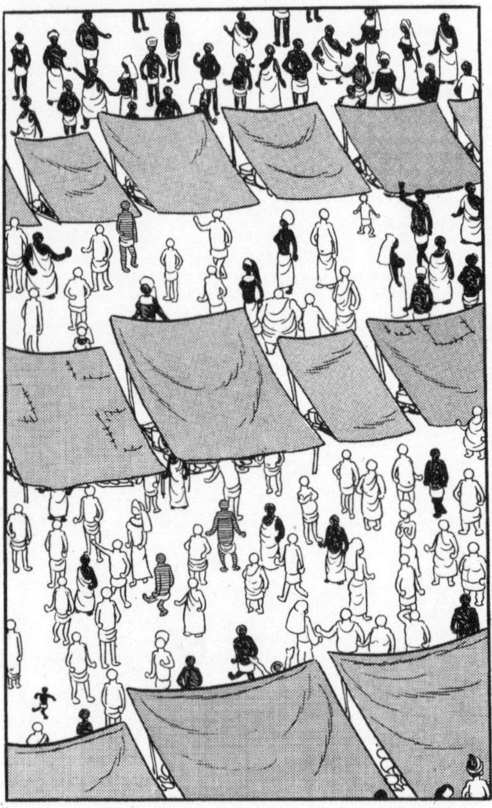

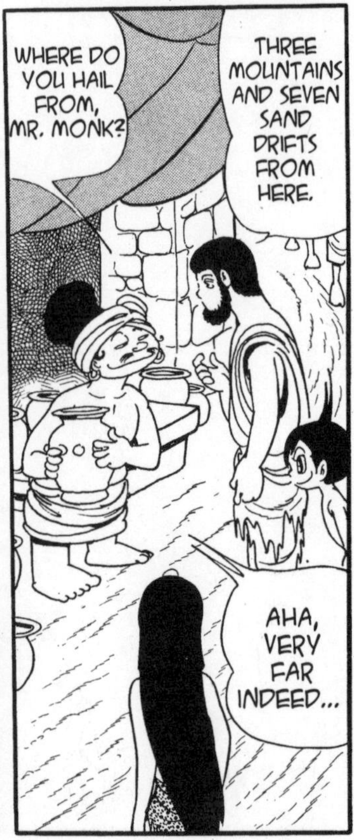
WHERE DO YOU HAIL FROM, MR. MONK?
THREE MOUNTAINS AND SEVEN SAND DRIFTS FROM HERE.
AHA, VERY FAR INDEED...

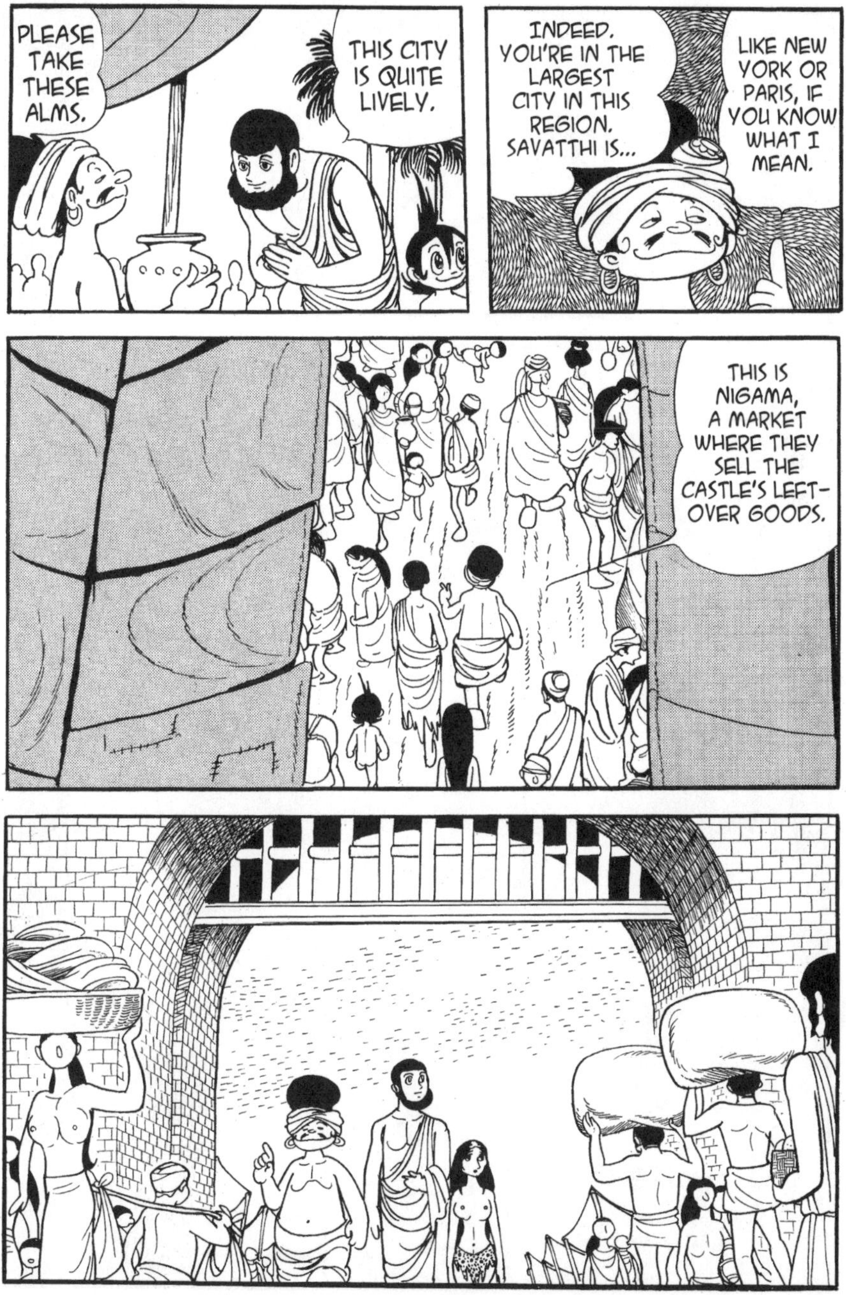
PLEASE TAKE THESE ALMS.
THIS CITY IS QUITE LIVELY.
INDEED. YOU'RE IN THE LARGEST CITY IN THIS REGION. SAVATTHI IS...
LIKE NEW YORK OR PARIS, IF YOU KNOW WHAT I MEAN.
THIS IS NIGAMA, A MARKET WHERE THEY SELL THE CASTLE'S LEFT-OVER GOODS.

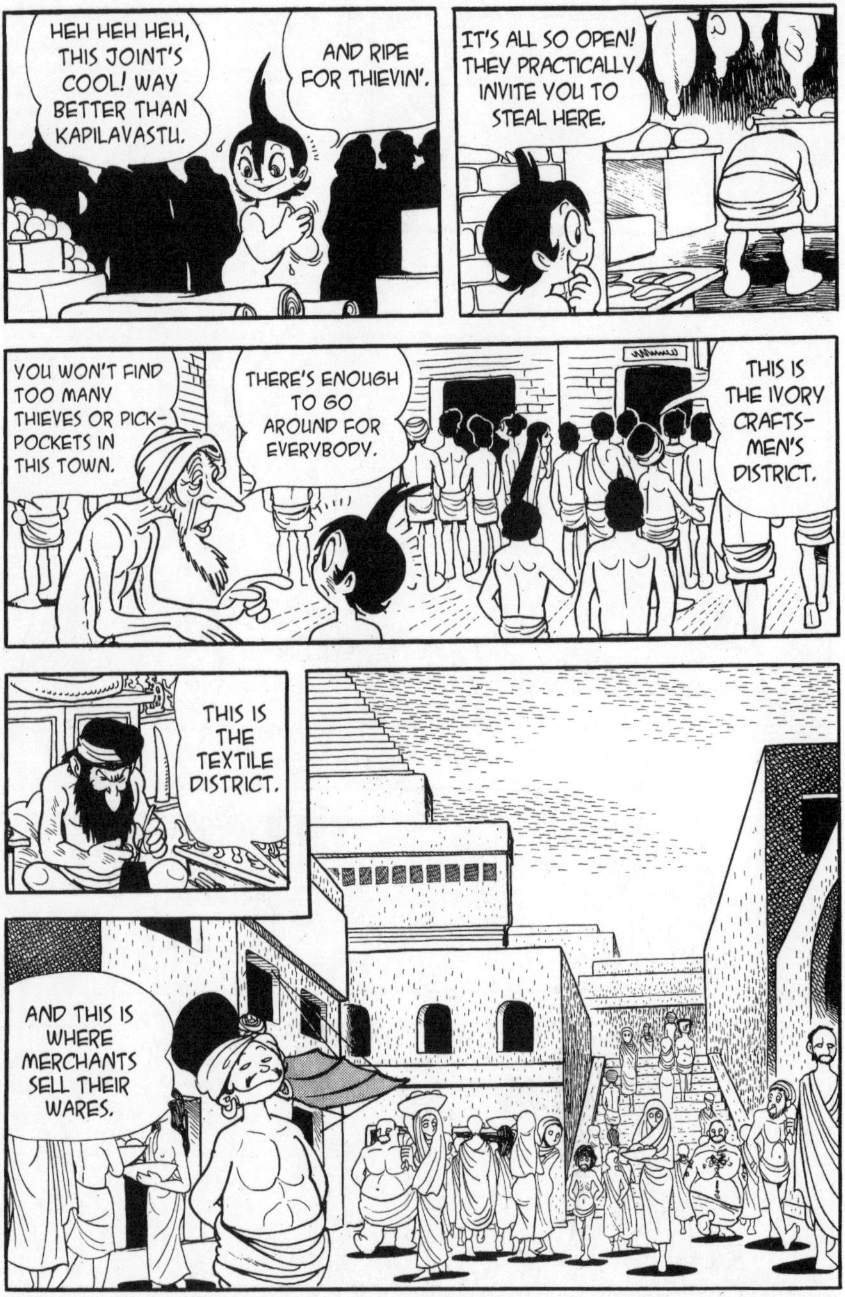
HEH HEH HEH, THIS JOINT'S COOL! WAY BETTER THAN KAPILAVASTU.
AND RIPE FOR THIEVIN'.
IT'S ALL SO OPEN! THEY PRACTICALLY INVITE YOU TO STEAL HERE.
YOU WON'T FIND TOO MANY THIEVES OR PICK-POCKETS IN THIS TOWN.
THERE'S ENOUGH TO GO AROUND FOR EVERYBODY.
THIS IS THE IVORY CRAFTS-MEN'S DISTRICT.
THIS IS THE TEXTILE DISTRICT.
AND THIS IS WHERE MERCHANTS SELL THEIR WARES.

A PARADE OF GENTRY.

YES. IT'S GENERAL BUDAI, A MAN OF GREAT INFLUENCE, AND HIS SON MASTER CHAPRA.

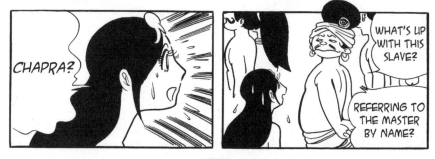

CHAPRA?

WHAT'S UP WITH THIS SLAVE?

REFERRING TO THE MASTER BY NAME?

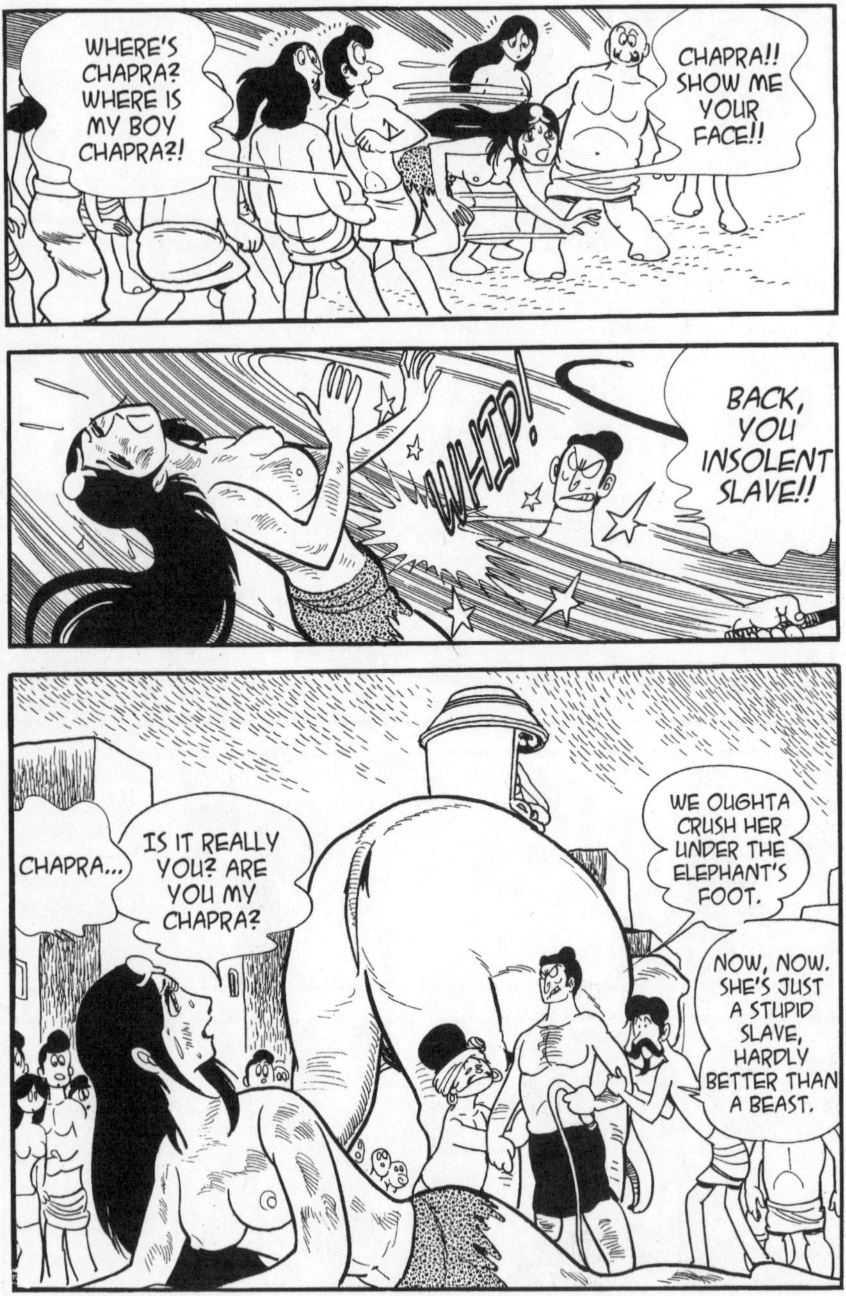
WHERE'S CHAPRA? WHERE IS MY BOY CHAPRA?!
CHAPRA!! SHOW ME YOUR FACE!!
WHIP!
BACK, YOU INSOLENT SLAVE!!
CHAPRA...
IS IT REALLY YOU? ARE YOU MY CHAPRA?
WE OUGHTA CRUSH HER UNDER THE ELEPHANT'S FOOT.
NOW, NOW. SHE'S JUST A STUPID SLAVE, HARDLY BETTER THAN A BEAST.

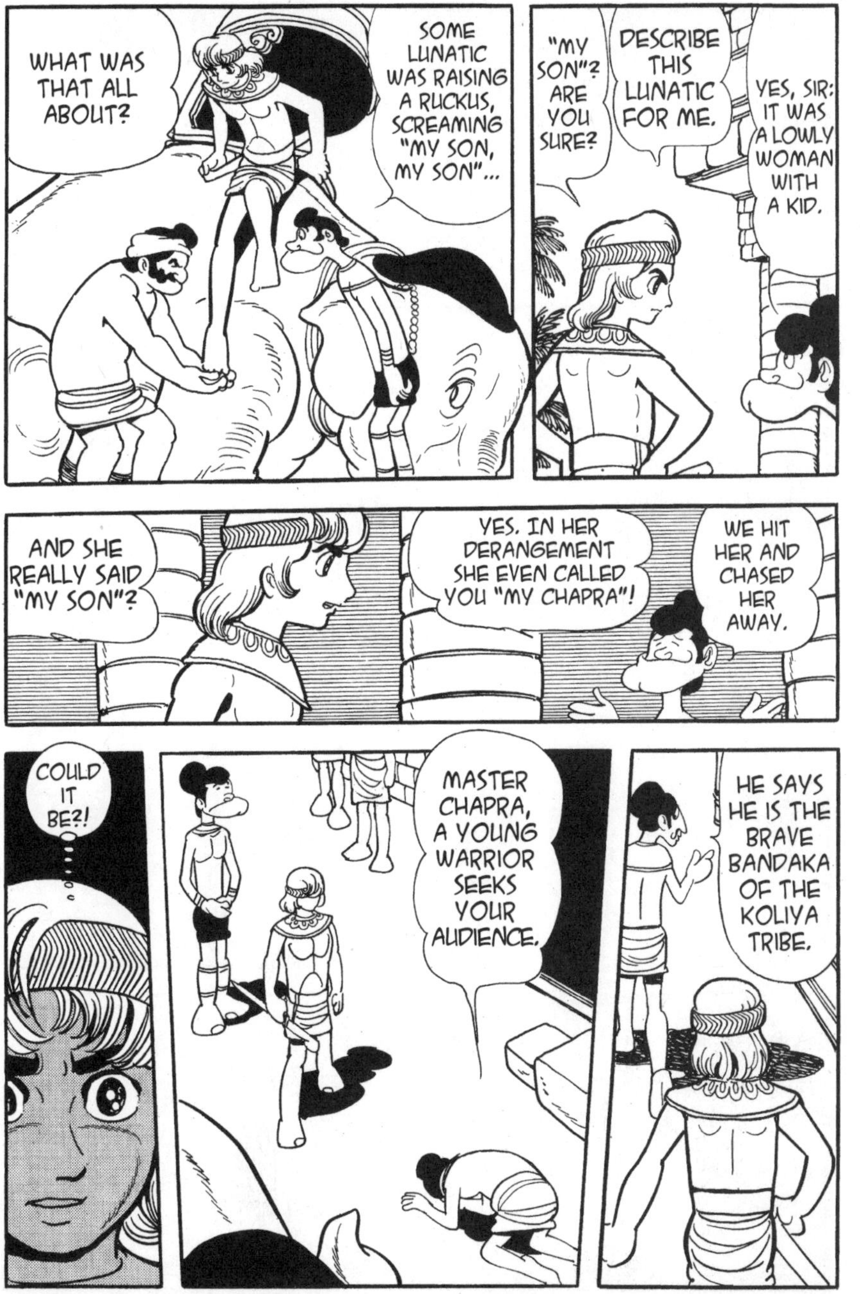
WHAT WAS THAT ALL ABOUT?
SOME LUNATIC WAS RAISING A RUCKUS, SCREAMING "MY SON, MY SON"...
"MY SON"? ARE YOU SURE?
DESCRIBE THIS LUNATIC FOR ME.
YES, SIR: IT WAS A LOWLY WOMAN WITH A KID.
AND SHE REALLY SAID "MY SON"?
YES. IN HER DERANGEMENT SHE EVEN CALLED YOU "MY CHAPRA"!
WE HIT HER AND CHASED HER AWAY.
COULD IT BE?!
MASTER CHAPRA, A YOUNG WARRIOR SEEKS YOUR AUDIENCE.
HE SAYS HE IS THE BRAVE BANDAKA OF THE KOLIYA TRIBE.

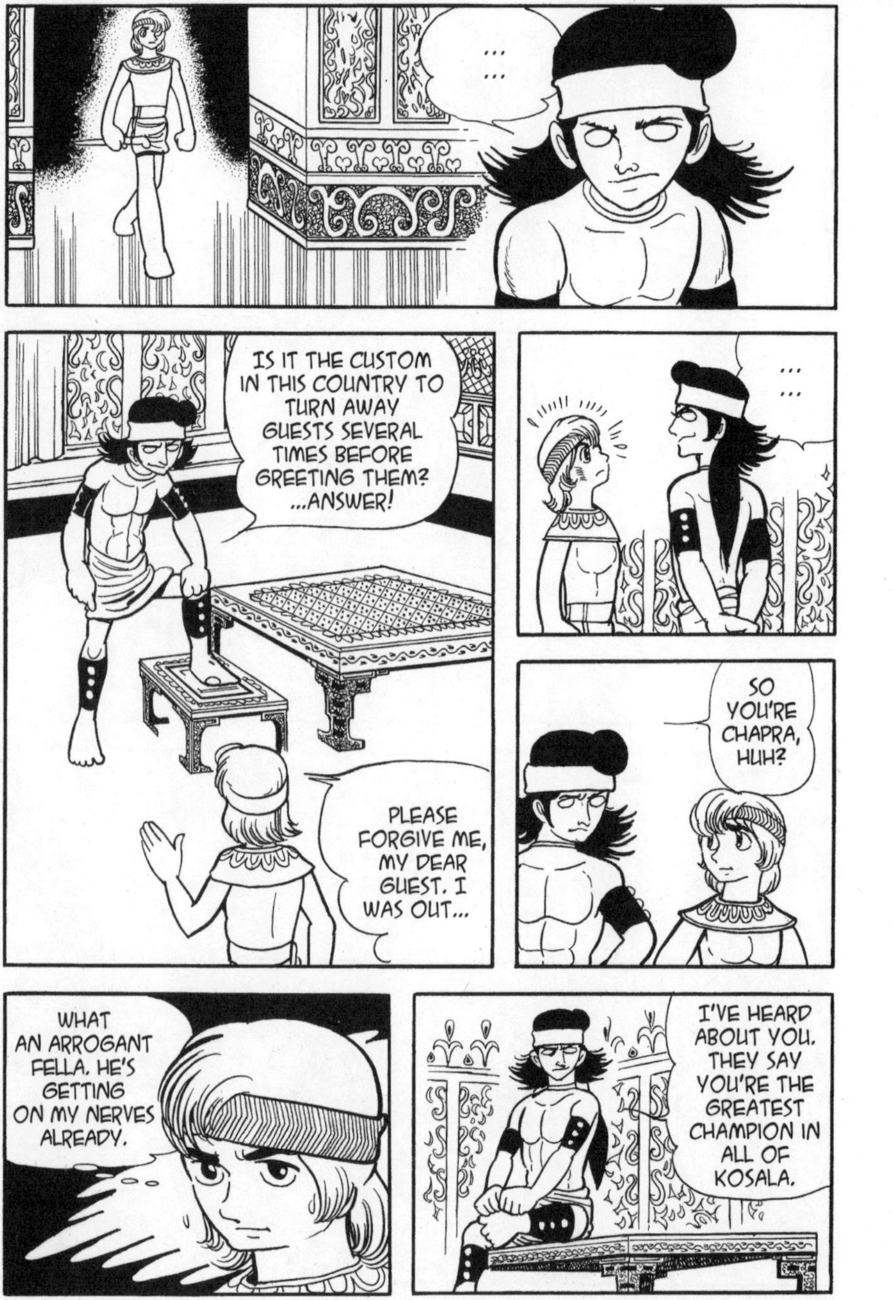
……
IS IT THE CUSTOM IN THIS COUNTRY TO TURN AWAY GUESTS SEVERAL TIMES BEFORE GREETING THEM? ...ANSWER!
PLEASE FORGIVE ME, MY DEAR GUEST. I WAS OUT...
……
SO YOU'RE CHAPRA, HUH?
WHAT AN ARROGANT FELLA. HE'S GETTING ON MY NERVES ALREADY.
I'VE HEARD ABOUT YOU. THEY SAY YOU'RE THE GREATEST CHAMPION IN ALL OF KOSALA.

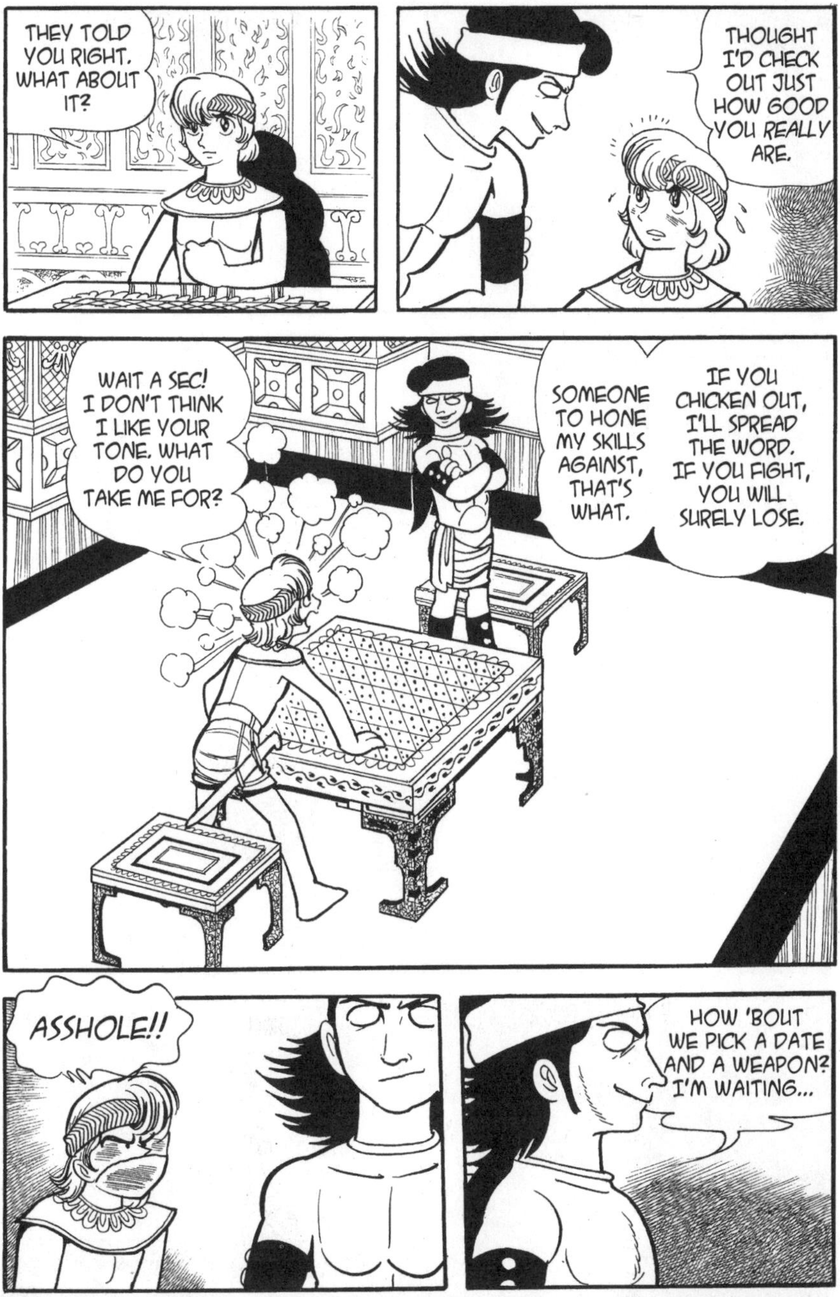
THEY TOLD YOU RIGHT. WHAT ABOUT IT?
THOUGHT I'D CHECK OUT JUST HOW GOOD YOU REALLY ARE.
WAIT A SEC! I DON'T THINK I LIKE YOUR TONE. WHAT DO YOU TAKE ME FOR?
SOMEONE TO HONE MY SKILLS AGAINST, THAT'S WHAT.
IF YOU CHICKEN OUT, I'LL SPREAD THE WORD. IF YOU FIGHT, YOU WILL SURELY LOSE.
ASSHOLE!!
HOW 'BOUT WE PICK A DATE AND A WEAPON? I'M WAITING...

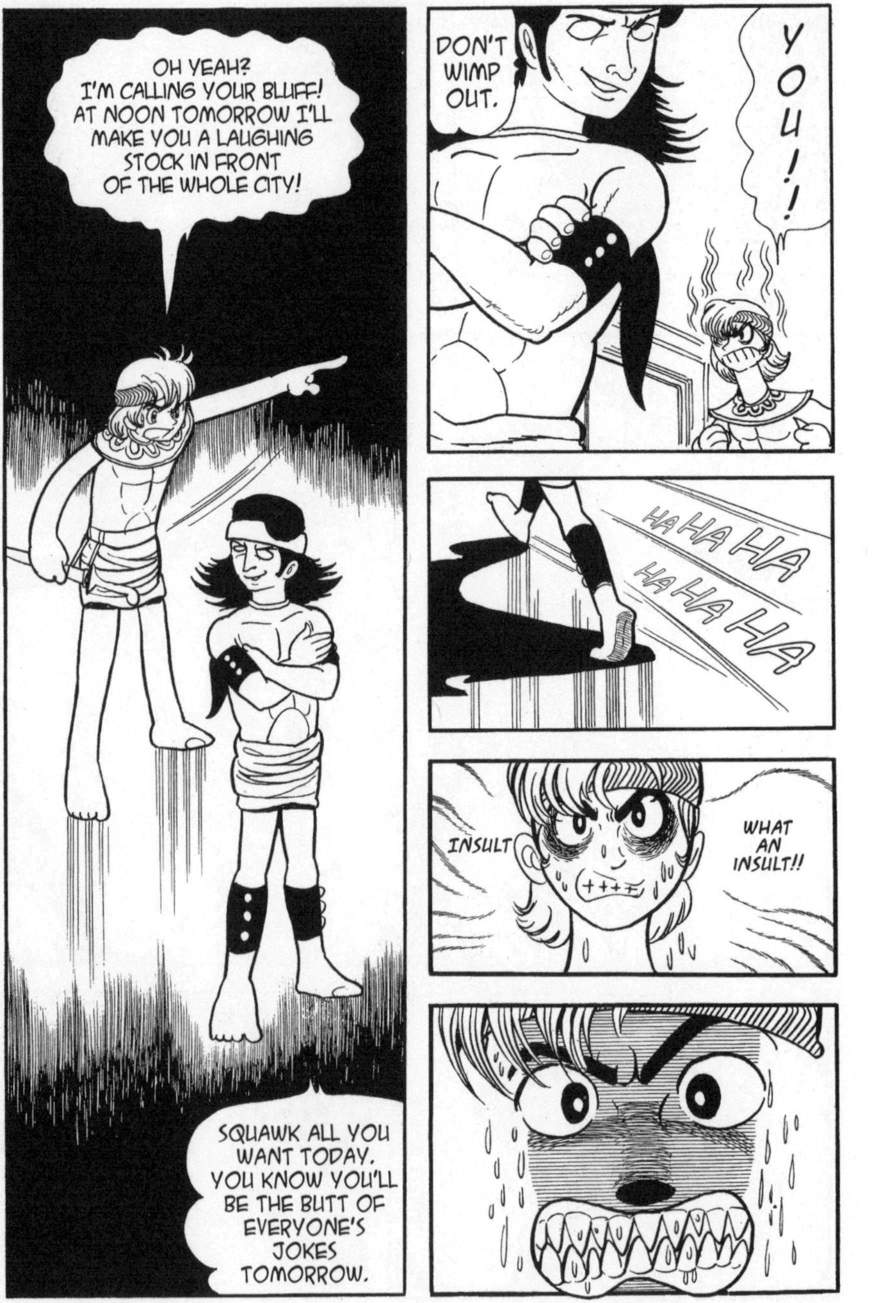
OH YEAH? I'M CALLING YOUR BLUFF! AT NOON TOMORROW I'LL MAKE YOU A LAUGHING STOCK IN FRONT OF THE WHOLE CITY!
SQUAWK ALL YOU WANT TODAY. YOU KNOW YOU'LL BE THE BUTT OF EVERYONE'S JOKES TOMORROW.
DON'T WIMP OUT.
YOU!!
HA HA HA HA
HA HA HA
INSULT
WHAT AN INSULT!!

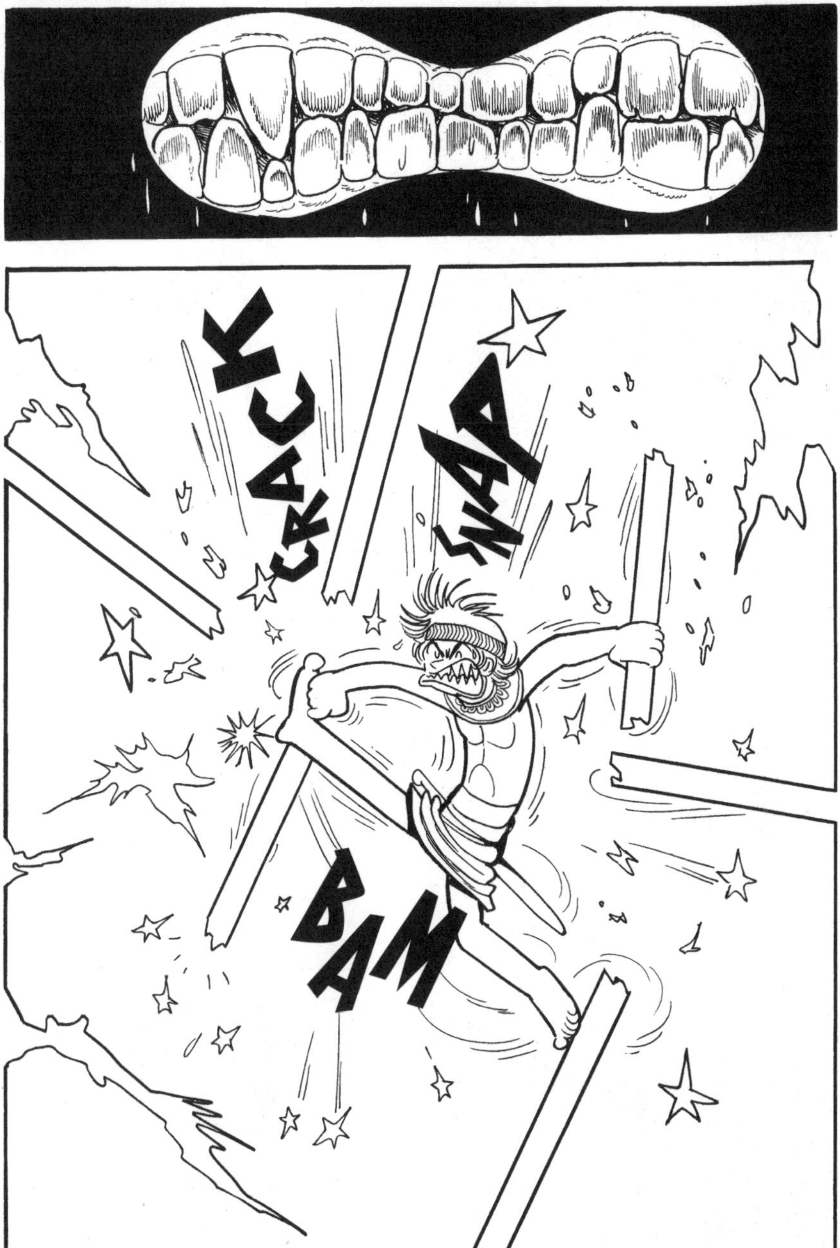
CRACK
SNAP
BAM

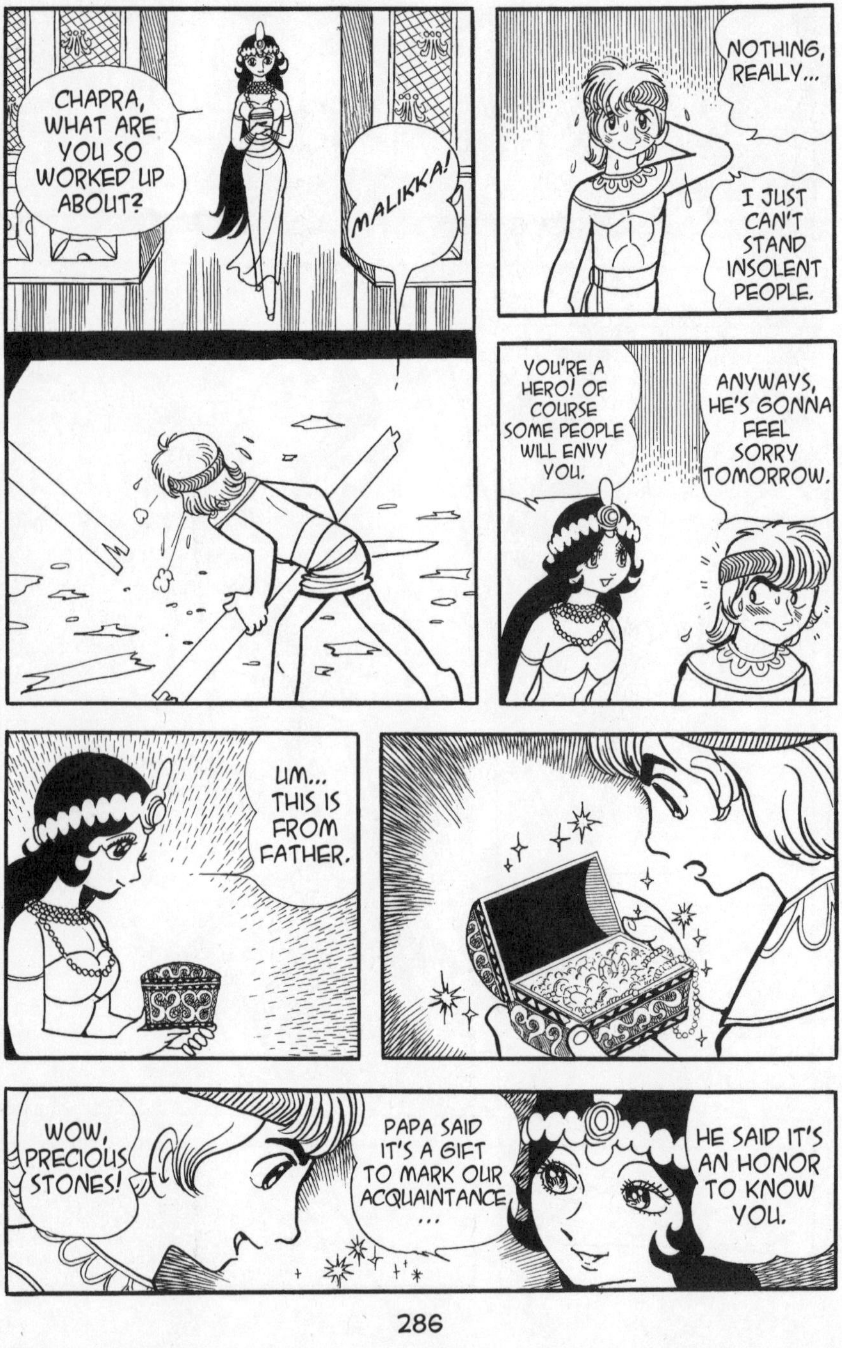
CHAPRA, WHAT ARE YOU SO WORKED UP ABOUT?
MALIKKA!
NOTHING, REALLY...
I JUST CAN'T STAND INSOLENT PEOPLE.
YOU'RE A HERO! OF COURSE SOME PEOPLE WILL ENVY YOU.
ANYWAYS, HE'S GONNA FEEL SORRY TOMORROW.
UM... THIS IS FROM FATHER.
WOW, PRECIOUS STONES!
PAPA SAID IT'S A GIFT TO MARK OUR ACQUAINTANCE...
HE SAID IT'S AN HONOR TO KNOW YOU.

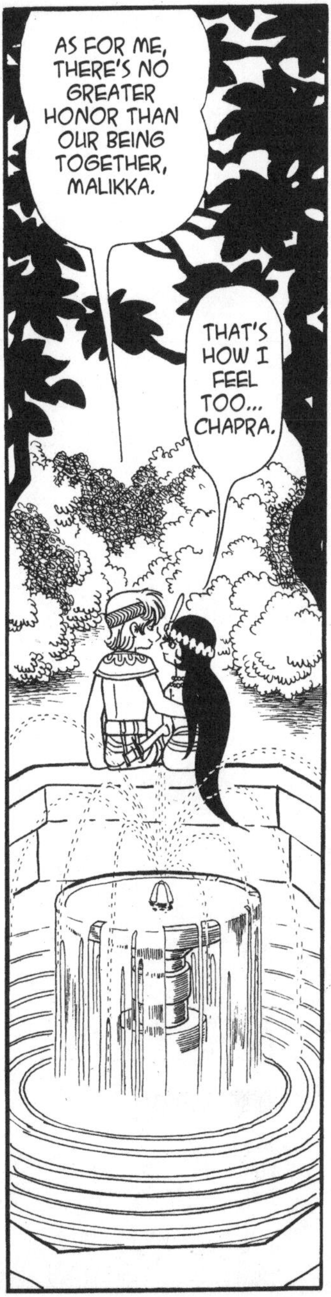
AS FOR ME, THERE'S NO GREATER HONOR THAN OUR BEING TOGETHER, MALIKKA.
THAT'S HOW I FEEL TOO... CHAPRA.
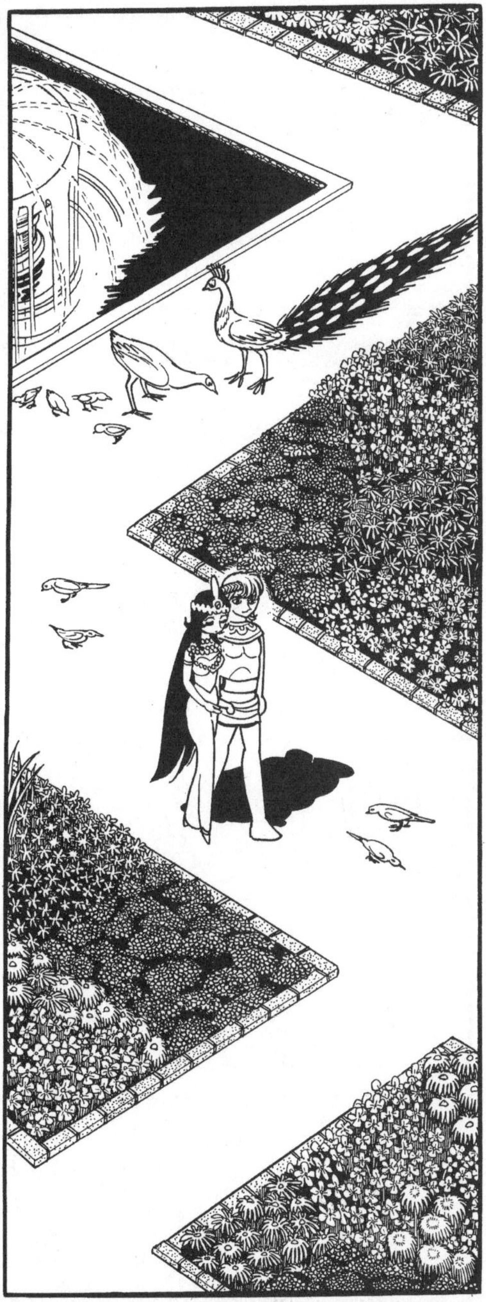

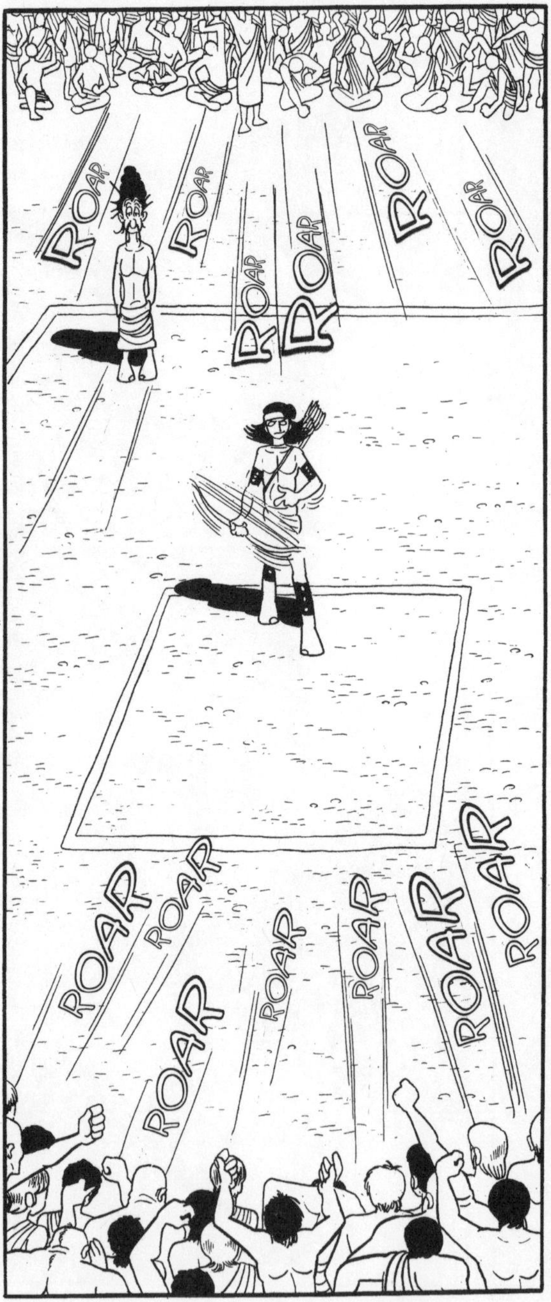
ROAR
ROAR
ROAR
ROAR
ROAR
ROAR
ROAR
ROAR
ROAR
ROAR
ROAR
ROAR
ROAR
ROAR
ROAR
ROAR
ROAR
ROAR

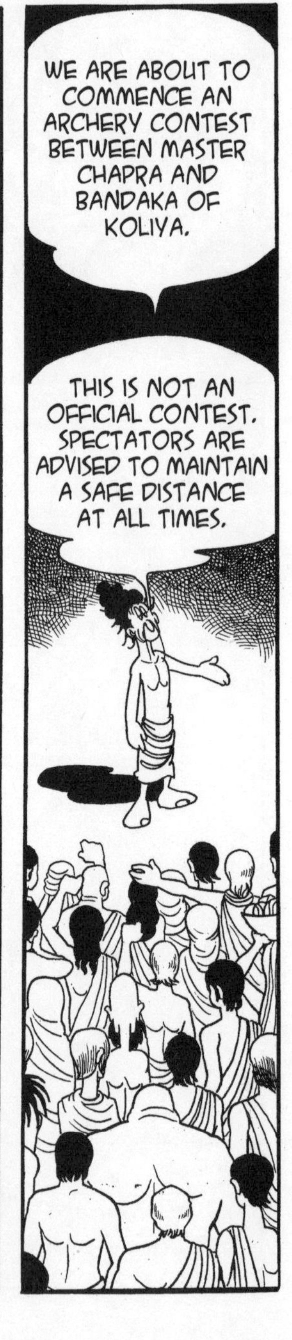
WE ARE ABOUT TO COMMENCE AN ARCHERY CONTEST BETWEEN MASTER CHAPRA AND BANDAKA OF KOLIYA.
THIS IS NOT AN OFFICIAL CONTEST. SPECTATORS ARE ADVISED TO MAINTAIN A SAFE DISTANCE AT ALL TIMES.

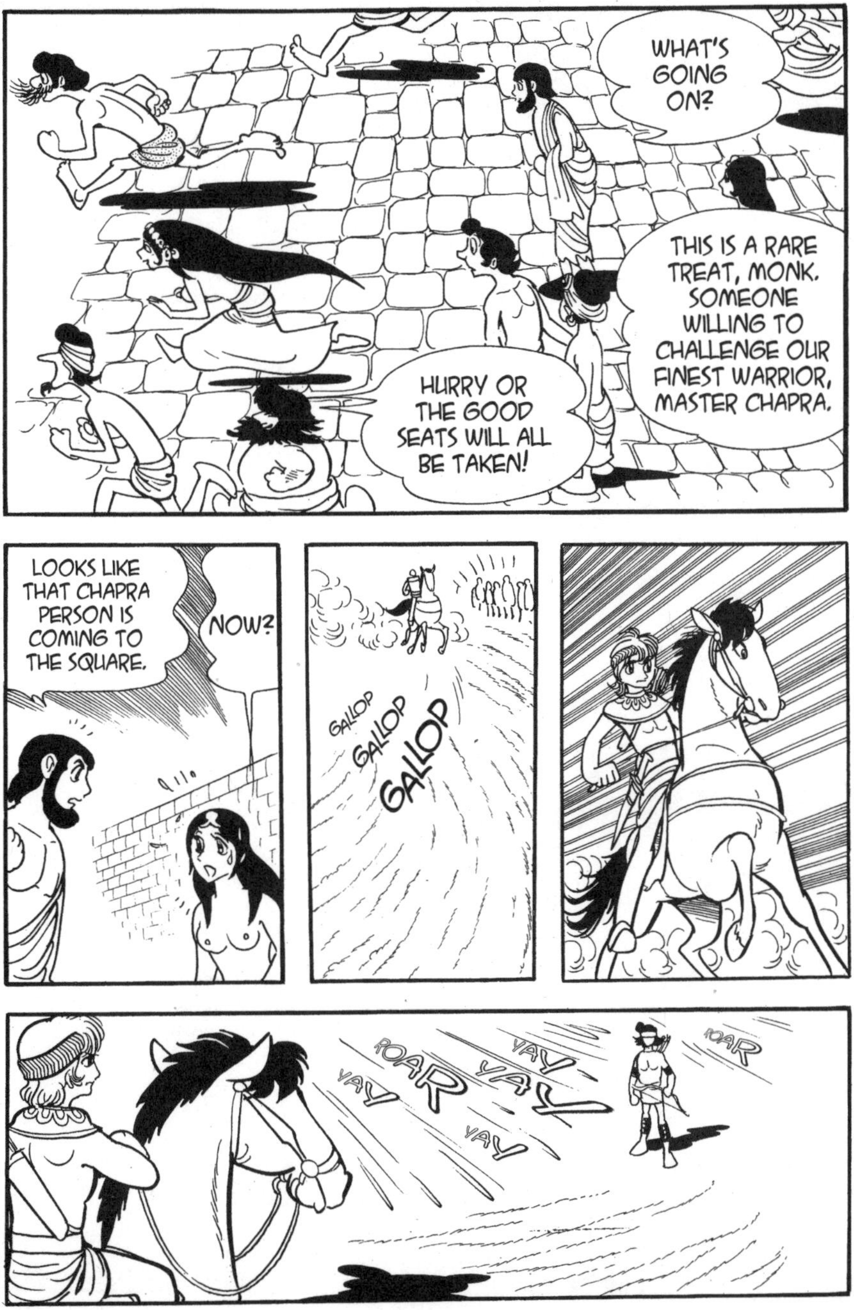
WHAT'S GOING ON?
THIS IS A RARE TREAT, MONK. SOMEONE WILLING TO CHALLENGE OUR FINEST WARRIOR, MASTER CHAPRA.
HURRY OR THE GOOD SEATS WILL ALL BE TAKEN!
LOOKS LIKE THAT CHAPRA PERSON IS COMING TO THE SQUARE.
NOW?
GALLOP
GALLOP
GALLOP
ROAR
YAY
YAY
ROAR
YAY
YAY
YAY
ROAR

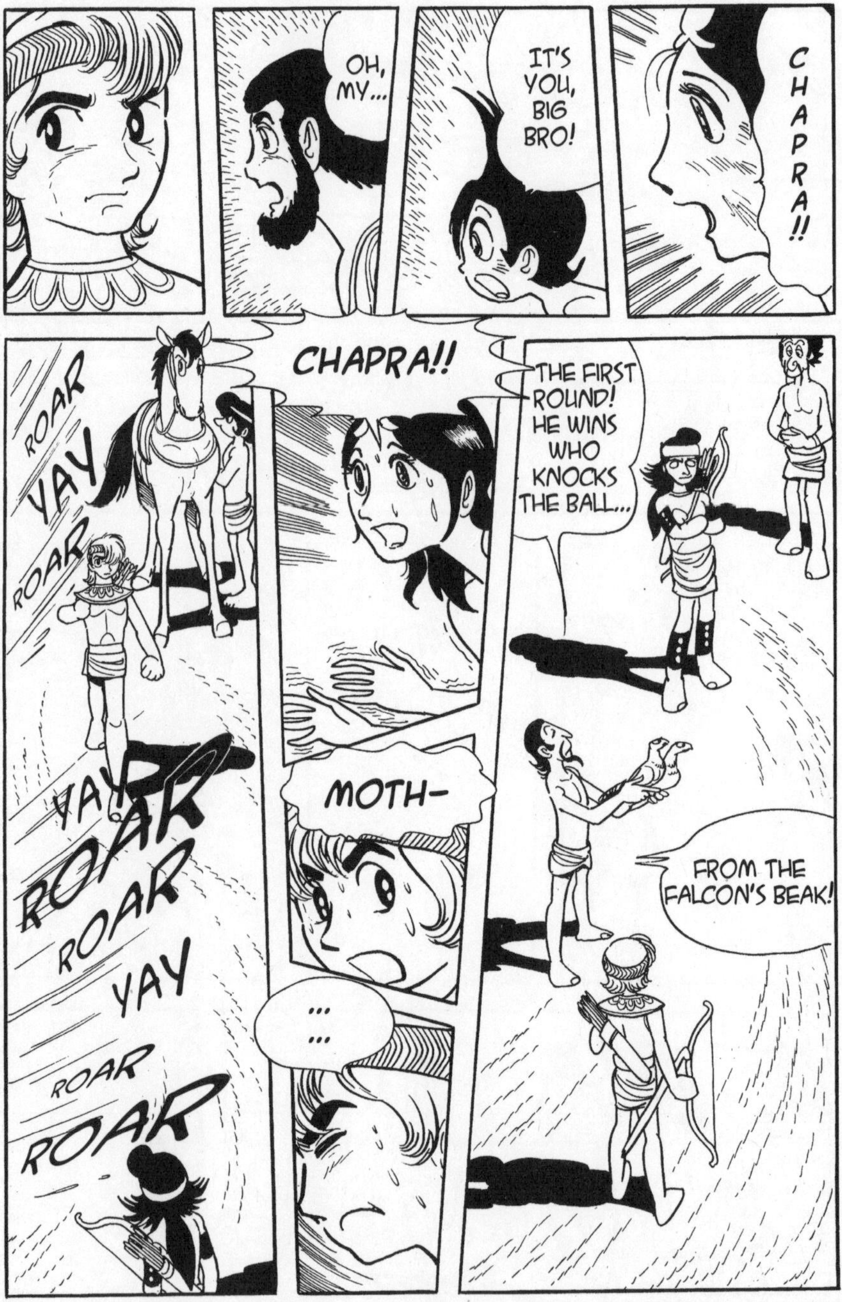
OH, MY...
IT'S YOU, BIG BRO!
CHAPRA!!
ROAR
YAY
ROAR
ROAR
YAY
ROAR
ROAR
YAY
ROAR
ROAR
CHAPRA!!
MOTH-
......
THE FIRST ROUND! HE WINS WHO KNOCKS THE BALL...
FROM THE FALCON'S BEAK!

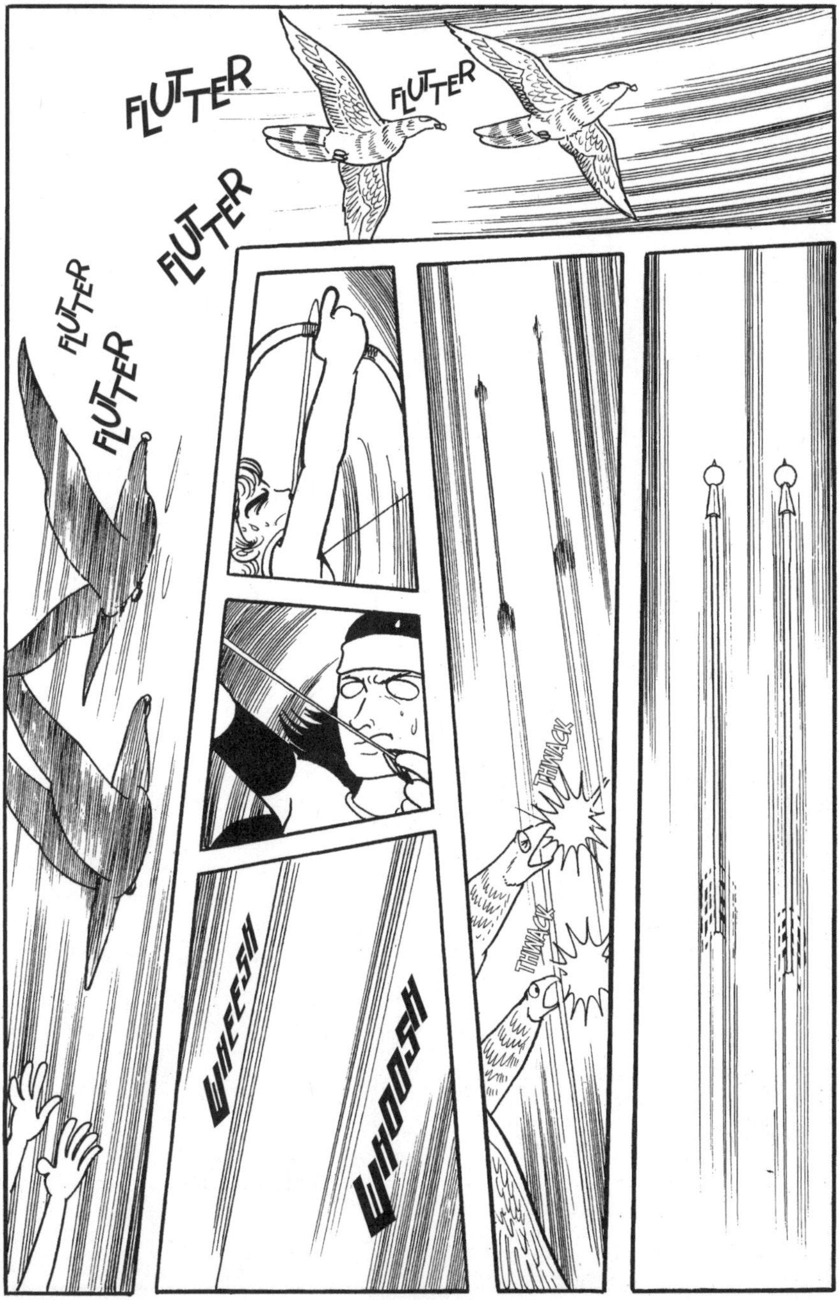
FLUTTER
FLUTTER
FLUTTER
FLUTTER
FLUTTER
WHEESH
WHOOSH
THWACK
THWACK

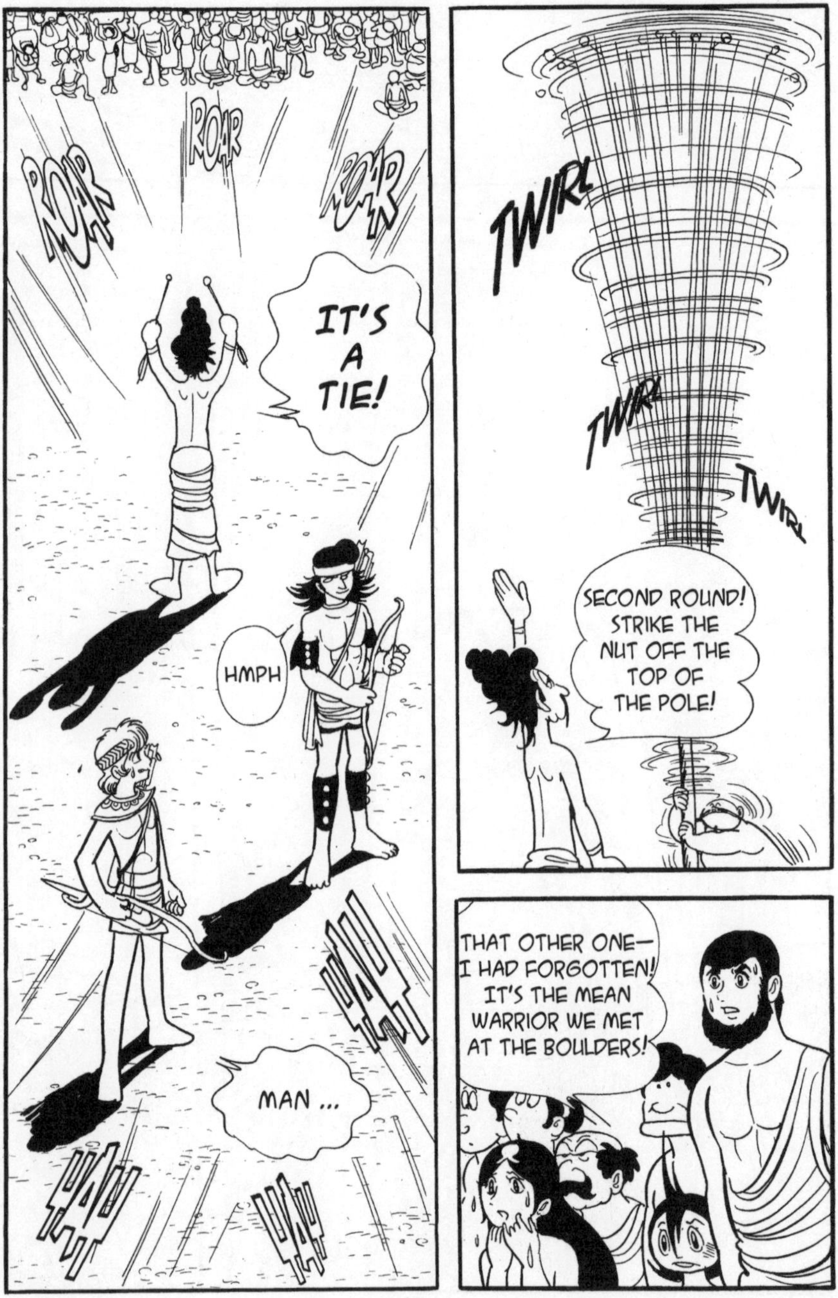
ROAR
ROAR
ROAR
IT'S A TIE!
HMPH
MAN ...
TWIRL
TWIRL
TWIRL
SECOND ROUND! STRIKE THE NUT OFF THE TOP OF THE POLE!
THAT OTHER ONE— I HAD FORGOTTEN! IT'S THE MEAN WARRIOR WE MET AT THE BOULDERS!

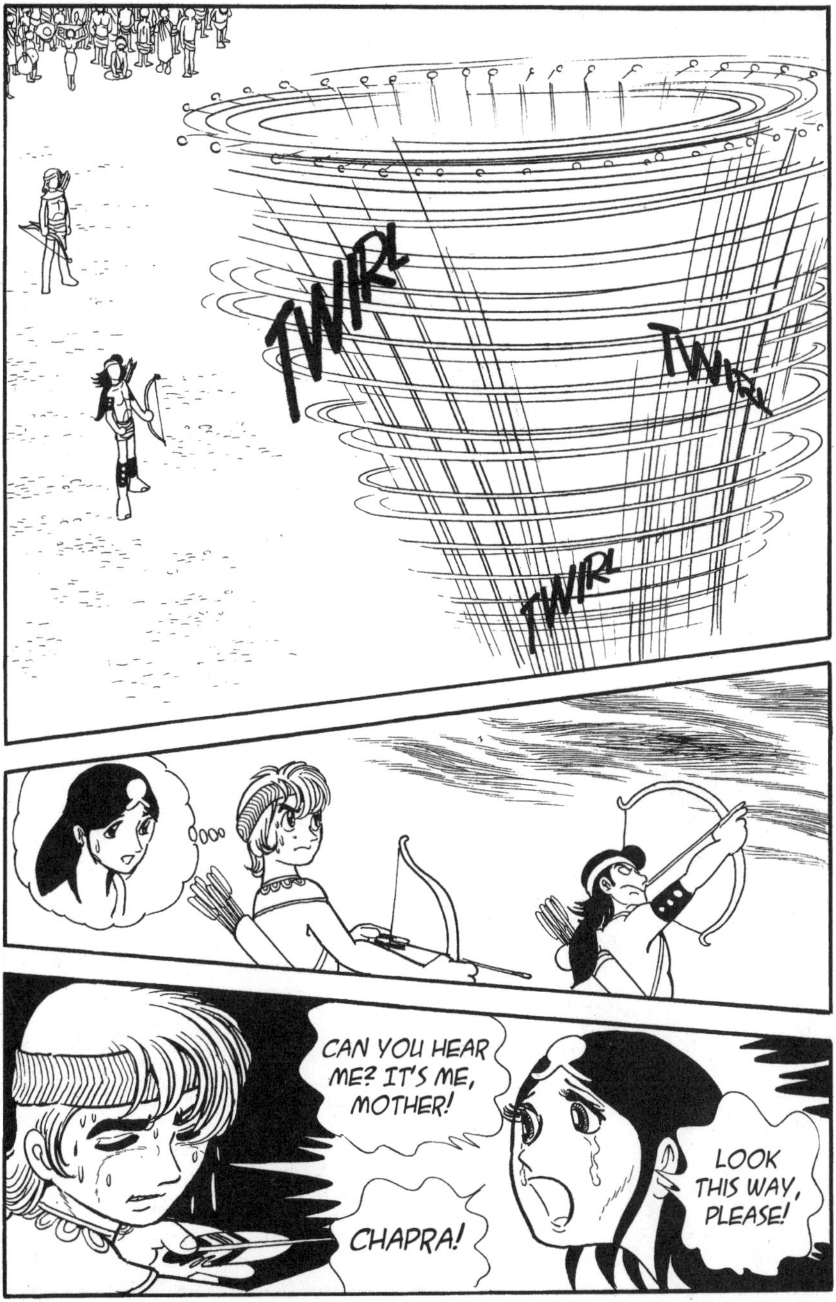
TWIRL
TWIRL
TWIRL
CAN YOU HEAR ME? IT'S ME, MOTHER!
CHAPRA!
LOOK THIS WAY, PLEASE!

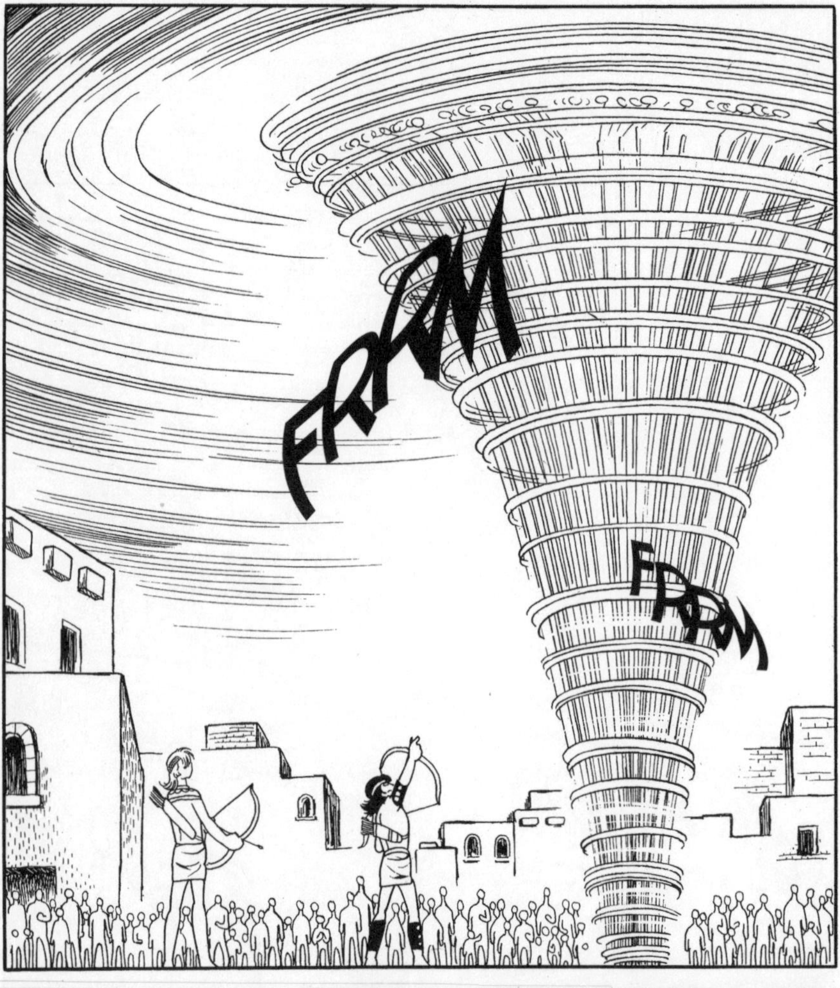
FRRM
FRRRM
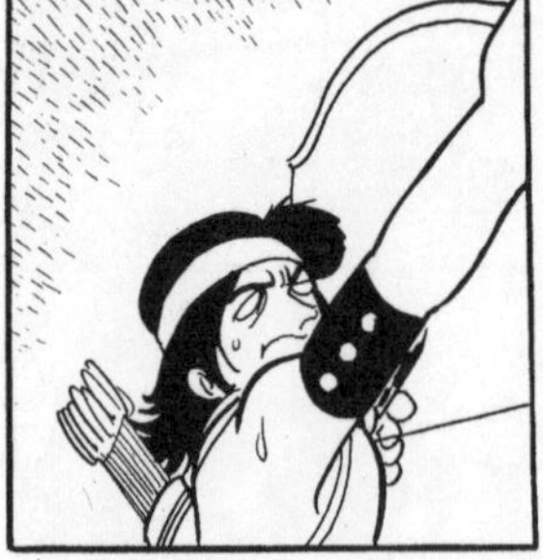
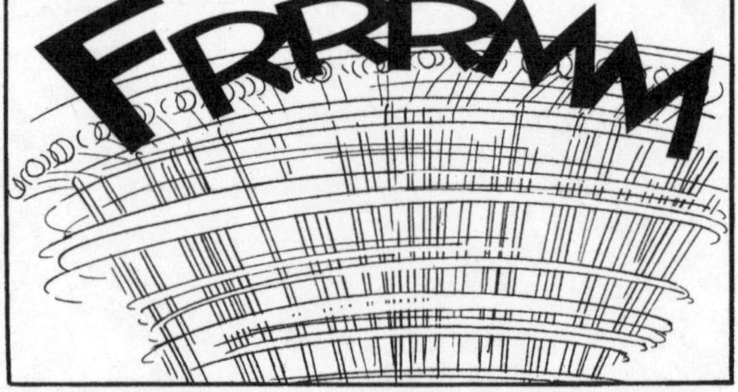
FRRRMMM

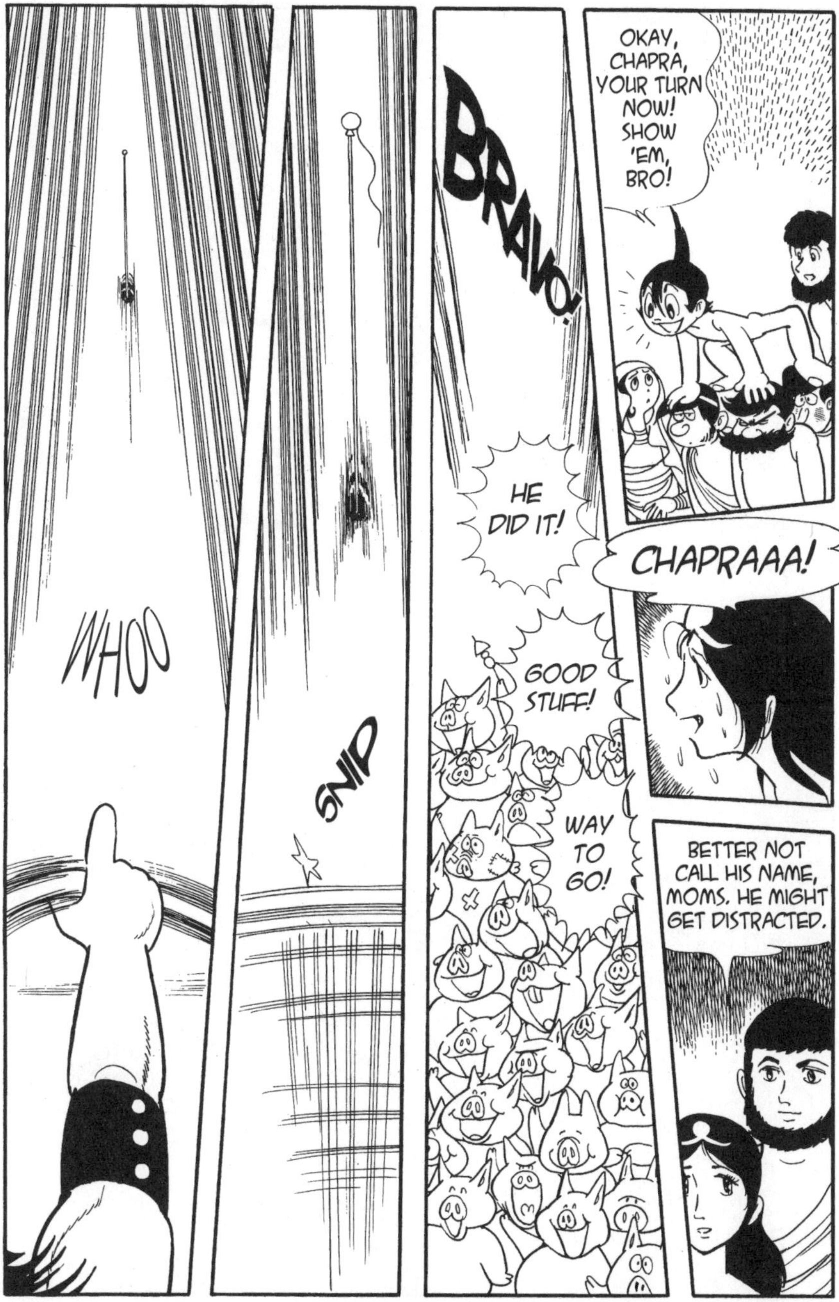
WHOO
SNIP
BRAVO!
HE DID IT!
GOOD STUFF!
WAY TO GO!
OKAY, CHAPRA, YOUR TURN NOW! SHOW 'EM, BRO!
CHAPRAAA!
BETTER NOT CALL HIS NAME, MOMS. HE MIGHT GET DISTRACTED.

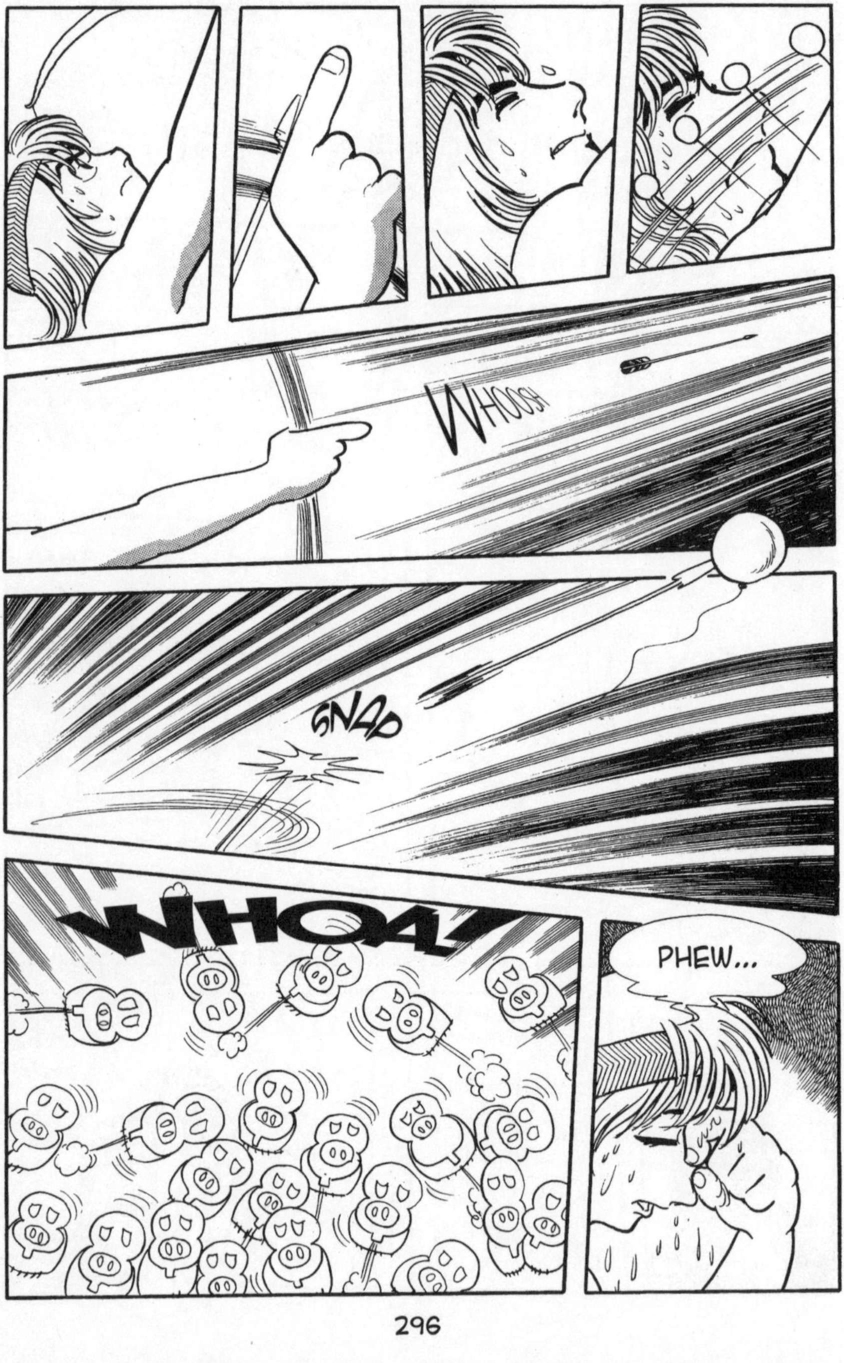
WHOOSH
SNAP
WHOA!
PHEW...

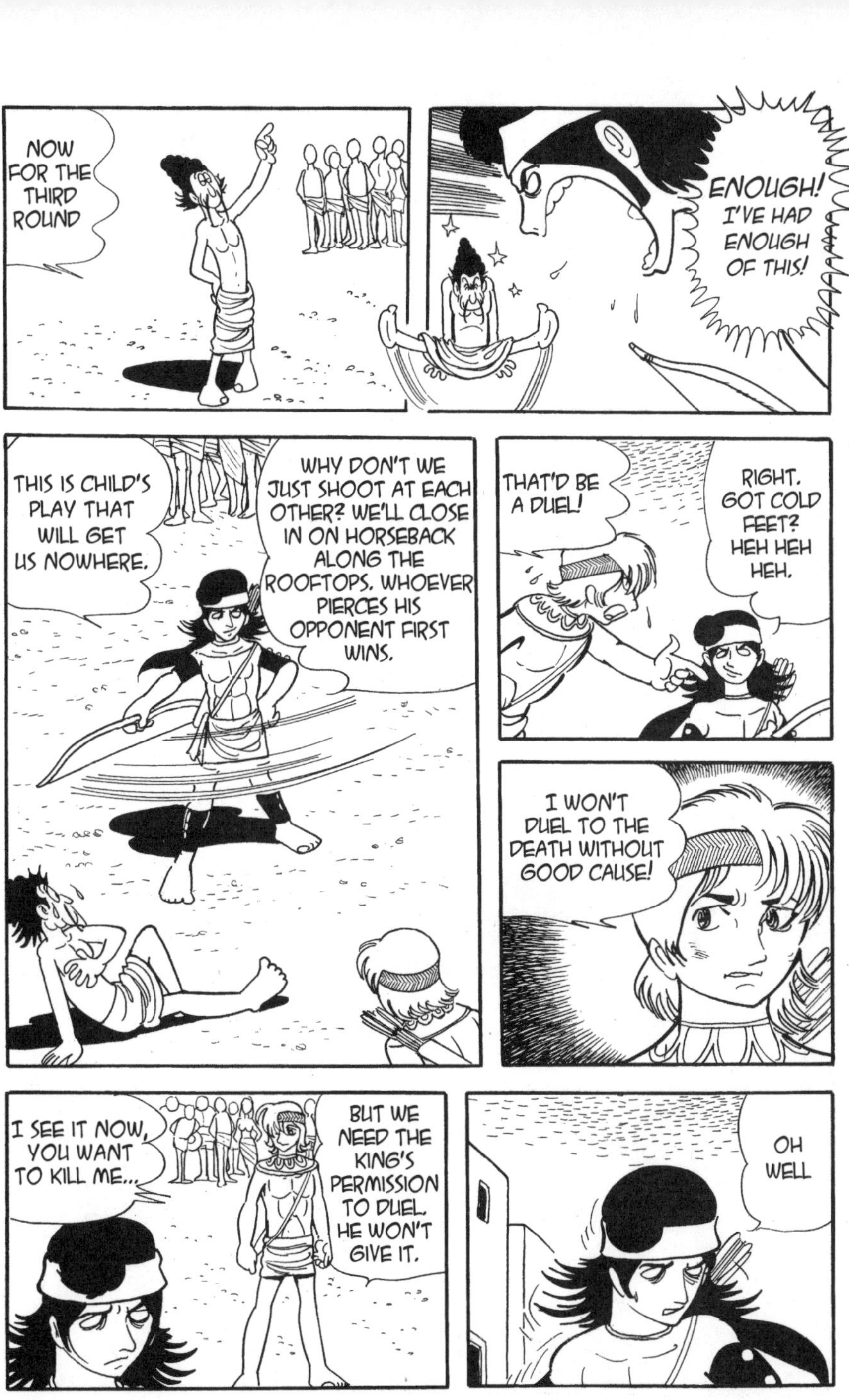
NOW FOR THE THIRD ROUND
ENOUGH! I'VE HAD ENOUGH OF THIS!
THIS IS CHILD'S PLAY THAT WILL GET US NOWHERE.
WHY DON'T WE JUST SHOOT AT EACH OTHER? WE'LL CLOSE IN ON HORSEBACK ALONG THE ROOFTOPS. WHOEVER PIERCES HIS OPPONENT FIRST WINS.
THAT'D BE A DUEL!
RIGHT. GOT COLD FEET? HEH HEH HEH.
I WON'T DUEL TO THE DEATH WITHOUT GOOD CAUSE!
I SEE IT NOW, YOU WANT TO KILL ME...
BUT WE NEED THE KING'S PERMISSION TO DUEL. HE WON'T GIVE IT.
OH WELL

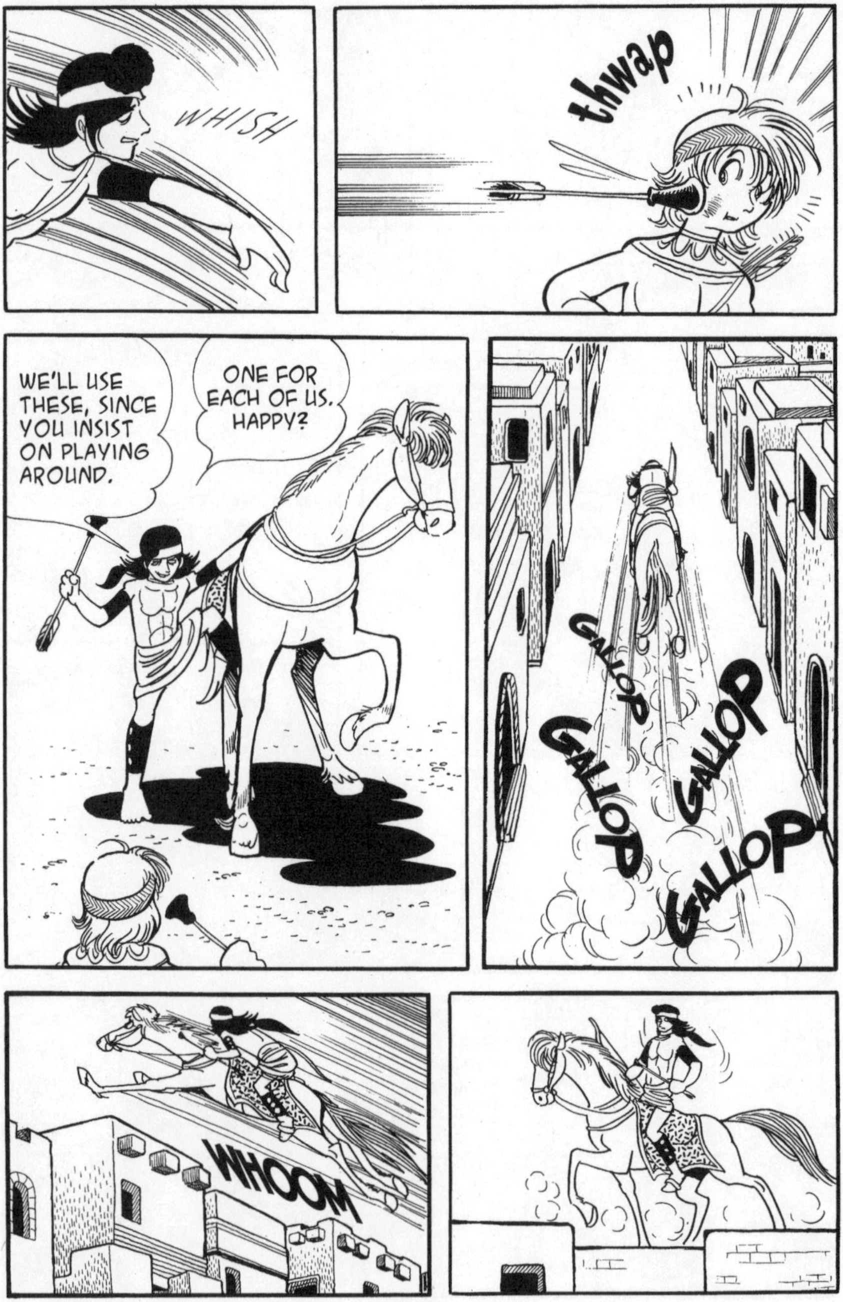
WHISH
thwap
WE'LL USE THESE, SINCE YOU INSIST ON PLAYING AROUND.
ONE FOR EACH OF US. HAPPY?
GALLOP
GALLOP
GALLOP
GALLOP
WHOOM

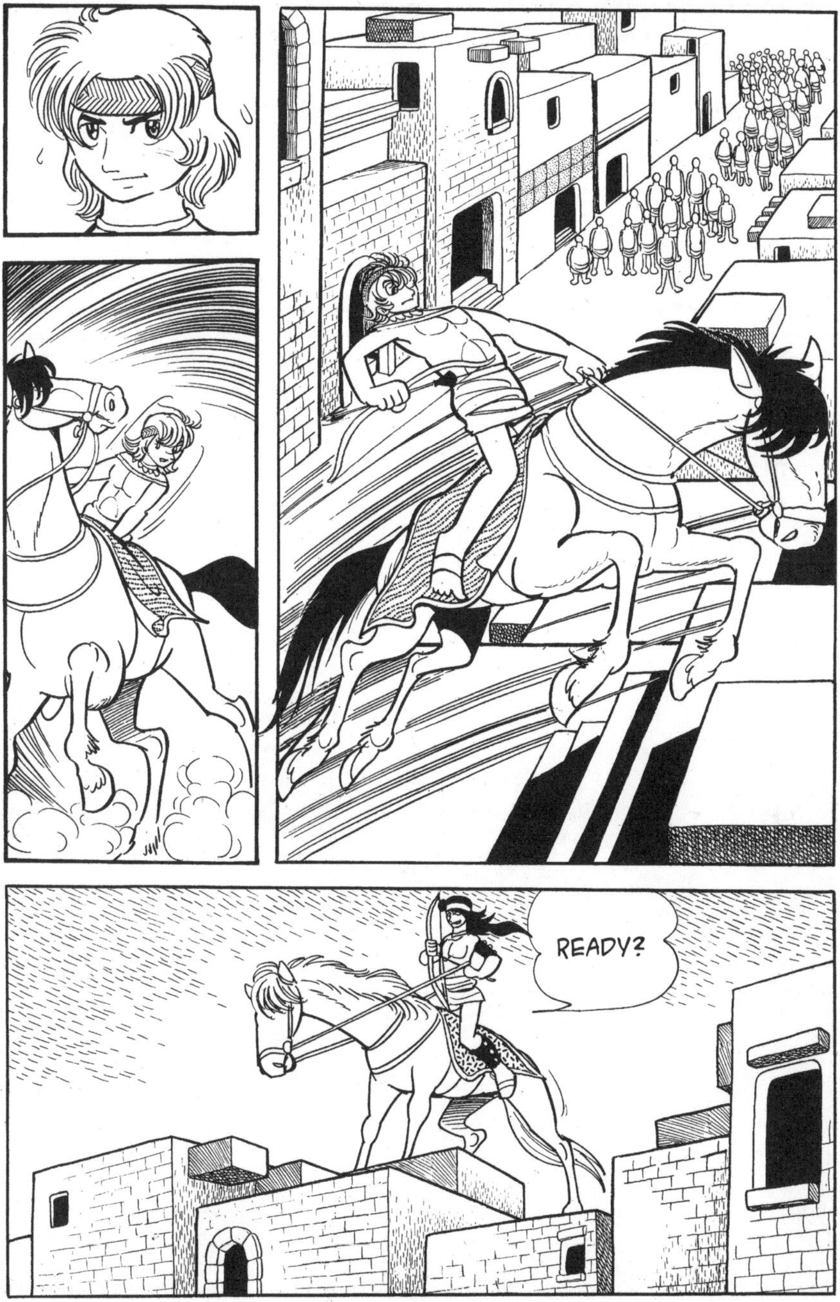
READY?

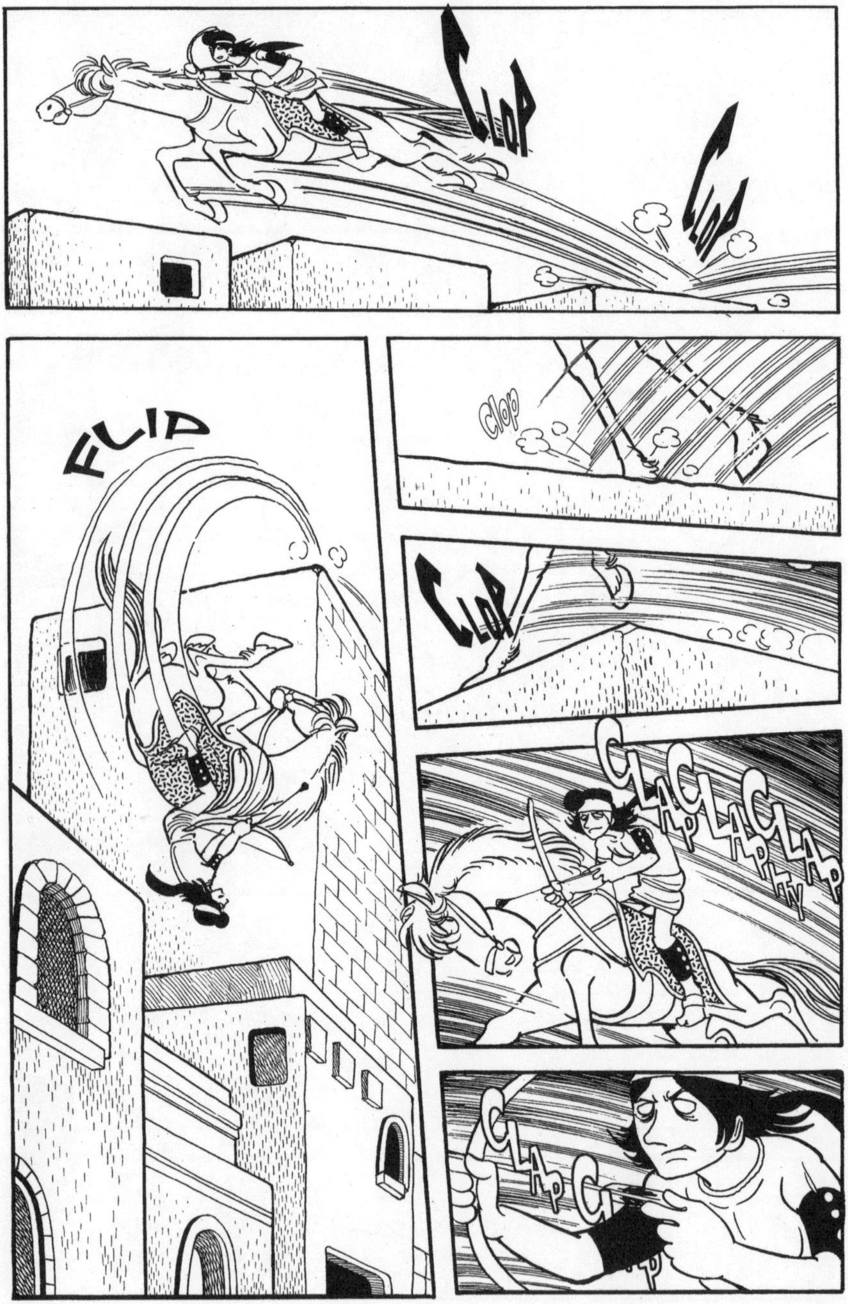
CLOP
CLOP
FLIP
Clop
CLOP
CLAP
CLAPPITY
CLAP
CLAP

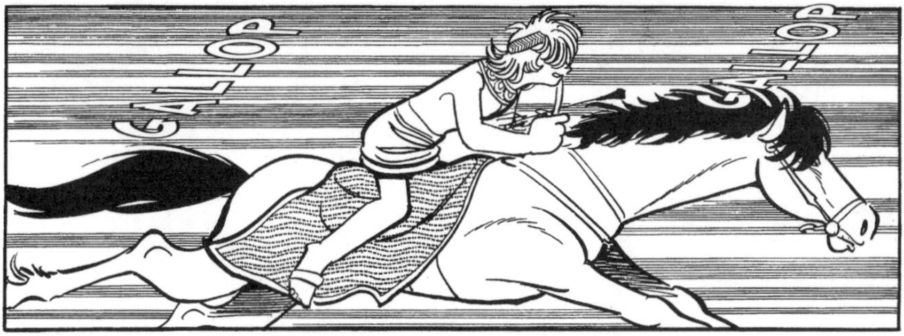
GALLOP
GALLOP
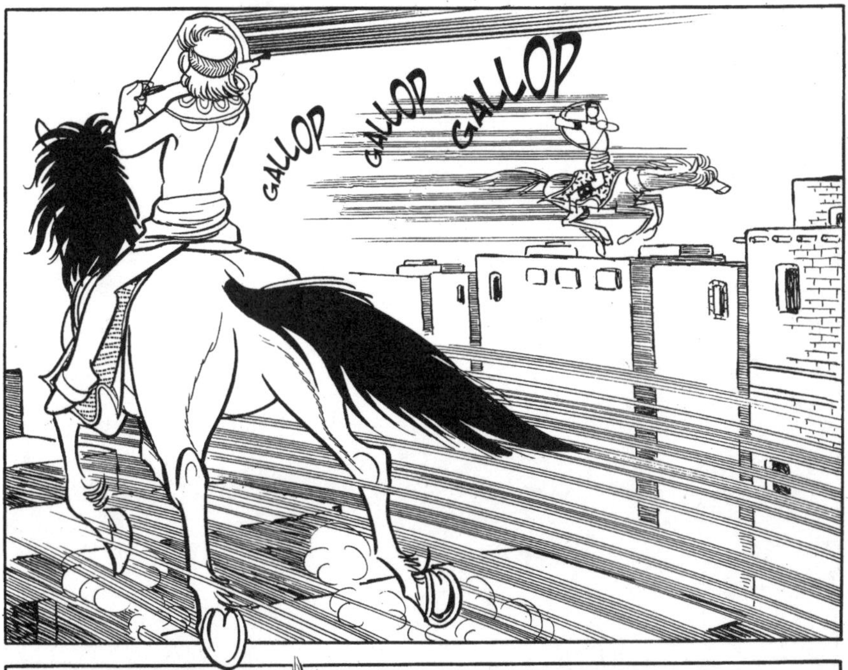
GALLOP
GALLOP
GALLOP
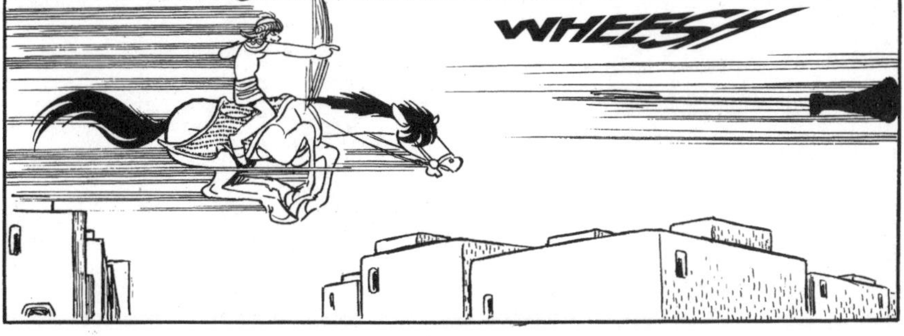
WHEESH

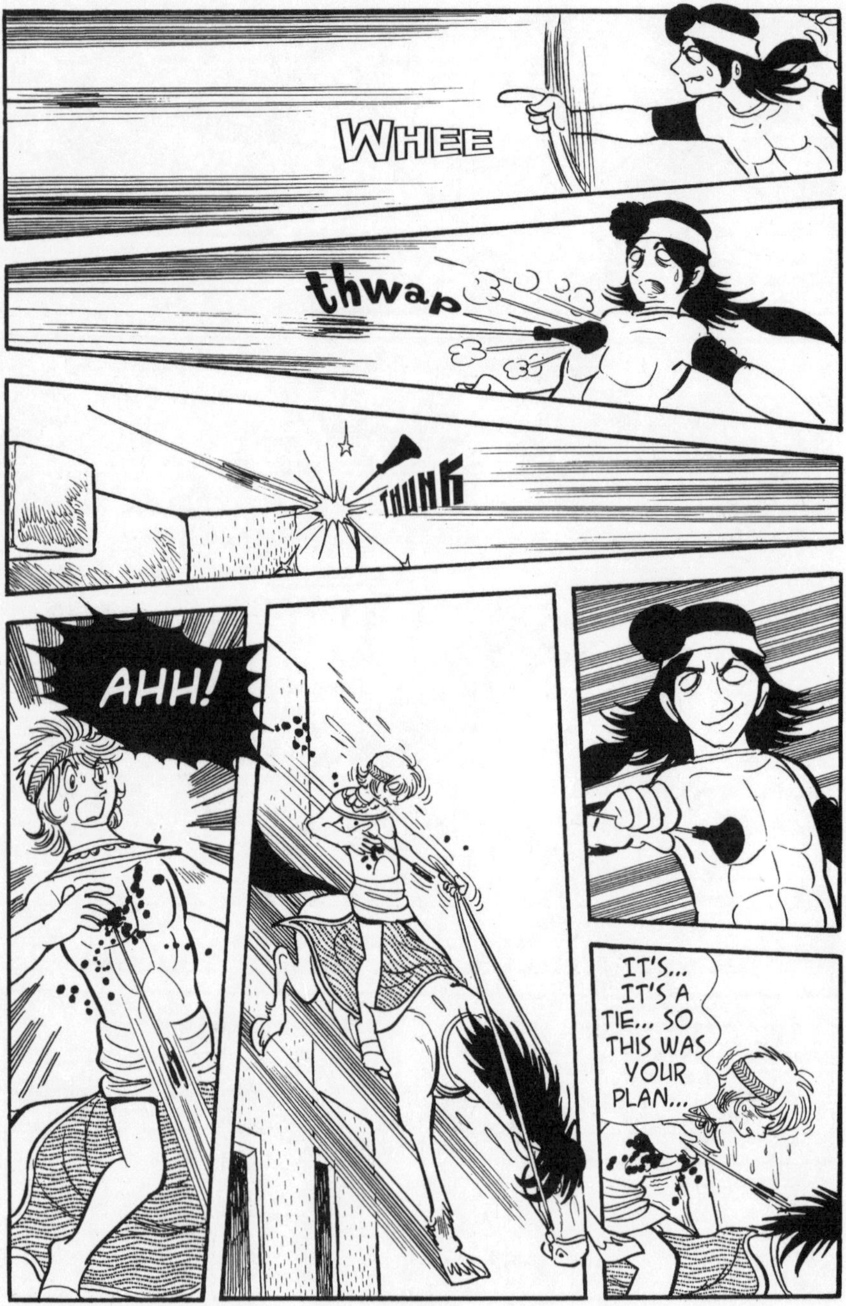
WHEE
thwap
THUNK
AHH!
IT'S... IT'S A TIE... SO THIS WAS YOUR PLAN...

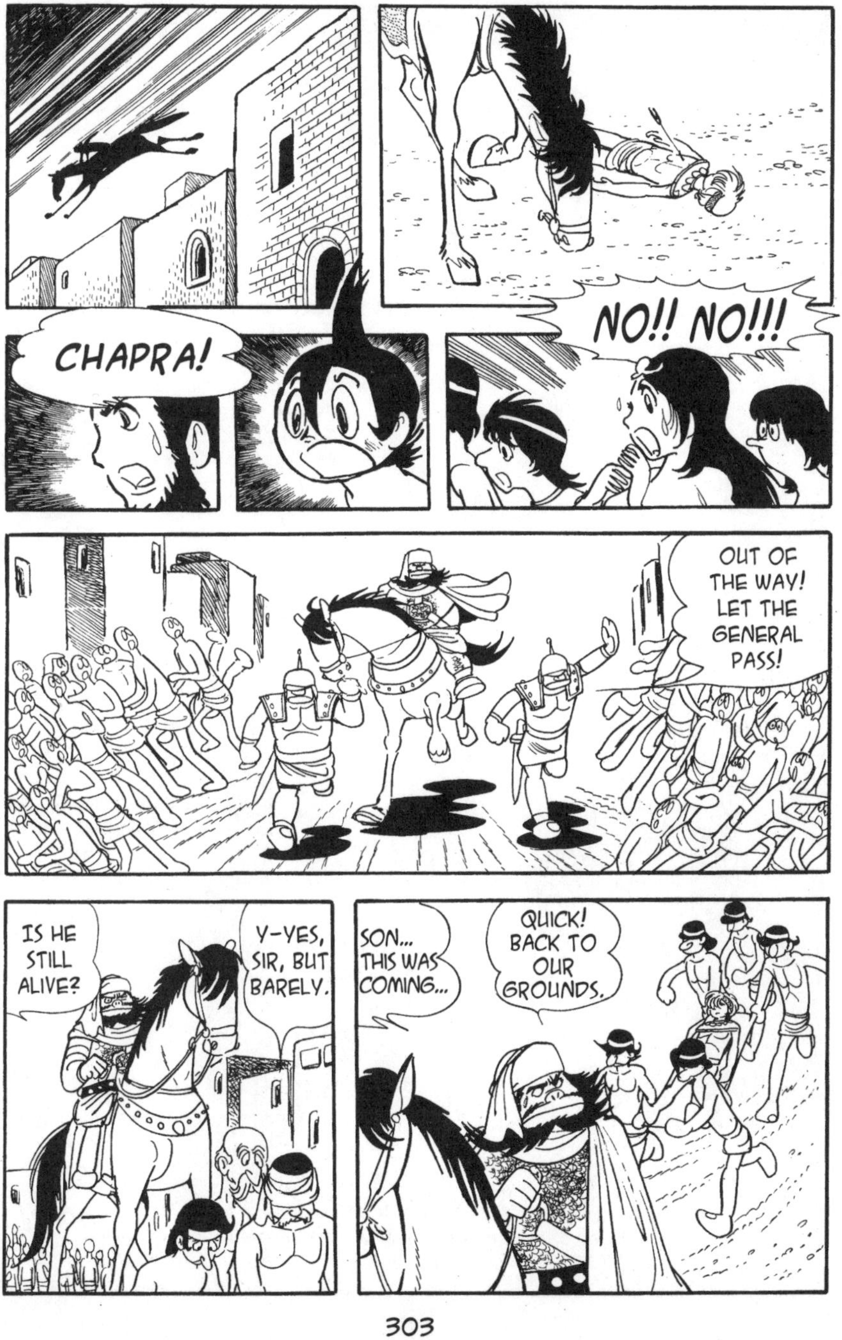
CHAPRA!
NO!! NO!!!
OUT OF THE WAY! LET THE GENERAL PASS!
IS HE STILL ALIVE?
Y-YES, SIR, BUT BARELY.
SON... THIS WAS COMING...
QUICK! BACK TO OUR GROUNDS.

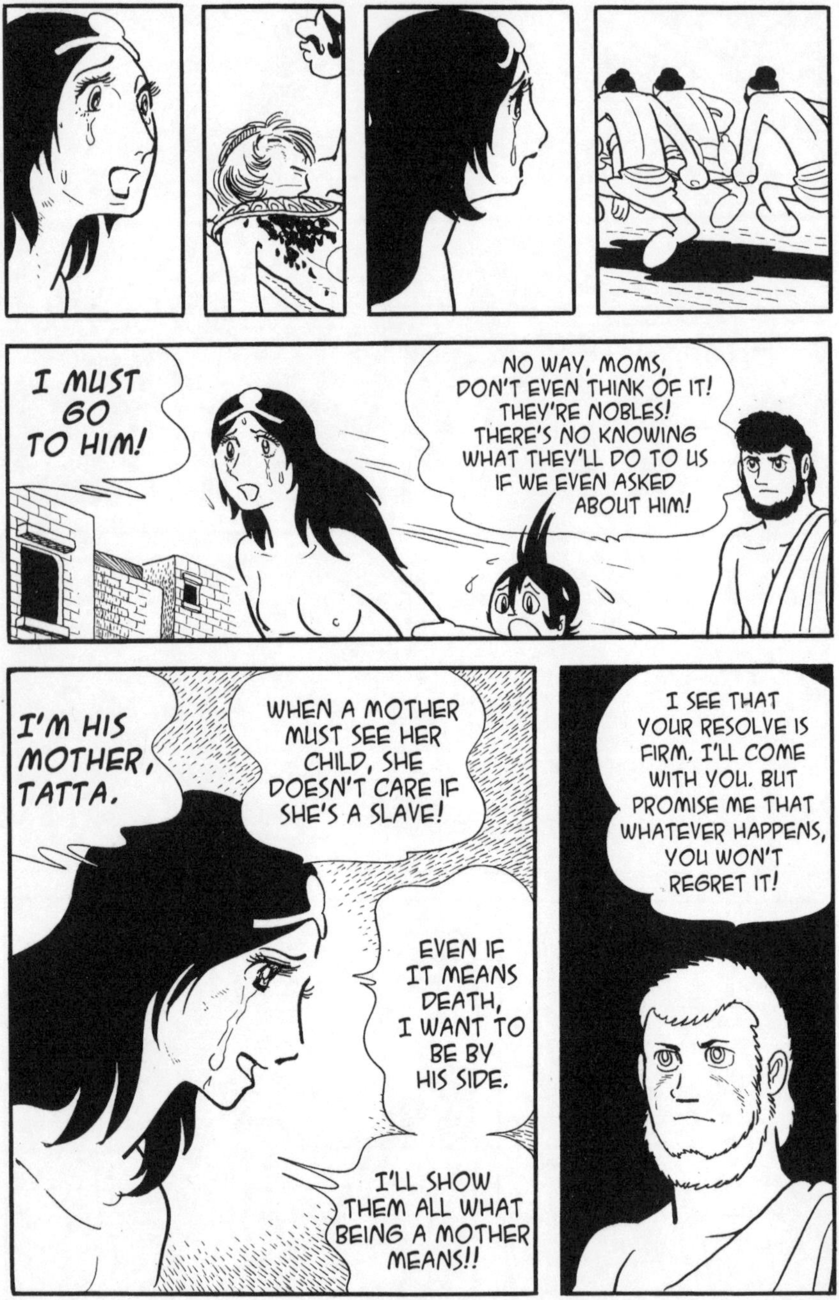
I MUST GO TO HIM!
NO WAY, MOMS, DON'T EVEN THINK OF IT! THEY'RE NOBLES! THERE'S NO KNOWING WHAT THEY'LL DO TO US IF WE EVEN ASKED ABOUT HIM!
I'M HIS MOTHER, TATTA.
WHEN A MOTHER MUST SEE HER CHILD, SHE DOESN'T CARE IF SHE'S A SLAVE!
EVEN IF IT MEANS DEATH, I WANT TO BE BY HIS SIDE.
I'LL SHOW THEM ALL WHAT BEING A MOTHER MEANS!!
I SEE THAT YOUR RESOLVE IS FIRM. I'LL COME WITH YOU. BUT PROMISE ME THAT WHATEVER HAPPENS, YOU WON'T REGRET IT!

CHAPTER NINE

ALL FOR A CURE

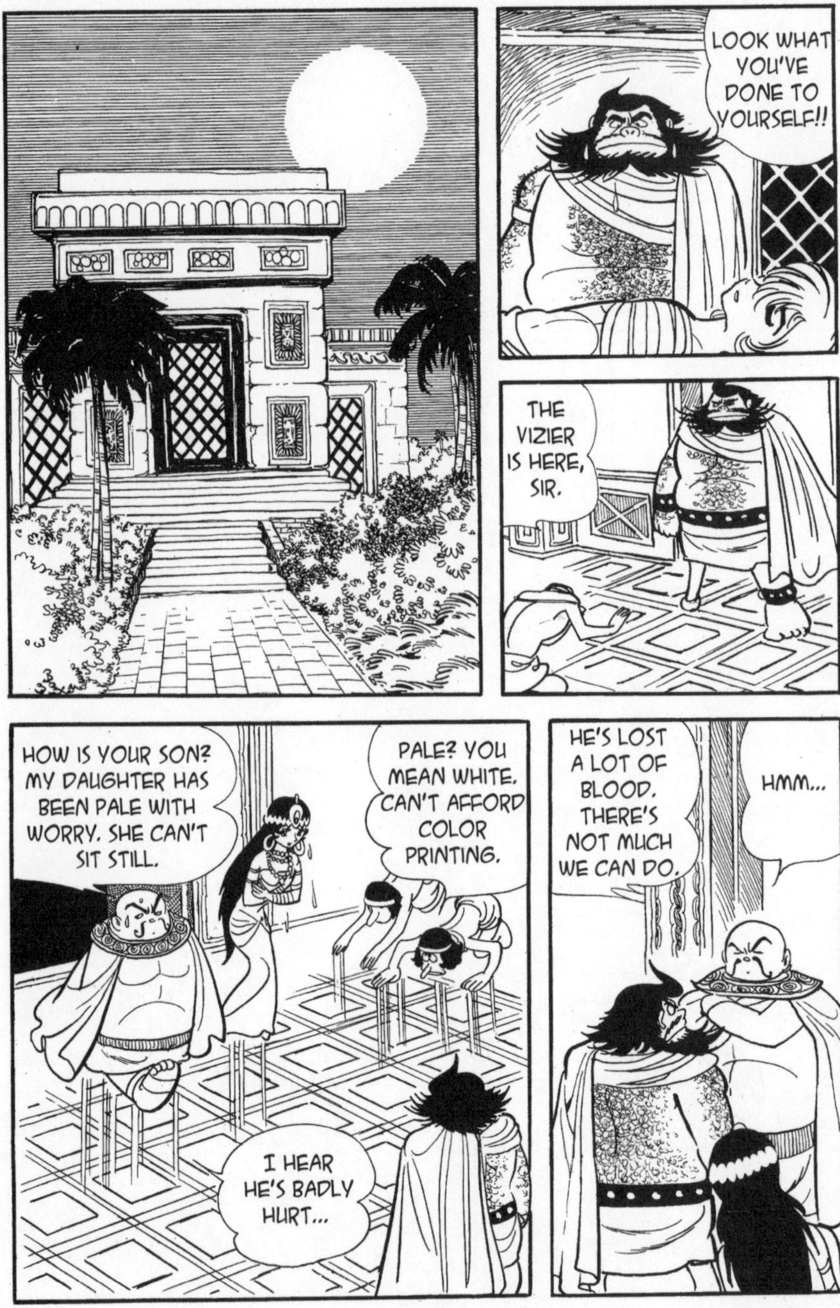
LOOK WHAT YOU'VE DONE TO YOURSELF!!
THE VIZIER IS HERE, SIR.
HOW IS YOUR SON? MY DAUGHTER HAS BEEN PALE WITH WORRY. SHE CAN'T SIT STILL.
PALE? YOU MEAN WHITE. CAN'T AFFORD COLOR PRINTING.
I HEAR HE'S BADLY HURT...
HE'S LOST A LOT OF BLOOD. THERE'S NOT MUCH WE CAN DO.
HMM...

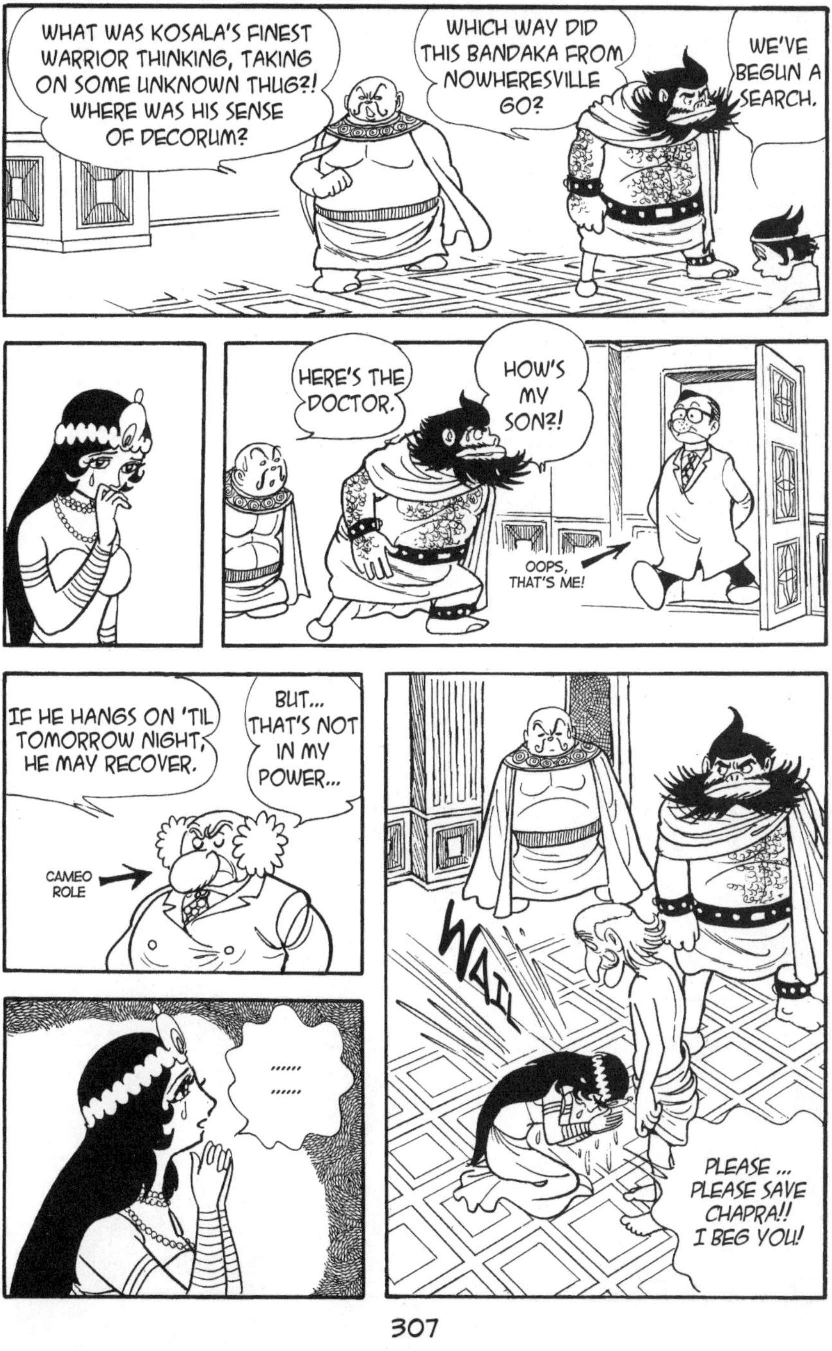
WHAT WAS KOSALA'S FINEST WARRIOR THINKING, TAKING ON SOME UNKNOWN THUG?! WHERE WAS HIS SENSE OF DECORUM?
WHICH WAY DID THIS BANDAKA FROM NOWHERESVILLE GO?
WE'VE BEGUN A SEARCH.
HERE'S THE DOCTOR.
HOW'S MY SON?!
OOPS, THAT'S ME!
IF HE HANGS ON 'TIL TOMORROW NIGHT, HE MAY RECOVER.
BUT... THAT'S NOT IN MY POWER...
CAMEO ROLE
......
......
WAIL
PLEASE ... PLEASE SAVE CHAPRA!! I BEG YOU!

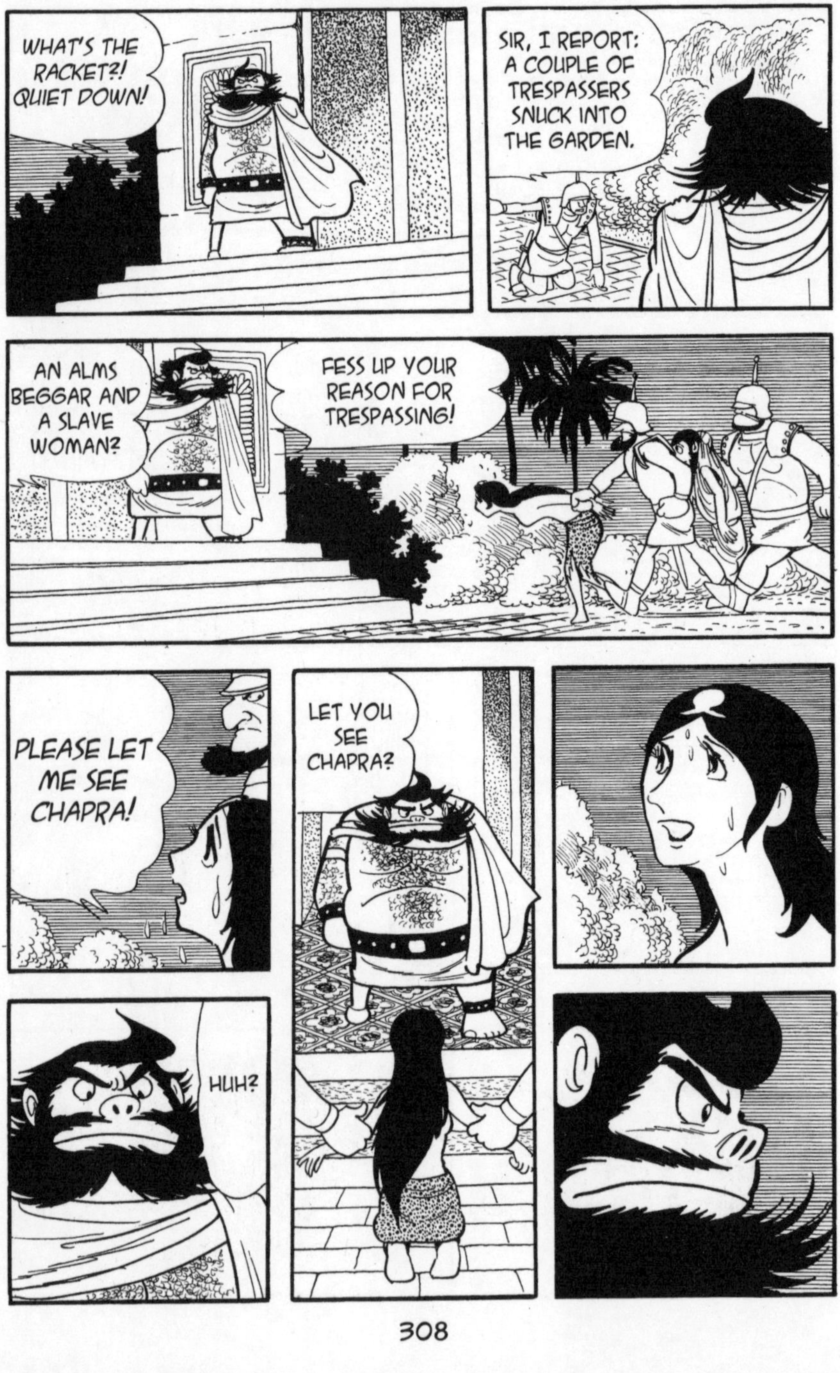
WHAT'S THE RACKET?! QUIET DOWN!
SIR, I REPORT: A COUPLE OF TRESPASSERS SNUCK INTO THE GARDEN.
AN ALMS BEGGAR AND A SLAVE WOMAN?
FESS UP YOUR REASON FOR TRESPASSING!
PLEASE LET ME SEE CHAPRA!
LET YOU SEE CHAPRA?
HUH?

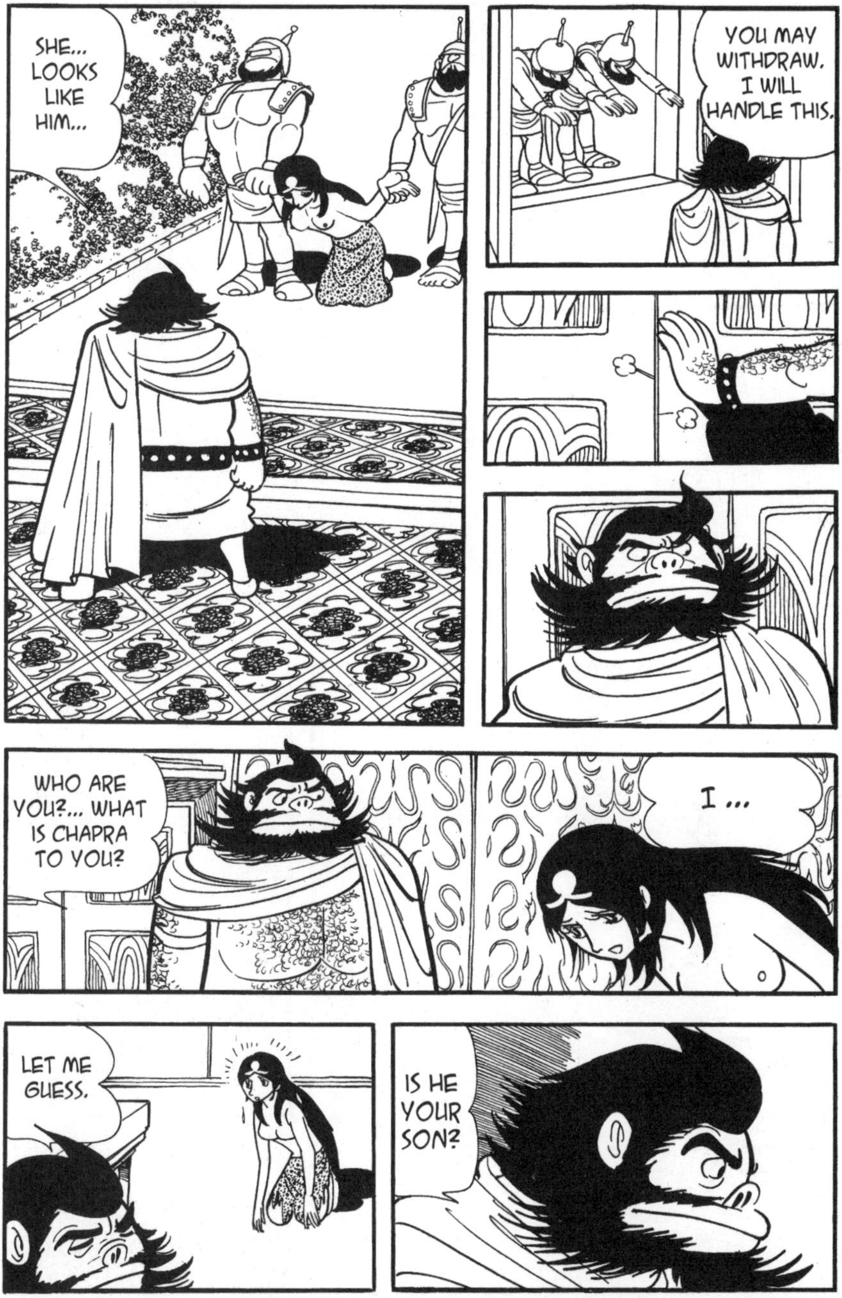
SHE... LOOKS LIKE HIM...
YOU MAY WITHDRAW. I WILL HANDLE THIS.
WHO ARE YOU?... WHAT IS CHAPRA TO YOU?
I...
LET ME GUESS.
IS HE YOUR SON?

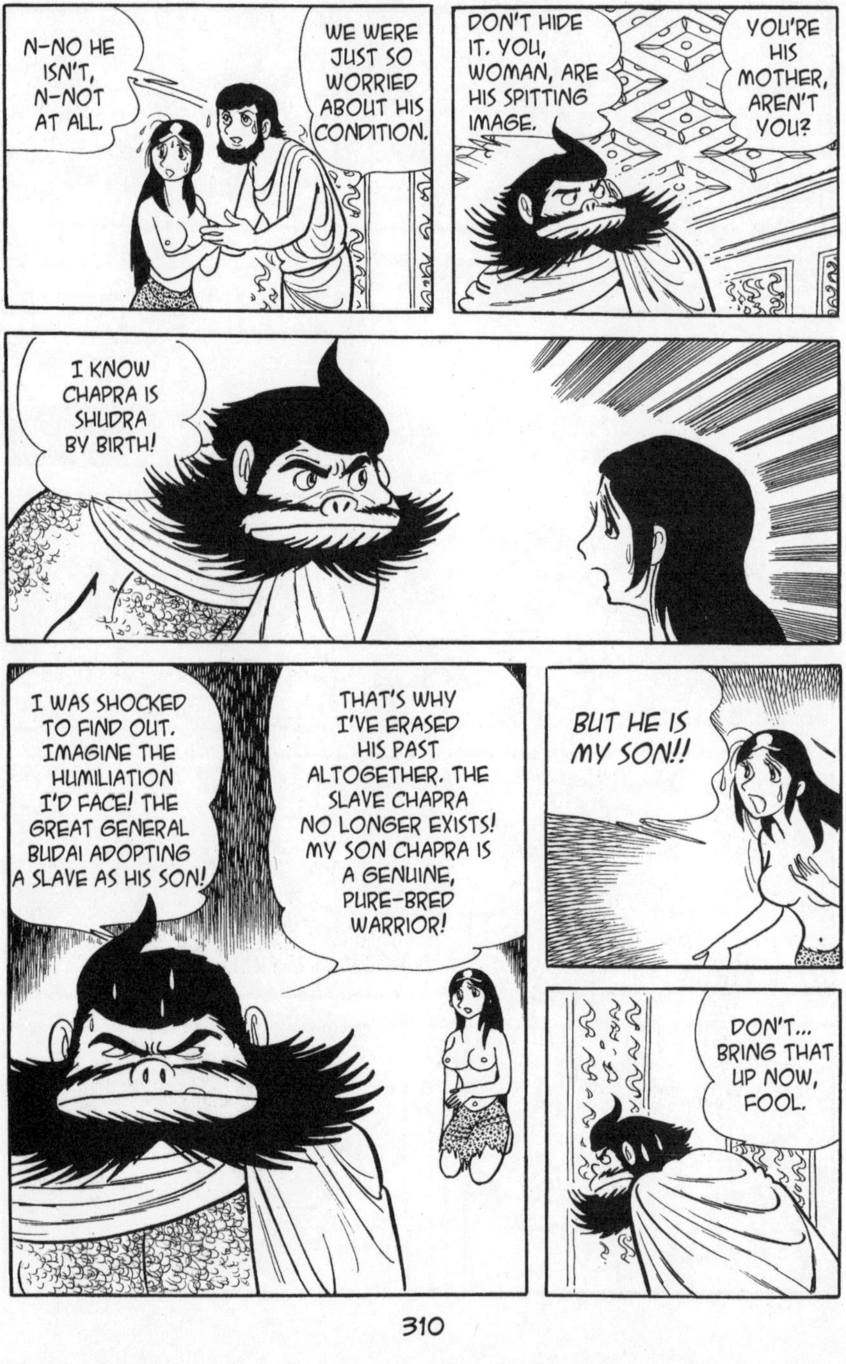
N-NO HE ISN'T, N-NOT AT ALL.
WE WERE JUST SO WORRIED ABOUT HIS CONDITION.
DON'T HIDE IT. YOU, WOMAN, ARE HIS SPITTING IMAGE.
YOU'RE HIS MOTHER, AREN'T YOU?
I KNOW CHAPRA IS SHUDRA BY BIRTH!
I WAS SHOCKED TO FIND OUT. IMAGINE THE HUMILIATION I'D FACE! THE GREAT GENERAL BUDAI ADOPTING A SLAVE AS HIS SON!
THAT'S WHY I'VE ERASED HIS PAST ALTOGETHER. THE SLAVE CHAPRA NO LONGER EXISTS! MY SON CHAPRA IS A GENUINE, PURE-BRED WARRIOR!
BUT HE IS MY SON!!
DON'T... BRING THAT UP NOW, FOOL.

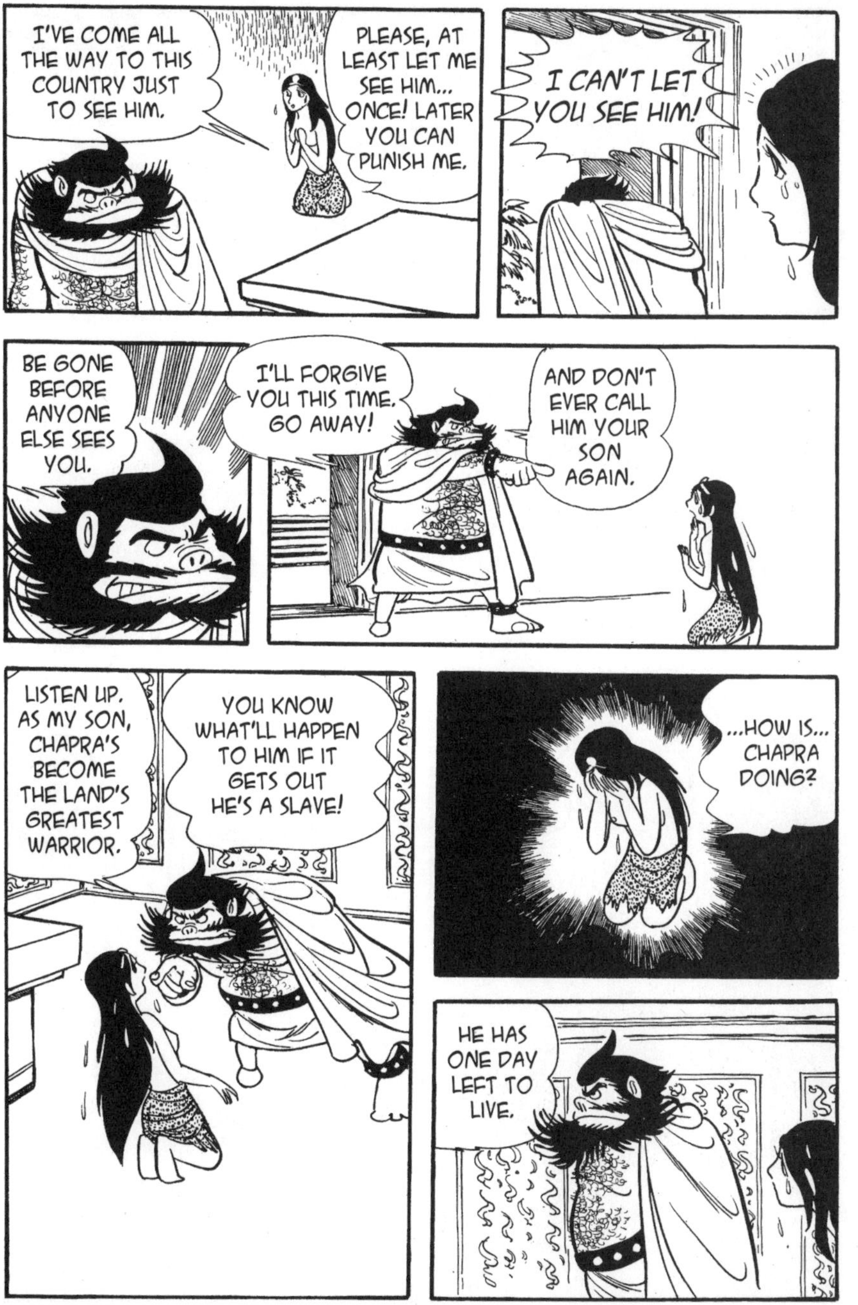

I'VE COME ALL THE WAY TO THIS COUNTRY JUST TO SEE HIM.
PLEASE, AT LEAST LET ME SEE HIM... ONCE! LATER YOU CAN PUNISH ME.
I CAN'T LET YOU SEE HIM!
BE GONE BEFORE ANYONE ELSE SEES YOU.
I'LL FORGIVE YOU THIS TIME. GO AWAY!
AND DON'T EVER CALL HIM YOUR SON AGAIN.
LISTEN UP. AS MY SON, CHAPRA'S BECOME THE LAND'S GREATEST WARRIOR.
YOU KNOW WHAT'LL HAPPEN TO HIM IF IT GETS OUT HE'S A SLAVE!
...HOW IS... CHAPRA DOING?
HE HAS ONE DAY LEFT TO LIVE.

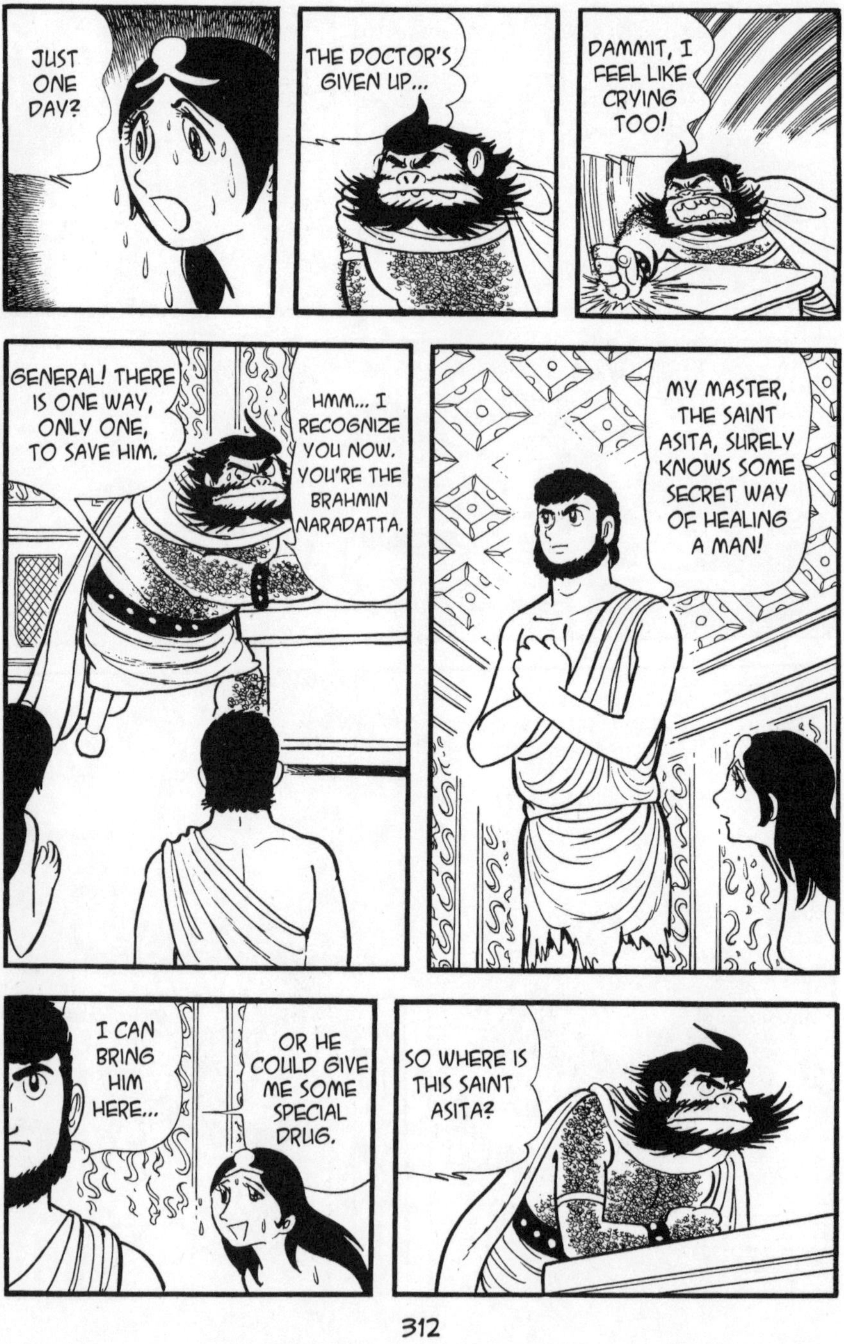
JUST ONE DAY?
THE DOCTOR'S GIVEN UP...
DAMMIT, I FEEL LIKE CRYING TOO!
GENERAL! THERE IS ONE WAY, ONLY ONE, TO SAVE HIM.
HMM... I RECOGNIZE YOU NOW. YOU'RE THE BRAHMIN NARADATTA.
MY MASTER, THE SAINT ASITA, SURELY KNOWS SOME SECRET WAY OF HEALING A MAN!
I CAN BRING HIM HERE...
OR HE COULD GIVE ME SOME SPECIAL DRUG.
SO WHERE IS THIS SAINT ASITA?

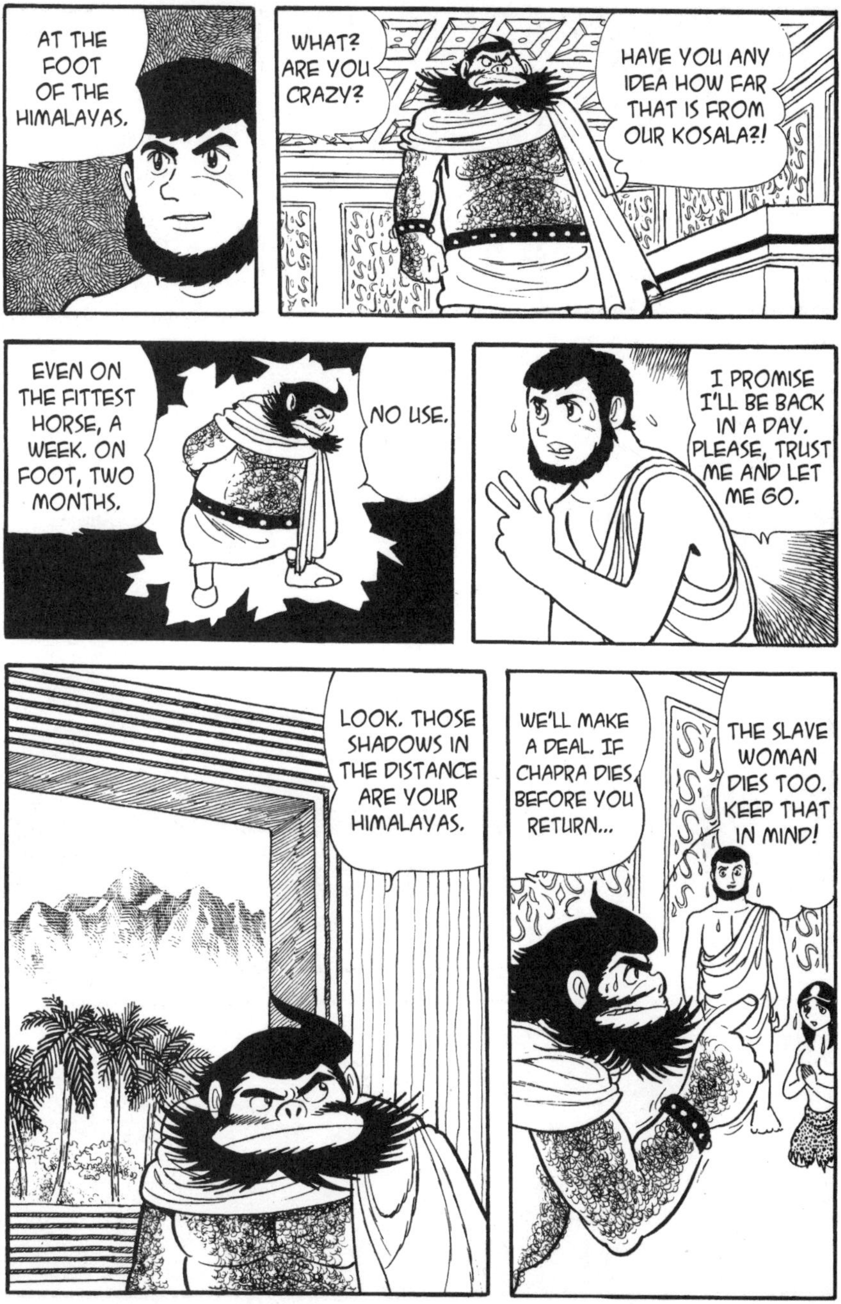
AT THE FOOT OF THE HIMALAYAS.
WHAT? ARE YOU CRAZY?
HAVE YOU ANY IDEA HOW FAR THAT IS FROM OUR KOSALA?!
EVEN ON THE FITTEST HORSE, A WEEK. ON FOOT, TWO MONTHS.
NO USE.
I PROMISE I'LL BE BACK IN A DAY. PLEASE, TRUST ME AND LET ME GO.
LOOK. THOSE SHADOWS IN THE DISTANCE ARE YOUR HIMALAYAS.
WE'LL MAKE A DEAL. IF CHAPRA DIES BEFORE YOU RETURN...
THE SLAVE WOMAN DIES TOO. KEEP THAT IN MIND!

AND IF I MAKE IT BACK IN TIME, AND CHAPRA IS SAVED...

WILL YOU GRANT HIS MOTHER HER REQUEST AND LET HER SEE HIM?

ALL RIGHT, I PROMISE. I'LL LET HER SEE HIM AND GRANT YOU A REWARD OF YOUR CHOOSING.

LOCK THIS WOMAN UP. THE MONK CAN GO.

NARADATTA

IT'S A GAMBLE. BUT DON'T WORRY.

314

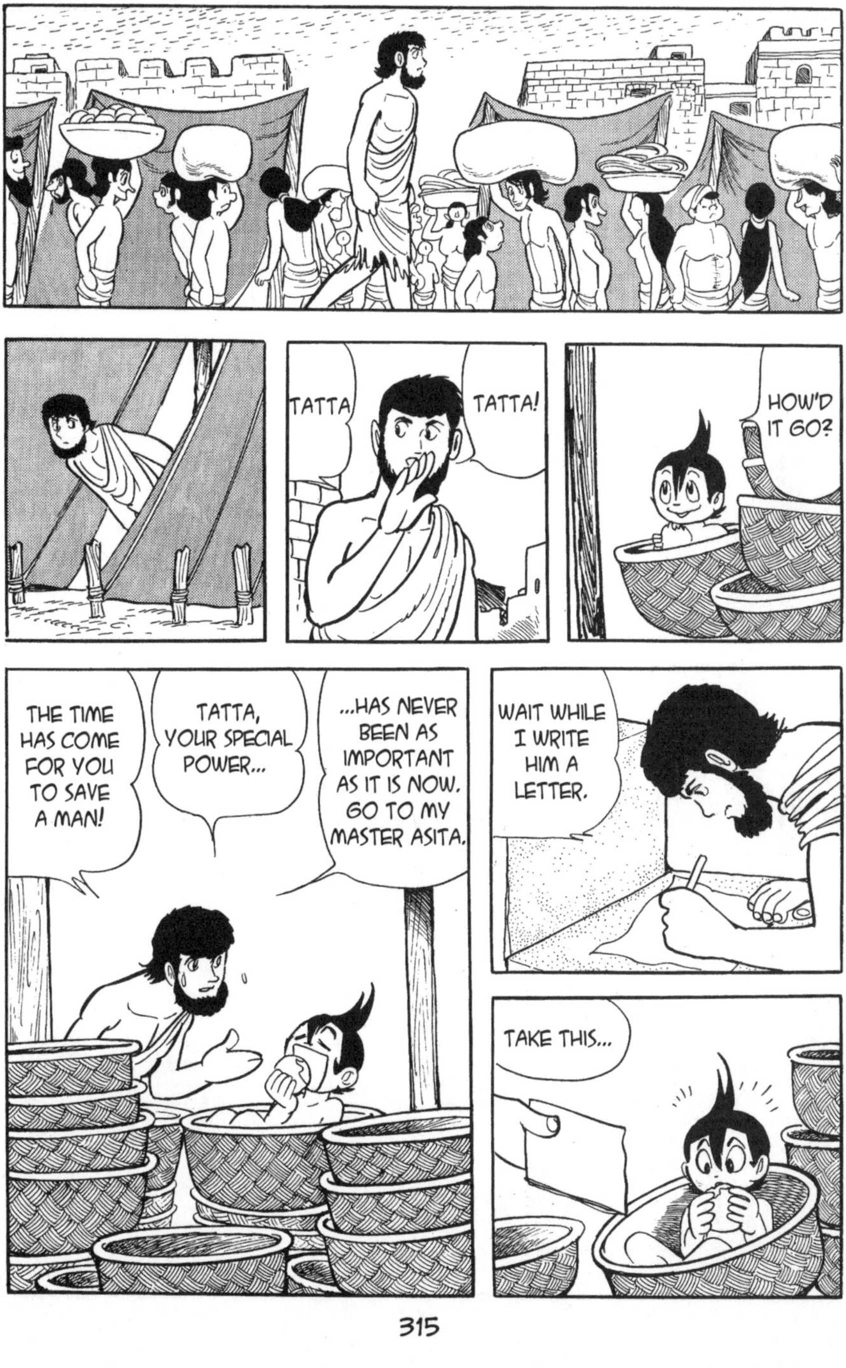
TATTA
TATTA!
HOW'D IT GO?
THE TIME HAS COME FOR YOU TO SAVE A MAN!
TATTA, YOUR SPECIAL POWER...
...HAS NEVER BEEN AS IMPORTANT AS IT IS NOW. GO TO MY MASTER ASITA.
WAIT WHILE I WRITE HIM A LETTER.
TAKE THIS...

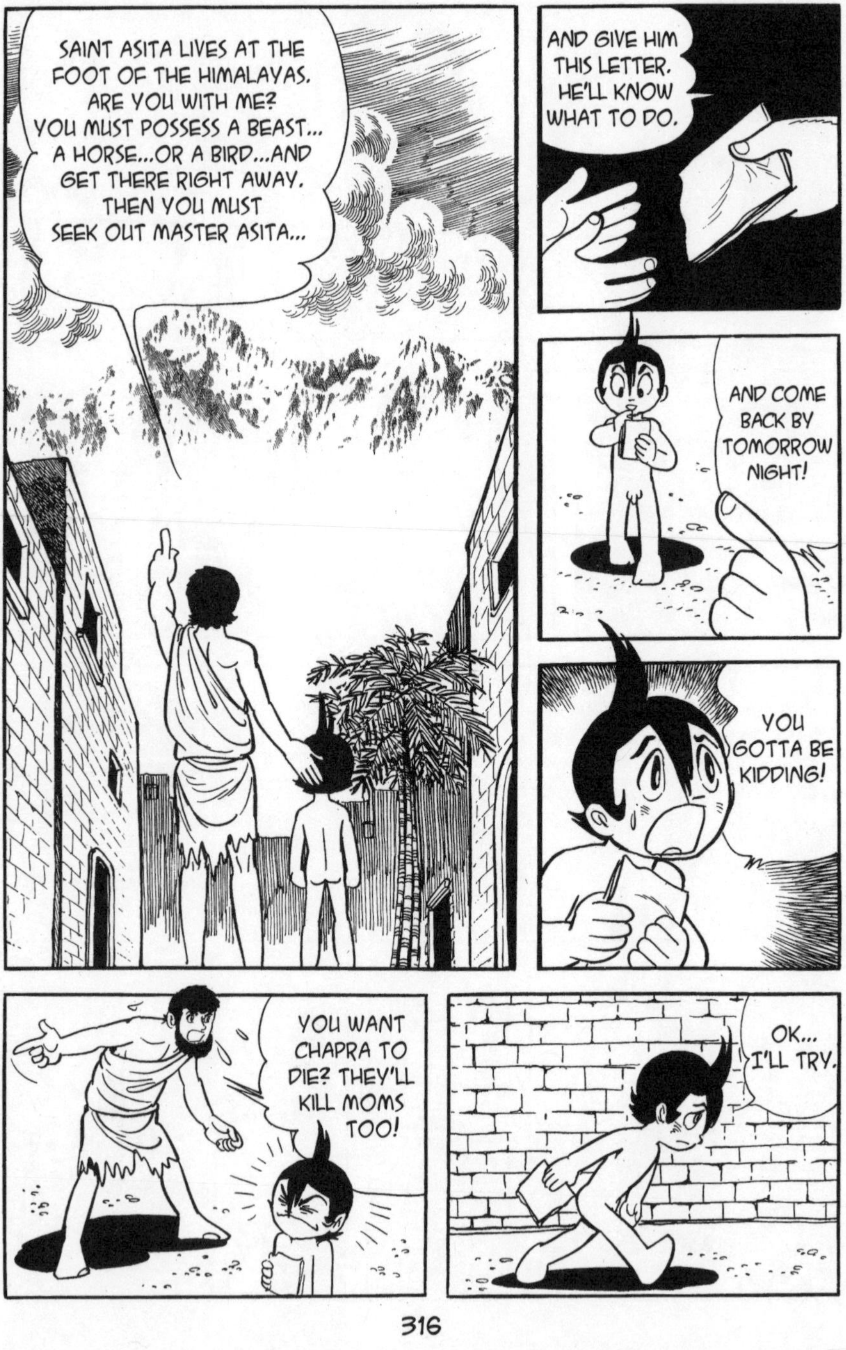
SAINT ASITA LIVES AT THE FOOT OF THE HIMALAYAS. ARE YOU WITH ME? YOU MUST POSSESS A BEAST... A HORSE...OR A BIRD...AND GET THERE RIGHT AWAY. THEN YOU MUST SEEK OUT MASTER ASITA...
AND GIVE HIM THIS LETTER. HE'LL KNOW WHAT TO DO.
AND COME BACK BY TOMORROW NIGHT!
YOU GOTTA BE KIDDING!
YOU WANT CHAPRA TO DIE? THEY'LL KILL MOMS TOO!
OK... I'LL TRY.

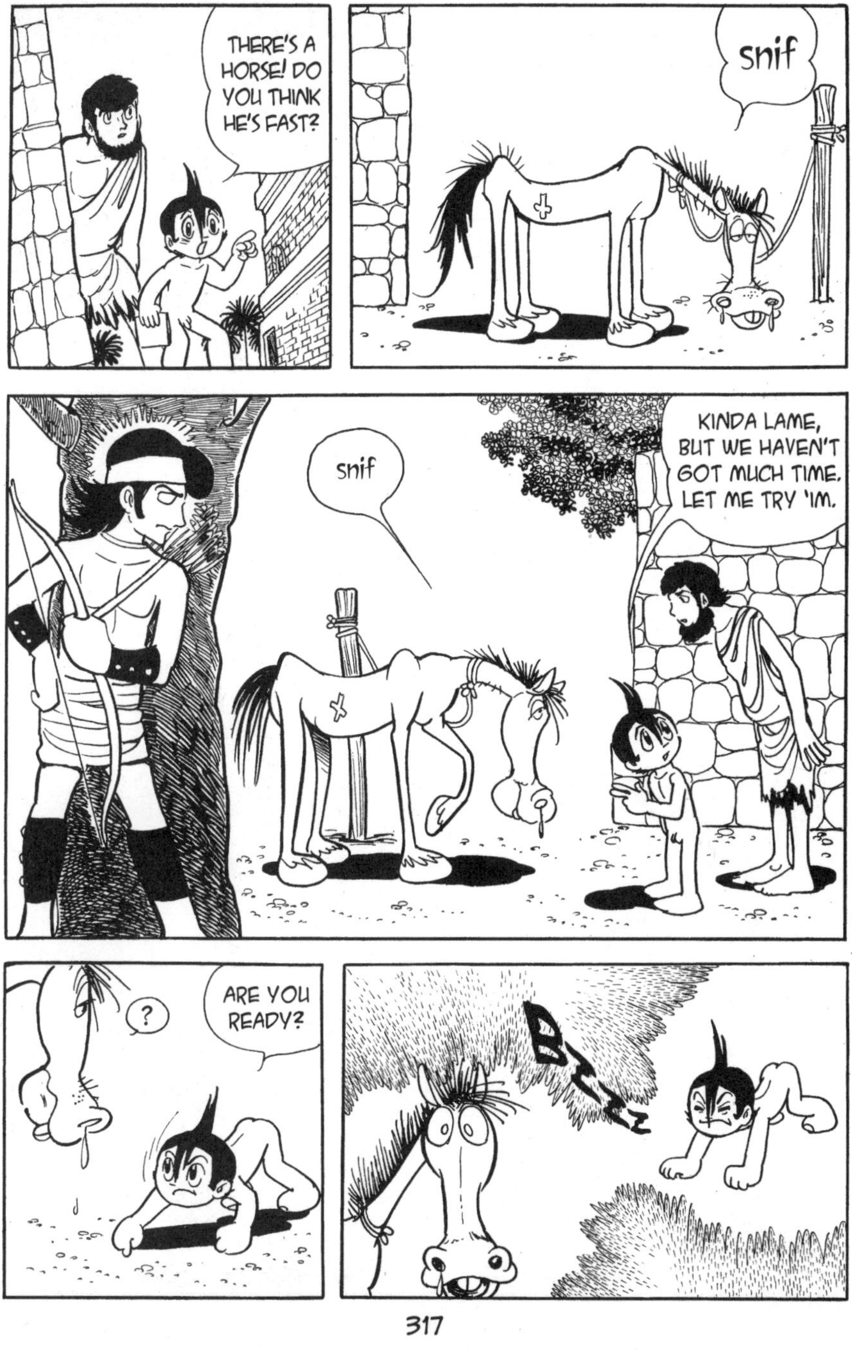
THERE'S A HORSE! DO YOU THINK HE'S FAST?
snif
snif
KINDA LAME, BUT WE HAVEN'T GOT MUCH TIME. LET ME TRY 'IM.
?
ARE YOU READY?

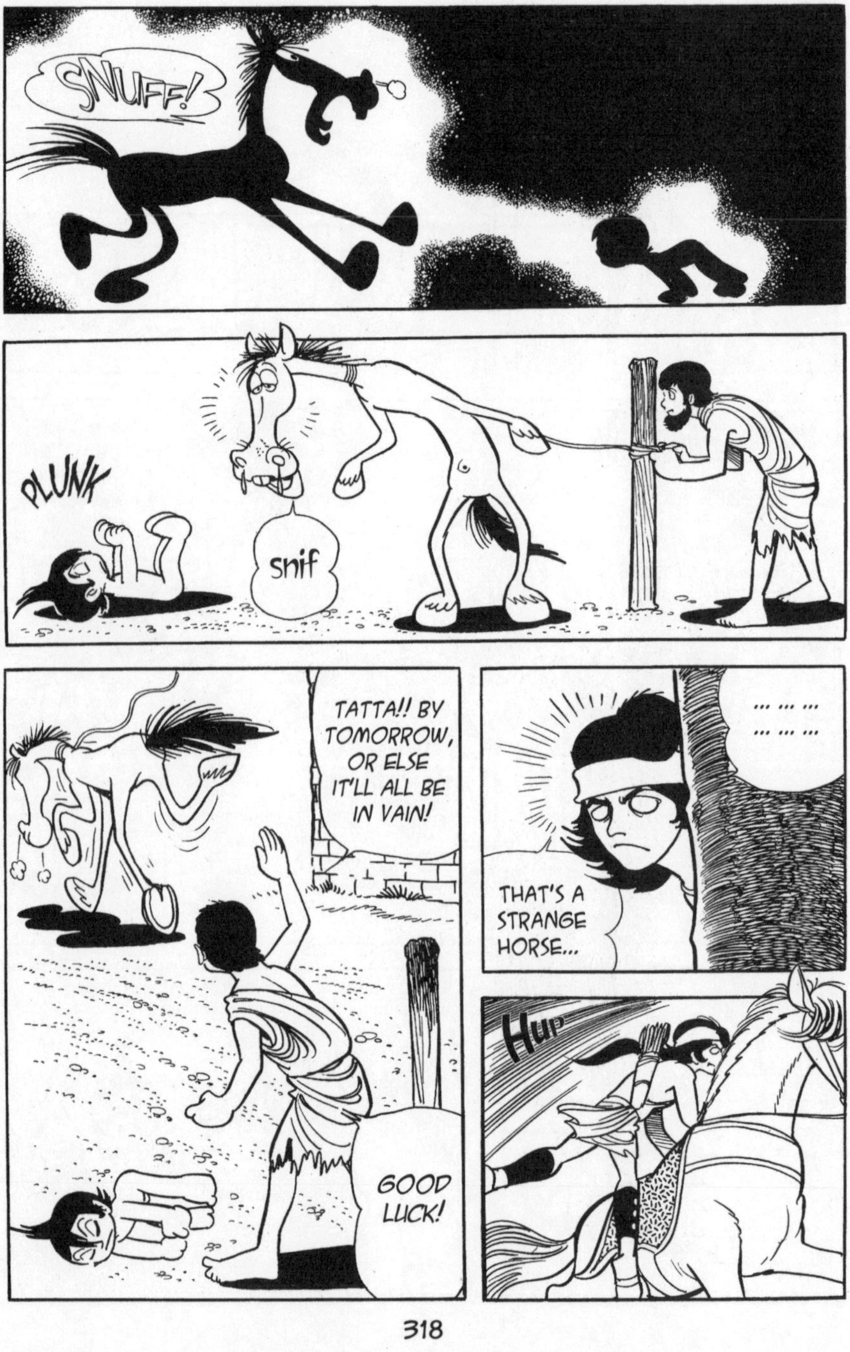
SNUFF!
PLUNK
snif
TATTA!! BY TOMORROW, OR ELSE IT'LL ALL BE IN VAIN!
GOOD LUCK!
... ...
... ...
THAT'S A STRANGE HORSE...
HUP

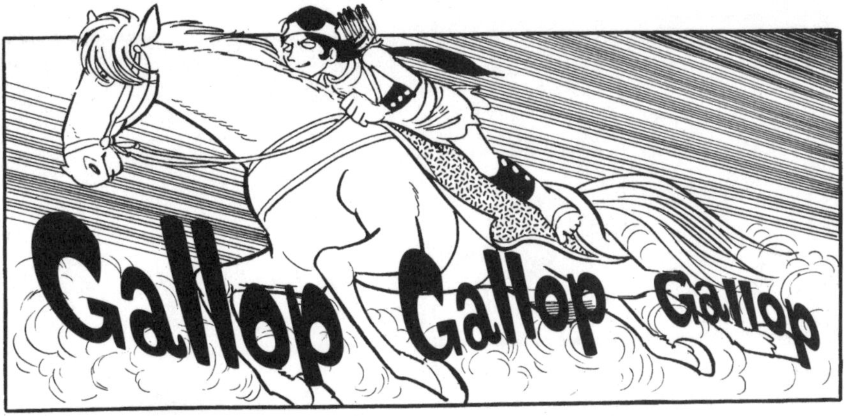
Gallop Gallop Gallop
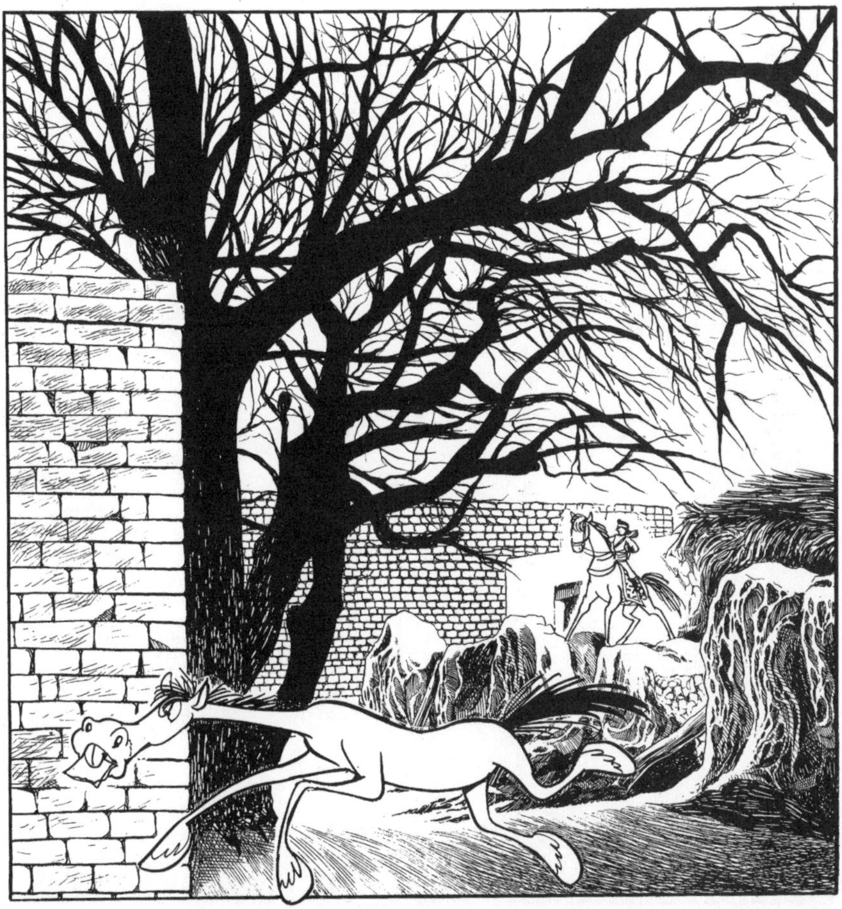

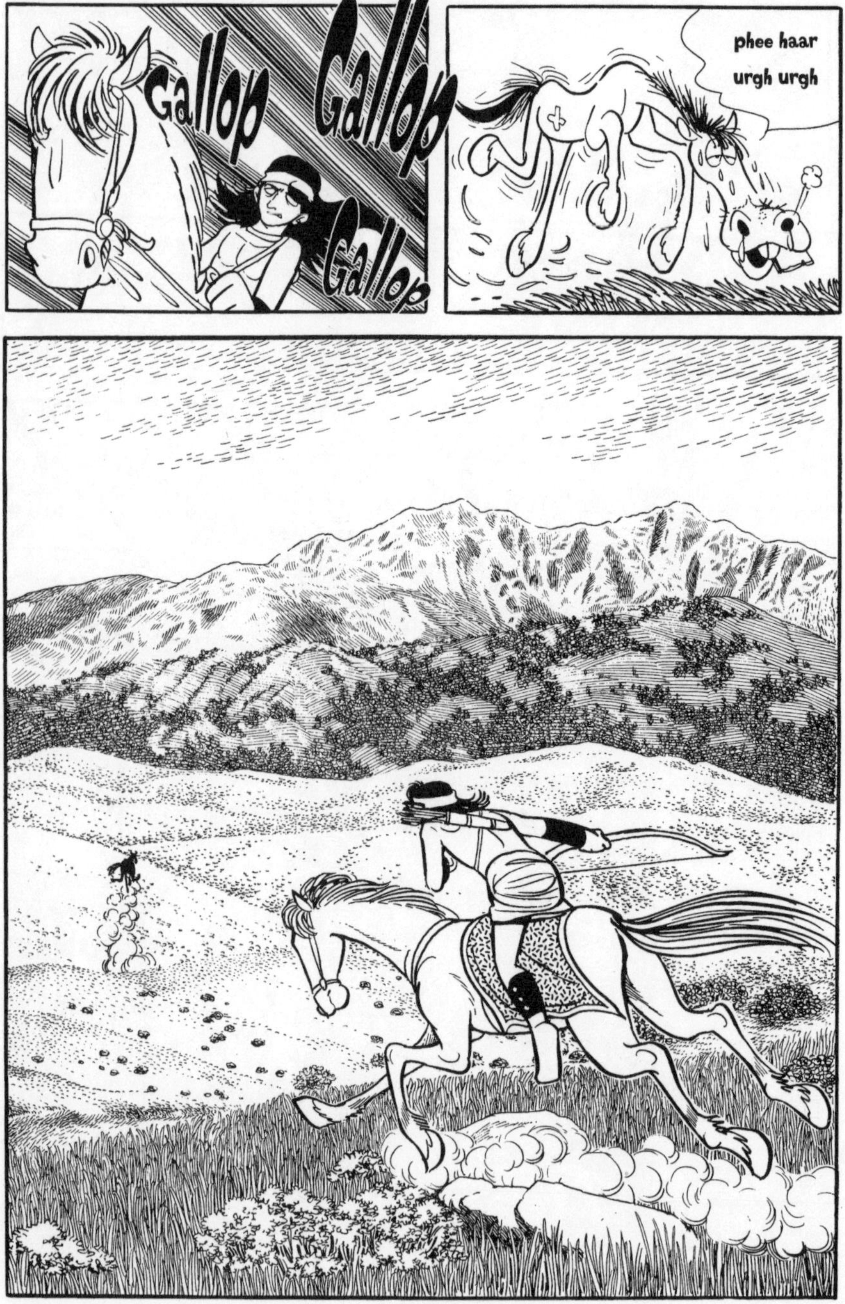
Gallop Gallop
Gallop
phee haar
urgh urgh

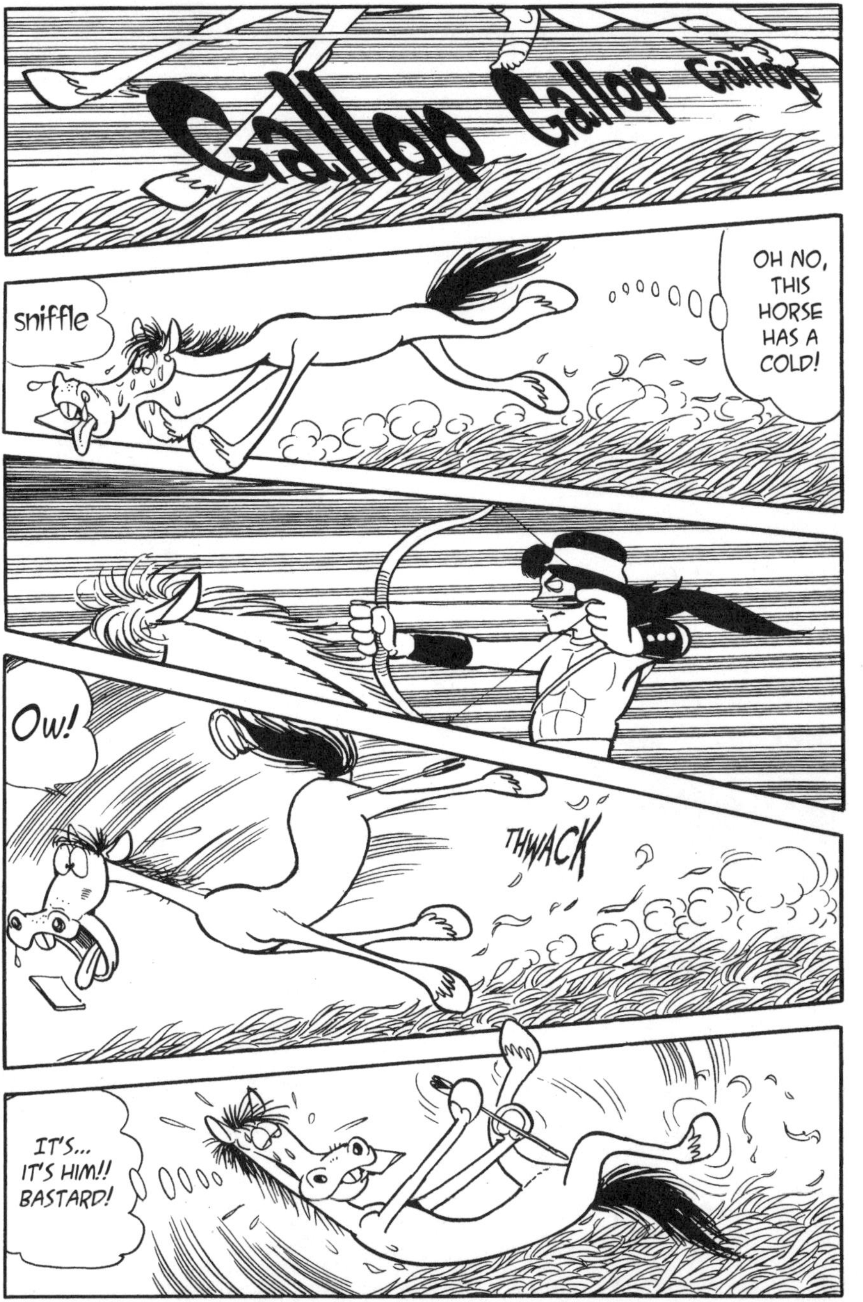
Gallop Gallop Gallop
sniffle
OH NO, THIS HORSE HAS A COLD!
Ow!
THWACK
IT'S... IT'S HIM!! BASTARD!

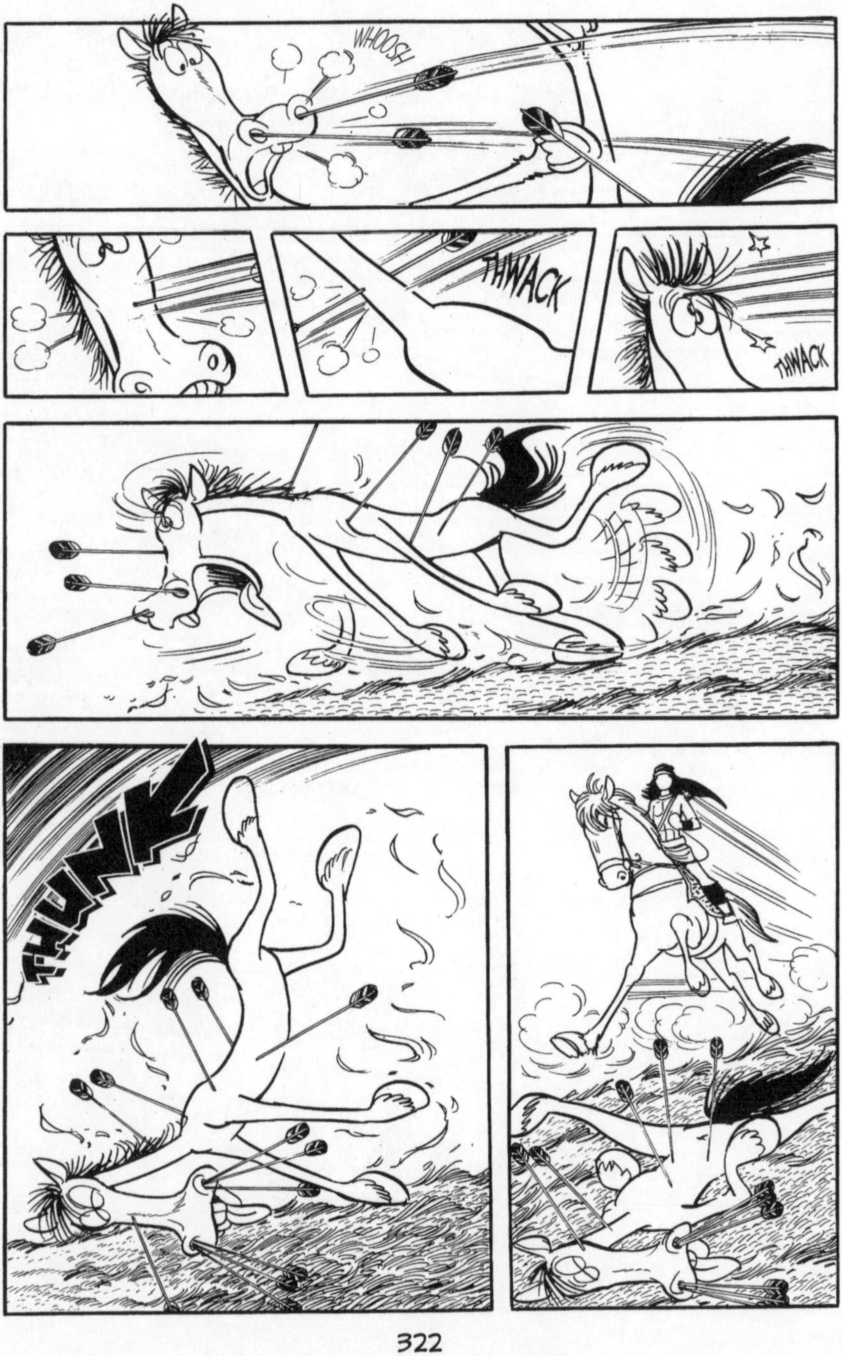
WHOOSH
THWACK
THWACK
THUNK

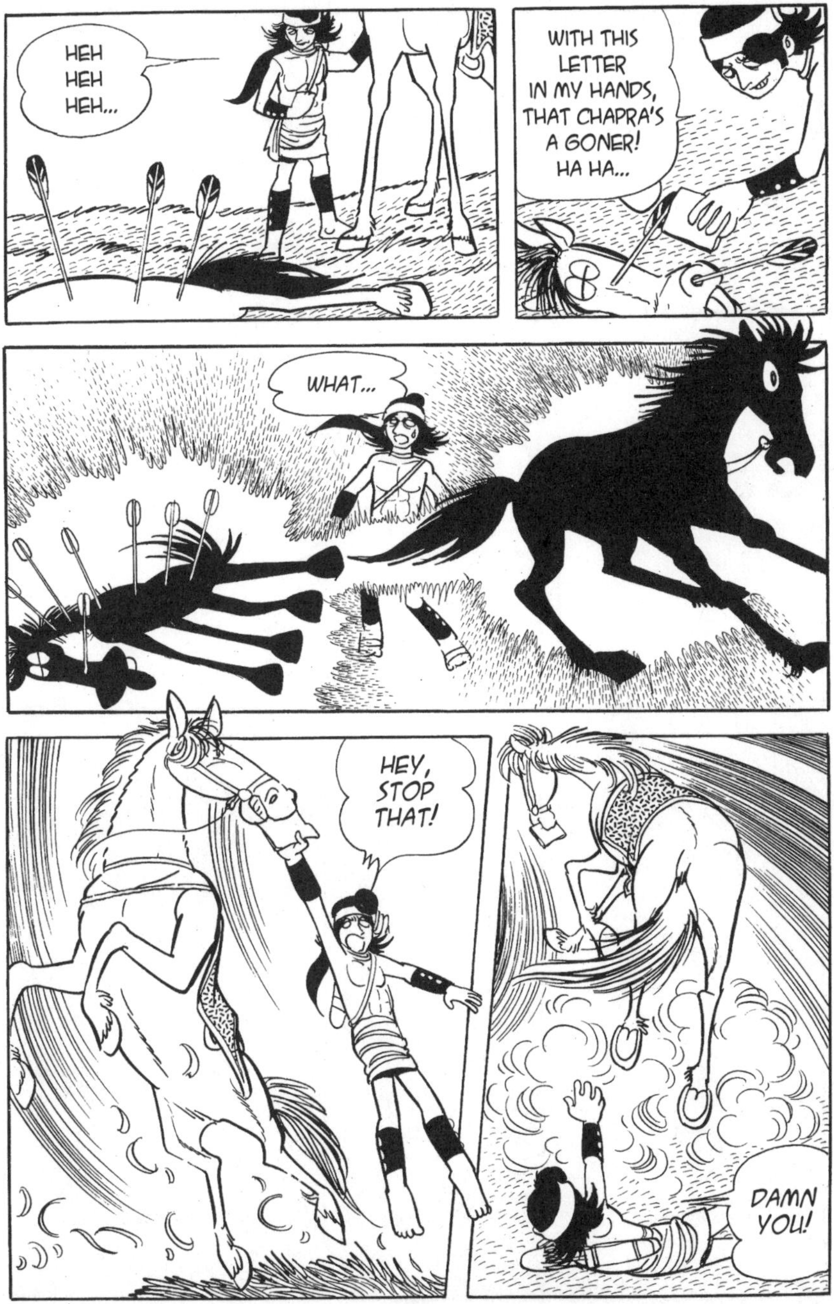
HEH
HEH
HEH...
WITH THIS LETTER IN MY HANDS, THAT CHAPRA'S A GONER! HA HA...
WHAT...
HEY, STOP THAT!
DAMN YOU!

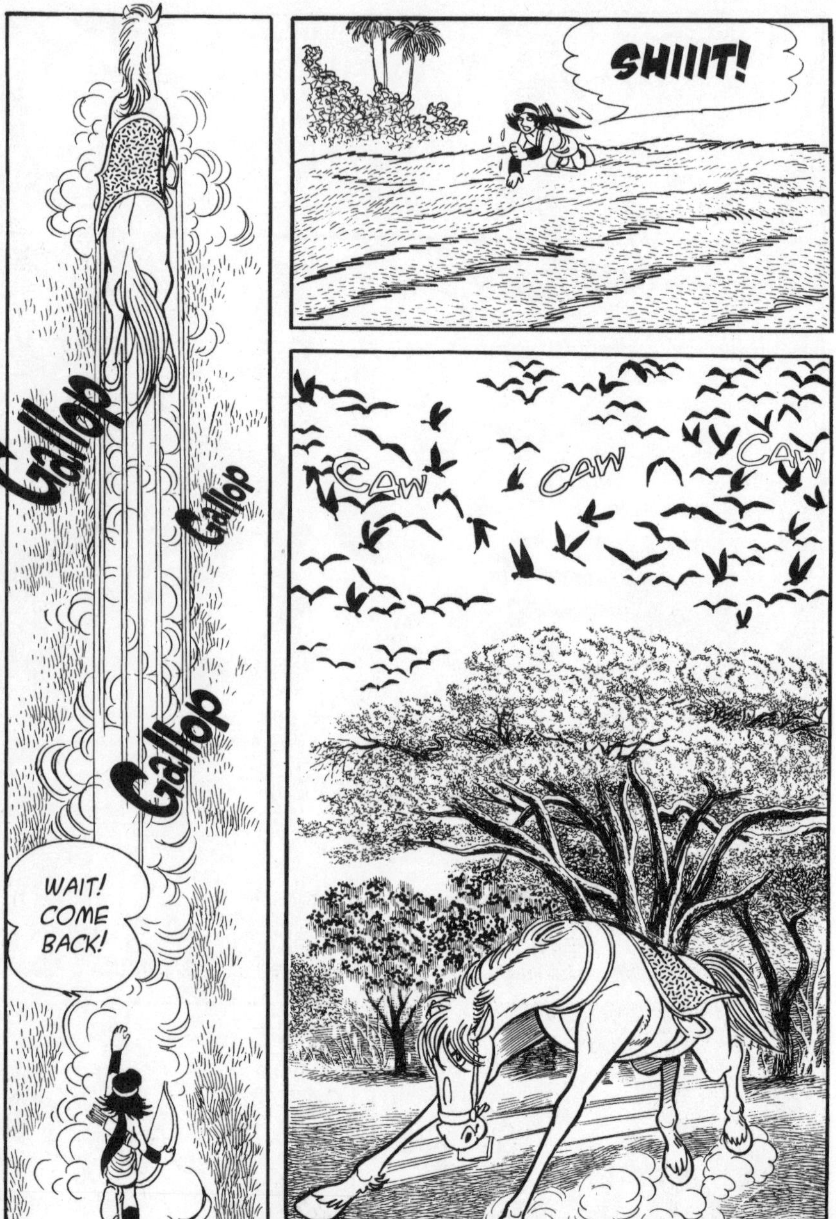
Gallop
Gallop
Gallop
WAIT! COME BACK!
SHIIIT!
CAW
CAW
CAW

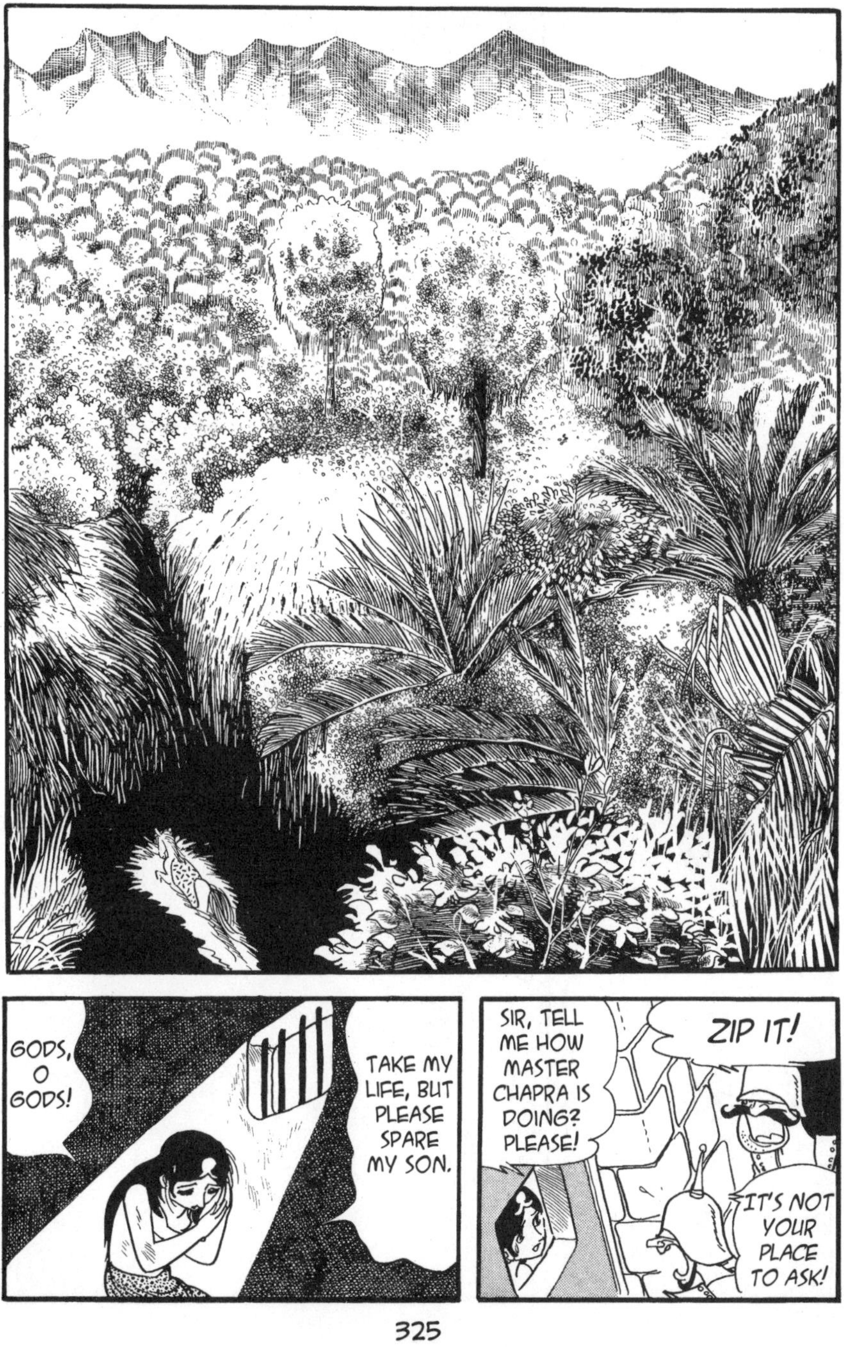
GODS, O GODS!
TAKE MY LIFE, BUT PLEASE SPARE MY SON.
SIR, TELL ME HOW MASTER CHAPRA IS DOING? PLEASE!
ZIP IT!
IT'S NOT YOUR PLACE TO ASK!

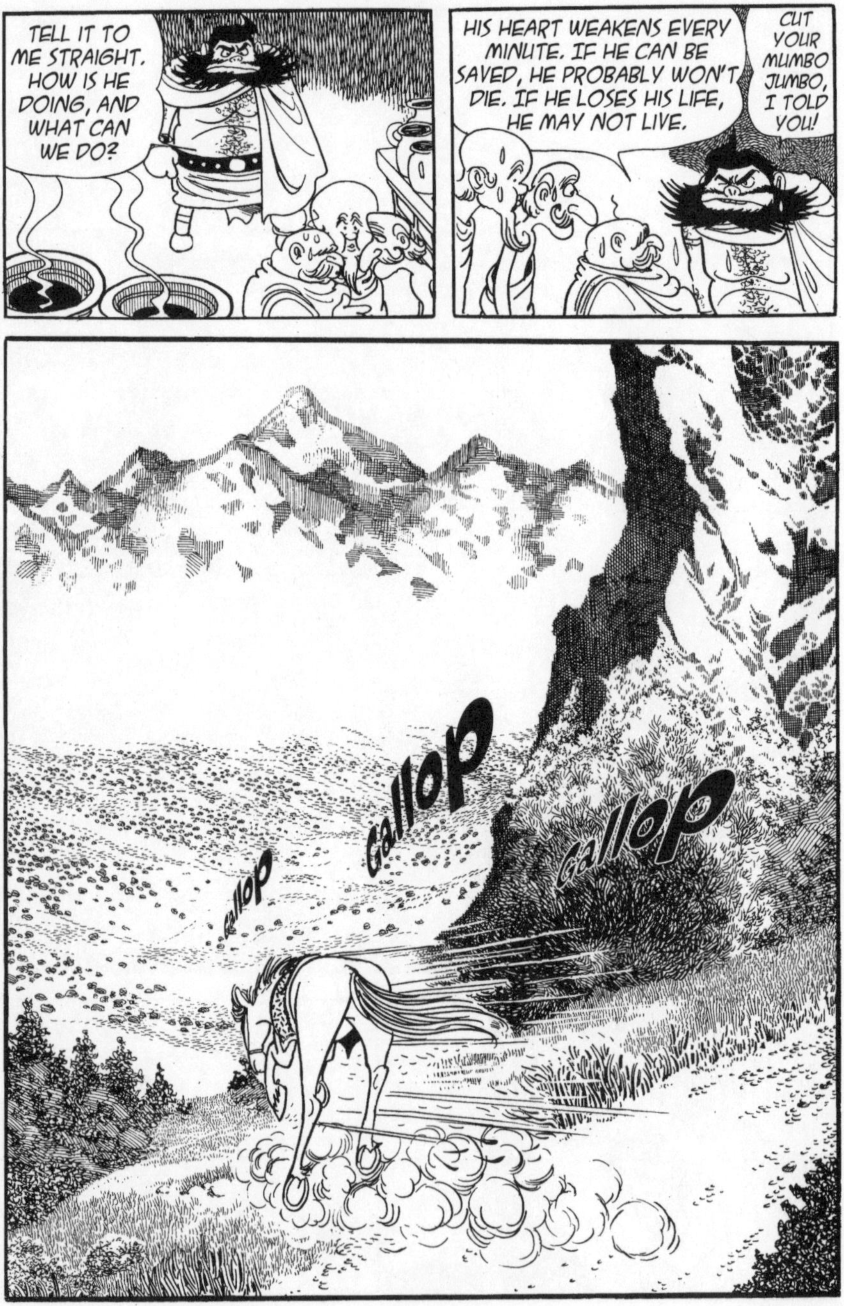
TELL IT TO ME STRAIGHT. HOW IS HE DOING, AND WHAT CAN WE DO?
HIS HEART WEAKENS EVERY MINUTE. IF HE CAN BE SAVED, HE PROBABLY WON'T DIE. IF HE LOSES HIS LIFE, HE MAY NOT LIVE.
CUT YOUR MUMBO JUMBO, I TOLD YOU!
Gallop
Gallop
Gallop

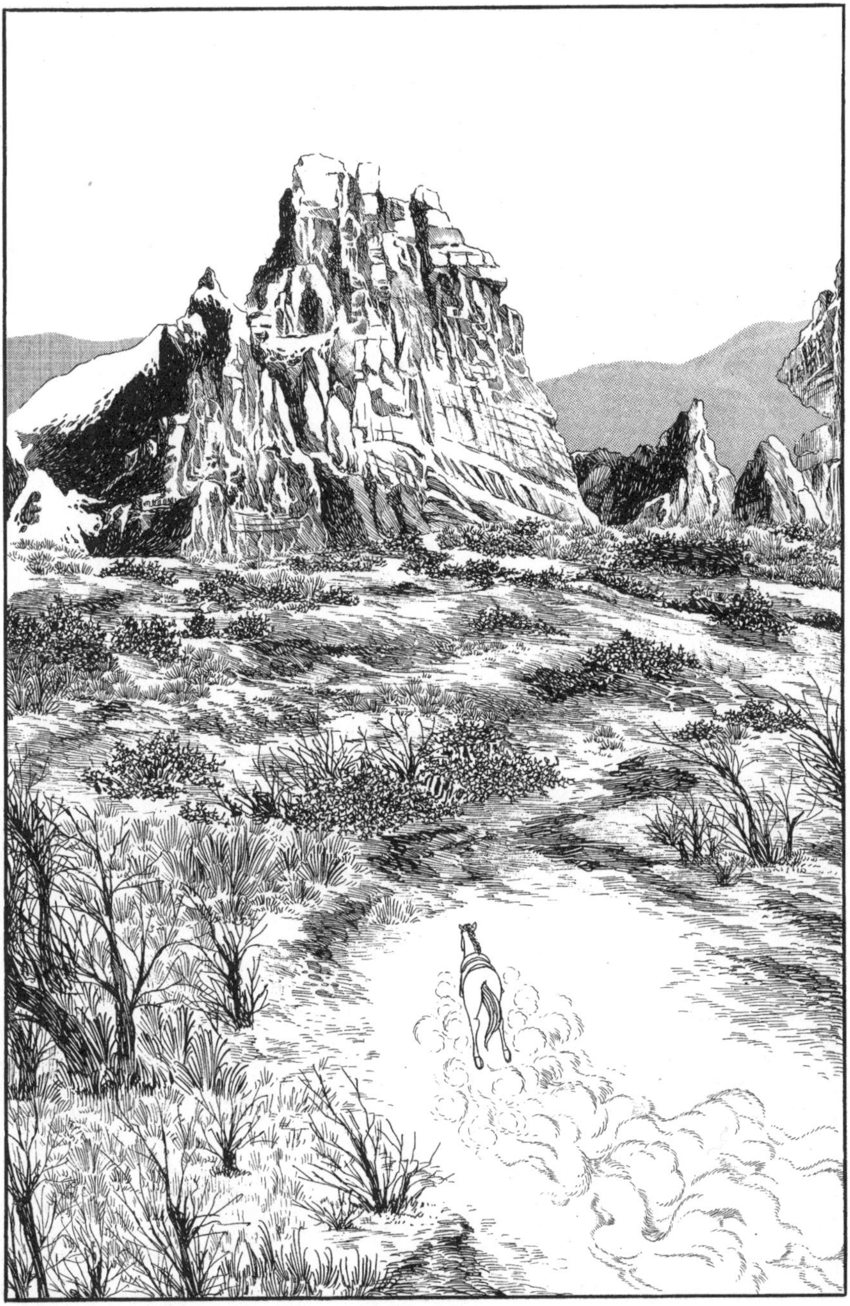

HEY, LOOK AT THAT! A HORSE WITH A LETTER.
A LETTER? IS IT A LOVE LETTER? FOR WHOM?
MASTER ASITA.
MASTER ASITA? HE'S AWAY.
MY POOR HORSE, I CAN TELL YOU'VE COME A LONG WAY, BUT MASTER ASITA IS AWAY.
ALL FOR NOUGHT.

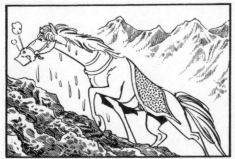

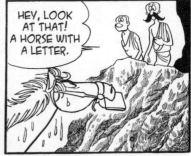

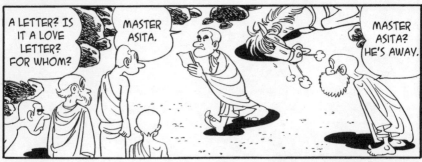

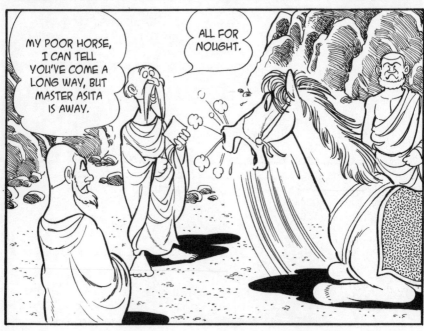

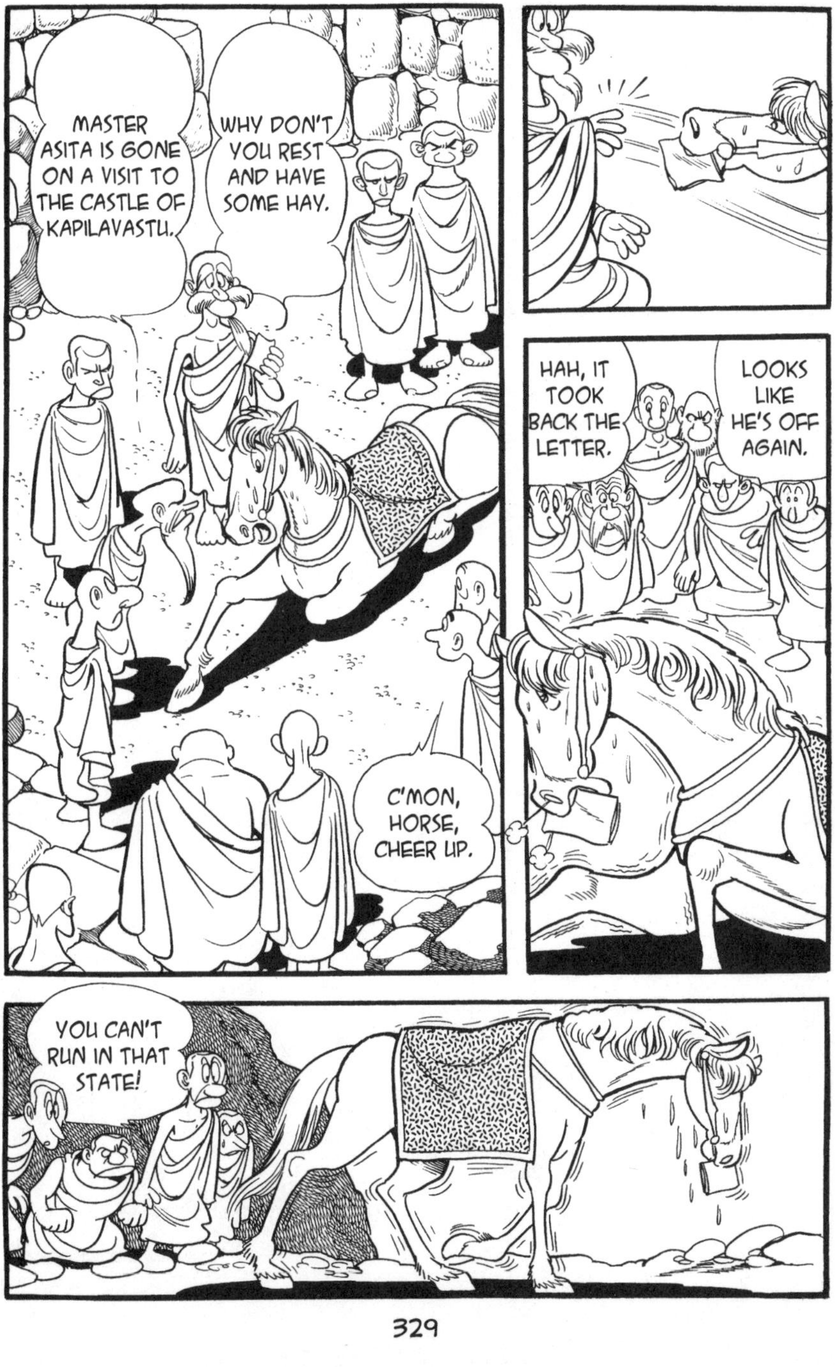
MASTER ASITA IS GONE ON A VISIT TO THE CASTLE OF KAPILAVASTU.
WHY DON'T YOU REST AND HAVE SOME HAY.
C'MON, HORSE, CHEER UP.
HAH, IT TOOK BACK THE LETTER.
LOOKS LIKE HE'S OFF AGAIN.
YOU CAN'T RUN IN THAT STATE!

HEY, WAIT. IT TAKES SEVERAL DAYS TO GO WHERE MASTER ASITA IS NOW.

OUCH, WHAT A STUBBORN HORSE.

DANG... IT'S GONE...

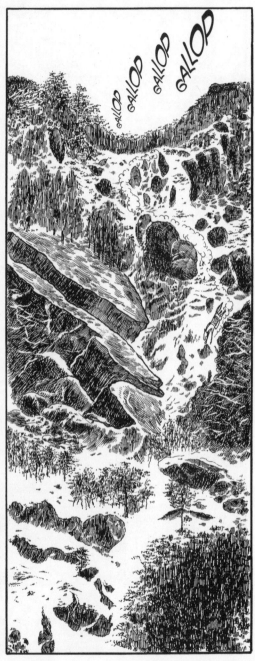

GALLOP GALLOP GALLOP GALLOP

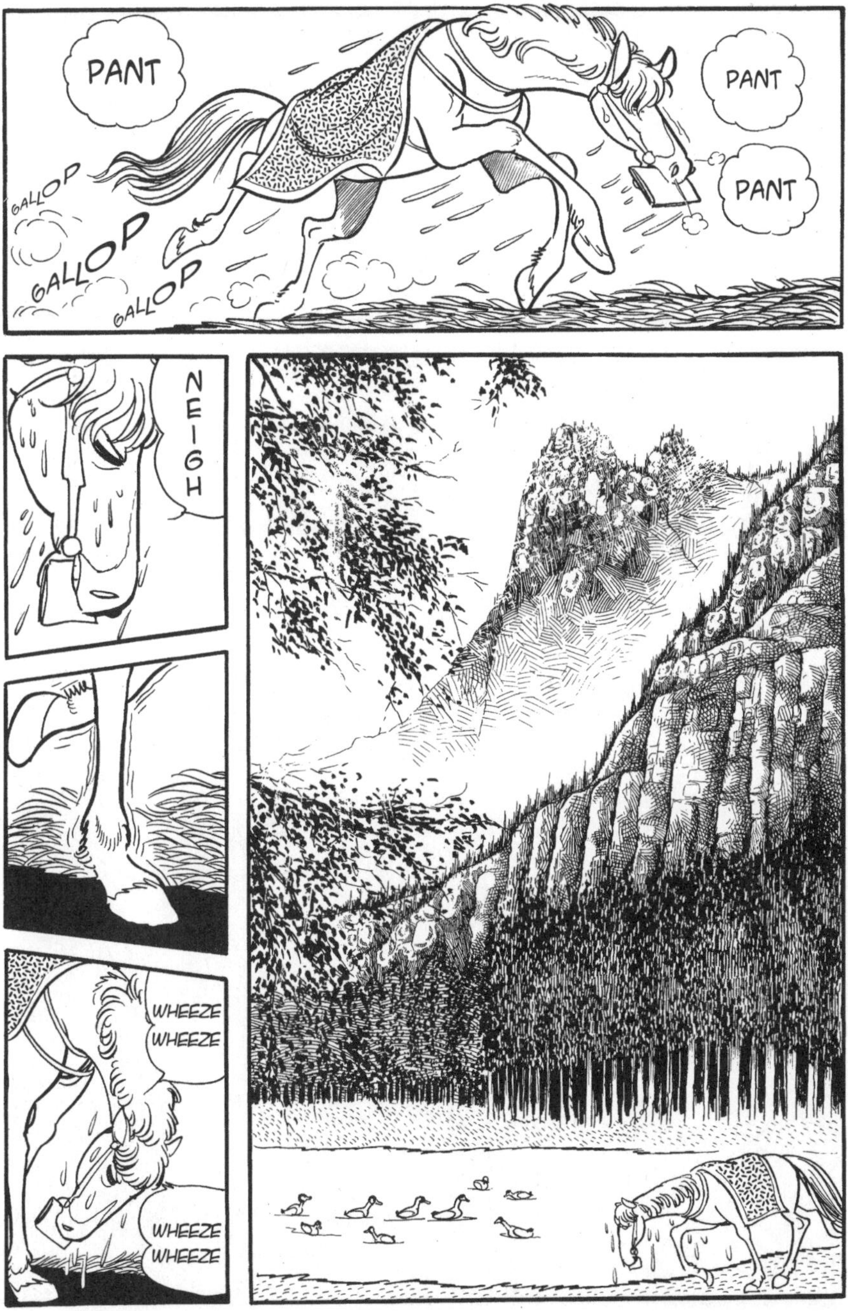
PANT
GALLOP
GALLOP
GALLOP
PANT
PANT
NEIGH
WHEEZE
WHEEZE
WHEEZE
WHEEZE

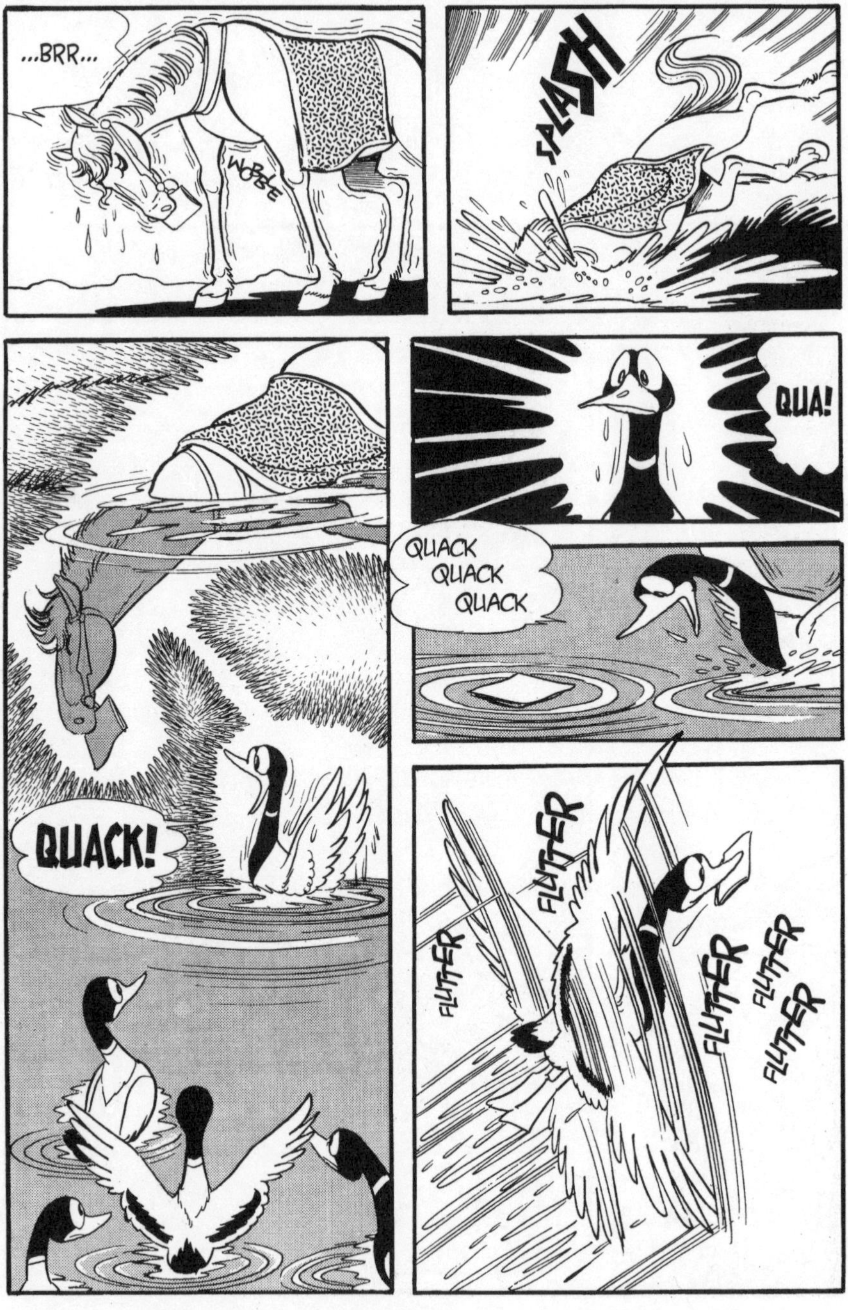
...BRR...
WOBBLE
SPLASH
QUACK!
QUA!
QUACK
QUACK
QUACK
FLUTTER
FLUTTER
FLUTTER
FLUTTER
FLUTTER

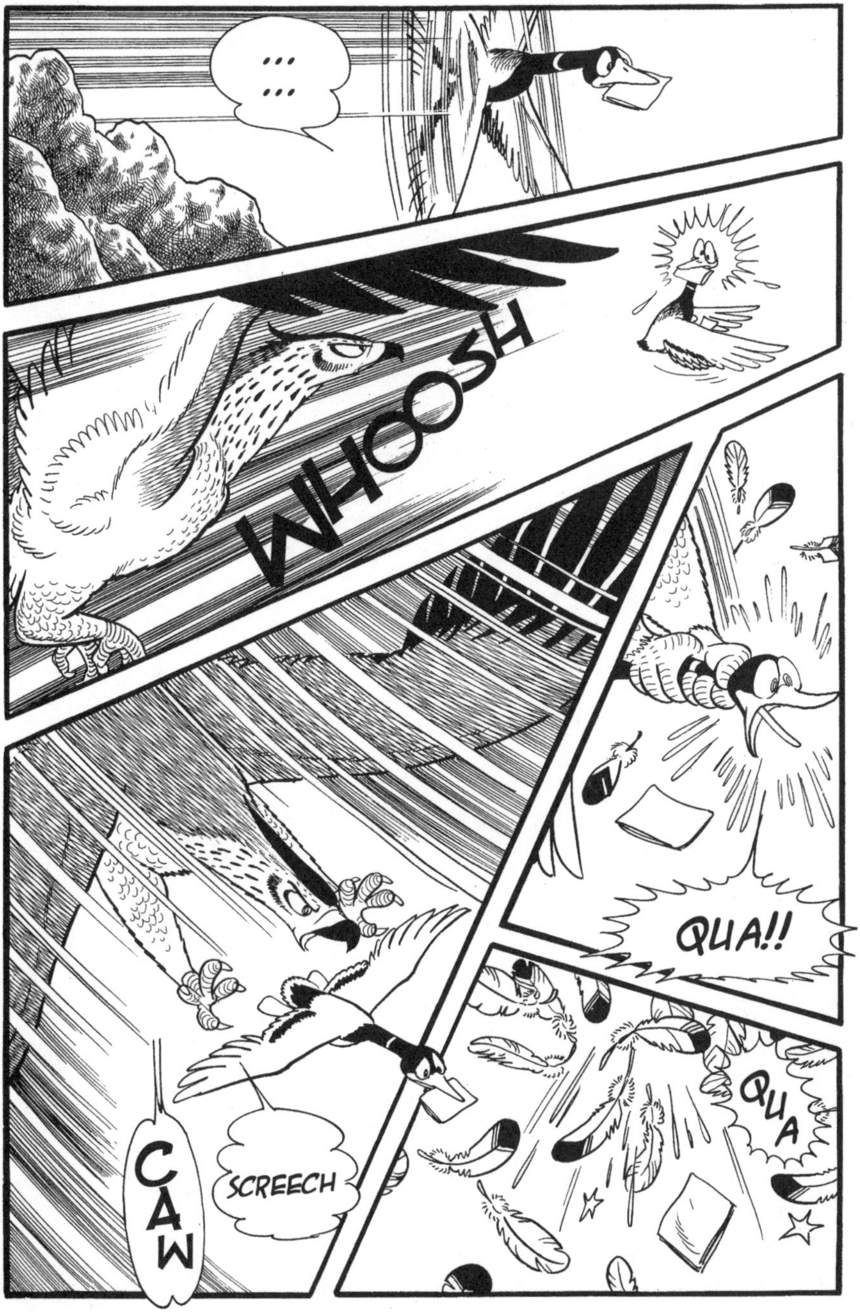
......
WHOOSH
QUA!!
CAW
SCREECH
QUA

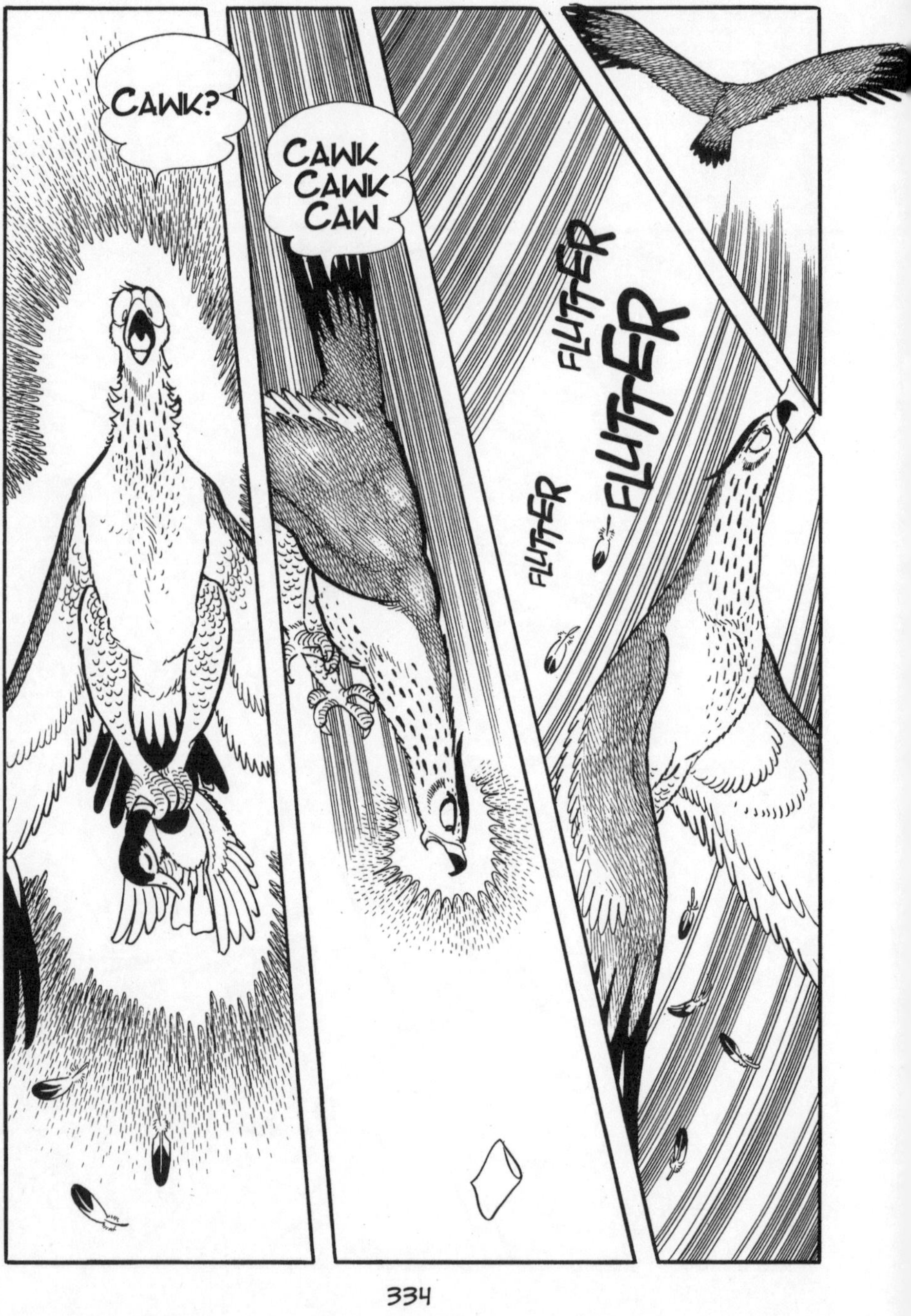
CAWK?
CAWK CAWK CAW
FLUTTER
FLUTTER
FLUTTER
FLUTTER

CHAPTER TEN

THE PROPHECY

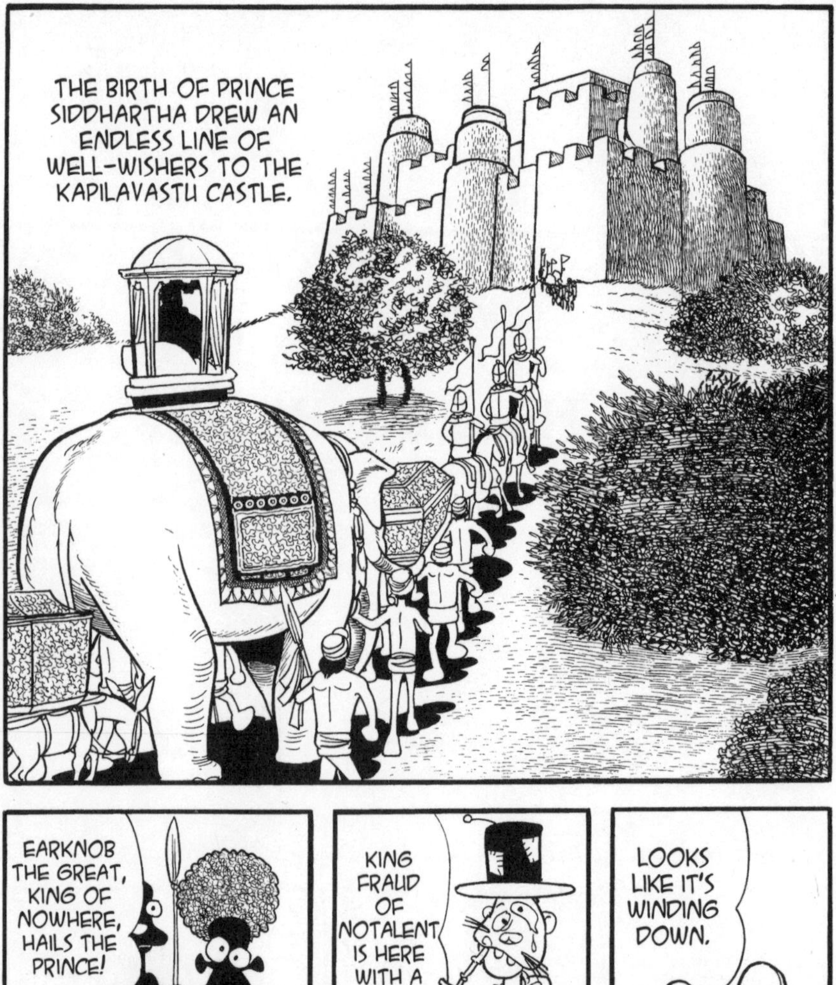
THE BIRTH OF PRINCE SIDDHARTHA DREW AN ENDLESS LINE OF WELL-WISHERS TO THE KAPILAVASTU CASTLE.
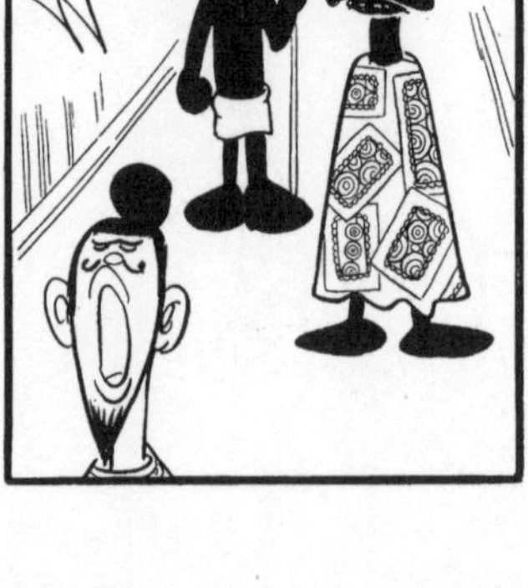
EARKNOB THE GREAT, KING OF NOWHERE, HAILS THE PRINCE!
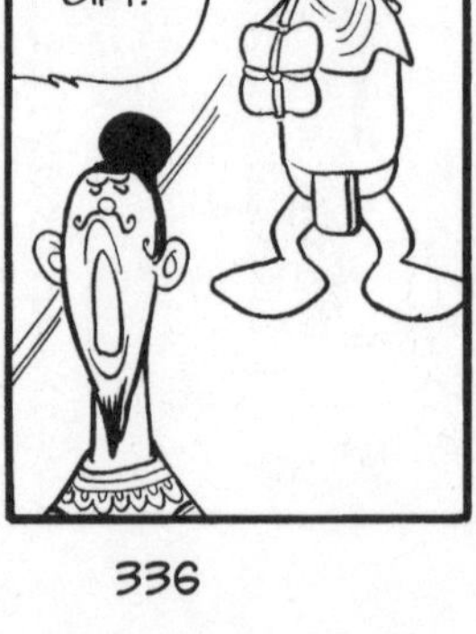
KING FRAUD OF NOTALENT IS HERE WITH A GIFT!
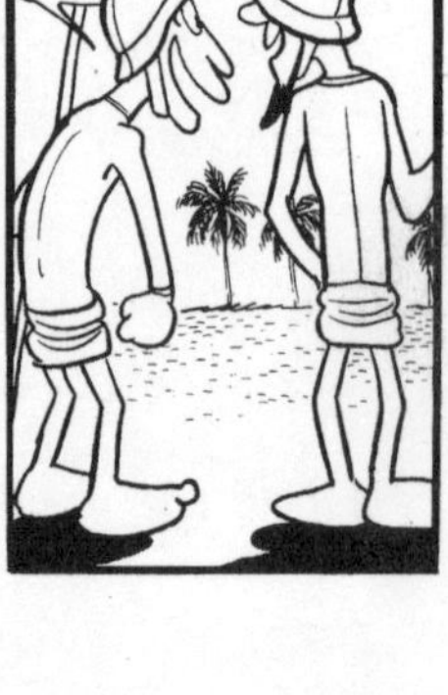
LOOKS LIKE IT'S WINDING DOWN.

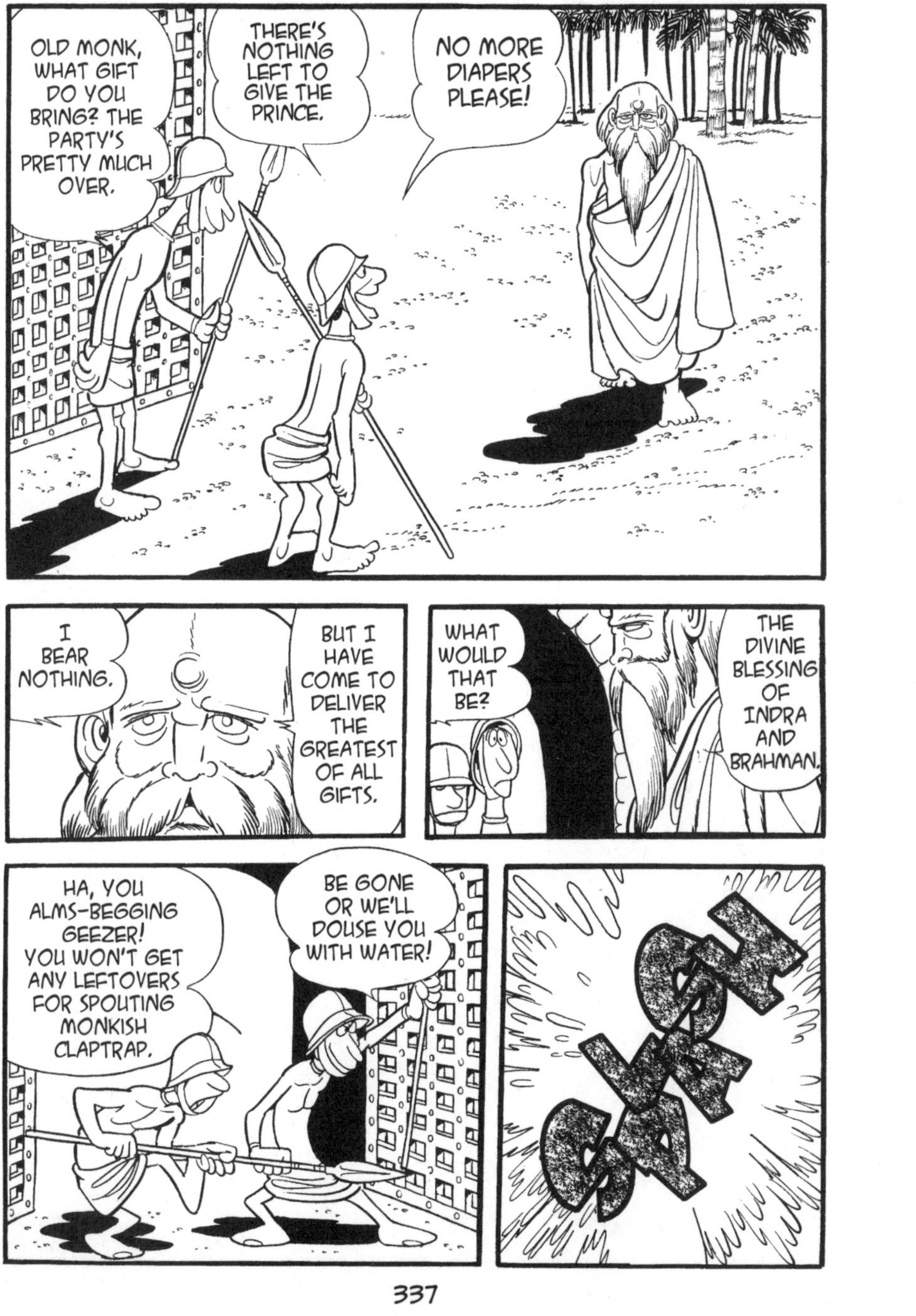
OLD MONK, WHAT GIFT DO YOU BRING? THE PARTY'S PRETTY MUCH OVER.
THERE'S NOTHING LEFT TO GIVE THE PRINCE.
NO MORE DIAPERS PLEASE!
I BEAR NOTHING.
BUT I HAVE COME TO DELIVER THE GREATEST OF ALL GIFTS.
WHAT WOULD THAT BE?
THE DIVINE BLESSING OF INDRA AND BRAHMAN.
HA, YOU ALMS-BEGGING GEEZER! YOU WON'T GET ANY LEFTOVERS FOR SPOUTING MONKISH CLAPTRAP.
BE GONE OR WE'LL DOUSE YOU WITH WATER!
SPLASH

... ...
... HUH?
WHERE'D ALL THE WATER GO?
DRY AS A BONE.
TELL THE KING THAT ASITA HAS COME. THAT'S ALL YOU'LL NEED TO SAY.
Y-Y-Y-YOUR H-H-HIGHNESS! A-A-A-ATISA, I MEAN ASATI, THAT'S TO SAY ATASI... IS ALL I NEED TO SAY!
YOU'RE NOT MAKING SENSE! RELAX!

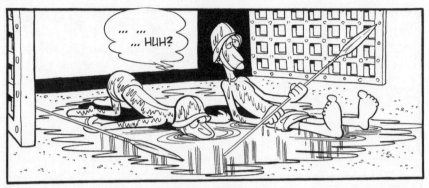

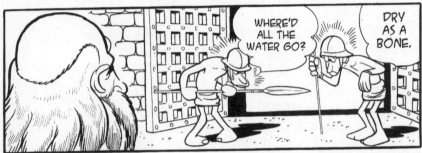

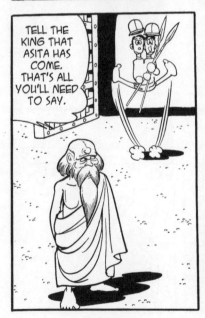

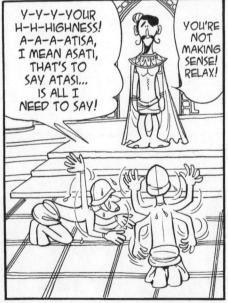

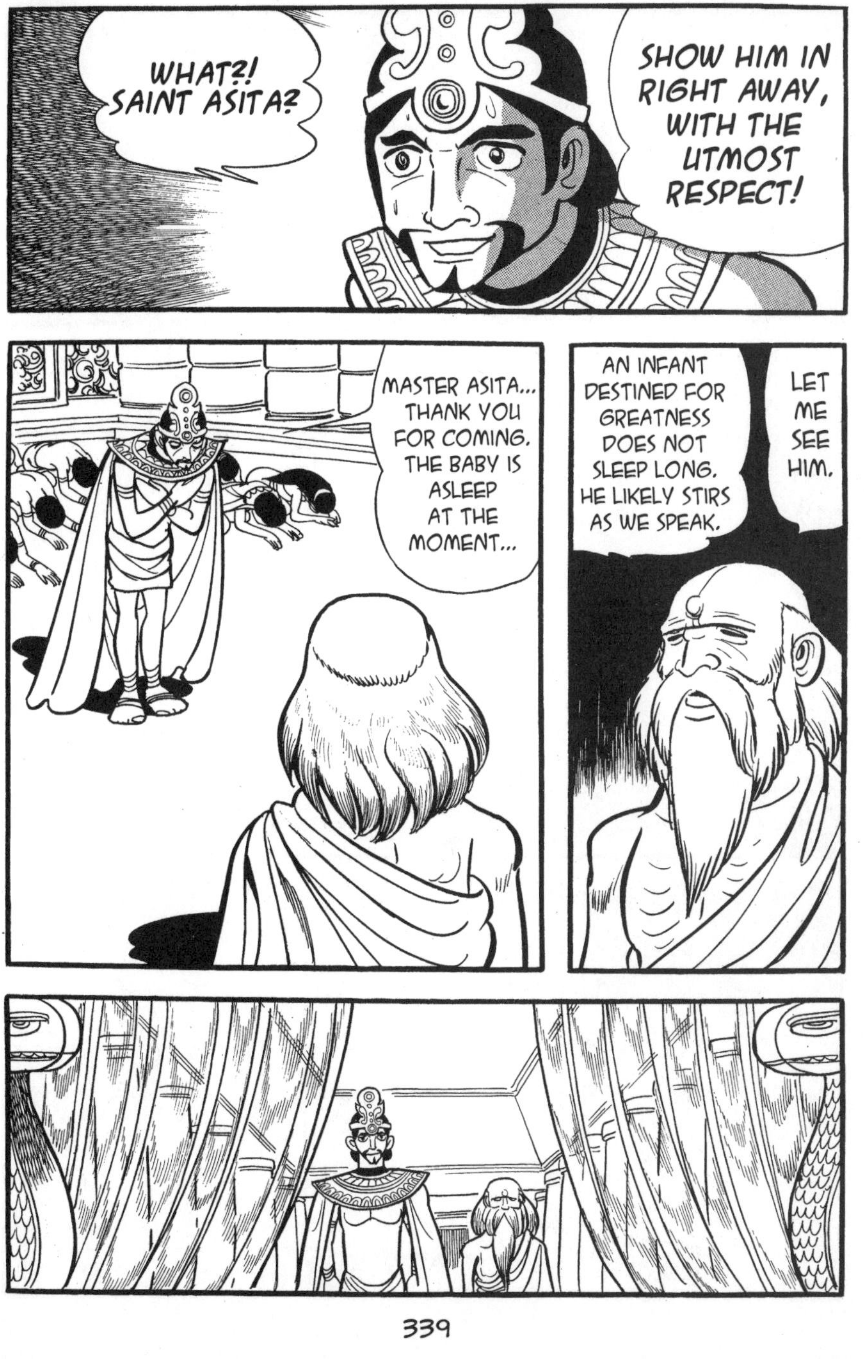
WHAT?! SAINT ASITA?
SHOW HIM IN RIGHT AWAY, WITH THE UTMOST RESPECT!
MASTER ASITA... THANK YOU FOR COMING. THE BABY IS ASLEEP AT THE MOMENT...
AN INFANT DESTINED FOR GREATNESS DOES NOT SLEEP LONG. HE LIKELY STIRS AS WE SPEAK.
LET ME SEE HIM.

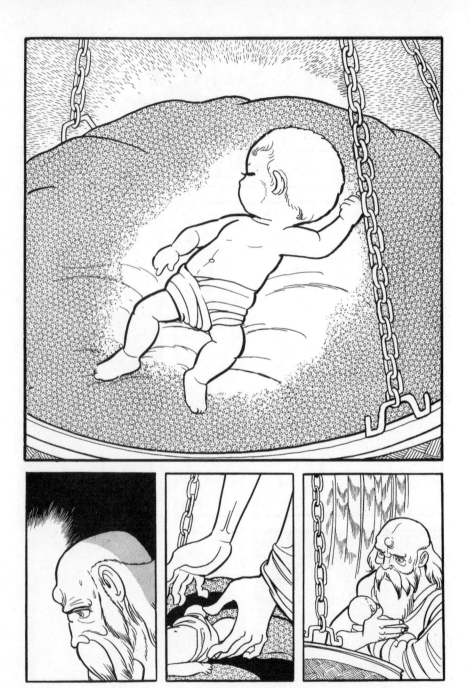

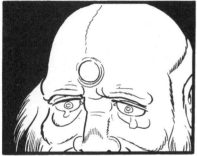

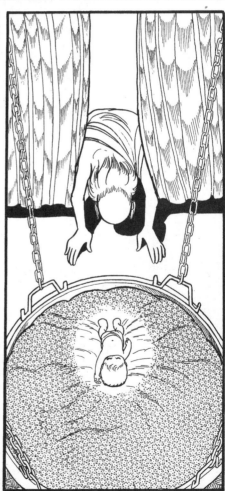

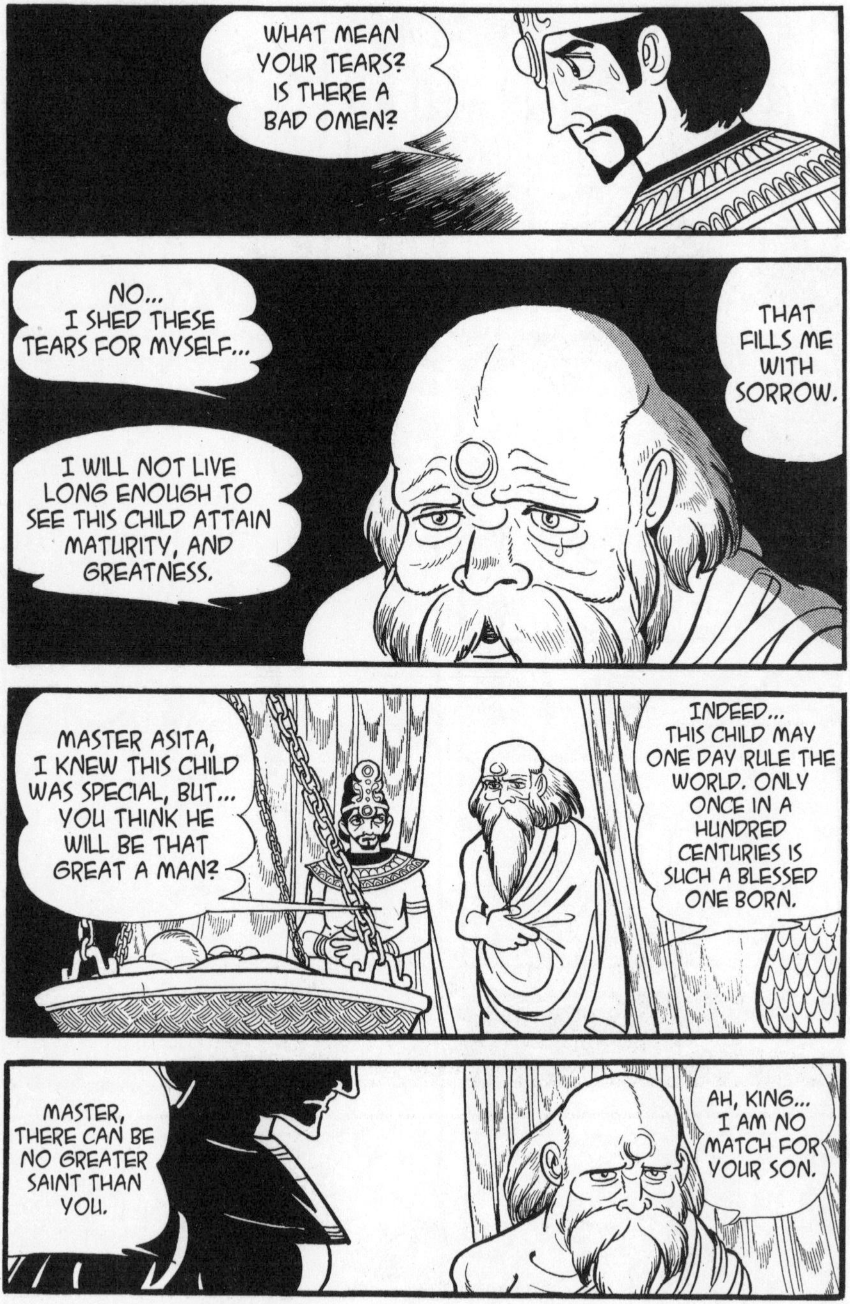
WHAT MEAN YOUR TEARS? IS THERE A BAD OMEN?
NO... I SHED THESE TEARS FOR MYSELF...
I WILL NOT LIVE LONG ENOUGH TO SEE THIS CHILD ATTAIN MATURITY, AND GREATNESS.
THAT FILLS ME WITH SORROW.
MASTER ASITA, I KNEW THIS CHILD WAS SPECIAL, BUT... YOU THINK HE WILL BE THAT GREAT A MAN?
INDEED... THIS CHILD MAY ONE DAY RULE THE WORLD. ONLY ONCE IN A HUNDRED CENTURIES IS SUCH A BLESSED ONE BORN.
MASTER, THERE CAN BE NO GREATER SAINT THAN YOU.
AH, KING... I AM NO MATCH FOR YOUR SON.

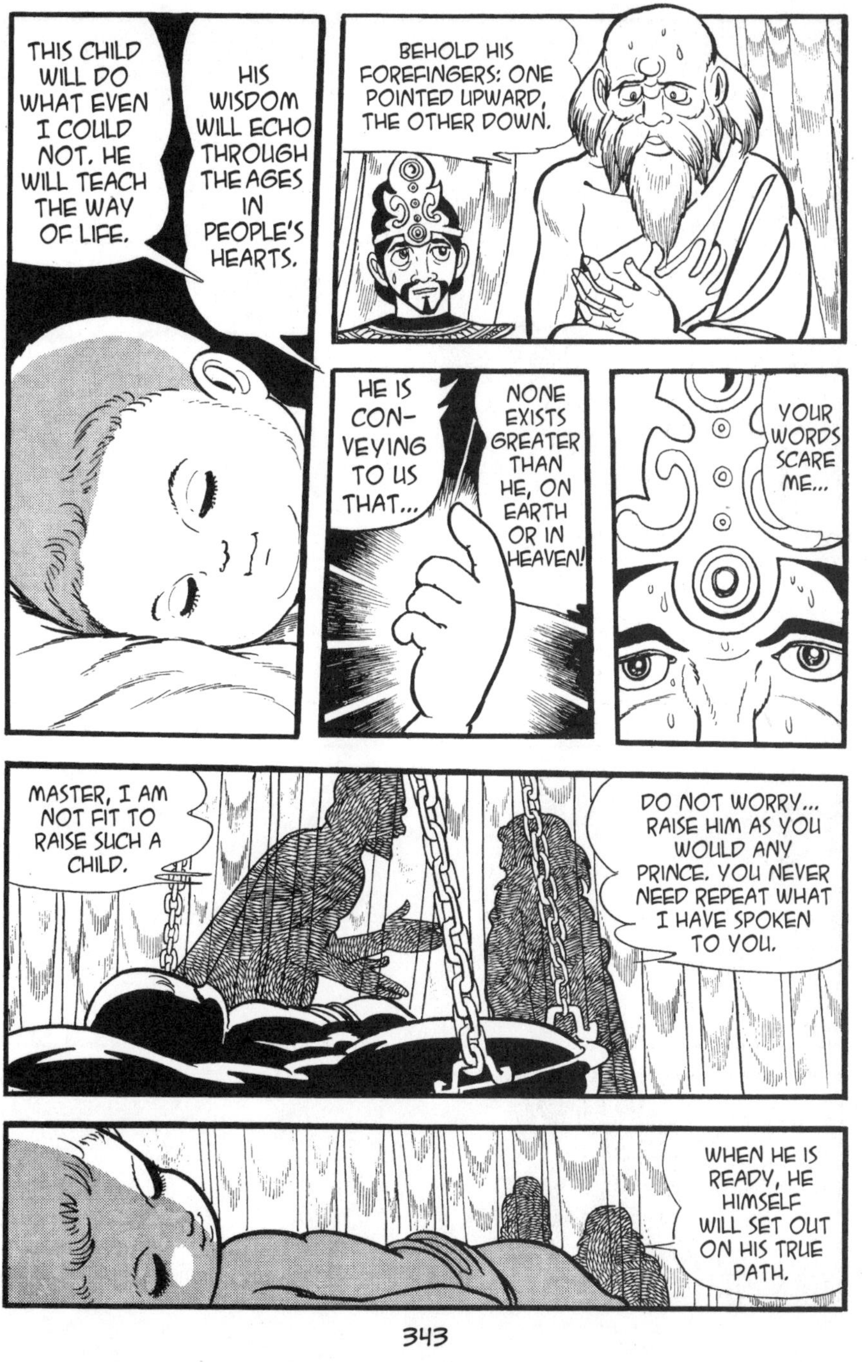
THIS CHILD WILL DO WHAT EVEN I COULD NOT. HE WILL TEACH THE WAY OF LIFE.
HIS WISDOM WILL ECHO THROUGH THE AGES IN PEOPLE'S HEARTS.
BEHOLD HIS FOREFINGERS: ONE POINTED UPWARD, THE OTHER DOWN.
HE IS CON-VEYING TO US THAT...
NONE EXISTS GREATER THAN HE, ON EARTH OR IN HEAVEN!
YOUR WORDS SCARE ME...
MASTER, I AM NOT FIT TO RAISE SUCH A CHILD.
DO NOT WORRY... RAISE HIM AS YOU WOULD ANY PRINCE. YOU NEVER NEED REPEAT WHAT I HAVE SPOKEN TO YOU.
WHEN HE IS READY, HE HIMSELF WILL SET OUT ON HIS TRUE PATH.

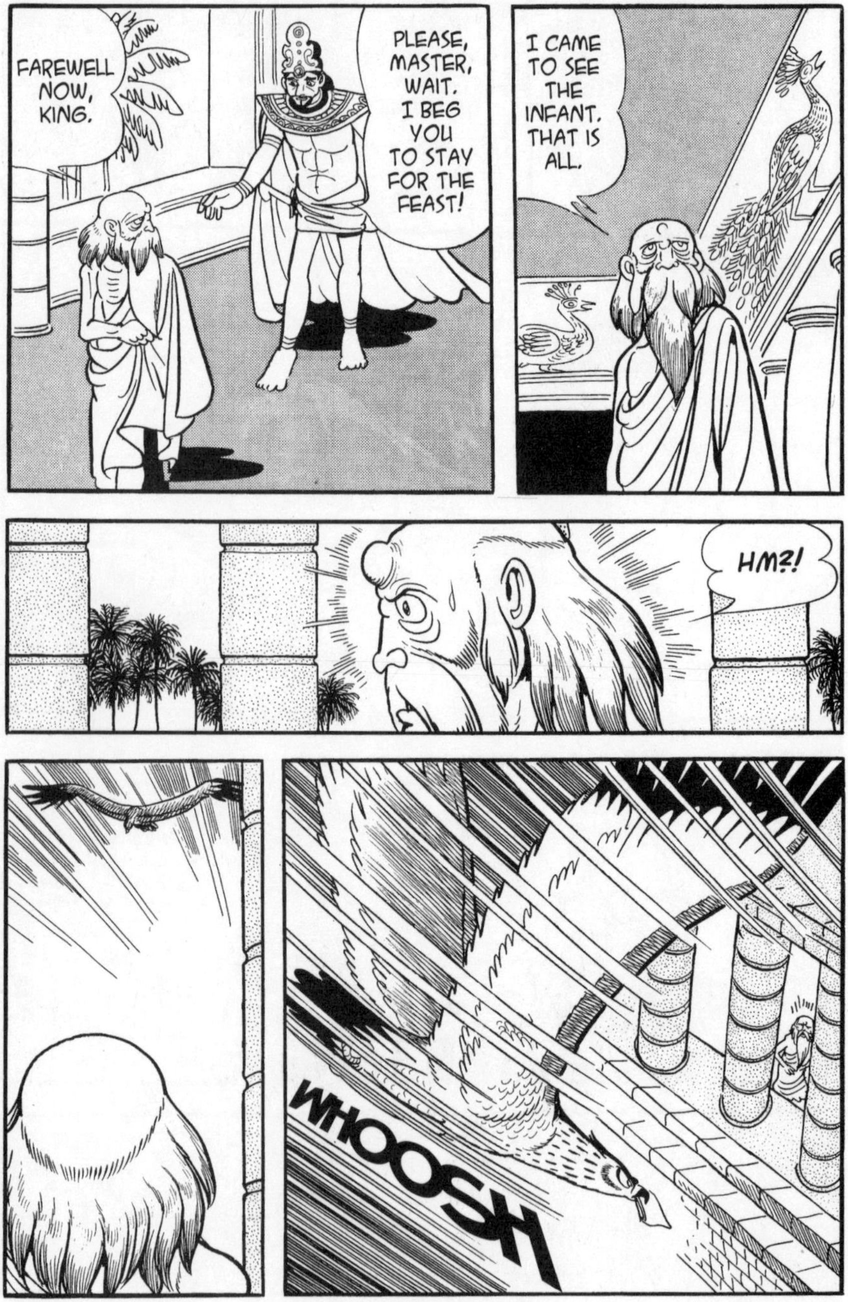
FAREWELL NOW, KING.
PLEASE, MASTER, WAIT. I BEG YOU TO STAY FOR THE FEAST!
I CAME TO SEE THE INFANT. THAT IS ALL.
HM?!
WHOOSH

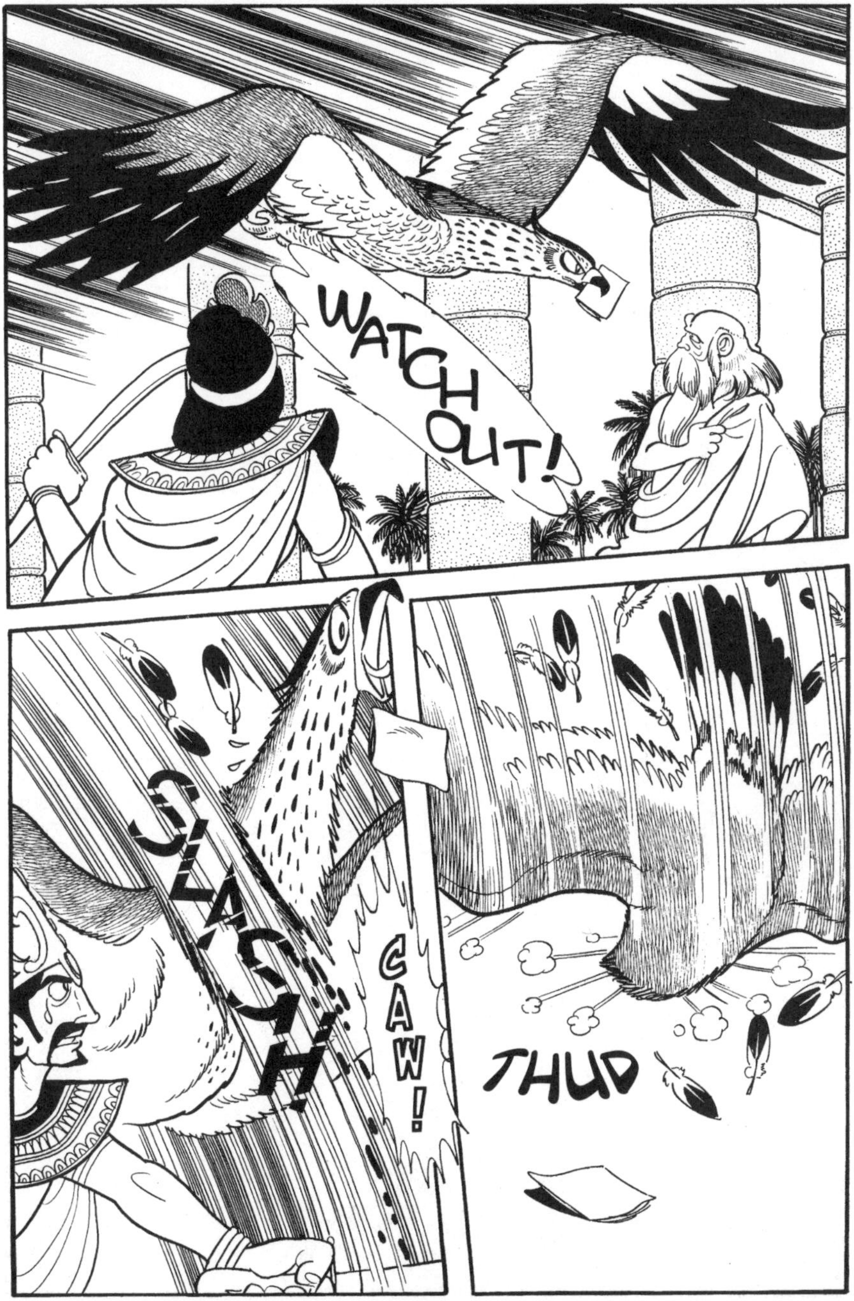
WATCH OUT!
SLASH!
CAW!
THUD

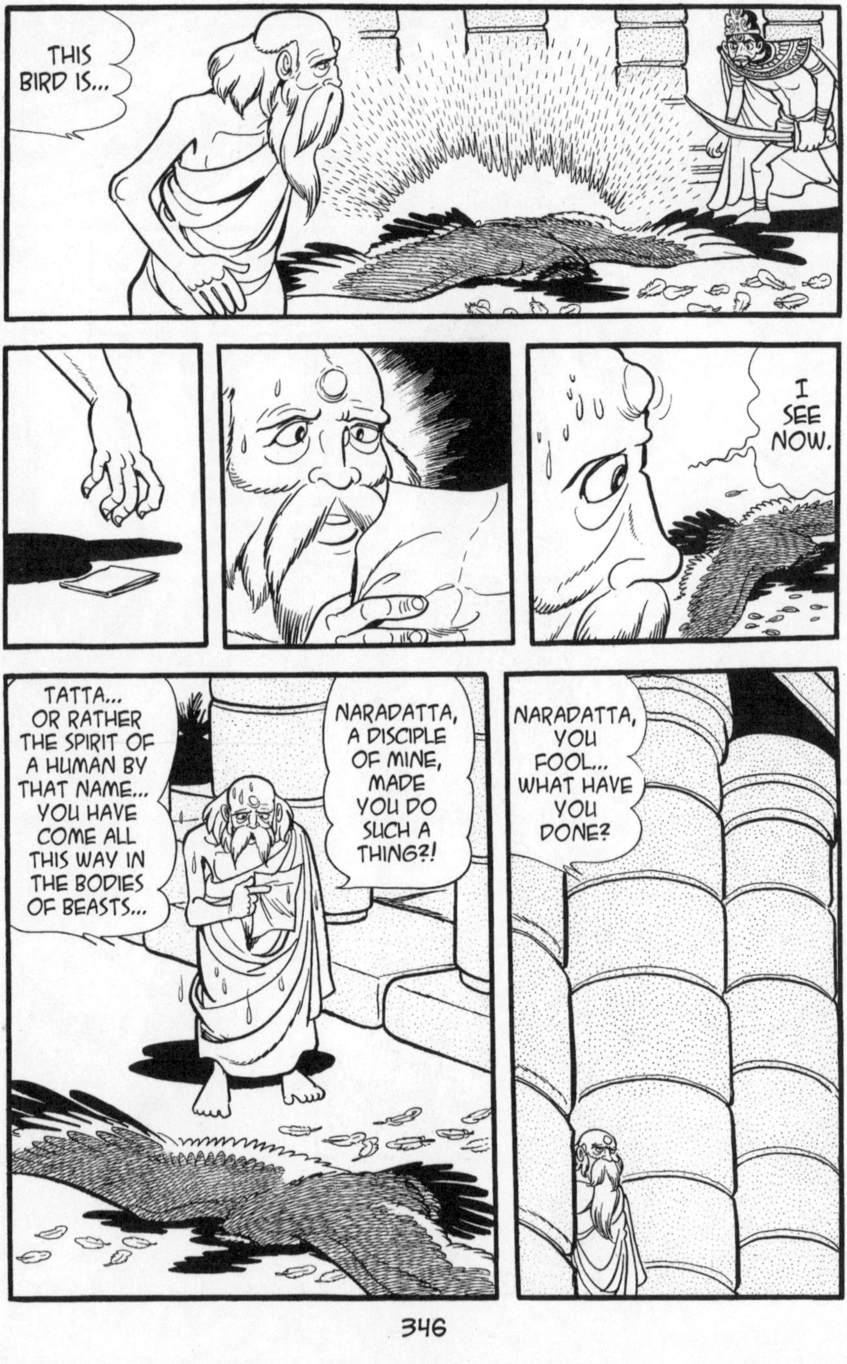
THIS BIRD IS...
I SEE NOW.
TATTA... OR RATHER THE SPIRIT OF A HUMAN BY THAT NAME... YOU HAVE COME ALL THIS WAY IN THE BODIES OF BEASTS...
NARADATTA, A DISCIPLE OF MINE, MADE YOU DO SUCH A THING?!
NARADATTA, YOU FOOL... WHAT HAVE YOU DONE?

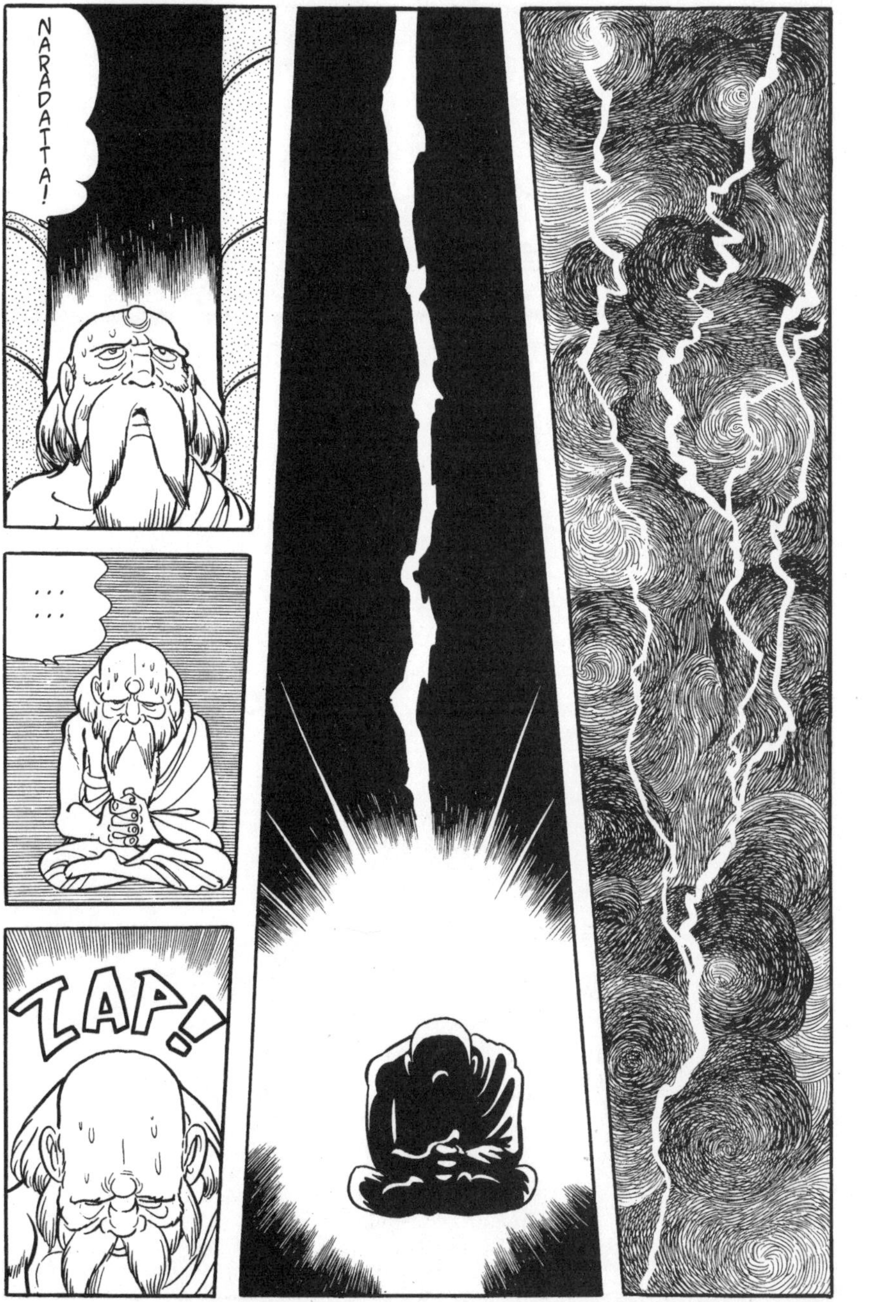
NARADATTA!
... ...
ZAP!

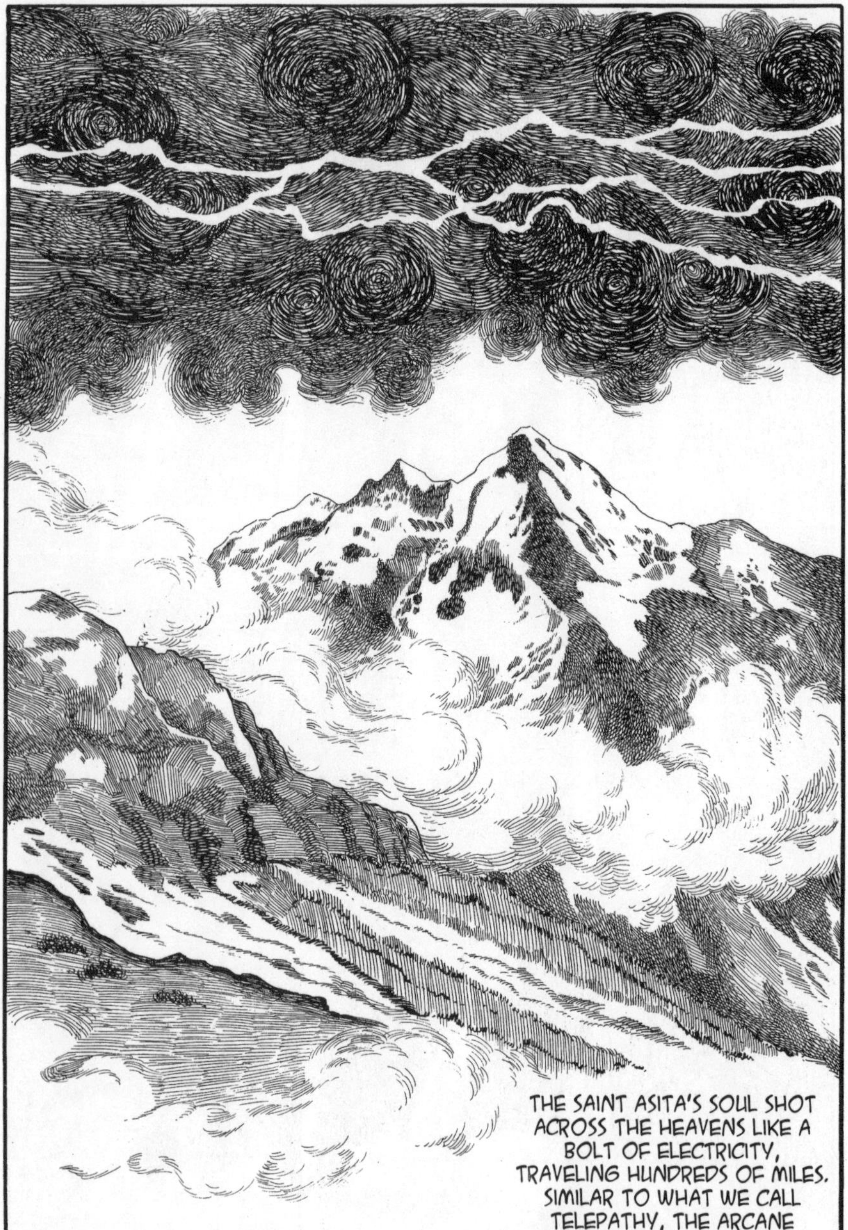
THE SAINT ASITA'S SOUL SHOT ACROSS THE HEAVENS LIKE A BOLT OF ELECTRICITY, TRAVELING HUNDREDS OF MILES. SIMILAR TO WHAT WE CALL TELEPATHY, THE ARCANE ART SENT A MESSAGE TO SOMEONE FAR AWAY.

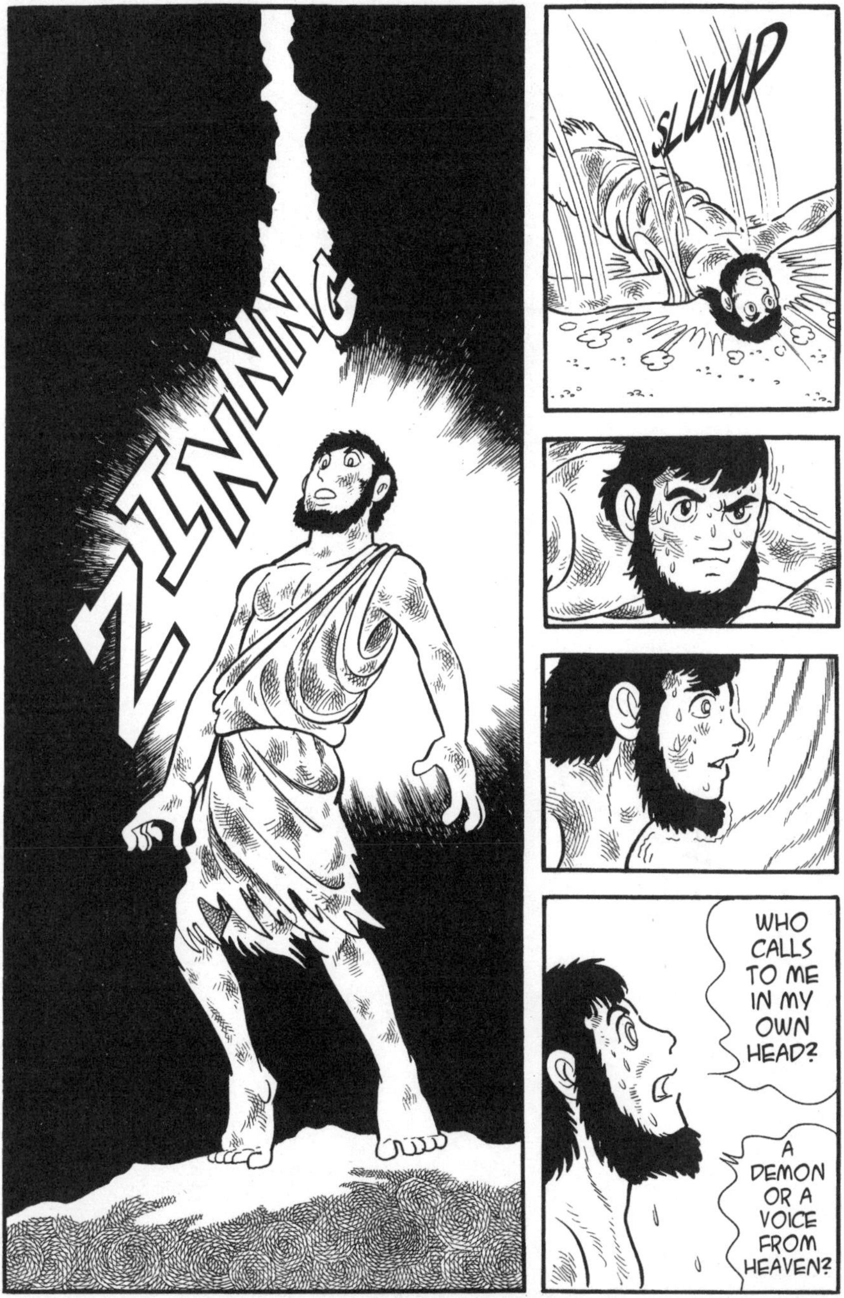
ZINNNG
SLUMP
WHO CALLS TO ME IN MY OWN HEAD?
A DEMON OR A VOICE FROM HEAVEN?

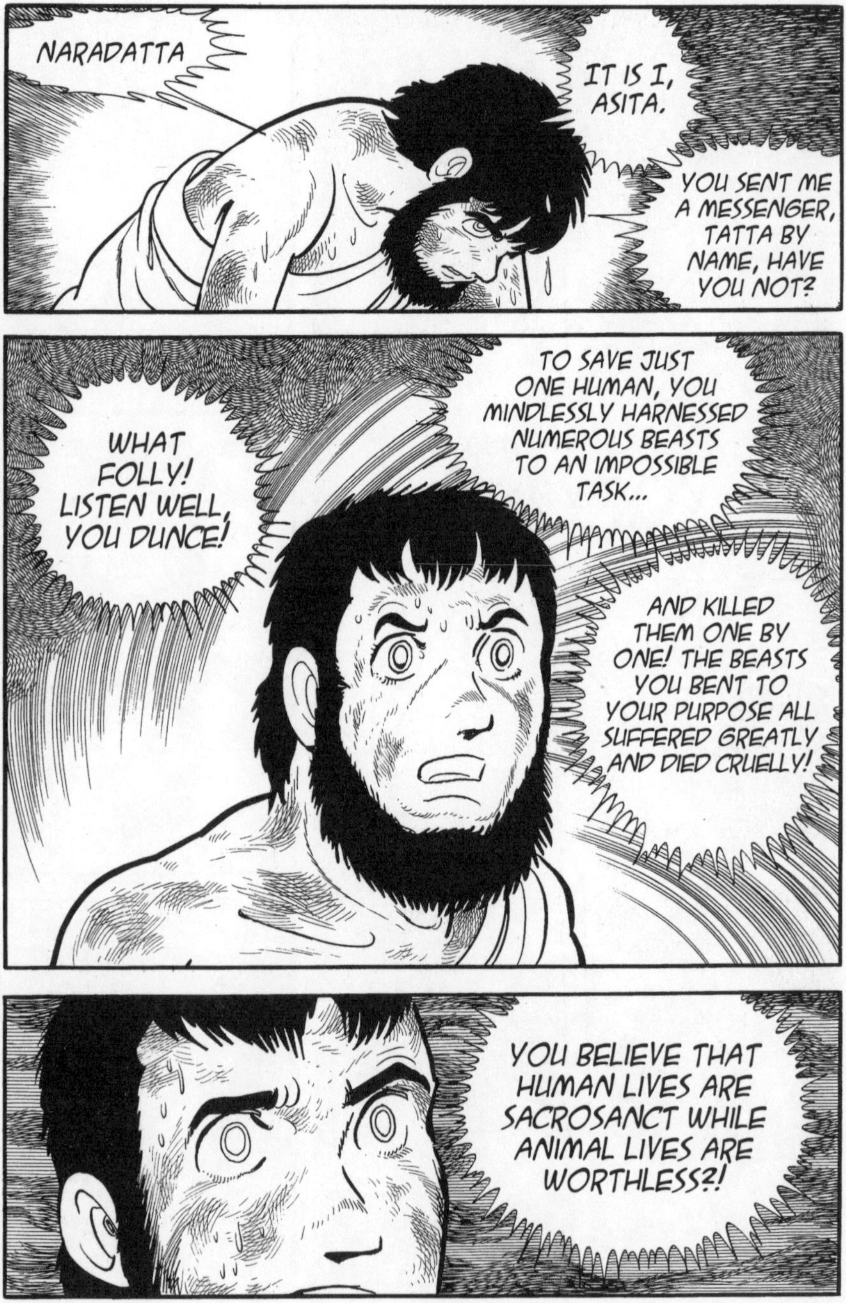
NARADATTA
IT IS I, ASITA.
YOU SENT ME A MESSENGER, TATTA BY NAME, HAVE YOU NOT?
WHAT FOLLY! LISTEN WELL, YOU DUNCE!
TO SAVE JUST ONE HUMAN, YOU MINDLESSLY HARNESSED NUMEROUS BEASTS TO AN IMPOSSIBLE TASK...
AND KILLED THEM ONE BY ONE! THE BEASTS YOU BENT TO YOUR PURPOSE ALL SUFFERED GREATLY AND DIED CRUELLY!
YOU BELIEVE THAT HUMAN LIVES ARE SACROSANCT WHILE ANIMAL LIVES ARE WORTHLESS?!

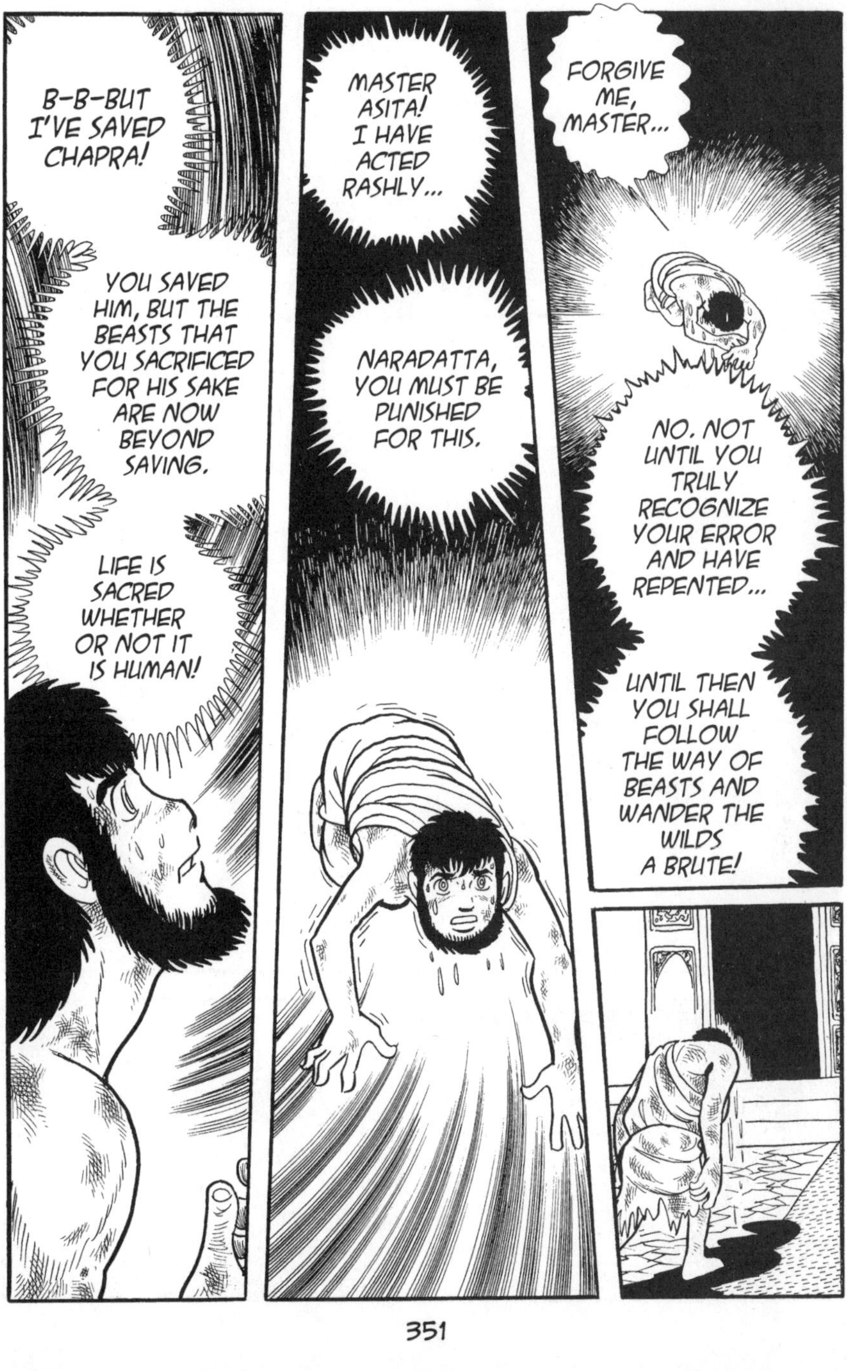
B-B-BUT I'VE SAVED CHAPRA!
YOU SAVED HIM, BUT THE BEASTS THAT YOU SACRIFICED FOR HIS SAKE ARE NOW BEYOND SAVING.
LIFE IS SACRED WHETHER OR NOT IT IS HUMAN!
MASTER ASITA! I HAVE ACTED RASHLY...
NARADATTA, YOU MUST BE PUNISHED FOR THIS.
FORGIVE ME, MASTER...
NO. NOT UNTIL YOU TRULY RECOGNIZE YOUR ERROR AND HAVE REPENTED...
UNTIL THEN YOU SHALL FOLLOW THE WAY OF BEASTS AND WANDER THE WILDS A BRUTE!

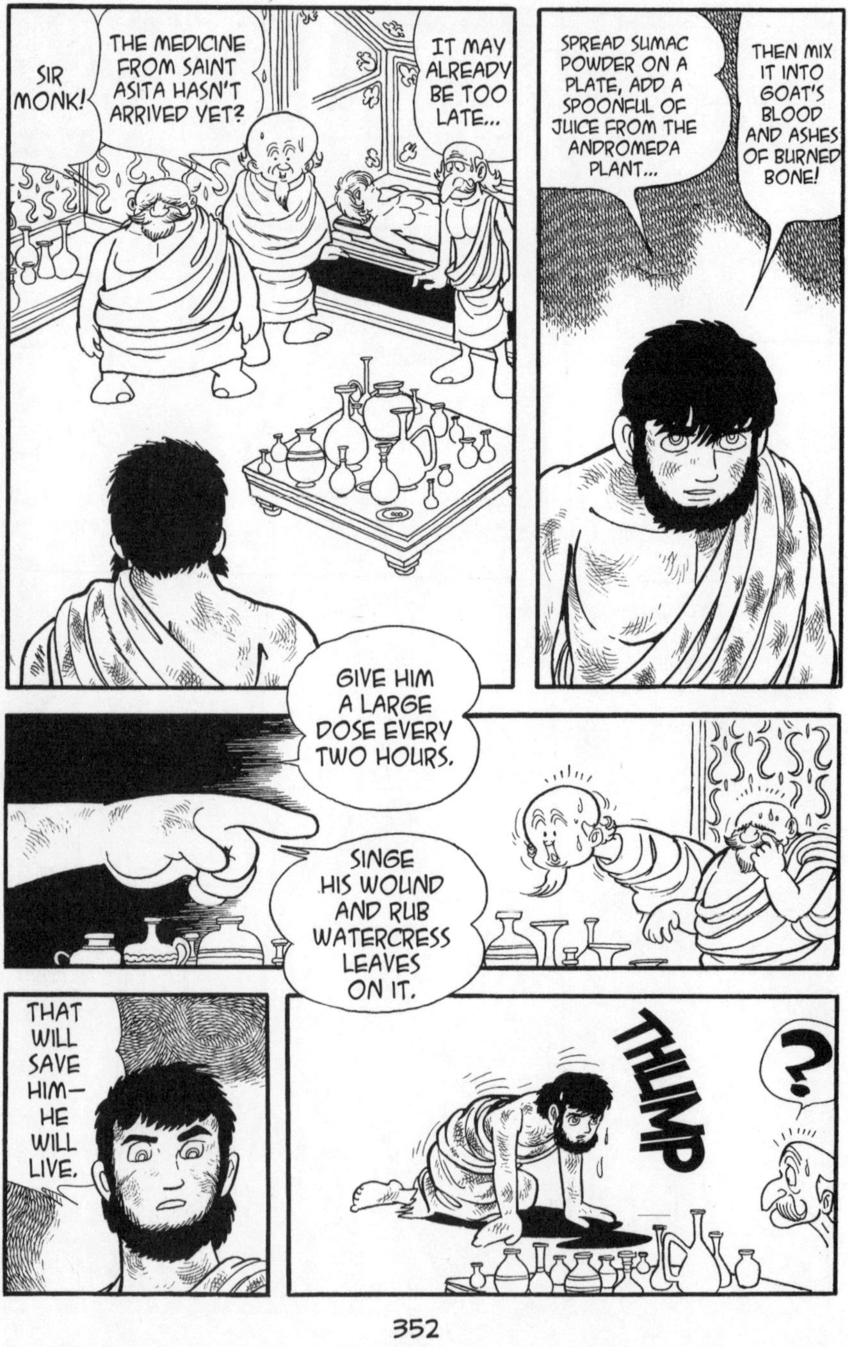
SIR MONK!
THE MEDICINE FROM SAINT ASITA HASN'T ARRIVED YET?
IT MAY ALREADY BE TOO LATE...
SPREAD SUMAC POWDER ON A PLATE, ADD A SPOONFUL OF JUICE FROM THE ANDROMEDA PLANT...
THEN MIX IT INTO GOAT'S BLOOD AND ASHES OF BURNED BONE!
GIVE HIM A LARGE DOSE EVERY TWO HOURS.
SINGE HIS WOUND AND RUB WATERCRESS LEAVES ON IT.
THAT WILL SAVE HIM—HE WILL LIVE.
THUMP
?

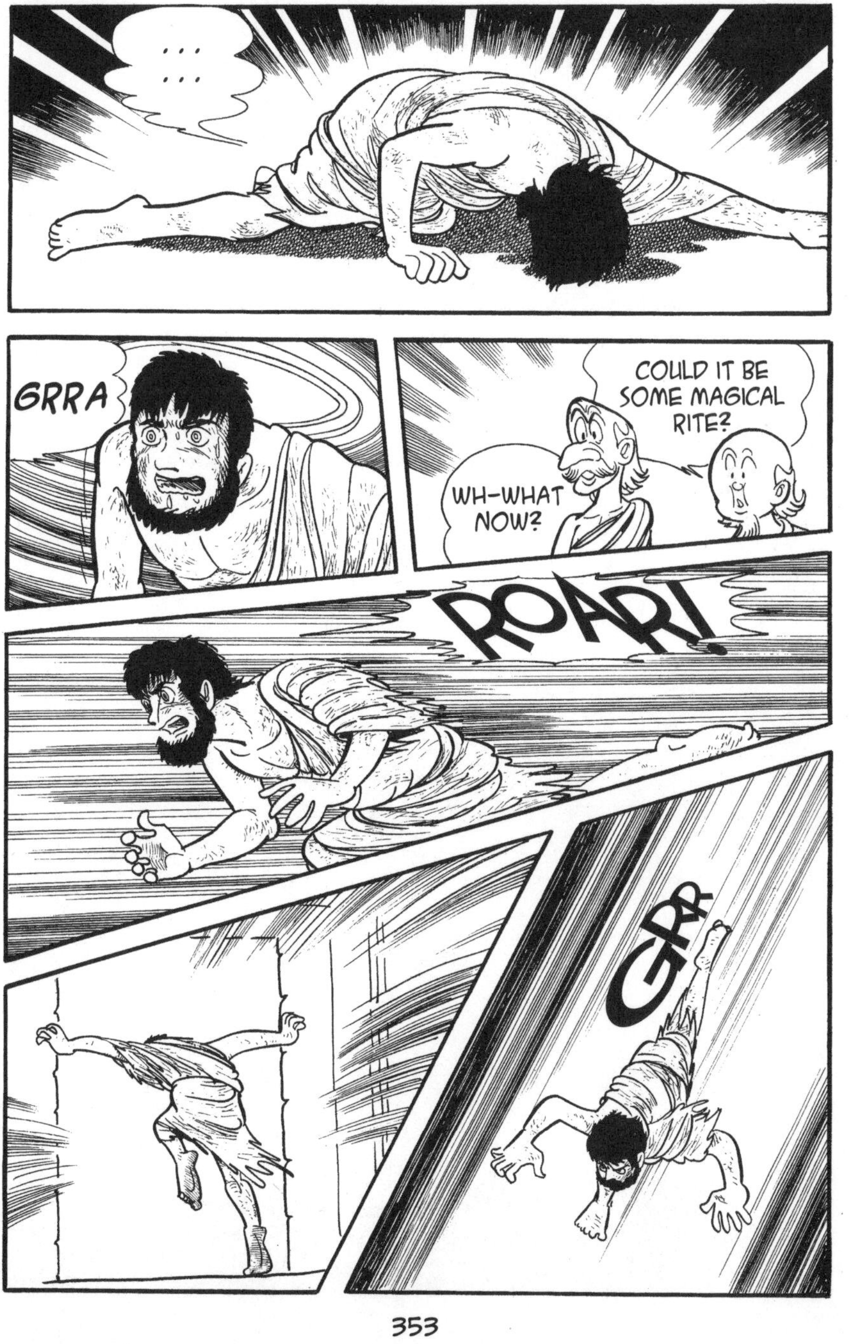
. . .
. . .
GRRA
COULD IT BE SOME MAGICAL RITE?
WH-WHAT NOW?
ROAR!
GRR

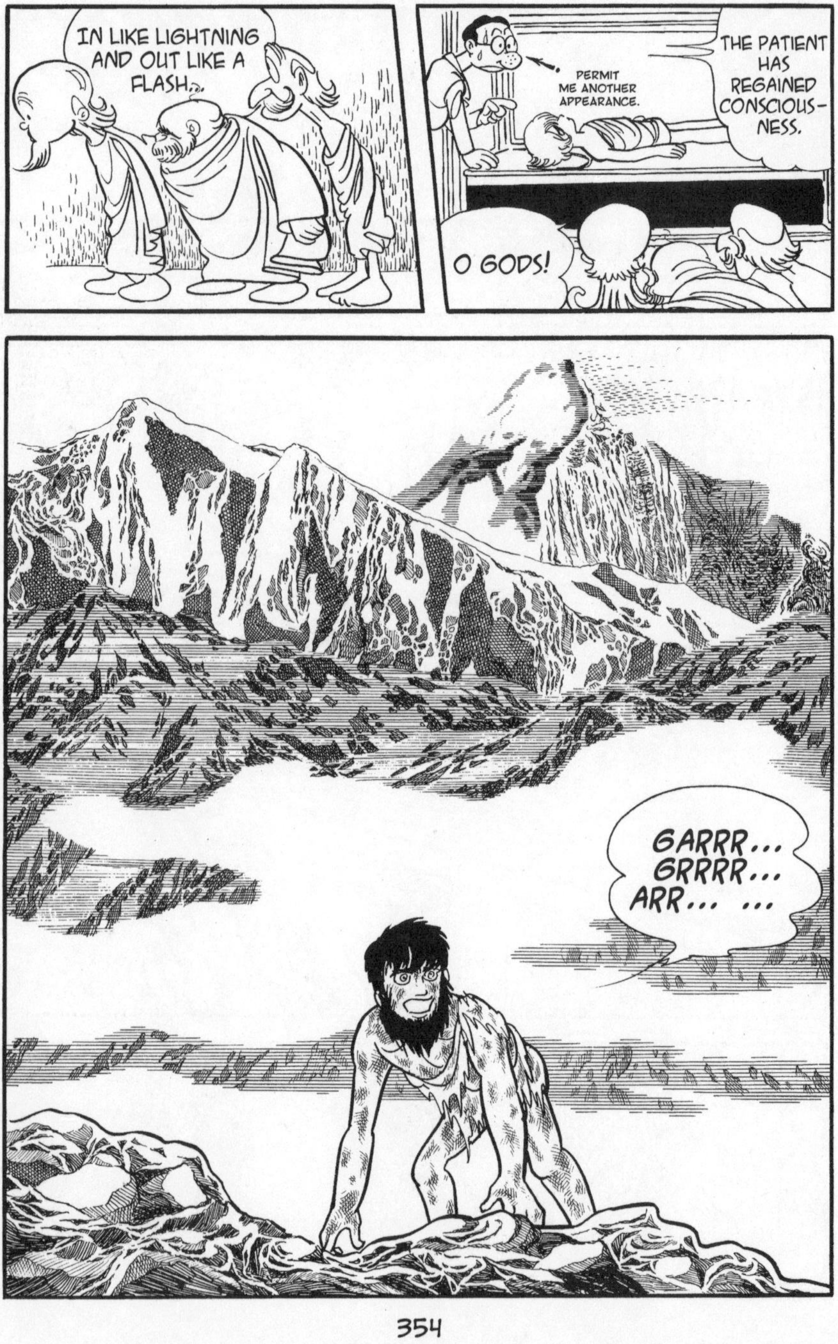
IN LIKE LIGHTNING AND OUT LIKE A FLASH...
THE PATIENT HAS REGAINED CONSCIOUS-NESS.
PERMIT ME ANOTHER APPEARANCE.
O GODS!
GARRR... GRRRR... ARR... ...

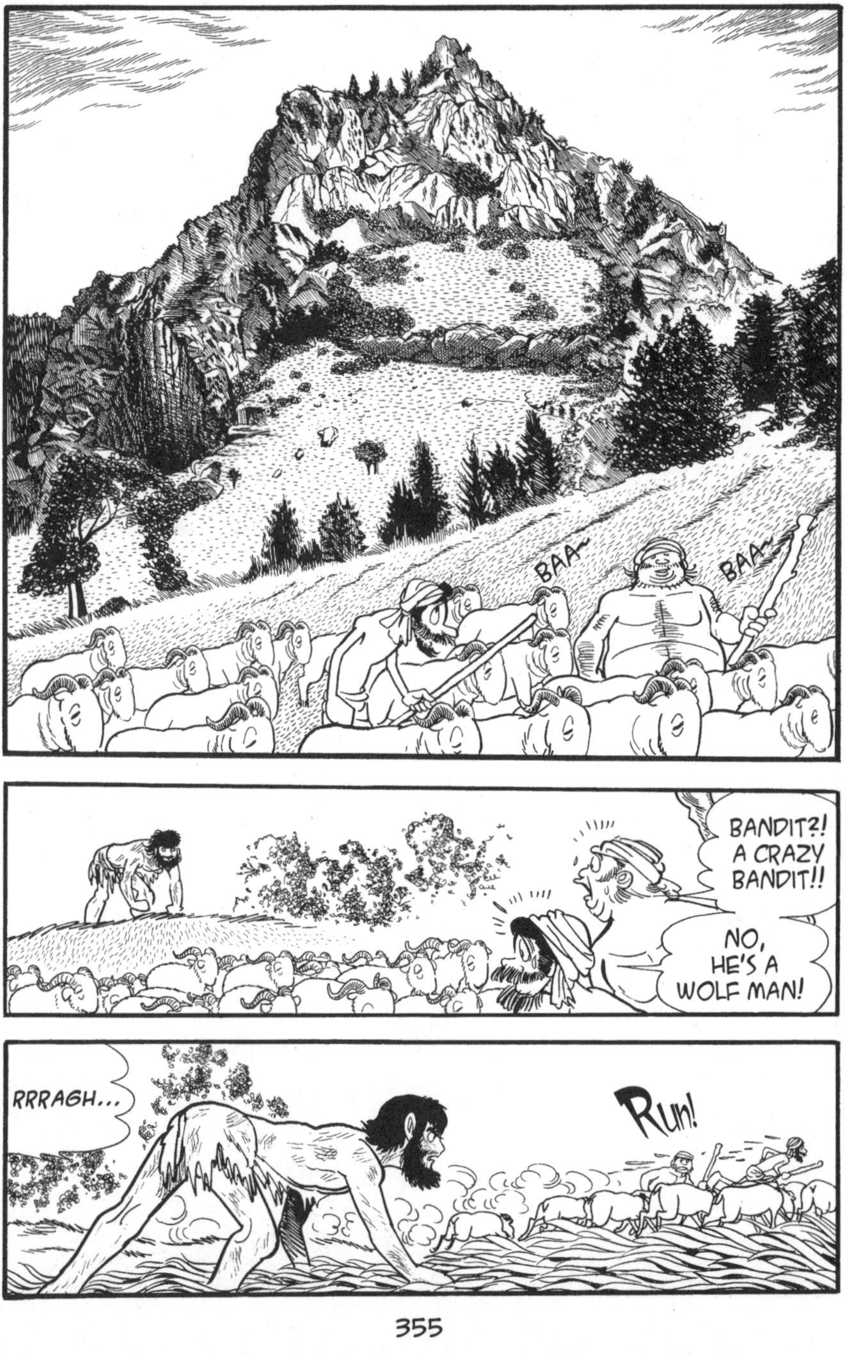
BAA~
BAA~
BANDIT?! A CRAZY BANDIT!!
NO, HE'S A WOLF MAN!
RRRAGH...
Run!

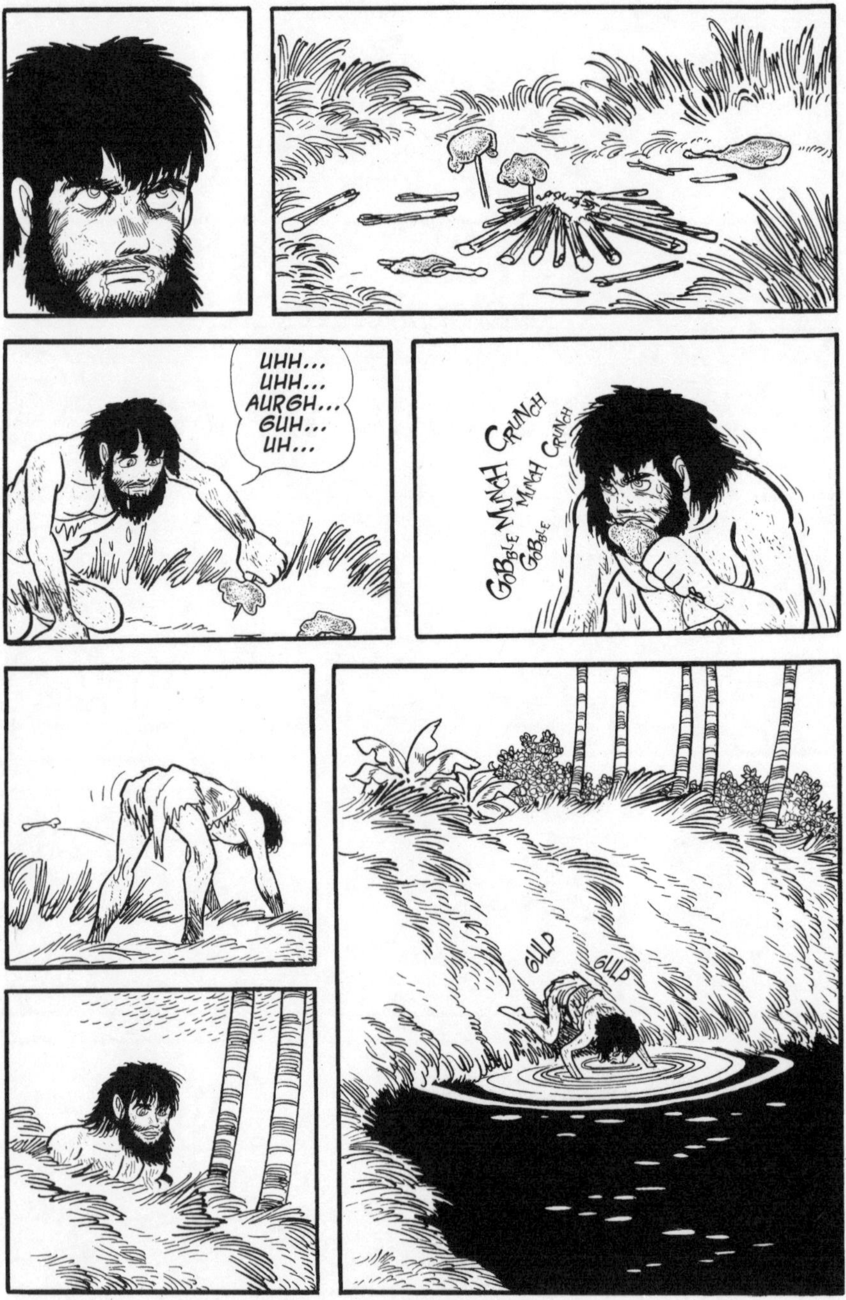
UHH... UHH... AURGH... GUH... UH...
GOBBLE MUNCH CRUNCH
GOBBLE MUNCH CRUNCH
GULP
GULP

CHAPTER ELEVEN

THE JUDGMENT

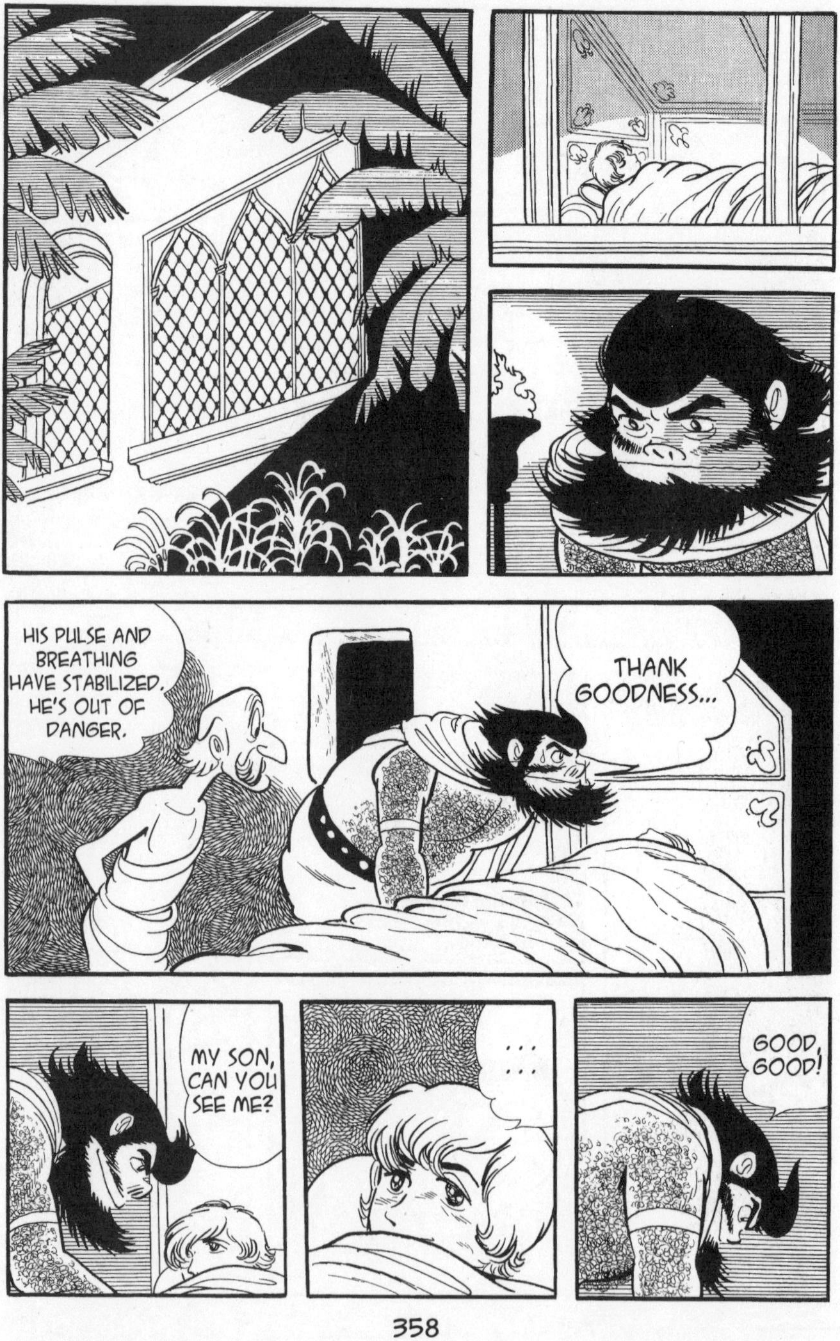

HIS PULSE AND BREATHING HAVE STABILIZED. HE'S OUT OF DANGER.
THANK GOODNESS...
MY SON, CAN YOU SEE ME?
... ...
GOOD, GOOD!

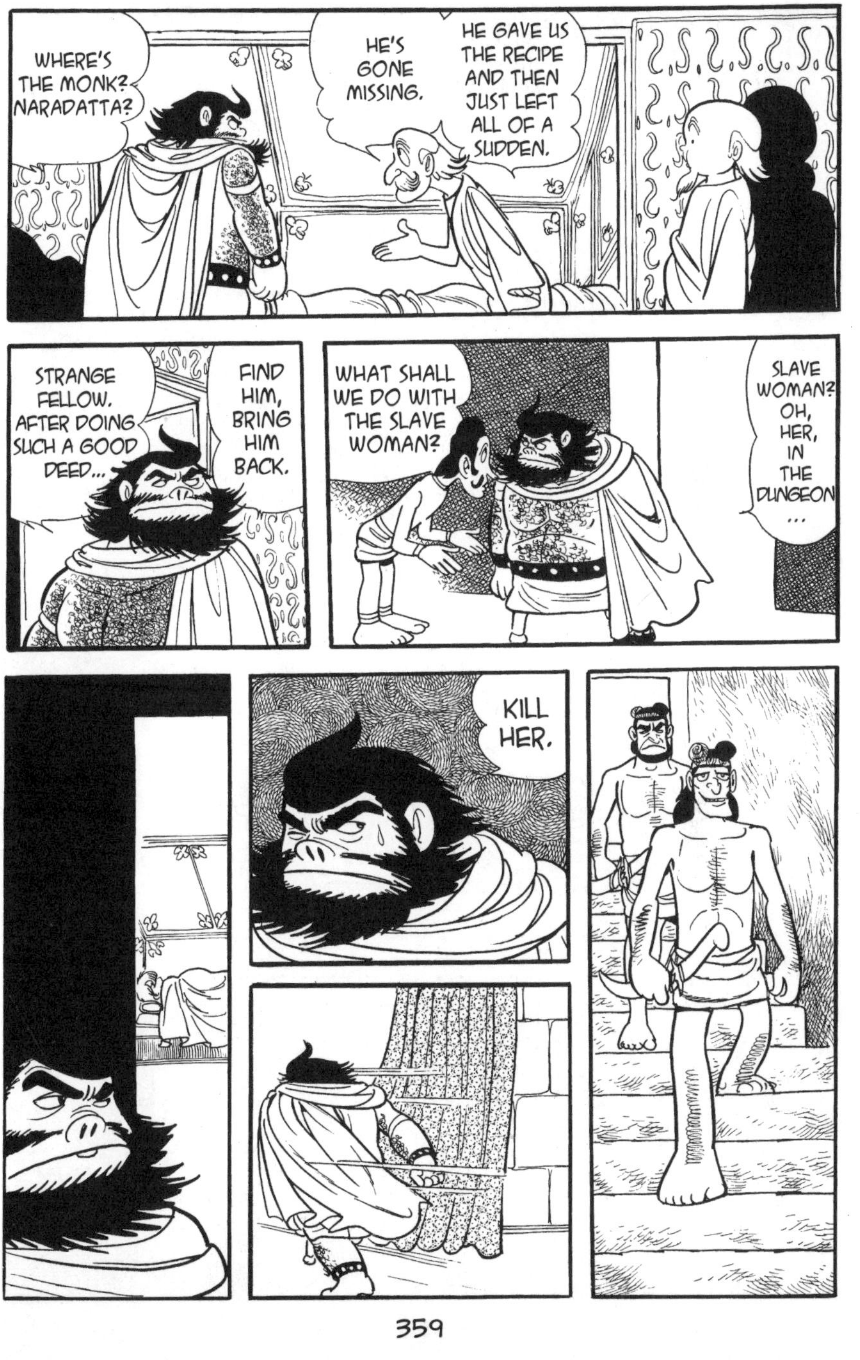
WHERE'S THE MONK? NARADATTA?
HE'S GONE MISSING.
HE GAVE US THE RECIPE AND THEN JUST LEFT ALL OF A SUDDEN.
STRANGE FELLOW. AFTER DOING SUCH A GOOD DEED...
FIND HIM, BRING HIM BACK.
WHAT SHALL WE DO WITH THE SLAVE WOMAN?
SLAVE WOMAN? OH, HER, IN THE DUNGEON ...
KILL HER.

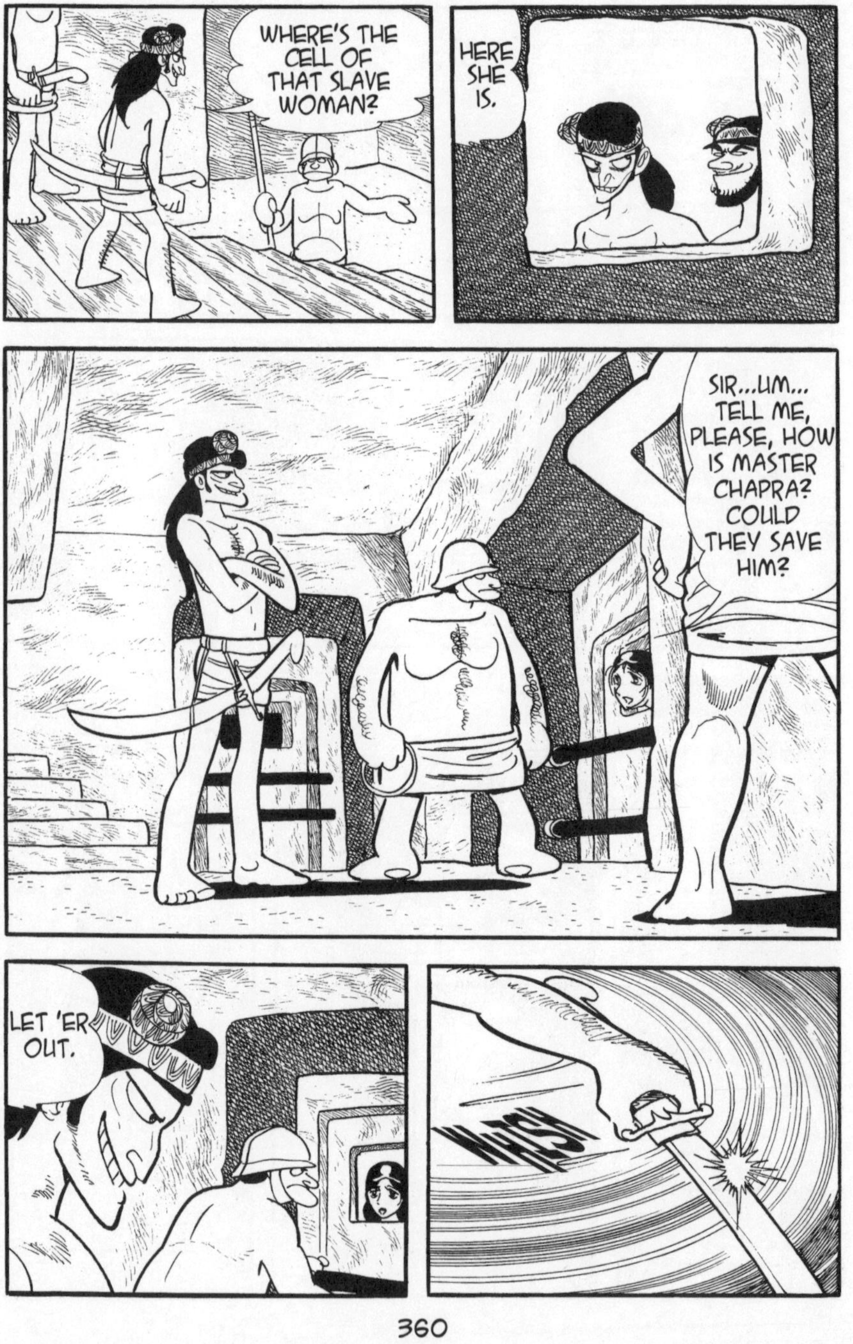
WHERE'S THE CELL OF THAT SLAVE WOMAN?
HERE SHE IS.
SIR...UM... TELL ME, PLEASE, HOW IS MASTER CHAPRA? COULD THEY SAVE HIM?
LET 'ER OUT.
WHISH

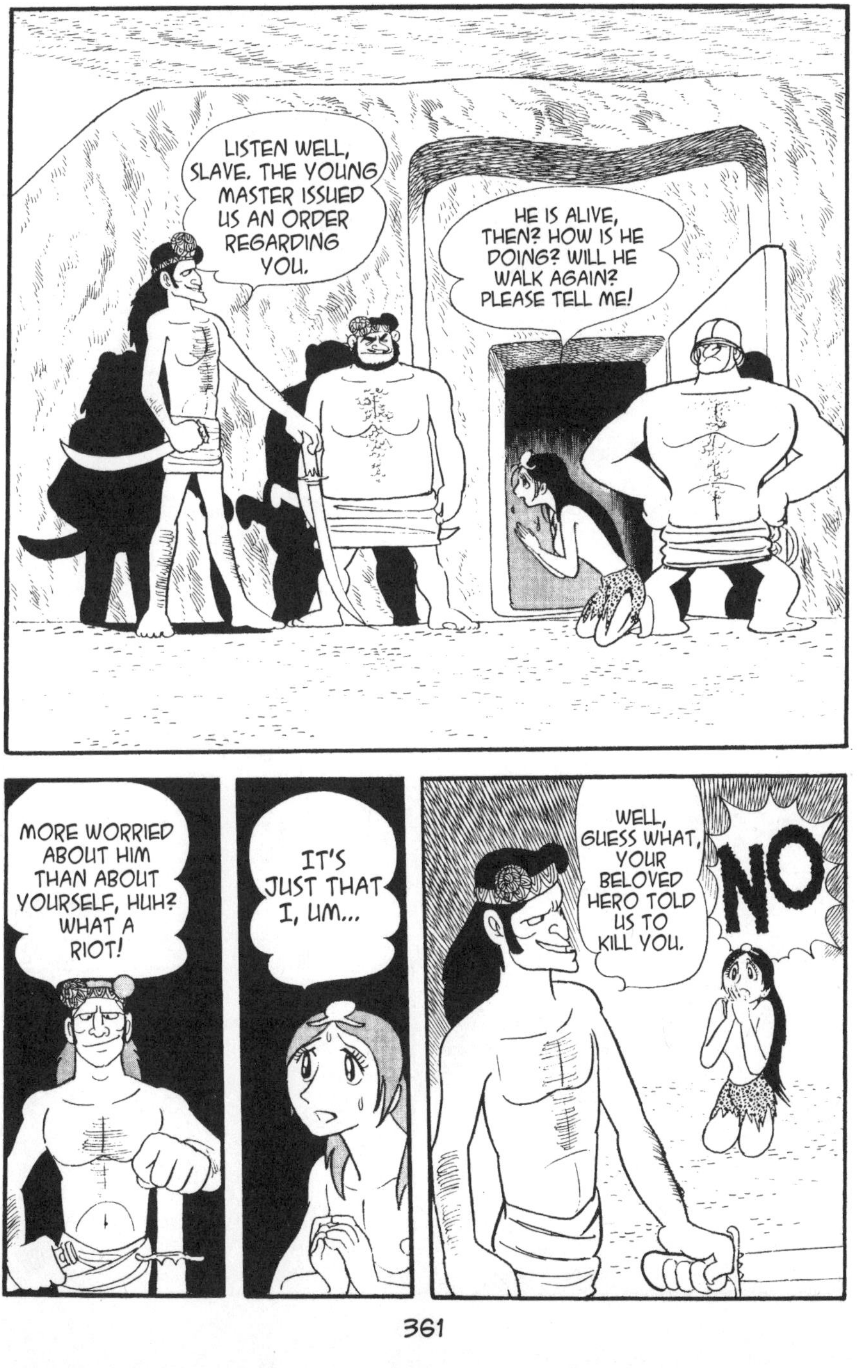
LISTEN WELL, SLAVE. THE YOUNG MASTER ISSUED US AN ORDER REGARDING YOU.
HE IS ALIVE, THEN? HOW IS HE DOING? WILL HE WALK AGAIN? PLEASE TELL ME!
MORE WORRIED ABOUT HIM THAN ABOUT YOURSELF, HUH? WHAT A RIOT!
IT'S JUST THAT I, UM...
WELL, GUESS WHAT, YOUR BELOVED HERO TOLD US TO KILL YOU.
NO

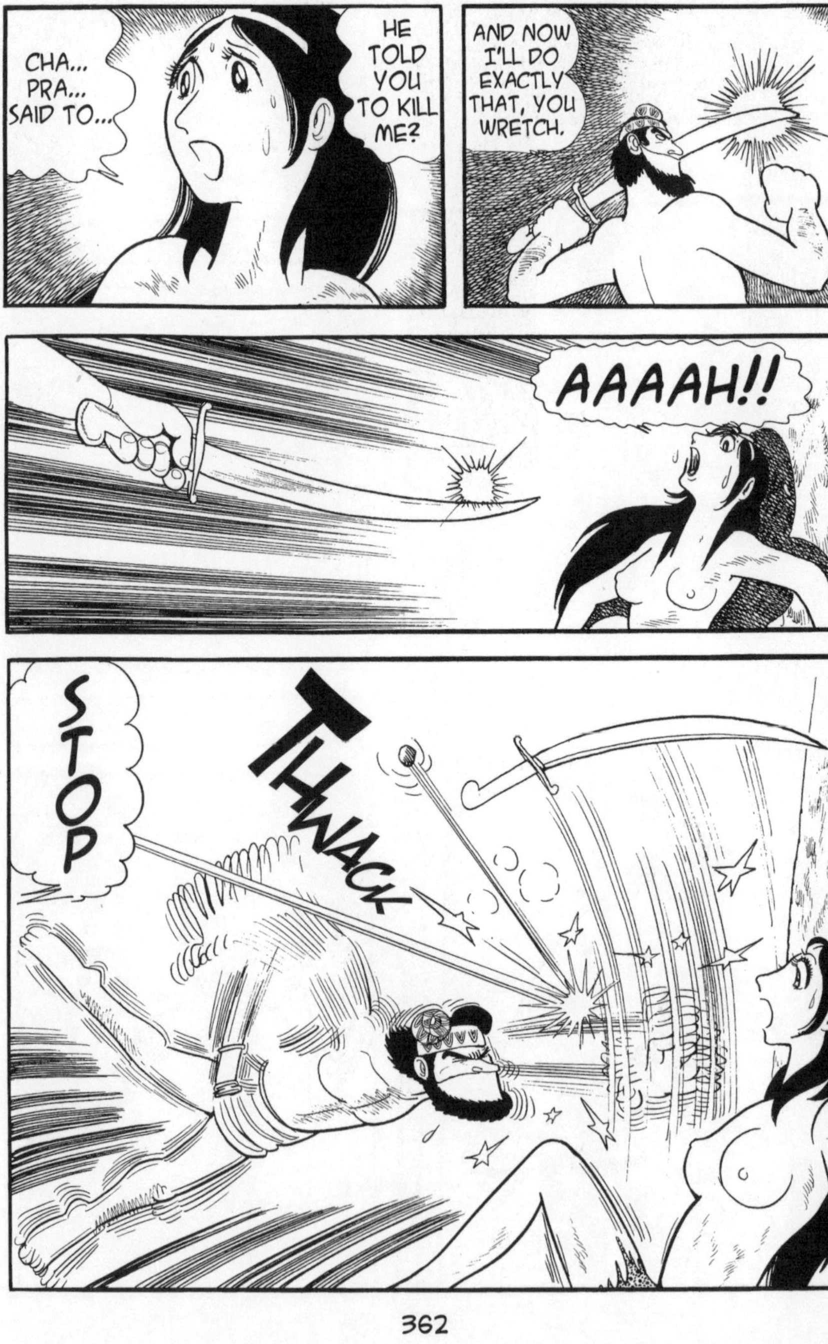
CHA... PRA... SAID TO...
HE TOLD YOU TO KILL ME?
AND NOW I'LL DO EXACTLY THAT, YOU WRETCH.
AAAAH!!
STOP
THWACK

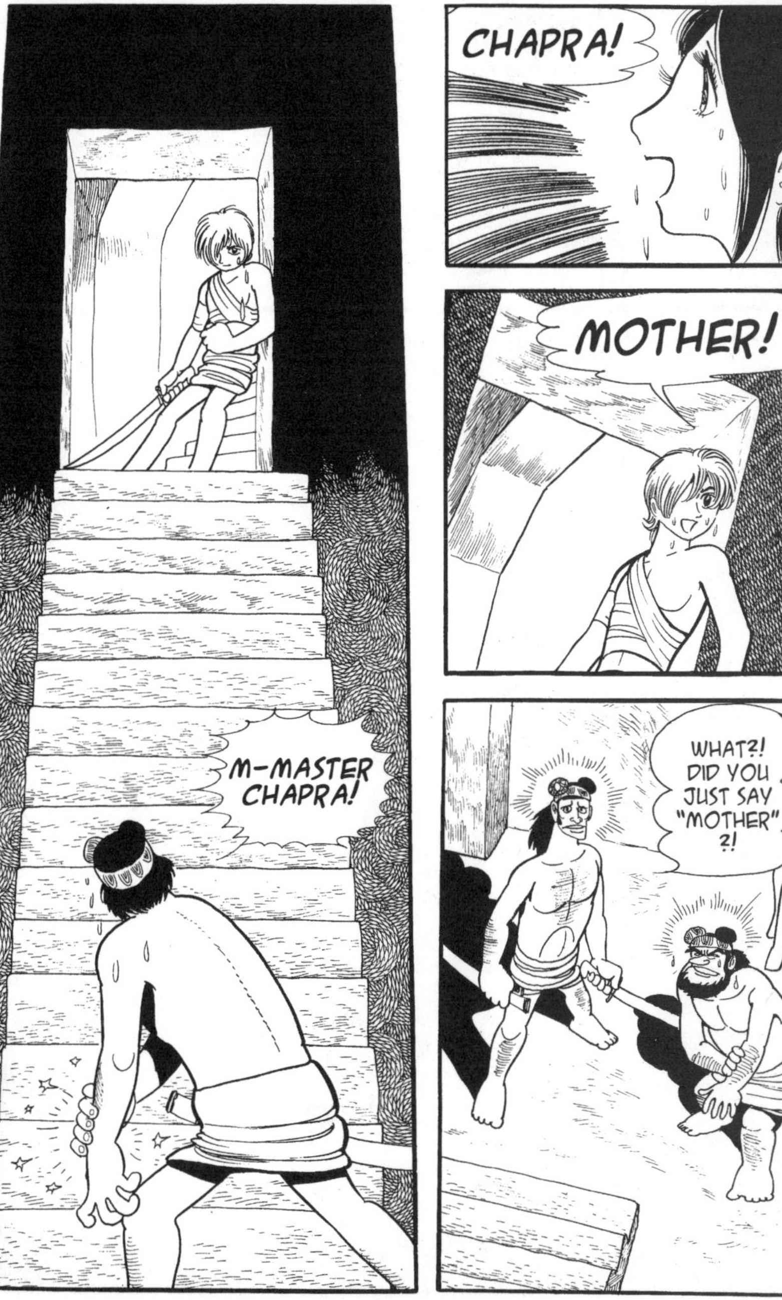
M-MASTER CHAPRA!
CHAPRA!
MOTHER!
WHAT?! DID YOU JUST SAY "MOTHER" ?!

AND NOW THAT YOU KNOW,

I'M SORRY BUT I'LL HAVE TO KILL YOU, MEN!

NO THANKS, MASTER, EVEN COMING FROM YOU, I'M GONNA HAVE TO PASS ON THAT.

GO AND REST, YOU'VE A BAD FEVER.

LET GO OF MOTHER. THAT'S AN ORDER!

MOTHER! WHY DO YOU CALL THIS SLAVE THAT?

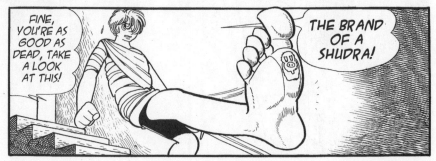

FINE, YOU'RE AS GOOD AS DEAD, TAKE A LOOK AT THIS!

THE BRAND OF A SHUDRA!

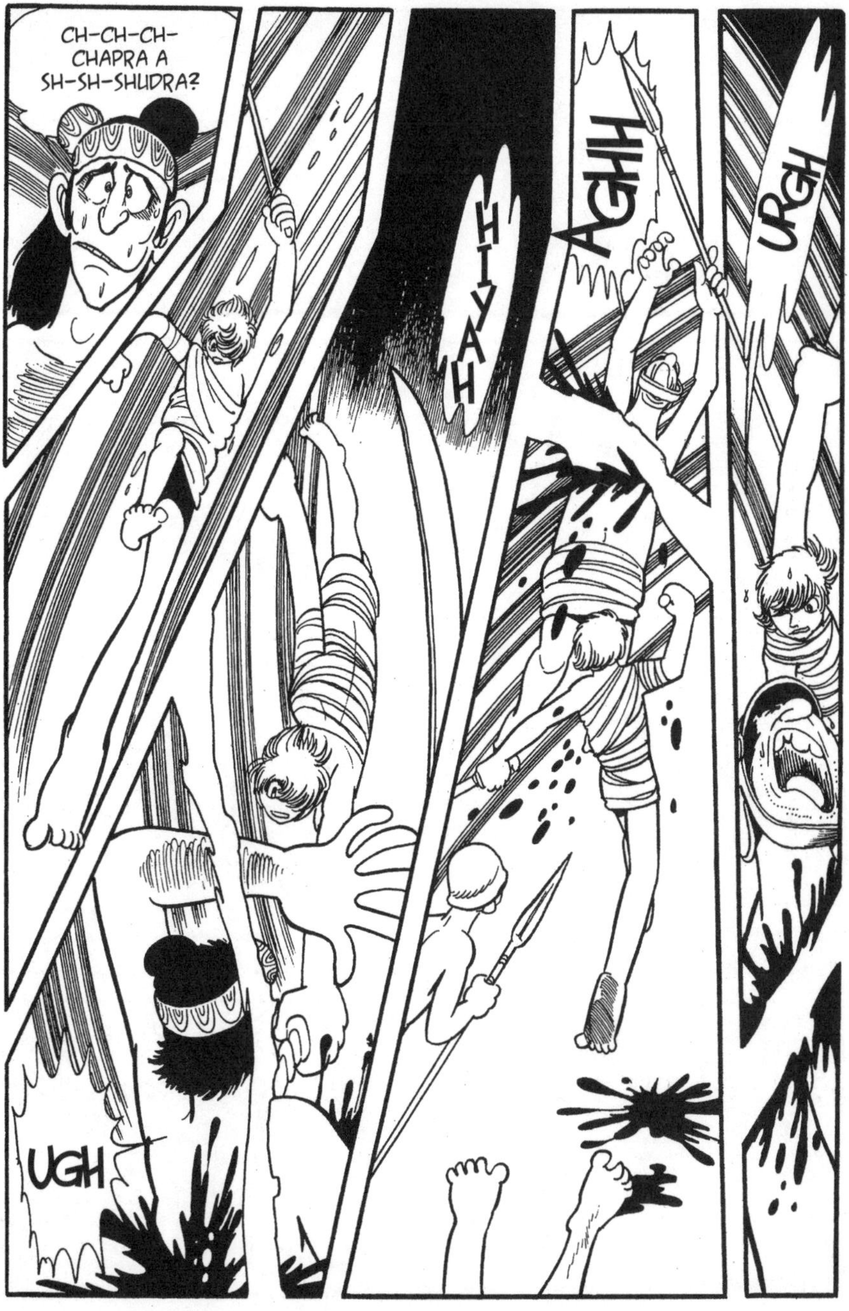
CH-CH-CH-
CHAPRA A
SH-SH-SHUDRA?
HIYAH
AGHH
URGH
UGH

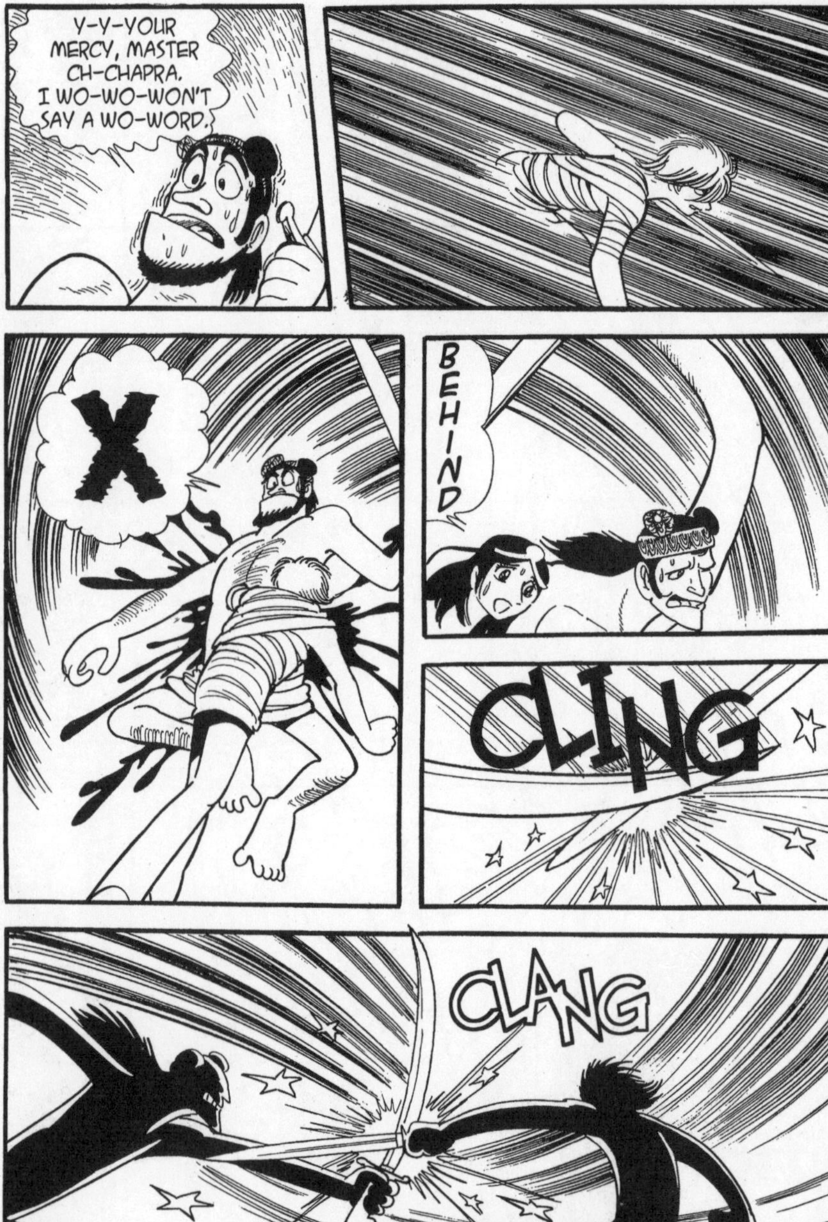
Y-Y-YOUR MERCY, MASTER CH-CHAPRA. I WO-WO-WON'T SAY A WO-WORD.
X
BEHIND
CLING
CLANG

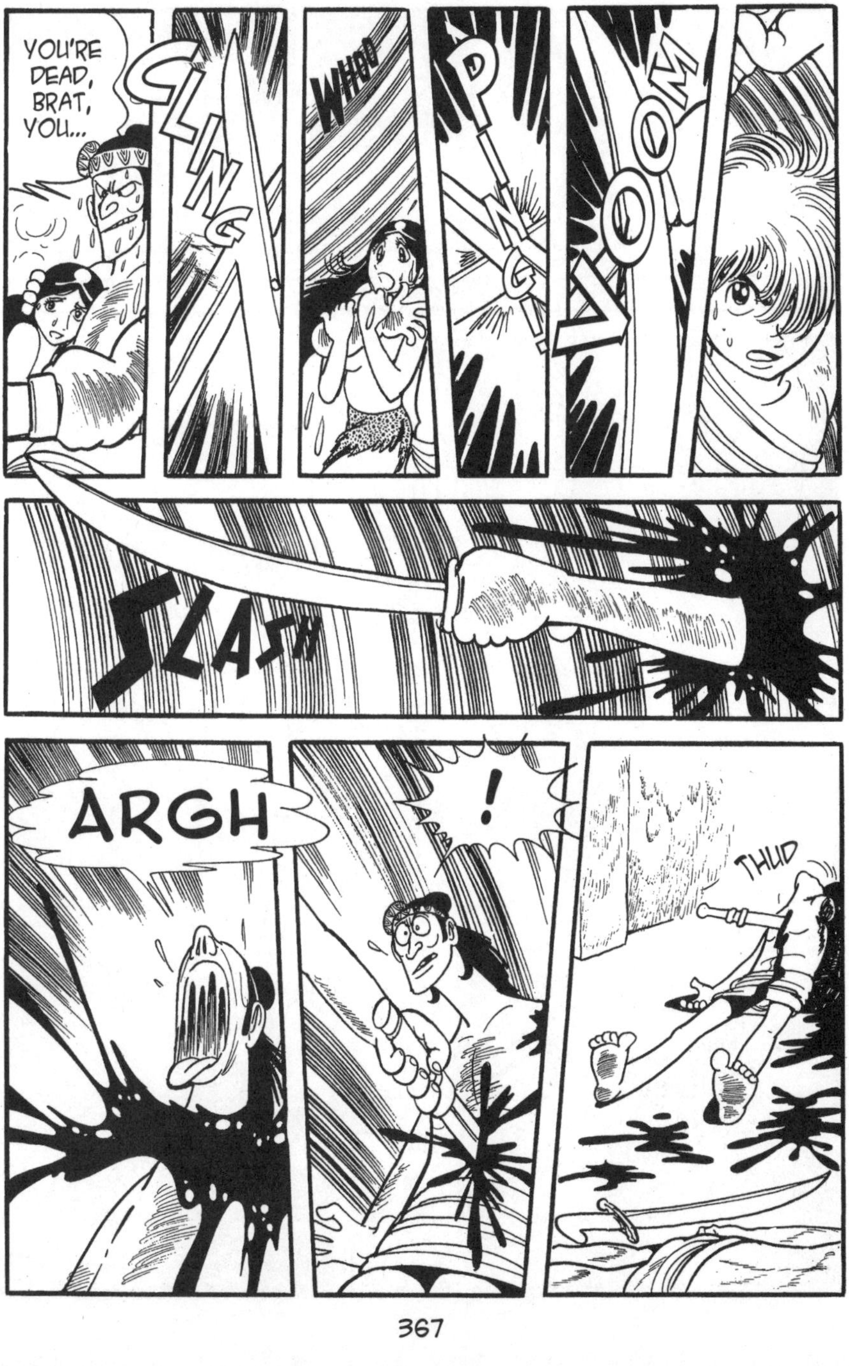

YOU'RE DEAD, BRAT, YOU...
CLING
WHOO
PING!
VOOM
SLASH
ARGH
!
THUD

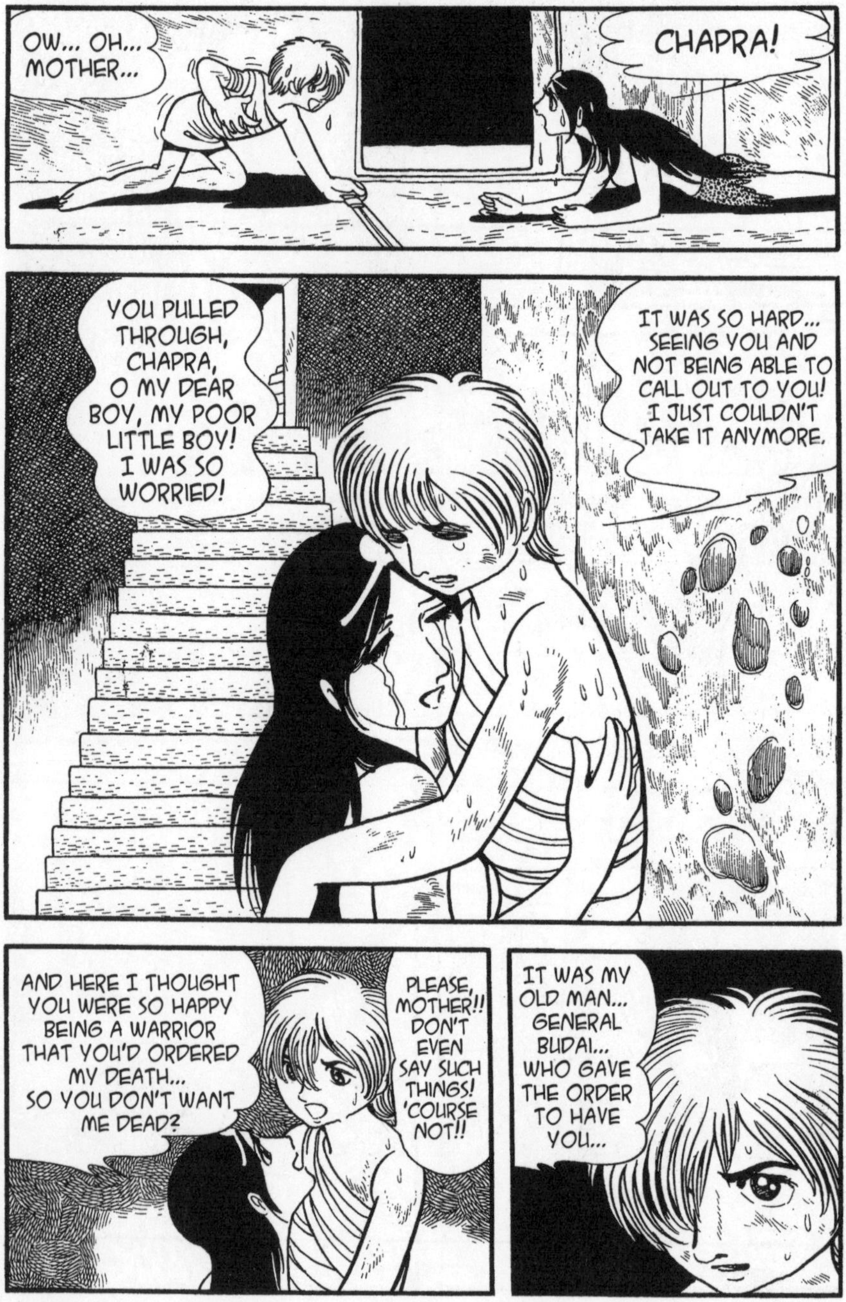
OW... OH... MOTHER...
CHAPRA!
YOU PULLED THROUGH, CHAPRA, O MY DEAR BOY, MY POOR LITTLE BOY! I WAS SO WORRIED!
IT WAS SO HARD... SEEING YOU AND NOT BEING ABLE TO CALL OUT TO YOU! I JUST COULDN'T TAKE IT ANYMORE.
AND HERE I THOUGHT YOU WERE SO HAPPY BEING A WARRIOR THAT YOU'D ORDERED MY DEATH... SO YOU DON'T WANT ME DEAD?
PLEASE, MOTHER!! DON'T EVEN SAY SUCH THINGS! 'COURSE NOT!!
IT WAS MY OLD MAN... GENERAL BUDAI... WHO GAVE THE ORDER TO HAVE YOU...

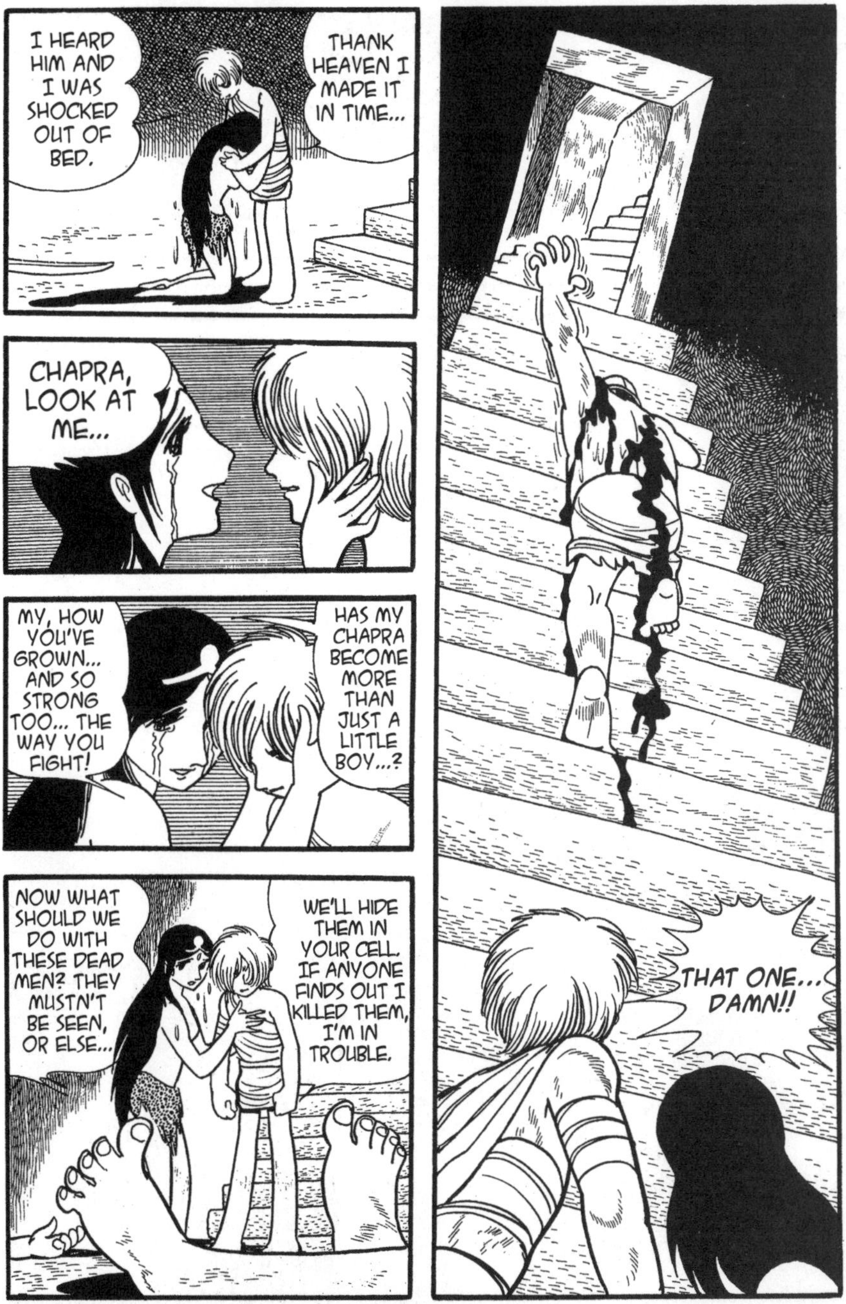
I HEARD HIM AND I WAS SHOCKED OUT OF BED.
THANK HEAVEN I MADE IT IN TIME...
CHAPRA, LOOK AT ME...
MY, HOW YOU'VE GROWN... AND SO STRONG TOO... THE WAY YOU FIGHT!
HAS MY CHAPRA BECOME MORE THAN JUST A LITTLE BOY...?
NOW WHAT SHOULD WE DO WITH THESE DEAD MEN? THEY MUSTN'T BE SEEN, OR ELSE...
WE'LL HIDE THEM IN YOUR CELL. IF ANYONE FINDS OUT I KILLED THEM, I'M IN TROUBLE.
THAT ONE... DAMN!!

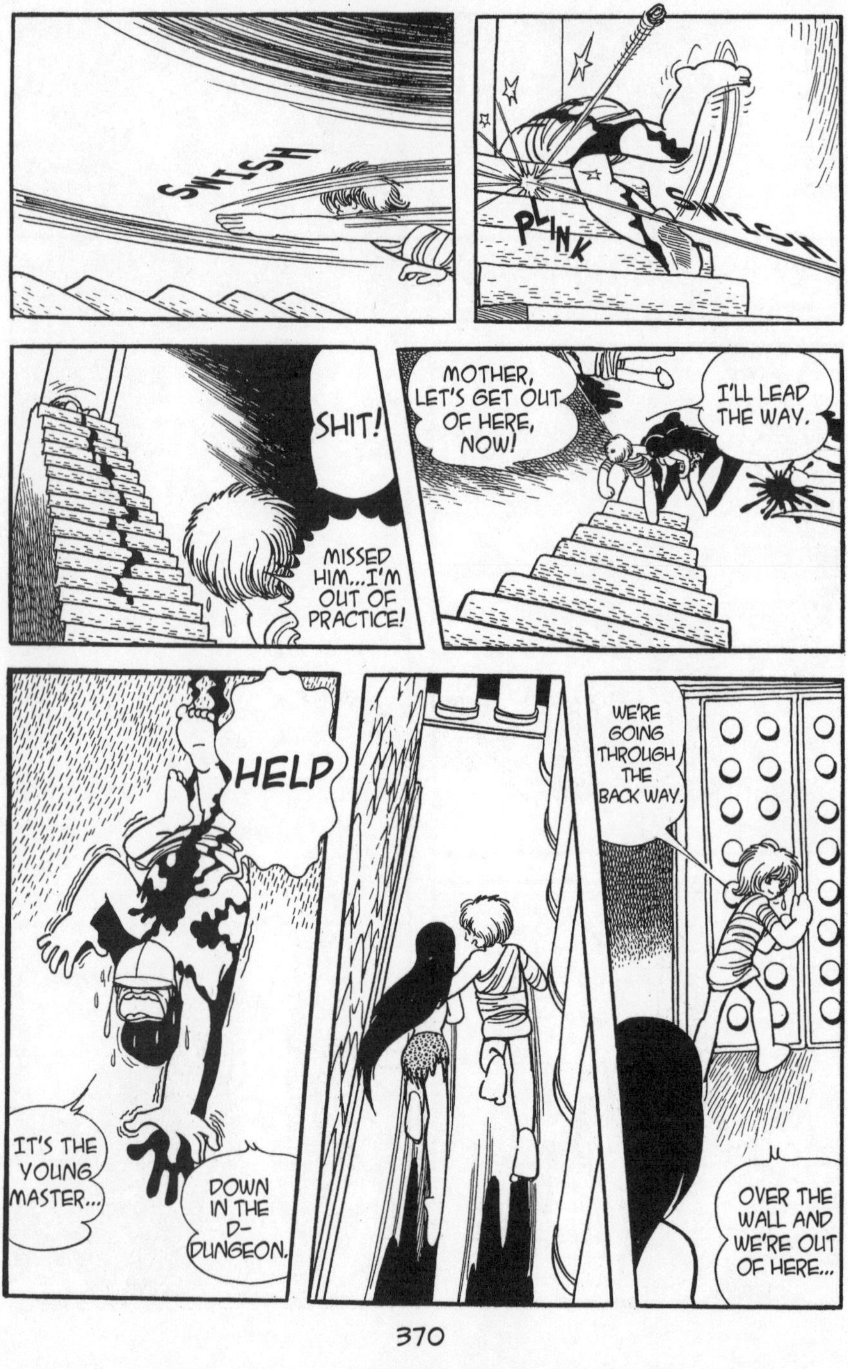
SWISH
SWISH
PLINK
SHIT!
MISSED HIM...I'M OUT OF PRACTICE!
MOTHER, LET'S GET OUT OF HERE, NOW!
I'LL LEAD THE WAY.
HELP
IT'S THE YOUNG MASTER...
DOWN IN THE D-DUNGEON.
WE'RE GOING THROUGH THE BACK WAY.
OVER THE WALL AND WE'RE OUT OF HERE...

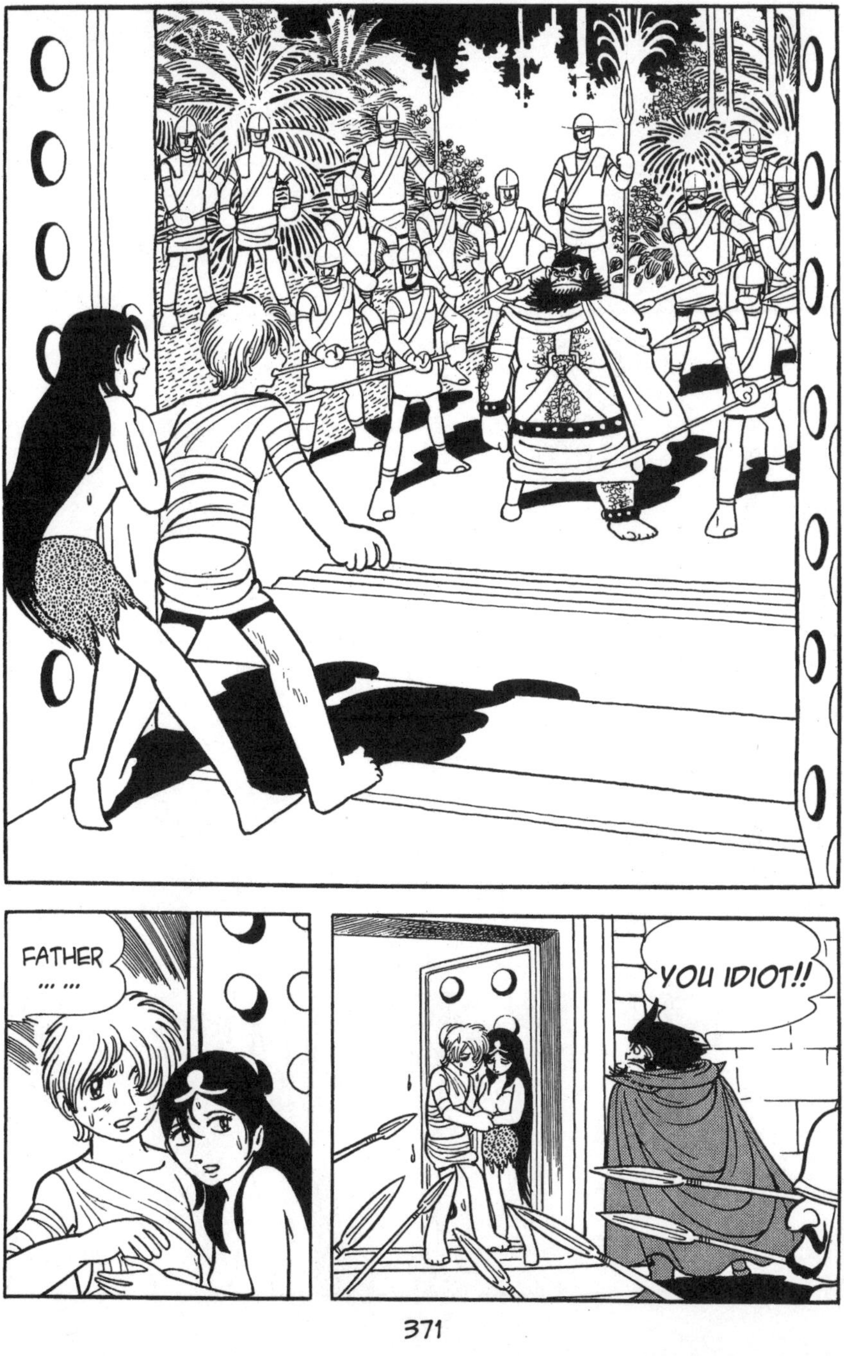
FATHER
... ...
YOU IDIOT!!

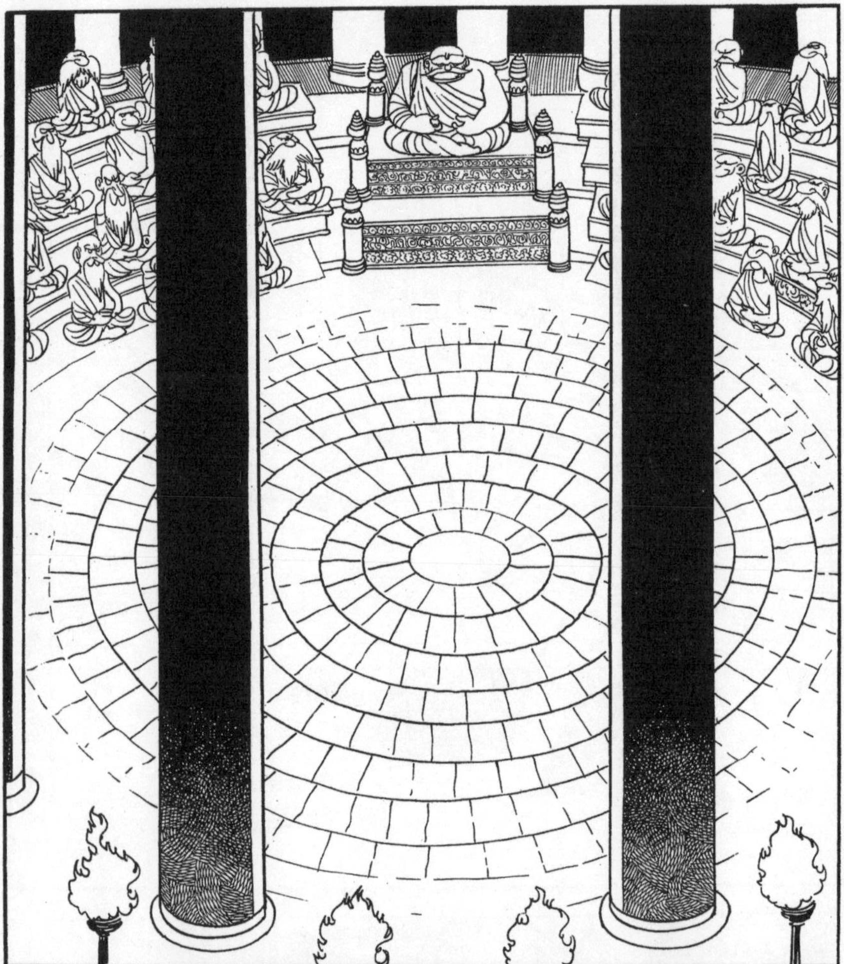

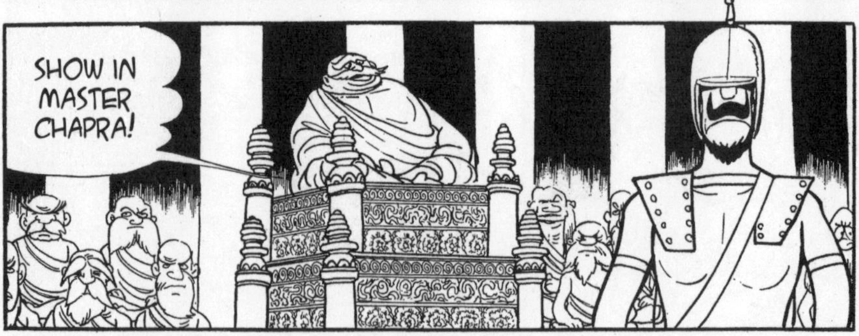
SHOW IN MASTER CHAPRA!

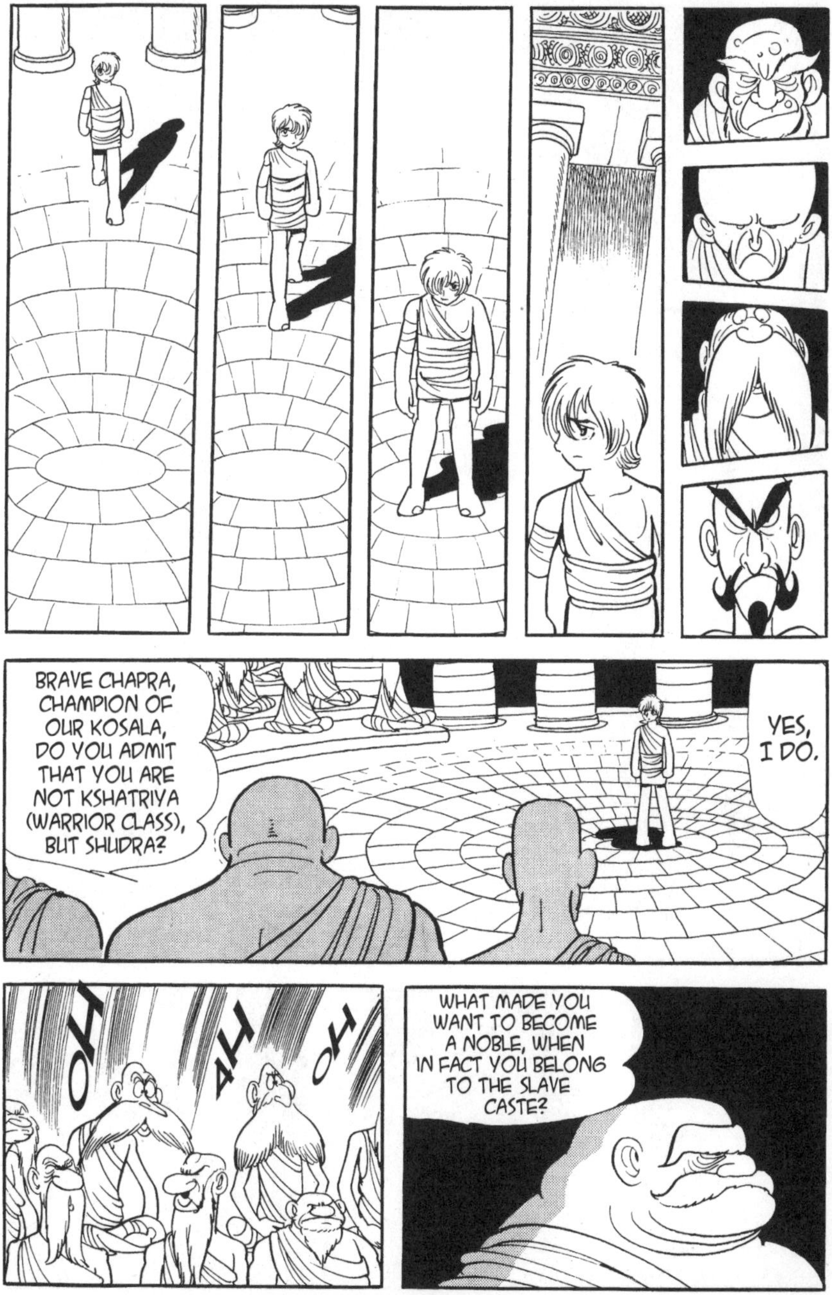
BRAVE CHAPRA, CHAMPION OF OUR KOSALA, DO YOU ADMIT THAT YOU ARE NOT KSHATRIYA (WARRIOR CLASS), BUT SHUDRA?
YES, I DO.
OH
AH
OH
WHAT MADE YOU WANT TO BECOME A NOBLE, WHEN IN FACT YOU BELONG TO THE SLAVE CASTE?

ARE YOU REALLY SO DIM, MY HONOR? WHAT'S WRONG WITH A SLAVE WANTING TO BECOME A NOBLE? NOTHING!

I DON'T BELIEVE I AM HEARING THIS!

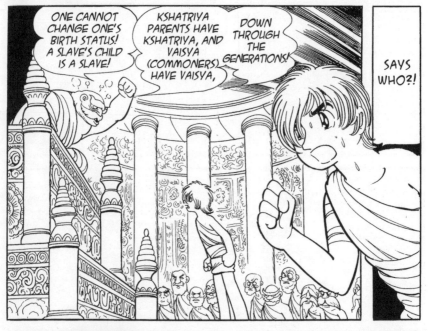

ONE CANNOT CHANGE ONE'S BIRTH STATUS! A SLAVE'S CHILD IS A SLAVE!

KSHATRIYA PARENTS HAVE KSHATRIYA, AND VAISYA (COMMONERS) HAVE VAISYA,

DOWN THROUGH THE GENERATIONS!

SAYS WHO?!

WHO? THAT IS THE WAY IT HAS ALWAYS BEEN.

AND SO WHO DECIDED IT HAD TO BE THAT WAY?

PEOPLE? OR WAS IT THE GODS?

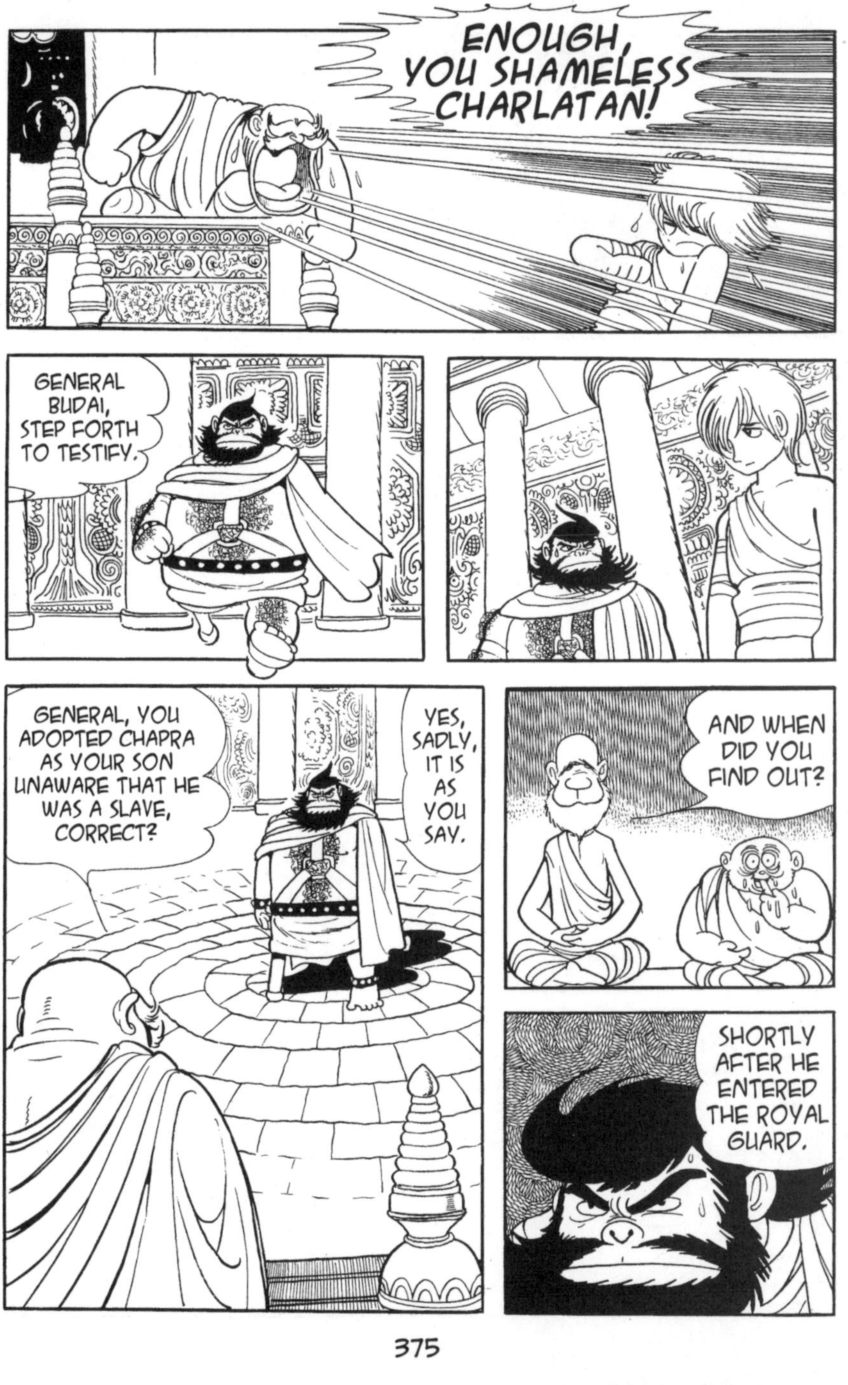
ENOUGH, YOU SHAMELESS CHARLATAN!
GENERAL BUDAI, STEP FORTH TO TESTIFY.
GENERAL, YOU ADOPTED CHAPRA AS YOUR SON UNAWARE THAT HE WAS A SLAVE, CORRECT?
YES, SADLY, IT IS AS YOU SAY.
AND WHEN DID YOU FIND OUT?
SHORTLY AFTER HE ENTERED THE ROYAL GUARD.

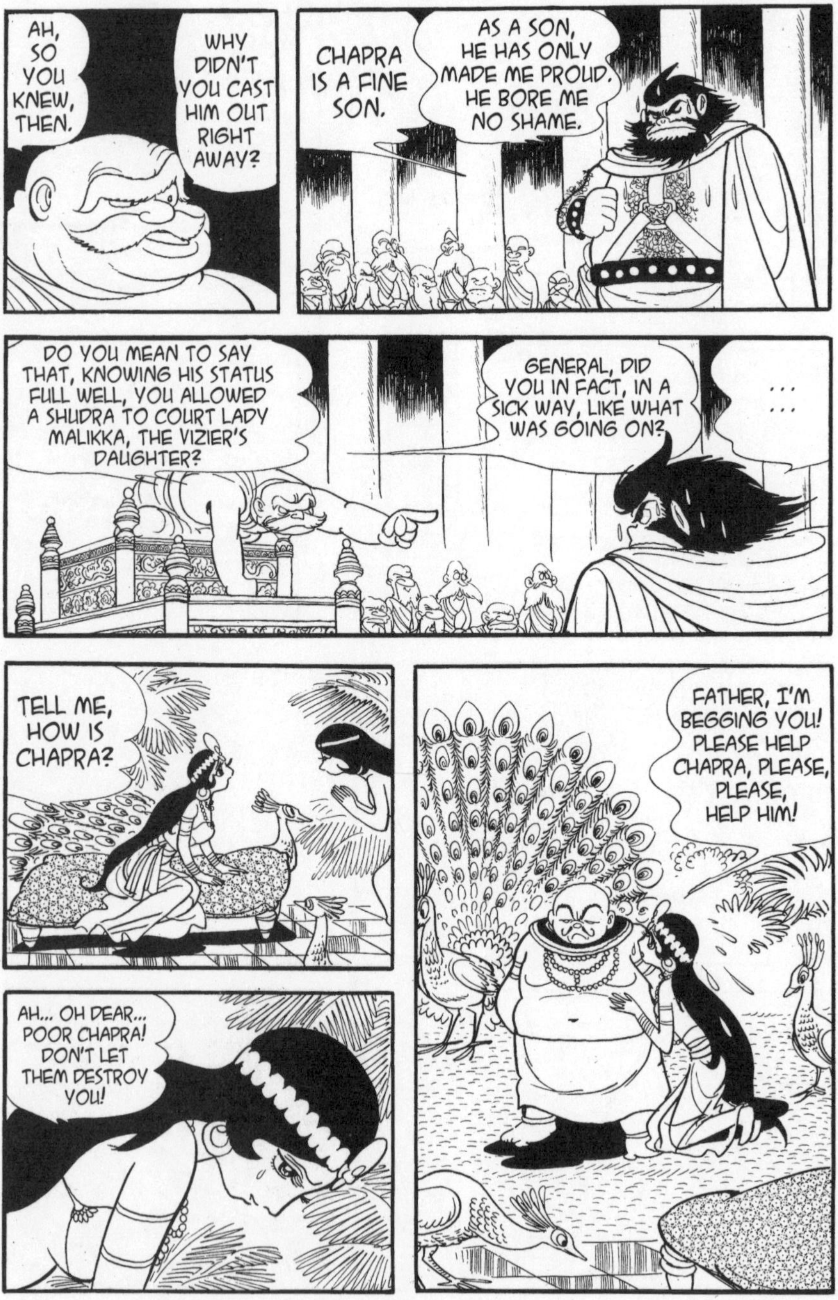
AH, SO YOU KNEW, THEN.
WHY DIDN'T YOU CAST HIM OUT RIGHT AWAY?
CHAPRA IS A FINE SON.
AS A SON, HE HAS ONLY MADE ME PROUD. HE BORE ME NO SHAME.
DO YOU MEAN TO SAY THAT, KNOWING HIS STATUS FULL WELL, YOU ALLOWED A SHUDRA TO COURT LADY MALIKKA, THE VIZIER'S DAUGHTER?
GENERAL, DID YOU IN FACT, IN A SICK WAY, LIKE WHAT WAS GOING ON?
... ...
TELL ME, HOW IS CHAPRA?
AH... OH DEAR... POOR CHAPRA! DON'T LET THEM DESTROY YOU!
FATHER, I'M BEGGING YOU! PLEASE HELP CHAPRA, PLEASE, PLEASE, HELP HIM!

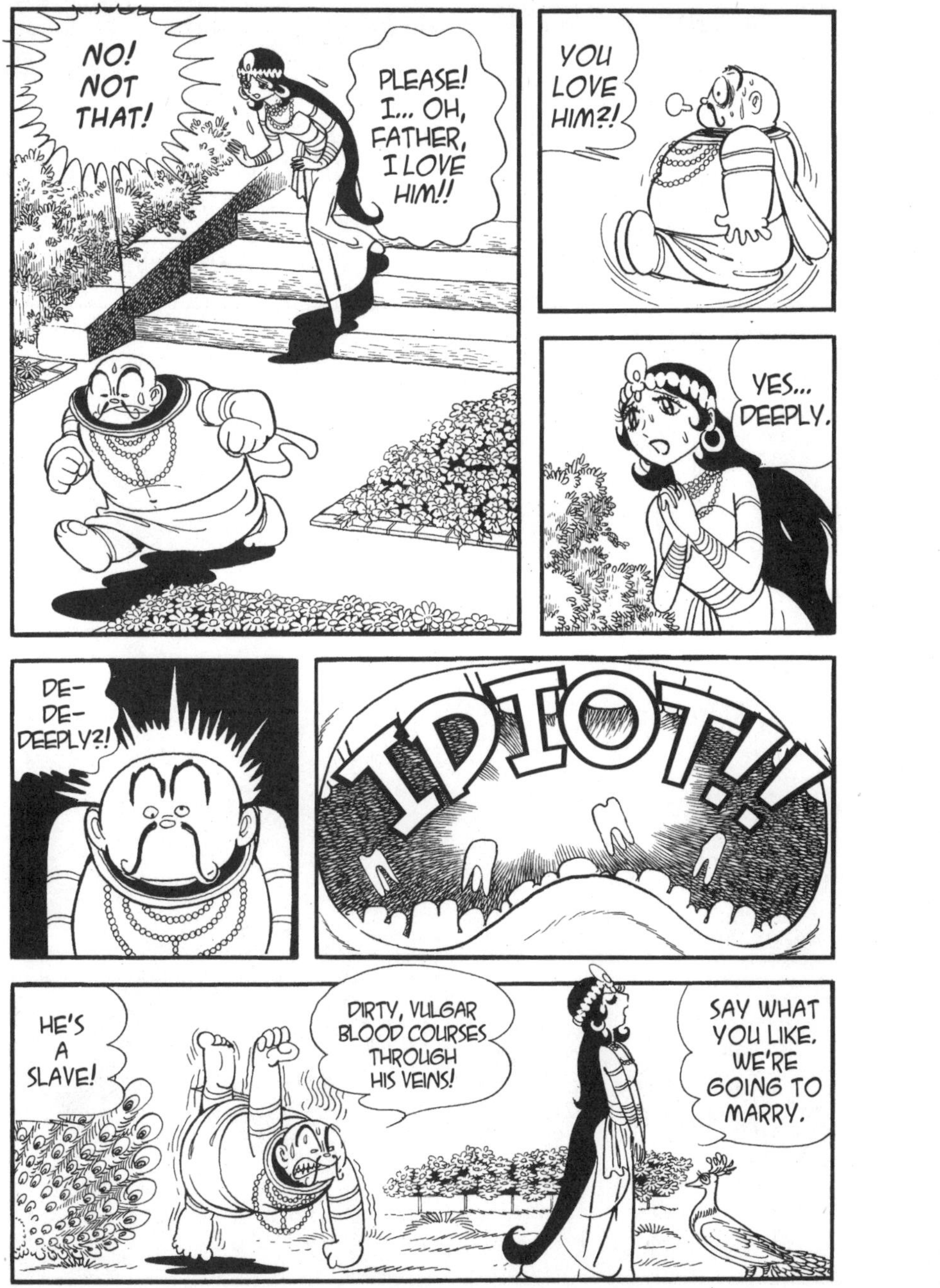
NO! NOT THAT!
PLEASE! I... OH, FATHER, I LOVE HIM!!
YOU LOVE HIM?!
YES... DEEPLY.
DE-DE-DEEPLY?!
IDIOT!!
HE'S A SLAVE!
DIRTY, VULGAR BLOOD COURSES THROUGH HIS VEINS!
SAY WHAT YOU LIKE. WE'RE GOING TO MARRY.

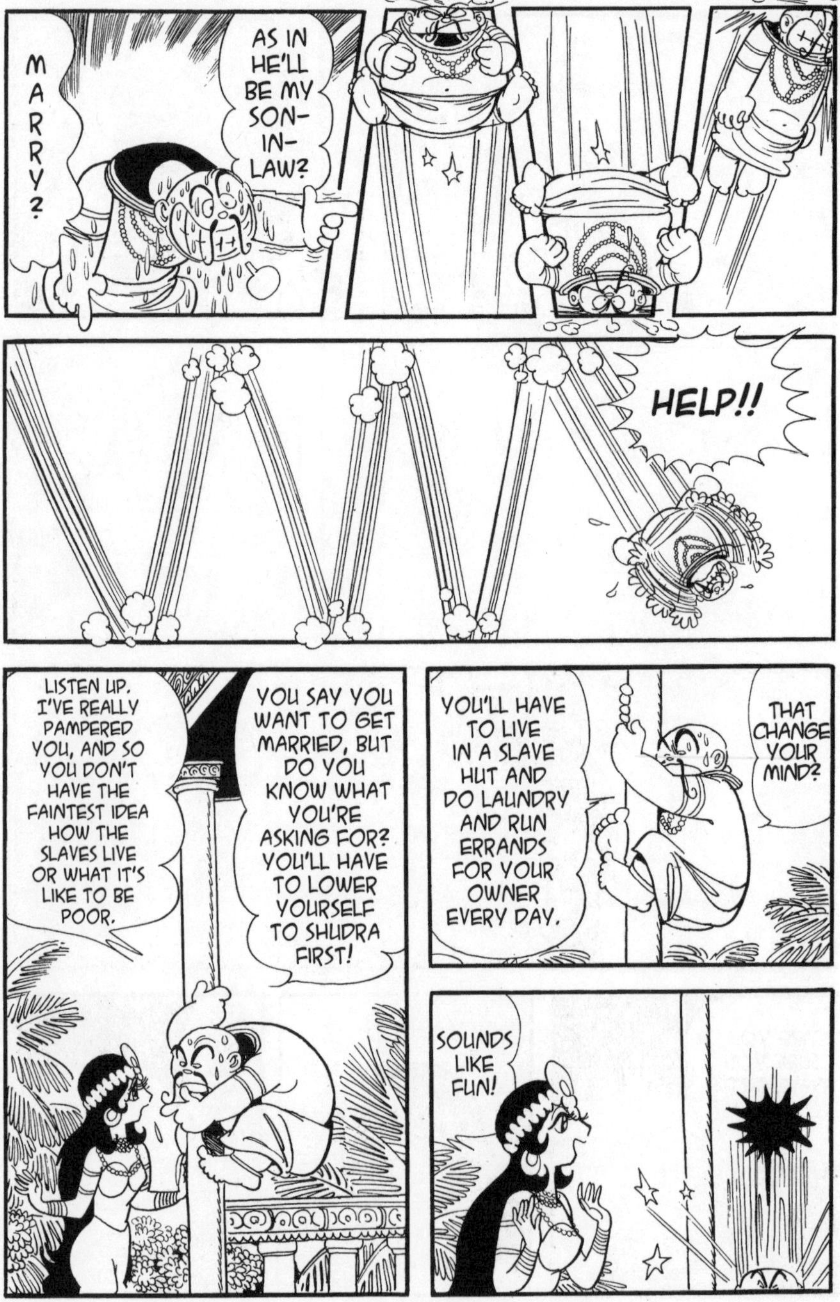
MARRY?
AS IN HE'LL BE MY SON-IN-LAW?
HELP!!
LISTEN UP. I'VE REALLY PAMPERED YOU, AND SO YOU DON'T HAVE THE FAINTEST IDEA HOW THE SLAVES LIVE OR WHAT IT'S LIKE TO BE POOR.
YOU SAY YOU WANT TO GET MARRIED, BUT DO YOU KNOW WHAT YOU'RE ASKING FOR? YOU'LL HAVE TO LOWER YOURSELF TO SHUDRA FIRST!
YOU'LL HAVE TO LIVE IN A SLAVE HUT AND DO LAUNDRY AND RUN ERRANDS FOR YOUR OWNER EVERY DAY.
THAT CHANGE YOUR MIND?
SOUNDS LIKE FUN!

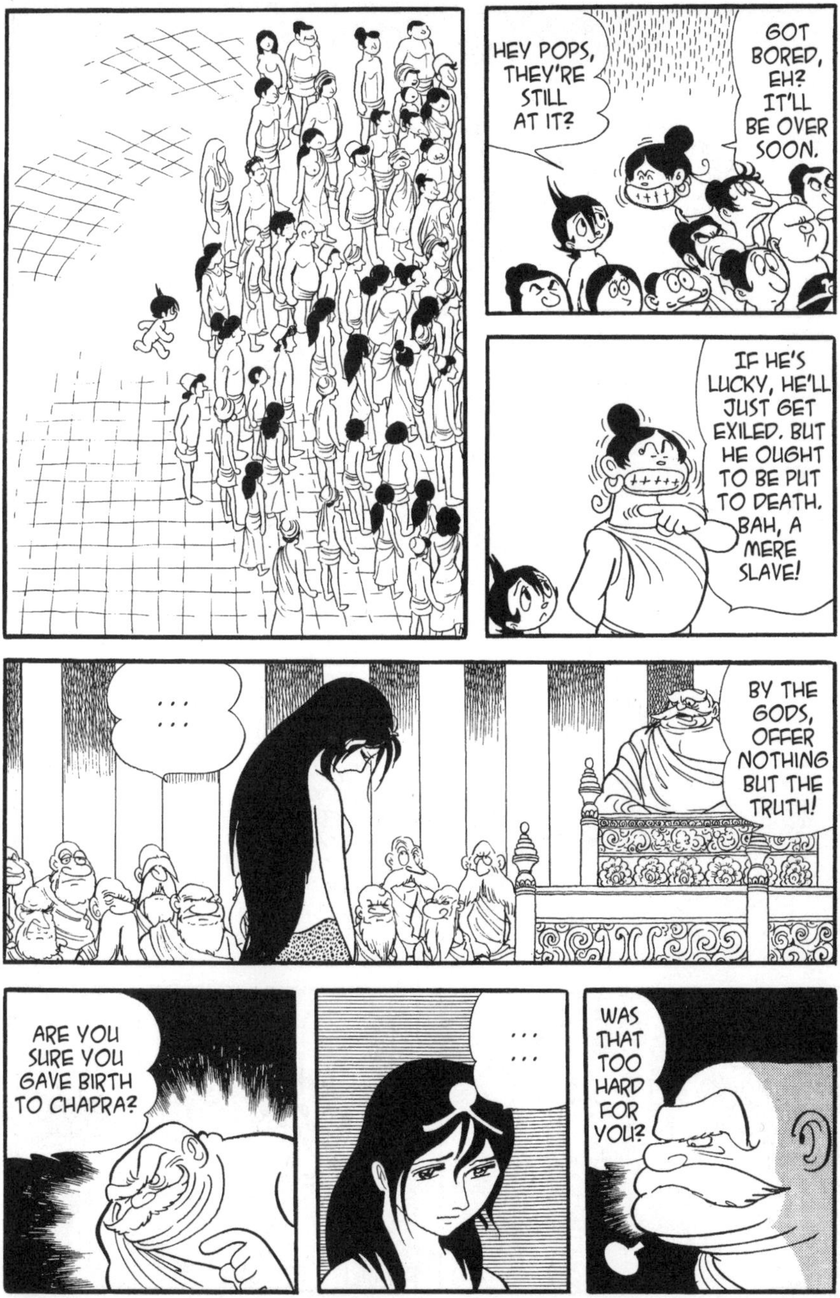
HEY POPS, THEY'RE STILL AT IT?
GOT BORED, EH? IT'LL BE OVER SOON.
IF HE'S LUCKY, HE'LL JUST GET EXILED. BUT HE OUGHT TO BE PUT TO DEATH. BAH, A MERE SLAVE!
... ...
BY THE GODS, OFFER NOTHING BUT THE TRUTH!
ARE YOU SURE YOU GAVE BIRTH TO CHAPRA?
... ...
WAS THAT TOO HARD FOR YOU?

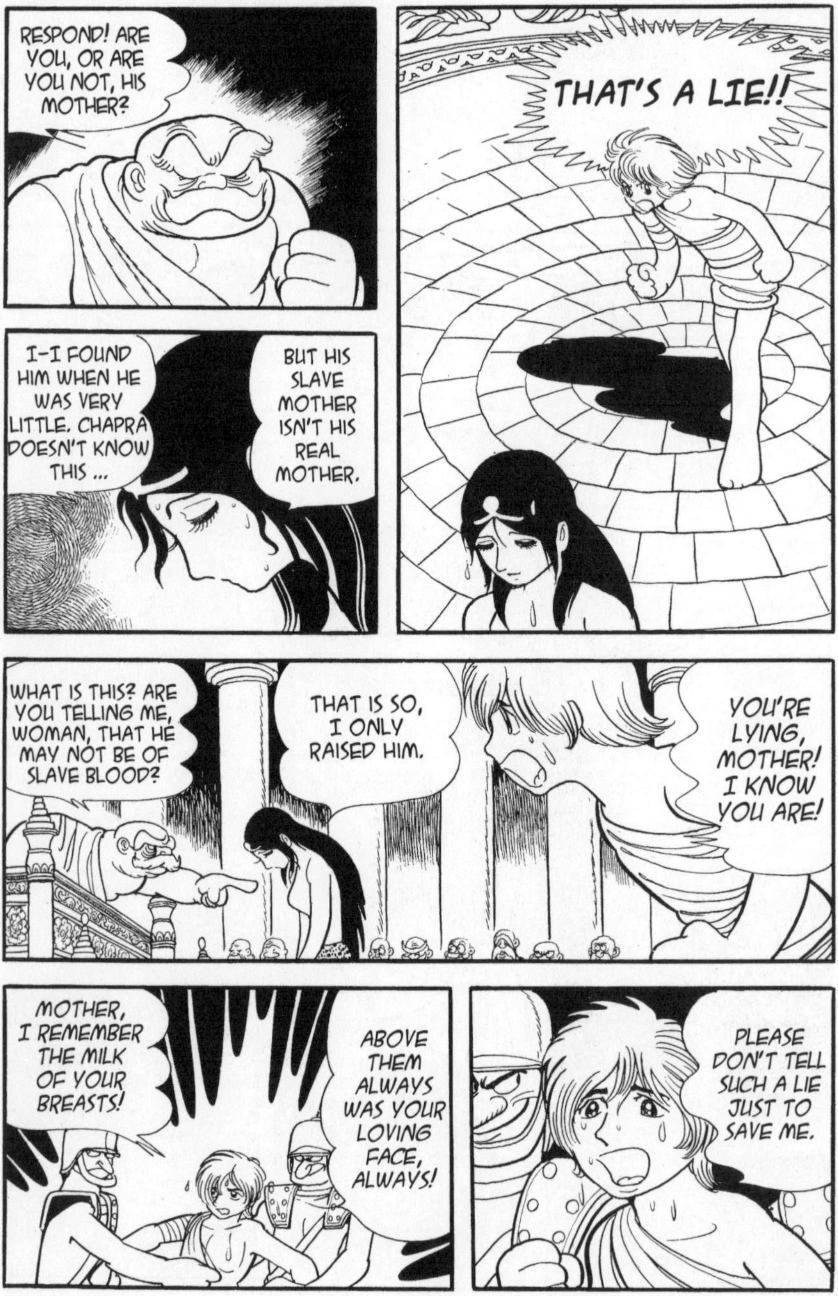

RESPOND! ARE YOU, OR ARE YOU NOT, HIS MOTHER?
THAT'S A LIE!!
I-I FOUND HIM WHEN HE WAS VERY LITTLE. CHAPRA DOESN'T KNOW THIS ...
BUT HIS SLAVE MOTHER ISN'T HIS REAL MOTHER.
WHAT IS THIS? ARE YOU TELLING ME, WOMAN, THAT HE MAY NOT BE OF SLAVE BLOOD?
THAT IS SO, I ONLY RAISED HIM.
YOU'RE LYING, MOTHER! I KNOW YOU ARE!
MOTHER, I REMEMBER THE MILK OF YOUR BREASTS!
ABOVE THEM ALWAYS WAS YOUR LOVING FACE, ALWAYS!
PLEASE DON'T TELL SUCH A LIE JUST TO SAVE ME.

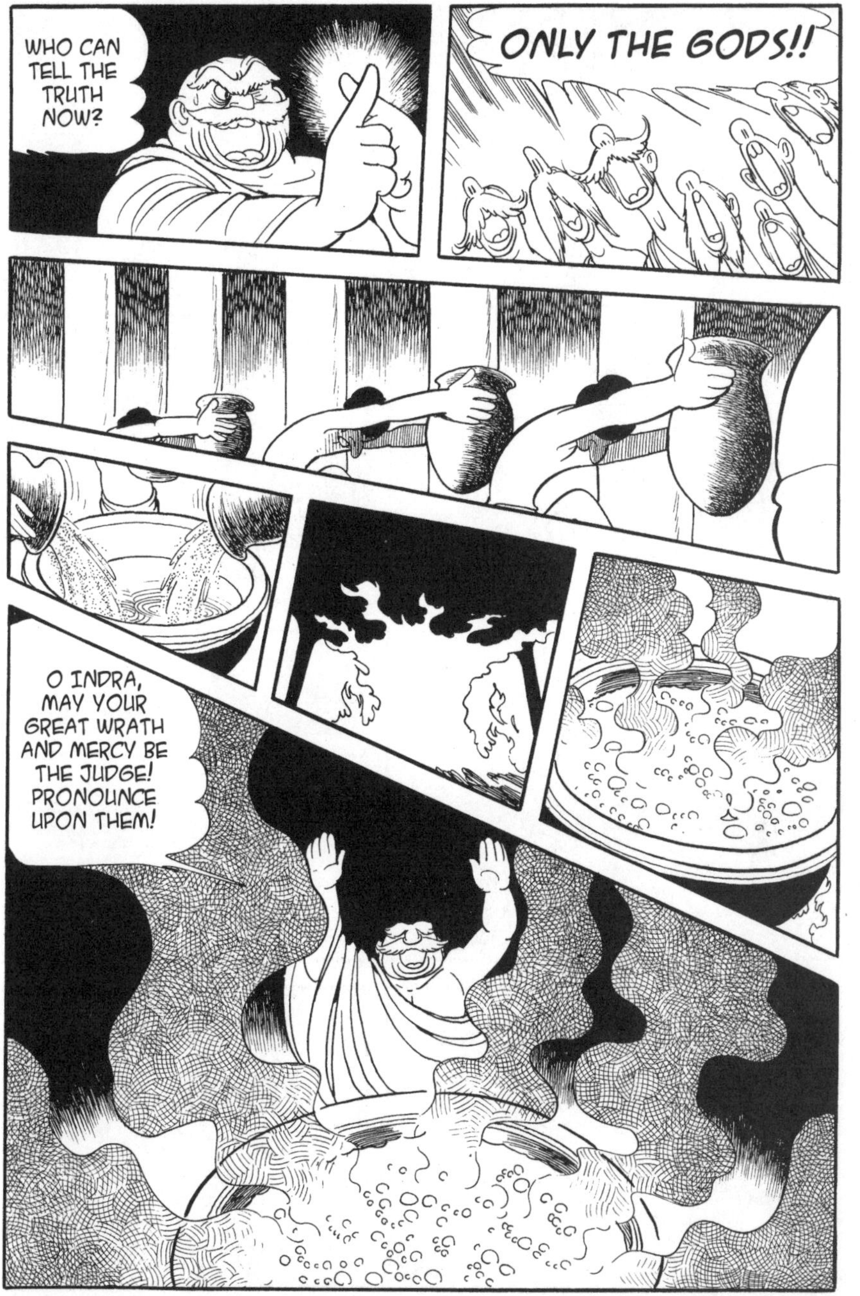
WHO CAN TELL THE TRUTH NOW?
ONLY THE GODS!!
O INDRA, MAY YOUR GREAT WRATH AND MERCY BE THE JUDGE! PRONOUNCE UPON THEM!

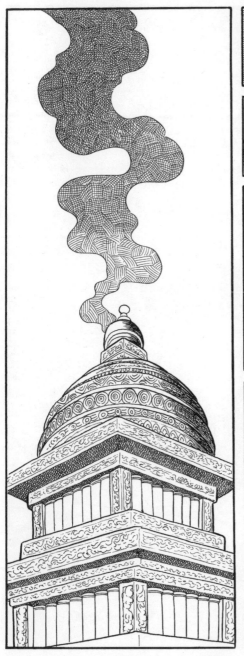

INDRA HAS BEEN CALLED UPON. THE VERDICT WILL BE IN VERY SOON.

THE VERDICT!

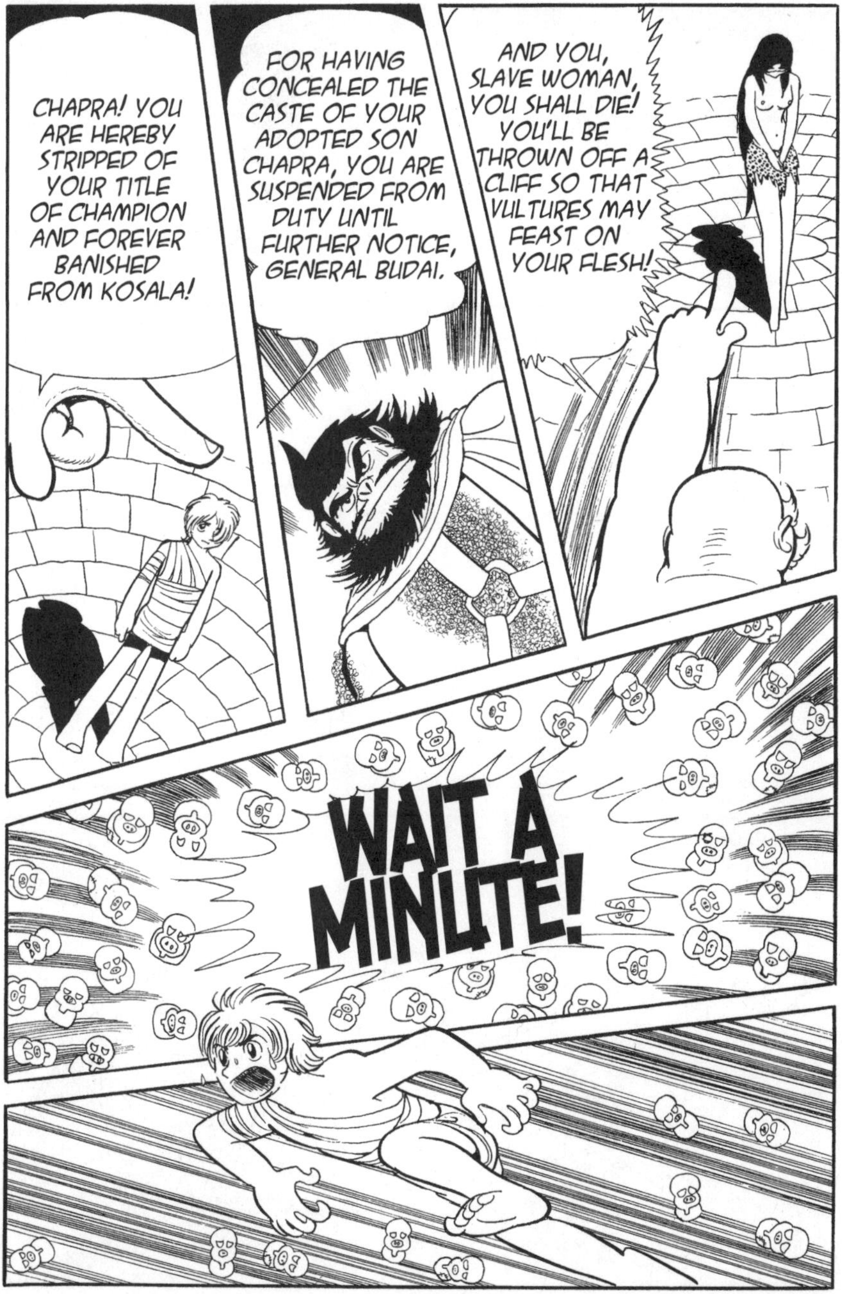
CHAPRA! YOU ARE HEREBY STRIPPED OF YOUR TITLE OF CHAMPION AND FOREVER BANISHED FROM KOSALA!
FOR HAVING CONCEALED THE CASTE OF YOUR ADOPTED SON CHAPRA, YOU ARE SUSPENDED FROM DUTY UNTIL FURTHER NOTICE, GENERAL BUDAI.
AND YOU, SLAVE WOMAN, YOU SHALL DIE! YOU'LL BE THROWN OFF A CLIFF SO THAT VULTURES MAY FEAST ON YOUR FLESH!
WAIT A MINUTE!

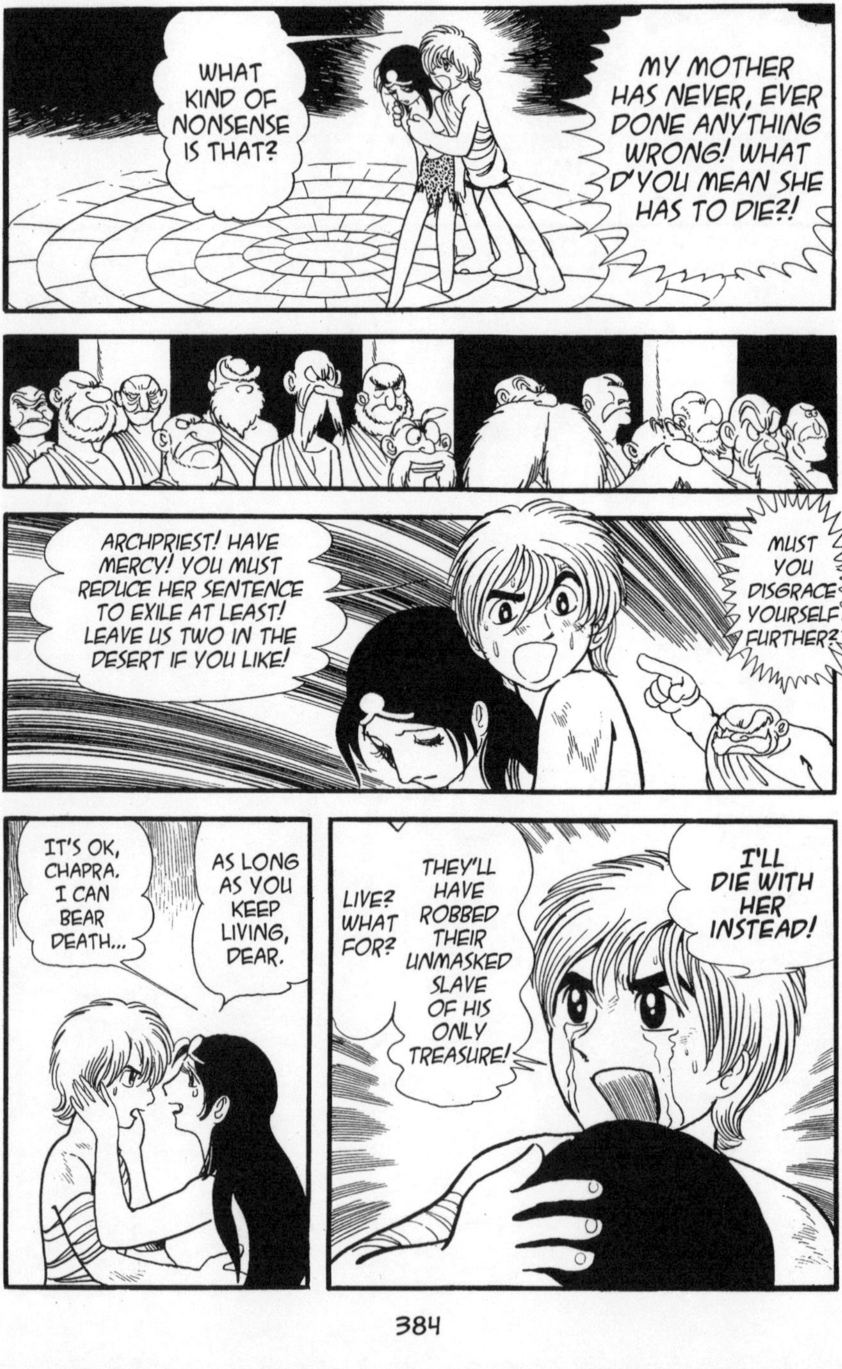

WHAT KIND OF NONSENSE IS THAT?
MY MOTHER HAS NEVER, EVER DONE ANYTHING WRONG! WHAT D'YOU MEAN SHE HAS TO DIE?!
ARCHPRIEST! HAVE MERCY! YOU MUST REDUCE HER SENTENCE TO EXILE AT LEAST! LEAVE US TWO IN THE DESERT IF YOU LIKE!
MUST YOU DISGRACE YOURSELF FURTHER?
IT'S OK, CHAPRA. I CAN BEAR DEATH...
AS LONG AS YOU KEEP LIVING, DEAR.
LIVE? WHAT FOR?
THEY'LL HAVE ROBBED THEIR UNMASKED SLAVE OF HIS ONLY TREASURE!
I'LL DIE WITH HER INSTEAD!

CHAPTER TWELVE

THE WALL OF DEATH

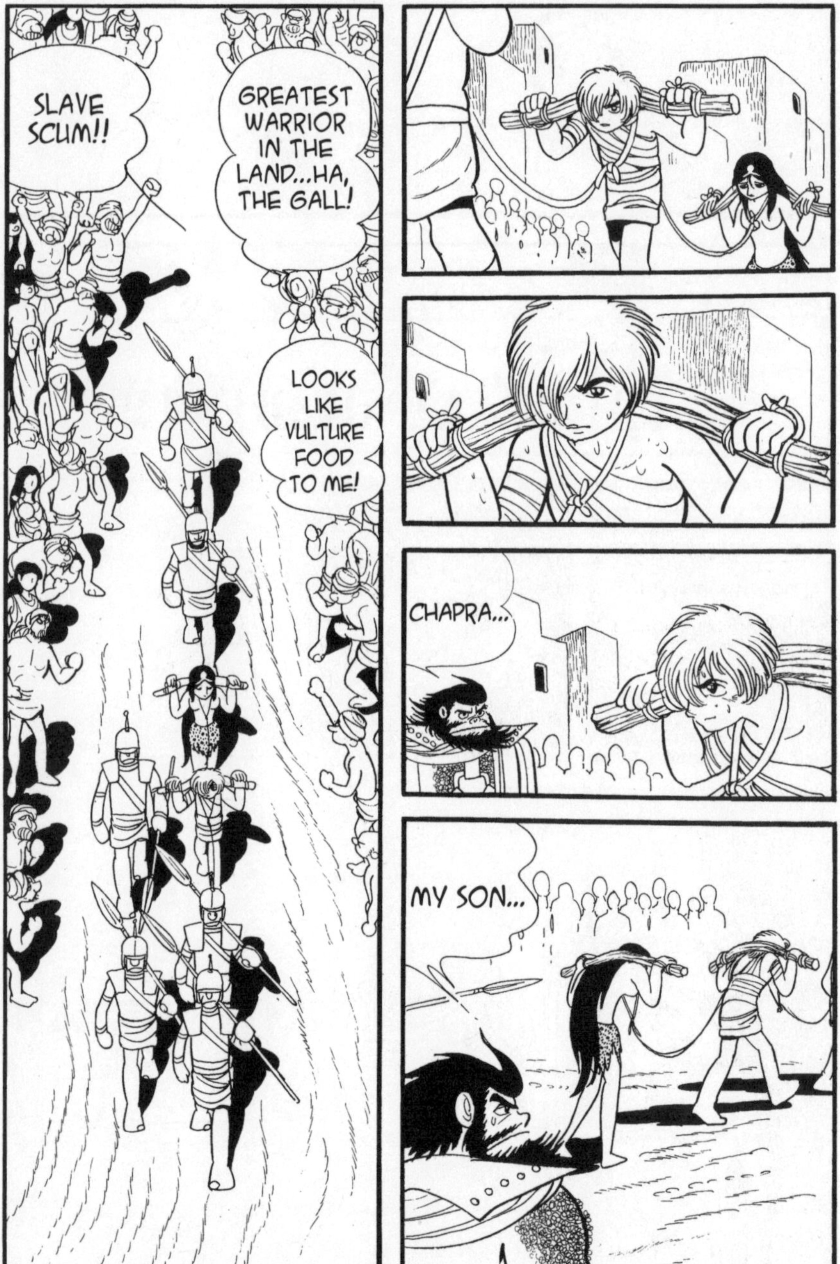
SLAVE SCUM!!
GREATEST WARRIOR IN THE LAND...HA, THE GALL!
LOOKS LIKE VULTURE FOOD TO ME!
CHAPRA...
MY SON...

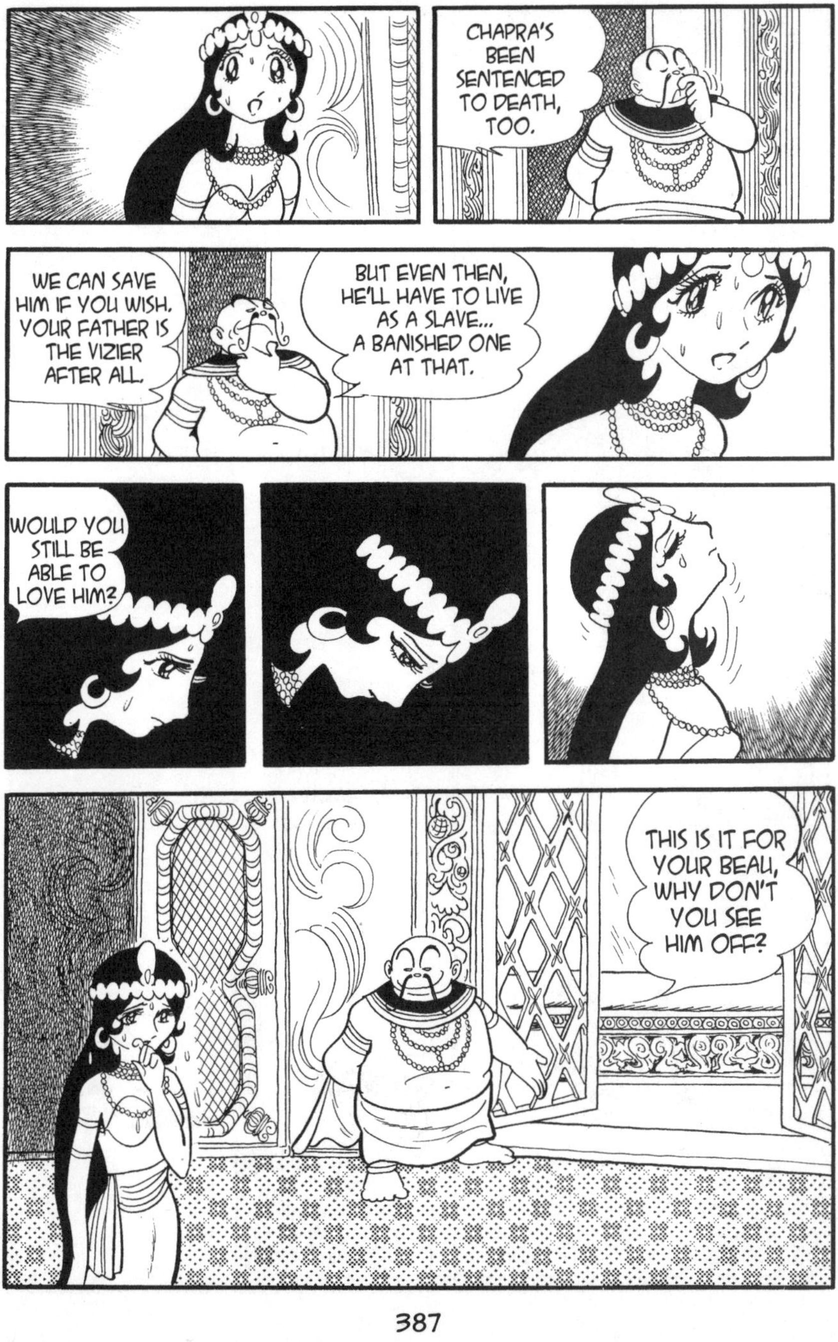
CHAPRA'S BEEN SENTENCED TO DEATH, TOO.
WE CAN SAVE HIM IF YOU WISH. YOUR FATHER IS THE VIZIER AFTER ALL.
BUT EVEN THEN, HE'LL HAVE TO LIVE AS A SLAVE... A BANISHED ONE AT THAT.
WOULD YOU STILL BE ABLE TO LOVE HIM?
THIS IS IT FOR YOUR BEAU, WHY DON'T YOU SEE HIM OFF?

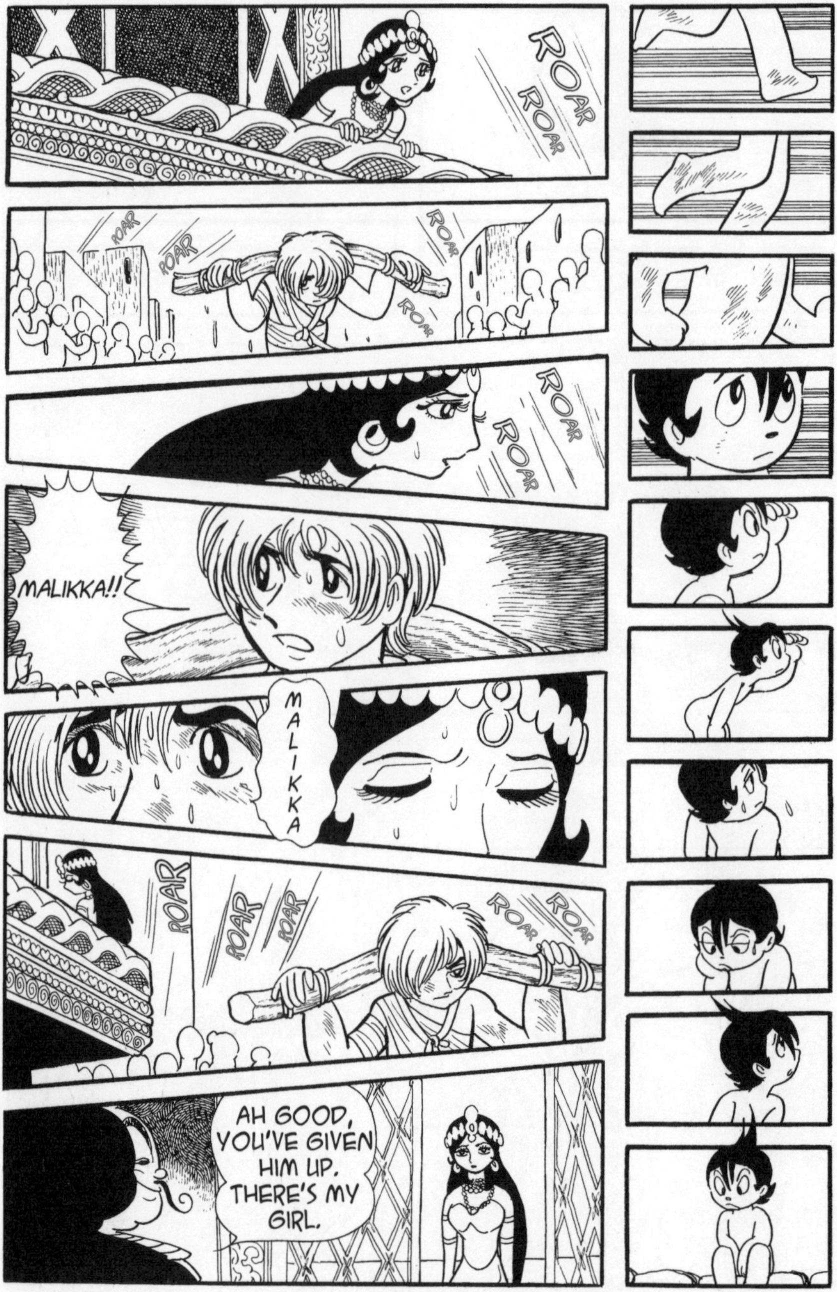
ROAR
ROAR
ROAR
ROAR
ROAR
ROAR
ROAR
ROAR
ROAR
ROAR
MALIKKA!!
MALIKKA
ROAR
ROAR
ROAR
ROAR
ROAR
AH GOOD, YOU'VE GIVEN HIM UP. THERE'S MY GIRL.

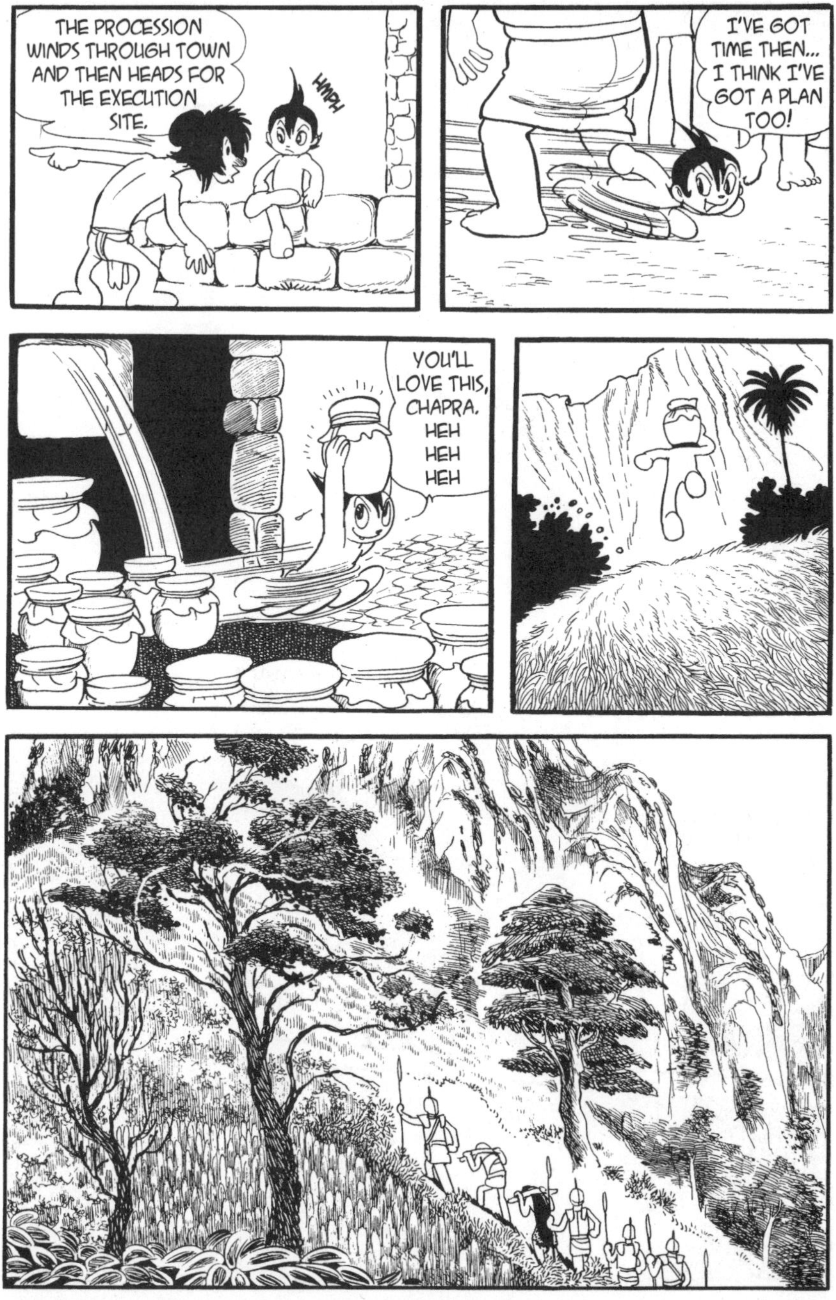
THE PROCESSION WINDS THROUGH TOWN AND THEN HEADS FOR THE EXECUTION SITE.
HMPH
I'VE GOT TIME THEN... I THINK I'VE GOT A PLAN TOO!
YOU'LL LOVE THIS, CHAPRA. HEH HEH HEH

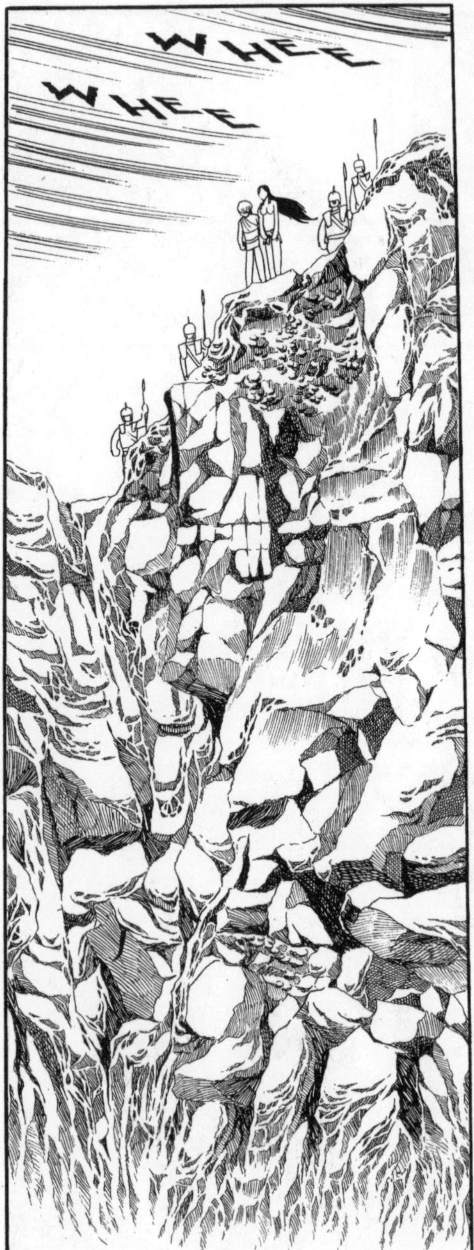
WHEE
WHEE

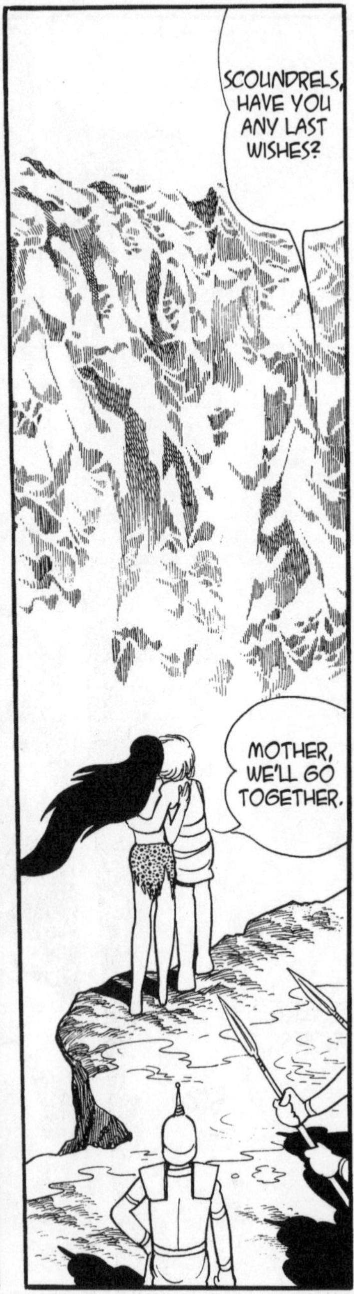
SCOUNDRELS, HAVE YOU ANY LAST WISHES?
MOTHER, WE'LL GO TOGETHER.

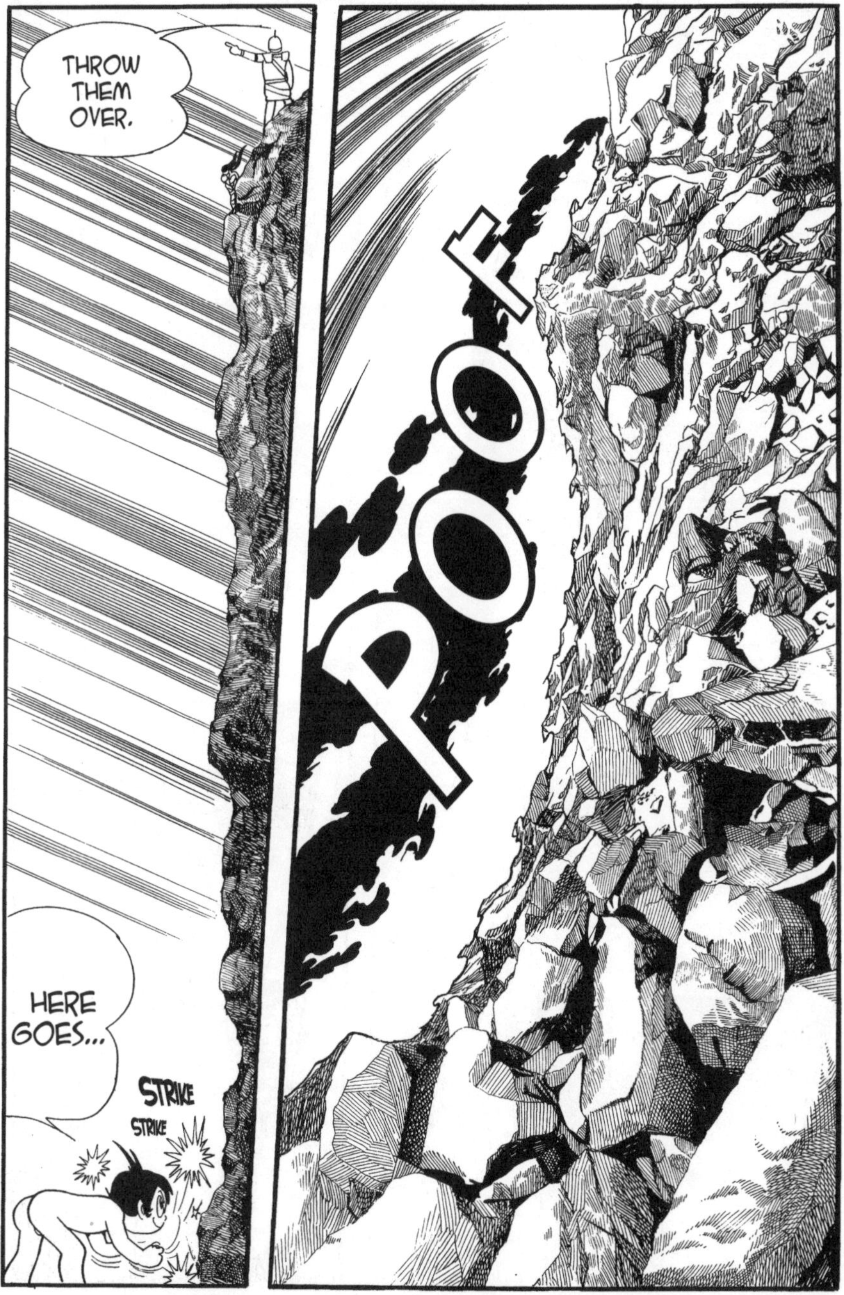
THROW THEM OVER.
HERE GOES...
STRIKE
STRIKE
POOF

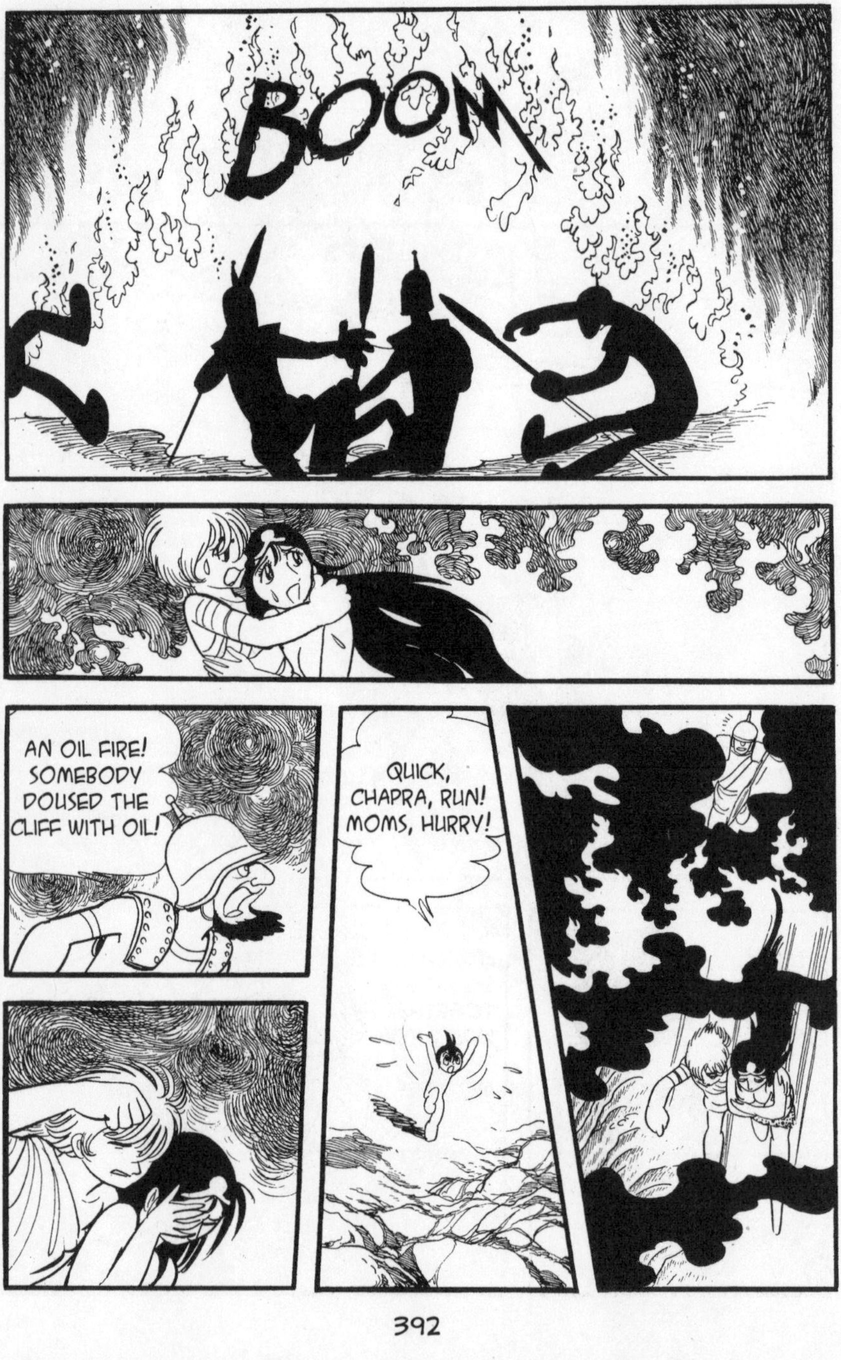
BOOM
AN OIL FIRE! SOMEBODY DOUSED THE CLIFF WITH OIL!
QUICK, CHAPRA, RUN! MOMS, HURRY!

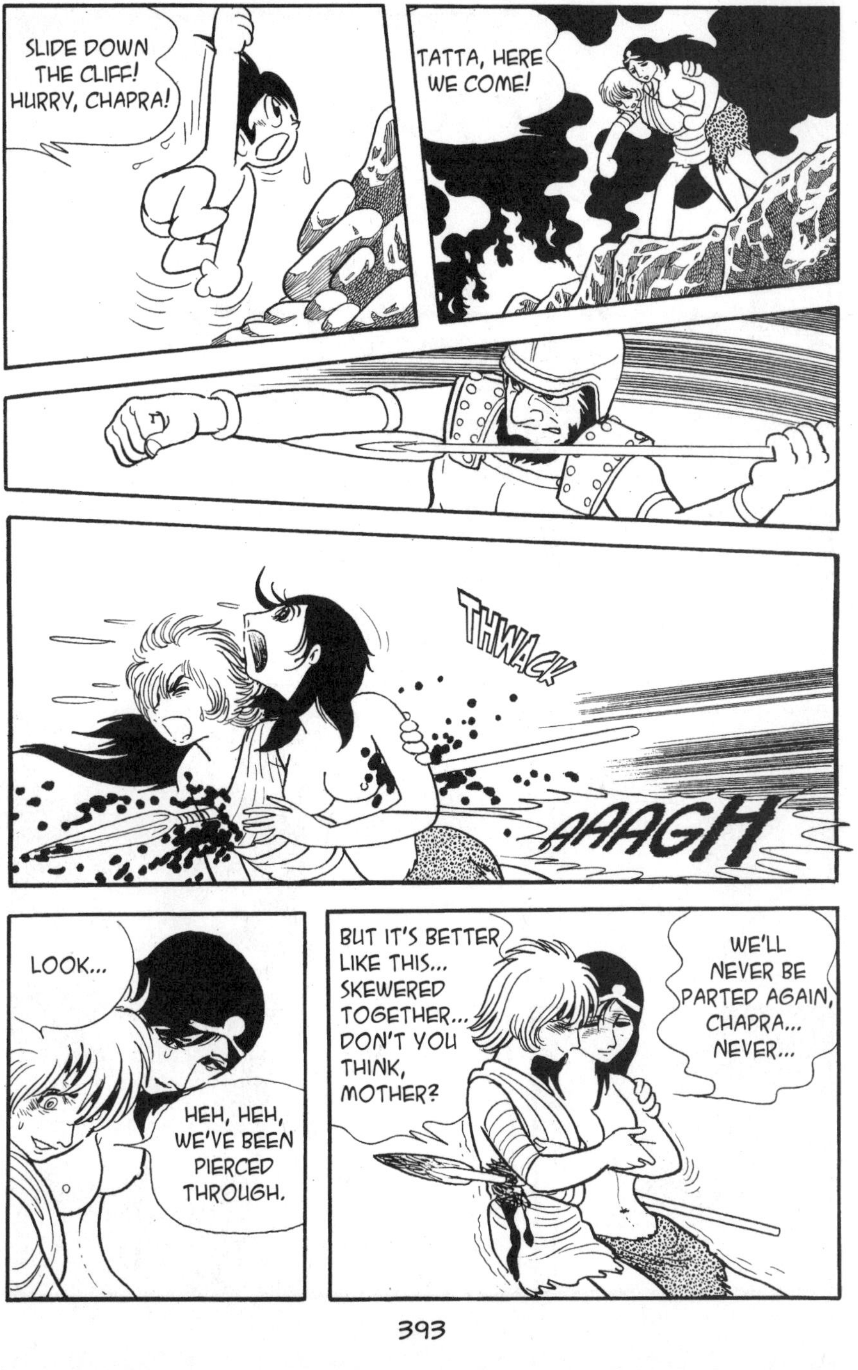
SLIDE DOWN THE CLIFF! HURRY, CHAPRA!
TATTA, HERE WE COME!
THWACK
AAAGH
LOOK...
HEH, HEH, WE'VE BEEN PIERCED THROUGH.
BUT IT'S BETTER LIKE THIS... SKEWERED TOGETHER... DON'T YOU THINK, MOTHER?
WE'LL NEVER BE PARTED AGAIN, CHAPRA... NEVER...

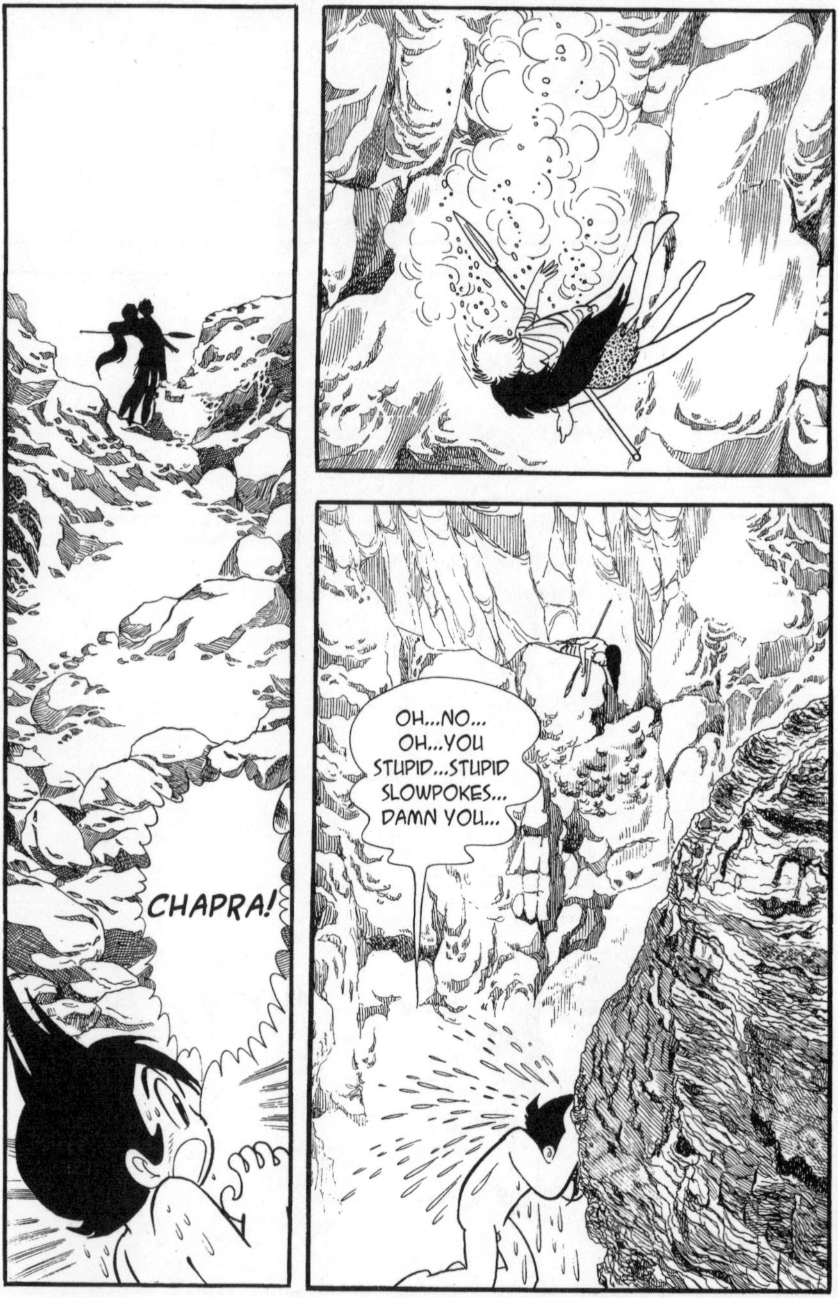
CHAPRA!
OH...NO... OH...YOU STUPID...STUPID SLOWPOKES... DAMN YOU...

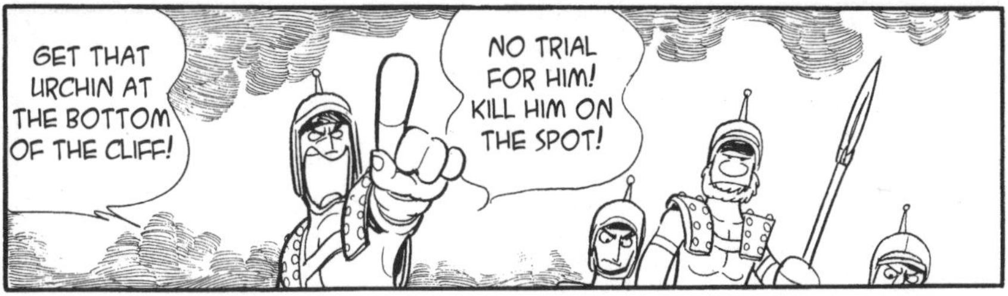
GET THAT URCHIN AT THE BOTTOM OF THE CLIFF!
NO TRIAL FOR HIM! KILL HIM ON THE SPOT!

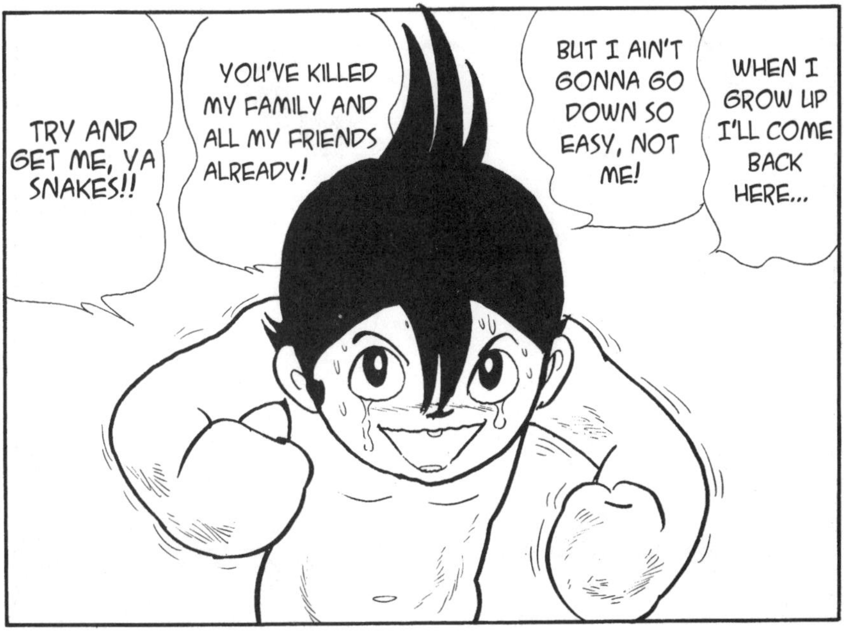
TRY AND GET ME, YA SNAKES!!
YOU'VE KILLED MY FAMILY AND ALL MY FRIENDS ALREADY!
BUT I AIN'T GONNA GO DOWN SO EASY, NOT ME!
WHEN I GROW UP I'LL COME BACK HERE...

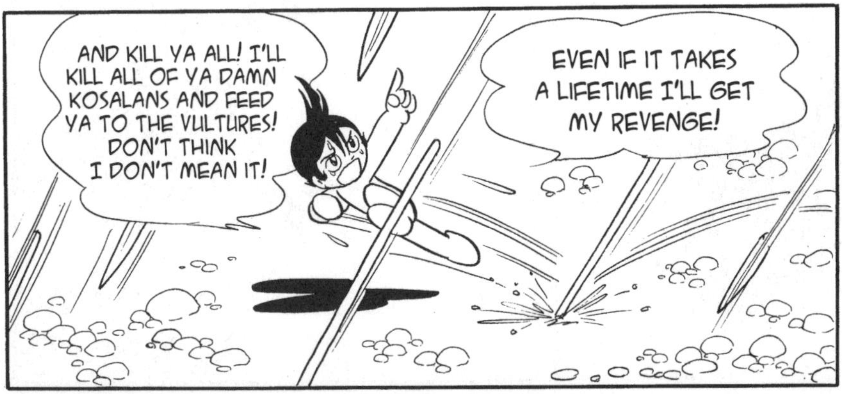
AND KILL YA ALL! I'LL KILL ALL OF YA DAMN KOSALANS AND FEED YA TO THE VULTURES! DON'T THINK I DON'T MEAN IT!
EVEN IF IT TAKES A LIFETIME I'LL GET MY REVENGE!

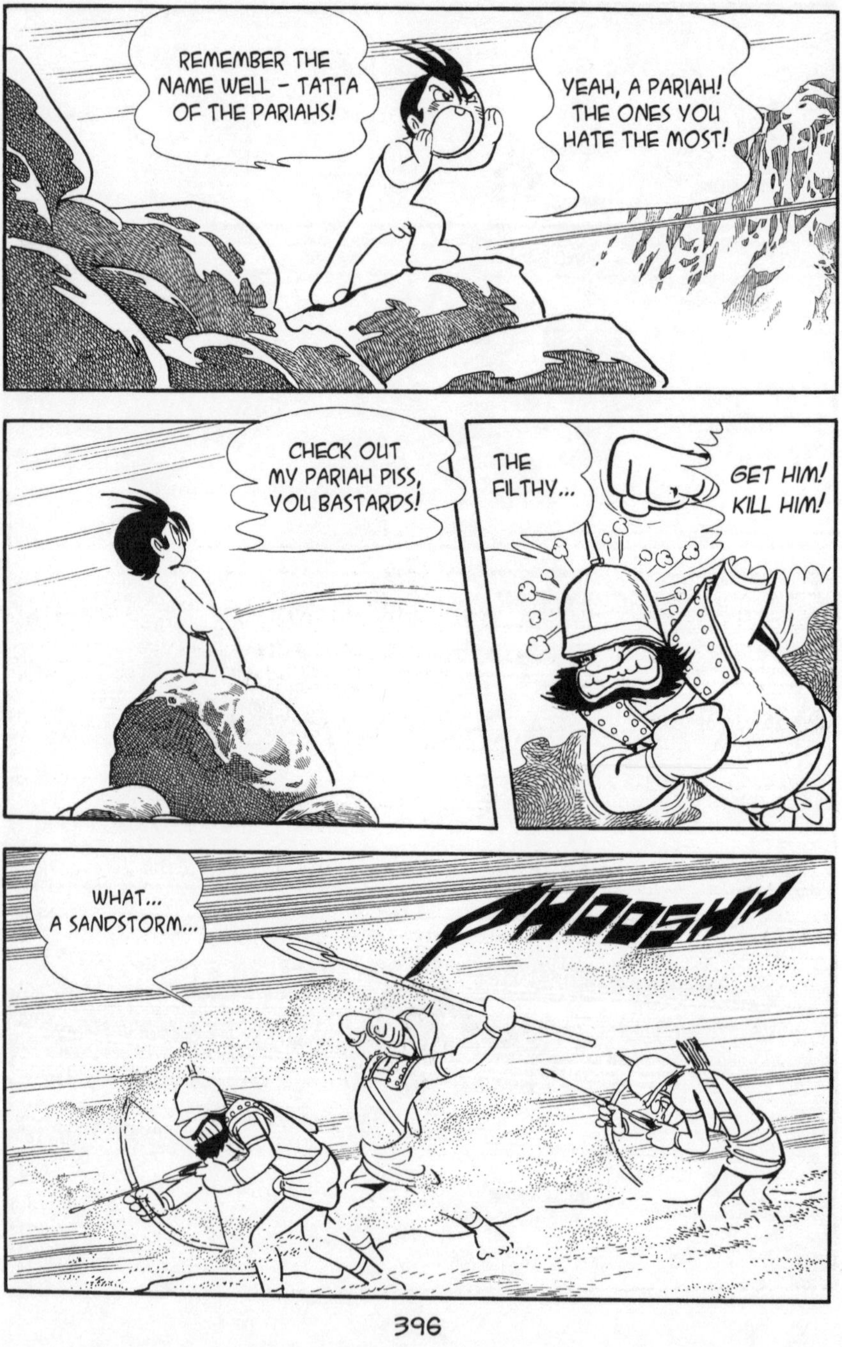
REMEMBER THE NAME WELL - TATTA OF THE PARIAHS!
YEAH, A PARIAH! THE ONES YOU HATE THE MOST!
CHECK OUT MY PARIAH PISS, YOU BASTARDS!
THE FILTHY...
GET HIM! KILL HIM!
WHAT... A SANDSTORM...
WHOOSHH

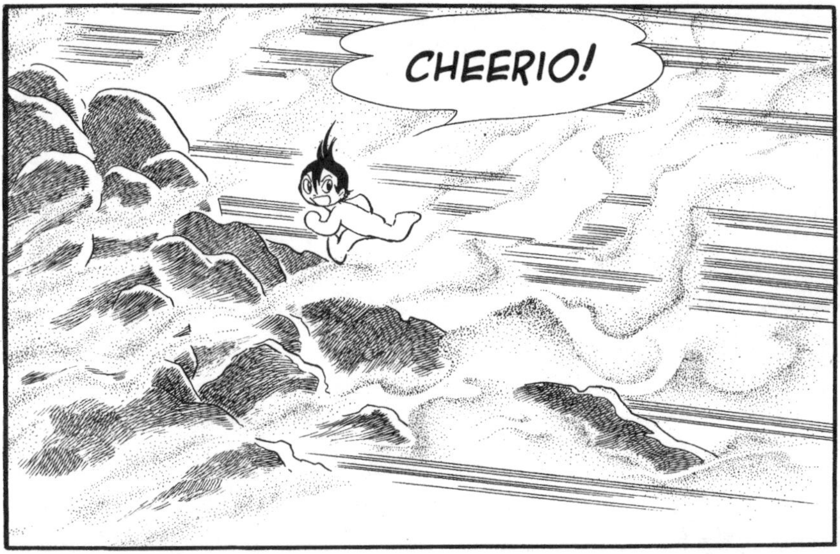
CHEERIO!
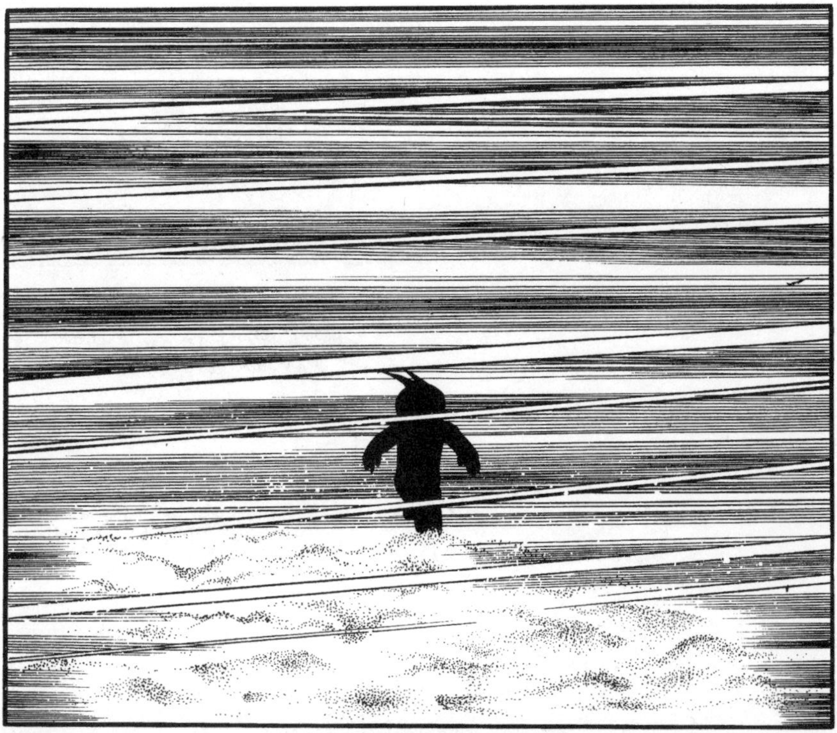

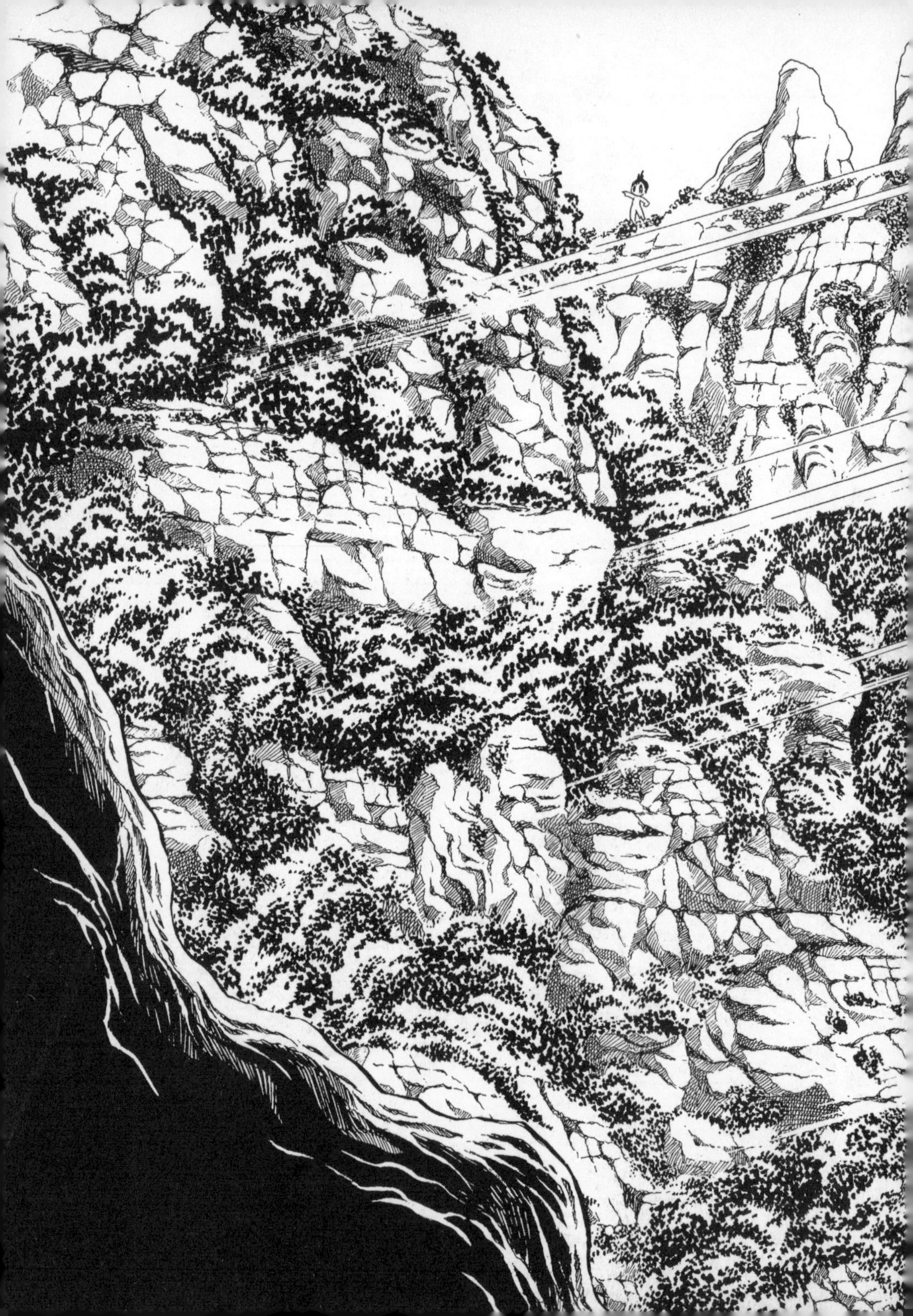

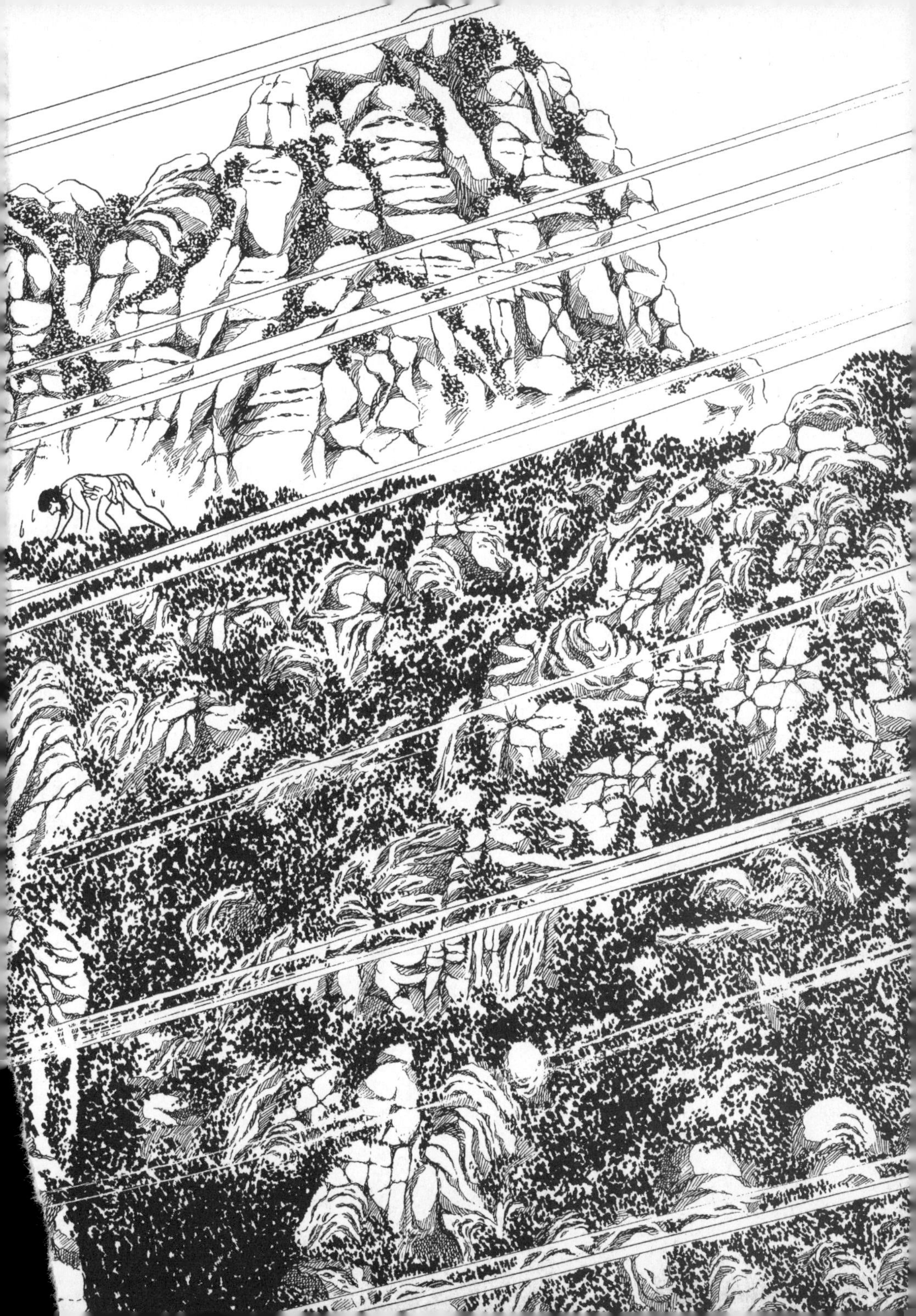

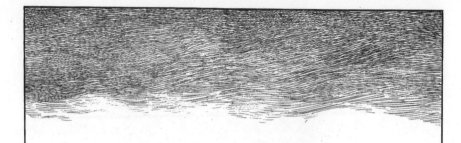

TATTA, VOWING REVENGE
ON KOSALA, TAKES TO THE
DISTANT MOUNTAINS...

NARADATTA, FALLEN TO THE
STATE OF A BEAST, SUFFERS IN
ATONEMENT FOR HIS SINS...

AND

THE ONE WHO
WAS BORN NEAR KAPILAVASTU...
THEIR DESTINIES UNFOLD IN
OUR NEXT VOLUMES.